Programming Abstractions in C++

Eric S. Roberts
Stanford University

Boston Columbus Indianapolis New York San Francisco Upper Saddle River

Amsterdam Cape Town Dubai London Madrid Milan Munich Paris Montreal Toronto

Delhi Mexico City Sao Paulo Sydney Hong Kong Seoul Singapore Taipei Tokyo

Editorial Director, ECS: Marcia Horton
Executive Editor: Tracy Johnson
Developmental and Copy Editor: Lauren Rusk
Editorial Assistants: Jenah Blitz-Stoehr
Director of Marketing: Christy Lesko
Marketing Manager: Yez Alayan
Director of Production: Erin Gregg
Managing Editor: Scott Disanno
Production Project Manager: Kayla Smith-Tarbox
Manufacturing Buyer: Linda Sager
Art Director/Cover Designer: Anthony Gemmellaro

Permissions Supervisor: Michael Joyce
Permissions Administrator: Jenell Forschler
Permissions Specialist: Jill Dougan, Electronic
    Publishing Services, Inc.
Director, Image Asset Services: Annie Atherton
Manager, Visual Research: Karen Sanatar
Image Permission Coordinator: Mary Young
Cover Printer: Lehigh Phoenix Color/Hagerstown
Media Project Manager: Renata Butera
Composition and Art: Eric Roberts
Text Printer: Courier Westford

Credits:
Cover: Bodleian Library at Oxford University © Shutterstock.
Page 67: Coin images. Reprinted with permission © United States Mint.
Page 182: Ant image. Reprinted with permission © paulrommer | Fotolia.com.
Page 251: Dürer's *Melencolia I* (1514). Reprinted with permission © Foto Marburg/Art Resource, NY.
Page 386: Fractal Tree photo. Reprinted with permission © Mark Wallinger.

Library of Congress Cataloging-in-Publication Data is available upon request.

10 9 8 7 6 5 4 3 2 1

ISBN 10: 0-13-345484-3

ISBN 13: 978-0-13345484-0

In loving memory of my father
James Stenius Roberts
(1924–2010)

To the Student

Over the last decade, the world of computing has grown vastly more exciting. The networked devices that most of us carry in our pockets have become faster, less expensive, and more powerful. Web-based services like Google and Wikipedia have put much of the world's information at our fingertips. Social networks have connected us with people throughout the world. Streaming technologies and faster hardware have made it possible to download music and video any time we want it.

These technologies, however, don't just happen; someone has to build them. Unfortunately, people with the necessary software-development skills are in short supply. At the center of the high-tech economy in Silicon Valley, companies cannot find the engineering talent they need to turn technological visions into reality. In particular, companies are desperate to find people who know how to develop and maintain large systems—software developers who understand such issues as data representation, efficiency, security, correctness, and modularity.

Although this book won't teach you everything you need to know about these topics and the broader field of computer science, it will give you a good start. At Stanford, over 1000 students a year take the course that uses this textbook. Many of those students find summer internships or industry jobs with no more background than working through this book provides. An even larger number of students continue on to more advanced courses that prepare them for the seemingly boundless opportunities that exist in this rapidly expanding field.

Beyond the opportunities they offer in the computing industry, the topics in this book are full of intellectual excitement. The algorithms and strategies you learn in this book—some of which were invented in the last decade while others have been around for more than 2000 years—are incredibly clever and stand as monuments to human creativity. They are also eminently practical and will help you become a much more sophisticated programmer.

As you study the material in this book, please keep in mind that programming is always a matter of learning by doing. Reading about an algorithmic technique does not mean that you will be able to apply that algorithm in practice. Your real learning will come from working through the exercises and debugging your early attempts at solving those problems. Programming can be frustrating at times, but the thrill of finding that last bug and watching your program work is so profound that it more than makes up for any difficulties you encounter along the way.

Eric Roberts
Stanford University
June 2013

To the Instructor

This text is intended for use in the second programming course in a typical college or university curriculum. It covers the material in a traditional CS2 course, as defined in the *Curriculum '78* report prepared by the Association for Computing Machinery (ACM). It therefore includes most of the topics specified for the CS102$_O$ and CS103$_O$ courses, as defined by the *Joint ACM/IEEE-CS Computing Curricula 2001* report and the material in the AL/Fundamental Data Structures and Algorithms unit from the draft release of *Computer Science Curricula 2013*.

The book adopts several pedagogical strategies that have proved to be extremely successful here at Stanford:

1. *A client-first approach to data structures.* The traditional CS2 curriculum typically consists of a sequential tour of the fundamental data structures. With this model, students learn how to use a particular structure, how to implement it, and what its performance characteristics are—all at the same time. By contrast, this book presents the full set of collection classes early and allows students to become familiar with those classes as clients. Once students have had time to assimilate that material, the book then explores the range of possible implementations and their associated computational characteristics. Adopting this strategy at Stanford has led to a significant improvement in student comprehension. Scores on examinations that require students to use collection classes have risen dramatically since the change.

2. *Late presentation of those C++ features that require a detailed understanding of the underlying machine.* Although the first two chapters offer students an overview of the primitive types and control structures available in C++, the initial presentation deliberately defers the topics—primarily pointers and arrays—that depend on an understanding of machine architecture. While those details are essential components of CS2, there is no need to burden students with them at the beginning of the course. Introducing collection classes early enables students to master several other equally important topics—including collection classes, recursion, object-oriented design, and algorithmic analysis—without having to struggle with low-level details at the same time.

3. *A portable library that enables the use of exciting graphical assignments.* One of the problems of using C++ as a teaching language is that the standard libraries do not offer any graphical capabilities. This book comes with a freely distributed, open-source library that supports graphics and interactivity in a simple, pedagogically appropriate way. The Stanford C++ library also includes simplified implementations of the collection classes that support a more logical and effective order of presentation.

Supplemental Resources

For students

The following items are available to all readers of this book at the Pearson web site (`http://www.pearsonhighered.com/ericroberts/`):

- Source code files for each example program in the book
- Full-color PDF versions of sample runs
- Answers to review questions

For instructors

The following items are available to qualified instructors from the Pearson web site (`http://www.pearsonhighered.com/ericroberts/`):

- Source code files for each example program in the book
- Full-color PDF versions of sample runs
- Answers to review questions
- Solutions to programming exercises
- PowerPoint lecture slides for each of the chapters

The Stanford C++ libraries

The Stanford C++ Libraries are freely available as an open-source development project. The header files, compiled libraries, and source code are available through GitHub (`http://www.github.com/eric-roberts/StanfordCPPLib`) or from my web site (`http://cs.stanford.com/~eroberts/StanfordCPPLib`).

Acknowledgments

This textbook has had an interesting evolutionary history that in some ways mirrors the genesis of the C++ language itself. Just as Bjarne Stroustrup's first version of C++ was implemented on top of the programming language C, this book began its life as my C-based textbook *Programming Abstractions in C,* published by the Pearson affiliate Addison-Wesley in 1998). A decade ago, my Stanford colleague Julie Zelenski updated it for use with the C++ programming language, which we began using in our introductory sequence during that year. Although the revised text worked well at the outset, our introductory courses evolved over the years to the point that a full rewrite was needed. This book is the result.

I want to thank my colleagues at Stanford over the last several years, starting with Julie Zelenski for her wonderful work on the initial C++ revision. My colleagues Keith Schwarz, Jerry Cain, Stephen Cooper, and Mehran Sahami have all made valuable contributions to the revision. And I also need to express my thanks to several generations of section leaders and my many students over the years, all of whom have helped make it so exciting to teach this material.

In addition, I want to express my gratitude to Marcia Horton, Tracy Johnson, and the other members of the team at Pearson for their support on this book as well as its predecessors over the years.

As always, the greatest thanks are due to my wife Lauren Rusk, who has again worked her magic as my developmental editor. Lauren's expertise has added considerable clarity and polish to the text. Without her, nothing would ever come out as well as it should.

Contents

Chapter 1
An Overview of C++

Out of these various experiments come programs. This is our experience: programs do not come out of the minds of one person or two people such as ourselves, but out of day-to-day work.

— Stokely Carmichael and Charles V. Hamilton,
Black Power, 1967

In Lewis Carroll's *Alice's Adventures in Wonderland,* the King asks the White Rabbit to "begin at the beginning and go on till you come to the end: then stop." Good advice, but only if you're starting from the beginning. This book is designed for a second course in computer science and therefore assumes that you have already begun your study of programming. At the same time, because first courses vary considerably in what they cover, it is difficult for a textbook author to rely on your having mastered any specific material. Some of you, for example, will already understand C++ control structures from prior experience with closely related languages such as C or Java. For others, however, the structure of C++ will seem unfamiliar. Because of this disparity in background, the best approach is to adopt the King's advice. This chapter therefore "begins at the beginning" and introduces you to those parts of the C++ language you will need to write simple programs.

1.1 Your first C++ program

As you will learn in more detail in the next section, C++ is an extension of an extremely successful programming language called C, which appeared in the early 1970s. In the book that serves as C's defining document, *The C Programming Language,* Brian Kernighan and Dennis Ritchie offer the following advice on the first page of Chapter 1:

> The only way to learn a new programming language is by writing programs in it. The first program to write is the same for all languages:
>
> *Print the words*
> ```
> hello, world
> ```
>
> This is the big hurdle; to leap over it you have to be able to create the program text somewhere, compile it successfully, load it, run it, and find out where the output went. With these mechanical details mastered, everything else is comparatively easy.

If you were to rewrite the "Hello World" program in C++, it would end up looking something like the code in Figure 1-1.

At this point, the important thing is not to understand exactly what all of the lines in this program mean. There will be plenty of time to master those details later. Your mission—and you *should* decide to accept it—is to get the **HelloWorld** program running. Type in the program exactly as it appears in Figure 1-1 and then figure out what you need to do to make it work. The exact steps you need to use depend on the programming environment you're using to create and run C++ programs. If you are using this textbook for a course, presumably your instructor will provide some reference material on the programming environments you are expected to use. If you are reading this book on your own, you'll need to refer to

FIGURE 1-1 The "Hello World" program

```
/*
 * File: HelloWorld.cpp
 * --------------------
 * This file is adapted from the example
 * on page 1 of Kernighan and Ritchie's
 * book The C Programming Language.
 */

#include <iostream>
using namespace std;

int main() {
   cout << "hello, world" << endl;
   return 0;
}
```

the documentation that comes with whatever programming environment you're using for C++.

When you get all these details worked out, you should see the output from the **HelloWorld** program on a window somewhere on your computer screen. On the Apple Macintosh on which I prepared this book, that window looks like this:

On your computer, the window will probably have a somewhat different appearance and may include additional status messages along with your program's cheery "hello, world" greeting. But the message will be there. And although it may not be true that "everything else is comparatively easy," you will have achieved a significant milestone.

1.2 The history of C++

In the early days of computing, programs were written in *machine language,* which consists of primitive instructions that can be executed directly by the machine. Programs written in machine language are difficult to understand, mostly because the structure of machine language reflects the design of the hardware rather than the needs of programmers. Worse still, each type of computing hardware has its own machine language, which means that a program written for one machine will not run on other types of hardware.

In the mid-1950s, a group of programmers under the direction of John Backus at IBM had an idea that profoundly changed the nature of computing. Would it be possible, Backus and his colleagues wondered, to write programs that resembled the mathematical formulas they were trying to compute and have the computer translate those formulas into machine language? In 1955, this team produced the initial version of FORTRAN (whose name is a contraction of *formula translation*), which was the first example of a ***higher-level programming language.***

Since that time, many new programming languages have been invented, most of which build on previous languages in an evolutionary way. C++ represents the joining of two branches in that evolution. One of its ancestors is a language called *C,* which was designed at Bell Laboratories by Dennis Ritchie in 1972 and then later revised and standardized by the American National Standards Institute (ANSI) in 1989. But C++ also descends from a family of languages designed to support a different style of programming—one that has dramatically changed the nature of software development in recent years.

The object-oriented paradigm

Over the last two decades, computer science and programming have gone through something of a revolution. Like most revolutions—whether political upheavals or the conceptual restructurings that Thomas Kuhn describes in his 1962 book *The Structure of Scientific Revolutions*—this change has been driven by the emergence of an idea that challenges an existing orthodoxy. Initially, the two ideas compete, and, at least for a while, the old order maintains its dominance. Over time, however, the strength and popularity of the new idea grows, until it begins to displace the older idea in what Kuhn calls a ***paradigm shift.*** In programming, the old order is represented by the ***procedural paradigm,*** in which programs consist of a collection of procedures and functions that operate on data. The new model is called the ***object-oriented paradigm,*** in which programs are viewed instead as a collection of data objects that embody particular characteristics and behavior.

The idea of object-oriented programming is not really all that new. The first object-oriented language was SIMULA, a language for coding simulations that was designed by the Scandinavian computer scientists Ole-Johan Dahl and Kristen Nygaard in 1967. With a design that was far ahead of its time, SIMULA anticipated many of the concepts that later became commonplace in programming, including the concept of abstract data types and much of the modern object-oriented paradigm. In fact, much of the terminology used to describe object-oriented languages comes from the original 1967 report on SIMULA.

Unfortunately, SIMULA did not generate a great deal of interest in the years after its introduction. The first object-oriented language to gain any significant following within the computing profession was Smalltalk, which was developed at the Xerox Palo Alto Research Center in the late 1970s. The purpose of Smalltalk, which is described in the book *Smalltalk-80: The Language and Its Implementation* by Adele Goldberg and David Robson, was to make programming accessible to a wider audience. As such, Smalltalk was part of a larger effort at Xerox PARC that gave rise to much of the modern user-interface technology that is now standard on personal computers.

Despite many attractive features and a highly interactive user environment that simplifies the programming process, Smalltalk never achieved much commercial success. The profession as a whole took an interest in object-oriented programming only when the central ideas were incorporated into variants of C, which had already become an industry standard. Although there were several parallel efforts to design an object-oriented language based on C, the most successful language was C++, which was developed by Bjarne Stroustrup at AT&T Bell Laboratories in the early 1980s. C++ includes standard C as a subset, which makes it possible to integrate C++ code into existing C programs in a gradual, evolutionary way.

Although object-oriented languages have gained some of their popularity at the expense of procedural languages, it would be a mistake to regard the object-oriented and procedural paradigms as mutually exclusive. Programming paradigms are not so much competitive as they are complementary. The object-oriented and the procedural paradigm—along with other important paradigms such as the functional programming style embodied in LISP—all have important applications in practice. Even within the context of a single application, you are likely to find a use for more than one approach. As a programmer, you must master many different paradigms, so that you can use the model that is most appropriate to the task at hand.

The evolution of C++

Like human languages, programming languages change over time. Over the years, C++ has evolved to meet the changing needs of its user community. The International Standards Organization (ISO), which oversees the development process for new versions of C++, issued major revisions of the language in 1998, 2003, and 2011. The most recent revision, which is called C++11 after the year in which the new standards were adopted, introduces many new features, including several that make C++ much easier to learn.

Although everyone will at some point be able to take advantage of the many features that C++11 provides, the unfortunate truth is that many compilers do not yet implement the C++11 standard. Until updated versions of the major compilers become available, you may be forced to follow the older C++ standard published in

2003. This book introduces C++11 features when they are appropriate, but always outlines a strategy for accomplishing the same result using an older compiler.

1.3 The compilation process

When you write a program in C++, your first step is to create a file, which is called a *source file,* that contains the text of your program. Before you can run your program, you need to translate the source file into an executable form. The first step in that process is to invoke a program called a *compiler,* which translates the source file into an *object file* containing the corresponding machine-language instructions. This object file is then combined with other object files to produce an *executable file* that can be run on the system. The other object files typically include predefined object files called *libraries,* which contain the machine-language instructions for various operations commonly required by programs. The process of combining all the individual object files into an executable file is called *linking.* The steps in the compilation process are illustrated in Figure 1-2.

As noted in the discussion of the **HelloWorld** program earlier in this chapter, the specific details of the compilation process vary from one machine to another. There is no way that a general textbook like this can tell you exactly what commands you should use to run a program on your system. The good news is that

FIGURE 1-2 **The compilation process**

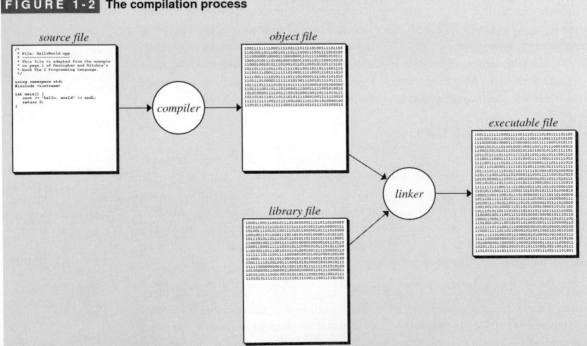

the C++ programs themselves will look the same. One of the advantages of programming in a higher-level language like C++ is that doing so allows you to ignore the particular characteristics of the hardware and create programs that will run on many different machines.

1.4 The structure of a C++ program

The best way to get a feeling for the C++ programming language is to look at some sample programs, even before you understand the details of the language. The **HelloWorld** program is a start, but it is so simple that it doesn't include many of the features you'd expect to see in a program. Since this book is designed for a second course in computer science, you've almost certainly written programs that read input from the user, store values in variables, use loops to perform repeated calculations, and make use of subsidiary functions to simplify the structure of the program. The **HelloWorld** program does none of these things. To illustrate more of the features of C++, Figure 1-3 shows the code for a program that lists powers of two and includes some annotations that describe the various parts of the program.

When you run the **PowersOfTwo** program shown in Figure 1-3, the computer begins by asking you for an exponent limit, which specifies how many powers of two the program should generate. If you type in 8, for example, the program will generate a list of the powers of two up to 2^8, as follows:

```
●○○                  PowersOfTwo
This program lists powers of two.
Enter exponent limit: 8
2 to the 0 = 1
2 to the 1 = 2
2 to the 2 = 4
2 to the 3 = 8
2 to the 4 = 16
2 to the 5 = 32
2 to the 6 = 64
2 to the 7 = 128
2 to the 8 = 256
```

This screen image shows what happens if you execute the **PowersOfTwo** program. Such images are called *sample runs.* In each sample run, input from the user appears in a lighter color so that you can distinguish input data from the output generated by the program.

As the annotations in Figure 1-3 indicate, the **PowersOfTwo** program is divided into several components, which are discussed in the next few sections.

FIGURE 1-3 The structure of a C++ program

```
/*
 * File: PowersOfTwo.cpp
 * ------------------------
 * This program generates a list of the powers of
 * two up to an exponent limit entered by the user.
 */                                                        }  program comments

#include <iostream>
using namespace std;                                       }  library inclusions

/* Function prototypes */

int raiseToPower(int n, int k);                            }  function prototype

/* Main program */

int main() {
   int limit;
   cout << "This program lists powers of two." << endl;
   cout << "Enter exponent limit: ";
   cin >> limit;
   for (int i = 0; i <= limit; i++) {                      }  main program
      cout << "2 to the " << i << " = "
           << raiseToPower(2, i) << endl;
   }
   return 0;
}

/*
 * Function: raiseToPower
 * Usage: int p = raiseToPower(n, k);
 * ------------------------------------                    }  function comment
 * Returns the integer n raised to the kth power.
 */

int raiseToPower(int n, int k) {
   int result = 1;
   for (int i = 0; i < k; i++) {                           }  function definition
      result *= n;
   }
   return result;
}
```

Comments

Much of the text in Figure 1-3 consists of English-language comments. A **comment** is text that is ignored by the compiler but which nonetheless conveys information to other programmers. A comment consists of text enclosed between the markers /* and */ and may continue over several lines. Alternatively, you can also specify single-line comments, which begin with the characters // and extend through the end of the line. This book uses the multiline /* ... */ comment form except when the comment marks some part of a program that is not yet complete. That strategy makes it easier to find unfinished parts of a program.

As you can see from Figure 1-3, the **PowersOfTwo** program includes a comment at the beginning that describes the program as a whole and one before the definition of **raiseToPower** that describes the operation of that function at a lower level of detail. In addition, the program includes a couple of one-line comments that act like section headings in English text.

Library inclusions

Modern programs are never written without using *libraries,* which are collections of previously written tools that perform useful operations. C++ defines several standard libraries, of which one of the most important is **iostream**. This library defines a set of simple input and output operations based on a data structure called a *stream,* which is a data structure used to manage the flow of information to or from some data source, such as the console or a file.

To gain access to the **iostream** library, your program must contain the line

```
#include <iostream>
```

This line instructs the C++ compiler to read the relevant definitions from what is called a *header file.* The angle brackets in this line indicate that the header file is a system library that is part of standard C++. Beginning in Chapter 2, you will also have occasion to use header files that you have written yourself or that come from other libraries. Those header files typically end with the suffix .h and are enclosed in quotation marks instead of angle brackets.

In C++, simply reading in the appropriate header file using **#include** is often not enough to give you access to a system library. To ensure that the names defined in different parts of a large system do not interfere with one another, the designers of C++ made it possible to segment code into structures called *namespaces,* each of which keeps track of its own set of names. The standard C++ libraries use a namespace called **std**, which means that you cannot refer to the names defined in standard header files like **iostream** unless you let the compiler know to which namespace those definitions belong.

Increasingly, professional C++ programmers specify the namespace explicitly by adding the prefix **std::** before each name that comes from the **std** namespace. If you adopt this approach, the first line of the **HelloWorld** program becomes

```
std::cout << "hello, world" << std::endl;
```

If you want to write code that looks like that of a professional, you can use this style. For someone just learning the language, all those `std::` tags make programs harder to read, so this book instead adopts the convention of adding the line

```
using namespace std;
```

at the end of the library inclusion section. At times—most importantly when you start to define your own library interfaces in Chapter 2—you will need to remember that the complete name of anything in the standard library namespace includes the `std::` prefix. For the moment, however, it is probably easiest to think of the

```
using namespace std;
```

as one of the incantations that the C++ compiler needs in order to work its magic on your code.

Function prototypes

Computation in a C++ program is carried out in the context of functions. A *function* is a named section of code that performs a specific operation. The **PowersOfTwo** program contains two functions—**main** and **raiseToPower**—each of which is described in more detail in one of the sections that follow. Although the definitions of these functions appear toward the end of the file, the **PowersOfTwo** program provides a concise description of the **raiseToPower** function just after the library inclusions. This concise form is called a *prototype* and makes it possible to make calls to that function before its actual definition appears.

A C++ prototype consists of the first line of the function definition followed by a semicolon, as illustrated by the prototype

```
int raiseToPower(int n, int k);
```

This prototype tells the compiler everything it needs to know about how to call that function when it appears in the code. As you will see in the expanded discussion of functions in Chapter 2, the prototype for **raiseToPower** indicates that the function takes two integers as arguments and returns an integer as its result.

You must provide the declaration or definition of each function before making any calls to that function. C++ requires such prototype declarations so the compiler can check whether calls to functions are compatible with the function definitions. If you accidentally supply the wrong number of arguments or if the arguments are of the wrong type, the compiler reports an error, which makes it easier to find such problems in your code.

The main program

Every C++ program must contain a function with the name **main**. This function specifies the starting point for the computation and is called when the program starts up. When **main** has finished its work and returns, execution of the program ends.

The first line of the **main** function in the **PowersOfTwo** program is an example of a *variable declaration,* which reserves space for a value used by the program. In this case, the line

        int limit;

introduces a new variable named **limit** capable of holding a value of type **int**, the standard type used to represent integers. The syntax of variable declarations is discussed in more detail in the section on "Variables" later in this chapter. For now, all you need to know is that this declaration creates space for an integer variable that you can then use in the body of the **main** function.

The next line of the **main** function is

        cout << "This program lists powers of two." << endl;

This line, which has the same effect as the single statement in **HelloWorld**, sends a message to the user indicating what the program does. The identifier **cout** refers to the *console output stream,* which is one of the facilities defined by the **iostream** interface. The effect of this statement is to take the characters enclosed in quotation marks and send them to the **cout** stream, along with the end-of-line sequence **endl**, which ensures that the next output operation will begin on a new line.

The next two lines ask the user to enter a value for the variable **limit**. The line

        cout << "Enter exponent limit: ";

also prints a message to the **cout** stream, just as the first line did. The purpose of this line is to let the user know what kind of input value is required. Such messages are generally known as *prompts.* When you print a prompt requesting input from the user, it is conventional to omit the **endl** value so that the prompt appears on the same line as the user input. When the computer executes this line of the program, it displays the prompt but leaves the console cursor—the blinking vertical bar or square that marks the current input position—at the end of the line, waiting for the user's value, as follows:

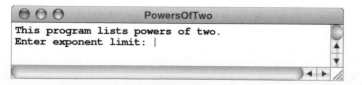

The actual request for the input value is the line

```
cin >> limit;
```

The identifier **cin** represents the **console input stream,** which is the counterpart to
cout for reading input from the user. This statement indicates that the next value
from the **cin** stream should be stored in the variable **limit**. Moreover, because
limit is declared as an integer variable, the **>>** operator automatically converts the
characters typed by the user into the appropriate integer. Thus, when the user types
8 and hits the RETURN key, the effect is to set **limit** to 8.

The next line of the **main** function is a **for** statement, which is used to repeat a
block of code. Like all control statements in C++, the **for** statement is divided into
a **header line,** which defines the nature of the control operation, and a **body,** which
indicates which statements are affected by the control operation. In this case, the
division looks like this:

```
for (int i = 0; i <= limit; i++) {        } header line
    cout << "2 to the " << i << " = "
        << raiseToPower(2, i) << endl;    } loop body
}
```

The header line—which you will have a chance to understand in more detail in the
section on "The **for** statement" later in this chapter—indicates that the statements
in the body, whatever they are, should be repeated for each value of i beginning
with 0 and continuing up to and including the value of **limit**. Each execution of
the body of the loop prints a single line showing the value of 2^i for the current value
of the variable i.

The single statement in the body of the loop is

```
cout << "2 to the " << i << " = "
    << raiseToPower(2, i) << endl;
```

This statement illustrates a couple of points. First, statements can be split across
more than one line; it is the semicolon that marks the end of the statement, and not
simply the end of the line. Second, this statement showcases the ability of the **cout**
stream to chain different output values together and to convert numeric quantities
into a printable form. The first part of the output is the character sequence

```
2 to the
```

This output is then followed by the value of the variable i, an equal sign surrounded
by spaces, the value of the function call

```
raiseToPower(2, i)
```

and finally the end-of-line marker. The spaces in the strings ensure that the numeric values do not run together.

Before the program can print the output line, however, it must invoke the **raiseToPower** function to see what the value should be. Calling **raiseToPower** suspends the execution of the **main** function, which then waits until the desired value is returned.

As is typically the case with functions, **raiseToPower** needs some information from the main program in order to do its work. If you think about what raising a number to a power involves, you quickly realize that **raiseToPower** needs to know the base, which in this case is the constant 2, and the exponent, which is currently stored in the variable **i**. That variable, however, is declared within the body of the **main** function and is accessible only within the main program. If **raiseToPower** is to have access to the value of the base and exponent, the main program must pass them as arguments to the function by including them in parentheses after the function name. Doing so copies those values into the corresponding parameters, as described in the next section.

As was true in the **HelloWorld** program as well, the final statement in **main** is

```
    return 0;
```

This statement indicates that the value of the **main** function is 0. By convention, C++ uses the value of the **main** function to report the status of the entire program. A value of 0 indicates success; any other value is taken as an indication of failure.

Function definitions

Because large programs are difficult to understand in their entirety, most programs are broken down into several smaller functions, each of which is easier to understand. In the **PowersOfTwo** program, the **raiseToPower** function is used to raise an integer to a power—an operation that is not built into C++ and must therefore be defined explicitly.

The first line of **raiseToPower** is the variable declaration

```
    int result = 1;
```

This declaration introduces a new variable named **result** capable of holding values of type **int** and initializes it to have the value 1.

The next statement in the function is a **for** loop—similar to the one you've already seen in the main program—that executes its body **k** times. The body of the **for** loop consists of the line

```
        result *= n;
```

which is C++ shorthand for the English sentence "Multiply **result** by **n**." Because the function initializes the value of **result** to 1 and then multiplies **result** by n a total of **k** times, the variable **result** ends up with the value n^k.

The last statement in **raiseToPower** is

```
    return result;
```

which indicates that the function should return **result** as the value of the function.

1.5 Variables

Data values in a program are usually stored in *variables,* which are named locations in memory capable of holding a particular data type. You have already seen examples of variables in the **PowersOfTwo** program and are almost certainly familiar with the basic concept from your earlier programming experience. The purpose of this section is to outline the rules for using variables in C++.

Variable declarations

In C++, you must *declare* each variable before you use it. The primary function of declaring a variable is to make an association between the *name* of the variable and the *type* of value that variable contains. The placement of the declaration in a program also determines the *scope* of the variable, which is the region in which that variable is accessible.

The usual syntax for declaring a variable is

```
    type namelist;
```

where *type* indicates the data type and *namelist* is a list of variable names separated by commas. In most cases, each declaration introduces a single variable name. For example, the function **main** in **PowersOfTwo** begins with the line

```
    int limit;
```

which declares the variable **limit** to be of type **int**. You can, however, declare several variable names at once, as in the following declaration, which declares three variables named **n1, n2,** and **n3**:

```
    double n1, n2, n3;
```

In this case, the variables are each declared to be of type **double**, which is the type C++ uses to represent numbers that can have fractional parts. The name *double* is short for *double-precision floating-point,* but there is no reason to worry about what all those terms mean. This declaration appears in the **AddThreeNumbers** program in Figure 1-4, which reads in three numbers and writes out their sum.

It is important to remember that both the name and the type of a variable remain fixed throughout its lifetime but that the value of that variable will typically change as the program runs. To emphasize the dynamic nature of the value of a variable, it often helps to diagram variables as boxes in which the name appears outside as a label on the box and the value appears inside. For example, you might diagram the declaration of `limit` like this:

limit

Assigning a value to `limit` overwrites any previous contents of the box, but does not change the name or the type.

In C++, the initial contents of a variable are undefined. If you want a variable to have a particular value, you need to initialize it explicitly. To do so, all you need to do is include an equal sign and a value after a variable name. Thus, the declaration

```
int result = 1;
```

FIGURE 1-4 **Program to add three numbers**

```
/*
 * File: AddThreeNumbers.cpp
 * --------------------------
 * This program adds three floating-point numbers and prints their sum.
 */

#include <iostream>
using namespace std;

int main() {
    double n1, n2, n3;
    cout << "This program adds three numbers." << endl;
    cout << "1st number: ";
    cin >> n1;
    cout << "2nd number: ";
    cin >> n2;
    cout << "3rd number: ";
    cin >> n3;
    double sum = n1 + n2 + n3;
    cout << "The sum is " << sum << endl;
    return 0;
}
```

is a shorthand for the following code, in which the declaration and assignment are separate:

```
int result;
result = 1;
```

An initial value specified as part of a declaration is called an ***initializer.***

Naming conventions

The names used for variables, functions, types, constants, and so forth are collectively known as ***identifiers.*** In C++, the rules for identifier formation are

1. The name must start with a letter or the underscore character (_).

2. All other characters in the name must be letters, digits, or the underscore. No spaces or other special characters are permitted in names.

3. The name must not be one of the reserved keywords listed in Table 1-1.

Uppercase and lowercase letters appearing in an identifier are considered to be different. Thus, the name **ABC** is not the same as the name **abc**. Identifiers can be of any length, but C++ compilers are not required to consider any more than the first 31 characters in determining whether two names are identical.

You can improve your programming style by adopting conventions for identifiers that help readers identify their function. In this text, names of variables and functions begin with a lowercase letter, such as **limit** or **raiseToPower**. The names of classes and other programmer-defined data types begin with an uppercase letter, as in **Direction** or **TokenScanner**. Constant values are written entirely in uppercase, as in **PI** or **HALF_DOLLAR**. Whenever an identifier consists of several English words run together, the usual convention is to capitalize the first letter of

TABLE 1-1	Reserved words in C++			
asm	do	inline	short	typeid
auto	double	int	signed	typename
bool	dynamic_cast	long	sizeof	union
break	else	mutable	static	unsigned
case	enum	namespace	static_cast	using
catch	explicit	new	struct	virtual
char	extern	operator	switch	void
class	false	private	template	volatile
const	float	protected	this	wchar_t
const_cast	for	public	throw	while
continue	friend	register	true	
default	goto	reinterpret_cast	try	
delete	if	return	typedef	

each word to make the name easier to read. Because that strategy doesn't work for constants, programmers use the underscore character to mark the word boundaries.

Local and global variables

Most variables are declared within the body of a function. Such variables are called *local variables.* The scope of a local variable extends to the end of the block in which it is declared. When the function is called, space for each local variable is allocated for the duration of that function call. When the function returns, all its local variables disappear.

If a variable declaration appears outside any function definition, that declaration introduces a *global variable.* The scope of a global variable is the remainder of the file in which it is declared, and it exists throughout the execution of a program. Global variables are therefore able to store values that persist across function calls. While that property may seem useful, the disadvantages of global variables easily outweigh their advantages. For one thing, global variables can be manipulated by any function in a program, and it is difficult to keep those functions from interfering with one another. Because of the problems they so often cause, global variables are not used in this text except to declare constants, as discussed in the following section. Although global variables may sometimes seem tempting, you will find it easier to manage the complexity of your programs if you avoid them.

Constants

As you write your programs, you will find that you often use the same constant many times in a program. If, for example, you are performing geometrical calculations that involve circles, the constant π comes up frequently. Moreover, if those calculations require high precision, you might actually need all the digits that fit into a value of type **double**, which means you would be working with the value 3.14159265358979323846. Writing that constant over and over again is tedious at best, and likely to introduce errors if you type it in by hand each time instead of cutting and pasting the value. It would be better if you could give this constant a name and then refer to it by that name everywhere in the program. You could, of course, simply declare **pi** as a local variable by writing

```
double pi = 3.14159265358979323846;
```

but you would then be able to use it only within the method in which it was defined. A better strategy is to declare a global constant named **PI** like this:

```
const double PI = 3.14159265358979323846;
```

The keyword **const** at the beginning of this declaration indicates that the value will not change after the variable is initialized, which ensures that the value remains constant. It would not be appropriate, after all, to change the value of π (despite the fact that a bill attempting to do just that was introduced in the Indiana State Legislature in 1897). The rest of the declaration consists of the type, the name, and the value, as before. The only difference is that the name is written entirely in upper case to be consistent with the C++ naming conventions for constants.

Using named constants offers several advantages. First, descriptive constant names make the program easier to read. More importantly, using constants can dramatically simplify the problem of maintaining the code for a program as it evolves. Even if the value of **PI** is unlikely to change, some "constants" in a program specify values that might change as the program evolves, even though they remain constant for a particular version of that program.

The importance of this principle is easiest to illustrate by historical example. Imagine for the moment that you are a programmer in the late 1960s working on the initial design of the *ARPANET,* the first large-scale computer network and the ancestor of today's Internet. Because resource constraints were quite serious at that time, you would need to impose a limit—as the actual designers of the ARPANET did in 1969—on the number of host computers that could be connected. In the early years of the ARPANET, that limit was 127 hosts. If C++ had existed in those days, you might have declared a constant that looked like this:

```
const int MAXIMUM_NUMBER_OF_HOSTS = 127;
```

At some later point, however, the explosive growth of networking would force you to raise this bound. That process would be relatively easy if you used named constants in your programs. To raise the limit on the number of hosts to 1023, it might well be sufficient to change this declaration so that it reads

```
const int MAXIMUM_NUMBER_OF_HOSTS = 1023;
```

If you used **MAXIMUM_NUMBER_OF_HOSTS** everywhere in your program to refer to that maximum value, making this change would automatically propagate to every part of the program in which the name was used.

Note that the situation would be entirely different if you had used the numeric constant 127 instead. In that case, you would need to search through the entire program and change all instances of 127 used for this purpose to the larger value. Some instances of 127 might well refer to other things than the limit on the number of hosts, and it would be just as important not to change any of those values. In the likely event that you made a mistake, you would have a very hard time tracking down the bug.

1.6 Data types

Each variable in a C++ program contains a value constrained to be of a particular type. You set the type of the variable as part of the declaration. So far, you have seen variables of type `int` and `double`, but these types merely scratch the surface of the types available in C++. Programs today work with many different data types, some of which are built into the language and some of which are defined as part of a particular application. Learning how to manipulate data of various types is an essential part of mastering the basics of any language, including C++.

The concept of a data type

In C++, every data value has an associated data type. From a formal perspective, a *data type* is defined by two properties: a *domain,* which is the set of values that belong to that type, and a *set of operations,* which defines the behavior of that type. For example, the domain of the type `int` includes all integers

$$. . . -9, -8, -7, -6, -5, -4, -3, -2, -1, 0, 1, 2, 3, 4, 5, 6, 7, 8, 9 . . .$$

and so on, up to the limits established by the hardware of the machine. The set of operations applicable to values of type `int` includes, for example, the standard arithmetic operations like addition and multiplication. Other types have a different domain and set of operations.

As you will learn in later chapters, much of the power of modern programming languages like C++ comes from the fact that you can define new data types from existing ones. To get that process started, C++ includes several fundamental types that are defined as part of the language. These types, which act as the building blocks for the type system as a whole, are called *atomic* or *primitive types.* These predefined types are grouped into five categories—integer, floating-point, Boolean, character, and enumerated types—which are discussed in the sections that follow.

Integer types

Although the concept of an integer seems like a simple one, C++ actually includes several different data types for representing integer values. In most cases, all you need to know is the type `int`, which corresponds to the standard representation of an integer on the computer system you are using. In certain cases, however, you need to be more careful. Like all data, values of type `int` are stored internally in storage units that have a limited capacity. Those values therefore have a maximum size, which limits the range of integers you can use. To get around this problem, C++ defines three integer types—`short`, `int`, and `long`—distinguished from each other by the size of their domains.

Unfortunately, the language definition for C++ does not specify an exact range for these three types. As a result, the range for the different integer types depends on the machine and the compiler you're using. In the early years of computing, the maximum value of type **int** was typically 32,767, which is very small by today's standards. If you had wanted, for example, to perform a calculation involving the number of seconds in a year, you could not have used type **int** on those machines, because that value (31,536,000) is considerably larger than 32,767. Modern machines tend to support larger integers, but the only properties you can count on are the following:

- The internal size of an integer cannot decrease as you move from **short** to **int** to **long**. A compiler designer for C++ could, for example, decide to make **short** and **int** the same size but could not make **int** smaller than **short**.

- The maximum value of type **int** must be at least 32,767 ($2^{15}-1$).

- The maximum value of type **long** must be at least 2,147,483,647 ($2^{31}-1$).

The designers of C++ could have chosen to define the allowable range of type **int** more precisely. For example, they could have declared—as the designers of Java did—that the maximum value of type **int** would be $2^{31}-1$ on every machine. Had they done so, it would be easier to move a program from one system to another and have it behave in the same way. The ability to move a program between different machines is called *portability,* which is an important consideration in the design of a programming language.

In C++, each of the integer types **int**, **long**, and **short** may be preceded by the keyword **unsigned**. Adding **unsigned** creates a new data type in which no negative values are allowed. Unsigned values also offer twice the range of positive values when compared to their signed counterparts. On modern machines, for example, the maximum value of type **int** is typically 2,147,483,647, but the maximum value of type **unsigned int** is 4,294,967,295. C++ allows the type **unsigned int** to be abbreviated to **unsigned**, and most programmers who use this type tend to follow this practice.

An integer constant is ordinarily written as a string of decimal digits. If the number begins with the digit 0, however, the compiler interprets the value as an octal (base 8) integer. Thus, the constant **040** is taken to be in octal and represents the decimal number 32. If you prefix a numeric constant with the characters **0x**, the compiler interprets that number as hexadecimal (base 16). Thus, the constant **0xFF** is equivalent to the decimal constant 255. You can explicitly indicate that an integer constant is of type **long** by adding the letter **L** at the end of the digit string. Thus, the constant **0L** is equal to 0, but the value is explicitly of type **long**. Similarly, if you use the letter **U** as a suffix, the constant is taken to be unsigned.

Floating-point types

Numbers that include a decimal fraction are called *floating-point numbers,* which are used to approximate real numbers in mathematics. C++ defines three different floating-point types: `float`, `double`, and `long double`. Although ANSI C++ does not specify the exact representation of these types, the way to think about the difference is that the longer types—where `long double` is longer than `double`, which is in turn longer than `float`—allow numbers to be represented with greater precision at the cost of occupying more memory space. Unless you are doing exacting scientific calculation, however, the differences between these types will not make a great deal of difference. In keeping with a common convention among C++ programmers, this text uses the type `double` as its standard floating-point type.

Floating-point constants in C++ are written with a decimal point. Thus, if `2.0` appears in a program, the number is represented internally as a floating-point value; if the programmer had written `2`, this value would be an integer. Floating-point values can also be written in a special programmer's style of scientific notation, in which the value is represented as a floating-point number multiplied by an integral power of 10. To write a number using this style, you write a floating-point number in standard notation, followed immediately by the letter `E` and an integer exponent, optionally preceded by a + or – sign. For example, the speed of light in meters per second can be written in C++ as

        `2.9979E+8`

where the `E` stands for the words *times 10 to the power.*

Boolean type

In the programs you write, it is often necessary to test a particular condition that affects the subsequent behavior of your code. Typically, that condition is specified using an expression whose value is either true or false. This data type—for which the only legal values are the constants `true` and `false`—is called *Boolean data,* after the mathematician George Boole, who developed an algebraic approach for working with such values.

In C++, the Boolean type is called `bool`. You can declare variables of type `bool` and manipulate them in the same way as other data objects. The operations that apply to the type `bool` are described in detail in the section entitled "Boolean operators" on page 34.

Characters

In the early days, computers were designed to work only with numeric data and were sometimes called **number crunchers** as a result. Modern computers, however, work less with numeric data than they do with text data, that is, any information composed of individual characters that appear on the keyboard and the screen. The ability of modern computers to process text data has led to the development of word processing systems, online reference libraries, electronic mail, social networks, and a seemingly infinite supply of exciting applications.

The most primitive elements of text data are individual characters, which are represented in C++ using the predefined data type **char**. The domain of type **char** is the set of symbols that can be displayed on the screen or typed on the keyboard: the letters, digits, punctuation marks, space, RETURN, and so forth. Internally, these values are represented inside the computer by assigning each character a numeric code. In most implementations of C++, the coding system used to represent characters is called **ASCII,** which stands for the **American Standard Code for Information Interchange.** The decimal values of the characters in the ASCII set are shown in Table 1-2, where the ASCII code for any character is the sum of the numbers at the beginning of its row and column.

Although it is important to know that characters are represented internally using a numeric code, it is not generally useful to know what numeric value corresponds

TABLE 1-2 ASCII character codes

	0	1	2	3	4	5	6	7	8	9
0x	\000	\001	\002	\003	\004	\005	\006	\a	\b	\t
1x	\n	\v	\f	\r	\016	\017	\020	\021	\022	\023
2x	\024	\025	\026	\027	\030	\031	\032	\033	\034	\035
3x	\036	\037	*space*	!	"	#	$	%	&	'
4x	(	)	*	+	,	−	.	/	0	1
5x	2	3	4	5	6	7	8	9	:	;
6x	<	=	>	?	@	A	B	C	D	E
7x	F	G	H	I	J	K	L	M	N	O
8x	P	Q	R	S	T	U	V	W	X	Y
9x	Z	[	\	]	^	_	`	a	b	c
10x	d	e	f	g	h	i	j	k	l	m
11x	n	o	p	q	r	s	t	u	v	w
12x	x	y	z	{	|	}	~	\177		

to a particular character. When you type the letter *A*, the hardware logic built into the keyboard automatically translates that character into the ASCII code 65, which is then sent to the computer. Similarly, when the computer sends the ASCII code 65 to the screen, the letter *A* appears.

You can write a character constant in C++ by enclosing the character in single quotes. Thus, the constant `'A'` represents the internal code of the uppercase letter *A*. In addition to the standard characters, C++ allows you to write special characters in a multicharacter form beginning with a backward slash (\). This form is called an *escape sequence.* Table 1-3 shows the escape sequences that C++ supports.

Strings

Characters are most useful when they are collected together into sequential units. In programming, a sequence of characters is called a *string.* So far, the strings you've seen in the `HelloWorld` and `PowersOfTwo` programs have been used simply to display messages on the screen, but strings have many more applications than that.

You write string constants in C++ by enclosing the characters contained within the string in double quotes. As with the data type `char`, C++ uses the escape sequences in Table 1-3 to represent special characters. If two or more string constants appear consecutively in a program, the compiler concatenates them together. The most important implication of this rule is that you can break a long string over several lines so that it doesn't run past the right margin of your program.

TABLE 1-3 Escape sequences

\a	Audible alert (beeps or rings a bell)
\b	Backspace
\f	Formfeed (starts a new page)
\n	Newline (moves to the beginning of the next line)
\r	Return (returns to the beginning of the current line without advancing)
\t	Tab (moves horizontally to the next tab stop)
\v	Vertical tab (moves vertically to the next tab stop)
\0	The *null character* (the character whose ASCII code is 0)
\\	The character \ itself
\'	The character ' (requires the backslash only in character constants)
\"	The character " (requires the backslash only in string constants)
\ddd	The character whose ASCII code is the octal number *ddd*

Since strings are essential to so many applications, all modern programming languages include special features for working with them. Unfortunately, C++ complicates the issue by defining two different string types: an older style inherited from C and a more sophisticated **string** library that supports the object-oriented paradigm. To minimize confusion, this text uses the **string** library wherever possible, and you should—for the most part—feel free to ignore the fact that two string models exist. The times when that complexity raises its ugly head are outlined in Chapter 3, which covers the **string** library in more detail. For the moment, you can simply imagine that C++ offers a built-in data type called **string** whose domain is the set of all sequences of characters. You can declare variables of type **string** and pass string values back and forth between functions as arguments and results.

The fact that **string** is a library type and not a built-in feature does have a few implications. If you use the type name **string** in a program, you need to add the **string** library to the list of **#include** lines, like this:

```
#include <string>
```

Moreover, because the **string** type is part of the standard library namespace, the compiler will recognize the type name only if you have included the line

```
using namespace std;
```

at the beginning of the file, as the programs in this book invariably do.

Enumerated types

As the discussion of ASCII codes in the preceding section makes clear, computers store character data in integer form by assigning a number to each character. This strategy of encoding data as integers by numbering the elements of the domain in fact represents a more general principle. C++ allows you to define new types by listing the elements in their domain. Such types are called ***enumerated types.***

The syntax for defining an enumerated type is

```
enum typename { namelist };
```

where *typename* is the name of the new type and *namelist* is a list of the constants in the domain, separated by commas. In this book, all type names start with an uppercase letter, and the names of the enumeration constants are written entirely in upper case. For example, the following definition introduces a new **Direction** type whose values are the four compass directions:

```
enum Direction { NORTH, EAST, SOUTH, WEST };
```

When the C++ compiler encounters this definition, it assigns values to the constant names by numbering them consecutively starting with 0. Thus, **NORTH** is assigned the value 0, **EAST** is assigned the value 1, **SOUTH** is assigned the value 2, and **WEST** is assigned the value 3.

C++ allows you to assign explicit underlying values to each of the constants of an enumerated type. For example, the type declaration

```
enum Coin {
    PENNY = 1,
    NICKEL = 5,
    DIME = 10,
    QUARTER = 25,
    HALF_DOLLAR = 50,
    DOLLAR = 100
};
```

introduces an enumerated type for U.S. coinage in which each constant is defined to equal the monetary value of that coin. If you supply values for some of the constants but not others, the C++ compiler will automatically choose values for the unassigned constants by numbering them consecutively after the last value you supplied. Thus, the type declaration

```
enum Month {
    JANUARY = 1,
    FEBRUARY,
    MARCH,
    APRIL,
    MAY,
    JUNE,
    JULY,
    AUGUST,
    SEPTEMBER,
    OCTOBER,
    NOVEMBER,
    DECEMBER
};
```

introduces a type for the months of the year in which **JANUARY** has the value 1, **FEBRUARY** has the value 2, and so forth up to **DECEMBER**, which has the value 12.

Compound types

The atomic types described in the preceding sections form the basis of a very rich type system that allows you to create new types from existing ones. Moreover, because C++ represents a synthesis of the object-oriented and procedural paradigms, the type system includes both objects and more traditional structures. Learning how to define and manipulate these types is, to a large extent, the theme of this entire book. It therefore does not make sense to squeeze a complete description of these types into Chapter 1. That's what the rest of the chapters are for.

Over many years of teaching this material at Stanford, we have discovered that you are much more likely to master the concepts of object-oriented programming if the details of defining classes and objects are presented *after* you have had a chance to use them in a high-level way. This book adopts that strategy and postpones any discussion of how to create your own objects until Chapter 6, at which point you will have had plenty of time to discover just how useful objects can be.

1.7 Expressions

Whenever you want a program to perform calculations, you need to write an expression that specifies the necessary operations in a form similar to that used for expressions in mathematics. For example, suppose that you wanted to solve the quadratic equation

$$ax^2 + bx + c = 0$$

As you know from high-school mathematics, this equation has two solutions given by the formula

$$x = \frac{-b \pm \sqrt{b^2 - 4ac}}{2a}$$

The first solution is obtained by using + in place of the ± symbol; the second is obtained by using – instead. In C++, you could compute the first of these solutions by writing the following expression:

```
(-b + sqrt(b * b - 4 * a * c)) / (2 * a)
```

There are a few differences in form: multiplication is represented explicitly by a *, division is represented by a /, and the square root function (which comes from a library called **<cmath>** described in Chapter 2) is written using the name **sqrt** rather than a mathematical symbol. Even so, the C++ form of the expression captures the intent of its mathematical counterpart in a way that is quite readable, particularly if you've written programs in any modern programming language.

In C++, an expression is composed of terms and operators. A *term,* such as the variables **a, b,** and **c** or the constants 2 and 4 in the preceding expression, represents a single data value and must be either a constant, a variable, or a function call. An *operator* is a character (or sometimes a short sequence of characters) that indicates a computational operation.   A list of the operators available in C++ appears in Table 1-4. The table includes familiar arithmetic operators like + and – along with several others that pertain only to types introduced in later chapters.

Precedence and associativity

The point of listing all the operators in a single table is to establish how they relate to one another in terms of *precedence,* which is a measure of how tightly an operator binds to its operands in the absence of parentheses. If two operators compete for the same operand, the one that appears higher in the precedence table is applied first. Thus, in the expression

```
(-b + sqrt(b * b - 4 * a * c)) / (2 * a)
```

the multiplications **b * b** and **4 * a * c** are performed before the subtraction because * has a higher precedence than –. It is, however, important to note that the – operator occurs in two forms. Operators that connect two operands are called *binary operators*; operators that take just one operand arc called *unary operators.* When a minus sign is written in front of a single operand, as in **-b**, it is interpreted as a unary operator signifying negation. When it appears between two operands, as it does inside the argument to **sqrt**, the minus sign is a binary operator signifying

TABLE. 1-4 Operators available in C++

Operators organized into precedence groups	Associativity
() [] -> .	*left*
unary operators: – ++ -- ! & * ~ *(type)* sizeof	*right*
* / %	*left*
+ –	*left*
<< >>	*left*
< <= > >=	*left*
== !=	*left*
&	*left*
^	*left*
|	*left*
&&	*left*
||	*left*
?:	*right*
= *op=*	*right*

subtraction. The precedence of the unary and binary versions of an operator are different and are listed separately in the precedence table.

If two operators have the same precedence, they are applied in the order specified by their *associativity,* which indicates whether that operator groups to the left or to the right. Most operators in C++ are *left-associative,* which means that the leftmost operator is evaluated first. A few operators—most notably the assignment operator discussed in its own section later in this chapter—are *right-associative,* which mean that they group from right to left. The associativity for each operator appears in Table 1-4.

The quadratic formula illustrates the importance of paying attention to precedence and associativity rules. Consider what would happen if you wrote the expression without the parentheses around **2 * a**, as follows:

```
(-b + sqrt(b * b - 4 * a * c)) / 2 * a
```

Without the parentheses, the division operator would be performed first because **/** and ***** have the same precedence and associate to the left. This example illustrates the use of the bug icon to mark code that is intentionally incorrect so that you won't copy it into your own programs.

Mixing types in an expression

In C++, you can write an expression that includes values of different numeric types. If C++ encounters an operator whose operands are of different types, the compiler automatically converts the operands to a common type by choosing the type that appears closest to the top of the hierarchy in Table 1-5. The result of applying the operation is always that of the arguments after any conversions are applied. This convention ensures that the result of the computation is as precise as possible.

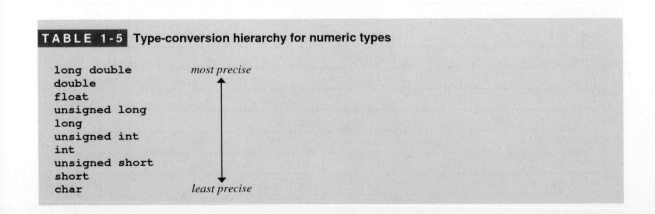

TABLE 1-5 Type-conversion hierarchy for numeric types

```
long double          most precise
double
float
unsigned long
long
unsigned int
int
unsigned short
short
char                 least precise
```

As an example, suppose that **n** is declared as an **int**, and **x** is declared as a **double**. The expression

    n + 1

is evaluated using integer arithmetic and produces a result of type **int**. The expression

    x + 1

however, is evaluated by converting the integer 1 to the floating-point value 1.0 and adding the results together using double-precision floating-point arithmetic, which results in a value of type **double**.

Integer division and the remainder operator

The fact that applying an operator to two integer operands generates an integer result leads to an interesting situation with respect to the division operator. If you write an expression like

    9 / 4

C++'s rules specify that the result of this operation must be an integer, because both operands are of type **int**. When C++ evaluates this expression, it divides 9 by 4 and discards any remainder. Thus, the value of this expression in C++ is 2, not 2.25.

If you want to compute the mathematically correct result of 9 divided by 4, at least one of the operands must be a floating-point number. For example, the three expressions

    9.0 / 4
    9 / 4.0
    9.0 / 4.0

each produce the floating-point value 2.25. The decimal fraction is thrown away only if both operands are of type **int**. The operation of discarding a decimal fraction is called *truncation.*

The / operator in C++ is closely associated with the % operator, which returns the remainder left over when the first operand is divided by the second. For example, the value of

    9 % 4

is 1, since 4 goes into 9 twice, with 1 left over. The following are some other examples of the % operator:

```
0 % 4  =  0             19 % 4  =  3
1 % 4  =  1             20 % 4  =  0
4 % 4  =  0           2001 % 4  =  1
```

The / and % operators are extremely useful in a wide variety of programming applications. You can, for example, use the % operator to test whether one number is divisible by another; to determine whether an integer **n** is divisible by 3, you just check whether the result of the expression **n % 3** is 0.

It is, however, important to use caution if either or both of the operands to / and % might be negative, because the results may differ from machine to machine. On most machines, division truncates its result toward 0, but this behavior is not actually guaranteed by the ANSI standard. In general, it is good programming practice to avoid—as this book does—using these operators with negative values.

Type casts

In C++, you can convert one type to another by using what is called a *type cast,* which specifies an explicit conversion action. In C++, type casts are usually written by specifying the name of the desired type, followed by the value you wish to convert in parentheses. For example, if **num** and **den** are declared as integers, you can compute the floating-point quotient by writing

```
quotient = double(num) / den;
```

The first step in evaluating the expression is to convert **num** to a **double**, after which the division is performed using floating-point arithmetic, as described in the section on "Mixing types in an expression" earlier in this chapter.

As long as the conversion moves upward in the hierarchy shown in Table 1-5, the conversion involves no loss of information. If, however, you convert a value of a more precise type to a less precise one, some information may be lost. For example, if you use a type cast to convert a value of type **double** to type **int**, any decimal fraction is simply dropped. Thus, the value of the expression

```
int(1.9999)
```

is the integer 1.

The assignment operator

In C++, assignment of values to variables is built into the structure of the expression. The = operator takes two operands, just like + or *. The left operand must indicate a value that can change, which is typically a variable name. When the assignment operator is executed, the expression on the right-hand side is evaluated, and the resulting value is then stored in the variable that appears on the left-hand side. Thus, if you evaluate an expression like

```
result = 1
```

the effect is that the value 1 is assigned to the variable **result**. In most cases, assignment expressions of this sort appear in the context of simple statements, which are formed by adding a semicolon after the expression, as in the line

```
result = 1;
```

Such statements are often called *assignment statements.*

The assignment operator converts the type of the value on the right-hand side so that it matches the declared type of the variable. Thus, if the variable **total** is declared to be of type **double**, and you write the assignment statement

```
total = 0;
```

C++ automatically converts the integer 0 into a **double** as part of making the assignment. If **n** is declared to be of type **int**, the assignment

```
n = 3.14159265;
```

has the effect of setting **n** to 3, because the value is truncated to fit in the integer variable.

Even though assignment operators usually occur in the context of simple statements, they can also be incorporated into larger expressions, in which case the result of applying the assignment operator is simply the value assigned. For example, the expression

```
z = (x = 6) + (y = 7)
```

has the effect of setting **x** to 6, **y** to 7, and **z** to 13. The parentheses are required in this example because the **=** operator has a lower precedence than **+**. Assignments that are written as part of larger expressions are called *embedded assignments.*

Although there are contexts in which embedded assignments are convenient, they often make programs more difficult to read because the assignment is easily overlooked in the middle of a complex expression. For this reason, this text limits the use of embedded assignments to a few special circumstances in which they seem to make the most sense. Of these, the most important is when you want to set several variables to the same value. C++'s definition of assignment as an operator makes it possible, instead of writing separate assignment statements, to write a single statement like

```
n1 = n2 = n3 = 0;
```

which has the effect of setting all three variables to 0. This statement works because C++ evaluates assignment operators from right to left. The entire statement is therefore equivalent to

```
n1 = (n2 = (n3 = 0));
```

C++ evaluates the expression **n3 = 0** first, which sets **n3** to 0. It also passes 0 along as the value of the assignment expression, which is then assigned to **n2** and subsequently to **n1**. Statements of this sort are called *multiple assignments.*

As a programming convenience, C++ allows you to combine assignment with a binary operator to produce a form called a *shorthand assignment.* For any binary operator *op*, the statement

    variable op= expression;

is equivalent to

    variable = variable op (expression);

where the parentheses are included to emphasize that the entire expression is evaluated before *op* is applied. Thus, the statement

```
balance += deposit;
```

is a shorthand for

```
balance = balance + deposit;
```

which adds **deposit** to **balance**.

Because this same shorthand applies to any binary operator in C++, you can subtract the value of **surcharge** from **balance** by writing

```
balance -= surcharge;
```

Similarly, you can divide the value of **x** by 10 using

```
x /= 10;
```

Increment and decrement operators

Beyond the shorthand assignment operators, C++ offers a further level of abbreviation for the particularly common programming operations of adding or subtracting 1 from a variable. Adding 1 to a variable is called **incrementing** it; subtracting 1 is called **decrementing** it. To indicate these operations in an extremely compact form, C++ uses the operators ++ and --. For example, in C++ the statement

```
x++;
```

has the same effect on the variable **x** as

```
x += 1;
```

which is itself short for

```
x = x + 1;
```

Similarly,

```
y--;
```

has the same effect as

```
y -= 1;
```

or

```
y = y - 1;
```

As it happens, these operators are more intricate than the preceding examples would suggest. To begin with, each of these operators can be written in two ways. The operator can come after the operand to which it applies, as in

```
x++
```

or before the operand, as in

```
++x
```

The first form, in which the operator follows the operand, is called the **suffix** form, the second, the **prefix** form.

If all you do is execute the ++ operator in isolation—as you do in the context of a separate statement or the standard **for** loop patterns—the prefix and suffix operators have precisely the same effect. You notice the difference only if you use these operators as part of a larger expression. Then, like all operators, the **++** operator returns a value, but the value depends on where the operator is written relative to the operand. The two cases are as follows:

x++   Calculates the value of **x** first, and then increments it. The value returned to the surrounding expression is the original value *before* the increment operation is performed.

++x   Increments the value of **x** first, and then uses the new value as the value of the **++** operation as a whole.

The **--** operator behaves similarly, except that the value is decremented rather than incremented.

You may wonder why would anyone use such an arcane feature. The **++** and **--** operators are certainly not essential. Moreover, there are not many circumstances in which programs that embed these operators in larger expressions are demonstrably better than those that use a simpler approach. On the other hand, **++** and **--** are firmly entrenched in the historical tradition shared by the languages C, C++, and Java. Programmers use them so frequently that they have become essential idioms in these languages. In light of their widespread use in programs, you need to understand these operators so that you can make sense of existing code.

Boolean operators

C++ defines three classes of operators that manipulate Boolean data: the relational operators, the logical operators, and the **?:** operator. The ***relational operators*** are used to compare two values. C++ defines six relational operators, as follows:

==	Equal
!=	Not equal
>	Greater than
<	Less than
>=	Greater than or equal to
<=	Less than or equal to

When you write programs that test for equality, be careful to use the **==** operator, which is composed of two equal signs. A single equal sign is the assignment operator. Since the double equal sign violates conventional mathematical usage, replacing it with a single equal sign is a particularly common mistake. This mistake can also be very difficult to track down, because the C++ compiler does not usually catch it as an error. A single equal sign turns the expression into an embedded assignment, which is perfectly legal in C++; it just isn't at all what you want.

The relational operators can be used to compare atomic data values like integers, floating-point numbers, Boolean values, and characters, but those operators can also be applied to many of the types supplied by libraries, such as **string**.

In addition to the relational operators, C++ defines three *logical operators* that take Boolean operands and combine them to form other Boolean values:

!	Logical *not* (**true** if the following operand is **false**)
&&	Logical *and* (**true** if both operands are **true**)
||	Logical *or* (**true** if either or both operands are **true**)

These operators are listed in decreasing order of precedence.

Although the operators **&&**, **||**, and **!** closely resemble the English words *and*, *or*, and *not*, it is important to remember that English can be somewhat imprecise when it comes to logic. To avoid that imprecision, it is often helpful to think of these operators in a more formal, mathematical way. Logicians define these operators using *truth tables,* which show how the value of a Boolean expression changes as the values of its operands change. The truth table in Table 1-6 illustrates the result for each of the logical operators, given all possible values of the variables **p** and **q**.

Whenever a C++ program evaluates an expression of the form

exp_1 **&&** exp_2

or

exp_1 **||** exp_2

the individual subexpressions are always evaluated from left to right, and evaluation ends as soon as the result is determined. For example, if exp_1 is **false** in the expression involving **&&**, there is no need to evaluate exp_2, since the final result will always be **false**. Similarly, in the example using **||**, there is no need to evaluate the second operand if the first operand is **true**. This style of evaluation, which stops as soon as the result is known, is called *short-circuit evaluation.*

TABLE 1-6 Truth table for the logical operators

p	q	p && q	p || q	!p
false	false	false	false	true
false	true	false	true	true
true	false	false	true	false
true	true	true	true	false

The C++ programming language includes another Boolean operator called `?:` that can be extremely useful in certain situations. In programming parlance, the name of this operator is always pronounced as *question-mark colon*, even though the two characters do not appear adjacent to each other in the code. Unlike the other operators in C++, `?:` is written in two parts and requires three operands. The general form of the operation is

> (*condition*) ? *exp*$_1$: *exp*$_2$

The parentheses are not technically required, but C++ programmers often include them to emphasize the boundaries of the conditional test.

When a C++ program encounters the `?:` operator, it first evaluates the condition. If the condition turns out to be **true**, *exp*$_1$ is evaluated and used as the value of the entire expression; if the condition is **false**, the value is the result of evaluating *exp*$_2$. For example, you can use the `?:` operator to assign to **max** either the value of **x** or the value of **y**, whichever is greater, as follows:

```
max = (x > y) ? x : y;
```

1.8 Statements

Programs in C++ are composed of functions, which are made up in turn of statements. As in most languages, statements in C++ fall into one of two principal classifications: *simple statements* that perform some action and *control statements* that affect the way in which other statements are executed. The sections that follow review the principal statement forms available in C++, giving you the tools you need to write your own programs.

Simple statements

The most common statement in C++ is the **simple statement,** which consists of an expression followed by a semicolon:

> *expression;*

In most cases, the expression is a function call, an assignment, or a variable followed by the increment or decrement operator.

Blocks

As C++ is defined, control statements typically apply to a single statement. When you are writing a program, you often want a particular control statement to apply to a whole group of statements. To indicate that a sequence of statements is part of a coherent unit, you can assemble those statements into a **block,** which is a collection of statements enclosed in curly braces, as follows:

```
{
      statement₁
      statement₂
      . . .
      statementₙ
}
```

When the C++ compiler encounters a block, it treats the entire block as a single statement. Thus, whenever the notation *statement* appears in a pattern for one of the control forms, you can substitute for it either a single statement or a block. To emphasize that they are statements as far as the compiler is concerned, blocks are sometimes referred to as *compound statements.* In C++, the statements in any block may be preceded by declarations of variables.

The statements in the interior of a block are usually indented relative to the enclosing context. The compiler ignores the indentation, but the visual effect is extremely helpful to the human reader, because it makes the structure of the program jump out at you from the format of the page. Empirical research has shown that indenting three or four spaces at each new level makes the program structure easiest to see; the programs in this text use three spaces for each new level. Indentation is critical to good programming, so you should strive to develop a consistent indentation style in your programs.

The `if` statement

In writing a program, you will often want to check whether some condition applies and use the result of that check to control the subsequent execution of the program. This type of program control is called *conditional execution.* The easiest way to express conditional execution in C++ is by using the `if` statement, which comes in two forms:

> `if` (*condition*) *statement*
>
> `if` (*condition*) *statement* `else` *statement*

You use the first form of the `if` statement when your solution strategy calls for a set of statements to be executed only if a particular Boolean condition is `true`. If the condition is `false`, the statements that form the body of the `if` statement are simply skipped. You use the second form of the `if` statement for situations in which the program must choose between two independent sets of actions according to the result of a test. This statement form is illustrated by the following code, which reports whether an integer `n` is even or odd:

```
if (n % 2 == 0) {
   cout << "That number is even." << endl;
} else {
   cout << "That number is odd." << endl;
}
```

As with any control statement, the statements controlled by the **if** statement can be either a single statement or a block. Even if the body of a control form is a single statement, you are free to enclose it in a block if you decide that doing so improves the readability of your code. The programs in this book enclose the body of every control statement in a block unless the entire statement—both the control form and its body—is so short that it fits on a single line.

The switch statement

The **if** statement is ideal for those applications in which the program logic calls for a two-way decision point: a condition is either **true** or **false**, and the program acts accordingly. Some applications, however, call for more complicated decision structures involving several mutually exclusive cases: in one case, the program should do *x;* in another case, it should do *y;* in a third, it should do *z;* and so forth. In many applications, the most appropriate statement to use for such situations is the **switch** statement, which has the following syntactic form:

```
switch (e) {
 case c₁:
    statements
    break;
 case c₂:
    statements
    break;
 . . . more case clauses . . .
 default:
    statements
    break;
}
```

The expression *e* is called the ***control expression.*** When the program executes a **switch** statement, it evaluates the control expression and compares it against the values c_1, c_2, and so forth, each of which must be a constant. If one of the constants matches the value of the control expression, the statements in the associated **case** clause are executed. When the program reaches the **break** statement at the end of the clause, the operations specified by that clause are complete, and the program continues with the statement that follows the entire **switch** statement.

The **default** clause is used to specify what action occurs if none of the constants match the value of the control expression. The **default** clause, however, is optional. If none of the cases match and there is no **default** clause, the program simply continues on with the next statement after the **switch** statement without taking any action at all. To avoid the possibility that the program might ignore an unexpected case, it is good programming practice to include a **default** clause in every **switch** statement unless you are certain you have enumerated all the possibilities.

The code pattern I've used to illustrate the syntax of the **switch** statement deliberately suggests that **break** statements are required at the end of each clause. In fact, C++ is defined so that if the **break** statement is missing, the program starts executing statements from the next clause after it finishes the selected one. While this design can be useful in some cases, it causes many more problems than it solves. To reinforce the importance of remembering to exit at the end of each **case** clause, the programs in this text include a **break** or **return** statement in each such clause.

The one exception to this rule is that multiple **case** lines specifying different constants can appear together, one after another, before the same statement group. For example, a **switch** statement might include the following code:

```
case 1:
case 2:
    statements
    break;
```

which indicates that the specified statements should be executed if the **select** expression is either 1 or 2. The C++ compiler treats this construction as two **case** clauses, the first of which is empty. Because the empty clause contains no **break** statement, a program that selects the first path simply continues on with the second clause. From a conceptual point of view, however, you are better off if you think of this construction as a single **case** clause representing two possibilities.

The constants in a **switch** statement must be a *scalar type,* which is defined in C++ as a type that uses an integer as its underlying representation. In particular, characters are often used as **case** constants, as illustrated by the following function, which tests to see if its argument is a vowel:

```
bool isVowel(char ch) {
   switch (ch) {
    case 'A': case 'E': case 'I': case 'O': case 'U':
    case 'a': case 'e': case 'i': case 'o': case 'u':
      return true;
    default:
      return false;
   }
}
```

Enumerated types also qualify as scalar types, as illustrated by the function

```
string directionToString(Direction dir) {
   switch (dir) {
    case NORTH: return "NORTH";
    case EAST: return "EAST";
    case SOUTH: return "SOUTH";
    case WEST: return "WEST";
    default: return "???";
   }
}
```

which converts a **Direction** value to a string. The **default** clause returns "???" if the internal value of **dir** does not match any of the **Direction** constants.

As a second example of using **switch** with enumerated types, the following function returns the number of days for a given month and year:

```
int daysInMonth(Month month, int year) {
   switch (month) {
    case APRIL:
    case JUNE:
    case SEPTEMBER:
    case NOVEMBER:
      return 30;
    case FEBRUARY:
      return (isLeapYear(year)) ? 29 : 28;
    default:
      return 31;
   }
}
```

This code assumes the existence of a function **isLeapYear(year)** that tests whether **year** is a leap year. You can implement **isLeapYear** using the logical operators **&&** and **||**, as follows:

```
bool isLeapYear(int year) {
   return ((year % 4 == 0) && (year % 100 != 0))
         || (year % 400 == 0);
}
```

This function simply encodes the rule for determining leap years: a leap year is any year divisible by 4, except for years ending in 00, in which case the year must be divisible by 400.

Functions that return Boolean values—like **isVowel** and **isLeapYear** in this section—are called ***predicate functions.*** Predicate functions play a useful role in programming, and you will encounter many of them in this text.

The while statement

In addition to the conditional statements **if** and **switch**, C++ includes several control statements that allow you to execute some part of the program multiple times to form a loop. Such control statements are called *iterative statements.* The simplest iterative statement in C++ is the **while** statement, which executes a statement repeatedly until a conditional expression becomes **false**. The general form for the **while** statement looks like this:

> **while** (*conditional-expression*) {
>   *statements*
> }

When a program encounters a **while** statement, it first evaluates the conditional expression to see whether it is **true** or **false**. If it is **false**, the loop ***terminates*** and the program continues with the next statement after the entire loop. If the condition is **true**, the entire body is executed, after which the program goes back to the beginning of the loop to check the condition again. A single pass through the statements in the body constitutes a *cycle* of the loop.

There are two important principles about the operation of a **while** loop:

1. The conditional test is performed before every cycle of the loop, including the first. If the test is **false** initially, the body of the loop is not executed at all.

2. The conditional test is performed only at the *beginning* of a loop cycle. If the condition becomes **false** at some point during the loop, the program won't notice that fact until it completes the entire cycle. At that point, the program evaluates the test condition again. If the condition is still **false**, the loop terminates.

The operation of the **while** loop is illustrated by the following function, which computes the sum of the digits in an integer:

```
int digitSum(int n) {
    int sum = 0;
    while (n > 0) {
        sum += n % 10;
        n /= 10;
    }
    return sum;
}
```

The function depends on the following observations:

- The expression n % 10 always returns the last digit in a positive integer n.
- The expression n / 10 returns a number without its final digit.

The while loop is designed for situations in which there is some test condition that can be applied at the beginning of a repeated operation, before any of the statements in the body of the loop are executed. If the problem you are trying to solve fits this structure, the while loop is the perfect tool. Unfortunately, many programming problems do not fit easily into the standard while loop structure. Instead of allowing a convenient test at the beginning of the operation, some problems are structured in such a way that the test you want to write to determine whether the loop is complete falls most naturally somewhere in the middle of the loop.

The most common example of such loops are those that read in data from the user until some special value, or *sentinel,* is entered to signal the end of the input. When expressed in English, the structure of the sentinel-based loop consists of repeating the following steps:

1. Read in a value.
2. If the value is equal to the sentinel, exit from the loop.
3. Perform whatever processing is required for that value.

Unfortunately, there is no test you can perform at the beginning of the loop to determine whether the loop is finished. The termination condition for the loop is reached when the input value is equal to the sentinel; in order to check this condition, the program must first read in some value. If the program has not yet read in a value, the termination condition doesn't make sense.

When some operations must be performed before you can check the termination condition, you have a situation that programmers call the *loop-and-a-half problem.* One strategy for solving the loop-and-a-half problem in C++ is to use the **break** statement, which, in addition to its use in the **switch** statement, has the effect of immediately terminating the innermost enclosing loop. Using **break**, it is possible to code the loop structure in a form that follows the natural structure of the problem, which is called the ***read-until-sentinel pattern:***

```
while (true) {
    Prompt user and read in a value.
    if (value == sentinel) break;
    Process the data value.
}
```

Note that the

```
while (true)
```

line itself seems to introduce an infinite loop because the value of the constant `true` can never become `false`. The only way this program can exit from the loop is by executing the `break` statement inside it. The `AddIntegerList` program in Figure 1-5 uses the read-until-sentinel pattern to compute the sum of a list of integers terminated by the sentinel value 0.

There are other strategies for solving the loop-and-a-half problem, most of which involve copying part of the code outside the loop or introducing additional Boolean variables. Empirical studies have demonstrated that students are more likely to write correct programs if they use a `break` statement to exit from the middle of the loop than if they are forced to use some other strategy. This evidence and my own experience have convinced me that using the read-until-sentinel pattern is the best solution to the loop-and-a-half problem.

The `for` statement

One of the most important control statements in C++ is the `for` statement, which is used in situations in which you want to repeat an operation a particular number of times. All modern programming languages have a statement that serves that purpose, but the `for` statement in the C family of languages is especially powerful and is useful in a wide variety of applications.

You have already seen two examples of the `for` loop in the `PowersOfTwo` program earlier in this chapter. The first appears in the main program, when it cycles through the desired values of the exponent. That loop looks like this:

```
for (int i = 0; i <= limit; i++) {
    cout << "2 to the " << i << " = "
        << raiseToPower(2, i) << endl;
}
```

FIGURE 1-5 Program to add a list of integers

```cpp
/*
 * File: AddIntegerList.cpp
 * -------------------------
 * This program adds a list of integers.  The end of the input is
 * indicated by entering a sentinel value, which is defined by
 * setting the value of the constant SENTINEL.
 */

#include <iostream>
using namespace std;

/*
 * Constant: SENTINEL
 * ------------------
 * Defines the value used to terminate the input list.  This value must
 * be chosen so that it is not one that could naturally appear in the
 * input data.  In the AddIntegerList application, the value 0 is an
 * appropriate sentinel because the user can simply skip any 0 values
 * in the input.
 */

const int SENTINEL = 0;

/* Main program */

int main() {
    cout << "This program adds a list of numbers." << endl;
    cout << "Use " << SENTINEL << " to signal the end." <<  endl;
    int total = 0;
    while (true) {
        int value;
        cout << " ? ";
        cin >> value;
        if (value == SENTINEL) break;
        total += value;
    }
    cout << "The total is " << total << endl;
    return 0;
}
```

The second example appears in the implementation of **raiseToPower** and has the following form:

```cpp
for (int i = 0; i < k; i++) {
    result *= n;
}
```

Each of these examples represents an idiomatic pattern that will come up often as you write your programs.

Of these two patterns, the second is more common. The general form of this pattern is

```
for (int var = 0; var < n; var++)
```

which has the effect of executing the body of the loop *n* times. You can substitute any variable name you want into this pattern, but that variable is often not used inside the body of the **for** loop at all, as is the case in **raiseToPower**.

The pattern from the main program counts from one value to another and has the following general form:

```
for (int var = start; var <= finish; var++)
```

In this pattern, the body of the **for** loop is executed with the variable *var* set to each value between *start* and *finish,* inclusive. Thus, you can use a **for** loop to have the variable **i** count from 1 to 100 like this:

```
for (int i = 1; i <= 100; i++)
```

You can also use the **for** loop pattern to implement the factorial function, which is defined as the product of the integers between 1 and *n* and is usually written in mathematics as *n*! The code is similar to the implementation of **raiseToPower**:

```
int fact(int n) {
   int result = 1;
   for (int i = 1; i <= n; i++) {
      result *= i;
   }
   return result;
}
```

In this implementation, the **for** loop ensures that the variable **i** counts from 1 to **n**. The body of the loop then updates the value of **result** by multiplying it by **i**, which takes on each of the desired values in turn.

The variable used in these **for** loop patterns is called an ***index variable.*** The convention of using single-letter names such as **i** and **j** for index variables dates back at least as far as the early versions of FORTRAN, which required integer variables to start with a predefined set of letters in the middle of the alphabet. Although short variable names are usually poor choices because they convey very little about the purpose of that variable, the fact that this naming convention exists makes such names appropriate in this context. Whenever you see the variable **i** or **j** in a **for** loop, you can be reasonably confident that the variable is counting through some range of values.

The **for** loop in C++, however, is considerably more general than the earlier examples suggest. The general form of the **for** loop pattern is

```
for (init; test; step) {
    statements
}
```

This code is equivalent to the following **while** statement

```
init;
while (test) {
    statements
    step;
}
```

The code fragment specified by *init,* which is typically a variable declaration, runs before the loop begins and is most often used to initialize an index variable. For example, if you write

```
for (int i = 0; . . .
```

the loop will begin by setting the index variable **i** to 0. If the loop begins

```
for (int i = -7; . . .
```

the variable **i** will start as **-7**, and so on.

The *test* expression is a conditional test written exactly like the test in a **while** statement. As long as the test expression is **true**, the loop continues. Thus, the loop

```
for (int i = 0; i < n; i++)
```

begins with **i** equal to 0 and continues as long as **i** is less than **n**, which turns out to represent a total of **n** cycles, with **i** taking on the values 0, 1, 2, and so on, up to the final value **n-1**. The loop

```
for (int i = 1; i <= n; i++)
```

begins with **i** equal to 1 and continues as long as **i** is less than or equal to **n**. This loop also runs for **n** cycles, with **i** taking on the values 1, 2, and so forth, up to **n**.

The *step* expression indicates how the value of the index variable changes from cycle to cycle. The most common form of step specification is to increment the index variable using the **++** operator, but this is not the only possibility. For example, one can count backward using the **--** operator, or count by twos using **+= 2** instead of **++**.

As an illustration of counting in the reverse direction, the program

```
int main() {
    for (int t = 10; t >= 0; t--) {
        cout << t << endl;
    }
    return 0;
}
```

generates the following sample run:

Each of the expressions in a **for** statement is optional, but the semicolons must appear. If *init* is missing, no initialization is performed. If *test* is missing, C++ assumes a value of **true**. If *step* is missing, no action occurs between loop cycles.

Summary

This chapter is itself a summary, which makes it hard to condense it to a few central points. Its purpose is to introduce you to the C++ programming language and give you a crash course in how to write simple programs in that language. The chapter focuses on the low-level structure of the language, concentrating on the concepts of *expressions* and *statements,* which together make it possible to define *functions*.

Important points in the chapter include:

- In the 30+ years of its existence, the C++ programming language has become one of the most widely used languages in the world.

- A typical C++ program consists of comments, library inclusions, program-level definitions, function prototypes, a function named **main** that is called when the program is started, and a set of auxiliary functions that work together with the main program to accomplish the required task.

- Variables in a C++ program must be declared before they are used. Most variables in C++ are *local variables,* which are declared within a function and can only be used inside the body of that function.

- A *data type* is defined by a domain of values and a set of operations. C++ includes several *primitive types* that allow programs to store common data values including integers, floating-point numbers, Booleans, and characters. As you will learn in later chapters, C++ also allows programmers to define new types from existing ones.

- The easiest way to perform input and output operations in C++ is to use the **iostream** library. This library defines three standard streams that refer to the console: **cin** for reading input data, **cout** for writing normal program output, and **cerr** for reporting error messages. Console input is traditionally performed using the **>>** operator, as in the statement

      cin >> limit;

  which reads a value from the console into the variable **limit**. Console output uses the **<<** operator, as illustrated by the line

      cout << "The answer is " << answer << endl;

  which displays the value of **answer** on the console along with an identifying label. The **endl** value ensures that the next console output appears on a new line.

- Expressions in C++ are written in a form similar to that in most programming languages, with individual terms connected by operators. A list of the C++ operators appears in Table 1-4 along with their *precedence* and *associativity*.

- Statements in C++ fall into two general categories: *simple statements* and *control statements*. A simple statement consists of an expression—typically an assignment or a function call—followed by a semicolon. The control statements described in this chapter are the **if**, **switch**, **while**, and **for** statements. The first two are used to express conditional execution, while the last two are used to specify repetition.

- C++ programs are typically subdivided into several functions. You can use the examples in this chapter as models for writing your own functions, or you can wait until functions are covered in more detail in Chapter 2.

Review questions

1. When you write a C program, do you prepare a source file or an object file?

2. What characters are used to mark comments in a C++ program?

3. In an **#include** line, the name of the library header file can be enclosed in either angle brackets or double quotation marks. What is the difference between the two forms of punctuation?

4. How would you define a constant called **CENTIMETERS_PER_INCH** with the value 2.54?

5. What is the name of the function that must be defined in every C++ program? What statement typically appears at the end of that function?

6. What is the purpose of **endl** when you are writing to the **cout** output stream?

7. Define each of the following terms for variables: *name, type, value,* and *scope.*

8. Indicate which of the following are legal variable names in C++:

   a.   **x**   g.   **total output**
   b.   **formula1**   h.   **aVeryLongVariableName**
   c.   **average_rainfall**   i.   **12MonthTotal**
   d.   **%correct**   j.   **marginal-cost**
   e.   **short**   k.   **b4hand**
   f.   **tiny**   l.   **_stk_depth**

9. What are the two attributes that define a data type?

10. How do the types **short**, **int**, and **long** differ?

11. What does ASCII stand for?

12. List all possible values of type **bool**.

13. What statements would you include in a program to read a value from the user and store it in the variable **x**, which is declared as a **double**?

14. Suppose that a function contains the following declarations:

    ```
    int i;
    double d;
    char c;
    string s;
    ```

    Write a statement that displays the values of each of these variables on the screen along with the name of the variable, so you can tell the values apart.

15. Indicate the values and types of the following expressions:

    a.   **2 + 3**   d.   **3 * 6.0**
    b.   **19 / 5**   e.   **19 % 5**
    c.   **19.0 / 5**   f.   **2 % 7**

16. What is the difference between the unary minus and the subtraction operator?

17. What does the term *truncation* mean?

18. What is a *type cast* and how do you indicate one in C++?

19. Calculate the result of each of the following expressions:

    a. `6 + 5 / 4 - 3`
    b. `2 + 2 * (2 * 2 - 2) % 2 / 2`
    c. `10 + 9 * ((8 + 7) % 6) + 5 * 4 % 3 * 2 + 1`
    d. `1 + 2 + (3 + 4) * ((5 * 6 % 7 * 8) - 9) - 10`

20. How do you specify a shorthand assignment operation?

21. What is the difference between the expressions `++x` and `x++`?

22. What is meant by *short-circuit evaluation?*

23. Write out the general syntactic form for each of the following control statements: `if`, `switch`, `while`, and `for`.

24. Describe in English the operation of the `switch` statement, including the role of the `break` statement at the end of each `case` clause.

25. What is a *sentinel?*

26. What `for` loop control line would you use in each of the following situations?

    a. Counting from 1 to 100
    b. Counting by sevens starting at 0 until the number has more than two digits
    c. Counting backward by twos from 100 to 0

▮▮▮ Exercises

1. Write a program that reads in a temperature in degrees Celsius and displays the corresponding temperature in degrees Fahrenheit. The conversion formula is

$$F = \tfrac{9}{5} C + 32$$

2. Write a program that converts a distance in meters to the corresponding English distance in feet and inches. The conversion factors you need are

    1 inch = 0.0254 meters
    1 foot = 12 inches

3. As mathematical historians have told the story, the German mathematician Carl Friedrich Gauss (1777–1855) began to show his mathematical talent at a very early age. When he was in elementary school, Gauss was asked by his teacher to compute the sum of the numbers between 1 and 100. Gauss is said to have

given the answer instantly: 5050. Write a program that computes the answer to the question Gauss's teacher posed.

4. Write a program that reads in a positive integer N and then calculates and displays the sum of the first N odd integers. For example, if N is 4, your program should display the value 16, which is $1 + 3 + 5 + 7$.

5. Write a program that reads in a list of integers from the user until the user enters the value 0 as a sentinel. When the sentinel appears, your program should display the largest value in the list, as illustrated in the following sample run:

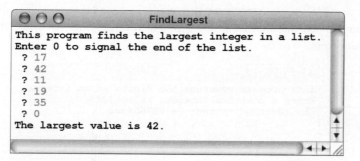

Be sure to define the sentinel value as a constant in a way that makes it easy to change. You should also make sure that the program works correctly if all the input values are negative.

6. For a slightly more interesting challenge, write a program that finds both the largest and the second-largest number in a list, prior to the entry of a sentinel. If you once again use 0 as the sentinel, a sample run of this program might look like this:

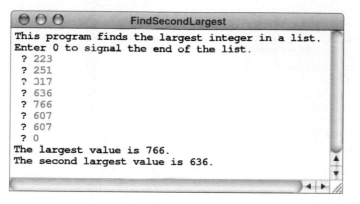

The values in this sample run are the number of pages in the British hardcover editions of J. K. Rowling's *Harry Potter* series. The output therefore tells us that the longest book (*Harry Potter and the Order of the Phoenix*) has 766 pages and the second-longest book (*Harry Potter and the Goblet of Fire*) weighs in at a mere 636 pages.

7. Using the **AddIntegerList** program from Figure 1-5 as a model, write a program **AverageList** that reads in a list of integers representing exam scores and then prints out the average. Because some unprepared student might actually get a score of 0, your program should use −1 as the sentinel to mark the end of the input.

8. Using the **digitSum** function from the section entitled "The **while** statement" as a model, write a program that reads in an integer and then displays the number that has the same digits in the reverse order, as illustrated by this sample run:

9. Every positive integer greater than 1 can be expressed as a product of prime numbers. This factorization is unique and is called the *prime factorization.* For example, the number 60 can be decomposed into the factors 2 × 2 × 3 × 5, each of which is prime. Note that the same prime can appear more than once in the factorization.

   Write a program to display the prime factorization of a number *n,* as illustrated by the following sample run:

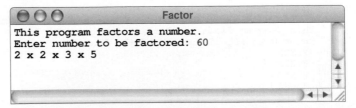

10. In 1979, Douglas Hofstadter, Professor of Cognitive Science at the University of Indiana, wrote *Gödel, Escher, Bach,* which he described as "a metaphorical fugue on minds and machines in the spirit of Lewis Carroll." The book won the Pulitzer Prize for Literature and has over the years become one of the classics of computer science. Much of its charm comes from the mathematical oddities and puzzles it contains, many of which can be expressed in the form of computer programs. Of these, one of the most interesting concerns the

sequence of numbers formed by repeatedly executing the following rules for some positive integer *n*:

* If *n* is equal to 1, you've reached the end of the sequence and can stop.
* If *n* is even, divide it by two.
* If *n* is odd, multiply it by three and add one.

Although it also goes by several other names, this sequence is often called the *hailstone sequence,* because the values tend to go up and down, much as hailstones do in the clouds in which they form.

Write a program that reads in a number from the user and then generates the hailstone sequence from that point, as in the following sample run:

```
● ● ●                    Hailstone
Enter a number: 15
15 is odd, so I multiply by 3 and add 1 to get 46.
46 is even, so I divide it by 2 to get 23.
23 is odd, so I multiply by 3 and add 1 to get 70.
70 is even, so I divide it by 2 to get 35.
35 is odd, so I multiply by 3 and add 1 to get 106.
106 is even, so I divide it by 2 to get 53.
53 is odd, so I multiply by 3 and add 1 to get 160.
160 is even, so I divide it by 2 to get 80.
80 is even, so I divide it by 2 to get 40.
40 is even, so I divide it by 2 to get 20.
20 is even, so I divide it by 2 to get 10.
10 is even, so I divide it by 2 to get 5.
5 is odd, so I multiply by 3 and add 1 to get 16.
16 is even, so I divide it by 2 to get 8.
8 is even, so I divide it by 2 to get 4.
4 is even, so I divide it by 2 to get 2.
2 is even, so I divide it by 2 to get 1.
```

As you can see, this program offers a narrative account of the process as it goes along, much as Hofstadter does in his book.

One of the fascinating things about the hailstone sequence is that no one has yet been able to prove that the process always stops. The number of steps in the process can get very large, but somehow it always seems to climb back down to one.

11. The German mathematician Leibniz (1646–1716) discovered the rather remarkable fact that the mathematical constant π can be computed using the following mathematical relationship:

$$\frac{\pi}{4} \cong 1 - \frac{1}{3} + \frac{1}{5} - \frac{1}{7} + \frac{1}{9} - \frac{1}{11} + \cdots$$

The formula to the right of the equal sign represents an infinite series; each fraction represents a term in that series. If you start with 1, subtract one-third, add one-fifth, and so on, for each of the odd integers, you get a number that gets closer and closer to the value of $\pi/4$ as you go along.

Write a program that calculates an approximation of π consisting of the first 10,000 terms in Leibniz's series.

12. You can also compute π by approximating the area bounded by a circular arc. Consider the following quarter circle:

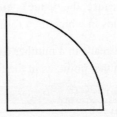

which has a radius r equal to two inches. From the formula for the area of a circle, you can easily determine that the area of the quarter circle should be π square inches. You can also approximate the area computationally by adding up the areas of a series of rectangles, where each rectangle has a fixed width and the height is chosen so that the circle passes through the midpoint of the top of the rectangle. For example, if you divide the area into 10 rectangles from left to right, you get the following diagram:

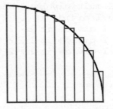

The sum of the areas of the rectangles approximates the area of the quarter circle. The more rectangles there are, the closer the approximation.

For each rectangle, the width w is a constant derived by dividing the radius by the number of rectangles. The height h, on the other hand, varies depending on the position of the rectangle. If the midpoint of the rectangle in the horizontal direction is given by x, the height of the rectangle can be computed using the **sqrt** function to express the distance formula

$$h = \sqrt{r^2 - x^2}$$

The area of each rectangle is then simply $h \times w$.

Write a program to compute the area of the quarter circle by dividing it into 10,000 rectangles.

Chapter 2
Functions and Libraries

Your library is your paradise.
— Desiderius Erasmus,
Fisher's Study at Rotterdam, 1524

As you know from the examples in Chapter 1, programs in C++ typically consist of a sequence of functions. This chapter looks more expansively at the concept of a function and the realization of that idea in C++. In addition, the chapter explores how functions can be stored in libraries, which makes it easier to use those functions in a variety of applications.

2.1 The idea of a function

When you are in the early stages of studying programming, your most important responsibility is to learn how to use functions effectively in programs. Fortunately, the concept of a function is likely to be familiar from mathematics, so you're probably not learning a new concept completely from scratch. At the same time, functions in C++ are much more general than their counterparts in mathematics, which means that you'll have to move beyond the mathematical conception and think more expansively about how you might use functions as a programmer. The sections that follow begin with the mathematical notion of a function and then generalize that concept to encompass the applications of functions in the programming domain.

Functions in mathematics

When you studied mathematics in high school, you almost certainly encountered the concept of a function. For example, you might have seen a function definition like

$$f(x) = x^2 + 1$$

which states that the function f transforms a number x into the square of x plus one. For any value of x, you can compute the value of the function simply by evaluating the formula that appears in the definition. Thus, the value of $f(3)$ is $3^2 + 1$, or 10.

Ever since the development of FORTRAN in the 1950s, programming languages have incorporated this mathematical approach to functions into their computational framework. For example, building on the examples of functions you saw in Chapter 1, you know that you can implement the function f in C++ like this:

```
double f(double x) {
   return x * x + 1;
}
```

This definition includes various bits of syntax that are absent from the mathematical formulation, but the basic idea is the same. The function **f** takes an input value represented by the variable **x** and returns as its output the value of the expression **x * x + 1**.

Functions in programming

In programming languages, the concept of a function is more general than in mathematics. Like their mathematical counterparts, functions in C++ can specify input values but don't need to do so. Similarly, functions in C++ aren't required to return results. The essential characteristic of a C++ function is that it associates a computational operation—specified by a block of code that forms the **body** of the function—with a particular name. Once a function has been defined, other parts of the program can trigger the associated operations by using only the function name. There is no need to repeat the code for the underlying operation, because the steps required to implement that operation are specified in the function body.

This model of functions in the context of programming makes it possible to define several terms that are essential to understanding how functions work in C++. First of all, a **function** is a block of code that has been organized into a separate unit and given a name. The act of using the name to invoke that code is known as **calling** that function. To specify a function call in C++, you write the name of the function, followed by a list of expressions enclosed in parentheses. These expressions, called **arguments,** allow the calling program to pass information to the function. If a function requires no information from its caller, it need not have any arguments, but an empty set of parentheses must appear in both the function definition and any calls to that function.

Once called, the function takes the data supplied as arguments, does its work, and then returns to the program at the point in the code from which the call was made. Remembering what the calling program was doing so that the program can get back to the precise location of the call is one of the essential characteristics of the function-calling mechanism. The operation of going back to the calling program is called **returning** from the function. As it returns, a function often passes a value back to its caller. This operation is called **returning a value.**

The advantages of using functions

Functions play several important roles in a programming language. First, defining functions makes it possible to write the code for an operation once but then use it many times. The ability to invoke the same sequence of instructions from many parts of a program can dramatically reduce its size. Having the code for a function appear in just one place also makes a program easier to maintain. If you need to make a change in the way a function operates, it is far easier to do so if the code appears only once than if the same operations are repeated throughout the code.

Defining a function is also valuable even if you use that function only once in a particular program. The most important role that functions play is that they make it possible to divide a large program into smaller, more manageable pieces. This process is called *decomposition.* As you almost certainly know from your prior experience with programming, writing a program as one monolithic block of code is a sure-fire recipe for disaster. What you want to do instead is subdivide the high-level problem into a set of lower-level functions, each of which makes sense on its own. Finding the right decomposition, however, turns out to be a challenging task that requires considerable practice. If you choose the individual pieces well, each one will have integrity as a unit and make the program as a whole much simpler to understand. If you choose unwisely, the decomposition can easily get in your way. There are no hard-and-fast rules for selecting a particular decomposition. Programming is an art, and you will learn to choose good decomposition strategies mostly through experience.

As a general rule, however, it makes sense to begin the decomposition process starting with the main program. At this level, you think about the problem as a whole and try to identify the major pieces of the entire task. Once you figure out what the big pieces of the program are, you can define them as independent functions. Since some of these functions may themselves be complicated, it is often appropriate to decompose them into still smaller ones. You can continue this process until every piece of the problem is simple enough to be solved on its own. This process is called *top-down design* or *stepwise refinement.*

Functions and algorithms

In addition to their role as a tool for managing complexity, functions are important in programming because they provide a basis for the implementation of *algorithms,* which are precisely specified strategies for solving computational problems. The term comes from the name of the ninth-century Persian mathematician Muḥammad ibn Mūsā al-Khwārizmī, whose treatise on mathematics entitled *Kitab al jabr w'al-muqabala* gave rise to the English word *algebra.* Mathematical algorithms, however, go back much further in history, and certainly extend at least as far as the early Greek, Chinese, and Indian civilizations.

One of the earliest known algorithms worthy of that distinction is named for the Greek mathematician Euclid, who lived in Alexandria during the reign of Ptolemy I (323–283 BCE). In his great mathematical treatise called *Elements,* Euclid outlines a procedure for finding the *greatest common divisor* (or *gcd* for short) of two integers x and y, which is defined to be the largest integer that divides evenly into both. For example, the gcd of 49 and 35 is 7, the gcd of 6 and 18 is 6, and the gcd of 32 and 33 is 1. In modern English, Euclid's algorithm can be described as follows:

1. Divide x by y and compute the remainder; call that remainder r.
2. If r is zero, the algorithm is complete, and the answer is y.
3. If r is not zero, set x to the old value of y, set y equal to r, and repeat the process.

You can easily translate this algorithmic description into the following code in C++:

```
int gcd(int x, int y) {
    int r = x % y;
    while (r != 0) {
        x = y;
        y = r;
        r = x % y;
    }
    return y;
}
```

Euclid's algorithm is considerably more efficient than any strategy you would be likely to discover on your own, and is still used today in a variety of practical applications, including the implementation of the cryptographic protocols that enable secure communication on the Internet.

At the same time, it is not easy to see exactly why the algorithm gives the correct result. Fortunately for those who rely on it in modern-day applications, Euclid was able to prove the correctness of his algorithm in *Elements,* Book VII, proposition 2. While it is not always necessary to have formal proofs of the algorithms that drive computer-based applications, such proofs make it possible for you to have more confidence in the correctness of those programs.

2.2 Libraries

When you write a C++ program, most of the code the computer executes is not the code you have written yourself, but the library code you've loaded along with your application. In a way, today's programs are like icebergs, in that most of the bulk lies hidden beneath the surface. If you want to become an effective C++ programmer, you need to spend at least as much time learning about the standard libraries as you do learning the language itself.

Every program you have seen in this book—all the way back to the tiny **HelloWorld** example at the beginning of Chapter 1—includes the **<iostream>** library, which gives the program access to the **cin** and **cout** streams. The details of how those streams are implemented aren't important to you when you are writing **HelloWorld** or **PowersOfTwo**. Those implementations, in fact, are not simply beyond your reach at the moment, but entirely beyond the scope of this book. In your role as a programmer, all that matters is that you know how to use these libraries and that the library implementations do what they're supposed to do.

Beginning programmers are sometimes uncomfortable with the idea of calling a function without understanding its underlying implementation. In fact, though, you've probably been doing precisely that in mathematics for a long time. In high school, you presumably encountered several functions that turned out to be useful even if you had no idea—and probably no interest—in how the values of that function are computed. In your algebra classes, for example, you learned about functions like logarithms and square root. If you took a trigonometry course, you worked with functions like sine and cosine. If you needed to know the value of one of these functions, you didn't compute the result by hand, but instead looked up the answer in a table or, more likely, typed the appropriate values into a calculator.

Writing programs requires much the same strategy. If you need to invoke some mathematical function, what you want to have is a library function that computes it with no more conceptual effort than it takes to press the correct key on a calculator. Fortunately, C++ has an extensive mathematical library called **<cmath>** that includes all the functions you are likely to need. The most common functions in the **<cmath>** library appear in Table 2-1. Don't worry if you have no idea what some

TABLE 2-1 Selected functions in the **<cmath>** library

General mathematical functions

abs (*x*)	Returns the absolute value of *x*.
sqrt (*x*)	Returns the square root of *x*.
floor (*x*)	Returns the largest integer less than or equal to *x* as a floating-point value.
ceil (*x*)	Returns the smallest integer greater than or equal to *x* as a floating-point value.

Logarithmic and exponential functions

exp (*x*)	Returns the exponential function of *x* (e^x).
log (*x*)	Returns the natural logarithm (base *e*) of *x*.
log10 (*x*)	Returns the common logarithm (base 10) of *x*.
pow (*x*, *y*)	Returns x^y.

Trigonometric functions

cos (*theta*)	Returns the cosine of the angle *theta*, measured in radians counterclockwise from the +*x* axis. You can convert from degrees to radians by multiplying by $\pi/180$.
sin (*theta*)	Returns the sine of the radian angle *theta*.
tan (*theta*)	Returns the tangent of the radian angle *theta*.
atan (*x*)	Returns the principal arctangent of *x*. The result is an angle expressed in radians between $-\pi/2$ and $+\pi/2$.
atan2 (*y*, *x*)	Returns the radian angle formed between the *x*-axis and the line extending from the origin through the point (*x*, *y*).

of the functions mean. This book requires very little mathematics and will explain any concepts beyond basic algebra as they come up.

Whenever a library makes some service available to the programs that include it, computer scientists say that the library **exports** that service. The `<iostream>` library, for example, exports the `cin` and `cout` streams; the `<cmath>` library exports the `sqrt` function, along with the other functions in Table 2-1.

One of the design goals of any library is to hide the complexity involved in the underlying implementation. By exporting the `sqrt` function, the designers of the `<cmath>` library made it far easier to write programs that use it. When you call the `sqrt` function, you don't need to have any idea how `sqrt` works internally. Those details are relevant only to the programmers who implemented the `<cmath>` library in the first place.

Knowing how to call the `sqrt` function and knowing how to implement it are both important skills. It is important to recognize, however, that those two skills— calling a function and implementing one—are to a large extent independent. Successful programmers often use functions that they wouldn't have a clue how to write. Conversely, programmers who implement a library function can never anticipate all the potential uses for that function.

To emphasize the difference in perspective between programmers who implement a library and those who use it, computer scientists have assigned names to programmers working in each of these roles. Naturally enough, a programmer who implements a library is called an ***implementer.*** Conversely, a programmer who calls functions provided by a library is called a ***client*** of that library. As you go through the chapters in this book, you will have a chance to look at several libraries from both of these perspectives, first as a client and later as an implementer.

2.3 Defining functions in C++

Although you saw several functions in Chapter 1 and even had a chance to write a few of your own in the exercises, it makes sense to review the rules for writing functions in C++ before going on to investigate how to use them most effectively. In C++, a function definition has the following syntactic form:

```
type name (parameters)  {
    . . . body . . .
}
```

In this example, *type* is the type returned by the function, *name* is the function name, and *parameters* is a list of declarations separated by commas, giving the type and name of each parameter to the function. A ***parameter*** is a placeholder for one of the arguments supplied in the function call. In most respects, a parameter acts just like a local variable. The only difference is that each parameter is initialized automatically to hold the value of the corresponding argument. If a function takes no parameters, the entire parameter list in the function header line is empty.

The body of the function is a block consisting of the statements that implement the function, along with the declarations of any local variables the function requires. For functions that return a value to their caller, at least one of the statements must be a **return** statement, which usually has the form

```
return expression;
```

Executing the **return** statement causes the function to return immediately to its caller, passing back the value of the expression as the value of the function.

Functions can return values of any type. The following function, for example, returns a Boolean value indicating whether the argument **n** is an even integer:

```
bool isEven(int n) {
    return n % 2 == 0;
}
```

Once you have defined this function, you can use it in an **if** statement like this:

```
if (isEven(i)) . . .
```

As noted in Chapter 1, functions that return Boolean results are called *predicate functions.*

Functions, however, do not need to return a value at all. A function that does not return a value and is instead executed for its effect is often called a *procedure.* Procedures are indicated in the definition of a function by using the reserved word **void** as the result type. Procedures ordinarily finish by reaching the end of the statements in the body. You can, however, signal early completion of a procedure by executing a **return** statement without a value expression, as follows:

```
return;
```

Function prototypes

When the C++ compiler encounters a function call in your program, it needs to have some information about that function in order to generate the correct code. In most cases, the compiler doesn't need to know all the steps that form the body of the function. All it really needs to know is what arguments the function requires and what type of value it returns. That information is usually provided by a *prototype,* which is simply the header line of the function followed by a semicolon.

You have already seen examples of prototypes in Chapter 1. The `PowersOfTwo` program in Figure 1-3, for example, provides the following prototype for the `raiseToPower` function:

```
int raiseToPower(int n, int k);
```

which tells the compiler that `raiseToPower` takes two integers as arguments and returns an integer as its result. The names of the parameters are optional in a prototype, but supplying them usually helps the reader.

If you always define functions before you call them, prototypes are not required. Some programmers organize their source files so that the low-level functions come at the beginning, followed by the intermediate-level functions that call them, with the main program coming at the very bottom. While this strategy can save a few prototype lines, it forces an order on the source file that often makes it harder for the reader to figure out what is going on. In particular, programs organized in this way end up reflecting the opposite of top-down design, since the most general functions appear at the end. In this text, every function other than `main` has an explicit prototype, which makes it possible to define those functions in any order.

Overloading

In C++, it is legal to give the same name to more than one function as long as the pattern of arguments is different. When the compiler encounters a call to a function with that name, it checks to see what arguments have been provided and chooses the version of the function that fits those arguments. Using the same name for more than one version of a function is called *overloading.* The pattern of arguments taken by a function—taking into account only the number and types of the arguments and not the parameter names—is called its *signature.*

As an example of overloading, the `<cmath>` library includes several versions of the function `abs`, one for each of the built-in arithmetic types. For instance, the library includes the function

```
int abs(int x) {
    return (x < 0) ? -x : x;
}
```

as well as the identically named function

```
double abs(double x) {
    return (x < 0) ? -x : x;
}
```

The only difference between these functions is that the first version takes an **int** as its argument and the second takes a **double**. The compiler chooses which of these versions to invoke by looking at the types of the arguments the caller provides. Thus, if **abs** is called with an **int**, the compiler invokes the integer-valued version of the functions and returns a value of type **int**. If, by contrast, the argument is of type **double**, the compiler chooses the version that takes a **double**.

The primary advantage of using overloading is that doing so makes it easier for you as a programmer to keep track of different function names for the same operation when that function is applied in slightly different contexts. If, for example, you need to call the absolute value function in C, which does not support overloading, you have to remember to call **fabs** for floating-point numbers and **abs** for integers. In C++, all you need to remember is the single function name **abs**.

Default parameters

C++ also makes it possible to specify that certain parameters are optional. The parameter variables still appear in the function header line, but the prototype for the function specifies the values that those parameters should have if they do not appear in the call. Such parameters are called *default parameters.*

To indicate that a parameter is optional, all you need to do is include an initial value in the declaration of that parameter in the function prototype. For example, if you were designing a set of functions to implement a word processor, you might define a procedure with the following prototype:

```
void formatInColumns(int nColumns = 2);
```

The **formatInColumns** procedure takes the number of columns as an argument, but the **= 2** in the prototype declaration means that this argument may be omitted. If you leave it out and call

```
formatInColumns();
```

the parameter variable **nColumns** will automatically be initialized to 2.

When you use default parameters, it helps to keep the following rules in mind:

- The specification of the default value appears only in the function prototype and not in the function definition.
- Any default parameters must appear at the end of the parameter list.

Default parameters tend to be overused in C++. It is always possible—and usually preferable—to achieve the same effect through overloading. Suppose, for example, that you want to define a procedure `setInitialLocation` that takes an *x* and a *y* coordinate as arguments. The prototype presumably looks like this:

```
void setInitialLocation(double x, double y);
```

Now suppose that you want to change this definition so that the initial location defaults to the origin (0, 0). One way to accomplish that goal is to add initializers to the prototype, like this:

```
void setInitialLocation(double x = 0, double y = 0);
```

While this definition has the desired effect, having it in place makes it possible to call `setInitialLocation` with one argument, which would almost certainly be confusing to anyone reading the code. It is almost certainly better to define an overloaded version of the function with the following implementation:

```
void setInitialLocation() {
    setInitialLocation(0, 0);
}
```

2.4 The mechanics of function calls

Although you can certainly get by with an intuitive understanding of how the function-calling process works, it sometimes helps—particularly when you start to work with recursive functions in Chapter 7—to understand precisely what happens when one function calls another in C++. The sections that follow describe the process in detail and then walk you through a simple example designed to help you visualize exactly what is going on.

The steps in calling a function

Whenever a function call occurs, the C++ compiler generates code to implement the following operations:

1. The calling function computes values for each argument using the bindings of local variables in its own context. Because the arguments are expressions, this computation can involve operators and other functions; the calling function evaluates these expressions before execution of the new function begins.

2. The system creates new space for all the local variables required by the new function, including any parameters. These variables are allocated together in a block, which is called a *stack frame.*

3. The value of each argument is copied into the corresponding parameter variable. For functions with more than one argument, these copies occur in order; the first argument is copied into the first parameter, and so forth. If necessary, the compiler generates automatic type conversions between the

argument values and the parameter variables, as it does in an assignment statement. For example, if you pass a value of type `int` to a function that expects a parameter of type `double`, the integer is converted into the equivalent floating-point value before it is copied into the parameter variable.

4. The statements in the function body are executed until the program encounters a `return` statement or there are no more statements to execute.

5. The value of the `return` expression, if any, is evaluated and returned as the value of the function. If necessary, the compiler performs automatic type conversions to ensure that the result is of the correct type. For example, if a `return` statement specifies a floating-point value in a function defined to return an `int`, the result is truncated to an integer.

6. The stack frame created for this function call is discarded. In the process, all local variables disappear.

7. The calling program continues, with the returned value substituted in place of the call.

Although this process may seem to make sense, you probably need to work through an example or two before you understand it thoroughly. Reading through the example in the next section will give you some insight into the process, but it is probably even more helpful to take one of your own programs and walk through it at the same level of detail. And while you can trace through a program on paper or a whiteboard, it may be better to get yourself a supply of 3×5 index cards and then use a card to represent each stack frame. The advantage of the index-card model is that you can create a stack of index cards that closely models the operation of the computer. Calling a function adds a card; returning from the function removes it.

The combinations function

The function-calling process is most easily illustrated in the context of a specific example. Suppose that you have a collection of six coins, which in the United States might be a penny, a nickel, a dime, a quarter, a half-dollar, and a dollar. Given those six coins, how many ways are there to choose two of them? As you can see from the full enumeration of the possibilities in Figure 2-1, the answer is 15. As a computer scientist, you should immediately think about the more general question: given a set containing n distinct elements, how many ways can you choose a subset with k elements? The answer to that question is computed by the *combinations function* $C(n, k)$, which is defined as follows:

$$C(n, k) = \frac{n!}{k! \times (n - k)!}$$

where the exclamation point indicates the factorial function, which is simply the product of the integers between 1 and the specified number, inclusive.

FIGURE 2-1   Illustration of the combinations function

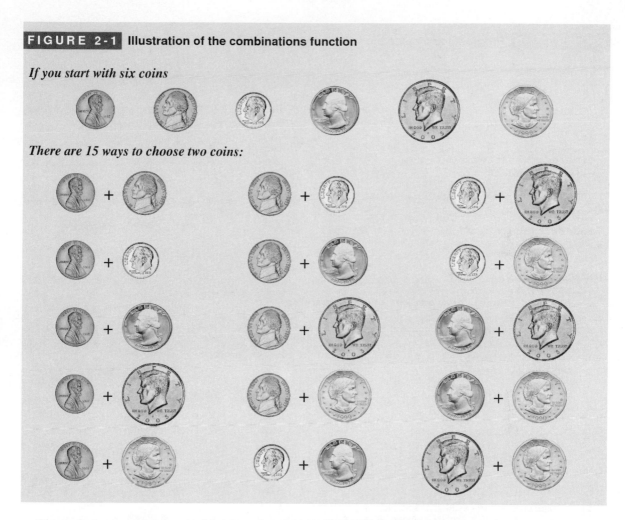

If you start with six coins

There are 15 ways to choose two coins:

The code to compute the combinations function in C++ appears in Figure 2-2, along with a main program that requests values of *n* and *k* from the user and then displays the value of $C(n, k)$. A sample run of the program might look like this:

```
○ ○ ○                   Combinations
Enter the number of objects (n):  6
Enter the number to be chosen (k):  2
C(n, k) = 15
```

As you can see from Figure 2-2, the **Combinations** program is divided into three functions. The **main** function implements the interaction with the user. The **combinations** function computes $C(n, k)$. Finally, the **fact** function, which is borrowed from Chapter 1, computes the factorials required for the computation.

FIGURE 2-2 Program to compute the combinations function

```
/*
 * File: Combinations.cpp
 * ------------------------
 * This program computes the mathematical function C(n, k) from
 * its mathematical definition in terms of factorials.
 */

#include <iostream>
using namespace std;

/* Function prototypes */

int combinations(int n, int k);
int fact(int n);

/* Main program */

int main() {
   int n, k;
   cout << "Enter the number of objects (n): ";
   cin >> n;
   cout << "Enter the number to be chosen (k): ";
   cin >> k;
   cout << "C(n, k) = " << combinations(n, k) << endl;
   return 0;
}

/*
 * Function: combinations(n, k)
 * Usage: int nWays = combinations(n, k);
 * -------------------------------------------
 * Returns the mathematical combinations function C(n, k), which is
 * the number of ways one can choose k elements from a set of size n.
 */

int combinations(int n, int k) {
   return fact(n) / (fact(k) * fact(n - k));
}

/*
 * Function: fact(n)
 * Usage: int result = fact(n);
 * ------------------------------
 * Returns the factorial of n, which is the product of all the
 * integers between 1 and n, inclusive.
 */

int fact(int n) {
   int result = 1;
   for (int i = 1; i <= n; i++) {
      result *= i;
   }
   return result;
}
```

Tracing the combinations function

While the **Combinations** program can be interesting in its own right, the purpose of this example is to illustrate the steps involved in executing functions. In C++, all programs begin by making a call to the function **main**. To implement a function call, the system—which encompasses both the operating system you're using and the hardware on which it runs—creates a new stack frame to keep track of the local variables that function declares. In the **Combinations** program, the **main** function declares two integers, **n** and **k**, so the stack frame must include space for these variables.

In the diagrams in this book, each stack frame appears as a rectangle surrounded by a double line. Each stack frame diagram shows the code for the function along with a pointing-hand icon that makes it easy to keep track of the current execution point. The frame also contains labeled boxes for each of the local variables. The stack frame for **main** therefore looks like this when execution begins:

```
int main() {
    int n, k;
☞  cout << "Enter the number of objects (n): ";
    cin >> n;
    cout << "Enter the number to be chosen (k): ";
    cin >> k;
    cout << "C(n, k) = " << combinations(n, k) << endl;
    return 0;
}
                                    k           n
```

From this point, the system executes the statements in order, printing out the prompts on the console, reading in the associated values from the user, and storing those values in the variables in that frame. If the user enters the values shown in the earlier sample run, the frame will look like this when it reaches the statement that displays the result:

```
int main() {
    int n, k;
    cout << "Enter the number of objects (n): ";
    cin >> n;
    cout << "Enter the number to be chosen (k): ";
    cin >> k;
☞  cout << "C(n, k) = " << combinations(n, k) << endl;
    return 0;
}
                                    k           n
                                    2           6
```

Before the program can complete the output line, it has to evaluate the call to `combinations(n, k)`. At this point, the function **main** is calling the function **combinations**, which means that the computer has to go through all the steps that are required in making a function call.

The first step is to evaluate the arguments in the context of the current frame. The variable **n** has the value 6, and the variable **k** has the value 2. These two arguments are then copied into the parameter variables **n** and **k** when the computer creates the **combinations** stack frame. The new frame gets stacked on top of the old one, which allows the computer to remember the values of the local variables in **main**, even though they are not currently accessible. The situation after creating the new frame and initializing the parameter variables looks like this:

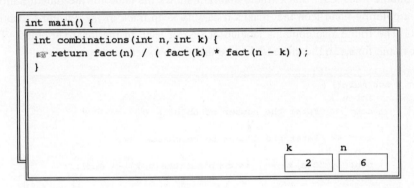

To compute the value of the **combinations** function, the program must make three calls to the function **fact**. In C++, those function calls can happen in any order, but it's easiest to process them from left to right. The first call, therefore, is the call to **fact(n)**. To evaluate this function, the system must create yet another stack frame, this time for the function **fact** with an argument value of 6:

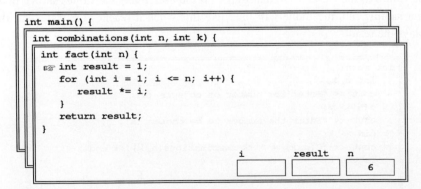

Unlike the earlier stack frames, the frame for **fact** includes both parameters and local variables. The parameter **n** is initialized to the value of the calling argument and therefore has the value 6. The two local variables, i and **result**, have not yet been initialized, but the system nonetheless needs to reserve space in the frame for those variables. Until you assign a new value to those variables, they will contain whatever data happened to be left over in the memory cells assigned to that stack frame, which is completely unpredictable. It is therefore important to initialize all local variables before you use them, ideally as part of the declaration.

The system then executes the statements in the function **fact**. In this instance, the body of the **for** loop is executed six times. On each cycle, the value of **result** is multiplied by the loop index i, which means that it will eventually hold the value 720 ($1\times2\times3\times4\times5\times6$ or 6!). When the program reaches the **return** statement, the stack frame looks like this:

```
int main() {
  int combinations (int n, int k) {
    int fact (int n) {
      int result = 1;
      for (int i = 1; i <= n; i++) {
        result *= i;
      }
   ☞ return result;
    }
```

	i	result	n
		720	6

In this diagram, the box for the variable i is empty, because the value of i is no longer defined at this point in the program. In C++, index variables declared in a **for** loop header are accessible only inside the loop body. Showing an empty box emphasizes the fact that the value of i is no longer available.

Returning from a function involves copying the value of the **return** expression (in this case the local variable **result**), into the point at which the call occurred. The frame for **fact** is then discarded, which leads to the following configuration:

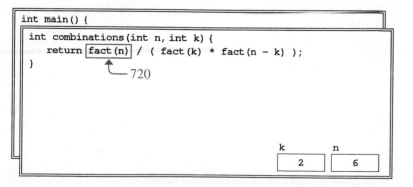

The next step in the process is to make a second call to **fact**, this time with the argument **k**. In the calling frame, **k** has the value 2. That value is then used to initialize the parameter **n** in the new stack frame, as follows:

```
int main() {
  int combinations(int n, int k) {
    int fact(int n) {
    ☞ int result = 1;
        for (int i = 1; i <= n; i++) {
          result *= i;
        }
        return result;
    }
                                    i        result     n
                                  [      ] [        ]  [  2  ]
```

The computation of **fact(2)** is a bit easier to perform in one's head than the earlier call to **fact(6)**. This time around, the value of **result** will be 2, which is then returned to the calling frame, like this:

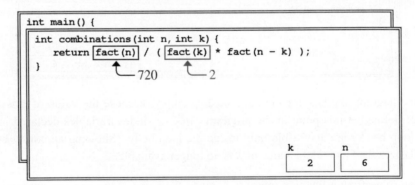

The code for **combinations** makes one more call to **fact**, this time with the argument **n - k**. As before, this call creates a new frame with **n** equal to 4:

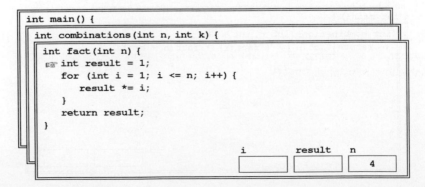

The value of **fact(4)** is $1 \times 2 \times 3 \times 4$, or 24. When this call returns, the system is able to fill in the last of the missing values in the calculation, as follows:

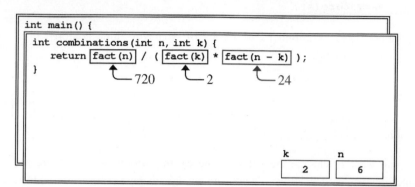

```
int main() {

  int combinations(int n, int k) {
      return  fact(n)  / ( fact(k)  *  fact(n - k) );
  }
              └─ 720      └─ 2        └─ 24



                                    k        n
                                    2        6
```

The computer then divides 720 by the product of 2 and 24 to get the answer 15. This value is then returned to the **main** function, which leads to the following state:

```
int main() {
    int n, k;
    cout << "Enter the number of objects (n): ";
    cin >> n;
    cout << "Enter the number to be chosen (k): ";
    cin >> k;
    cout << "C(n, k) = " << combinations(n, k)  << endl;
    return 0;
}                              └─ 15  k        n
                                      2        6
```

From this point, all that remains is to generate the output line and return from the **main** function, which completes the execution of the program.

2.5 Reference parameters

In C++, whenever you pass a simple variable from one function to another, the function gets a copy of the calling value. Assigning a new value to the parameter as part of the function changes the local copy but has no effect on the calling argument. For example, if you try to implement a procedure that initializes a variable to zero using the code

```
void setToZero(int var) {
    var = 0;
}
```

that procedure ends up having no effect whatever. If you call

```
setToZero(x);
```

the parameter **var** is initialized to a copy of whatever value is stored in **x**. The assignment statement

```
var = 0;
```

inside the function sets the local copy to 0 but leaves **x** unchanged in the calling program.

If you want to change the value of the calling argument—and there are often compelling reasons for doing so—you can change the parameter from the usual kind of C++ parameter (which is called a *value parameter*) into a *reference parameter* by adding an ampersand between the type and the name in the function header. Unlike value parameters, reference parameters are not copied. What happens instead is that the function receives a reference to the original variable, which means that the memory used for that variable is shared between the function and its caller. The new version of **setToZero** looks like this:

```
void setToZero(int & var) {
    var = 0;
}
```

This style of parameter passing is known as *call by reference.* When you use call by reference, the argument corresponding to the reference parameter must be an assignable value, such as a variable name. Although calling **setToZero(x)** would correctly set the integer variable **x** to 0, it would be illegal to call **setToZero(3)** because **3** is not assignable.

In C++, one of the most common uses of call by reference occurs when a function needs to return more than one value to the calling program. A single result can easily be returned as the value of the function itself. If you need to return more than one result from a function, the return value is no longer appropriate. The standard approach to solving the problem is to turn that function into a procedure and pass values back and forth through the argument list.

As an example, suppose that you are writing a program to solve the quadratic equation

$$ax^2 + bx + c = 0$$

Because of your commitment to good programming style, you want to structure that program into three phases as illustrated in the following flowchart:

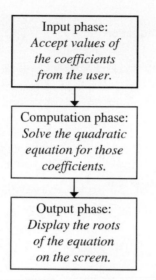

The **Quadratic** program in Figure 2-3 shows how call by reference makes it possible to decompose the quadratic equation problem in this way. Each of the functions in Figure 2-3 corresponds to one of the phases in the flowchart. The main program provides information to the function using conventional parameters. Whenever a function needs to get information back to the main program, it uses reference parameters. The **solveQuadratic** function uses parameters of each type. The parameters **a**, **b**, and **c** represent input to the function and give it access to the three coefficients. By contrast, the parameters **x1** and **x2** are output parameters that allow the program to pass back the two roots of the quadratic equation.

The **Quadratic** program also introduces a new strategy for reporting errors. Whenever the code encounters a condition that makes further progress impossible, it calls a function named **error** that prints a message indicating the nature of the problem and then terminates the execution of the program. The code for **error** looks like this:

```
void error(string msg) {
   cerr << msg << endl;
   exit(EXIT_FAILURE);
}
```

The code for **error** uses two features of C++ that have not yet made their appearance in this book: the **cerr** output stream and the **exit** function. The **cerr** stream is similar to **cout**, but is reserved for reporting errors. The **exit** function terminates the execution of the main program immediately, using the value of the parameter to report the program status. The constant **EXIT_FAILURE** is defined in the **<cstdlib>** library and is used to indicate that some kind of failure occurred.

FIGURE 2-3 **FIGURE 2-3** Program to solve the quadratic equation

```cpp
/*
 * File: Quadratic.cpp
 * --------------------
 * This program finds roots of the quadratic equation
 *
 *         2
 *     a x    + b x  +  c = 0
 *
 * If a is 0 or if the equation has no real roots, the
 * program prints an error message and exits.
 */

#include <iostream>
#include <cstdlib>
#include <cmath>
using namespace std;

/* Function prototypes */

void getCoefficients(double & a, double & b, double & c);
void solveQuadratic(double a, double b, double c,
                       double & x1, double & x2);
void printRoots(double x1, double x2);
void error(string msg);

/* Main program */

int main() {
   double a, b, c, r1, r2;
   getCoefficients(a, b, c);
   solveQuadratic(a, b, c, r1, r2);
   printRoots(r1, r2);
   return 0;
}

/*
 * Function: getCoefficients
 * Usage: getCoefficients(a, b, c);
 * ------------------------------------
 * Reads the coefficients of a quadratic equation into the
 * reference parameters a, b, and c.
 */

void getCoefficients(double & a, double & b, double & c) {
   cout << "Enter coefficients for the quadratic equation:" << endl;
   cout << "a: ";
   cin >> a;
   cout << "b: ";
   cin >> b;
   cout << "c: ";
   cin >> c;
}
```

FIGURE 2-3 Program to solve the quadratic equation (continued)

```
/*
 * Function: solveQuadratic
 * Usage: solveQuadratic(a, b, c, x1, x2);
 * -------------------------------------------
 * Solves a quadratic equation for the coefficients a, b, and c.  The
 * roots are returned in the reference parameters x1 and x2.
 */

void solveQuadratic(double a, double b, double c,
                    double & x1, double & x2) {
   if (a == 0) error("The coefficient a must be nonzero.");
   double disc = b * b - 4 * a * c;
   if (disc < 0) error("This equation has no real roots.");
   double sqrtDisc = sqrt(disc);
   x1 = (-b + sqrtDisc) / (2 * a);
   x2 = (-b - sqrtDisc) / (2 * a);
}

/*
 * Function: printRoots
 * Usage: printRoots(x1, x2);
 * ----------------------------
 * Displays x1 and x2, which are the roots of the quadratic equation.
 */

void printRoots(double x1, double x2) {
   if (x1 == x2) {
      cout << "There is a double root at " << x1 << endl;
   } else {
      cout << "The roots are " << x1 << " and " << x2 << endl;
   }
}

/*
 * Function: error
 * Usage: error(msg);
 * --------------------
 * Writes the string msg to the cerr stream and then exits the program
 * with a standard status value indicating that a failure has occurred.
 */

void error(string msg) {
   cerr << msg << endl;
   exit(EXIT_FAILURE);
}
```

The **error** function, of course, is useful in many applications beyond the one that solves quadratic equations. Although you could easily copy the code into another program, it would make much more sense to save the **error** function in a library. In the following section, you'll have a chance to do precisely that.

◼ 2.6 Interfaces and implementations

When you define a library in C++, you need to supply two parts. First, you must define the *interface,* which provides the information clients need to use the library but leaves out the details about how the library works. Second, you need to provide the *implementation,* which specifies the underlying details. A typical interface will export several definitions, which are typically functions, types, or constants. Each individual definition is called an *interface entry.*

In C++, the interface and implementation are usually written as two separate files. The name of the interface file ends with **.h**, which marks it as a *header file.* The implementation appears in a file with the same root, but with the suffix **.cpp**. Following this convention, the **error** library is defined in the file **error.h** and implemented in the file **error.cpp**.

Defining the error library

The contents of the **error.h** interface appear in Figure 2-4. As you can see, the file consists mostly of comments. The only other parts of the interface are the prototype for the **error** function and three additional lines that are often referred to as *interface boilerplate,* which is a patterned set of lines that appears in every

FIGURE 2-4 Interface for the error library

```
/*
 * File: error.h
 * --------------
 * This file defines a simple function for reporting errors.
 */

#ifndef _error_h
#define _error_h

/*
 * Function: error
 * Usage: error(msg);
 * --------------------
 * Writes the string msg to the cerr stream and then exits the program
 * with a standard status code indicating failure.  The usual pattern for
 * using error is to enclose the call to error inside an if statement that
 * checks for a particular condition, which might look something like this:
 *
 *     if (divisor == 0) error("Division by zero");
 */

void error(std::string msg);

#endif
```

interface. In this interface, the boilerplate consists of the **#ifndef** and **#define** lines at the beginning of the interface and the matching **#endif** line at the end. These lines make sure that the compiler doesn't compile the same interface twice. The **#ifndef** directive checks whether the **_error_h** symbol has been defined. When the compiler reads this interface for the first time, the answer is no. The next line, however, defines that symbol. Thus, if the compiler is later asked to read the same interface, the **_error_h** symbol will already be defined, and the compiler will skip over the contents of the interface this time around. In this book, the symbol in the **#ifndef** line always consists of an underscore followed by the name of the interface file, with a second underscore replacing the dot in the filename.

The prototype for **error**, however, looks slightly different when it appears in interface form. The parameter declaration now uses the type name **std::string** to indicate that **string** comes from the **std** namespace. Interfaces are typically read before the **using namespace std** line and therefore cannot use identifiers from that namespace without explicitly including the **std::** qualifier.

The **error.cpp** implementation appears in Figure 2-5. Comments in the implementation are intended for programmers responsible for maintaining the library and are often less extensive than those in the interface. Here, the body of the

---

FIGURE 2-5 Implementation of the error library

```
/*
 * File: error.cpp
 * ----------------
 * This file implements the error.h interface.
 */

#include <iostream>
#include <cstdlib>
#include <string>
#include "error.h"
using namespace std;

/*
 * Implementation notes: error
 * ----------------------------
 * This function writes out the error message to the cerr stream and
 * then exits the program.  The EXIT_FAILURE constant is defined in
 * <cstdlib> to represent a standard failure code.
 */

void error(string msg) {
   cerr << msg << endl;
   exit(EXIT_FAILURE);
}
```

error function is all of two lines long, and the purpose of each of those lines is instantly recognizable to any C++ programmer.

Exporting types

The **error.h** interface described in the preceding section exports a single function and nothing else. Most of the interfaces you will use in C++ also export data types. Most of these types will be *classes,* which are the foundation of the object-oriented type system that C++ provides. Given that you won't learn how to define your own classes until Chapter 6, it is premature to introduce class-based examples at this point in the text. What does make sense is to create an interface that exports one of the enumerated types introduced in Chapter 1, such as the **Direction** type used to encode the four standard compass points:

```
enum Direction { NORTH, EAST, SOUTH, WEST };
```

The simplest approach to making this type accessible through a library interface would be to write a **direction.h** interface that contained only this line along with the usual interface boilerplate. If you were to adopt that strategy, you wouldn't need to supply an implementation at all.

It is more useful, however, to have this interface export some simple functions for working with **Direction** values. For example, it would be useful to export the **directionToString** function defined on page 40, which returns the name of a direction given the enumerated value. For some of the programs that appear later in this book, it will be useful to have functions **leftFrom** and **rightFrom** that return the **Direction** value that results from turning 90 degrees in the specified direction, so that, for example, **leftFrom(NORTH)** returns **WEST**. If you add these functions to the **direction.h** interface, you will also need to supply a **direction.cpp** file to implement the functions. Those files appear in Figures 2-6 and 2-7.

The implementations of **leftFrom** and **rightFrom** require some subtlety that is worth a little explanation. While C++ lets you freely convert an enumerated value to an integer, conversions in the opposite direction—from an integer to the corresponding value of an enumerated type—require a type cast. This fact is illustrated by the implementation of **rightFrom**, which looks like this:

```
Direction rightFrom(Direction dir) {
   return Direction((dir + 1) % 4);
}
```

FIGURE 2-6   Interface for the direction library

```
/*
 * File: direction.h
 * ------------------
 * This interface exports an enumerated type called Direction whose
 * elements are the four compass points: NORTH, EAST, SOUTH, and WEST.
 */

#ifndef _direction_h
#define _direction_h

#include <string>

/*
 * Type: Direction
 * ---------------
 * This enumerated type is used to represent the four compass directions.
 */

enum Direction { NORTH, EAST, SOUTH, WEST };

/*
 * Function: leftFrom
 * Usage: Direction newdir = leftFrom(dir);
 * ----------------------------------------
 * Returns the direction that is to the left of the argument.
 * For example, leftFrom(NORTH) returns WEST.
 */

Direction leftFrom(Direction dir);

/*
 * Function: rightFrom
 * Usage: Direction newdir = rightFrom(dir);
 * -----------------------------------------
 * Returns the direction that is to the right of the argument.
 * For example, rightFrom(NORTH) returns EAST.
 */

Direction rightFrom(Direction dir);

/*
 * Function: directionToString
 * Usage: string str = directionToString(dir);
 * --------------------------------------------
 * Returns the name of the direction as a string.
 */

std::string directionToString(Direction dir);

#endif
```

FIGURE 2-7 Implementation of the direction library

```
/*
 * File: direction.cpp
 * ---------------------
 * This file implements the direction.h interface.
 */

#include <string>
#include "direction.h"
using namespace std;

/*
 * Implementation notes: leftFrom, rightFrom
 * ------------------------------------------
 * These functions use the remainder operator to cycle through the
 * internal values of the enumeration type.  Note that the leftFrom
 * function cannot subtract 1 from the direction because the result
 * might then be negative; adding 3 achieves the same effect but
 * ensures that the values remain positive.
 */

Direction leftFrom(Direction dir) {
   return Direction((dir + 3) % 4);
}

Direction rightFrom(Direction dir) {
   return Direction((dir + 1) % 4);
}

/*
 * Implementation notes: directionToString
 * ----------------------------------------
 * Most C++ compilers require the default clause to make sure that this
 * function always returns a string, even if the direction is not one
 * of the legal values.
 */

string directionToString(Direction dir) {
   switch (dir) {
    case NORTH: return "NORTH";
    case EAST: return "EAST";
    case SOUTH: return "SOUTH";
    case WEST: return "WEST";
    default: return "???";
   }
}
```

The arithmetic operators in the expression

```
(dir + 1) % 4
```

automatically convert the **Direction** value to its underlying representation as an integer: 0 for **NORTH**, 1 for **EAST**, 2 for **SOUTH**, and 3 for **WEST**. Turning right from one of these compass points corresponds to adding one to the underlying value, with the exception of turning right from **WEST**, when it is necessary to cycle back to the value 0 to indicate the direction **NORTH**. As is so often the case in situations that involve cyclical structures, using the **%** operator eliminates the need for special-case testing. Before the function returns, however, the function must use a type cast to convert the result of the arithmetic expression to the **Direction** value that **rightFrom** is defined to return.

As a cautionary reminder about the dangers of using **%** with negative numbers, the **leftFrom** function cannot be defined as

```
Direction leftFrom(Direction dir) {
    return Direction((dir - 1) % 4);
}
```

The problem with this implementation arises when you call **leftFrom(NORTH)**. When **dir** has the value **NORTH**, the expression

```
(dir - 1) % 4
```

has the value −1 on most machines, which is not a legal **Direction**. Fortunately, it is easy to fix the problem by coding **leftFrom** like this:

```
Direction leftFrom(Direction dir) {
    return Direction((dir + 3) % 4);
}
```

Exporting constant definitions

In addition to functions and types, interfaces often export constant definitions so that several clients can share that constant without redefining it in every source file. If, for example, you are writing programs that involve geometrical calculations, it is useful to have a definition of the mathematical constant π, which, given the usual conventions for constants, would presumably be named **PI**. If you declared **PI** as a constant in the fashion introduced in Chapter 1, you would write

```
const double PI = 3.14159265358979323846;
```

In C++, constants written in this form are private to the source file that contains them and cannot be exported through an interface. To export the constant **PI**, you need to add the keyword **extern** to both its definition and the prototype declaration in the interface. This strategy is illustrated by the **gmath.h** interface in Figure 2-8, which exports **PI** along with some simple functions that simplify working with angles in degrees. The corresponding implementation appears in Figure 2-9.

FIGURE 2-8 Simplified interface for the gmath library

```
/*
 * File: gmath.h
 * --------------
 * This file exports the constant PI along with a few degree-based
 * trigonometric functions, which are typically easier to use than
 * their radian-based counterparts in <cmath>.
 */

#ifndef _gmath_h
#define _gmath_h

/* Constants */

extern const double PI;              /* The mathematical constant pi */

/*
 * Function: sinDegrees
 * Usage: double sine = sinDegrees(angle);
 * ----------------------------------------
 * Returns the trigonometric sine of angle expressed in degrees.
 */

double sinDegrees(double angle);

/*
 * Function: cosDegrees
 * Usage: double cosine = cosDegrees(angle);
 * ------------------------------------------
 * Returns the trigonometric cosine of angle expressed in degrees.
 */

double cosDegrees(double angle);

/*
 * Function: toDegrees
 * Usage: double degrees = toDegrees(radians);
 * -------------------------------------------
 * Converts an angle from radians to degrees.
 */

double toDegrees(double radians);

/*
 * Function: toRadians
 * Usage: double radians = toRadians(degrees);
 * -------------------------------------------
 * Converts an angle from degrees to radians.
 */

double toRadians(double degrees);

#endif
```

FIGURE 2-9 Implementation of the gmath library

```cpp
/*
 * File: gmath.cpp
 * ----------------
 * This file implements the gmath.h interface.  In all cases, the
 * implementation for each function requires only one line of code,
 * which makes detailed documentation unnecessary.
 */

#include <cmath>

#include "gmath.h"
extern const double PI = 3.14159265358979323846;

double sinDegrees(double angle) {
    return sin(toRadians(angle));
}

double cosDegrees(double angle) {
    return cos(toRadians(angle));
}

double toDegrees(double radians) {
    return radians * 180 / PI;
}

double toRadians(double degrees) {
    return degrees * PI / 180;
}
```

2.7 Principles of interface design

One of the reasons that programming is difficult is that programs reflect the complexity of the underlying application. As long as computers are used to solve problems of ever-increasing sophistication, the process of programming will of necessity become more sophisticated as well.

Writing a program to solve a large or difficult problem forces you to manage a staggering amount of complexity. There are algorithms to design, special cases to consider, user requirements to meet, and innumerable details to get right. To make programming manageable, you must reduce the complexity of the programming process as much as possible. Functions reduce some of the complexity; libraries offer a similar reduction in programming complexity but at a higher level of detail. A function gives its caller access to a set of steps that together implement a single operation. A library gives its client access to a set of functions and types that implement what computer scientists describe as a *programming abstraction.* The extent to which a particular abstraction simplifies the programming process, however, depends on how well you have designed its interface.

To design an effective interface, you must balance several criteria. In general, you should try to develop interfaces that are

- *Unified.* An interface should define a consistent abstraction with a clear unifying theme. If a function does not fit that theme, it should be defined elsewhere.

- *Simple.* To the extent that the underlying implementation is itself complex, the interface must seek to hide that complexity from the client.

- *Sufficient.* When clients use an abstraction, the interface must provide sufficient functionality to meet their needs. If some critical operation is missing from an interface, clients may decide to abandon it and develop their own, more powerful abstraction. As important as simplicity is, the designer must avoid simplifying an interface to the point that it becomes useless.

- *General.* A well-designed interface should be flexible enough to meet the needs of many different clients. An interface that performs a narrowly defined set of operations for one client is not as useful as one that can be used in many different situations.

- *Stable.* The functions defined in an interface should continue to have precisely the same structure and effect even if the underlying implementation changes. Making changes in the behavior of an interface forces clients to change their programs, which compromises the value of interface.

The sections that follow discuss each of these criteria in detail.

The importance of a unifying theme

Unity gives strength.

—Aesop, *The Bundle of Sticks,* ~600 BCE

A central feature of a well-designed interface is that it presents a unified and consistent abstraction. In part, this criterion implies that the functions in a library should be chosen so that they reflect a coherent theme. Thus, the **<cmath>** library exports mathematical functions, the **<iostream>** library exports the **cin**, **cout**, and **cerr** streams along with the operators that perform input and output, and the **error.h** interface introduced in section 2.6 exports a function for reporting errors. Each interface entry exported by these libraries fits the purpose of that interface. For example, you would not expect to find **sqrt** in the **<string>** library since it fits much more naturally into the framework of the **<cmath>** library.

The principle of a unifying theme also influences the design of the functions within a library interface. The functions within an interface should behave in as consistent a way as possible. For example, all the functions in the **<cmath>** library measure angles in radians. If some functions measured angles in degrees, clients would have to remember what units to use for each function.

Simplicity and the principle of information hiding

Embrace simplicity.
—Lao-tzu, *The Way of Lao-tzu,* ~550 BCE

Because a primary goal of using interfaces is to reduce the complexity of the programming process, it makes sense that simplicity is a desirable criterion in the design of an interface. In general, an interface should be as easy to use as possible. The underlying implementation may perform extremely intricate operations, but the client should be able to think about those operations in a simple, more abstract way.

To a certain extent, an interface acts as a reference guide to a particular library abstraction. When you want to know how to use the **error** function, you consult the **error.h** interface to find out how to do so. The interface contains precisely the information that you, as a client, need to know—and no more. For clients, getting too much information can be as bad as getting too little, because additional detail is likely to make the interface more difficult to understand. Often, the real value of an interface lies not in the information it *reveals* but rather in the information it *hides*.

When you design an interface, you should try to protect the client from as many of the complicating details of the implementation as possible. In that respect, it is perhaps best to think of an interface not primarily as a communication channel between the client and the implementation, but instead as a wall that divides them.

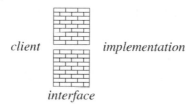

client   *implementation*

interface

Like the wall that divided the lovers Pyramus and Thisbe in Greek mythology, the wall representing an interface contains a chink that allows the client and the implementation to communicate. In programming, that chink consists of the interface entries that allow the client and implementation to communicate. The main purpose of the wall, however, is to keep the two sides apart. Because we conceive of it as lying at the border of the abstraction represented by the library, an interface is sometimes called an ***abstraction boundary.*** Ideally, all the complexity involved in the realization of a library lies on the implementation side of the wall. The interface is successful if it keeps that complexity away from the client side. Keeping details confined to the implementation is called ***information hiding.***

The principle of information hiding has important practical implications for interface design. When you write an interface, you should be sure you don't reveal details of the implementation, even in the commentary. Especially if you are writing an interface and an implementation at the same time, you may be tempted to describe in your interface all the clever ideas you used in the implementation. Try to resist that temptation. The interface is written for the benefit of the client and should contain only what the client needs to know.

Similarly, you should design the functions in an interface so that they are as simple as possible. If you can reduce the number of arguments or find a way to eliminate confusing special cases, it will be easier for the client to understand how to use those functions. Moreover, it is good practice to limit the total number of functions exported by an interface, so that the client does not become lost in a mass of functions, unable to make sense of the whole.

Meeting the needs of your clients

Everything should be as simple as possible, but no simpler.

—attributed to Albert Einstein

Simplicity is only part of the story. You can easily make an interface simple just by throwing away any parts of it that are hard or complicated. There is a good chance that doing so will also make the interface useless. Sometimes clients need to perform tasks that have some inherent complexity. Denying your clients the tools they require just to make the interface simpler is not an effective strategy. Your interface must provide sufficient functionality to serve the clients' needs. Learning to strike the right balance between simplicity and completeness in interface design is one of the fundamental challenges in programming.

In many cases, the clients of an interface are concerned not only with whether a particular function is available but also with the efficiency of its implementation. For example, if you are developing a system for air-traffic control and need to call functions provided by a library interface, those functions must return the correct answer quickly. Late answers may be just as devastating as wrong answers.

For the most part, efficiency is a concern associated with the implementation rather than the interface. Even so, you will often find it valuable to think about implementation strategies while you are designing the interface itself. Suppose, for example, that you are faced with a choice of two designs. If you determine that one of them would be much easier to implement efficiently, it makes sense—assuming there are no compelling reasons to the contrary—to choose that design.

The advantages of general tools

Give us the tools and we will finish the job.

— Winston Churchill, BBC broadcast, 1941

An interface that is perfectly adapted to a particular client's needs may not be useful to others. A good library abstraction serves the needs of many different clients. To do so, it must be general enough to solve a wide range of problems and not be limited to one highly specific purpose. By choosing a design that offers flexibility, you can create interfaces that are widely used.

The desire to ensure that an interface remains general has an important practical implication. When you are writing a program, you will often discover that you need a particular tool. If you decide that the tool is important enough to go into a library, you then need to change your mode of thought. When you design the interface for that library, you have to forget about the original application and instead design your interface for a more general audience.

The value of stability

People change and forget to tell each other. Too bad— causes so many mistakes.

—Lillian Hellman, *Toys in the Attic,* 1959

Interfaces have another property that makes them critically important to programming: they tend to be stable over long periods of time. Stable interfaces can dramatically simplify the problem of system maintenance by establishing clear boundaries of responsibility. As long as the interface does not change, both implementers and clients are relatively free to make changes on their own side of the abstraction boundary.

For example, suppose that you are the implementer of the `<cmath>` library. In the course of your work, you discover a clever new algorithm for calculating the `sqrt` function that cuts in half the time required to calculate a square root. If you can say to your clients that you have a new implementation of `sqrt` that works just as it did before, only faster, they will probably be pleased. If, on the other hand, you were to say that the name of the function had changed or that its use involved certain new restrictions, your clients would be justifiably annoyed. To use your "improved" implementation of square root, they would be forced to change their programs. Changing programs is a time-consuming, error-prone activity, and many clients would happily give up the extra efficiency for the convenience of being able to leave their programs alone.

Interfaces simplify the task of program maintenance only if they remain stable. Programs change frequently as new algorithms are discovered or as the requirements of applications change. Throughout such evolution, however, the interfaces must remain as constant as possible. In a well-designed system, changing the details of an implementation is a straightforward process. The complexity involved in making that change is localized on the implementation side of the abstraction boundary. On the other hand, changing an interface often produces a global upheaval that requires changing every program that depends on it. Thus, interface changes should be undertaken very rarely and then only with the active participation of clients.

Some interface changes are more drastic than others. For example, adding an entirely new function to an interface is usually a relatively straightforward process, since no clients already depend on that function. Changing an interface in such a way that existing programs will continue to run without modification is called *extending* the interface. If you find that you need to make evolutionary changes over the lifetime of an interface, it is usually best to make those changes by extension.

■ 2.8 Designing a random number library

The easiest way to appreciate the principles of interface design is to go through a simple design exercise. To this end, this section goes through the design process that led to the development of the `random.h` interface in the Stanford libraries, which makes it possible to write programs that make seemingly random choices. Being able to simulate random behavior is necessary, for example, if you want to write a computer game that involves flipping a coin or rolling a die, but is also useful in more practical contexts, as well. Programs that simulate such random events are called *nondeterministic* programs.

Getting a computer to behave in a random way involves a certain amount of complexity. For the benefit of client programmers, you want to hide this complexity behind an interface. In this section, you will have the opportunity to focus your attention on that interface from several different perspectives: that of the interface designer, the implementer, and the client.

Random versus pseudorandom numbers

Partly because early computers were used primarily for numerical applications, the idea of generating randomness using a computer is often expressed in terms of being able to generate a *random number* in a particular range. From a theoretical perspective, a number is random if there is no way to determine in advance what value it will have among a set of equally probable possibilities. For example, rolling a die generates a random number between 1 and 6. If the die is fair, there is no way to predict which number will come up. The six possible values are equally likely.

Although the idea of a random number makes intuitive sense, it is a difficult notion to represent inside a computer. Computers operate by following a sequence of instructions in memory and therefore function in a deterministic mode. How is it possible to generate unpredictable results by following a deterministic set of rules?

If a number is the result of a deterministic process, any user should be able to work through that same set of rules and anticipate the computer's response.

Yet computers do in fact use a deterministic procedure to generate what we call random numbers. This strategy works because, even though the user could, in theory, follow the same set of rules and anticipate the computer's response, no one actually bothers to do so. In most practical applications, it doesn't matter if the numbers are truly random; all that matters is that the numbers *appear* to be random. For numbers to appear random, they should (1) behave like random numbers from a statistical point of view and (2) be sufficiently difficult to predict in advance that no user would bother. "Random" numbers generated by an algorithmic process inside a computer are referred to as *pseudorandom numbers* to underscore the fact that no truly random activity is involved.

Pseudorandom numbers in the standard libraries

The `<cstdlib>` library exports a low-level function called `rand` that produces pseudorandom numbers. The prototype for `rand` is

```
int rand();
```

which indicates that `rand` takes no arguments and returns an integer. Each call to `rand` produces a different value that is difficult for clients to predict and therefore appears to be random. The result of `rand` is guaranteed to be nonnegative and no larger than the constant `RAND_MAX`, which is also defined in `<cstdlib>`. Thus, each time you call `rand`, it returns a different integer between 0 and `RAND_MAX`, inclusive.

If you want to get a feel for how the `rand` function works, one strategy is to write a simple program to test it. The `RandTest` program in Figure 2-10 displays the value of `RAND_MAX` and then prints out the result of calling `rand` ten times. A sample run of the program looks like this:

```
⊖ ⊖ ⊖                    RandTest
On this computer, RAND_MAX is 2147483647
The first 10 calls to rand:
1103527590
 377401575
 662824084
1147902781
2035015474
 368800899
1508029952
 486256185
1062517886
 267834847
```

```
FIGURE 2-10    Program to test the rand function

/*
 * File: RandTest.cpp
 * --------------------
 * This program tests the random number generator in C++ and produces
 * the values used in the examples in the text.
 */

#include <iostream>
#include <iomanip>
#include <cstdlib>
using namespace std;

const int N_TRIALS = 10;

int main() {
   cout << "On this computer, RAND_MAX is " << RAND_MAX << endl;
   cout << "The first " << N_TRIALS << " calls to rand:" << endl;
   for (int i = 0; i < N_TRIALS; i++) {
      cout << setw(10) << rand() << endl;
   }
   return 0;
}
```

As you can see, the value of **rand** is always positive, and never larger than the value of **RAND_MAX**. The values, moreover, appear to jump around unpredictably within that range, which is exactly what you want from a pseudorandom process.

Given that the C++ libraries include a function for generating pseudorandom numbers, it is reasonable to ask why one would bother to develop a new interface to support this process. The answer, in part, is that the **rand** function itself does not return a value that clients are likely to use in its original form. For one thing, the value of **RAND_MAX** depends on the hardware and software environment. On most systems, **RAND_MAX** is defined to be the largest positive integer, which is typically 2,147,483,647, but it may have different values on different systems. Moreover, even if you could count on **RAND_MAX** having that particular value, there are few (if any) applications where what you would need is a random number between 0 and 2,147,483,647. As a client, you are much more likely to want values that fall into some other range, usually a much smaller one. For example, if you are trying to simulate flipping a coin, you want a function that has only two outcomes: heads and tails. Similarly, if you are trying to represent rolling a die, you need to produce a random integer between 1 and 6. If you are trying to simulate processes in the physical world, you will often need to produce random values over a continuous range, where the result needs to be represented as a **double** rather than an **int**. If you could design an interface that was well suited to the needs of such clients, that interface would be much more flexible and easy to use.

Another reason to design a higher-level interface is that using the low-level functions from **<cstdlib>** introduces several complexities—as you will discover when you turn your attention to the implementation—that clients would be happy to ignore. Part of your job as an interface designer is to hide as much complexity from clients as possible. Defining a higher-level **random.h** interface makes that possible, because all the complexity can be localized within the implementation.

Choosing the right set of functions

As an interface designer, one of your primary challenges is choosing what functions to export. Although interface design turns out to be more of an art than a science, there are some general principles you can apply, including those outlined in section 2.7. In particular, the functions you export through **random.h** should be simple and should hide as much of the underlying complexity as possible. They should also provide the functionality necessary to meet the needs of a wide range of clients, which means that you need to have some idea of what operations clients are likely to need. Understanding those needs depends in part on your own experience, but often requires interacting with potential clients to get a better sense of their requirements.

From my own experience with programming, I know that the operations clients expect from an interface like **random.h** include the following:

- *Selecting a random integer in a specified range.* If you want, for example, to simulate the process of rolling a standard six-sided die, you need to choose a random integer between 1 and 6.

- *Choosing a random real number in a specified range.* If you want to position an object at a random point in space, you need to choose random *x* and *y* coordinates within whatever limits are appropriate to the application.

- *Simulating a random event with a specific probability.* If you want to simulate flipping a coin, you need to generate the value *heads* with probability 0.5, which corresponds to 50 percent of the time.

Translating these conceptual operations into a set of function prototypes is a relatively straightforward task. The first three functions—**randomInteger**, **randomReal**, and **randomChance**—in the **random.h** interface correspond to these three operations. The complete interface, which also exports a function called **setRandomSeed** described later in the chapter, appears in Figure 2-11.

FIGURE 2-11 Interface for the random number library

```
/*
 * File: random.h
 * ----------------
 * This file exports functions for generating pseudorandom numbers.
 */

#ifndef _random_h
#define _random_h

/*
 * Function: randomInteger
 * Usage: int n = randomInteger(low, high);
 * ------------------------------------------
 * Returns a random integer in the range low to high, inclusive.
 */

int randomInteger(int low, int high);

/*
 * Function: randomReal
 * Usage: double d = randomReal(low, high);
 * ------------------------------------------
 * Returns a random real number in the half-open interval [low, high).  A
 * half-open interval includes the first endpoint but not the second, which
 * means that the result is always greater than or equal to low but
 * strictly less than high.
 */

double randomReal(double low, double high);

/*
 * Function: randomChance
 * Usage: if (randomChance(p)) ...
 * ----------------------------------
 * Returns true with the probability indicated by p.  The argument p must
 * be a floating-point number between 0 (never) and 1 (always).  For
 * example, calling randomChance(.30) returns true 30 percent of the time.
 */

bool randomChance(double p);

/*
 * Function: setRandomSeed
 * Usage: setRandomSeed(seed);
 * ----------------------------
 * Sets the internal random number seed to the specified value.  You can
 * use this function to set a specific starting point for the pseudorandom
 * sequence or to ensure that program behavior is repeatable during the
 * debugging phase.
 */

void setRandomSeed(int seed);

#endif
```

As you can see from either the comments or the prototype in Figure 2-11, the **randomInteger** function takes two integer arguments and returns an integer in that range. If you wanted to simulate a die roll, you would call

```
randomInteger(1, 6)
```

To simulate a spin on a European roulette wheel (American wheels have both a 0 and a 00 slot in addition to the numbers from 1 to 36), you would call

```
randomInteger(0, 36)
```

The function **randomReal** is conceptually similar to **randomInteger**. It takes two floating-point values, **low** and **high**, and returns a floating-point value r subject to the condition that **low** $\leq r <$ **high**. For example, calling **randomReal(0, 1)** returns a random number that can be as small as 0 but is always strictly less than 1. In mathematics, a range of real numbers that can be equal to one endpoint but not the other is called a *half-open interval.* On a number line, a half-open interval is marked using an open circle to show that the endpoint is excluded, like this:

In mathematics, the standard convention is to use square brackets to indicate closed ends of intervals and parentheses to indicate open ones, so that the notation [0, 1) indicates the half-open interval corresponding to this diagram.

The function **randomChance** is used to simulate random events that occur with some fixed probability. In accord with the conventions of statistics, a probability is represented as a number between 0 and 1, where 0 means that the event never occurs and 1 means that it always does. Calling **randomChance(p)** returns **true** with probability **p**. Thus, calling **randomChance(0.75)** returns **true** 75 percent of the time.

You can use **randomChance** to simulate flipping a coin, as illustrated by the following function, which returns **"heads"** or **"tails"** with equal probability:

```
string flipCoin() {
   if (randomChance(0.50)) {
      return "heads";
   } else {
      return "tails";
   }
}
```

Constructing a client program

One of the best ways to validate the design of an interface is to write applications that use it. The program in Figure 2-12, for example, uses the **randomInteger** function to play the casino game called *craps*. The rules for craps appear in the comments at the beginning of the program, although you would probably want the program to explain the rules to the user as well. In this example, the printed instructions have been omitted to save space.

Although the **Craps.cpp** program is nondeterministic and will produce different outcomes each time, one possible sample run looks like this:

```
●○○                    Craps
This program plays a game of craps.
Rolling the dice . . .
You rolled 5 and 5 - that's 10.
Your point is 10.
Rolling the dice . . .
You rolled 4 and 1 - that's 5.
Rolling the dice . . .
You rolled 4 and 6 - that's 10.
You made your point.  You win.
```

Implementing the random number library

Up to now, this chapter has looked only at the design of the **random.h** interface. Before you can actually use that interface in a program, it is necessary to write the corresponding **random.cpp** implementation. All you know at this point is that you have a function **rand** in the **<cstdlib>** library that generates a random integer between 0 and a positive constant called **RAND_MAX**, which is some point on a number line that looks like this:

To simulate the die roll, for example, what you need to do is transform that random integer into one of the following discrete outcomes:

As it happens, there are many bad strategies for performing this transformation. A surprising number of textbooks, for example, suggest code that looks like this:

```
int die = rand() % 6 + 1;
```

FIGURE 2-12 Program to play the casino game of craps

```cpp
/*
 * File: Craps.cpp
 * ----------------
 * This program plays the casino game called craps, which is
 * played using a pair of dice.  At the beginning of the game,
 * you roll the dice and compute the total.  If your first roll
 * is 7 or 11, you win with what gamblers call a "natural."
 * If your first roll is 2, 3, or 12, you lose by "crapping
 * out."  In any other case, the total from the first roll
 * becomes your "point," after which you continue to roll
 * the dice until one of the following conditions occurs:
 *
 * a) You roll your point again, in which case you win.
 * b) You roll a 7, in which case you lose.
 *
 * Other rolls, including 2, 3, 11, and 12, have no effect
 * during this phase of the game.
 */

#include <iostream>
#include "random.h"
using namespace std;

/* Function prototypes */

bool tryToMakePoint(int point);
int rollTwoDice();

/* Main program */

int main() {
   cout << "This program plays a game of craps." << endl;
   int point = rollTwoDice();
   switch (point) {
    case 7: case 11:
      cout << "That's a natural.  You win." << endl;
      break;
    case 2: case 3: case 12:
      cout << "That's craps.  You lose." << endl;
      break;
    default:
      cout << "Your point is " << point << "." << endl;
      if (tryToMakePoint(point)) {
         cout << "You made your point.  You win." << endl;
      } else {
         cout << "You rolled a seven.  You lose." << endl;
      }
   }
   return 0;
}
```

FIGURE 2-12 Program to play the casino game of craps (continued)

```
/*
 * Function: tryToMakePoint
 * Usage: flag = tryToMakePoint(point);
 * ------------------------------------
 * Rolls the dice repeatedly until you either make your point or roll a 7.
 * The function returns true if you make your point and false if a 7 comes
 * up first.
 */

bool tryToMakePoint(int point) {
   while (true) {
      int total = rollTwoDice();
      if (total == point) return true;
      if (total == 7) return false;
   }
}

/*
 * Function: rollTwoDice
 * Usage: total = rollTwoDice();
 * ------------------------------
 * Simulates the process of rolling two dice.  The individual values of the
 * dice are printed on cout along with the sum, which is returned as the
 * value of the function.
 */

int rollTwoDice() {
   cout << "Rolling the dice . . ." << endl;
   int d1 = randomInteger(1, 6);
   int d2 = randomInteger(1, 6);
   int total = d1 + d2;
   cout << "You rolled " << d1 << " and " << d2
        << " - that's " << total << "." << endl;
   return total;
}
```

This code looks reasonable on the surface. The **rand** function always returns a positive integer, so the remainder on division by six must be an integer between 0 and 5. Adding one to that value gives an integer in the desired range of 1 to 6.

The problem here is that **rand** guarantees only that the value it produces is uniformly distributed over the range from 0 to **RAND_MAX**. There is, however, no guarantee that the remainders on division by six will be at all random. In fact, early versions of **rand** distributed with the Unix operating system generated values that alternated between odd and even values, despite the fact that those values did fall uniformly over the range. Taking the remainder on division by six would also alternate between even and odd values, which hardly fits any reasonable definition of random behavior. If nothing else, it would be impossible to roll doubles on successive die rolls, given that one die would always be even and the other would always be odd.

What you want to do instead is divide the integers between 0 and **RAND_MAX** into six equal-sized segments that correspond to the different outcomes, as follows:

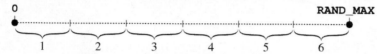

In the more general case, you need to divide the number line between 0 and **RAND_MAX** into *k* equal intervals, where *k* is the number of possible outcomes in the desired range. Once you've done that, all you need to do is map the interval number into the value the client wants.

The process of transforming the result of the **rand** function into an integer in a finite range can be understood most easily if you decompose it into the following four-step process:

1. *Normalize* the integer result from **rand** by converting it into a floating-point number *d* in the range $0 \le d < 1$.

2. *Scale* the value *d* by multiplying it by the size of the desired range, so that it spans the correct number of integers.

3. *Translate* the value by adding in the lower bound so that the range begins at the desired point.

4. *Convert* the number to an integer by calling the function **floor** from **<cmath>**, which returns the largest integer that is smaller than its argument.

These phases are illustrated in Figure 2-13, which also traces one possible path through the process. If the initial call to **rand** returns 848,256,064 and **RAND_MAX** has its most common value of 2,147,483,647, the normalization process produces a value close to 0.4 (the values in Figure 2-13 have been rounded to a single digit after the decimal point to make them fit in the diagram). Multiplying this value by 6 in the scaling step gives 2.4, which is then shifted to 3.4 in the translation step. In the conversion step, calling **floor** on 3.4 yields the value 3.

Writing the code to implement this process is not as easy as it might appear, because there are several pitfalls that can easily trap the insufficiently careful programmer. Consider, for example, just the normalization step. You can't convert the result of **rand** to a floating-point value in the half-open interval [0, 1) by calling

```
double d = double(rand()) / RAND_MAX;
```

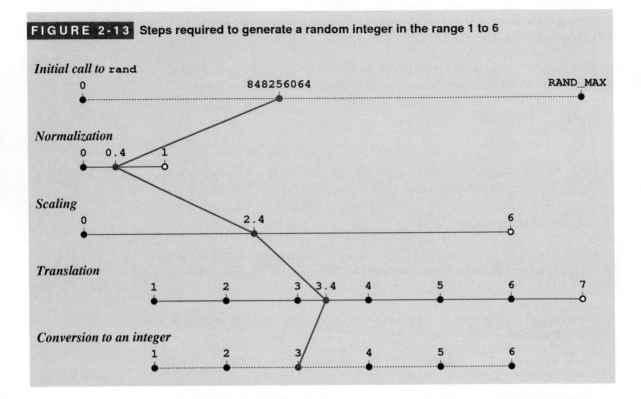

FIGURE 2-13   Steps required to generate a random integer in the range 1 to 6

Initial call to `rand`

Normalization

Scaling

Translation

Conversion to an integer

The problem here is that **rand** might return the value **RAND_MAX**, which would mean that the variable **d** would be assigned the value 1.0, which is specifically excluded from the half-open interval. What's worse is that you also can't write

```
double d = double(rand()) / (RAND_MAX + 1);
```

although the problem in this case is more subtle. As noted earlier, **RAND_MAX** is typically chosen to be the largest positive value of type **int**. If that is indeed the case, adding one to it cannot possibly produce a value in the integer range.

To fix these problems, what you need to do instead is perform the addition using type **double** instead of **int**, as follows:

```
double d = rand() / (double(RAND_MAX) + 1);
```

A similar problem arises in the scaling step. Mathematically, the number of integer values in the inclusive range from **low** to **high** is given by the expression **high - low + 1**. That calculation, however, overflows the range of an integer if **high** is a large positive number and **low** is a negative number with a large absolute magnitude. Thus, this expression must be evaluated using double precision as well.

Taking these complexities into account, the implementation of `randomInteger` looks like this:

```
int randomInteger(int low, int high) {
   double d = rand() / (double(RAND_MAX) + 1);
   double s = d * (double(high) - low + 1);
   return int(floor(low + s));
}
```

The implementations of `randomReal` and `randomChance` are relatively simple, given that you've already had to work out the complexities for `randomInteger`:

```
double randomReal(double low, double high) {
   double d = rand() / (double(RAND_MAX) + 1);
   double s = d * (high - low);
   return low + s;
}

bool randomChance(double p) {
   return randomReal(0, 1) < p;
}
```

Initializing the random number seed

Unfortunately, the implementations of the `randomInteger`, `randomReal`, and `randomChance` functions from the preceding section don't quite work exactly the way clients would want. The problem is that—far from producing unpredictable results—programs that use these functions always produce exactly the same results. If, for example, you were to run the `Craps` program twenty times in succession, you would see exactly the same output each time. So much for randomness.

To figure out why the implementation is behaving in this way, it helps to go back to the `RandTest` program and run it again. This time, the output is

```
⊝ ⊝ ⊝                    RandTest
On this computer, RAND_MAX is 2147483647
The first 10 calls to rand:
1103527590
 377401575
 662824084
1147902781
2035015474
 368800899
1508029952
 486256185
1062517886
 267834847
```

The output is the same as the first time around. In fact, the **RandTest** program produces identical output *every* time because the designers of the C++ library (and the earlier C libraries on which these libraries are based) decided that **rand** should return the *same* random sequence each time a program is run.

At first, it may be hard to understand why a function that is supposed to return a random number always returns the same sequence of values. After all, deterministic behavior of this sort seems to run counter to the whole idea of randomness. There is, however, a good reason for this behavior: programs that behave deterministically are easier to debug.

To get a sense of why such repeatability is important, imagine that you have written a program to play an intricate game, such as Monopoly. As is always the case with newly written programs, the odds are good that your program will have a few bugs. In a complex program, bugs can be relatively obscure, in the sense that they occur only in rare situations. Suppose you are playing the game and discover that the program is starting to behave in a bizarre way. As you begin to debug the program, it would be very convenient if you could regenerate the same state and take a closer look at what is going on. Unfortunately, if the program is running in a random way, a second run of the program will behave differently from the first. Bugs that showed up the first time may not occur on the second pass. The designers of the original C libraries therefore concluded that it had to be possible to use **rand** in a deterministic way in order to support debugging.

At the same time, it also has to be possible to use **rand** so that it *doesn't* always deliver the same results. To understand how to implement this behavior, it helps to understand how **rand** works internally. The **rand** function generates each new random value by applying a set of mathematical calculations to the last value it produced. Because you don't know what those calculations are, it is best to think of the entire operation as a black box where old numbers go in on one side and new pseudorandom numbers pop out on the other. Since the first call to **rand** produces the value 1103527590, the second call to **rand** corresponds to putting 1103527590 into one end of the black box and having 377401575 pop out on the other side:

$$1103527590 \longrightarrow \boxed{\texttt{rand}} \longrightarrow 377401575$$

On the next call to **rand**, the implementation puts 377401575 into the black box, which returns 662824084:

$$377401575 \longrightarrow \boxed{\texttt{rand}} \longrightarrow 662824084$$

This same process is repeated on each call to **rand**. The computation inside the black box is designed so that (1) the numbers are uniformly distributed over the legal range, and (2) the sequence goes on for a long time before it begins to repeat.

But what about the first call to **rand**—the one that returns 1103527590? The implementation must have a starting point. There must be an integer s_0 that goes into the black box and produces 1103527590:

$$s_0 \longrightarrow \boxed{\textbf{rand}} \longrightarrow 1103527590$$

This initial value—the value that is used to get the entire process started—is called the *seed* for the random number generator. In the **<cstdlib>** library, you can set that seed explicitly by calling **srand**(*seed*).

As you know from the multiple runs of the **RandTest** program, the C++ library sets the initial seed to a constant value every time a program is started, which is why **rand** always generates the same sequence of values. That behavior, however, makes sense only during the debugging phase. Most modern languages change the default behavior so that the functions in the random-number library return *different* results on each run unless the programmer specifies otherwise. That design is considerably simpler for clients, and it makes sense to incorporate that design change into the **random.h** interface. It is still necessary to allow clients to generate a repeatable sequence of values, because doing so simplifies the debugging process. The need to provide that option is the reason for the inclusion in the interface of the **setRandomSeed** function. During the debugging phase, you can add the line

```
    setRandomSeed(1);
```

at the beginning of the **main** program. The calls to the other entries exported by the **random.h** interface will then produce the repeatable sequence of values generated by using 1 as the initial seed. When you are convinced that the program is working, you can remove this line to restore unpredictable behavior.

To implement this change, the functions **randomInteger**, **randomReal**, and **randomChance** must first check to see whether the random number seed has already been initialized and, if not, set it to some starting value that would be difficult for users to predict, which is usually taken from the value of the system clock. Because that value is different each time you run a program, the random number sequence changes as well. In C++, you can retrieve the current value of the system clock by calling the function **time** and then converting the result to an integer. This technique allows you to write the following statement, which has the effect of initializing the pseudorandom number generator to an unpredictable point:

```
    srand(int(time(NULL)));
```

Although it requires only a single line, the operation to set the random seed to an unpredictable value based on the system clock is quite obscure. If this line were to appear in the client program, the client would have to understand the concept of a random number seed, along with the functions **srand** and **time** and the constant **NULL** (which you will learn about in Chapter 11). To make things as easy as possible for the client, you need to hide this complexity away.

The situation becomes even more complicated when you realize that this initialization step must be performed once—and only once—before delivering up the results of any of the other functions. To ensure that the initialization code doesn't get executed every time, you need a Boolean flag to record whether that initialization has been performed. Unfortunately, it doesn't work to declare that flag as a global variable, because C++ does not specify the order in which global variables are initialized. If you declare other global values whose initial values were produced by the random-library library, there is no way to ensure that the initialization flag has been set correctly.

In C++, the best strategy is to declare the initialization flag inside the context of the function that checks to see whether the necessary initialization has already been performed. That variable, however, can't be declared as a traditional local variable, because doing so would mean that a new variable would be created on every call. To make this strategy work, you need to mark the flag as **static**, as shown in the following implementation:

```
void initRandomSeed() {
   static bool initialized = false;
   if (!initialized) {
      srand(int(time(NULL)));
      initialized = true;
   }
}
```

When it is marked with the keyword **static**, the variable **initialized** becomes a *static local variable.* Like any local variable, a static local variable is accessible only within the body of the function; the difference with a static local variable is that the compiler allocates only one copy of that variable, which is then shared by all calls to **initRandomSeed**. The rules of C++ ensure that static local variables are initialized exactly once and, moreover, that the initialization occurs before the function containing them is called. Defining **initRandomSeed** represents the final step in coding the **random.cpp** implementation, which appears in Figure 2-14.

My goal in going through the code for the **random.cpp** implementation is not for you to master all of its intricacies. What I hope to do instead is convince you why it is important for you as a client of **random.h** *not* to have to understand all those details. The code in **random.cpp** is subtle and contains many potential pitfalls that are likely to ensnare the programmer who tries to implement these functions from scratch. The primary purpose of library interfaces is to hide precisely this sort of complexity.

```
FIGURE 2-14  Implementation of the random number library
```

```
/*
 * File: random.cpp
 * ----------------
 * This file implements the random.h interface.
 */

#include <cstdlib>
#include <cmath>
#include <ctime>
#include "random.h"
using namespace std;

/* Private function prototype */

void initRandomSeed();

/*
 * Implementation notes: randomInteger
 * ------------------------------------
 * The code for randomInteger produces the number in four steps:
 *
 * 1. Generate a random real number d in the range [0 .. 1).
 * 2. Scale the number to the range [0 .. N) where N is the number of values.
 * 3. Translate the number so that the range starts at the appropriate value.
 * 4. Convert the result to the next lower integer.
 *
 * The implementation is complicated by the fact that both the expression
 *
 *     RAND_MAX + 1
 *
 * and the expression for the number of values
 *
 *     high - low + 1
 *
 * can overflow the integer range.  These calculations must therefore be
 * performed using doubles instead of ints.
 */

int randomInteger(int low, int high) {
   initRandomSeed();
   double d = rand() / (double(RAND_MAX) + 1);
   double s = d * (double(high) - low + 1);
   return int(floor(low + s));
}
```

☞

FIGURE 2-14 Implementation of the random number library (continued)

```
/*
 * Implementation notes: randomReal
 * ---------------------------------
 * The code for randomReal is similar to that for randomInteger,
 * without the final conversion step.
 */

double randomReal(double low, double high) {
   initRandomSeed();
   double d = rand() / (double(RAND_MAX) + 1);
   double s = d * (high - low);
   return low + s;
}

/*
 * Implementation notes: randomChance
 * -----------------------------------
 * The code for randomChance calls randomReal(0, 1) and then checks
 * whether the result is less than the requested probability.
 */

bool randomChance(double p) {
   initRandomSeed();
   return randomReal(0, 1) < p;
}

/*
 * Implementation notes: setRandomSeed
 * ------------------------------------
 * The setRandomSeed function simply forwards its argument to srand.
 * The call to initRandomSeed is required to set the initialized flag.
 */

void setRandomSeed(int seed) {
   initRandomSeed();
   srand(seed);
}

/*
 * Implementation notes: initRandomSeed
 * -------------------------------------
 * The initRandomSeed function declares a static variable that keeps track
 * of whether the seed has been initialized.  The first time initRandomSeed
 * is called, initialized is false, so the seed is set to the current time.
 */

void initRandomSeed() {
   static bool initialized = false;
   if (!initialized) {
      srand(int(time(NULL)));
      initialized = true;
   }
}
```

◼️ 2.9 Introduction to the Stanford libraries

Up to this point, the programs in this book have used only standard features of C++. For that reason, these programs should work with any C++ compiler on any type of hardware. Unfortunately, the standard C++ libraries do not include all the features that you would want as a programmer. Even though almost all modern applications use graphical displays, the standard libraries offer no graphical capabilities. Every modern operating system provides libraries that support drawing pictures on the screen, but those libraries are different for each machine. In order to create applications that are as interesting as those you are accustomed to using, you will need to use nonstandard libraries somewhere along the way.

As part of the supporting material for this textbook, Stanford University provides a set of libraries that make learning to program in C++ both easier and more enjoyable. Those libraries include, for example, a graphics package that works the same way on the most common computing platforms. The Stanford libraries also provide a home for the libraries developed in this chapter. After going to all the effort of defining and implementing interfaces like **error.h**, **direction.h**, **gmath.h**, and **random.h**, it doesn't make sense to abandon those tools or even to force potential clients to copy the associated code. Since every one of those interfaces will come in handy for certain applications, it makes sense to include the interfaces as part of a library. Creating a compiled library, however, is beyond the scope of this text, mostly because the details of doing so differ from machine to machine. The Stanford web site for this book includes a precompiled version of these libraries for all the major platforms that students are likely to use. You can download those libraries from the web along with the **.h** files that define the library interfaces. It might take a little time to figure out how to use the Stanford libraries in the programming environment in which you're working, but that effort will quickly repay itself many times over.

A library to simplify input and output

In addition to the library interfaces introduced in this chapter, the Stanford libraries include several other interfaces that will make programming somewhat easier. Of these, the most important is the **simpio.h** interface, which simplifies the process of getting input from the user. Instead of the lines

```
int limit;
cout << "Enter exponent limit: ";
cin >> limit;
```

using **simpio.h** allows you to collapse this set of operations into a single line:

```
int limit = getInteger("Enter exponent limit: ");
```

Although the code for the `simpio.h` strategy is considerably shorter, its real advantage is that the `getInteger` function checks the user's input for errors. Suppose, for example, that your program is in the process of executing the line

```
int n = getInteger("Enter an integer: ");
```

The implementation of `getInteger` displays the prompt string and waits for user input, like this:

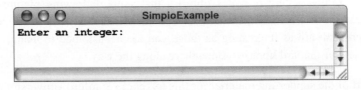

If the user intends to type 120 but mistakenly types a minus sign in place of the zero, `getInteger` will notice that the input is not a legal integer and give the user another chance to enter the correct value, as shown in the following sample run:

```
⊖ ○ ⊖                    SimpioExample
Enter an integer: 12-
Illegal integer format.  Try again.
Enter an integer: 120
```

The `>>` operator, by contrast, does not check for this type of error. If the user entered `12-` in response to the statement

```
cin >> n;
```

the variable **n** would get the value 12, leaving the minus sign in the input stream.

In addition to `getInteger`, the `simpio.h` interface also exports a `getReal` function for reading a floating-point value and a `getLine` function for reading an entire line as a string. You will learn how to implement these functions in Chapter 4, but you can use them now to get in the habit.

The Stanford libraries also include a console library, which creates a console window on the screen as soon as your program starts up. Having this window appear automatically solves the problem that Dennis Ritchie identified in *The C Programming Language* when he wrote that one of the harder challenges in running a program is to "find out where the output went." To use this library, all you have to do is add the line

```
#include "console.h"
```

at the beginning of your program. If this line appears, the program creates the console. If the line is missing, the program works the way it always did.

Graphical programs in the Stanford libraries

One of the challenges of using C++ as a teaching language is that C++ doesn't offer a standard graphics library. Although it is perfectly possible to learn about data structures and algorithms without using graphics, having a graphics library makes the process a lot more enjoyable. And because you're likely to learn things more easily if you can have a little fun along the way, the Stanford libraries include a library package that supports two-dimensional graphics on most common platforms.

The primary interface to the graphics library is **gwindow.h**, which exports a class called **GWindow** that represents a graphics window. To draw graphics on the screen, you need to declare a **GWindow** and then invoke methods on that object. Although the **GWindow** class exports a much larger set of methods, the programs in this book use only the methods shown in Table 2-2. Almost every graphics package supports methods that look very similar to the ones in this table, and it should be easy to adapt the examples in this text to work with other graphics libraries.

Figure 2-15 shows a simple graphics application, which is designed to illustrate the methods in Table 2-2 rather than to draw anything useful. The output of the program appears in Figure 2-16 at the top of page 111.

TABLE 2-2 Methods in the GWindow class that are used in this text

`GWindow gw;` `GWindow gw(width, height);`	Creates a graphics window, which is conventionally stored in a variable named **gw**. That variable must be passed by reference to any functions that perform graphical operations. If *width* and *height* are omitted, the constructor creates a window with a default size of 500×300 pixels.
`gw.drawLine(x_0, y_0, x_1, y_1)`	Draws a line from the point (x_0, y_0) to the point (x_1, y_1).
`gw.drawPolarLine(x, y, r, theta)`	Draws a line from the point (x, y) that extends r pixel units at angle *theta* relative to the +x axis. This method is described in more detail in Chapter 8.
`gw.drawRect(x, y, width, height)`	Draws the frame of the rectangle with the specified bounds.
`gw.fillRect(x, y, width, height)`	Fills the rectangle with the specified bounds.
`gw.drawOval(x, y, width, height)`	Draws the frame of the oval inscribed in the specified rectangle.
`gw.fillOval(x, y, width, height)`	Fills the oval inscribed in the specified rectangle.
`gw.setColor(color)`	Sets the current color. The *color* parameter is a string that names a color. A list of defined color names appears in the web-based documentation.
`gw.getWidth()`	Returns the width of the graphics window in pixels.
`gw.getHeight()`	Returns the height of the graphics window in pixels.

FIGURE 2-15 Code for the GraphicsExample program

```cpp
/*
 * File: GraphicsExample.cpp
 * --------------------------
 * This program illustrates the use of graphics using the GWindow class.
 */

#include "gwindow.h"

/* Prototypes */

void drawDiamond(GWindow & gw);
void drawRectangleAndOval(GWindow & gw);

/* Main program */

int main() {
   GWindow gw;
   drawDiamond(gw);
   drawRectangleAndOval(gw);
   return 0;
}

/*
 * Function: drawDiamond
 * Usage: drawDiamond(gw);
 * -----------------------
 * Draws a diamond connecting the midpoints of the window edges.
 */

void drawDiamond(GWindow & gw) {
   double width = gw.getWidth();
   double height = gw.getHeight();
   gw.drawLine(0, height / 2, width / 2, 0);
   gw.drawLine(width / 2, 0, width, height / 2);
   gw.drawLine(width, height / 2, width / 2, height);
   gw.drawLine(width / 2, height, 0, height / 2);
}

/*
 * Function: drawRectangleAndOval
 * Usage: drawRectangleAndOval(gw);
 * --------------------------------
 * Draws a blue rectangle and a gray oval inscribed in the diamond.
 */

void drawRectangleAndOval(GWindow & gw) {
   double width = gw.getWidth();
   double height = gw.getHeight();
   gw.setColor("BLUE");
   gw.fillRect(width / 4, height / 4, width / 2, height / 2);
   gw.setColor("GRAY");
   gw.fillOval(width / 4, height / 4, width / 2, height / 2);
}
```

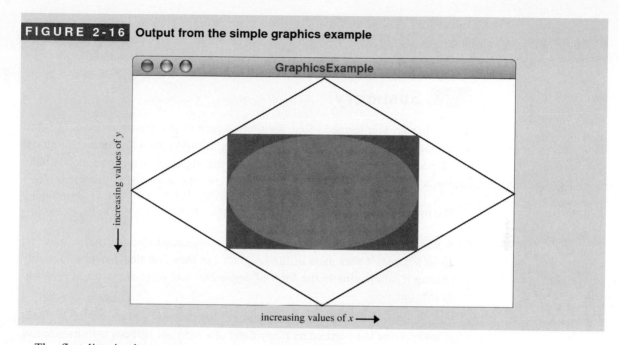

FIGURE 2-16 **Output from the simple graphics example**

The first line in the **GraphicsExample** program declares a **GWindow** object, which implements the graphical operations. The simplest form of the declaration is

```
GWindow gw;
```

which creates a small graphics window and displays it on the screen. You can, however, specify the window size by invoking an alternate form of the constructor:

```
GWindow gw(width, height);
```

The parameters *width* and *height* are measured in units called ***pixels***, which are the individual dots that cover the surface of the display screen.

All graphical operations are implemented as methods applied to the **GWindow** stored in the variable **gw**. For that reason, any piece of code that uses graphics must have access to that variable. If you decompose your program into several functions, you will typically need to pass the value of **gw** as a reference parameter to any function that needs access to the graphical capabilities of the window.

Coordinates in the graphics window are represented using a pair of values (x, y) where the x and y values represent the distance in that dimension from the ***origin,*** which is the point $(0, 0)$ in the upper left corner of the window. As in traditional Cartesian coordinates, the value for x increases as you move rightward across the window. Having the location of the origin in the upper left corner, however, means that the y value increases as you move downward, which is precisely opposite to the conventions used in the usual Cartesian plane. Computer-based graphics packages invert the *y* coordinate because doing so is more natural for text. If *y* values increase downward, successive lines of text appear at increasing values of *y*.

Summary

In this chapter, you learned about *functions*, which enable you to refer to an entire set of operations by using a simple name. By allowing the programmer to ignore the internal details and concentrate only on the effect of a function as a whole, functions are an essential tool for reducing the conceptual complexity of programs.

The important points introduced in this chapter include:

- A *function* is a block of code that has been organized into a separate unit and given a name. Other parts of the program can then *call* that function, possibly passing it information in the form of *arguments* and receiving a result *returned* by that function.

- Functions serve several useful purposes in programming. Allowing the same set of instructions to be shared by many parts of a program reduces both its size and its complexity. More importantly, functions make it possible to *decompose* large programs into smaller, more manageable pieces. Functions also serve as the basis for implementing *algorithms,* which are precisely specified strategies for solving computational problems.

- Functions become even more useful when they are collected into a *library,* which can then be shared by many different applications. Each library typically defines several functions that share a single conceptual framework. In computer science, the process of making a function available through a library is called *exporting* that function.

- The **<cmath>** library exports several functions that are likely to be familiar from mathematics, including functions like **sqrt**, **sin**, and **cos**. As a client of the **<cmath>** library, you need to know how to call these functions, but do not need to know the details of how they work.

- In C++, functions must be declared before they are used. A function declaration is called a *prototype*. In addition to the prototype, functions have an *implementation*, which specifies the individual steps that function contains.

- A function that returns a value must have a **return** statement that specifies the result. Functions may return values of any type. Functions that return Boolean values play an important role in programming and are called *predicate functions*.

- A function that returns no result and is executed only for its effect is called a *procedure*.

- C++ allows you to define several functions with the same name as long as the compiler can use the number and types of the arguments to determine which function is required. This process is called *overloading*. The argument pattern that distinguishes each of the overloaded variants is called a *signature*. C++ also makes it possible to specify *default parameters,* which are used if the client omits the corresponding arguments from the call.

- Variables declared with a function are *local* to that function and cannot be used outside of it. Internally, all the variables declared within a function are stored together in a *stack frame*.

- When you call a function, the arguments are evaluated in the context of the caller and then copied into the *parameter variables* specified in the function prototype. The association of arguments and parameters always follows the order in which the variables appear in each of the lists.

- C++ makes it possible for a function and its caller to share the value of a parameter variable by marking it with the ampersand character (`&`). This style of parameter transmission is referred to as *call by reference.*

- When a function returns, it continues from precisely the point at which the call was made. The computer refers to this point as the *return address* and keeps track of it in the stack frame.

- Programmers who create a library are its *implementers;* programmers who make use of one are called its *clients*. The connection between the implementer and the client is called an *interface*. Interfaces typically export functions, types, and constants, which are collectively known as *interface entries.*

- In C++, interfaces are stored in *header files,* which typically end with a `.h` suffix. Every interface should include several lines of *interface boilerplate* to ensure that the compiler reads the interface only once.

- When you design an interface, you must balance several criteria. Well-designed interfaces are *unified, simple, sufficient, general,* and *stable.*

- The `random.h` interface exports several functions that make it easy to simulate random behavior.

- The interfaces defined in this chapter—`error.h`, `direction.h`, `gmath.h`, and `random.h`—are exported as part of a Stanford library package so that clients can use them without having to rewrite the necessary code. The Stanford library also defines several other useful interfaces, including a simplified input/output library (`simpio.h`), a library to produce an interactive console (`console.h`), and a library to display graphical windows on the screen (`gwindow.h`).

Review questions

1. Explain in your own words the difference between a *function* and a *program*.

2. Define the following terms as they apply to functions: *call, argument, return*.

3. True or false: Every function in a C++ program requires a prototype.

4. What is the prototype of the function `sqrt` in the `<cmath>` library?

5. Can there be more than one `return` statement in the body of a function?

6. What is a *predicate function?*

7. What is meant by the term *overloading?* How does the C++ compiler use *signatures* to implement overloading?

8. How do you specify a default value for a parameter?

9. True or false: It is possible to specify a default value for the first parameter to a function without specifying a default value for the second.

10. What is a *stack frame?*

11. Describe the process by which *arguments* are associated with *parameters*.

12. Variables declared within a function are said to be *local variables*. What is the significance of the word *local* in this context?

13. What does the term *call by reference* mean?

14. How do you indicate *call by reference* in a C++ program?

15. Define the following terms in the context of libraries: *client, implementation, interface*.

16. If you were writing an interface called `mylib.h`, what lines would you include as the interface boilerplate?

17. Describe the process used to export a constant definition as part of an interface.

18. What criteria are identified in this chapter as central to the process of interface design?

19. Why is it important for an interface to be stable?

20. What is meant by the term *pseudorandom number?*

21. On most computers, how is the value of **RAND_MAX** chosen?

22. What four steps are necessary to convert the result of **rand** into an integer value with a different range?

23. How would you use the **randomInteger** function to generate a pseudorandom number between 1 and 100?

24. By executing each of the statements in the implementation by hand, determine whether the **randomInteger** function works with negative arguments. What are the possible results of calling the function **randomInteger(-5, 5)**?

25. Assuming that **d1** and **d2** have already been declared as variables of type **int**, could you use the multiple assignment statement

        d1 = d2 = RandomInteger(1, 6);

    to simulate the process of rolling two dice?

26. True or false: The **rand** function ordinarily generates the same sequence of random numbers every time a program is run.

27. What is meant by the term *seed* in the context of random numbers?

28. What suggestion does this chapter offer for debugging a program involving random numbers?

29. What functions are defined in the final version of the **random.h** interface? In what context would you use each function?

■ Exercises

1. If you did not do so the first time around, rewrite the Celsius-to-Fahrenheit program from exercise 1 in Chapter 1 so that it uses a function to perform the conversion.

2. Reimplement the distance-conversion program from exercise 2 in Chapter 1 so that it uses a function. In this case, the function must produce both the number of feet and the number of inches, which means that you need to use call by reference to return these values.

3. When a floating-point number is converted to an integer in C++, the value is truncated by throwing away any fraction. Thus, when 4.99999 is converted to an integer, the result is 4. In many cases, it would be useful to have the option of rounding a floating-point value to the nearest integer. Given a positive floating-point number x, you can round it to the closest integer by adding 0.5 and then truncating the result to an integer. Because truncation always moves toward zero, rounding negative numbers requires you to subtract 0.5, rather than adding it.

    Write a function `roundToNearestInt(x)` that rounds the floating-point number `x` to the nearest integer. Show that your function works by writing a suitable main program to test it.

4. If you have been outside in cold, windy weather, you know that your perception of the cold depends on the wind speed as well as the temperature. The faster the wind blows, the colder you feel. To quantify the how wind affects temperature perception, the National Weather Service reports the *wind chill*, which is illustrated on their website as shown in Figure 2-17.

FIGURE 2-17   Wind chill as a function of temperature and wind speed

Wind (mph)	Calm	40	35	30	25	20	15	10	5	0	-5	-10	-15	-20	-25	-30	-35	-40	-45
5		36	31	25	19	13	7	1	-5	-11	-16	-22	-28	-34	-40	-46	-52	-57	-63
10		34	27	21	15	9	3	-4	-10	-16	-22	-28	-35	-41	-47	-53	-59	-66	-72
15		32	25	19	13	6	0	-7	-13	-19	-26	-32	-39	-45	-51	-58	-64	-71	-77
20		30	24	17	11	4	-2	-9	-15	-22	-29	-35	-42	-48	-55	-61	-68	-74	-81
25		29	23	16	9	3	-4	-11	-17	-24	-31	-37	-44	-51	-58	-64	-71	-78	-84
30		28	22	15	8	1	-5	-12	-19	-26	-33	-39	-46	-53	-60	-67	-73	-80	-87
35		28	21	14	7	0	-7	-14	-21	-27	-34	-41	-48	-55	-62	-69	-76	-82	-89
40		27	20	13	6	-1	-8	-15	-22	-29	-36	-43	-50	-57	-64	-71	-78	-84	-91
45		26	19	12	5	-2	-9	-16	-23	-30	-37	-44	-51	-58	-65	-72	-79	-86	-93
50		26	19	12	4	-3	-10	-17	-24	-31	-38	-45	-52	-60	-67	-74	-81	-88	-95
55		25	18	11	4	-3	-11	-18	-25	-32	-39	-46	-54	-61	-68	-75	-82	-89	-97
60		25	17	10	3	-4	-11	-19	-26	-33	-40	-48	-55	-62	-69	-76	-84	-91	-98

Temperature (°F)

Frostbite Times   30 minutes   10 minutes   5 minutes

Wind Chill (°F) = $35.74 + 0.6215T - 35.75(V^{0.16}) + 0.4275T(V^{0.16})$

Where, T = Air Temperature (°F)   V = Wind Speed (mph)   *Effective 11/01/01*

Source: National Weather Service

As you can see at the bottom of Figure 2-17, the National Weather Service calculates wind chill using the formula

$$35.74 + 0.6215\,t - 35.75\,v^{0.16} + 0.4275\,t\,v^{0.16}$$

where t is the Fahrenheit temperature and v is the wind speed in miles per hour.

Write a function **windChill** that takes the values of t and v and returns the wind chill. In doing so, your function should take account of two special cases:

- If there is no wind, **windChill** should return the original temperature t.

- If the temperature is greater than 40° F, the wind chill is undefined, and your function should call **error** with an appropriate message.

Although it will be easier to write such an application once you learn how to format numeric data in Chapter 4, you already know enough to align the columns of the wind-chill table as shown in Figure 2-17. If you're up for a challenge, write a main program that uses **windChill** to produce that table.

5. Greek mathematicians took a special interest in numbers that are equal to the sum of their *proper divisors,* which is simply any divisor less than the number itself. They called such numbers *perfect numbers.* For example, 6 is a perfect number because it is the sum of 1, 2, and 3, which are the integers less than 6 that divide evenly into 6. Similarly, 28 is a perfect number because it is the sum of 1, 2, 4, 7, and 14.

    Write a predicate function **isPerfect** that takes an integer **n** and returns **true** if **n** is perfect, and **false** otherwise. Test your implementation by writing a main program that uses the **isPerfect** function to check for perfect numbers in the range 1 to 9999 by testing each number in turn. When a perfect number is found, your program should display it on the screen. The first two lines of output should be 6 and 28. Your program should find two other perfect numbers in the range as well.

6. An integer greater than 1 is said to be *prime* if it has no divisors other than itself and one. The number 17, for example, is prime, because there are no numbers other than 1 and 17 that divide evenly into it. The number 91, however, is not prime because it is divisible by 7 and 13. Write a predicate method **isPrime(n)** that returns **true** if the integer **n** is prime, and **false** otherwise. To test your algorithm, write a main program that lists the prime numbers between 1 and 100.

7. Even though clients of the **<cmath>** library typically don't need to understand how functions like **sqrt** work internally, the implementers of that library have

to be able to design an effective algorithm and write the necessary code. If you were asked to implement the **sqrt** function without using the library version, there are many strategies you could adopt. One of the easiest strategies to understand is *successive approximation,* in which you make a guess at the solution and then refine that guess by choosing new values that move closer to the solution.

You can use successive approximation to determine the square root of x by adopting the following strategy:

1.   Begin by guessing that the square root is $x / 2$. Call that guess g.

2.   The actual square root must lie between g and x / g. At each step in the successive approximation, generate a new guess by averaging g and x / g.

3.   Repeat step 2 until the values g and x / g are as close together as the precision of the hardware allows. In C++, the best way to check for this condition is to test whether the average is equal to either of the values used to generate it.

Use this strategy to write your own implementation of the **sqrt** function.

8.   Although Euclid's algorithm for calculating the greatest common divisor is one of the oldest to be dignified with that term, there are other algorithms that date back many centuries. In the Middle Ages, one of the problems that required sophisticated algorithmic thinking was determining the date of Easter, which falls on the first Sunday after the first full moon following the vernal equinox. Given this definition, the calculation involves interacting cycles of the day of the week, the orbit of the moon, and the passage of the sun through the zodiac. Early algorithms for solving this problem date back to the third century and are described in the writings of the eighth-century scholar known as the Venerable Bede. In 1800, the German mathematician Carl Friedrich Gauss published an algorithm for determining the date of Easter that was purely computational in the sense that it relied on arithmetic rather than looking up values in tables. His algorithm—translated from the German—appears in Figure 2-18.

Write a procedure

```
void findEaster(int year, string & month, int & day);
```

that returns the Easter date for **year** in the reference parameters **month** and **day**.

Unfortunately, the algorithm in Figure 2-18 only works for years in the 18th and 19th centuries. It is easy, however, to search the web for extensions that work for all years. Once you have completed your implementation of Gauss's algorithm, undertake the necessary research to find a more general approach.

FIGURE 2-18 Gauss's algorithm for computing the date of Easter

I.   Divide the number of the year for which one wishes to calculate Easter by 19, by 4, and by 7, and call the remainders of these divisions *a*, *b*, and *c*, respectively. If the division is even, set the remainder to 0; the quotients are not taken into account. Precisely the same is true of the following divisions.

II.   Divide the value 19*a* + 23 by 30 and call the remainder *d*.

III. Finally, divide 2*b* + 4*c* + 6*d* + 3, or 2*b* + 4*c* + 6*d* + 4, choosing the former for years between 1700 and 1799 and the latter for years between 1800 and 1899, by 7 and call the remainder *e*.

Then Easter falls on March 22 + *d* + *e*, or when *d* + *e* is greater than 9, on April *d* + *e* − 9.

Translated from Karl Friedrich Gauss, "Berechnung des Osterfestes," August 1800
`http://gdz.sub.uni-goettingen.de/no_cache/dms/load/img/?IDDOC=137484`

---

9. The combinations function $C(n, k)$ described in this chapter determines the number of ways you can choose k values from a set of n elements, ignoring the order of the elements. If the order of the value matters—so that, in the case of the coin example, choosing a quarter first and then a dime is seen as distinct from choosing a dime and then a quarter—you need to use a different function, which computes the number of ***permutations,*** which are all the ways of ordering k elements taken from a collection of size n. This function is denoted as $P(n, k)$, and has the following mathematical formulation:

$$P(n, k) = \frac{n!}{(n-k)!}$$

Although this definition is mathematically correct, it is not well suited to implementation in practice because the factorials involved can get much too large to store in an integer variable, even when the answer is small. For example, if you tried to use this formula to calculate the number of ways to select two cards from a standard 52-card deck, you would end up trying to evaluate the following fraction:

$$\frac{80{,}658{,}175{,}170{,}943{,}878{,}571{,}660{,}636{,}856{,}403{,}766{,}975{,}289{,}505{,}440{,}883{,}277{,}824{,}000{,}000{,}000{,}000}{30{,}414{,}093{,}201{,}713{,}378{,}043{,}612{,}608{,}166{,}064{,}768{,}844{,}377{,}641{,}568{,}960{,}512{,}000{,}000{,}000{,}000}$$

even though the answer is the much more manageable 2652 (52 × 51).

Write a function **permutations(n, k)** that computes the $P(n, k)$ function without calling the **fact** function. Part of your job in this problem is to figure out how to compute this value efficiently. To do so, you will probably find it useful to play around with some relatively small values to get a sense of how the factorials in the numerator and denominator of the formula behave.

10. The $C(n, k)$ function from the text and the $P(n, k)$ function from the preceding exercise appear often in computational mathematics, particularly in an area called **combinatorics,** which is concerned with counting the ways objects can be combined. Now that you have C++ implementations for each of these functions, it might be worth putting them in a library so that you can use them in many different applications.

Write the files **combinatorics.h** and **combinatorics.cpp** for a library that exports the functions **permutations** and **combinations**. When you write the implementation, make sure to rewrite the code for the **combinations** function so that it uses the efficiency enhancements suggested for permutations in exercise 9.

11. Using the **direction.h** interface as an example, design and implement a **calendar.h** interface that exports the **Month** type from Chapter 1, along with the functions **daysInMonth** and **isLeapYear**, which also appear in that chapter. Your interface should also export a **monthToString** function that returns the constant name for a value of type **Month**. Test your implementation by writing a main program that asks the user to enter a year and then prints the number of days in each month of that year, as in the following sample run:

```
●  ○  ○                TestCalendar
Enter a year: 2012
JANUARY has 31 days.
FEBRUARY has 29 days.
MARCH has 31 days.
APRIL has 30 days.
MAY has 31 days.
JUNE has 30 days.
JULY has 31 days.
AUGUST has 31 days.
SEPTEMBER has 30 days.
OCTOBER has 31 days.
NOVEMBER has 30 days.
DECEMBER has 31 days.
```

12. Write a program **RandomAverage** that repeatedly generates a random real number between 0 and 1 and then displays the average after a specified number of trials entered by the user.

13.   *I shall never believe that God plays dice with the world.*
                                        —Albert Einstein, 1947

Despite Einstein's metaphysical objections, the current models of physics, and particularly of quantum theory, are based on the idea that nature does indeed involve random processes. A radioactive atom, for example, does not decay for any specific reason that we mortals understand. Instead, that atom has a random probability of decaying within a particular period of time. Sometimes it does, sometimes it doesn't, and there is no way to know for sure.

Because physicists consider radioactive decay a random process, it is not surprising that random numbers can be used to simulate it. Suppose you start with a collection of atoms, each of which has a certain probability of decaying in any unit of time. You can then approximate the decay process by taking each atom in turn and deciding randomly whether it decays, considering the probability.

Write a program that simulates the decay of a sample that contains 10,000 atoms of radioactive material, where each atom has a 50 percent chance of decaying in a year. The output of your program should show the number of atoms remaining at the end of each year, which might look something like this:

```
⊖ ◯ ◯              RadioactiveDecay
There are 10000 atoms initially.
There are 4957 atoms at the end of year 1.
There are 2484 atoms at the end of year 2.
There are 1215 atoms at the end of year 3.
There are 612 atoms at the end of year 4.
There are 296 atoms at the end of year 5.
There are 143 atoms at the end of year 6.
There are 66 atoms at the end of year 7.
There are 37 atoms at the end of year 8.
There are 15 atoms at the end of year 9.
There are 8 atoms at the end of year 10.
There are 2 atoms at the end of year 11.
There are 0 atoms at the end of year 12.
```

As the numbers indicate, roughly half the atoms in the sample decay each year. In physics, the conventional way to express this observation is to say that the sample has a *half-life* of one year.

14. Random numbers offer yet another strategy for approximating the value of π. Imagine that you have a dartboard hanging on your wall that consists of a circle painted on a square backdrop, as in the following diagram:

What happens if you throw a whole bunch of darts completely randomly, ignoring any darts that miss the board altogether? Some of the darts will fall inside the gray circle, but some will be outside the circle in the white corners of the square. If the throws are random, the ratio of the number of darts landing inside the circle to the total number of darts hitting the square should be approximately equal to the ratio between the two areas. The ratio of the areas is independent of the actual size of the dartboard, as illustrated by the formula

$$\frac{darts\ falling\ inside\ the\ circle}{darts\ falling\ inside\ the\ square} \cong \frac{area\ inside\ the\ circle}{area\ inside\ the\ square} = \frac{\pi r^2}{4r^2} = \frac{\pi}{4}$$

To simulate this process in a program, imagine that the dart board is drawn on the standard Cartesian coordinate plane with its center at the origin and a radius of 1 unit. The process of throwing a dart randomly at the square can be modeled by generating two random numbers, x and y, each of which lies between −1 and +1. This (x, y) point always lies somewhere inside the square. The point (x, y) lies inside the circle if

$$\sqrt{x^2 + y^2} < 1$$

This condition, however, can be simplified considerably by squaring each side of the inequality, which yields the following more efficient test:

$$x^2 + y^2 < 1$$

If you perform this simulation many times and compute what fraction of the darts fall inside the circle, the result will be an approximation of $\pi/4$.

Write a program that simulates throwing 10,000 darts and then uses the simulation technique described in this exercise to generate and display an approximate value of π. Don't worry if your answer is correct only in the first few digits. The strategy used in this problem is not particularly accurate, even though it occasionally proves useful as an approximation technique. In mathematics, this technique is called **Monte Carlo integration**, after the capital city of Monaco, famous for its casinos.

15. *Heads. . . .*
Heads. . . .
Heads. . . .
A weaker man might be moved to re-examine his faith, if in nothing else at least in the law of probability.
—Tom Stoppard, *Rosencrantz and Guildenstern Are Dead,* 1967

Write a program that simulates flipping a coin repeatedly and continues until three consecutive heads have been tossed. At that point, your program should display the total number of coin flips that were made. The following is one possible sample run of the program:

```
○ ○ ○              ConsecutiveHeads
heads
tails
heads
tails
tails
heads
heads
heads
It took 8 flips to get 3 consecutive heads.
```

16. Use the graphics library to draw a rainbow that looks something like this:

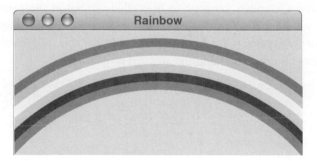

Starting at the top, the six bands in the rainbow are red, orange, yellow, green, blue, and magenta, respectively; cyan makes a lovely color for the sky.

17. Use the graphics library to write a program that draws a checkerboard on the graphics window. Your picture should include the red and black pieces, as they exist at the beginning of the game, like this:

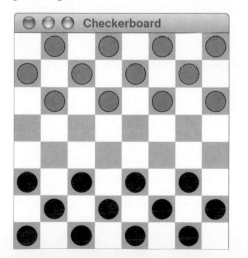

18. One of the principles that defines Taoist philosophy is that dichotomies do not have sharp boundaries, and that there is mixing even between categories that most people see as opposites. This idea is captured in the Yin-Yang symbol, in which each region contains a bit of the other color:

Write a graphics program to draw this symbol at the center of an empty graphics window. The challenge is to decompose the drawing in such a way that you can create it using only the methods in Table 2-2, which do not include facilities for drawing and filling arcs and semicircles.

Chapter 3
Strings

Whisper music on those strings.

— T. S. Eliot, *The Waste Land,* 1922

Up to now, most of the programming examples you have seen in this book have used numbers as their basic data type. These days, computers work less with numeric data than with ***text data,*** which is a generic term for information composed of individual characters. The ability of modern computers to process text data has led to the development of text messaging, electronic mail, word processing systems, online reference libraries, and a wide variety of other useful applications.

This chapter introduces the C++ `<string>` library, which provides a convenient abstraction for working with strings of characters. Having this library in your toolbox will make it much easier to write interesting applications. This chapter also introduces the notion of a ***class,*** which is the term computer scientists have adopted for data types that support the object-oriented programming paradigm. Although C++ defines a more primitive string type, most text-processing applications work instead with objects of a class called `string`. Working with the `string` class in this chapter will increase your understanding of classes and provide the foundation you need to define your own classes in Chapter 6.

▉▉▉ 3.1 Using strings as abstract values

Conceptually, a *string* is simply a sequence of characters. For example, the string `"hello, world"` is a sequence of 12 characters including ten letters, a comma, and a space. In C++, the `string` class and its associated operations are defined in the `<string>` library, and you must therefore include this library in any source file that manipulates string data.

In Chapter 1, you learned that data types are defined by two properties: a *domain* and a *set of operations*. For strings, the domain is easy to identify: the domain of type `string` is the set of all sequences of characters. A more interesting problem is to identify the appropriate set of operations. Early versions of C++ followed the lead of the older C language and offered little support for manipulating strings. The only facilities were low-level operations that required you to understand the underlying representation. The designers of C++ soon solved that problem by introducing a `string` class that enables clients to work at a more abstract level.

For the most part, you can use `string` as a primitive data type in much the same way that you use types like `int` and `double`. You can, for example, declare a variable of type `string` and assign it an initial value, as you would with a numeric variable. When you declare a `string` variable, you typically specify its initial value as a ***string literal,*** which is a sequence of characters enclosed in double quotation marks. For example, the declaration

```
const string ALPHABET = "ABCDEFGHIJKLMNOPQRSTUVWXYZ";
```

sets the constant `ALPHABET` to a 26-character string containing the uppercase letters.

You can also use the operators **>>** and **<<** to read and write data values of type **string**, although doing so requires some caution. For example, you could make the **Hello** program more conversational by rewriting the **main** function like this:

```
int main() {
    string name;
    cout << "Enter your name: ";
    cin >> name;
    cout << "Hello, " << name << "!" << endl;
    return 0;
}
```

This program reads a string from the user into the variable **name** and then includes that name as part of the greeting, as shown in the following sample run:

```
○ ○ ○              HelloName
Enter your name: Eric
Hello, Eric!
```

This program, however, behaves in a somewhat surprising way if you enter a user's full name instead of the first name alone. For example, if I had typed my full name in response to the prompt, the sample run would look like this:

```
○ ○ ○              HelloName
Enter your name: Eric Roberts
Hello, Eric!
```

Even though the program contains no code to take the two pieces of my name apart, it somehow still uses only my first name when it prints its greeting. How does the program know to be so colloquial?

Answering this question requires you to understand in more detail how the **>>** operator behaves when you use it to read a string value. Although you might expect it to read an entire line of input, the **>>** operator stops as soon as it hits the first *whitespace character,* which is defined to be any character that appears as blank space on the display screen. The most common whitespace character is the space character itself, but the set of whitespace characters also includes tabs and the characters that mark the end of a line.

If you want to read a string that contains whitespace characters, you can't use the >> operator. The standard approach is to call the function

```
getline(cin, str);
```

which reads an entire line from the console input stream **cin** into the variable **str**, which is passed by reference. Incorporating **getline** into the **HelloName** program gives rise to the code shown in Figure 3-1 and enables the program to display the full name of the user, as follows:

In practice, reading a complete line is a much more common operation than reading a substring bounded by whitespace characters. As a result, programs that need to read a string from the user are far more likely to use the **getline** function (or the **getLine** function from **simpio.h** introduced in section 2.9) than the **>>** operator.

FIGURE 3-1 An interactive version of the "Hello World" program

```
/*
 * File: HelloName.cpp
 * -------------------
 * This program extends the classic "Hello world" program by asking
 * the user for a name, which is then used as part of the greeting.
 * This version of the program reads a complete line into name and
 * not just the first word.
 */

#include <iostream>
#include <string>
using namespace std;

int main() {
   string name;
   cout << "Enter your full name: ";
   getline(cin, name);
   cout << "Hello, " << name << "!" << endl;
   return 0;
}
```

3.2 String operations

If you need to perform more complex operations using the **<string>** library, you will discover that the data type **string** doesn't behave in precisely the same way that more traditional types do. One of the major differences is in the syntax used to invoke function calls. For example, if you were assured that the **<string>** library exports a function named **length**, you might imagine that the way to determine the length of a string **str** would be to use a statement like this:

```
int nChars = length(str);
```

As the bug icon emphasizes, this statement is incorrect in C++. The problem with this expression is that the data type **string** is not a traditional type but is instead an example of a *class,* which is probably easiest to define informally as a template that describes a set of values together with an associated set of operations. In the language of object-oriented programming, the values that belong to a class are called *objects.* A single class can give rise to many different objects; each such object is said to be an *instance* of that class.

The operations that apply to instances of a class are called *methods.* In C++, methods look and behave much like traditional functions, although it helps to give them a new name to emphasize that there are differences. Unlike functions, methods are tightly coupled to the class to which they belong. In cases where it is useful to emphasize the distinction, traditional functions are sometimes called *free functions* because they are not bound to a particular class.

In the object-oriented world, objects communicate by sending information and requests from one object to another. Collectively, these transmissions are called *messages.* The act of sending a message corresponds to having one object invoke a method that belongs to a different object. For consistency with the conceptual model of sending messages, the object that initiates the method is called the *sender,* and the object that is the target of that transmission is called the *receiver.* In C++, sending a message is specified using the following syntax:

>   *receiver . name* (*arguments*)

The object-oriented version of the statement that sets **nChars** to the length of the string object **str** is therefore

```
int nChars = str.length();
```

Table 3-1 lists the most common methods exported by the **<string>** library, all of which use the receiver syntax.

TABLE 3-1 Common methods in the `<string>` library

String operators

str_1 + str_2	Concatenates str_1 and str_2 end to end and returns a new string containing the combined characters. Either string can be replaced by a character, but numeric types are not allowed.
str += str_2	Appends a copy of str_2 to the end of str. C++ overloads this operator so that str_2 can be a character value as well.
str_1 == str_2 str_1 != str_2 str_1 < str_2 str_1 <= str_2 str_1 > str_2 str_1 >= str_2	These operators compare str_1 and str_2. The comparison is performed using *lexicographic order,* which is the order defined by the underlying ASCII codes.
$str[k]$	Returns the character at index position k in str as an assignable value. The `[]` operator does not check to see whether k is in range.

Methods that leave the receiver string unchanged

str.`length`()	Returns the number of characters in str.
str.`at`(k)	Returns the character at index position k in str. In contrast to the `[]` operator, `at` generates an exception if k is out of range.
str.`substr`(pos, n)	Returns a new string made of characters starting at pos in str and extending for n characters or up to the end of the string. The second parameter is optional. If n is missing, the substring always extends to the end of the string.
str.`compare`(str_2)	Compares the receiver string str with str_2 and returns an integer that is 0 if the two strings are equal, negative if str precedes str_2, and positive if str follows str_2 in lexicographic order. Because C++ overloads the relational operators, programmers rarely call `compare` explicitly.
str.`find`($pattern$, pos)	Searches the receiver string str for $pattern$, starting at position pos. The function returns the first index at which $pattern$ (which can be either a character or a string) appears; if $pattern$ does not appear, `find` returns the constant `string::npos`. The second argument is optional; if it is missing, `find` starts at the beginning of the string.

Methods that destructively modify the receiver string

str.`erase`(pos, n)	Deletes n characters from str starting at pos.
str.`insert`(pos, str_2)	Inserts a copy of str_2 into str starting at pos.
str.`replace`(pos, n, str_2)	Replaces the n characters in str starting at pos with a copy of str_2.

Methods for creating C++ and C-style strings

`string`($carray$)	Returns a C++ string containing the same characters as $carray$.
`string`(n, ch)	Returns a C++ string containing n copies of the character ch.
str.`c_str`()	Returns a C-style character array containing the same characters as str.

Operator overloading

As you can see from the first section of Table 3-1, the `<string>` library redefines several of the standard operators using an extremely powerful C++ feature called *operator overloading,* which redefines the behavior of operators depending on the types of their operands. In the `<string>` library, the most important overloaded operator is the **+** sign. When **+** is applied to numbers, it performs addition. When **+** is applied to strings, it performs *concatenation,* which is just a fancy word for joining the two strings together end to end.

You can also use the shorthand **+=** form to concatenate new text to the end of an existing string. Both the **+** and **+=** operators allow concatenation of strings or single characters, as illustrated by the following example, which sets the string variable `str` to the string `"abcd"`:

```
string str = "abc";
str += 'd';
```

Those of you who are familiar with Java may expect the **+** operator to support values of other types by converting those values to strings and then concatenating them together. That feature, however, is not available in C++, which treats any attempt to use the **+** operator with incompatible operands as an error.

C++ also overloads the relational operators so that you can compare string values much more conveniently than you can in many other languages, including C and Java. For example, you can use the following code to check whether the value of `str` is equal to `"quit"`:

```
if (str == "quit") . . .
```

The relational operators compare strings using *lexicographic order,* which is the order defined by the underlying ASCII codes. Lexicographic order means that case is significant, so `"abc"` is not equal to `"ABC"`.

Selecting characters from a string

In C++, positions within a string are numbered starting from 0. For example, the characters in the string `"hello, world"` are numbered as in the following diagram:

h	e	l	l	o	,		w	o	r	l	d
0	1	2	3	4	5	6	7	8	9	10	11

The position number written underneath each character is called its *index.*

The `<string>` library offers two different mechanisms for selecting individual characters from a string. One approach is to supply the index inside square brackets after the string. For example, if the string variable **str** contains **"hello, world"**, the expression

      str[0]

selects the character **'h'** at the beginning of the string. Although C++ programmers tend to use the square-bracket syntax for its expressiveness, it is arguably better to call the **at** method instead. The expressions **str[i]** and **str.at(i)** have almost the same meaning in C++; the only difference is that **at** checks to make sure the index is in range.

No matter which syntax you use, selecting an individual character in a string returns a direct reference to the character in the string, which allows you to assign a new value to that character. For example, you can use either the statement

      str[0] = 'H';

or the statement

      str.at(0) = 'H';

to change the value of the string from **"hello, world"** to **"Hello, world"**. Partly because the second form generates confusion by suggesting that it is possible to assign a value to the result of any function and partly because experience has shown that students have more trouble understanding examples written using **at**, I have chosen to use bracket selection for the programming examples in this book, despite the lack of range-checking.

Although index positions in strings are conceptually integers, the **string** class complicates matters by using the type **size_t** to represent both index positions and lengths in a string. If you want to be slavishly correct in your coding, you should use that type (which is automatically defined when you include the **<string>** header file) every time you store a string index in a variable. At Stanford, we have found that the additional conceptual complexity of using **size_t** makes programs harder to understand and have therefore chosen to use **int** instead. Using **int** works just fine unless your strings are longer than 2,147,483,647 characters long, although you may get a warning message from some compilers.

String assignment

C++ does take some steps to mitigate the conceptual problems that follow from allowing the client to change individual characters in an existing string. In particular, C++ redefines assignment for strings so that assigning one string to another copies the underlying characters. For example, the assignment statement

```
    str2 = str1;
```

overwrites any previous contents of **str2** with a copy of the characters contained in
str1. The variables **str1** and **str2** therefore remain independent, which means
that changing the characters in **str1** does not affect **str2**. Similarly, C++ copies
the characters in any string passed as a value parameter. Thus, if a function makes
changes to an argument that happens to be a string, those changes are not reflected
in the calling function unless the string parameter is passed by reference.

Extracting parts of a string

While concatenation makes longer strings from shorter pieces, you often need to do
the reverse: separate a string into the shorter pieces it contains. A string that is part
of a longer string is called a ***substring.*** The **string** class exports a method called
substr that takes two parameters: the index of the first character you want to select
and the desired number of characters. Calling **str.substr(start, n)** creates a
new string by extracting **n** characters from **str** starting at the index position
specified by **start**. For example, if **str** contains the string **"hello, world"**, the
method call

```
    str.substr(1, 3)
```

returns the three-character substring **"ell"**. Because indices in C++ begin at 0, the
character at index position 1 is the character **'e'**.

The second argument in the **substr** method is optional. If it is missing, **substr**
returns the substring that starts at the specified position and continues through the
end of the string. Thus, calling

```
    str.substr(7)
```

returns the string **"world"**. Similarly, if **n** is supplied but fewer than **n** characters
follow the specified starting position, **substr** returns characters only up to the end
of the original string.

The following function uses **substr** to return the second half of the parameter
str, which is defined to include the middle character if the length of **str** is odd:

```
    string secondHalf(string str) {
       return str.substr(str.length() / 2);
    }
```

Searching within a string

From time to time, you will find it useful to search a string to see whether it
contains a particular character or substring. To make such search operations

possible, the **string** class exports a method called **find**, which comes in several forms. The simplest form of the call is

> **str.find**(*search*);

where *search* is the content you're looking for, which can be either a string or a character. When called, the **find** method searches through **str** looking for the first occurrence of the search value. If the search value is found, **find** returns the index position at which the match begins. If the character does not appear before the end of the string, **find** returns the constant **string::npos**. Unlike the constants you saw in Chapter 1, the identifier **npos** is defined as part of the **string** class and therefore requires the **string::** qualifier whenever it appears.

The **find** method also takes an optional second argument that indicates the index position at which to start the search. The effect of both styles of the **find** method is illustrated by the following examples, which assume that the variable **str** contains the string **"hello, world"**:

```
str.find('o')      →   4
str.find('o', 5)   →   8
str.find('x')      →   str::npos
```

As with string comparison, the methods for searching a string consider uppercase and lowercase characters to be different.

Iterating through the characters in a string

Even though the methods exported by the **string** class provide the tools you need to implement string applications from scratch, it is usually easier to write programs by adapting existing code examples that implement particularly common operations. In programming terminology, such illustrative examples are called *patterns*. When you work with strings, one of the most important patterns involves iterating through the characters in a string, which requires the following code:

```
for (int i = 0; i < str.length(); i++) {
    . . . body of loop that manipulates str[i] . . .
}
```

On each loop cycle, the selection expression **str[i]** refers to the ith character in the string. Because the purpose of the loop is to process every character, the loop continues until **i** reaches the length of the string. Thus, you can count the number of spaces in a string by using the following function:

```
int countSpaces(string str) {
   int nSpaces = 0;
   for (int i = 0; i < str.length(); i++) {
      if (str[i] == ' ') nSpaces++;
   }
   return nSpaces;
}
```

For some applications, you will find it useful to iterate through a string in the opposite direction, starting with the last character and continuing backward until you reach the first. This style of iteration uses the following **for** loop:

```
for (int i = str.length() - 1; i >= 0; i--)
```

Here, the index **i** begins at the last index position, which is one less than the length of the string, and then decreases by one on each cycle, down to and including the index position 0.

Assuming that you understand the syntax and semantics of the **for** statement, you could work out the patterns for each iteration direction from first principles each time this pattern comes up in an application. Doing so, however, would slow you down enormously. These iteration patterns are worth memorizing so that you don't have to waste any time thinking about them. Whenever you recognize that you need to cycle through the characters in a string, some part of your nervous system between your brain and your fingers should be able to translate that idea effortlessly into the following line:

```
for (int i = 0; i < str.length(); i++)
```

For some applications, you will need to modify the basic iteration pattern to start or end the iteration at a different index position. For example, the following function checks to see whether a string begins with a particular prefix:

```
bool startsWith(string str, string prefix) {
   if (str.length() < prefix.length()) return false;
   for (int i = 0; i < prefix.length(); i++) {
      if (str[i] != prefix[i]) return false;
   }
   return true;
}
```

This code begins by checking to make sure that **str** is not shorter than **prefix** (in which case, the result must certainly be **false**) and then iterates through the characters in **prefix** rather than the string as a whole.

As you read through the code for the **startsWith** function, it is useful to pay attention to the placement of the two **return** statements. The code returns **false** from *inside* the loop, as soon as it discovers the first difference between the string and the prefix. The code returns **true** from *outside* the loop, after it has checked every character in the prefix without finding any differences. You will encounter examples of this basic pattern over and over again as you read through this book.

The **startsWith** function and the similar **endsWith** function that you will have a chance to write in exercise 1 turn out to be very useful, even though they are not part of the standard **<string>** library in C++. They are thus ideal candidates for inclusion in a library of string functions that you create for yourself by applying the same techniques used in Chapter 2 to define the **error** library. The Stanford libraries include an interface called **strlib.h** that exports several useful string functions. The contents of that interface are described in more detail in section 3.7.

Growing a string through concatenation

The other pattern that it's important to memorize as you learn how to work with strings involves creating a new string one character at a time. The loop structure itself will depend on the application, but the general pattern for creating a string by concatenation looks like this:

```
string str = "";
for (whatever loop header line fits the application)  {
    str += the next substring or character;
}
```

As a simple example, the following method returns a string consisting of **n** copies of the character **ch**:

```
string repeatChar(int n, char ch) {
    string str = "";
    for (int i = 0; i < n; i++) {
        str += ch;
    }
    return str;
}
```

The **repeatChar** function is useful if, for example, you need to generate some kind of section separator in console output. One strategy to accomplish this goal would be to use the statement

```
cout << repeatChar(72, '-') << endl;
```

which prints a line of 72 hyphens.

Many string-processing functions use the iteration and concatenation patterns together. For example, the following function reverses the argument string so that, for example, calling **reverse("desserts")** returns **"stressed"**:

```
string reverse(string str) {
    string rev = "";
    for (int i = str.length() - 1; i >= 0; i--) {
        rev += str[i];
    }
    return rev;
}
```

3.3 The <cctype> library

Since strings are composed of characters, it is often useful to have tools for working with those individual characters, and not just the string as a whole. The **<cctype>** library exports a variety of functions that work with characters, the most common of which appear in Table 3-2.

The first section of Table 3-2 defines a set of predicate functions to test whether a character belongs to a particular category. Calling **isdigit(ch)**, for example, returns **true** if **ch** is one of the digit characters in the range between **'0'** and **'9'**.

TABLE 3-2 Selected functions in the **<cctype>** library

Predicate functions for testing character type

isalpha(*ch*)	Returns **true** if *ch* is an alphabetic character.
isupper(*ch*)	Returns **true** if *ch* is an uppercase alphabetic character.
islower(*ch*)	Returns **true** if *ch* is a lowercase alphabetic character.
isdigit(*ch*)	Returns **true** if *ch* is a digit (**'0'**-**'9'**).
isxdigit(*ch*)	Returns **true** if *ch* is a hexadecimal digit (**'0'**-**'9'**, **'A'**-**'F'**, **'a'**-**'f'**).
isalnum(*ch*)	Returns **true** if *ch* is *alphanumeric*, which means that it is either a letter or a digit.
ispunct(*ch*)	Returns **true** if *ch* is a punctuation symbol.
isspace(*ch*)	Returns **true** if *ch* is a *whitespace character*. These characters are **' '** (the space character), **'\t'**, **'\n'**, **'\f'**, **'\v'**, or **'\r'**, all of which appear as blank space.
isprint(*ch*)	Returns **true** if *ch* is any printable character.

Functions for case conversion

toupper(*ch*)	Returns *ch* converted to upper case (or *ch* itself if *ch* is not a letter).
tolower(*ch*)	Returns *ch* converted to lower case (or *ch* itself if *ch* is not a letter).

Similarly, calling **isspace(ch)** returns **true** if **ch** is any of the characters that appear as white space on a display screen, such as spaces and tabs. The functions in the second section of Table 3-2 make it easy to convert between uppercase and lowercase letters. Calling **toupper('a')**, for instance, returns the character **'A'**. If the argument to either the **toupper** or **tolower** function is not a letter, the function returns its argument unchanged, so that **tolower('7')** returns **'7'**.

The functions in the **<cctype>** library often come in handy when you are working with strings. The following function, for example, returns **true** if the argument **str** is a nonempty string of digits, which means that it represents an integer:

```
bool isDigitString(string str) {
   if (str.length() == 0) return false;
   for (int i = 0; i < str.length(); i++) {
      if (!isdigit(str[i])) return false;
   }
   return true;
}
```

Similarly, the following function returns **true** if the strings **s1** and **s2** are equal, ignoring differences in case:

```
bool equalsIgnoreCase(string s1, string s2) {
   if (s1.length() != s2.length()) return false;
   for (int i = 0; i < s1.length(); i++) {
      if (tolower(s1[i]) != tolower(s2[i])) return false;
   }
   return true;
}
```

The implementation of **equalsIgnoreCase** returns **false** as soon as it finds the first character position that doesn't match, but must wait until it reaches the end of the loop to return **true**.

3.4 Modifying the contents of a string

Unlike other languages such as Java, C++ allows you to change the characters in a string by assigning new values to a particular index position. That fact makes it possible to design your own string functions that change the content of a string in much the same way that the **erase**, **insert**, and **replace** methods do. In most cases, however, it is better to write functions so that they return a transformed version of a string without changing the original.

As an illustration of how these two approaches differ, suppose that you want to design a string counterpart to the **toupper** function in the **<cctype>** library that converts every lowercase character in a string to its uppercase equivalent. One approach is to implement a procedure that changes the contents of the argument string, as follows:

```
void toUpperCaseInPlace(string & str) {
   for (int i = 0; i < str.length(); i++) {
      str[i] = toupper(str[i]);
   }
}
```

An alternative strategy is to write a function that returns an uppercase copy of its argument without changing the original. If you use the iteration and concatenation patterns, such a function might look like this:

```
string toUpperCase(string str) {
   string result = "";
   for (int i = 0; i < str.length(); i++) {
      result += toupper(str[i]);
   }
   return result;
}
```

The strategy that modifies the string in place is more efficient, but the second is more flexible and less likely to cause unexpected results. Having the first version, however, makes it possible to code the second in a more efficient way:

```
string toUpperCase(string str) {
   toUpperCaseInPlace(str);
   return str;
}
```

In this implementation, C++ automatically copies the argument string because it is passed by value. Given that **str** is no longer connected to the argument string in the caller's domain, it is perfectly acceptable to modify it in place and then return a copy back to the caller.

3.5 The legacy of C-style strings

In its early years, C++ succeeded in part because it includes all of C as a subset, thereby making it possible to evolve gradually from one language to the other. That design decision, however, means that C++ includes some aspects of C that no longer make sense in a modern object-oriented language, but nonetheless need to be maintained for compatibility.

In C, strings are implemented as low-level arrays of characters, which offer none of the high-level facilities that make the **string** class so useful. Unfortunately, the decision to keep C++ compatible with C means that C++ must support both styles. String literals, for example, are implemented using the older C-based style. For the most part, you can ignore this historical detail because C++ automatically converts a string literal to a C++ string whenever the compiler can determine that what you want is a C++ string. If you initialize a string using the line

```
string str = "hello, world";
```

C++ automatically converts the C-style string literal **"hello, world"** to a C++ **string** object, because you've told the compiler that **str** is a **string** variable. By contrast, C++ does not allow you to write the declaration

```
string str = "hello" + ", " + "world";
```

even though it seems as if this statement would have the same ultimate effect. The problem here is that this version of the code tries to apply the **+** operator to string literals, which are not C++ **string** objects.

If you need to get around this problem, you can explicitly convert a string literal to a string object by calling **string** on the literal. For example, the following line correctly converts **"hello"** to a C++ **string** object and then uses concatenation to complete the calculation of the initial value:

```
string str = string("hello") + ", " + "world";
```

Another problem that arises from having two different representations for strings is that some C++ libraries require the use of C-style strings instead of the more modern C++ **string** class. If you use these library abstractions in the context of an application that uses C++ strings, you must at some point convert the C++ string objects into their older, C-style counterparts. Specifying that conversion is simple enough: all you have to do is apply the **c_str** method to the C++ version of a string to obtain its C-style equivalent. The more important problem, however, is that having to master two different representations for strings increases the conceptual complexity of C++, thereby making it harder to learn.

◼ 3.6 Writing string applications

Although they are useful to illustrate how particular string functions work, the string examples you have seen so far are too simple to give you much insight into how to write a significant string-processing application. This section addresses that deficiency by developing two applications that manipulate string data.

Recognizing palindromes

A *palindrome* is a word that reads identically backward and forward, such as *level* or *noon*. The goal of this section is to write a predicate function `isPalindrome` that checks whether a string is a palindrome. Calling `isPalindrome("level")` should return `true`; calling `isPalindrome("xyz")` should return `false`.

As with most programming problems, there are several reasonable strategies for solving this problem. In my experience, the approach that most students are likely to try first uses a `for` loop to run through each index position in the first half of the string. At each position, the code then checks to see whether that character matches the one that appears in the symmetric position relative to the end of the string. Adopting that strategy leads to the following code:

```
bool isPalindrome(string str) {
   int n = str.length();
   for (int i = 0; i < n / 2; i++) {
      if (str[i] != str[n - i - 1]) return false;
   }
   return true;
}
```

Given the string functions you've already encountered in this chapter, you can also code `isPalindrome` in the following, much simpler form:

```
bool isPalindrome(string str) {
   return str == reverse(str);
}
```

Of these two implementations, the first is more efficient. The second version has to construct a new string that is the reverse of the original; worse still, it does so by concatenating the characters together one at a time, which means that the program creates as many intermediate string values as there are characters in the original string. The first version doesn't have to create any strings at all. It does its work by selecting and comparing characters, which turn out to be less costly operations.

Despite this difference in efficiency, the second coding has many advantages, particularly as an example for new programmers. For one thing, it takes advantage of existing code by making use of the **reverse** function. For another, it hides the complexity involved in calculating index positions required by the first version. It takes at least a minute or two for most students to figure out why the code includes the selection expression `str[n - i - 1]` or why it is appropriate to use the `<` operator in the `for` loop test, as opposed to `<=`. By contrast, the line

```
return str == reverse(str);
```

reads almost as fluidly as English: a string is a palindrome if it is equal to the same string in reverse order.

Particularly as you are learning about programming, it is much more important to work toward the clarity of the second implementation than the efficiency of the first. Given the speed of modern computers, it is almost always worth sacrificing a few machine cycles to make a program easier to understand.

Translating English to Pig Latin

To give you more of a sense of how to implement string-processing applications, this section describes a C++ program that reads a line of text from the user and then translates each word in that line from English to Pig Latin, a made-up language familiar to most children in the English-speaking world. In Pig Latin, words are formed from their English counterparts by applying the following rules:

1. If the word contains no vowels, no translation is done, which means that the Pig Latin word is the same as the original.

2. If the word begins with a vowel, the Pig Latin translation consists of the original word followed by the suffix *way.*

3. If the word begins with a consonant, the Pig Latin translation is formed by extracting the string of consonants up to the first vowel, moving that collection of consonants to the end of the word, and then adding the suffix *ay.*

As an example, suppose that the English word is *scram.* Because the word begins with a consonant, you divide it into two parts: one consisting of the letters before the first vowel and one consisting of that vowel and the remaining letters:

You then interchange these two parts and add *ay* at the end, as follows:

| am | scr | ay |

Thus the Pig Latin word for *scram* is *amscray.* For a word that begins with a vowel, such as *apple,* you simply add *way* to the end, which leaves you with *appleway.*

The code for the **PigLatin** program appears in Figure 3-2. The main program reads a line of text from the user and then calls **lineToPigLatin** to translate that line into Pig Latin. The **lineToPigLatin** function then calls **wordToPigLatin** to convert each word to its Pig Latin equivalent. Characters that are not part of a word are copied directly to the output line so that punctuation and spacing remain unaffected.

FIGURE 3-2 Program to translate English to Pig Latin

```
/*
 * File: PigLatin.cpp
 * --------------------
 * This program converts lines from English to Pig Latin.
 * This dialect of Pig Latin applies the following rules:
 *
 * 1. If the word contains no vowels, return the original
 *    word unchanged.
 *
 * 2. If the word begins with a consonant, extract the set
 *    of consonants up to the first vowel, move that set
 *    of consonants to the end of the word, and add "ay".
 *
 * 3. If the word begins with a vowel, add "way" to the
 *    end of the word.
 */

#include <iostream>
#include <string>
#include <cctype>
using namespace std;

/* Function prototypes */

string lineToPigLatin(string line);
string wordToPigLatin(string word);
int findFirstVowel(string word);
bool isVowel(char ch);

/* Main program */

int main() {
   cout << "This program translates English to Pig Latin." << endl;
   string line;
   cout << "Enter English text: ";
   getline(cin, line);
   string translation = lineToPigLatin(line);
   cout << "Pig Latin output: " << translation << endl;
   return 0;
}
```

FIGURE 3-2   Program to translate English to Pig Latin (continued)

```
/*
 * Function: lineToPigLatin
 * Usage: string translation = lineToPigLatin(line);
 * ---------------------------------------------------
 * Translates each word in the line to Pig Latin, leaving all other
 * characters unchanged.  The variable start keeps track of the index
 * position at which the current word begins.  As a special case,
 * the code sets start to -1 to indicate that the beginning of the
 * current word has not yet been encountered.
 */

string lineToPigLatin(string line) {
   string result;
   int start = -1;
   for (int i = 0; i < line.length(); i++) {
      char ch = line[i];
      if (isalpha(ch)) {
         if (start == -1) start = i;
      } else {
         if (start >= 0) {
            result += wordToPigLatin(line.substr(start, i - start));
            start = -1;
         }
         result += ch;
      }
   }
   if (start >= 0) result += wordToPigLatin(line.substr(start));
   return result;
}

/*
 * Function: wordToPigLatin
 * Usage: string translation = wordToPigLatin(word);
 * ---------------------------------------------------
 * Translates a word from English to Pig Latin using the rules
 * specified in the text.  The translated word is returned as the
 * value of the function.
 */

string wordToPigLatin(string word) {
   int vp = findFirstVowel(word);
   if (vp == -1) {
      return word;
   } else if (vp == 0) {
      return word + "way";
   } else {
      string head = word.substr(0, vp);
      string tail = word.substr(vp);
      return tail + head + "ay";
   }
}
```

☞

FIGURE 3-2   **Program to translate English to Pig Latin (continued)**

```
/*
 * Function: findFirstVowel
 * Usage: int k = findFirstVowel(word);
 * -----------------------------------------
 * Returns the index position of the first vowel in word.  If
 * word does not contain a vowel, findFirstVowel returns -1.
 */

int findFirstVowel(string word) {
   for (int i = 0; i < word.length(); i++) {
      if (isVowel(word[i])) return i;
   }
   return -1;
}

/*
 * Function: isVowel
 * Usage: if (isVowel(ch)) . . .
 * ------------------------------
 * Returns true if the character ch is a vowel.
 */

bool isVowel(char ch) {
   switch (ch) {
     case 'A': case 'E': case 'I': case 'O': case 'U':
     case 'a': case 'e': case 'i': case 'o': case 'u':
       return true;
     default:
       return false;
   }
}
```

A sample run of the program might look like this:

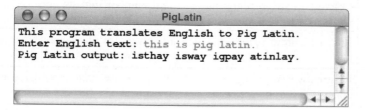

It is worth taking a careful look at the implementations of `lineToPigLatin` and `wordToPigLatin` in Figure 3-2. The `lineToPigLatin` function finds the word boundaries in the input, which provides a useful pattern for separating a string into individual words. The `wordToPigLatin` function uses `substr` to extract pieces of the English word and then uses concatenation to put them back together in their Pig Latin form. In Chapter 6, you will learn about a more general facility called a *token scanner* that divides a string into its logically connected parts.

3.7 The `strlib.h` library

As I've noted from time to time in the text, several of the functions in this chapter seem ideal for inclusion in a library. Once you have written these functions as part of one application, it would be wasteful not to use them in other applications that need to perform the same operations. While functions like **wordToPigLatin** are unlikely to show up anywhere else, you will often have occasion to use functions like **toUpperCase** and **startsWith**. To avoid having to rewrite them or having to cut-and-paste the code, it makes sense to put those functions into a library so that you always have them available.

The Stanford libraries distributed with the book include an interface called **strlib.h** that exports the functions shown in Table 3-3. You can see on this list several functions whose definitions appear in this chapter. In the exercises, you will have a chance to fill in the definitions of some of the others, including **endsWith** and **trim**. The first four functions in Table 3-3, all of which are concerned with converting numeric values to string form, require techniques that are beyond the limits of your knowledge of C++, but only for the moment. In Chapter 4, you will learn how to use a new data type called a *stream,* which will make it easy to implement these functions.

TABLE 3-3   Functions exported by the `strlib.h` interface

integerToString (*n*)	Converts an integer into the corresponding string of digits.
stringToInteger (*str*)	Converts a string of digits into an integer.
realToString (*d*)	Converts a floating-point number into the corresponding string form.
stringToReal (*str*)	Converts a string representing a real number into its corresponding value.
toUpperCase (*str*)	Returns a new string in which all lowercase characters have been converted into their uppercase equivalents.
toLowerCase (*str*)	Returns a new string in which all uppercase characters have been converted into their lowercase equivalents.
equalsIgnoreCase (*s₁*, *s₂*)	Returns **true** if s_1 and s_2 are equal, discounting differences in case.
startsWith (*str*, *prefix*)	Returns **true** if the string *str* starts with the specified prefix, which may be either a string or a character.
endsWith (*str*, *suffix*)	Returns **true** if the string *str* ends with the specified suffix, which may be either a string or a character.
trim (*str*)	Returns a new string after removing any whitespace characters from the beginning and end of the argument.

Summary

In this chapter, you have learned how to use the **<string>** library, which makes it possible to write string-processing functions without worrying about the details of the underlying representation. The important points in this chapter include:

- The **<string>** library exports a class called **string** that represents a sequence of characters. Although C++ also includes a more primitive string type to maintain compatibility with the C programming language, it is best to use the **string** class in any programs that you write.

- If you use the **>>** extraction operator to read string data, the input stops at the first *whitespace character.* If you want to read an entire line of text from the user, it is usually better to use the **getline** function from the standard C++ libraries.

- The most common methods exported by the **string** class appear in Table 3-1 on page 130. Because **string** is a class, the methods use the *receiver syntax* instead of the traditional functional form. Thus, to obtain the length of a string stored in the variable **str**, you need to invoke **str.length()**.

- Several of the methods exported by the **string** class destructively modify the receiver string. Giving clients free access to methods that change the internal state of an object makes it harder to protect that object's integrity. The programs in this book therefore minimize the use of these methods.

- The **string** class uses *operator overloading* to simplify many common string operations. For strings, the most important operators are **+** (for concatenation), **[]** (for selection), and the relational operators.

- The standard pattern for iterating through the characters in a string is

```
for (int i = 0; i < str.length(); i++) {
    . . . body of loop that manipulates str[i] . . .
}
```

- The standard pattern for growing a string by concatenation is

```
string str = "";
for (whatever loop header line fits the application) {
    str += the next substring or character;
}
```

- The **<cctype>** library exports several functions for working with individual characters. The most important of these functions appear in Table 3-2.

Review questions

1. What is the difference between a *character* and a *string?*

2. True or false: If you execute the lines

   ```
   string line;
   cin >> line;
   ```

   the program will read an entire line of data from the user and store it in the variable `line`.

3. Which arguments to the `getline` function are passed by reference?

4. What is the difference between a *method* and a *free function?*

5. True or false: In C++, you can determine the length of the string stored in the variable `str` by calling `length(str)`.

6. If you call `s1.replace(0, 1, s2)`, which string is the *receiver?*

7. What is the effect of the `+` operator when it is used with two string operands?

8. When C++ evaluates the expression `s1 < s2`, what rule does the `string` class use to compare the string values?

9. What two syntactic forms does this chapter describe for selecting an individual character from a string? How do these two syntactic forms differ in their implementation?

10. When you select an individual character from a C++ string, you can use either the `at` method or the standard subscript notation in which the index is enclosed in square brackets. From the client's perspective, what is the difference between these two options?

11. True or false: If you assign the value of the string variable `s1` to the string variable `s2`, the `string` class copies the characters so that subsequent changes to the characters in one string will not affect the characters in the other.

12. True or false: The index positions in a string begin at 0 and extend up to the length of the string minus 1.

13. What are the arguments to the `substr` method? What happens if you omit the second argument?

14. Describe how the **compare** method uses the return value to indicate the relative ordering of two strings. Why is this method rarely used in practice?

15. What value does the **find** method return to indicate that the search string does not appear?

16. What is the significance of the optional second argument to the **find** method?

17. Suppose that you have declared and initialized the variables **s** and **t** like this:

```
string s = "ABCDE"
string t = "";
```

    Given these declarations, what is the effect of each of the following calls:

    a. `s.length()`
    b. `t.length()`
    c. `s[2]`
    d. `s + t`
    e. `t += 'a'`
    f. `s.replace(0, 2, "Z")`
    g. `s.substr(0, 3)`
    h. `s.substr(4)`
    i. `s.substr(3, 9)`
    j. `s.substr(3, 3)`

18. What is the pattern for iterating through each character in a string?

19. How does the pattern in question 18 change if you want to iterate through the characters in reverse order, starting with the last character and ending with the first?

20. What is the pattern for growing a string through concatenation?

21. What is the result of each of the following calls to the **<cctype>** library:

    a. `isdigit(7)`
    b. `isdigit('7')`
    c. `isalnum(7)`
    d. `toupper(7)`
    e. `toupper('A')`
    f. `tolower('A')`

22. Why does C++ support both a **string** class and a more primitive string type?

23. How can you convert a primitive string value to a C++ string? How can you specify a conversion in the opposite direction?

Exercises

1. Implement the function **endsWith(str, suffix)**, which returns **true** if **str** ends with **suffix**. Like its **startsWith** counterpart, the **endsWith** function should allow the second argument to be either a string or a character.

2.　The **strlib.h** function exports a function **trim(str)** that returns a new string formed by removing all whitespace characters from the beginning and end of **str**. Write the corresponding implementation.

3.　Without using the built-in string method **substr**, implement a free function **substr(str, pos, n)** that returns the substring of **str** beginning at position **pos** and containing at most **n** characters. Make sure that your function correctly applies the following rules:

- If **n** is missing or greater than the length of the string, the substring should extend to the end of the original string.

- If **pos** is greater than the length of the string, **substr** should call **error** with an appropriate message.

4.　Implement a function **capitalize(str)** that returns a string in which the initial character is capitalized (if it is a letter) and all other letters are converted to lower case. Characters other than letters are not affected. For example, both **capitalize("BOOLEAN")** and **capitalize("boolean")** should return the string **"Boolean"**.

5.　In most word games, each letter in a word is scored according to its point value, which is inversely proportional to its frequency in English words. In Scrabble™, the points are allocated as follows:

Points	Letters
1	A, E, I, L, N, O, R, S, T, U
2	D, G
3	B, C, M, P
4	F, H, V, W, Y
5	K
8	J, X
10	Q, Z

For example, the word **"FARM"** is worth 9 points in Scrabble: 4 for the *F*, 1 each for the *A* and the *R*, and 3 for the *M*. Write a program that reads in words and prints their score in Scrabble, not counting any of the other bonuses that occur in the game. You should ignore any characters other than uppercase letters in computing the score. In particular, lowercase letters are assumed to represent blank tiles, which can stand for any letter but have a score of 0.

6.　An **_acronym_** is a word formed by combining, in order, the initial letters of a series of words. For example, the word *scuba* is an acronym formed from the first letters in *self-contained underwater breathing apparatus.* Similarly, *AIDS* is an acronym for *Acquired Immune Deficiency Syndrome.* Write a function **acronym** that takes a string and returns the acronym formed from that string. To ensure that your function treats hyphenated compounds like *self-contained* as two words, it should define the beginning of a word as any alphabetic character that appears either at the beginning of the string or after a nonalphabetic character.

7. Write a function

    ```
    string removeCharacters(string str, string remove);
    ```

    that returns a new string consisting of the characters in **str** after removing all instances of the characters in **remove**. For example, if you call

    ```
    removeCharacters("counterrevolutionaries", "aeiou")
    ```

    the function should return **"cntrrvltnrs"**, which is the original string after removing all of its vowels.

8. Modify your solution to exercise 7 so that, instead of using a function that returns a new string, you define a function **removeCharactersInPlace** that removes the letters from the string passed as the first argument.

9. *The waste of time in spelling imaginary sounds and their history (or etymology as it is called) is monstrous in English . . .*
    —George Bernard Shaw, 1941

    In the early part of the 20th century, there was considerable interest in both England and the United States in simplifying the rules used for spelling English words, which has always been a difficult proposition. One suggestion advanced as part of this movement was to eliminate all doubled letters, so that *bookkeeper* would be written as *bokeper* and *committee* would become *comite*. Write a function **removeDoubledLetters(str)** that returns a new string in which any duplicated characters in **str** have been replaced by a single copy.

10. Write a function

    ```
    string replaceAll(string str, char c1, char c2);
    ```

    that returns a copy of **str** with every occurrence of **c1** replaced by **c2**. For example, calling

    ```
    replaceAll("nannies", 'n', 'd');
    ```

    should return **"daddies"**.

Once you have coded and tested this function, write an overloaded version

```
string replaceAll(string str, string s1, string s2);
```

that replaces all instances of the string **s1** with the replacement string **s2**.

11.   The concept of a palindrome is often extended to full sentences by ignoring punctuation and differences in the case of letters. For example, the sentence

Madam, I'm Adam.

is a sentence palindrome, because if you look only at the letters and ignore any distinction between uppercase and lowercase letters, it reads identically backward and forward.

Write a predicate function **isSentencePalindrome(str)** that returns **true** if the string **str** fits this definition of a sentence palindrome. For example, you should be able to use your function to write a main program capable of producing the following sample run:

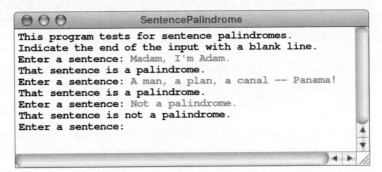

12.   Write a function **createRegularPlural(word)** that returns the plural of **word** formed by following these standard English rules:

a.   If the word ends in *s, x, z, ch,* or *sh,* add *es* to the word.

b.   If the word ends in a *y* preceded by a consonant, change the *y* to *ies*.

c.   In all other cases, add just an *s*.

Write a test program and design a set of test cases to verify that your program works.

13.   Like most other languages, English includes two types of numbers. The **cardinal numbers** (such as *one, two, three,* and *four*) are used in counting; the **ordinal numbers** (such as *first, second, third,* and *fourth*) are used to indicate a position in a sequence. In text, ordinals are usually indicated by writing the digits in the number, followed by the last two letters of the English word that

names the corresponding ordinal. Thus, the ordinal numbers *first, second, third,* and *fourth* often appear in print as *1st, 2nd, 3rd,* and *4th.* The ordinals for 11, 12, and 13, however, are *11th, 12th,* and *13th.* Devise a rule that determines what suffix should be added to each number, and then use this rule to write a function `createOrdinalForm(n)` that returns the ordinal form of the number **n** as a string.

14. When large numbers are written on paper, it is traditional—at least in the United States—to use commas to separate the digits into groups of three. For example, the number one million is usually written in the following form:

    1,000,000

    To make it easier for programmers to display numbers in this fashion, implement a function

    ```
    string addCommas(string digits);
    ```

    that takes a string of decimal digits representing a number and returns the string formed by inserting commas at every third position, starting on the right. For example, if you were to execute the main program

    ```
    int main() {
       while (true) {
          string digits;
          cout << "Enter a number: ";
          getline(cin, digits);
          if (digits == "") break;
          cout << addCommas(digits) << endl;
       }
       return 0;
    }
    ```

    your implementation of the **addCommas** function should be able to produce the following sample run:

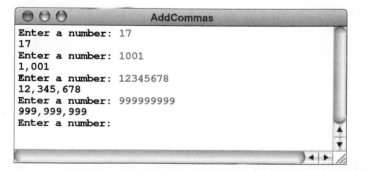

15. As written, the `PigLatin` program in Figure 3-2 behaves oddly if you enter a string that includes words beginning with an uppercase letter. For example, if you were to capitalize the first word in the sentence and the name of the Pig Latin language, you would see the following output:

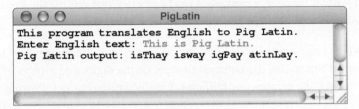

Rewrite the `wordToPigLatin` function so that any word that begins with a capital letter in the English line still begins with a capital letter in Pig Latin. Thus, after you make the necessary changes in the program, the output should look like this:

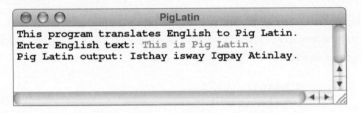

16. Most people—at least those in English-speaking countries—have played the Pig Latin game at some point in their lives. There are other invented "languages" in which words are created using some simple transformation of English. One such language is called *Obenglobish,* in which words are created by adding the letters *ob* before the vowels (*a, e, i, o,* and *u*) in an English word. For example, under this rule, the word *english* gets the letters *ob* added before the *e* and the *i* to form *obenglobish,* which is how the language got its name.

In official Obenglobish, the `ob` characters are added only before vowels that are pronounced, which means that a word like *game* would become *gobame* rather than *gobamobe* because the final *e* is silent. While it is impossible to implement this rule perfectly, you can do a pretty good job by adopting the rule that the *ob* should be added before every vowel in the English word *except*

- Vowels that follow other vowels

- An *e* that occurs at the end of the word

Write a function **obenglobish** that takes an English word and returns its Obenglobish equivalent, using the translation rule given above. For example, if you used your function with the main program

```
int main() {
    while (true) {
        string word = getLine("Enter a word: ");
        if (word == "") break;
        string trans = obenglobish(word);
        cout << word << " -> " << trans << endl;
    }
    return 0;
}
```

you should be able to generate the following sample run:

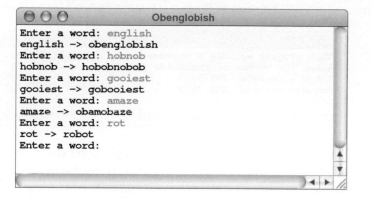

```
Enter a word: english
english -> obenglobish
Enter a word: hobnob
hobnob -> hobobnobob
Enter a word: gooiest
gooiest -> gobooiest
Enter a word: amaze
amaze -> obamobaze
Enter a word: rot
rot -> robot
Enter a word:
```

17. If you played around with codes and ciphers as a child, the odds are good that you at some point used a *cyclic cipher*—which is often called a *Caesar cipher* because the Roman historian Suetonius records that Julius Caesar used this technique—in which you replace each letter in the original message by the letter that appears a fixed distance ahead in the alphabet. As an example, suppose that you wanted to encode a message by shifting every letter ahead three places. In this cipher, each A becomes a D, B becomes E, and so on. If you reach the end of the alphabet, the process cycles around to the beginning, so that X becomes A, Y becomes B, and Z becomes C.

To implement a Caesar cipher, you should first define a function

```
string encodeCaesarCipher(string str, int shift);
```

that returns a new string formed by shifting every letter in **str** forward the number of letters indicated by **shift**, cycling back to the beginning of the alphabet if necessary. After you have implemented **encodeCaesarCipher**, write a program that generates the following sample run:

```
● ○ ○                    CaesarCipher
This program encodes a message using a Caesar cipher.
Enter the number of character positions to shift: 13
Enter a message: This is a secret message.
Encoded message: Guvf vf n frperg zrffntr.
```

Note that the transformation applies only to letters; any other characters are copied unchanged to the output. Moreover, the case of letters is unaffected: lowercase letters come out as lowercase, and uppercase letters come out as uppercase. You should also write your program so that a negative value of **shift** means that letters are shifted toward the beginning of the alphabet instead of toward the end, as illustrated by the following sample run:

```
● ○ ○                    CaesarCipher
This program encodes a message using a Caesar cipher.
Enter the number of character positions to shift: -1
Enter a message: IBM 9000
Encoded message: HAL 9000
```

18. Although they are certainly simple, Caesar ciphers are also extremely easy to break. There are, after all, only 25 values for the number of characters to shift. If you want to break a Caesar cipher, all you have to do is try each of the 25 possibilities and see which one translates the original message into something readable. A better scheme is to allow each letter in the original message to be represented by an arbitrary letter instead of one a fixed distance from the original. In this case, the key for the encoding operation is a translation table that shows what each of the 26 letters becomes in the encrypted form. Such a coding scheme is called a *letter-substitution cipher.*

The key in a letter-substitution cipher is a 26-character string that indicates the translation for each character in the alphabet in order. For example, the key **"QWERTYUIOPASDFGHJKLZXCVBNM"** indicates that the encoding process should use the following translation rule:

```
A B C D E F G H I J K L M N O P Q R S T U V W X Y Z
↓ ↓ ↓ ↓ ↓ ↓ ↓ ↓ ↓ ↓ ↓ ↓ ↓ ↓ ↓ ↓ ↓ ↓ ↓ ↓ ↓ ↓ ↓ ↓ ↓ ↓
Q W E R T Y U I O P A S D F G H J K L Z X C V B N M
```

Write a program that implements encryption using a letter-substitution cipher. Your program should be able to duplicate the following sample run:

```
 ⊖ ○ ◯              LetterSubstitutionCipher
 Letter substitution cipher.
 Enter a 26-letter key: QWERTYUIOPASDFGHJKLZXCVBNM
 Enter a message: WORKERS OF THE WORLD UNITE!
 Encoded message: VGKATKL GY ZIT VGKSR XFOZT!
```

19. Using the definition of keys for letter-substitution ciphers as described in the preceding exercise, write a function **invertKey** that takes an encryption key and returns the 26-letter key necessary to decrypt a message encoded with that encryption key.

20.

There is no gene for the human spirit.

—Tagline for the 1997 film *GATTACA*

The genetic code for all living organisms is carried in its DNA—a molecule with the remarkable capacity to replicate its own structure. The DNA molecule itself consists of a long strand of chemical bases wound together with a similar strand in a double helix. DNA's ability to replicate comes from the fact that its four constituent bases—adenosine, cytosine, guanine, and thymine—combine with each other only in the following ways:

- Cytosine on one strand links only with guanine on the other, and vice versa.

- Adenosine links only with thymine, and vice versa.

Biologists abbreviate the names of the bases by writing only the initial letter: **A**, **C**, **G**, or **T**.

Inside the cell, a DNA strand acts as a template to which other DNA strands can attach themselves. As an example, suppose that you have the following DNA strand, in which the position of each base has been numbered as it would be in a C++ string:

Your mission in this exercise is to determine where a shorter DNA strand can attach itself to the longer one. If, for example, you were trying to find a match for the strand

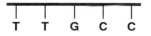

the rules for DNA dictate that this strand can bind to the longer one only at position 1:

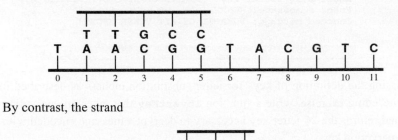

By contrast, the strand

T G C

matches at either position 2 or position 7.

Write a function

```
int findDNAMatch(string s1, string s2, int start = 0);
```

that returns the first position at which the DNA strand **s1** can attach to the strand **s2**. As in the **find** method for the **string** class, the optional **start** parameter indicates the index position at which the search should start. If there is no match, **findDNAMatch** should return −1.

Chapter 4
Streams

We will not be satisfied until justice rolls down like waters and righteousness like a mighty stream.

— Reverend Martin Luther King, Jr.
"I Have a Dream," August 28, 1963
(paraphrasing Amos 5:24)

Ever since **HelloWorld** back in Chapter 1, the programs in this book have made use of an important data structure called a *stream,* which C++ uses to manage the flow of information to or from some data source. In the earlier chapters, you have used the **<<** and **>>** operators and have already had occasion to use the three standard streams exported by the **<iostream>** library: **cin**, **cout**, and **cerr**. You have, however, only scratched the surface of what you can do even with the standard streams. To write C++ programs that move beyond the simple examples you have seen up to now, you will have to learn more about streams and how to use them to create more sophisticated applications. This chapter begins by giving you more insight into the features provided by the **<<** and **>>** operators. It then moves on to introduce the notion of *data files* and shows you how to implement file-processing applications. The chapter then concludes by exploring the structure of the C++ stream classes as a representative example of inheritance hierarchies in an object-oriented language.

4.1 Formatted output

The easiest way to generate formatted output in C++ is to use the **<<** operator. This operator is called the ***insertion operator*** because it has the effect of inserting data into a stream. The operand on the left is the output stream; the operand on the right is the data you want to insert into that stream. The **<<** operator is overloaded so that the operand on the right can be a string or any primitive value. If this operand is not a string, the **<<** operator converts it to string form before sending it to the output stream. This feature makes it easy to display the values of variables, because C++ handles the output conversion automatically.

C++ makes generating output even more convenient by having the **<<** operator return the value of the stream. This design decision makes it possible to chain several output operations together, as you have already seen in several examples in this text. Suppose, for example, that you want to display the value of the variable **total** on an output line that begins with some text telling the user what that value represents. In C++, you start with the expression

```
cout << "The total is "
```

which copies the characters in the string **"The total is "** to the **cout** stream. To insert the decimal representation of the value in **total**, all you need to do is chain on another instance of the **<<** operator like this:

```
cout << "The total is " << total
```

This expression has the intended effect because the **<<** operator returns the stream. Thus, the left operand of the second **<<** is simply **cout**, which means that the value of `total` is displayed at that point in the output. Finally, you can signal the end of the line by inserting the value `endl` using yet another instance of the `<<` operator:

```
cout << "The total is " << total << endl;
```

If `total` contains the value 42, the resulting output looks like this on the console:

Even though you have been using statements like this one since the beginning of this book, knowing that the `<<` operator propagates the value of `cout` through the expression as it moves along the chain of insertion operators may help you to appreciate how output works in C++.

Although it seems as if it might be a simple string constant, the `endl` value used to signal the end of an output line is actually an example of something that C++ calls a *manipulator,* which is just a fancy name for a special type of value used to control formatting. The C++ libraries export a variety of manipulators that you can use to specify the format for output values, the most common of which appear in Table 4-1. For the most part, these manipulators are automatically available when you include the `<iostream>` library. The only exceptions are the manipulators that take parameters, such as `setw(`*n*`)`, `setprecision(`*digits*`)`, and `setfill(`*ch*`)`. To use these manipulators, you need to include `<iomanip>` as well.

Manipulators typically have the effect of setting properties of the output stream in a way that changes the formatting of subsequent output. As the individual entries in Table 4-1 make clear, some manipulators are *transient,* which means that they affect only the next data value that appears. Most, however, are *persistent,* which means that they remain in effect until they are explicitly changed.

One of the most common applications of manipulators involves specifying a field width to support tabular output. Suppose, for example, that you want to rewrite the `PowersOfTwo` program from Chapter 1 so that the numbers in the table are aligned in columns. To do so, all you need to do is add the appropriate manipulators in the output statement, which will look something like this:

```
cout << right << setw(2) << i
          << setw(8) << raiseToPower(2, i) << endl;
```

TABLE 4-1   Output manipulators

`endl`	Inserts an end-of-line sequence into the output stream and ensures that the characters in the output are written to the destination stream.
`setw(n)`	Sets the width of the next field to *n* characters. If the value requires fewer characters, extra space is added to fill the field. This property is ***transient***, which means that it affects only the next value inserted into the stream.
`setprecision(digits)`	Sets the precision for the stream to *digits*. The interpretation of the precision specification depends on other stream settings. If you have set the mode to `fixed` or `scientific`, *digits* specifies the number of digits after the decimal point. If neither of these modes are set, *digits* indicates the number of significant digits, irrespective of where those digits appear. This property is ***persistent***, which means that it remains in effect for the stream until it is explicitly changed.
`setfill(ch)`	Sets the fill character for the stream to *ch*. By default, spaces are added to the output if additional characters are necessary to fill the field width established by `setw`. Calling `setfill` makes it possible to change that character. For example, calling `setfill('0')` means that fields will be filled with zeroes. This property is persistent.
`left`	Specifies that fields should be aligned on the left, which means that any fill characters are inserted *after* the value. This property is persistent.
`right`	Specifies that fields should be aligned on the right, which means that any fill characters are inserted *before* the value. This property is persistent.
`fixed`	Specifies that subsequent floating-point output should be displayed in full, without using scientific notation. By default, floating point values are displayed in the most compact form. This property is persistent.
`scientific`	Specifies that subsequent floating-point output should always appear in scientific notation. This property is persistent.
`showpoint` `noshowpoint`	These manipulators control whether a decimal point should appear in floating-point numbers, even if the value is equal to an integer. You can use `showpoint` to force inclusion of the decimal point and later restore the default behavior with `noshowpoint`. This property is persistent.
`showpos` `noshowpos`	These manipulators control whether a plus sign is printed before positive values. By default, positive values are printed without a sign. This property is persistent.
`uppercase` `nouppercase`	These manipulators control the case of any letters generated as part of numeric conversion, such as the `E` in scientific notation. By default, these characters appear in lower case. This property is persistent.
`boolalpha` `noboolalpha`	These manipulators control the format of `bool` values, which are ordinarily displayed (for historical reasons) using their internal numeric representation. Using the `boolalpha` manipulator causes them to appear instead as `true` and `false`. This property is persistent.

This statement prints the value of **i** in a field of width 2 and the value of the function **raiseToPower(2, i)** in a field of width 8. Both fields are justified on the right because the effect of the **right** manipulator is persistent. If you used this line to display the powers of two between 0 and 16, the output would look like this:

```
 ◯ ◯ ◯                    PowersOfTwo
This program lists powers of two.
Enter exponent limit: 16
  0       1
  1       2
  2       4
  3       8
  4      16
  5      32
  6      64
  7     128
  8     256
  9     512
 10    1024
 11    2048
 12    4096
 13    8192
 14   16384
 15   32768
 16   65536
```

Understanding the use of the **setprecision(***digits***)** manipulator is complicated by the fact that the interpretation of the argument depends on other mode settings for the stream. In the absence of any specifications to the contrary, C++ represents floating-point numbers using either decimal or scientific notation, choosing the representation that is more compact. The fact that C++ can choose either of these representations makes sense if all you care about is seeing the value. If, however, you want to control the output more precisely, you need to indicate which of these formats you want C++ to use. The **fixed** manipulator specifies that floating-point values should always appear as a string of digits with a decimal point in the appropriate position. Conversely, the **scientific** manipulator specifies that values should always use the programming form of scientific notation in which the exponent is separated from the value by the letter **E**. Each of these formats interprets the **setprecision** manipulator in a slightly different way, which makes it harder to provide a concise description of how **setprecision** works.

As is often the case in programming, one of the best ways to understand how some highly detailed aspect of a library works is to write simple test programs that allow you to see what happens on the screen. The **PrecisionExample** program in Figure 4-1 shows how three constants—the mathematical constant π, the speed of light in meters per second, and the fine-structure constant that characterizes the strength of electrical interaction—appear using different floating-point modes and precision. The output of the program appears in Figure 4-2.

FIGURE 4-1 Program to explore the behavior of setprecision

```cpp
/*
 * File: PrecisionExample.cpp
 * --------------------------
 * This program demonstrates various options for floating-point output
 * by displaying three different constants (pi, the speed of light in
 * meters/second, and the fine-structure constant).  These constants
 * are chosen because they illustrate a range of exponent scales.
 */

#include <iostream>
#include <iomanip>
#include <cmath>
using namespace std;

/* Constants */

const double PI = 3.14159265358979323846;
const double SPEED_OF_LIGHT = 2.99792458E+8;
const double FINE_STRUCTURE = 7.2573525E-3;

/* Function prototypes */

void printPrecisionTable();

/* Main program */

int main() {
   cout << uppercase << right;
   cout << "Default format:" << endl << endl;
   printPrecisionTable();
   cout << endl << "Fixed format:" << fixed << endl << endl;
   printPrecisionTable();
   cout << endl << "Scientific format:" << scientific << endl << endl;
   printPrecisionTable();
   return 0;
}

/*
 * Function: printPrecisionTable
 * -----------------------------
 * Generates a simple precision table for the current cout settings.
 */

void printPrecisionTable() {
   cout << " prec |      pi      | speed of light | fine structure" << endl;
   cout << "------+--------------+----------------+----------------" << endl;
   for (int prec = 0; prec <= 6; prec += 2) {
      cout << setw(4) << prec << "  |";
      cout << " " << setw(12) << setprecision(prec) << PI << " |";
      cout << " " << setw(16) << setprecision(prec) << SPEED_OF_LIGHT << " |";
      cout << " " << setw(14) << setprecision(prec) << FINE_STRUCTURE << endl;
   }
}
```

FIGURE 4-2 Sample run illustrating floating-point output

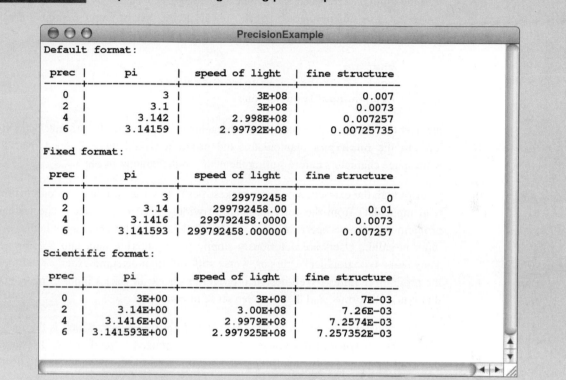

```
                              PrecisionExample
Default format:

prec |        pi      |    speed of light    |  fine structure
-----+----------------+----------------------+--------------------
  0  |             3  |               3E+08  |         0.007
  2  |           3.1  |               3E+08  |         0.0073
  4  |         3.142  |           2.998E+08  |         0.007257
  6  |       3.14159  |         2.99792E+08  |         0.00725735

Fixed format:

prec |        pi      |    speed of light    |  fine structure
-----+----------------+----------------------+--------------------
  0  |             3  |         299792458    |            0
  2  |          3.14  |         299792458.00  |         0.01
  4  |        3.1416  |         299792458.0000|         0.0073
  6  |      3.141593  |       299792458.000000|         0.007257

Scientific format:

prec |        pi      |    speed of light    |  fine structure
-----+----------------+----------------------+--------------------
  0  |         3E+00  |               3E+08  |         7E-03
  2  |      3.14E+00  |            3.00E+08  |         7.26E-03
  4  |    3.1416E+00  |          2.9979E+08  |         7.2574E-03
  6  |  3.141593E+00  |        2.997925E+08  |         7.257352E-03
```

Although the mechanisms for formatted input and output (which computer scientists often abbreviate as *I/O*) in any programming language can be quite useful, they also tend to be detail-ridden. In general, it makes sense to learn how to perform a few of the most common formatting tasks but to look up the details of other, less common operations only when you need to use them.

4.2 Formatted input

Formatted input in C++ is enabled by the operator **>>**, which you have already used in a variety of programs. This operator is called the *extraction operator,* because it is used to extract formatted data from an input stream. Up to now, you have used the **>>** operator to request input values from the console, typically by writing a sequence of statements such as the following lines from the **PowersOfTwo** program from Chapter 1:

```
int limit;
cout << "Enter exponent limit: ";
cin >> limit;
```

By default, the **>>** operator skips over whitespace characters before trying to read the input data. If necessary, you can change this behavior by using the **skipws** and **noskipws** manipulators, which appear in the list of input manipulators in Table 4-2. For example, if you execute the lines

```
char ch;
cout << "Enter a single character: ";
cin >> noskipws >> ch;
```

the user can then enter a space or tab character in response to the prompt. Had you left out the **noskipws** manipulator, the program would have skipped over the whitespace characters before storing the next input character in **ch**.

Although the extraction operator makes it easy to write simple test programs that read input data from the console, it is not widely used in practice. The primary problem with the **>>** operator is that it offers little support for checking whether user input is valid. Users are notoriously sloppy when entering data into a computer. They make typographical errors or, worse still, fail to understand exactly what input the program requires. Well-designed programs check the user's input to make sure that it is well-formed and that it makes sense in context.

Unfortunately, the **>>** operator is simply not up to this task, which is the reason behind the existence of the **simpio.h** library introduced in section 2-9. If you use the facilities provided by this library, the code to read a value from the user shrinks from three lines to one:

```
int limit = getInteger("Enter exponent limit: ");
```

As noted in Chapter 2, the **getInteger** function also implements the necessary error checking internally, making it much safer to use as well. You'll have a chance to see how **getInteger** is implemented later in this chapter, after which it won't seem so mysterious.

TABLE 4-2 Input manipulators

skipws noskipws	These manipulators control whether the extraction operator skips over whitespace characters before reading a value. If you specify **noskipws**, the extraction operator treats all characters (including whitespace characters) as part of the input field. You can later use **skipws** to restore the default behavior. This property is persistent.
ws	Reads characters from the input stream until some character appears that is not in the whitespace category. The effect of this manipulator is therefore to skip over any spaces, tabs, and newlines in the input. Unlike **skipws** and **noskipws**, which change the behavior of the stream for subsequent input operations, the **ws** manipulator takes effect immediately.

4.3 Data files

Whenever you want to store information on the computer for longer than the running time of a program, the usual approach is to collect the data into a logically cohesive whole and store it on a permanent storage medium as a ***file***. Ordinarily, a file is stored using magnetic or optical media, such as the hard disk installed inside your computer or a portable flash drive or memory stick. The specific details of the medium, however, are not critical; the important point is that the permanent data objects you store on the computer—documents, games, executable programs, source code, and the like—are all stored in the form of files.

On most systems, files come in a variety of types. For example, in the programming domain, you work with source files, object files, and executable files, each of which has a distinct representation. When you use a file to store data for use by a program, that file usually consists of text and is therefore called a ***text file***. You can think of a text file as a sequence of characters stored in a permanent medium and identified by a file name. The name of the file and the characters it contains have the same relationship as the name of a variable and its contents.

As an example, the following text file contains the first stanza of Lewis Carroll's nonsense poem "Jabberwocky," which appears in *Through the Looking Glass:*

```
Jabberwocky.txt
```
```
'Twas brillig, and the slithy toves
Did gyre and gimble in the wabe;
All mimsy were the borogoves,
And the mome raths outgrabe.
```

The name of the file is `Jabberwocky.txt`, and the contents of the file consist of the four lines of characters that comprise the first stanza of the poem.

When you look at a file, it is often convenient to regard it as a two-dimensional structure: a sequence of lines composed of individual characters. Internally, however, text files are represented as a one dimensional sequence of characters. In addition to the printing characters you can see, files also contain a newline character that marks the end of each line.

In many respects, text files are similar to strings. Each consists of an ordered collection of characters with a specified endpoint. On the other hand, strings and files differ in several important respects. The most important difference is the permanence of the data. A string is stored temporarily in the computer's memory while a program runs; a file is stored permanently on a long-term storage device until it is explicitly deleted. There is also a difference regarding how you refer to individual characters in strings and files. Because each character in a string has an index, you can process those characters in any order simply by choosing the appropriate sequence of index values. By contrast, characters in a text file tend to be processed sequentially. Programs that work with file data typically start at the beginning of the file and then work their way—either reading existing characters from an input file or writing new ones to an output file—to the end of the file.

Using file streams

As you will discover in section 4.4, the C++ stream library exports several classes that form a hierarchical structure. To help you make sense of that structure as a whole, it is useful to start with two stream classes—**ifstream** and **ofstream**—exported by the **<fstream>** library. Once you are familiar with those examples, it will be easier to generalize from that experience to understand the stream hierarchy as a whole.

The most common methods that apply to file streams appear in Table 4-3. Studying this table, however, is not likely to be as helpful to you as learning a few simple patterns for working with files. File processing in any language tends to be idiomatic in the sense that you need to learn a general strategy and then apply that strategy in the applications you write. C++ is no exception to this rule.

Reading or writing a file in C++ requires the following steps:

1. *Declare a stream variable to refer to the file.* Programs that work with files typically declare a stream variable for each active file. Thus, if you are writing a program that reads an input file and then manipulates the data to produce an output file, you need to declare two variables, as follows:

   ```
   ifstream infile;
   ofstream outfile;
   ```

2. *Open the file.* Before you can use a stream variable, you need to establish an association between that variable and an actual file. This operation is called *opening* the file and is performed by calling the stream method **open**. For example, if you want to read the text contained in the **Jabberwocky.txt** file, you open the file by executing the method call

   ```
   infile.open("Jabberwocky.txt");
   ```

   Because the stream libraries predate the introduction of the **string** class, the **open** method expects a C-style string as the file name. A string literal is therefore acceptable as is. If, however, the name of the file is stored in a **string** variable named **filename**, you will need to open the file like this:

   ```
   infile.open(filename.c_str());
   ```

TABLE 4-3 Useful methods in the stream classes

Methods supported by all streams

stream.**fail**()	Returns **true** if the stream is in a failure state. This condition usually occurs when you try to read data past the end of the file, but may also indicate an integrity error in the data.
stream.**eof**()	Returns **true** if the stream is positioned at the end of the file. Given the semantics of the C++ stream library, the **eof** method is useful *only* after a call to **fail**. At that point, calling **eof** allows you to test whether the failure indication was caused by reaching the end of the file.
stream.**clear**()	Resets the status bits associated with the stream. You must call this method whenever you need to reuse a stream after a failure has occurred.
if (*stream*) . . .	Checks whether the stream is valid. For the most part, this test has the same effect as calling **if** (!*stream*.**fail**()).

Methods supported by all file streams

stream.**open** (*filename*)	Attempts to open the named file and attach it to the stream. The direction is determined by the stream type: input streams are opened for input, output streams for output. The *filename* parameter is a C-style string, which means that you will need to call **c_str** on any C++ string. You can check whether the **open** method fails by calling **fail**.
stream.**close**()	Closes the file attached to the stream.

Methods supported by all input streams

stream >> *variable*	Reads formatted data into a variable. The data format is controlled by the variable type and whatever input manipulators are in effect.
stream.**get** (*var*)	Reads the next character into the character variable *var*, which is passed by reference. The return value is the stream itself, with the **fail** flag set if there are no more characters.
stream.**get** ()	Returns the next character in the stream. The return value is an integer, which makes it possible to identify the end-of-file character, which is represented by the constant **EOF**.
stream.**unget** ()	Backs up the internal pointer of the stream so that the last character read will be read again by the next call to **get**.
getline (*stream*, *str*)	Reads the next line of input from *stream* into the string *str*. The **getline** function returns the stream, which simplifies the end-of-file test.

Methods supported by all output streams

stream << *expression*	Writes formatted data to an output stream. The data format is controlled by the expression type and whatever output manipulators are in effect.
stream.**put** (*ch*)	Writes the character *ch* to the output stream.

If the requested file is missing, the stream will record that error and let you check for it by calling the predicate method **fail**. It is your responsibility as a programmer to recover from such failures, and you will learn various strategies for doing so later in this chapter.

3. *Transfer the data.* Once you have opened the data files, you then use the appropriate stream operations to perform the actual I/O operations. Depending on the application, you can choose any of several strategies to transfer the file data. At the simplest level, you can read or write files character by character. In some cases, however, it is more convenient to process files line by line. At a still higher level, you can choose to read and write formatted data, which allows you to intermix numeric data with strings and other data types. The details of each of these strategies appear in the sections that follow.

4. *Close the file.* When you have finished all data transfers, you need to indicate that fact to the file system by calling the stream method **close**, as follows:

```
infile.close();
```

This operation, which is called *closing* the file, breaks the association between a stream and the actual file.

Single character I/O

In many applications, the best way to process the data in a text file is to go through the contents of the file one character at a time. Input streams in the C++ library support reading a single character using a method called **get**, which exists in two forms. The simplest strategy is to use the first form of the **get** method listed in Table 4-3, which stores the next character from the stream in a variable passed by reference, as shown in the following code that reads the first character from the **infile** stream into the variable **ch**:

```
char ch;
infile.get(ch);
```

For most applications, of course, the goal is not to read a single character, but to read successive characters, one at a time, as you go through the file. C++ makes this operation easy by allowing streams to be used in conditional contexts. The general pattern for reading all the characters in a file looks like this:

```
char ch;
while (infile.get(ch)) {
    Perform some operation on the character.
}
```

The **get** method reads the next character into the variable **ch** and returns the stream. That stream, in turn, is interpreted as **true** if the **get** operation succeeds and as **false** if it fails, presumably because no characters remain in the file. The effect, therefore, is to execute the body of the **while** loop once for each character until the stream reaches the end of the file.

Although this strategy is extremely simple, many C++ programmers use the version of **get** that returns a character, mostly because that strategy was available even back in the days of C programming. This form of the **get** method has the following prototype:

```
int get();
```

At first glance, the result type seems odd. The prototype indicates that **get** returns an **int**, even though it would seem more appropriate for the method to return a **char**. The reason for this design decision is that returning a character would make it harder for a program to detect the end of the input file. There are only 256 possible character codes, and a data file might contain any of those values. There is no value—or at least no value of type **char**—that you could use as a sentinel to indicate the end-of-file condition. Defining **get** so that it returns an integer means that the implementation can return a value outside the range of legal character codes to indicate the end-of-file condition. That value has the symbolic name of **EOF**.

If you use this form of the **get** method, the code pattern to read an entire file character by character looks like this:

```
while (true) {
    int ch = infile.get();
    if (ch == EOF) break;
    Perform some operation on the character.
}
```

This implementation uses the read-until-sentinel pattern that was introduced in the **AddList** program from Chapter 1. The body of the **while** loop reads the next character into the integer variable **ch** and then exits the loop if **ch** is the end-of-file sentinel.

Many C++ programmers, however, implement this loop in the following slightly shorter but decidedly more cryptic form:

```
int ch;
while ((ch = infile.get()) != EOF) {
    Perform some operation on the character.
}
```

In this form of the code, the test expression for the **while** loop uses embedded assignment to combine the operations of reading in a character and testing for the end-of-file condition. When C++ evaluates this test, it begins by evaluating the subexpression

```
ch = infile.get()
```

which reads a character and assigns it to **ch**. Before executing the loop body, the program then goes on to make sure the result of the assignment is not **EOF**. The parentheses around the assignment are required; without them, the expression would incorrectly assign to **ch** the result of comparing the character against **EOF**. Because this idiom occurs frequently in existing C++ code, you need to recognize and understand it when it appears. In your own code, it is far easier to use the simpler idiom based on the call-by-reference version of **get**.

For output streams, the **put** method takes a **char** value as its argument and writes that character to the stream. A typical call to **put** therefore looks like this:

```
outfile.put(ch);
```

As an example of the use of **get** and **put**, the **ShowFileContents** program in Figure 4-3 displays the contents of a text file on the console. Assuming that the **Jabberwocky.txt** file exists, a sample run of this program might look like this:

The code in Figure 4-3 also includes the function **promptUserForFile**, which asks the user to enter a file name and then opens that file for input. If the file does not exist or cannot be opened for some reason, **promptUserForFile** asks the user for a new file name, continuing that process until the **open** call succeeds. This design allows the program to recover gracefully if the user enters an invalid file name. For example, if the user forgot to include the **.txt** extension the first time around, the first few lines of the console output would look like this:

FIGURE 4-3   **Program to show the contents of a file**

```cpp
/*
 * File: ShowFileContents.cpp
 * ---------------------------
 * This program displays the contents of a file chosen by the user.
 */

#include <iostream>
#include <fstream>
#include <string>
using namespace std;

/* Function prototypes */

string promptUserForFile(ifstream & infile, string prompt = "");

/* Main program */

int main() {
   ifstream infile;
   promptUserForFile(infile, "Input file: ");
   char ch;
   while (infile.get(ch)) {
      cout.put(ch);
   }
   infile.close();
   return 0;
}

/*
 * Function: promptUserForFile
 * Usage: string filename = promptUserForFile(infile, prompt);
 * ----------------------------------------------------------------
 * Asks the user for the name of an input file and opens the reference
 * parameter infile using that name, which is returned as the result of
 * the function.  If the requested file does not exist, the user is
 * given additional chances to enter a valid file name.  The optional
 * prompt argument is used to give the user more information about the
 * desired input file.
 */

string promptUserForFile(ifstream & infile, string prompt) {
   while (true) {
      cout << prompt;
      string filename;
      getline(cin, filename);
      infile.open(filename.c_str());
      if (!infile.fail()) return filename;
      infile.clear();
      cout << "Unable to open that file.  Try again." << endl;
      if (prompt == "") prompt = "Input file: ";
   }
}
```

Although the logic behind the implementation of **promptUserForFile** is easy to follow, there are a few important details that are worth mentioning. The **open** call, for example, needs to use **c_str** to convert the C++ string stored in **filename** to the old-style C string that the stream library requires. Similarly, the call to **clear** inside the **while** loop is necessary to ensure that the failure status indicator in the stream is reset before the user enters a new file name.

When you are reading character data from an input file, you will sometimes find yourself in the position of not knowing that you should stop reading characters until you have already read more than you need. Consider, for example, what happens when the C++ extraction operator tries to read an integer, which is represented as a string of decimal digits. The library implementation cannot know that the number is finished until it reads a character that is *not* a digit. That character, however, may be part of some subsequent input, and it is essential not to lose that information.

C++ solves this problem for input streams by exporting a method called **unget** that has the following form:

```
infile.unget();
```

The effect of this call is to "push" the most recent character back into the input stream so that it is returned on the next call to **get**. The specifications for the C++ library guarantee that it will always be possible to push one character back into the input file, but you should not rely on being able to read several characters ahead and then push them all back. Fortunately, being able to push back one character is sufficient in the vast majority of cases.

Line-oriented I/O

Because files are usually subdivided into individual lines, it is often useful to read an entire line of data at a time. The stream function that performs this operation is called **getline**, which is not the same as the **getLine** function from **simpio.h** even though they serve a similar purpose. The **getline** function—which is defined as a free function rather than a method—takes two references parameters: the input stream from which the line is read and a string variable into which the result is written. Calling

```
getline(infile, str);
```

copies the next line of the file into the variable **str**, up to but not including the newline character that signals the end of the line. Like **get**, the **getline** function returns the input stream, which makes it easy to test for the end-of-file condition. All you have to do is use the **getline** call itself as a test expression.

The `getline` function makes it possible to rewrite the `ShowFileContents` program so that the program reads the file one line at a time. If you adopt this approach, the `while` loop in the main program looks like this:

```
string line;
while (getline(infile, line)) {
   cout << line << endl;
}
```

The `while` loop reads each line of data from the file into the string variable `line` until the stream reaches the end of the file. For each line, the body of the loop uses the `<<` operator to send the line to `cout`, followed by a newline character.

Formatted I/O

In addition to the character-by-character and line-by-line approaches to processing files, it is also possible to use the `<<` and `>>` operators on file streams, just as you have already had occasion to do with the console streams. Suppose, for example, that you want to revise the `AddIntegerList` program from Figure 1-5 so that it takes its input from a data file instead of from the console. The simplest approach is to open a data file for input and use the resulting `ifstream` instead of `cin` to read the input values.

The only other change you need to make is in the code that exits the loop when the input is complete. The console version of the program uses a sentinel value to indicate the end of the input. For the version that reads from a file, the loop should continue until there are no more data values to read. The easiest way to test for that condition is to use the `>>` operator as a test. Since `>>` returns the stream, it will indicate the end-of-file condition by setting the `fail` flag, which C++ then interprets as `false`.

If you make these changes to the original code, the program looks like this:

```
int main() {
   ifstream infile;
   promptUserForFile(infile, "Input file: ");
   int total = 0;
   int value;
   while (infile >> value) {
      total += value;
   }
   infile.close();
   cout << "The sum is " << total << endl;
   return 0;
}
```

Unfortunately, this implementation strategy is less than ideal, even if it is technically correct. If all the numbers are formatted in exactly the right way, the program will get the right answer. If, however, there are extraneous characters in the file, the loop will exit before all the input values have been read. Worse still, the program will give no indication that an error has occurred.

The crux of the problem is that the extraction operator in the expression

```
infile >> value;
```

will set the failure indicator in either of two cases:

1.   Reaching the end of the file, at which point there are no more values to read.

2.   Trying to read data from the file that cannot be converted to an integer.

You can differentiate these two cases by checking to make sure the end of the file has been reached when the loop exits. For example, you can let the user know if a data error has occurred by adding the following lines after the **while** loop:

```
if (!infile.eof()) {
    error("Data error in file");
}
```

The error doesn't provide the user with much guidance as to the source of the error, but at least it's better than nothing.

Another problem is that the extraction operator is overly permissive in terms of the formats it allows. Unless you specify otherwise, the **>>** operator will accept any sequence of whitespace characters as data separators. Thus, the input file need not contain one value per line, but can instead be formatted in any of a number of ways. For example, if you wanted to use your application to add the first five integers, it would not be necessary to enter the data with one value per line, as illustrated by the following data file:

It would work just as well—and might indeed be more convenient—to put the values on a single line like this:

One problem with having so much flexibility is that it becomes harder to detect certain kinds of formatting errors. What would happen, for example, if you accidentally included a space in one of the integers? As things stand, the **SumIntegerFile** application would simply read the digits before and after the space as two separate values. In such cases, it is often better to insist on more rigid formatting rules to improve data integrity.

In the **SumIntegerFile** application, it probably makes sense to insist that the data values appear one per line, as in the first sample file. Unfortunately, enforcing that restriction is difficult if the only tools you have are file streams and the extraction operator. One way to start would be to read the data file one line at a time and then convert each line to an integer before adding it to the total. If you were to adopt this approach, the main program would look like this:

```
int main() {
    ifstream infile;
    promptUserForFile(infile, "Input file: ");
    int total = 0;
    string line;
    while (getline(infile, line)) {
        total += stringToInteger(line);
    }
    infile.close();
    cout << "The sum is " << total << endl;
    return 0;
}
```

The only thing that's missing is the implementation of **stringToInteger**.

Although the C++ libraries include a function called **atoi** that converts a string to an integer, that function predates the **<string>** library and therefore requires the use of C strings, which are much less convenient to use. It would be great if you could find a way to implement that conversion while remaining entirely in the C++ domain. You know that the C++ libraries must contain the necessary code, because the **>>** operator has to perform that conversion when it reads an integer from a file. If there were a way to use that same code to read an integer from a string, the implementation of **stringToInteger** would follow immediately as a result. As you will learn in the following section, the C++ stream libraries provide precisely that capability, which will turn out to be useful in a wide variety of applications.

String streams

Given that files and strings are both sequences of characters, it seems reasonable to think that programming languages might allow you to treat them symmetrically. C++ provides that capability through the **<sstream>** library, which exports several classes that allow you to associate a stream with a string value in much the same way that the **<fstream>** library allows you to associate a stream with a file. The **istringstream** class is the counterpart of **ifstream** and makes it possible to use stream operators to read data from a string. For output, the **ostringstream** class works very much like **ofstream** except that the output is directed to a string rather than a file.

The existence of the **istringstream** class makes it possible to implement the **stringToInteger** method described in the last section as follows:

```
int stringToInteger(string str) {
    istringstream stream(str);
    int value;
    stream >> value >> ws;
    if (stream.fail() || !stream.eof()) {
        error("stringToInteger: Illegal integer format");
    }
    return value;
}
```

The first line of the function introduces an important feature of variable declarations that you have not yet seen. If you are declaring an object, C++ allows you to supply arguments after the variable name that control how that object is initialized. In this implementation, the line

```
istringstream stream(str);
```

declares a variable named **stream** and initializes it to an **istringstream** object that is already set up to read data from the string variable **str**. The next two lines

```
int value;
stream >> value >> ws;
```

read an integer value from that stream and store it in the variable **value**. In this implementation, whitespace characters are allowed either before or after the value. The first **>>** operator automatically skips over any whitespace characters that appear before the value; the **ws** manipulator at the end of the line reads any whitespace characters that follow the value, thereby ensuring that the stream will be positioned correctly at the end of the line if the input is correctly formatted. The lines

```
if (stream.fail() || !stream.eof()) {
    error("stringToInteger: Illegal integer format");
}
```

then check to make sure that the input is valid. If the string cannot be parsed as an integer, `stream.fail()` will return `true`, thereby triggering the error message. If, however, the string begins with a number but then contains additional characters, `stream.eof()` will be `false`, which also triggers the error message.

If you need to convert in the other direction, you can use the `ostringstream` class. The following function, for example, converts an integer into a string of decimal digits:

```
string integerToString(int n) {
    ostringstream stream;
    stream << n;
    return stream.str();
}
```

The `<<` operator in the second line converts the value into its decimal representation just as it would for a file. In this case, however, the output is directed to a string stored internally as part of the `ostringstream` object. The `str` function in the `return` statement copies the value of that internal string so that it can be returned to the caller. It is interesting to note that converting in this direction is substantially easier because it is no longer necessary to take account of formatting errors.

A more robust strategy for console input

String streams also offer a solution to the problem of checking whether user input is properly formed. As discussed in the section on "Formatted input" earlier in the chapter, the `>>` operator does not check the user's input for errors. Consider, for example, what happens if you ask the user for an integer value using the following statements from the `PowersOfTwo` program:

```
int limit;
cout << "Enter exponent limit: ";
cin >> limit;
```

If the user enters a valid integer, everything is fine. But what would happen if the user tried to enter the value 16 but slipped down one row on the keyboard and typed the letter `t` instead of the digit `6`? In an ideal world, the program would look at the input `1t` and complain about its validity. Unfortunately, if you use the extraction operator in C++, that error will go undetected. When the program is asked to read a value into the integer variable `limit`, the `>>` operator reads characters until it finds one that is illegal in an integer field. Input therefore stops on the `t`, but the value `1` is still a legal integer, so the program keeps right on going with `limit` equal to 1.

The most effective way to ensure that user input is valid is to read an entire line as a string and then convert that string to an integer. This strategy is embodied in the function **getInteger** shown in Figure 4-4. This function reads an integer from the user just as the **>>** operator does but also makes sure that the integer is valid. The logic of **getInteger** is similar to that used in the **stringToInteger** function from the preceding section. The only major difference is that **getInteger** gives the user a chance to reenter a corrected value instead of terminating the program with an error message, as illustrated in the following sample run:

```
PowersOfTwo
This program lists powers of two.
Enter exponent limit: 1t
Illegal integer format. Try again.
Enter exponent limit: 16
```

As this example makes clear, **getInteger** finds the typographical error in the first input line and then asks the user for a new value. When the user presses RETURN after correctly typing the value 16, **getInteger** returns this value to the caller.

FIGURE 4-4 Function to read an integer from the console

```
/*
 * Function: getInteger
 * Usage: int n = getInteger(prompt);
 * -------------------------------------
 * Requests an integer value from the user.  The function begins by
 * printing the prompt string on the console and then waits for the
 * user to enter a line of input data.  If that line contains a
 * single integer, the function returns the corresponding integer
 * value.  If the input is not a legal integer or if extraneous
 * characters (other than whitespace) appear on the input line,
 * the implementation gives the user a chance to reenter the value.
 */

int getInteger(string prompt) {
   int value;
   string line;
   while (true) {
      cout << prompt;
      getline(cin, line);
      istringstream stream(line);
      stream >> value >> ws;
      if (!stream.fail() && stream.eof()) break;
      cout << "Illegal integer format. Try again." << endl;
   }
   return value;
}
```

As you can see from the code in Figure 4-4, the `getInteger` function takes a prompt string, which it then displays to the user before reading the input line. This design decision follows directly from the fact that the `getInteger` function needs that information in order to repeat the prompt string if an error occurs.

The `getInteger` function is a more reliable tool for reading integer data than the `>>` operator. For that reason, it makes sense to use `getInteger` instead of `>>` in any application that requires checking for errors. As you already know from Chapter 2, the Stanford libraries include `getInteger` as part of the `simpio` library.

4.4 Class hierarchies

When the designers of C++ undertook the task of modernizing the input/output libraries, they chose to adopt an object-oriented approach. One implication of that decision is that the data types in the stream libraries are implemented as *classes*. Classes have a number of advantages over older strategies for representing data. Of these, the most important is that classes provide a framework for *encapsulation*, which is the process of combining the data representation and the associated operations into a coherent whole that reveals as few details as possible about the underlying structure. The classes you have already seen in this chapter illustrate encapsulation well. When you use these classes, you have no idea how they are implemented. As a client, all you need to know is what methods are available for those classes and how to call them.

Object-oriented programming offers other important advantages besides encapsulation. In particular, classes in an object-oriented language form a hierarchy in which each class automatically acquires the characteristics of the classes that precede it in the hierarchy. This property is called *inheritance.* Although C++ tends to use inheritance less frequently than many object-oriented languages do, it is nonetheless one of the features that sets the object-oriented paradigm apart from earlier programming models.

Biological hierarchies

The class structure of an object oriented language is similar in many ways to the biological classification system developed by the eighteenth-century Swedish botanist Carl Linnaeus as a way to represent the structure of the biological world. In Linnaeus's conception, living things are first subdivided into *kingdoms.* The original system contained only the plant and animal kingdoms, but there are some forms of life—such as fungi and bacteria—that don't fit well in either category and now occupy kingdoms of their own. Each kingdom is then further broken down into the hierarchical categories of *phylum, class, order, family, genus,* and *species.* Every living species fits at the bottom of this hierarchy but also belongs to some category at each higher level.

This biological classification system is illustrated in Figure 4-5, which shows the classification of the common black garden ant, which has the scientific name of *Lasius niger,* corresponding to its genus and species. This species of ant, however, is also part of the family *Formicidae,* which is the classification that actually identifies it as an ant. If you move upward in the hierarchy from there, you discover that *Lasius niger* is also of the order *Hymenoptera* (which includes bees and wasps), the class *Insecta* (which consists of the insects), and the phylum *Arthropoda* (which includes, for example, shellfish and spiders).

FIGURE 4-5 Class hierarchies in the biological world

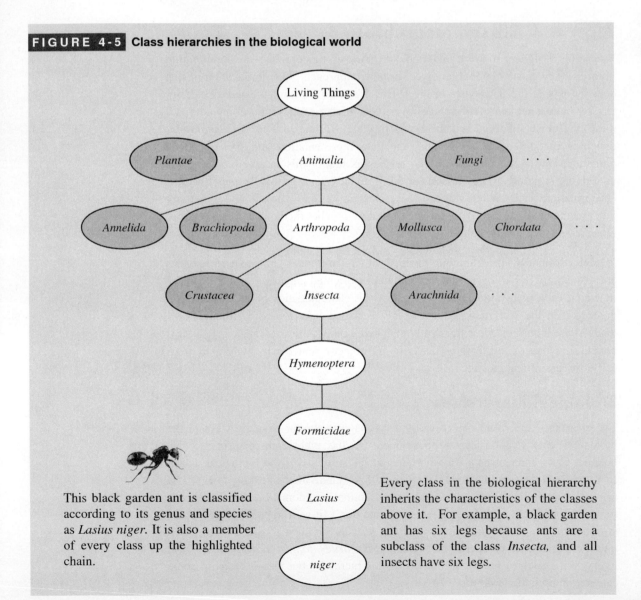

This black garden ant is classified according to its genus and species as *Lasius niger*. It is also a member of every class up the highlighted chain.

Every class in the biological hierarchy inherits the characteristics of the classes above it. For example, a black garden ant has six legs because ants are a subclass of the class *Insecta,* and all insects have six legs.

One of the properties that makes this biological classification system useful is that all living things belong to a category at every level in the hierarchy. Each individual life form therefore belongs to several categories simultaneously and inherits the properties that are characteristic of each one. The species *Lasius niger,* for example, is an ant, an insect, an arthropod, and an animal—all at the same time. Moreover, each individual ant shares the properties that it inherits from each of those categories. One of the defining characteristics of the class *Insecta* is that insects have six legs. All ants must therefore have six legs because ants are members of that class.

The biological metaphor also helps to illustrate the distinction between classes and objects. Although every common black garden ant has the same biological classification, there are many individuals of the common-black-garden-ant variety. Thus, each of the ants

is an instance of *Lasius niger.* In the language of object-oriented programming, *Lasius niger* is a class and each individual ant is an object.

The stream class hierarchy

The classes in the stream libraries form hierarchies that are in many ways similar to the biological hierarchy introduced in the preceding section. So far, you have seen two types of input streams—**ifstream** and **istringstream**—and two types of output streams—**ofstream** and **ostringstream**—that in each pairing share a common set of operations. In C++, these classes form the hierarchy shown in Figure 4-6. At the top of the hierarchy is the class **ios**, which represents a general

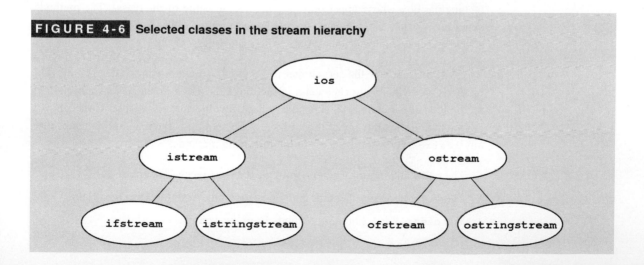

FIGURE 4-6 Selected classes in the stream hierarchy

stream type that can be used for any kind of I/O. The hierarchy is then subdivided into two categories—**istream** and **ostream**—that generalize the notions of input stream and output stream, respectively. The C++ file and string stream classes then fall naturally into the appropriate position in this hierarchy, as shown.

Figure 4-6 provides a useful framework for introducing some of the terminology associated with object-oriented programming. In this diagram, which was drawn using the same geometrical structure as the evolutionary diagram in Figure 4-5, each class is a *subclass* of the class that appears above it in the hierarchy. Thus, **istream** and **ostream** are both subclasses of **ios**. In the opposite direction, **ios** is called a *superclass* of both **istream** and **ostream**. Similar relationships exist at different levels of this diagram. For example, **ifstream** is a subclass of **istream**, and **ostream** is a superclass of **ofstream**.

The relationship between subclasses and superclasses is in many ways best conveyed by the English words *is a*. Every **ifstream** object is also an **istream** and, continuing up the hierarchy, an **ios**. As in the biological hierarchy, this relationship implies that the characteristics of any class are inherited by its subclasses. In C++, these characteristics correspond to the methods and other definitions associated with the class. Thus, if the **istream** class exports a particular method, that method is automatically available to any **ifstream** or **istringstream** object. More globally, any methods exported by the **ios** class are available to every class in the hierarchy shown in Figure 4-6.

Although simple diagrams that show only the relationships among classes are valuable in their own right, it is useful to expand them to include the methods exported at each level, as shown in Figure 4-7. This enhanced diagram adopts parts of a standard methodology for illustrating class hierarchies called the ***Universal Modeling Language,*** or ***UML*** for short. In UML, each class appears as a rectangular box whose upper portion contains the name of the class. The methods exported by that class appear in the lower portion. UML diagrams use open arrowheads to point from subclasses to their superclasses.

UML diagrams of the sort shown in Figure 4-7 make it easy to determine what methods are available to each class in the diagram. Because each class inherits the methods of every class in its superclass chain, an object of a particular class can call any method defined in any of those classes. For example, the diagram indicates that any **ifstream** object has access to the following methods:

- The **open** and **close** methods from the **ifstream** class itself

- The **get** and **unget** methods and the **>>** operator from the **istream** class

- The **clear**, **fail**, and **eof** methods from the **ios** class

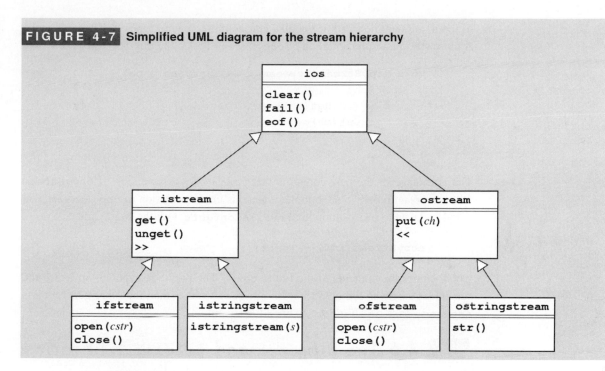

FIGURE 4-7 Simplified UML diagram for the stream hierarchy

Choosing the right level in the stream hierarchy

One of the most important decisions you need to make when using object hierarchies is that of choosing the right level at which to work. As a general rule, it is best to write your code so that it uses the most general level in the hierarchy that supports the operations you need. Adopting this rule ensures that your code is as flexible as possible in that it supports the widest range of types.

As an example, you will often find it useful to define a **copyStream** method that copies all the characters from one input stream to another. If you had come up with this idea as you were working with file streams, you might have been tempted to implement the method as follows:

```
void copyStream(ifstream & infile, ofstream & outfile) {
    while (true) {
        int ch = infile.get();
        if (ch == EOF) break;
        outfile.put(ch);
    }
}
```

Although this implementation is not technically incorrect, it is certainly problematic enough to justify the bug icon. The problem is that the method works only for file streams, even though the code would have been perfectly appropriate for any type of input and output stream if you had chosen more general types for the arguments. A more flexible implementation of **copyStream** looks like this:

```
void copyStream(istream & is, ostream & os) {
   char ch;
   while (is.get(ch)) {
      os.put(ch);
   }
}
```

The advantage of the new coding is that you can use this version of **copyStream** with all stream types. For example, given this implementation of **copyStream**, you could replace the **while** loop in **ShowFileContents** with the single line

```
copyStream(infile, cout);
```

which copies the contents of the file to **cout**. The previous version—in which the second argument is declared to be an **ofstream** rather than the more general class **ostream**—fails because **cout** is not a file stream.

4.5 The `simpio.h` and `filelib.h` libraries

Chapter 3 introduced several new functions that were useful enough to package as the **strlib.h** library. In this chapter, you have seen several useful tools for working with streams that have also made their way into two interfaces in the Stanford library: the **simpio.h** interface introduced in Chapter 2 and a **filelib.h** interface for the methods that are more closely related to files.

Although it is possible to list the contents of each of those interfaces in tables of the sort used in this book, most modern interfaces are not described on paper. With the expansion of the web, programmers use online reference materials more often than printed ones. Figure 4-8, for example, shows the web-based documentation for the **simpio.h** library.

While the tabular description fits well on the printed page and the web-based documentation is ideal for online browsing, you also have another option for learning what resources are available in an interface: you can read the **.h** file. If an interface is designed and documented effectively, reading the **.h** file can provide all the information you need. In any event, reading **.h** files is a programming skill that you will need to cultivate if you want to become proficient in C++.

To give yourself some practice in reading interfaces, you should look at the **filelib.h** interface supplied with the Stanford libraries. That interface includes the **promptUserForFile** function developed in this chapter, along with a number of other functions that will likely come in handy when you work with files.

FIGURE 4-8 Online documentation for the `simpio.h` interface

⊝ ⊜ ◯   simpio.h

simpio.h

This interface exports a set of functions that simplify input/output operations in C++ and provide some error-checking on console input.

Functions

getInteger(prompt)	Reads a complete line from **cin** and tries to scan it as an integer.
getReal(prompt)	Reads a complete line from **cin** and tries to scan it as a floating-point number.
getLine(prompt)	Reads a line of text from **cin** and returns that line as a string.

Function detail

---

int getInteger(string prompt = "");

Reads a complete line from **cin** and scans it as an integer. If the scan succeeds, the integer value is returned. If the argument is not a legal integer or if extraneous characters (other than whitespace) appear in the string, the user is given a chance to reenter the value. If supplied, the optional **prompt** string is printed before reading the value.

Usage:

```
int n = getInteger(prompt);
```

---

double getReal(string prompt = "");

Reads a complete line from **cin** and scans it as a floating-point number. If the scan succeeds, the floating-point value is returned. If the input is not a legal number or if extraneous characters (other than whitespace) appear in the string, the user is given a chance to reenter the value. If supplied, the optional **prompt** string is printed before reading the value.

Usage:

```
double x = getReal(prompt);
```

---

string getLine(string prompt = "");

Reads a line of text from **cin** and returns that line as a string. The newline character that terminates the input is not stored as part of the return value. If supplied, the optional **prompt** string is printed before reading the value.

Usage:

```
string line = getLine(prompt);
```

Summary

In this chapter, you have learned how to use the libraries in the stream hierarchy to support input/output operations involving the console, strings, and data files. Important points in this chapter include:

- The `<iostream>` library exports three standard streams: `cin`, `cout`, and `cerr`.

- The `<iomanip>` library makes it possible to control the output format. This library exports a set of *manipulators*, the most important of which appear in Table 4-1. The `<iomanip>` library includes manipulators for input as well, but these are less important in practice.

- The `<fstream>` library in C++ supports the reading and writing of data files. The most important methods that apply to file streams are listed in Table 4-3.

- The C++ stream libraries allow you to choose any of several different strategies when reading a file. You can read the file character by character using the `get` methods, line by line using the `getline` method, or as formatted data using the `>>` extraction operator.

- The `<sstream>` library makes it possible to use the `>>` and `<<` operators to read and write string data.

- The classes in the stream library form a hierarchy in which subclasses inherit the behavior of their superclasses. When you design functions to work with streams, it is important to choose the most general level of the hierarchy for which the necessary operations are defined.

- At various points in the first three chapters, the text defines new functions that are likely to prove useful in many different contexts. These functions are exported through several interfaces that constitute the Stanford C++ libraries, which makes sure they are available without forcing you to copy the code.

Review questions

1. What are the three standard file streams defined by the `<iostream>` library?

2. What are the formal names for the `<<` and `>>` operators?

3. What value do the `<<` and `>>` operators return? Why is this value important?

4. What is a *manipulator?*

5. What is the difference between a *transient* and a *persistent* property?

6. In your own words, describe how the `fixed` and `scientific` manipulators change the format for floating-point output. What happens if you don't specify either of these options?

7.   Suppose that the constant **PI** has been defined as

            const double PI = 3.14159265358979323846;

      What output manipulators would you use to produce each line of the following
      sample run:

8.   What is the purpose of the types **ifstream** and **ofstream**?

9.   The argument to **open** must be a C-style string. How does this requirement
      affect the code you write to open a file?

10.   How can you determine if an **open** operation on a stream was successful?

11.   When you are using the **get** method to read a file character by character, how
      do you detect the end of a file?

12.   Why is the return type of **get** declared as **int** instead of **char**?

13.   What is the purpose of the **unget** method?

14.   When you are using the **getline** method to read a file line by line, how do
      you detect the end of the file?

15.   What classes does the **<sstream>** library support? How do these classes
      differ from the ones provided in **<fstream>**?

16.   What is meant by the following terms: *subclass, superclass,* and *inheritance?*

17   True or false: The **stream** class hierarchy of Figure 4-7 shows that **istream**
      is a subclass of **istringstream**.

18.   Why does the **copyStream** function take arguments of type **istream** and
      ostream instead of **ifstream** and **ofstream**?

19.   What are the advantages of using the **getInteger** and **getReal** functions
      from **simpio.h** over using the **>>** extraction operator?

20.   If this text does not describe the functions exported by a library in tabular
      form, what options do you have for learning how to use that library?

▮▮▮ Exercises

1. The `<iomanip>` library gives programmers more control over output format, which makes it easy, for example, to create formatted tables. Write a program that displays a table of trigonometric sines and cosines that looks like this:

```
 ● ○ ●                        TrigTable
 theta |  sin(theta)  |  cos(theta)  |
 ------+------------+------------+
   -90  | -1.0000000 |  0.0000000 |
   -75  | -0.9659258 |  0.2588190 |
   -60  | -0.8660254 |  0.5000000 |
   -45  | -0.7071068 |  0.7071068 |
   -30  | -0.5000000 |  0.8660254 |
   -15  | -0.2588190 |  0.9659258 |
     0  |  0.0000000 |  1.0000000 |
    15  |  0.2588190 |  0.9659258 |
    30  |  0.5000000 |  0.8660254 |
    45  |  0.7071068 |  0.7071068 |
    60  |  0.8660254 |  0.5000000 |
    75  |  0.9659258 |  0.2588190 |
    90  |  1.0000000 |  0.0000000 |
```

   The numeric columns should all be aligned on the right, and the columns containing the trigonometric functions (which are listed here for angles at 15-degree intervals) should all have seven digits after the decimal point.

2. In exercise 4 in Chapter 2, you wrote a function `windChill` that calculated the wind chill for a given temperature and wind velocity. Write a program that uses this function to display these values in tabular form, as illustrated by the table from the National Weather Service shown in Figure 2-17 on page 116.

3. Write a program that prints the longest line in a file chosen by the user. If several lines are all equally long, your program should print the first such line.

4. Write a program that reads a file and reports how many lines, words, and characters appear in it. For the purposes of this program, a word consists of a consecutive sequence of any characters except whitespace characters. As an example, suppose that the file **Lear.txt** contains the following passage from Shakespeare's *King Lear*:

   Lear.txt

   ```
   Poor naked wretches, wheresoe'er you are,
   That bide the pelting of this pitiless storm,
   How shall your houseless heads and unfed sides,
   Your loop'd and window'd raggedness, defend you
   From seasons such as these?  O, I have ta'en
   Too little care of this!
   ```

your program should be able to generate the following sample run:

```
 ● ● ●                    FileCounts
Input file: Lear.txt
Chars: 254
Words:   43
Lines:    6
```

The counts in the output should be displayed in a column that is aligned on the right but which expands to fit the data. For example, if you have a file containing the full text of George Eliot's *Middlemarch,* the output of your program should look like this:

```
 ● ● ●                    FileCounts
Input file: Middlemarch.txt
Chars: 1796948
Words:   316689
Lines:    34037
```

5. The **filelib.h** interface exports several functions that make it easy to work with filenames. In particular, the functions **getRoot** and **getExtension** divide a filename into its *root,* which is the part before the dot that specifies the name, and the *extension,* which indicates its type. For example, given the filename **Middlemarch.txt**, the root is **Middlemarch** and the extension is **.txt** (note that **filelib.h** defines the extension to include the dot). Write the code necessary to implement these functions. To find out how to handle special cases, such as filenames that don't include a dot, you can read through the **filelib.h** interface or consult the online documentation.

6. Another useful function in **filelib.h** is

    ```
    string defaultExtension(string filename, string ext);
    ```

    which adds **ext** to the end of **filename** if it doesn't already have an extension. For example,

    ```
    defaultExtension("Shakespeare", ".txt")
    ```

    would return **"Shakespeare.txt"**. If **filename** already has an extension, that name is returned unchanged, so that

    ```
    defaultExtension("library.h", ".cpp")
    ```

    would ignore the specified extension and return **"library.h"** unchanged. If, however, **ext** includes a star before the dot, **defaultExtension** removes any existing extension from **filename** and adds the new one (minus the star). Thus,

```
defaultExtension("library.h", "*.cpp")
```

would return **"library.cpp"**. Write the code for **defaultExtension** so that it behaves as described in this exercise.

7. On occasion, publishers find it useful to evaluate layouts and stylistic designs without being distracted by the actual words. To do so, they sometimes typeset sample pages in such a way that all of the original letters are replaced with random letters. The resulting text has the spacing and punctuation structure of the original, but no longer conveys any meaning that might get in the way of the design. The publishing term for text that has been replaced in this way is *greek,* presumably after the old saying "It's all Greek to me," which is itself adapted from a line from Shakespeare's *Julius Caesar.*

Write a program that reads characters from an input file and displays them on the console after making the appropriate random substitutions. Your program should replace every uppercase character in the input with a random uppercase character and every lowercase character with a random lowercase one. Nonalphabetic characters should remain unchanged. For example, suppose that the input file **Troilus.txt** contains the following text from Shakespeare's *Troilus and Cressida:*

Troilus.txt
```
Ay, Greek; and that shall be divulged well
In characters as red as Mars his heart
Inflamed with Venus:
```

Your program should generate output that looks something like this:

```
Greek
Input file: Troilus.txt
Ne, Inyes; fmd ckhj zntqt uv dqijxnkp uyww
Rt pkjfvkmzdf yt kut ya Itgp byi blxod
Ogmgmkwl jjbe Nscku:
```

8. Even though comments are essential for human readers, the compiler simply ignores them. If you are writing a compiler, you therefore need to be able to recognize and eliminate comments that occur in a source file.

Write a function

```
void removeComments(istream & is, ostream & os);
```

that copies characters from the input stream `is` to the output stream `os`, except for characters that appear inside C++ comments. Your implementation should recognize both comment conventions:

- Any text beginning with `/*` and ending with `*/`, possibly many lines later.

- Any text beginning with `//` and extending through the end of the line.

The real C++ compiler needs to check to make sure that these characters are not contained inside quoted strings, but you should feel free to ignore that detail. The problem is tricky enough as it stands.

9.
> *Books were bks and Robin Hood was Rbinhd. Little Goody Two Shoes lost her Os and so did Goldilocks, and the former became a whisper, and the latter sounded like a key jiggled in a lck. It was impossible to read "cockadoodledoo" aloud, and parents gave up reading to their children, and some gave up reading altogether. . . .*
>
> —James Thurber, *The Wonderful O,* 1957

In James Thurber's children's story *The Wonderful O,* the island of Ooroo is invaded by pirates who set out to banish the letter *O* from the alphabet. Such censorship would be much easier with modern technology. Write a program that asks the user for an input file, an output file, and a string of letters to be eliminated. The program should then copy the input file to the output file, deleting any of the letters that appear in the string of censored letters, no matter whether they appear in uppercase or lowercase form.

As an example, suppose that you have a file containing the first few lines of Thurber's novel, as follows:

`TheWonderfulO.txt`

```
Somewhere a ponderous tower clock slowly
dropped a dozen strokes into the gloom.
Storm clouds rode low along the horizon,
and no moon shone.  Only a melancholy
chorus of frogs broke the soundlessness.
```

If you run your program with the input

it should write the following file:

```
TheWnderful.txt
```
```
Smewhere a pnderus twer clck slwly
drpped a dzen strkes int the glm.
Strm cluds rde lw alng the hrizn,
and n mn shne.  nly a melanchly
chrus f frgs brke the sundlessness.
```

If you tried to get greedy and banish all the vowels by entering **aeiou** in response to the prompt, the contents of the output file would be

```
Smwhr  pndrs twr clck slwly
drppd  dzn strks nt th glm.
Strm clds rd lw lng th hrzn,
nd n mn shn.  nly  mlnchly
chrs f frgs brk th sndlssnss.
```

10. Some files use tab characters to align data into columns. Doing so, however, can cause problems for applications that are unable to work directly with tabs. For these applications, it is useful to have access to a program that replaces tabs in an input file with the number of spaces required to reach the next tab stop. In programming, tab stops are usually set at every eight columns. For example, suppose that the input file contains a line of the form

```
abc ———┤ pqrst —┤ xyz
```

where the ———┤ symbol represents the space taken up by a tab, which differs depending on its position in the line. If the tab stops are set every eight spaces, the first tab character must be replaced by five spaces and the second tab character by three.

Write a program that copies an input file to an output file, replacing all tab characters by the appropriate number of spaces.

11. Using the functions **stringToInteger** and **integerToString** as a model, write the code necessary to implement **stringToReal** and **realToString**.

12. Complete the implementation of the **simpio.h** interface by implementing the functions **getReal** and **getLine**.

Chapter 5
Collections

In this way I have made quite a valuable collection.

— Mark Twain, *A Tramp Abroad,* 1880

As you know from your programming experience, data structures can be assembled to form hierarchies. The atomic data types like `int`, `char`, `double` represent the basic building blocks of those hierarchies. To represent more complex information, you combine the atomic types to form larger structures. These larger structures can then be assembled into even larger ones in an open-ended process. Collectively, these assemblages are called *data structures.*

As you learn more about programming, you will discover that particular data structures are so useful that they are worth studying in their own right. Moreover, it is usually far more important to know how to use those structures effectively than it is to understand their underlying representation. For example, even though a string might be represented inside the machine as an array of characters, it also has an abstract behavior that transcends that representation. A type defined in terms of its behavior rather than its representation is called an *abstract data type,* which is often abbreviated to *ADT.* Abstract data types are central to the object-oriented style of programming, which encourages programmers to think about data structures in a holistic way.

This chapter introduces five classes—`Vector`, `Stack`, `Queue`, `Map`, and `Set`—each of which represents an important abstract data type. Each of these classes, moreover, contains a collection of values of some simpler type. Such classes are therefore called *collection classes.* For the moment, you don't need to understand how these classes are implemented, because your primary focus is on learning how to use these classes as a client. In later chapters, you'll have a chance to explore a variety of implementation strategies and learn about the algorithms and data structures necessary to make the implementations efficient.

Separating the behavior of a class from its underlying implementation is a fundamental technique of object-oriented programming. As a design strategy, maintaining that separation offers the following advantages:

- *Simplicity.* Hiding the internal representation from the client means that there are fewer details for the client to understand.

- *Flexibility.* Because a class is defined in terms of its public behavior, the programmer who implements a class is free to change its underlying private representation. As with any abstraction, it is appropriate to change the implementation as long as the interface remains the same.

- *Security.* The interface boundary acts as a wall that protects the implementation and the client from each other. If a client program has access to the representation, it can change the values in the underlying data structure in unexpected ways. Making the data private in a class prevents the client from making such changes.

To use any of the collection classes introduced in this chapter, you must include the appropriate interface, just as you would for any of the libraries from the earlier chapters. The interface for each of the collection classes is simply the name of the class spelled with a lowercase initial letter and followed with the extension `.h` at the end. For example, in order to use the `Vector` class in a program, you must add the following line at the beginning of your source file:

```
#include "vector.h"
```

The collection classes used in this book are inspired by and draw much of their structure from a more advanced set of classes available for C++ called the *Standard Template Library*, or *STL* for short. Although the STL is enormously powerful, it is more difficult to understand, no matter whether you approach it as a client or as an implementer. One of the advantages of using the simplified version is that you can understand the entire implementation by the time you finish this book. Knowing how the implementation works gives you greater insight into what the Standard Template Library is doing for you behind the scenes.

5.1 The Vector class

One of the most valuable collection classes is the `Vector` class, which provides a facility similar to the arrays you have almost certainly encountered in your earlier experience with programming. Arrays have been around since the early days of programming. Like most languages, C++ supports arrays, and you will have the chance to learn how C++ arrays work in Chapter 11. Arrays in C++, however, have a number of weaknesses, including the following:

- Arrays are allocated with a fixed size that you can't subsequently change.

- Even though arrays have a fixed size, C++ does not make that size available to the programmer. As a result, programs that work with arrays typically need an additional variable to keep track of the number of elements.

- Traditional arrays offer no support for inserting and deleting elements.

- C++ does not check that the elements you select are actually present in the array. For example, if you create an array with 25 elements and then try to select the value at index position 50, C++ will simply look at the memory addresses at which element 50 *would* appear if it existed.

The `Vector` class solves each of these problems by reimplementing the array concept in the form of an abstract data type. You can use the `Vector` class in place of arrays in any application, usually with surprisingly few changes in the source code and at most a minor reduction in efficiency. In fact, once you have the `Vector` class, it's unlikely that you will have much occasion to use arrays at all, unless you actually have to *implement* classes like `Vector`, which, not surprisingly, uses arrays in its underlying structure. As a client of the **Vector** class, however, you are not interested in that underlying structure and can leave the array mechanics to the programmers who implement the abstract data type.

As a client of the **Vector** class, you are concerned with a different set of issues and need to answer the following questions:

1.   How is it possible to specify the type of object contained in a **Vector**?

2.   How does one create an object that is an instance of the **Vector** class?

3.   What methods exist in the **Vector** class to implement its abstract behavior?

The next three sections explore the answers to each of these questions in turn.

Specifying the base type of a Vector

In C++, collection classes specify the type of object they contain by including the type name in angle brackets following the class name. For example, the class **Vector<int>** represents a vector whose elements are integers, **Vector<char>** specifies a vector whose elements are single characters, and **Vector<string>** specifies one in which the elements are strings. The type enclosed within the angle brackets is called the **base type** for the collection.

Classes that include a base-type specification are called **parameterized classes** in the object-oriented community. In C++, parameterized classes are more often called **templates,** which reflects the fact that C++ compilers treat **Vector<int>**, **Vector<char>**, and **Vector<string>** as independent classes that share a common structure. The name **Vector** acts as a template for generating a whole family of classes, in which the only difference is what type of value the vector contains. For now, all you need to understand is how to *use* templates; the process of implementing basic templates is described in Chapter 14.

Declaring a Vector object

One of the philosophical principles behind abstract data types is that clients should be able to think of them as if they were built-in primitive types. Thus, just as you would declare an integer variable by writing a declaration such as

```
int n;
```

it ought to be possible to declare a new vector by writing

```
Vector<int> vec;
```

In C++, that is precisely what you do. That declaration introduces a new variable named **vec**, which is—as the template marker in angle brackets indicates—a vector of integers.

Vector operations

When you declare a **Vector** variable, it starts out as an *empty vector,* which means that it contains no elements. Since an empty vector is not particularly useful, one of the first things you need to learn is how to add new elements to a **Vector** object. The usual approach is to invoke the **add** method, which adds a new element at the end of the **Vector**. For example, if **vec** is an empty vector of integers as declared in the preceding section, executing the code

```
vec.add(10);
vec.add(20);
vec.add(40);
```

changes **vec** into a three-element vector containing the values 10, 20, and 40. As with the characters in a string, C++ numbers the elements of a vector starting with 0, which means that you could diagram the contents of **vec** like this:

```
vec
┌──────┬──────┬──────┐
│  10  │  20  │  40  │
└──────┴──────┴──────┘
    0      1      2
```

Unlike the more primitive array type that will be introduced in Chapter 11, the size of a vector is not fixed, which means that you can add additional elements at any time. Later in the program, for example, you could call

```
vec.add(50);
```

which would add the value 50 to the end of the vector, like this:

```
vec
┌──────┬──────┬──────┬──────┐
│  10  │  20  │  40  │  50  │
└──────┴──────┴──────┴──────┘
    0      1      2      3
```

The **insert** method allows you to add new elements in the middle of a vector. The first argument to **insert** is an index number, and the new element is inserted before that position. For example, calling

```
vec.insert(2, 30);
```

inserts the value 30 before index position 2, as follows:

vec

10	20	30	40	50
0	1	2	3	4

Internally, the implementation of the **Vector** class has to expand the array storage and move the values 40 and 50 over one position to make room for the 30. From your perspective as a client, the implementation simply takes care of such details, and you don't need to understand how it does so.

The **Vector** class also lets you remove elements. For example, calling

```
vec.remove(0);
```

removes the element from position 0, leaving the following values:

vec

20	30	40	50
0	1	2	3

Once again, the implementation shifts the elements to close the gap left by the deleted value.

The **Vector** class includes two methods for selecting and modifying individual elements. The **get** method takes an index number and returns the value in that index position. For example, given the value of **vec** shown in the most recent diagram, calling **vec.get(2)** would return the value 40.

Symmetrically, you can use the **set** method to change the value of an existing element. For example, calling

```
vec.set(3, 70);
```

changes the value in index position 3 from 50 to 70, like this:

vec

20	30	40	70
0	1	2	3

The **get**, **set**, **insert**, and **remove** methods all check to make sure that the index value you supply is valid for the vector. For example, if you were to call **vec.get(4)** in this vector, the **get** method would call **error** to report that the index value 4 is too large for a vector in which the index values run from 0 to 3. For **get**, **set**, and **remove**, the **Vector** implementation checks that the index is greater than or equal to 0 and less than the number of elements. The **insert** method allows the index to be equal to the number of elements, in which case the new value is added at the end of the array, just as it is with **add**.

The operation of testing whether an index is valid is called ***bounds-checking.*** Bounds-checking makes it easier to catch programming errors that can often go unnoticed when you work with traditional arrays.

Selecting elements in a vector

Even though the **get** and **set** methods are easy to use, hardly anyone actually calls these methods. One of the characteristics of C++ that sets it apart from most other languages is that classes can override the definition of the standard operators. This feature makes it possible for the **Vector** class to support the more traditional syntax of using square brackets to specify the desired index. Thus, to select the element at position **i**, you can use the expression **vec[i]**, just as you would with a traditional array. You can, moreover, change the value of that element by assigning a new value to **vec[i]**. For example, you can set element 3 in **vec** to 70 by writing

```
vec[3] = 70;
```

The resulting syntax is marginally shorter than calling **set**, but is more evocative of the array operations that the **Vector** class is designed to emulate.

The index used to select an element from an array can be any expression that evaluates to an integer. One of the most common index expressions is the index of a **for** loop that cycles through each of the index values is order. The general pattern for cycling through the index positions in a vector looks like this:

```
for (int i = 0; i < vec.size(); i++) {
    loop body
}
```

Inside the loop body, you can refer to the current element as **vec[i]**.

As an example, the following code writes out the contents of the vector **vec** as a comma-separated list enclosed in square brackets:

```
cout << "[";
for (int i = 0; i < vec.size(); i++) {
    if (i > 0) cout << ", ";
    cout << vec[i];
}
cout << "]" << endl;
```

If you were to execute this code given the most recent contents of **vec**, you would see the following output on the screen:

```
    ⊙ ○ ○                    PrintVector
  [20, 30, 40, 70]
```

Passing a `Vector` object as a parameter

The code at the end of the preceding section is so useful (particularly when you're debugging and need to see what values a vector contains), that it is worth defining a function for this purpose. At one level, encapsulating the code inside a function is easy; all you have to do is add the appropriate function header, like this:

```
void printVector(Vector<int> & vec) {
   cout << "[";
   for (int i = 0; i < vec.size(); i++) {
      if (i > 0) cout << ", ";
      cout << vec[i];
   }
   cout << "]" << endl;
}
```

The header line, however, involves one subtlety that you have to understand before you can use collection classes effectively. As described in Chapter 2, the **&** before the parameter name indicates that the argument **vec** is passed by reference, which means that the value in the function is shared with the value in the caller. Call-by-reference is more efficient than C++'s default model of call-by-value, which requires copying every element in the vector. In the **printVector** example, there is no reason to make that copy. Using call-by-reference—particularly for large data structures like the collection classes—can therefore save a substantial amount of execution time.

Perhaps more importantly, using call-by-reference makes it possible to write functions that change the contents of a vector. As an example, the following function deletes any zero-valued elements from a vector of integers:

```
void removeZeroElements(Vector<int> & vec) {
   for (int i = vec.size() - 1; i >= 0; i--) {
      if (vec[i] == 0) vec.remove(i);
   }
}
```

The **for** loop cycles through each element and checks whether its value is 0. If so, the function calls **remove** to delete that element from the vector. To ensure that removing an element doesn't change the positions of elements that have not yet been checked, the **for** loop starts at the end of the vector and runs backwards.

This function depends on the use of call-by-reference. If you left out the ampersand in this header line, **removeZeroElements** would have no effect at all. The code would remove the zero elements from the local copy of **vec**, but not from the vector the caller supplied. When **removeZeroElements** returned, that copy would go away, leaving the original vector unchanged. This kind of error is easy to make, and you should learn to look for it when your programs go awry.

The **ReverseFile** program in Figure 5-1 shows a complete C++ program that uses **Vector** to display the lines from a file in reverse order. You will find that the functions **promptUserForFile** and **readEntireFile** come in handy in a variety of applications. For this reason, both of these functions—along with many other useful functions for working with files—are included in the **filelib.h** library.

Creating a Vector of a predefined size

The examples you have seen up to this point start out with an empty vector and then add elements to it, one at a time. In many applications, building up a vector one element at a time is tedious, particularly if you know the size of the vector in advance. In such cases, it makes more sense to specify the number of elements as part of the declaration.

As an example, suppose that you want to create a vector to hold the scores for each hole on an 18-hole golf course. The strategy you already know is to create an empty **Vector<int>** and then add 18 elements to it using a **for** loop, as follows:

```
const int N_HOLES = 18;

Vector<int> golfScores;
for (int i = 0; i < N_HOLES; i++) {
   golfScores.add(0);
}
```

A better approach is to include the size as a parameter to the declaration like this:

```
Vector<int> golfScores(N_HOLES);
```

This declaration creates a **Vector<int>** with **N_HOLES** elements, each of which is initialized to 0 for a **Vector** of type **int**. The effect of these two code fragments is the same. Each of them creates a **Vector<int>** filled with 18 zero values. The first form requires the client to initialize the elements; the second hands that responsibility off to the **Vector** class itself.

FIGURE 5-1 **Program to display the lines of a file in reverse order**

```cpp
/*
 * File: ReverseFile.cpp
 * ----------------------
 * This program displays the lines of an input file in reverse order.
 */

#include <iostream>
#include <fstream>
#include <string>
#include "filelib.h"
#include "vector.h"
using namespace std;

/* Function prototypes */

void readEntireFile(istream & is, Vector<string> & lines);

/* Main program */

int main() {
   ifstream infile;
   Vector<string> lines;
   promptUserForFile(infile, "Input file: ");
   readEntireFile(infile, lines);
   infile.close();
   for (int i = lines.size() - 1; i >= 0; i--) {
      cout << lines[i] << endl;
   }
   return 0;
}

/*
 * Function: readEntireFile
 * Usage: readEntireFile(is, lines);
 * ----------------------------------
 * Reads the entire contents of the specified input stream into the
 * string vector lines.  The client is responsible for opening and
 * closing the stream.
 */

void readEntireFile(istream & is, Vector<string> & lines) {
   string line;
   while (getline(is, line)) {
      lines.add(line);
   }
}
```

As a more significant example of when you might want to declare a vector of a constant size, consider the **LetterFrequency** program in Figure 5-2, which counts how often each of the 26 letters appears in a data file. Those counts are maintained in the variable **letterCounts**, which is declared as follows:

```
Vector<int> letterCounts(26);
```

Each element in this vector contains the count of the letter at the corresponding index in the alphabet, with the number of *A*s in **letterCounts[0]**, the number of *B*s in **letterCounts[1]**, and so on. For each letter in the file, all the program has to do is increment the value at the appropriate index position in the vector, which

FIGURE 5-2 Program to count letter frequencies in a file

```cpp
/*
 * File: LetterFrequency.cpp
 * -----------------------
 * This program counts the frequency of letters in a data file.
 */

#include <iostream>
#include <iomanip>
#include <fstream>
#include <cctype>
#include "filelib.h"
#include "vector.h"
using namespace std;

/* Constants */

static const int COLUMNS = 7;

/* Main program */

int main() {
   Vector<int> letterCounts(26);
   ifstream infile;
   promptUserForFile(infile, "Input file: ");
   char ch;
   while (infile.get(ch)) {
      if (isalpha(ch)) {
         letterCounts[toupper(ch) - 'A']++;
      }
   }
   infile.close();
   for (char ch = 'A'; ch <= 'Z'; ch++) {
      cout << setw(COLUMNS) << letterCounts[ch - 'A'] << " " << ch << endl;
   }
   return 0;
}
```

the program can compute arithmetically from the ASCII code of the character. This calculation occurs in the statement

```
letterCounts[toupper(ch) - 'A']++;
```

Subtracting the ASCII value `'A'` from the uppercase character code gives the index of the character `ch` in the alphabet. This statement then updates the count by incrementing that element of the vector.

The remainder of the program is mostly concerned with formatting the output so that the letter counts are properly aligned in columns. As an example, here is what the `LetterCounts` program produces if you run it on a file containing the text of George Eliot's *Middlemarch:*

```
●○○                    LetterFrequency
Input file: Middlemarch.txt
 114157 A
  23269 B
  34031 C
  61046 D
 166989 E
  30826 F
  30055 G
  89636 H
  99651 I
   1695 J
  11010 K
  56865 L
  37816 M
  96887 N
 108561 O
  21922 P
   1441 Q
  79808 R
  88555 S
 123433 T
  40647 U
  12792 V
  34508 W
   2069 X
  28700 Y
    249 Z
```

Constructors for the Vector class

The sample programs you've seen so far in this chapter declare vectors in two different ways. The `ReverseFile` program in Figure 5-1 defines an empty vector of strings using the declaration

```
Vector<string> lines;
```

The `LetterFrequency` program declares a vector containing 26 zeroes like this:

```
Vector<int> letterCounts(26);
```

As it happens, there is more going on in these declarations than meets the eye. When you declare a variable of a primitive type, as in

```
double total;
```

C++ does not make any attempt to initialize that variable. The memory used to hold the variable **total** continues to have whatever value happened to be there before the declaration, which can easily lead to unexpected results. For this reason, declarations of primitive variables usually include an explicit initializer that sets the variable to the desired starting value, as in

```
double total = 0.0;
```

The situation is different when you declare a variable to be an instance of a C++ class. In that case, C++ automatically initializes that variable by invoking a special method called a *constructor*. For example, in the declaration

```
Vector<string> lines;
```

C++ calls the **Vector** constructor, which initializes the variable **lines** to be an empty vector that belongs to the parameterized class **Vector<string>**. The declaration

```
Vector<int> letterCounts(26);
```

calls a different version of the constructor to initialize a **Vector<int>** with 26 elements.

The C++ compiler determines which version of the constructor to call by looking at the arguments appearing in the declaration, just as it does for overloaded functions. The declaration of **lines** provides no arguments, which tells the compiler to invoke the constructor that takes no arguments, which is called the *default constructor.* The declaration of **letterCounts** provides an integer argument, which tells the compiler to invoke the version of the constructor that takes an integer indicating the vector size. The two versions of the **Vector** constructor appear—along with a complete list of the **Vector** methods—in Table 5-1.

If you look closely at the constructor descriptions in Table 5-1, you'll discover that the second form of the constructor accepts an optional argument indicating the initial value to use for each of the elements. That argument is usually omitted, in which case the initial value for the elements is the *default value* for the base type, which is 0 for numeric types, the constant **false** for type **bool**, and the character

TABLE 5-1 Entries in the `vector.h` interface

Constructors

`Vector<type>()`	Creates an empty vector.
`Vector<type>(n, value);`	Creates a vector with *n* elements, each of which is initialized to *value*, or, if *value* is missing, to the default value for that type.

Methods

`size()`	Returns the number of elements in the vector.
`isEmpty()`	Returns **true** if the vector is empty.
`get(index)`	Returns the element at the specified index position. Attempting to get the value of an element outside the vector bounds generates an error.
`set(index, value)`	Sets the element at the specified index to the new value. Attempting to set the value of an element outside the vector bounds generates an error.
`add(value)`	Adds a new element at the end of the vector.
`insertAt(index, value)`	Inserts the new value before the specified index position.
`removeAt(index)`	Deletes the element at the specified index position.
`clear()`	Removes all elements from the vector.

Operators

`vec[index]`	Selects the element at the specified index position. Selecting an element outside the vector bounds generates an error.
$v_1 + v_2$	Concatenates v_1 and v_2 and returns a new vector containing the combined elements.
`vec += e_1, e_2, ...`	Adds the elements e_1, e_2, and so on, to the end of the vector.

whose ASCII value is 0 for type **char**. For classes, the default value is produced by calling the default constructor.

Vector operators

In addition to the methods listed in Table 5-1, the **Vector** class also defines several operators that apply to vector objects. You have already seen the use of square brackets, which make it possible to select objects from a vector using the traditional selection syntax for arrays. The **Vector** class also defines the operators **+** and **+=** as shorthand forms for concatenating two vectors and for adding elements to an existing vector.

The **+** operator on vectors is defined so that it works exactly the way it does for strings. If the character vectors **v1** and **v2** contain the values

v1

'A'	'B'	'C'
0	1	2

and

v2

'D'	'E'
0	1

evaluating the expression **v1 + v2** creates a new five-element vector, as follows:

'A'	'B'	'C'	'D'	'E'
0	1	2	3	4

The **+=** operator adds elements to the end of an existing vector, but is also useful if you need to initialize the contents of a vector. For example, you can declare and initialize the vector **v1** like this:

```
Vector<char> v1;
v1 += 'A', 'B', 'C';
```

If you are using C++11, which is the new C++ standard released in 2011, you can simplify this initialization, as follows:

```
Vector<char> v1 = { 'A', 'B', 'C' };
```

Representing two-dimensional structures

The type parameter used in the **Vector** class can be any C++ type and may itself be a parameterized type. In particular, you can create a two-dimensional structure by declaring a **Vector** whose base type is itself a **Vector**. The declaration

```
Vector< Vector<int> > sudoku(9, Vector<int>(9));
```

initializes the variable **sudoku** to a **Vector** of nine elements, each of which is itself a **Vector** of nine elements. The base type of the inner vector is **int**, and the base type of the outer vector is **Vector<int>**. The type of the whole assemblage is therefore

```
Vector< Vector<int> >
```

Although some C++ compilers have been extended so that the spaces are optional, this declaration adheres to the C++ standard by including spaces around the inner type parameter. The spaces ensure that the angle brackets for the type parameters are interpreted correctly. If you instead write the declaration as

```
Vector<Vector<int>> sudoku(9, Vector<int>(9));
```

many C++ compilers will interpret the `>>` as a single operator and be unable to compile this line.

The `Grid` class in the Stanford libraries

Although using nested vectors makes it possible to represent two-dimensional structures, that strategy is by no means convenient. To simplify the development of applications that need to work with two-dimensional structures, the Stanford version of the collection class library includes a class called `Grid`, even though there is no direct counterpart for this class in the Standard Template Library. The entries exported by `grid.h` appear in Table 5-2.

TABLE 5-2 Entries exported by the `grid.h` interface

Constructors

`Grid<type>()`	Creates an empty grid. Clients who use the default constructor must specify the grid dimensions by calling `resize`.
`Grid<type>(rows, cols)`	Creates a grid with the specified number of rows and columns. Each element is initialized to the default value for the type.

Methods

`numRows()`	Returns the number of horizontal rows.
`numCols()`	Returns the number of vertical columns.
`inBounds(row, col)`	Returns `true` if the specified row and column coordinates are inside the grid.
`get(row, col)`	Returns the element of the grid that appears at the specified row and column.
`set(row, col, value)`	Sets the element at the specified grid coordinates to the new value.
`resize(rows, cols)`	Changes the dimensions of the grid as specified by the *rows* and *cols* parameters. Any previous contents of the grid are discarded.

Operators

`grid[row][col]`	Selects the element at the specified row and column position in the grid.

5.2 The Stack class

When measured in terms of the operations it supports, the simplest collection class is the **Stack** class, which—despite its simplicity—turns out to be useful in a variety of programming applications. Conceptually, a **stack** provides storage for a collection of data values, subject to the restriction that values must be removed from a stack in the opposite order from which they were added. This restriction implies that the last item added to a stack is always the first item that gets removed.

In light of their importance in computer science, stacks have a terminology of their own. Adding a new value to a stack is called **pushing** that value; removing the most recent item from a stack is called **popping** the stack. Moreover, the order in which stacks are processed is sometimes called **LIFO**, which stands for "last in, first out."

A common (but possibly apocryphal) explanation for the words *stack, push,* and *pop* is that the stack model is derived from the way plates are stored in a cafeteria. Particularly, if you are in a cafeteria in which customers pick up their own plates at the beginning of a buffet line, those plates are placed in spring-loaded columns that make it easy for people in line to take the top plate, as illustrated in the following diagram:

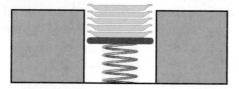

When a dishwasher adds a new plate, it goes on the top of the stack, pushing the others down slightly as the spring is compressed, as shown:

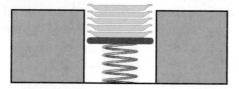

Customers can take plates only from the top of the stack. When they do, the remaining plates pop back up. The last plate added to the stack is the first one a customer takes.

The primary reason that stacks are important in programming is that nested function calls behave in a stack-oriented fashion. For example, if the main program calls a function named **f**, a stack frame for **f** gets pushed on top of the stack frame for **main**, as illustrated by the following diagram:

```
int main() {
  void f() {
    ☞ cout << "This is the function f" << endl;
      g();
  }
```

If **f** calls **g**, a new stack frame for **g** is pushed on top of the frame for **f**, as follows:

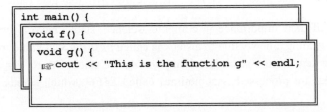

```
int main() {
  void f() {
    void g() {
      ☞ cout << "This is the function g" << endl;
    }
```

When **g** returns, its frame is popped off the stack, restoring **f** to the top of the stack as shown in the original diagram.

The structure of the Stack class

Like **Vector** and **Grid**, **Stack** is a collection class that requires you to specify the element type. For example, **Stack<int>** represents a stack whose elements are integers, and **Stack<string>** represents one in which the elements are strings. Similarly, if you define the classes **Plate** and **Frame**, you can create stacks of these objects using the classes **Stack<Plate>** and **Stack<Frame>**. The list of entries exported by the **stack.h** interface appears in Table 5-3.

TABLE 5-3 Entries exported by the **stack.h** interface

Constructor

Stack<*type*>()	Creates an empty stack capable of holding values of the specified type.

Methods

size()	Returns the number of elements currently on the stack.
isEmpty()	Returns **true** if the stack is empty.
push(*value*)	Pushes *value* on the stack so that it becomes the topmost element.
pop()	Pops the topmost value from the stack and returns it to the caller. Calling **pop** on an empty stack generates an error.
peek()	Returns the topmost value on the stack without removing it. Calling **peek** on an empty stack generates an error.
clear()	Removes all the elements from a stack.

Stacks and pocket calculators

One interesting application of stacks is in electronic calculators, where stacks are used to store intermediate results of a calculation. Although stacks play a central role in the operation of most calculators, that role is easiest to see in early scientific calculators that required users to enter expressions in *reverse Polish notation,* or *RPN.*

In reverse Polish notation, operators are entered after the operands to which they apply. For example, to compute the result of the expression

        8.5 * 4.4 + 6.9 / 1.5

on an RPN calculator, you would enter the operations in the following order:

    8.5 (ENTER) 4.4 (*) 6.9 (ENTER) 1.5 (/) (+)

When the **ENTER** button is pressed, the calculator takes the previous value and pushes it on a stack. When an operator button is pressed, the calculator first checks whether the user has just entered a value and, if so, automatically pushes it on the stack. It then computes the result of applying the operator by

- Popping the top two values from the stack
- Applying the arithmetic operation indicated by the button to these values
- Pushing the result back on the stack

Except when the user is actually typing in a number, the calculator display shows the value at the top of the stack. Thus, at each point in the operation, the calculator display and stack contain the values shown in Figure 5-3.

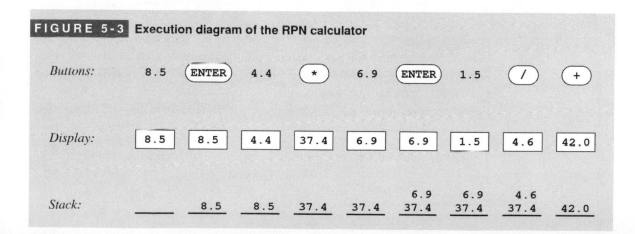

FIGURE 5-3 **Execution diagram of the RPN calculator**

Buttons:	8.5	ENTER	4.4	*	6.9	ENTER	1.5	/	+
Display:	8.5	8.5	4.4	37.4	6.9	6.9	1.5	4.6	42.0
Stack:	___	8.5	8.5	37.4	37.4	6.9 / 37.4	6.9 / 37.4	4.6 / 37.4	42.0

Implementing the RPN calculator in C++ requires making some changes in the user-interface design. In a real calculator, the digits and operations appear on a keypad. In this implementation, it is easier to imagine that the user enters lines on the console, where those lines take one of the following forms:

- A floating-point number
- An arithmetic operator chosen from the set **+**, **−**, *****, and **/**
- The letter **Q**, which causes the program to quit
- The letter **H**, which prints a help message
- The letter **C**, which clears any values left on the stack

A sample run of the calculator program might therefore look like this:

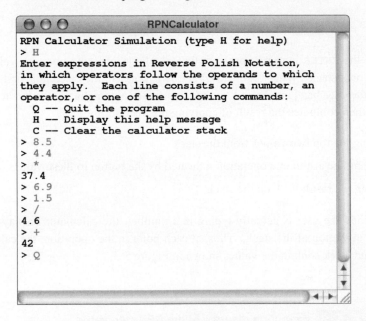

```
RPN Calculator Simulation (type H for help)
> H
Enter expressions in Reverse Polish Notation,
in which operators follow the operands to which
they apply.  Each line consists of a number, an
operator, or one of the following commands:
  Q -- Quit the program
  H -- Display this help message
  C -- Clear the calculator stack
> 8.5
> 4.4
> *
37.4
> 6.9
> 1.5
> /
4.6
> +
42
> Q
```

Because the user enters each number on a separate line terminated with the RETURN key, there is no need for any counterpart to the calculator's ENTER button, which really serves only to indicate that a number is complete. The calculator program can simply push the numbers on the stack as the user enters them. When the calculator reads an operator, it pops the top two elements from the stack, applies the operator, displays the result, and then pushes the result back on the stack.

The complete implementation of the calculator application appears in Figure 5-4.

FIGURE 5-4   Program to implement a simple RPN calculator

```cpp
/*
 * File: RPNCalculator.cpp
 * -------------------------
 * This program simulates an electronic calculator that uses
 * reverse Polish notation, in which the operators come after
 * the operands to which they apply.  Information for users
 * of this application appears in the helpCommand function.
 */

#include <iostream>
#include <cctype>
#include <string>
#include "error.h"
#include "simpio.h"
#include "stack.h"
#include "strlib.h"
using namespace std;

/* Function prototypes */

void applyOperator(char op, Stack<double> & operandStack);
void helpCommand();

/* Main program */

int main() {
   cout << "RPN Calculator Simulation (type H for help)" << endl;
   Stack<double> operandStack;
   while (true) {
      string line = getLine("> ");
      if (line.length() == 0) line = "Q";
      char ch = toupper(line[0]);
      if (ch == 'Q') {
         break;
      } else if (ch == 'C') {
         operandStack.clear();
      } else if (ch == 'H') {
         helpCommand();
      } else if (isdigit(ch)) {
         operandStack.push(stringToReal(line));
      } else {
         applyOperator(ch, operandStack);
      }
   }
   return 0;
}
```

FIGURE 5-4 Program to implement a simple RPN calculator (continued)

```
/*
 * Function: applyOperator
 * Usage: applyOperator(op, operandStack);
 * ---------------------------------------------
 * Applies the operator to the top two elements on the operand stack.
 * Because the elements on the stack are popped in reverse order,
 * the right operand is popped before the left operand.
 */

void applyOperator(char op, Stack<double> & operandStack) {
   double result;
   double rhs = operandStack.pop();
   double lhs = operandStack.pop();
   switch (op) {
    case '+': result = lhs + rhs; break;
    case '-': result = lhs - rhs; break;
    case '*': result = lhs * rhs; break;
    case '/': result = lhs / rhs; break;
    default:  error("Illegal operator");
   }
   cout << result << endl;
   operandStack.push(result);
}

/*
 * Function: helpCommand
 * Usage: helpCommand();
 * ------------------------
 * Generates a help message for the user.
 */

void helpCommand() {
   cout << "Enter expressions in Reverse Polish Notation," << endl;
   cout << "in which operators follow the operands to which" << endl;
   cout << "they apply.  Each line consists of a number, an" << endl;
   cout << "operator, or one of the following commands:" << endl;
   cout << "  Q -- Quit the program" << endl;
   cout << "  H -- Display this help message" << endl;
   cout << "  C -- Clear the calculator stack" << endl;
}
```

5.3 The Queue class

As you learned in section 5.2, the defining feature of a stack is that the last item pushed is always the first item popped. As noted in the introduction to that section, this behavior is often referred to in computer science as *LIFO*, which is an acronym for the phrase "last in, first out." The LIFO discipline is useful in programming contexts because it reflects the operation of function calls; the most recently called function is the first to return. Relatively few real-world situations, however, follow this "last in, first out" model. Indeed, in human society, our collective notion of fairness assigns some priority to being first, as expressed in the maxim "first come, first served." In programming, the usual phrasing of this ordering strategy is "first in, first out," which is traditionally abbreviated as *FIFO*.

A data structure that stores items using a FIFO discipline is called a *queue.* The fundamental operations on a queue—which are analogous to the `push` and `pop` operations for stacks—are called `enqueue` and `dequeue`. The `enqueue` operation adds a new element to the end of the queue, which is traditionally called its *tail.* The `dequeue` operation removes the element at the beginning of the queue, which is called its *head.*

The conceptual difference between these structures can be illustrated most easily with a diagram. In a stack, the client must add and remove elements from the same end of the internal data structure, as follows:

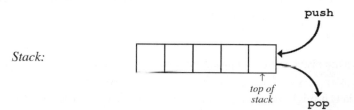

In a queue, the client adds elements at one end and removes them from the other, like this:

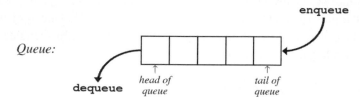

As you might expect from the fact that the models are so similar, the structure of the `Queue` class looks very much like its `Stack` counterpart. The list of entries in Table 5-4 bears out that supposition. The only differences are in the terminology, which reflects the difference in the ordering of the elements.

TABLE 5-4   Entries exported by the `queue.h` interface

Constructor

`Queue<type>()`	Creates an empty queue capable of holding values of the specified type.

Methods

`size()`	Returns the number of elements currently in the queue.
`isEmpty()`	Returns `true` if the queue is empty.
`enqueue(value)`	Adds *value* to the tail of the queue.
`dequeue()`	Removes the element at the head of the queue and returns that element to the caller. Calling `dequeue` on an empty queue generates an error.
`peek()`	Returns the value at the head of the queue without removing that value from the queue. Calling `peek` on an empty queue generates an error.
`clear()`	Removes all the elements from a queue.

The queue data structure has many applications in programming. Not surprisingly, queues turn up in many situations in which it is important to maintain a first-in/first-out discipline in order to ensure that service requests are treated fairly. For example, if you are working in an environment in which a single printer is shared among several computers, the printing software is usually designed so that all print requests are entered in a queue. Thus, if several users decide to enter print requests, the queue structure ensures that each user's request is processed in the order received.

Queues are also common in programs that simulate the behavior of waiting lines. For example, if you wanted to decide how many cashiers you needed in a supermarket, it might be worth writing a program that could simulate the behavior of customers in the store. Such a program would almost certainly involve queues, because a checkout line operates in a first-in/first-out way. Customers who have completed their purchases arrive in the checkout line and wait for their turn to pay. Each customer eventually reaches the front of the line, at which point the cashier totals up the purchases and collects the money. Because simulations of this sort represent an important class of application programs, it is worth spending a little time understanding how such simulations work.

Simulations and models

Beyond the world of programming, there are an endless variety of real-world events and processes that—although they are undeniably important—are nonetheless too complicated to understand completely. For example, it would be very useful to know how various pollutants affect the ozone layer and how the resulting changes in the ozone layer affect the global climate. Similarly, if economists and political leaders had a more complete understanding of exactly how the national economy works, it would be possible to evaluate whether a cut in the capital-gains tax would spur investment or whether it would exacerbate the existing disparities of wealth and income.

When faced with such large-scale problems, it is usually necessary to come up with an idealized *model,* which is a simplified representation of some real-world process. Most problems are far too complex to allow for a complete understanding. There are just too many details. The reason to build a model is that, despite the complexity of a particular problem, it is often possible to make certain assumptions that allow you to simplify a complicated process without affecting its fundamental character. If you can come up with a reasonable model for a process, you can often translate the dynamics of the model into a program that captures the behavior of that model. Such a program is called a *simulation.*

It is important to remember that creating a simulation is usually a two-step process. The first step consists of designing a conceptual model for the real-world behavior you are trying to simulate. The second consists of writing a program that implements the conceptual model. Because errors can occur in both steps of the process, maintaining a certain skepticism about simulations and their applicability to the real world is probably wise. In a society conditioned to believe the "answers" delivered by computers, it is critical to recognize that the simulations can never be better than the models on which they are based.

The waiting-line model

Suppose that you want to design a simulation that models the behavior of a supermarket waiting line. By simulating the waiting line, you can determine some useful properties of waiting lines that might help a company make decisions such as how many cashiers are needed, how much space needs to be reserved for the line itself, and so forth.

The first step in the process of writing a checkout-line simulation is to develop a model for the waiting line, in which you identify any simplifying assumptions. For example, to make the initial implementation of the simulation as simple as possible, you might begin by assuming that there is one cashier who serves customers from a single queue. You might then assume that customers arrive with a random probability and enter the queue at the end of the line. Whenever the cashier is free and someone is waiting in line, the cashier begins to serve that customer. After an appropriate service period—which you must also model in some way—the cashier completes the transaction with the current customer and is then free to serve the next customer in the queue.

Discrete time

Another assumption often required in a model is some limitation on the level of accuracy. In the context of the checkout-line simulation, the time a customer spends being served by the cashier will clearly vary within some limits. One customer might spend two minutes; another might spend six. It is important, however, to consider whether measuring time in minutes allows the simulation to be sufficiently precise. If you had a sufficiently accurate stopwatch, you might discover that a customer actually spent 3.14159265 minutes. The question you need to resolve is how precise you have to be.

For most models, and particularly for those intended for simulation, it is useful to introduce the simplifying assumption that all events within the model happen in discrete integral time units. Using discrete time assumes that you can find a time unit that—for the purpose of the model—you can treat as indivisible. In general, the time units used in a simulation must be small enough that the probability of more than one event occurring during a single time unit is negligible. In the checkout-line simulation, for example, minutes may not be accurate enough; two customers could easily arrive in the same minute. On the other hand, you could probably get away with using seconds as the time unit and discount the possibility that two customers arrive in precisely the same second.

The sections that follow adopt the strategy of measuring time in seconds. In general, however, there is no reason you have to measure time in conventional units. When you write a simulation, you can define the unit of time in any way that fits the structure of the model. For example, you could define a time unit to be five seconds and then run the simulation as a series of five-second intervals.

Events in simulated time

One of the advantages of using discrete time units is that doing so makes it possible to work with variables of type **int** instead of the less efficient type **double**. A more important advantage of discrete time is that it allows you to structure the simulation as a loop in which each time unit represents a single cycle. When you approach the problem in this way, a simulation program has the following form:

```
for (int time = 0; time < SIMULATION_TIME; time++) {
    Execute one cycle of the simulation.
}
```

Within the body of the loop, the program performs the operations necessary to advance through one unit of simulated time.

Think for a moment about what events might occur during each time unit of the checkout-line simulation. One possibility is that a new customer might arrive.

Another is that the cashier might finish with the current customer and go on to serve the next person in line. These events bring up some interesting issues. To complete the model, you need to say something about how often customers arrive and how much time they spend at the cash register. You could (and probably should) gather approximate data by watching a real checkout line in a store. Even if you collect that information, however, you need to simplify it to a form that (1) captures enough of the real-world behavior to be useful and (2) is easy to understand in terms of the model. For example, your surveys might show that customers arrive at the line on average once every 20 seconds. This average arrival rate is certainly useful input to the model. On the other hand, you would not have much confidence in a simulation in which customers arrived exactly once every 20 seconds. Such an implementation would violate the real-world condition that customer arrivals have some random variability and that they sometimes bunch together.

For this reason, the arrival process is usually modeled by specifying the probability that an arrival takes place in any discrete time unit instead of the average time between arrivals. For example, if your studies indicated that a customer arrived once every 20 seconds, the average probability of a customer arriving in any particular second would be 1/20 or 0.05. If you assume that arrivals occur randomly with an equal probability in each unit of time, the arrival process forms a pattern that mathematicians call a *Poisson distribution* after the French mathematician Siméon Poisson (1781–1840).

You might also choose to make simplifying assumptions about how long it takes to serve a particular customer. For example, the program will be easier to write if you assume that the service time required for each customer is uniformly distributed within a certain range. If you do, you can use the **randomInteger** function from the **random.h** interface to pick the service time.

Implementing the simulation

Even though it is longer than the other programs in this chapter, the code for the simulation program is reasonably easy to write. The code for the **CheckoutLine** program appears in Figure 5-5. The core of the simulation is a loop that runs for the number of seconds indicated by the parameter **SIMULATION_TIME**. In each second, the simulation performs the following operations:

1. Check whether a customer has arrived and, if so, add that person to the queue.

2. If the cashier is busy, note that the cashier has spent another second with the current customer. Eventually, the required service time will be complete, which will free the cashier.

3. If the cashier is free, serve the next customer in the waiting line.

FIGURE 5-5 Program to simulate a checkout line

```
/*
 * File: CheckoutLine.cpp
 * ----------------------
 * This program simulates a checkout line, such as one you
 * might encounter in a grocery store.  Customers arrive at
 * the checkout stand and get in line.  Those customers wait
 * in the line until the cashier is free, at which point
 * they are served and occupy the cashier for some period
 * of time.  After the service time is complete, the cashier
 * is free to serve the next customer in the line.
 *
 * In each unit of time, up to the constant SIMULATION_TIME,
 * the following operations are performed:
 *
 * 1. Determine whether a new customer has arrived.
 *    New customers arrive randomly, with a probability
 *    determined by the constant ARRIVAL_PROBABILITY.
 *
 * 2. If the cashier is busy, note that the cashier has
 *    spent another minute with that customer.  Eventually,
 *    the customer's time request is satisfied, which frees
 *    the cashier.
 *
 * 3. If the cashier is free, serve the next customer in line.
 *    The service time is taken to be a random period between
 *    MIN_SERVICE_TIME and MAX_SERVICE_TIME.
 *
 * At the end of the simulation, the program displays the
 * simulation constants and the following computed results:
 *
 * o  The number of customers served
 * o  The average time spent in line
 * o  The average number of people in line
 */

#include <iostream>
#include <iomanip>
#include "queue.h"
#include "random.h"
using namespace std;

/* Constants */

const double ARRIVAL_PROBABILITY = 0.05;
const int MIN_SERVICE_TIME =  5;
const int MAX_SERVICE_TIME = 15;
const int SIMULATION_TIME = 2000;

/* Function prototypes */

void runSimulation(int & nServed, int & totalWait, int & totalLength);
void printReport(int nServed, int totalWait, int totalLength);
```

FIGURE 5-5 Program to simulate a checkout line (continued)

```
/* Main program */

int main() {
   int nServed;
   int totalWait;
   int totalLength;
   runSimulation(nServed, totalWait, totalLength);
   printReport(nServed, totalWait, totalLength);
   return 0;
}

/*
 * Function: runSimulation
 * Usage: runSimulation();
 * ------------------------
 * Runs the actual simulation.  This function returns the results
 * of the simulation through the reference parameters, which record
 * the number of customers served, the total number of seconds that
 * customers were waiting in a queue, and the sum of the queue length
 * in each time step.
 */

void runSimulation(int & nServed, int & totalWait, int & totalLength) {
   Queue<int> queue;
   int timeRemaining = 0;
   nServed = 0;
   totalWait = 0;
   totalLength = 0;
   for (int t = 0; t < SIMULATION_TIME; t++) {
      if (randomChance(ARRIVAL_PROBABILITY)) {
         queue.enqueue(t);
      }
      if (timeRemaining > 0) {
         timeRemaining--;
      } else if (!queue.isEmpty()) {
         totalWait += t - queue.dequeue();
         nServed++;
         timeRemaining = randomInteger(MIN_SERVICE_TIME, MAX_SERVICE_TIME);
      }
      totalLength += queue.size();
   }
}
```

FIGURE 5-5 **Program to simulate a checkout line (continued)**

```
/*
 * Function: printReport
 * Usage: printReport(nServed, totalWait, totalLength);
 * ----------------------------------------------------
 * Reports the results of the simulation in tabular format.
 */

void printReport(int nServed, int totalWait, int totalLength) {
   cout << "Simulation results given the following constants:"
        << endl;
   cout << fixed << setprecision(2);
   cout << "   SIMULATION_TIME:     " << setw(4)
        << SIMULATION_TIME << endl;
   cout << "   ARRIVAL_PROBABILITY: " << setw(7)
        << ARRIVAL_PROBABILITY << endl;
   cout << "   MIN_SERVICE_TIME:    " << setw(4)
        << MIN_SERVICE_TIME << endl;
   cout << "   MAX_SERVICE_TIME:    " << setw(4)
        << MAX_SERVICE_TIME << endl;
   cout << endl;
   cout << "Customers served:      " << setw(4) << nServed << endl;
   cout << "Average waiting time:  " << setw(7)
        << double(totalWait) / nServed << " seconds" << endl;
   cout << "Average queue length:  " << setw(7)
        << double(totalLength) / SIMULATION_TIME << " people" << endl;
}
```

The waiting line itself is represented, naturally enough, as a queue. The value stored in the queue is the time at which that customer arrived in the queue, which makes it possible to determine how many seconds that customer spent in line before reaching the head of the queue.

The simulation is controlled by the following constants:

- **SIMULATION_TIME**—This constant specifies the duration of the simulation.

- **ARRIVAL_PROBABILITY**—This constant indicates the probability that a new customer will arrive at the checkout line during a single unit of time. In keeping with standard statistical convention, the probability is expressed as a real number between 0 and 1.

- **MIN_SERVICE_TIME**, **MAX_SERVICE_TIME**—These constants define the legal range of customer service time. For any particular customer, the amount of time spent with the cashier is determined by picking a random integer in this range.

When the simulation is complete, the program reports the simulation constants along with the following results:

- The number of customers served
- The average amount of time customers spent in the waiting line
- The average length of the waiting line

For example, the following sample run shows the results of the simulation for the indicated constant values:

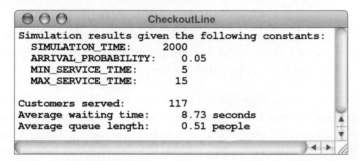

```
○ ○ ○                    CheckoutLine
Simulation results given the following constants:
   SIMULATION_TIME:      2000
   ARRIVAL_PROBABILITY:     0.05
   MIN_SERVICE_TIME:        5
   MAX_SERVICE_TIME:       15

Customers served:        117
Average waiting time:       8.73 seconds
Average queue length:       0.51 people
```

The behavior of the simulation depends significantly on the values of the constants used to control it. Suppose, for example, that the probability of a customer arriving increases from 0.05 to 0.10. Running the simulation with these parameters gives the following results:

```
○ ○ ○                    CheckoutLine
Simulation results given the following constants:
   SIMULATION_TIME:      2000
   ARRIVAL_PROBABILITY:     0.10
   MIN_SERVICE_TIME;        5
   MAX_SERVICE_TIME:       15

Customers served:        176
Average waiting time:      68.95 seconds
Average queue length:       6.49 people
```

As you can see, doubling the probability of arrival causes the average waiting time to grow from under nine seconds to more than a minute, which is obviously a dramatic increase. The reason for the poor performance is that the arrival rate in the second run of the simulation means that new customers arrive at the same rate at which they are served. When this arrival level is reached, the length of the queue and the average waiting time both begin to grow very quickly. Simulations of this sort make it possible to experiment with different parameter values. Those experiments, in turn, make it possible to identify potential sources of trouble in the corresponding real-world systems.

5.4 The Map class

This section introduces another generic collection called a *map,* which is conceptually similar to a dictionary. A dictionary allows you to look up a word to find its meaning. A map is a generalization of this idea that provides an association between an identifying tag called a *key* and an associated *value,* which may be a much larger and more complicated structure. In the dictionary example, the key is the word you're looking up, and the value is its definition.

Maps have many applications in programming. For example, an interpreter for a programming language needs to be able to assign values to variables, which can then be referenced by name. A map makes it easy to maintain the association between the name of a variable and its corresponding value. When they are used in this context, maps are often called *symbol tables.*

In addition to the **Map** class described in this section, the Stanford libraries offer a **HashMap** class that has almost the same structure and behavior. The **HashMap** class is more efficient but somewhat less convenient to use for certain applications. For now, it's best to focus on the **Map** class until you understand how maps work in general. You'll have a chance to learn about the differences between these two implementations of the map concept in Chapters 15 and 16.

The structure of the Map class

As with the collection classes introduced earlier in this chapter, **Map** is implemented as a template class that must be parameterized with both the key type and the value type. For example, if you want to simulate a dictionary in which individual words are associated with their definitions, you can start by declaring a **dictionary** variable as follows:

```
Map<string,string> dictionary;
```

Similarly, if you are implementing a programming language, you can use a **Map** to store the values of floating-point variables by associating variable names and values, as follows:

```
Map<string,double> symbolTable;
```

These definitions create empty maps that contain no keys and values. In either case, you would subsequently need to add key/value pairs to the map. In the case of the dictionary, you could read the contents from a data file. For the symbol table, you would add new associations whenever an assignment statement appeared.

The most common methods used with the **Map** class appear in Table 5-5. Of these methods, the ones that implement the fundamental behavior of the map concept are **put** and **get**. The **put** method creates an association between a key and a value. Its operation is analogous to assigning a value to a variable in C++: if there is a value already associated with the key, the old value is replaced by the new one. The **get** method retrieves the value most recently associated with a particular key and therefore corresponds to the act of using a variable name to retrieve its value. If no value appears in the map for a particular key, calling **get** with that key returns the default value for the value type. You can check whether a key exists in a map by calling the **containsKey** method, which returns **true** or **false** depending on whether the specified key has been defined.

A few simple diagrams may help to illustrate the operation of the **Map** class in more detail. Suppose that you have declared the **symbolTable** variable to be a **Map<string,double>** as you saw earlier in the section. That declaration creates

TABLE 5-5   **Entries exported by the map.h interface**

Constructors

Map<*key type*, *value type*> **()**	Creates an empty map associating keys and values.

Methods

size()	Returns the number of key/value pairs contained in the map.
isEmpty()	Returns **true** if the map is empty.
put (*key*, *value*)	Associates the specified key and value in the map. If *key* has no previous definition, a new entry is added; if a previous association exists, the old value is discarded and replaced by the new one.
get (*key*)	Returns the value currently associated with *key* in the map. If *key* is not defined, **get** returns the default value for the value type.
remove (*key*)	Removes *key* from the map along with any associated value. If *key* does not exist, this call leaves the map unchanged.
containsKey (*key*)	Checks to see whether *key* is associated with a value. If so, this method returns **true**; if not, it returns **false**.
clear()	Removes all the key/value pairs from the map.

Operators

map [*key*]	Selects the value associated with *key* in the map, in much the same way that the **get** method does. If the key does not exist in the map, the selection operator creates a new entry and sets its value to the default for that type. Maps that use square brackets to select and change the values assigned to particular keys are often called *associative arrays*.

an empty map with no associations, as represented by the following diagram that contains an empty set of bindings:

symbolTable

Once you have the map, you can use **put** to establish new associations. For example, if you called

```
symbolTable.put("pi", 3.14159);
```

the conceptual effect would be to add an association between the key **"pi"** and the value 3.14159, as follows:

symbolTable
| pi = 3.14159 |

Similarly, calling

```
symbolTable.put("e", 2.71828);
```

would add a new association between the key **"e"** and the value 2.71828, like this:

symbolTable
| pi = 3.14159 |
| e = 2.71828 |

You could then use **get** to retrieve these values. Calling **symbolTable.get("e")** would return the value 2.71828, and calling **symbolTable.get("e")** would return 3.14159.

Although it hardly makes sense in the case of mathematical constants, you could change the values in the map by making additional calls to **put**. You could, for example, reset the value associated with **"pi"** (as an 1897 bill before the Indiana State General Assembly sought to do) by calling

```
symbolTable.put("pi", 3.0);
```

which would leave the map in the following state:

symbolTable
| pi = 3.0 |
| e = 2.71828 |

At this point, calling **symbolTable.containsKey("pi")** would return **true**; by contrast, calling **symbolTable.containsKey("x")** would return **false**.

Using maps in an application

If you fly at all frequently, you quickly learn that every airport in the world has a three-letter code assigned by the International Air Transport Association (IATA). For example, John F. Kennedy airport in New York City is assigned the three-letter code JFK. Other codes, however, are considerably harder to recognize. Most web-based travel systems offer some means of looking up these codes as a service to their customers.

Suppose that you have been asked to write a simple C++ program that reads a three-letter airport code from the user and responds with the location of that airport. The data you need is in the form of a text file called **AirportCodes.txt**, which contains a list of the several thousand airport codes that IATA has assigned. Each line of the file consists of a three-letter code, an equal sign, and the location of the airport. If the file were sorted in descending order by passenger traffic in 2009, as compiled by Airports Council International, the file would begin with the lines in Figure 5-6.

The existence of the **Map** class makes this application extremely easy to write. The entire application fits on a single page, as shown in Figure 5-7.

FIGURE 5-6 Beginning of a data file containing airport codes and locations

```
AirportCodes.txt
ATL=Atlanta, GA, USA
ORD=Chicago, IL, USA
LHR=London, England, United Kingdom
HND=Tokyo, Japan
LAX=Los Angeles, CA, USA
CDG=Paris, France
DFW=Dallas/Ft Worth, TX, USA
FRA=Frankfurt, Germany
PEK=Beijing, China
MAD=Madrid, Spain
DEN=Denver, CO, USA
AMS=Amsterdam, Netherlands
JFK=New York, NY, USA
HKG=Hong Kong, Hong Kong
LAS=Las Vegas, NV, USA
IAH=Houston, TX, USA
PHX=Phoenix, AZ, USA
BKK=Bangkok, Thailand
SIN=Singapore, Singapore
MCO=Orlando, FL, USA
  .
  .
  .
```

FIGURE 5-7 Program to look up three-letter airport codes

```
/*
 * File: AirportCodes.cpp
 * -----------------------
 * This program looks up a three-letter airport code in a Map object.
 */

#include <iostream>
#include <fstream>
#include <string>
#include "error.h"
#include "map.h"
#include "strlib.h"
using namespace std;

/* Function prototypes */

void readCodeFile(string filename, Map<string,string> & map);

/* Main program */

int main() {
   Map<string,string> airportCodes;
   readCodeFile("AirportCodes.txt", airportCodes);
   while (true) {
      string line;
      cout << "Airport code: ";
      getline(cin, line);
      if (line == "") break;
      string code = toUpperCase(line);
      if (airportCodes.containsKey(code)) {
        cout << code << " is in " << airportCodes.get(code) << endl;
      } else {
        cout << "There is no such airport code" << endl;
      }
   }
   return 0;
}

void readCodeFile(string filename, Map<string,string> & map) {
   ifstream infile;
   infile.open(filename.c_str());
   if (infile.fail()) error("Can't read the data file");
   string line;
   while (getline(infile, line)) {
      if (line.length() < 4 || line[3] != '=') {
         error("Illegal data line: " + line);
      }
      string code = toUpperCase(line.substr(0, 3));
      map.put(code, line.substr(4));
   }
   infile.close();
}
```

The main program in the **AirportCodes** application reads in three-letter codes, looks up the corresponding location, and then prints the location on the console, as shown in the following sample run:

```
Airport code: LHR
LHR is in London, England, United Kingdom
Airport code: SFO
SFO is in San Francisco, CA, USA
Airport code: XXX
There is no such airport code
Airport code:
```

Maps as associative arrays

The **Map** class overloads the square bracket operators used for array selection so that the statement

```
map[key] = value;
```

acts as shorthand for

```
map.put(key, value);
```

Similarly, the expression **map[key]** returns the value from **map** associated with **key** in exactly the same way that **map.get(key)** does. While these shorthand forms of the **put** and **get** methods are undoubtedly convenient, the use of array notation for maps may be surprising, given that maps and arrays seem to be entirely different in their structure. If you think about maps and arrays more abstractly, however, they turn out to be more alike than you might at first suspect.

The insight necessary to unify these two seemingly different structures is that you can think of arrays as structures that map index positions to elements. Suppose, for example, that you have an array—or, equivalently, a vector—containing a set of scores such as those you might assign for a gymnastics match:

scores

9.2	9.9	9.7	8.9	9.5
0	1	2	3	4

This array maps the key 0 into the value 9.2, the key 1 into 9.9, the key 2 into 9.7, and so forth. Thus, you can think of an array as simply a map with integer keys. Conversely, you can think of a map as an array that uses the key type as an index, which is precisely what the overloaded selection syntax for the **Map** class suggests.

Using array syntax to perform map operations is becoming increasingly common in programming languages even beyond the C++ domain. Many popular scripting languages implement all arrays internally as maps, which makes it possible to use index values that are not necessarily integers. Arrays implemented using maps as their underlying representation are called **associative arrays.**

5.5 The Set class

One of the most useful collection classes is the **Set** class, which exports the entries shown in Table 5-6. This class is used to model the mathematical abstraction of a *set,* which is a collection in which the elements are unordered and in which each value appears only once. Sets turn out to be extremely useful in many algorithmic

TABLE 5-6 Entries exported by the set.h interface

Constructor

Set <*type*> ()	Creates an empty set containing values of the specified type.

Methods

size ()	Returns the number of elements in the set.
isEmpty ()	Returns **true** if the set is empty.
add (*value*)	Adds the value to the set. If the value is already in the set, no error is generated, and the set remains unchanged.
remove (*value*)	Removes the value to the set. If the value is not present, no error is generated, and the set remains unchanged.
contains (*value*)	Returns **true** if the value is in the set.
clear ()	Removes all elements from the set.
isSubsetOf (*set*)	Returns **true** if this set is a subset of the set passed as an argument.
first ()	Returns the first element of the set in the ordering specified for its value type.

Operators

s_1 + s_2	Returns the **union** of s_1 and s_2, which consists of the elements in either or both of the original sets.
s_1 * s_2	Returns the **intersection** of s_1 and s_2, which consists of the elements common to both of the original sets.
s_1 − s_2	Returns the **set difference** of s_1 and s_2, which consists of the all elements in s_1 that are not present in s_2.
s_1 += s_2 s_1 −= s_2 s_1 *= s_2	The +, −, and * operators can be combined with assignment just as they can with numeric values. For += and −=, the value s_2 can be a set, a single value, or a list of values separated by commas.

applications and are therefore worth a chapter of their own. Even before you have a chance to read the more detailed account in Chapter 17, it is worth presenting a few examples of sets so you can get a better sense of how sets work and how they might be useful in applications.

Implementing the `<cctype>` library

In Chapter 3, you learned about the `<cctype>` library, which exports several predicate functions that test the type of a character. Calling `isdigit(ch)`, for example, tests whether the character `ch` is one of the digit characters. You could implement the `isdigit` function by testing the character code for `ch` against a simple range of values, as follows:

```
bool isdigit(ch) {
    return ch >= '0' && ch <= '9';
}
```

The situation gets a little more complicated with some of the other functions. Implementing `ispunct` in this same style would be more difficult because the punctuation characters are spread over several intervals of the ASCII range. Things would be a lot easier if you could simply define a set of all the punctuation marks, in which case all you would need to do to implement `ispunct(ch)` is check whether the character `ch` is in that set.

A set-based implementation of the predicate functions from `<cctype>` appears in Figure 5-8. The code creates a `Set<char>` for each of the character types and then defines the predicate functions so that they simply invoke `contains` on the appropriate set. For example, to implement `isdigit`, the cctype implementation defines a set containing the digit characters, like this:

```
const Set<char> DIGIT_SET = setFromString("0123456789");
```

The `setFromString` function, which appears at the bottom of Figure 5-8, is a simple helper function that creates a set by adding each of the characters in the argument string. This function makes it very easy to define sets like the set of punctuation characters simply by listing the characters that fit that description.

One of the advantages of working with sets is that doing so makes it easier to think in terms of abstract, high-level operations. While most of the sets in `cctype.cpp` use `setFromString` to create the set from the actual characters, a few use the `+` operator, which is overloaded to return the union of two sets. For example, once you have defined the sets `LOWER_SET` and `UPPER_SET` so that they contain the lowercase and uppercase letters, you can define `ALPHA_SET` by writing

```
const Set<char> ALPHA_SET = LOWER_SET + UPPER_SET;
```

FIGURE 5-8 Set-based implementation of <cctype>

```
/*
 * File: cctype.cpp
 * ----------------
 * This program simulates the <cctype> interface using sets of characters.
 */

#include <string>
#include "cctype.h"
#include "set.h"
using namespace std;

/* Function prototypes */

Set<char> setFromString(string str);

/*
 * Constant sets
 * -------------
 * These sets are initialized to contain the characters in the
 * corresponding character class.
 */

const Set<char> DIGIT_SET = setFromString("0123456789");
const Set<char> LOWER_SET = setFromString("abcdefghijklmnopqrstuvwxyz");
const Set<char> UPPER_SET = setFromString("ABCDEFGHIJKLMNOPQRSTUVWXYZ");
const Set<char> PUNCT_SET = setFromString("!\"#$%&'()*+,-./:;<=>?@[\\]^_`{|}");
const Set<char> SPACE_SET = setFromString(" \t\v\f\n\r");
const Set<char> XDIGIT_SET = setFromString("0123456789ABCDEFabcdef");
const Set<char> ALPHA_SET = LOWER_SET + UPPER_SET;
const Set<char> ALNUM_SET = ALPHA_SET + DIGIT_SET;
const Set<char> PRINT_SET = ALNUM_SET + PUNCT_SET + SPACE_SET;

/* Exported functions */

bool isalnum(char ch) { return ALNUM_SET.contains(ch); }
bool isalpha(char ch) { return ALPHA_SET.contains(ch); }
bool isdigit(char ch) { return DIGIT_SET.contains(ch); }
bool islower(char ch) { return LOWER_SET.contains(ch); }
bool isprint(char ch) { return PRINT_SET.contains(ch); }
bool ispunct(char ch) { return PUNCT_SET.contains(ch); }
bool isspace(char ch) { return SPACE_SET.contains(ch); }
bool isupper(char ch) { return UPPER_SET.contains(ch); }
bool isxdigit(char ch) { return XDIGIT_SET.contains(ch); }

/* Helper function to create a set from a string of characters */

Set<char> setFromString(string str)  {
   Set<char> set;
   for (int i = 0; i < str.length(); i++) {
      set.add(str[i]);
   }
   return set;
}
```

Creating a word list

In the discussion of the **Map** class earlier in the chapter, one of the examples used to explain the underlying concept was that of a dictionary in which the keys are individual words and the corresponding values are the definitions. In some applications, such as a spelling checker or a program that plays Scrabble, you don't need to know the definition of a word. All you need to know is whether a particular combination of letters is a legal word. For such applications, the **Set** class is an ideal tool. Instead of a map containing both words and definitions, all you need is a **Set<string>** whose elements are the legal words. A word is legal if it is contained in the set, and illegal if it is not.

A set of words with no associated definitions is called a *lexicon.* If you have a text file named **EnglishWords.txt** containing all the words in English, one word per line, you could create an English lexicon using the following code:

```
Set<string> lexicon;
ifstream infile;
infile.open("EnglishWords.txt");
if (infile.fail()) error("Can't open EnglishWords.txt");
string word;
while (getline(infile, word)) {
   lexicon.add(word);
}
infile.close();
```

The **Lexicon** class in the Stanford libraries

Although the **Set** class works reasonably well as the underlying representation for a lexicon, it is not particularly efficient. Because having an efficient representation for lexicons opens up many exciting possibilities for programming projects, the Stanford libraries include a **Lexicon** class, which is essentially a specialized version of **Set** optimized for storing sets of words. The entries exported by the **Lexicon** class appear in Table 5-7. As you can see, these entries are largely the same as those for **Set**.

The library distribution also includes a data file called **EnglishWords.dat**, which is a compiled representation of a lexicon containing a reasonably complete list of English words. Programs that use the English lexicon conventionally initialize it using the declaration

```
Lexicon english("EnglishWords.dat");
```

In word games like Scrabble, it is useful to memorize as many two-letter words as you can, because knowing the two-letter words makes it easier to attach new

TABLE 5-7   Entries exported by the `lexicon.h` interface

Constructors

`Lexicon()`	Creates an empty lexicon.
`Lexicon(file)`	Initializes a lexicon by reading data from a file.

Methods

`size()`	Returns the number of words in the lexicon.
`isEmpty()`	Returns **true** if the lexicon is empty.
`add(word)`	Adds a new word to the lexicon, if that word is not already present. All words in a lexicon are stored in lower case.
`addWordsFromFile(file)`	Adds all the words in the named file to the lexicon. The file must either be a text file, in which case the words are listed on separate lines, or a compiled data file specifically formatted for the lexicon.
`contains(word)`	Returns **true** if *word* is in the lexicon.
`containsPrefix(prefix)`	Returns **true** if any of the words in the lexicon start with the specified prefix.
`clear()`	Removes all the words from a lexicon.

words to the existing words on the board. Given that you have a lexicon containing English words, you could create such a list by generating all two-letter strings and then using the lexicon to check which of the resulting combinations are actually words. The code to do so appears in Figure 5-9.

As you will discover in the following section, it is also possible to solve this problem by going through the lexicon and printing out the words whose length is two. However, given that there are more than 100,000 English words in the lexicon and only 676 (26 × 26) combinations of two letters, the strategy used in Figure 5-9 is more efficient.

5.6 Iterating over a collection

The **TwoLetterWords** program introduced in Figure 5-9 produces a list of the two-letter words by generating every possible combination of two letters and then looking up each one to see whether that two-letter string appears in the lexicon of English words. Another strategy that accomplishes the same result is to go through every word in the lexicon and display the words whose length is equal to 2. To do so, all you need is some way of stepping through each word in a **Lexicon** object, one word at a time.

FIGURE 5-9 Program to generate a list of all the two-letter English words

```cpp
/*
 * File: TwoLetterWords.cpp
 * ---------------------------
 * This program generates a list of the two-letter English words.
 */

#include <iostream>
#include "lexicon.h"
using namespace std;

int main() {
   Lexicon english("EnglishWords.dat");
   string word = "xx";
   for (char c0 = 'a'; c0 <= 'z'; c0++) {
      word[0] = c0;
      for (char c1 = 'a'; c1 <= 'z'; c1++) {
         word[1] = c1;
         if (english.contains(word)) {
            cout << word << endl;
         }
      }
   }
   return 0;
}
```

Iterating through the elements is a fundamental operation for any collection class. Moreover, if the package of collection classes is well designed, clients should be able to use the same strategy to perform that operation, no matter whether they are cycling through all elements in a vector or grid, all keys in a map, or all words in a lexicon. The Standard Template Library offers a powerful mechanism called an *iterator* for doing just that. Unfortunately, understanding the standard iterators depends on being familiar with certain low-level details of C++, most notably the concept of pointers. Given that one of the goals of this text is to defer covering those details until you understand the high-level ideas, introducing standard iterators would have the effect of dragging in a large amount of complexity to achieve a goal that is in fact quite simple. All you really need is some way to express the algorithmic idea suggested by the following pseudocode:

> *For each element in a particular collection {*
>   *Process that element*
> *}*

Most modern languages define a syntactic form that expresses precisely that idea. Unfortunately, the syntax of C++ does not yet include such a facility, although one has been proposed for a future release. The good news, however, is that it is possible to use the macro-definition capabilities of the C++ preprocessor to achieve exactly what you would like to see in the language. Although the implementation is beyond the scope of this text, the collection classes—both those in the Standard Template Library and the simplified versions used in this text—support a new control pattern called a ***range-based `for` loop*** that has the following form:

```
for (type variable : collection) {
    body of the loop
}
```

For example, if you want to iterate through all the words in the English lexicon and select only those containing two letters, you can write

```
for (string word : english) {
    if (word.length() == 2) {
        cout << word << endl;
    }
}
```

The range-based **for** loop is a new feature of C++11, which is the new C++ standard released in 2011. Because this standard is so recent, the C++11 extensions have not yet been incorporated into all C++ programming, including several of the leading ones. If you are working with an older compiler, you won't be able to use the range-based **for** loop in its standard form. But there's no need to despair. The Stanford C++ libraries include an interface called **foreach.h** that uses the C++ preprocessor to define a **foreach** macro with a very similar form:

```
foreach (type variable in collection) {
    body of the loop
}
```

The only differences are the name of the keyword and the use of the keyword **in** rather than a colon. Like the range-based **for** loop, **foreach** works with the collection classes in both the Stanford and the STL implementations.

Iteration order

When you use the range-based **for** loop, it is sometimes useful to understand the order in which it processes the individual values. There is no universal rule. Each collection class defines its own policy about iteration order, usually based on considerations of efficiency. The classes you've already seen make the following guarantees about the order of values:

- When you iterate through the elements of the **Vector** class, the range-based **for** loop delivers the elements in order by index position, so that the element in position 0 comes first, followed by the element in position 1, and so on, up to the end of the vector. The iteration order is therefore the same as that produced by the traditional **for** loop pattern:

```
for (int i = 0; i < vec.size(); i++) {
    code to process vec[i]
}
```

- When you iterate through the elements of the **Grid** class, the range-based **for** loop cycles first through the elements of row 0 in order, then the elements of row 1, and so forth. This iteration strategy for **Grid** is thus analogous to using the following **for** loop:

```
for (int row = 0; row < grid.numRows(); row++) {
    for (int col = 0; col < grid.numCols(); col++) {
        code to process grid[row][col]
    }
}
```

This order, in which the **row** subscript appears in the outer loop, is called *row-major order.*

- When you iterate through the elements of the **Map** class, the range-based **for** loop returns the keys in the natural order for the key type. For example, a **Map** whose keys are integers will process the keys in ascending numerical order. A **Map** whose keys are strings will process the keys in *lexicographic order,* which is the order determined by comparing the underlying ASCII codes.

- When you iterate through the elements of a **Set** or a **Lexicon**, the range-based **for** loop always returns the elements in the natural order for the value type. In the **Lexicon** class, the range-based **for** loop returns the words in lower case.

- You cannot use the range-based **for** loop in conjunction with the **Stack** and **Queue** classes. Allowing unrestricted access to these structures would violate the principle that only one element (the element at the top of a stack or the one at the head of a queue) is visible at a particular time.

Pig Latin revisited

When you convert English to Pig Latin as described in section 3.2, most words turn into something that sounds vaguely Latinate but certainly distinct from conventional English. There are, however, a few words whose Pig Latin equivalents just happen to be English words. For example, the Pig Latin translation of *trash* is *ashtray,* and the translation for *entry* is *entryway.* Such words are not all that common; in the lexicon stored in **EnglishWords.dat**, there are only 27 words with that property out of over 100,000 English words. Given the range-based **for** loop and the **translateWord** function from the **PigLatin** program from Chapter 3, it is easy to write a program that lists all such words, as shown in Figure 5-10.

FIGURE 5-10 **Program to list words that remain English words in Pig Latin**

```
/*
 * File: PigEnglish.cpp
 * --------------------
 * This program finds all English words that remain words when
 * you convert them to Pig Latin, such as "trash" (which becomes
 * "ashtray") and "entry" (which becomes "entryway").  The code
 * ignores words containing no vowels (mostly Welsh-derived
 * words like "cwm"), which don't change form under the Pig Latin
 * rules introduced in Chapter 3.
 */

#include <iostream>
#include <string>
#include <cctype>
#include "lexicon.h"
using namespace std;

/* Function prototypes */

string wordToPigLatin(string word);
int findFirstVowel(string word);
bool isVowel(char ch);

/* Main program */

int main() {
   cout << "This program finds words that remain words"
        << " when translated to Pig Latin." << endl;
   Lexicon english("EnglishWords.dat");
   for (string word : english) {
      string pig = wordToPigLatin(word);
      if (pig != word && english.contains(pig)) {
         cout << word << " -> " << pig << endl;
      }
   }
   return 0;
}

/* The code for the helper functions appears in Figure 3-2 */
```

Computing word frequencies

The **WordFrequency** program in Figure 5-11 is another application in which iteration plays an important role. Given the tools you have at your disposal from earlier examples, the necessary code is quite straightforward. The strategy for dividing a line into words is similar to what you have already seen in the **PigLatin** program from Chapter 3. To keep track of the mapping between words and their associated counts, a **Map<string,int>** is precisely what you need.

FIGURE 5-11 Program to compute word frequencies

```
/*
 * File: WordFrequency.cpp
 * ------------------------
 * This program computes the frequency of words in a text file.
 */

#include <iostream>
#include <fstream>
#include <iomanip>
#include <string>
#include <cctype>
#include "filelib.h"
#include "map.h"
#include "strlib.h"
#include "vector.h"
using namespace std;

/* Function prototypes */

void countWords(istream & stream, Map<string,int> & wordCounts);
void displayWordCounts(Map<string,int> & wordCounts);
void extractWords(string line, Vector<string> & words);

/* Main program */

int main() {
   ifstream infile;
   Map<string,int> wordCounts;
   promptUserForFile(infile, "Input file: ");
   countWords(infile, wordCounts);
   infile.close();
   displayWordCounts(wordCounts);
   return 0;
}

/*
 * Function: countWords
 * Usage: countWords(stream, wordCounts);
 * ------------------------------------------
 * Counts words in the input stream, storing the results in wordCounts.
 */

void countWords(istream & stream, Map<string,int> & wordCounts) {
   Vector<string> lines, words;
   readEntireFile(stream, lines);
   for (string line : lines) {
      extractWords(line, words);
      for (string word : words) {
         wordCounts[toLowerCase(word)]++;
      }
   }
}
```

FIGURE 5-11 Program to compute word frequencies (continued)

```cpp
/*
 * Function: displayWordCounts
 * Usage: displayWordCounts(wordCount);
 * -----------------------------------------
 * Displays the count associated with each word in the wordCount map.
 */

void displayWordCounts(Map<string,int> & wordCounts) {
   for (string word : wordCounts) {
      cout << left << setw(15) << word
           << right << setw(5) << wordCounts[word] << endl;
   }
}

/*
 * Function: extractWords
 * Usage: extractWords(line, words);
 * -----------------------------------
 * Extracts words from the line into the string vector words.
 */

void extractWords(string line, Vector<string> & words) {
   words.clear();
   int start = -1;
   for (int i = 0; i < line.length(); i++) {
      if (isalpha(line[i])) {
         if (start == -1) start = i;
      } else {
         if (start >= 0) {
            words.add(line.substr(start, i - start));
            start = -1;
         }
      }
   }
   if (start >= 0) words.add(line.substr(start));
}
```

Computing word frequencies turns out to be useful for applications in which the use of such modern tools might at first seem surprising. Over the last few decades, for example, computer analysis has become central to resolving questions of disputed authorship. There are several plays from the Elizabethan era that might have been written by Shakespeare, even though they are not part of the traditional canon. Conversely, several Shakespearean plays that are attributed to Shakespeare have parts that don't sound like his other works and may have in fact been written by someone else. To resolve such questions, Shakespearean scholars often compute the frequency of particular words that appear in the text and see whether those frequencies match what we expect to find based on an analysis of Shakespeare's known works.

Suppose, for example, that you have a text file containing a passage from Shakespeare, such as the following well-known lines from Act 5 of *Macbeth:*

```
Macbeth.txt
```

```
Tomorrow, and tomorrow, and tomorrow
Creeps in this petty pace from day to day
```

If you are trying to determine the relative frequency of words in Shakespeare's writing, you can use the **WordFrequency** program to count how many times each word appears in the data file. Thus, given the file **Macbeth.txt**, you would like your program to produce something like the following output:

```
WordFrequency
Input file: Macbeth.txt
and           2
creeps        1
day           2
from          1
in            1
pace          1
petty         1
this          1
to            1
tomorrow      3
```

Summary

This chapter introduced the C++ classes **Vector**, **Stack**, **Queue**, **Map**, and **Set**, which together represent a powerful framework for storing collections. For the moment, you have looked at these classes only as a client. In subsequent chapters, you will have a chance to learn more about how they are implemented. Given that you will be implementing them as you complete the text, the classes presented here have been simplified to some extent from the **vector**, **stack**, **queue**, **map**, and **set** classes in the Standard Template Library, although they export a very similar collection of methods.

Important points in this chapter include:

- Data structures defined in terms of their behavior rather their representation are called *abstract data types.* Abstract data types have several important advantages over more primitive data structures. These advantages include simplicity, flexibility, and security.

- Classes that contain other objects as elements of an integral collection are called *collection classes.* In C++, collection classes are defined using a *template* or *parameterized type,* in which the type name of the element appears in angle brackets after the name of the collection class. For example, the class **Vector<int>** signifies a vector containing values of type **int**.

- The **Vector** class is an abstract data type that behaves in much the same fashion as a one-dimensional array but is much more powerful. Unlike an array, a **Vector** can grow dynamically as elements are added and removed. The **Vector** class is also more secure, because it checks to make sure that all indices are in range. Although you can create a two-dimensional structure using a vector of vectors, it is often easier to use the **Grid** class in the Stanford libraries.

- The **Stack** class represents a collection of objects whose behavior is defined by the property that items are removed from a stack in the opposite order from which they were added: last in, first out (LIFO). The fundamental operations on a stack are **push**, which adds a value to the stack, and **pop**, which removes and returns the value most recently pushed.

- The **Queue** class is similar to the **Stack** class except for the fact that elements are removed from a queue in the same order in which they were added: first in, first out (FIFO). The fundamental operations on a queue are **enqueue**, which adds a value to the end of a queue, and **dequeue**, which removes and returns the value from the front.

- The **Map** class makes it possible to associate *keys* with *values* in a way that makes it possible to retrieve those associations efficiently. The fundamental operations on a map are **put**, which adds a key/value pair, and **get**, which returns the value associated with a particular key.

- The **Set** class represents a collection in which the elements are unordered and in which each value appears only once, as with sets in mathematics. The fundamental operations on a set include **add**, which stores a new element in the set and **contains**, which checks to see whether an element is in the set.

- With the exception of **Stack** and **Queue**, all collection classes support the **foreach** pattern, which makes it easy to cycle through the elements of the collection. Each collection defines its own iteration order, as described in the section on "Iteration order" on page 238.

- In addition to the **Map** and **Set** classes, the Stanford libraries export the closely related classes **HashMap** and **HashSet**. The only difference between **Map** and **HashMap** (or between **Set** and **HashSet**) is the order in which the range-based **for** loop iterates through the elements. The **Map** and **Set** classes step through the elements in increasing order as defined by the value type. The **HashMap** and **HashSet** classes are more efficient, but step through elements in a seemingly random order.

Review questions

1. True or false: An abstract data type is one defined in terms of its behavior rather than its representation.

2. What three advantages does this chapter cite for separating the behavior of a class from its underlying implementation?

3. What is the STL?

4. If you want to use the **Vector** class in a program, what **#include** line do you need to add to the beginning of your code?

5. List at least three advantages of the **Vector** class over the more primitive array mechanism available in C++.

6. What is meant by the term *bounds-checking?*

7. What is a *parameterized type?*

8. What type name would you use to store a vector of Boolean values?

9. True or false: The default constructor for the **Vector** class creates a vector with ten elements, although you can make it longer later.

10. How would you initialize a **Vector<int>** with 20 elements, all equal to 0?

11. What method do you call to determine the number of elements in a **Vector**?

12. If a **Vector** object has *N* elements, what is the legal range of values for the first argument to **insert**? What about for the argument to **remove**?

13. What feature of the **Vector** class makes it possible to avoid explicit use of the **get** and **set** methods?

14. Why is it important to pass vectors and other collection objects by reference?

15. What declaration would you use to initialize a variable called **chessboard** to an 8×8 grid, each of whose elements is a character?

16. Given the **chessboard** variable from the preceding exercise, how would you assign the character **'R'** (which stands for a white rook in standard chess notation) to the squares in the lower left and lower right corners of the board?

17. What do the acronyms *LIFO* and *FIFO* stand for? How do these terms apply to stacks and queues?

18. What are the names of the two fundamental operations for a stack?

19. What are the names for the corresponding operations for a queue?

20. What does the **peek** operation do in each of the **Stack** and **Queue** classes?

21. Describe in your own words what is meant by the term *discrete time* in the context of a simulation program.

22. What are the two type parameters used with the **Map** class?

23. What happens if you call **get** for a key that doesn't exist in a map?

24. What are the syntactic shorthand forms for **get** and **put** that allow you to treat maps as associative arrays?

25. Why do the Stanford libraries include a separate **Lexicon** class even though it is easy to implement a lexicon using the **Set** class?

26. What are the two kinds of data files supported by the constructor for the **Lexicon** class?

27. What is the general form of the range-based **for** loop pattern?

28. What reason does the chapter offer for disallowing the use of the range-based **for** loop with the **Stack** and **Queue** classes?

29. Describe the order in which the range-based **for** loop processes elements for each of the collection classes introduced in this chapter.

Exercises

1. Write the overloaded functions

```
void readVector(istream & is, Vector<int> & vec);
void readVector(istream & is, Vector<double> & vec);
void readVector(istream & is, Vector<string> & vec);
```

each of which reads lines from the input stream specified by **is** into the vector **vec**. In the input stream, each element of the vector appears on a line of its own. The function should read elements until it encounters a blank line or the end of the file.

To illustrate the operation of this function, suppose that you have the data file

```
SquareAndCubeRoots.txt
1.0000
1.4142
1.7321
2.0000

1.0000
1.2599
1.4422
1.5874
1.7100
1.8171
1.9129
2.0000
```

and that you have opened **infile** as an **ifstream** on that file. In addition, suppose that you have declared the variable **roots** as follows:

```
Vector<double> roots;
```

The first call to **readVector(infile, roots)** should initialize **roots** so that it contains the four elements shown at the beginning of the file. The second call should change the value of **roots** so that it contains the eight elements shown at the end of the file. Calling **readVector** a third time should set **roots** to an empty vector.

2.   In statistics, a collection of data values is often referred to as a ***distribution.*** One of the primary goals of statistical analysis is to find ways to compress the complete set of data into summary statistics that express properties of the distribution as a whole. The most common statistical measure is the ***mean,*** which is simply the traditional average. For the distribution $x_1, x_2, x_3, \ldots, x_n$, the mean is usually represented by the symbol $\bar{x}$. Write a function

```
double mean (Vector<double> & data);
```

that returns the mean of the data in the vector.

3.   Another common statistical measure is the ***standard deviation,*** which provides an indication of how much the values in a distribution $x_1, x_2, x_3, \ldots, x_n$ differ from the mean. In mathematical form, the standard deviation (σ) is expressed as follows, at least if you are computing the standard deviation of a complete distribution as opposed to a sample:

$$\sigma = \sqrt{\frac{\sum_{i=1}^{n}(\bar{x} - x_i)^2}{n}}$$

The Greek letter sigma (Σ) indicates a summation of the quantity that follows, which in this case is the square of the difference between the mean and each individual data point. Write a function

```
double stddev(Vector<double> & data);
```

that returns the standard deviation of the data distribution.

4. A *histogram* is a graph that displays a set of values by dividing the data into separate ranges and then indicating how many data values fall into each range. For example, given the set of exam scores

100, 95, 47, 88, 86, 92, 75, 89, 81, 70, 55, 80

a traditional histogram would have the following form:

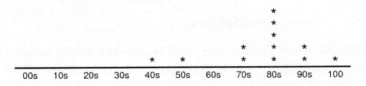

The asterisks in the histogram indicate one score in the 40s, one score in the 50s, five scores in the 80s, and so forth.

When you generate histograms using a computer, however, it is much easier to display them sideways on the page, as in this sample run:

```
●●●                    Histogram
00s:
10s:
20s:
30s:
40s: *
50s: *
60s:
70s: **
80s: *****
90s: **
100: *
```

Write a program that reads in a vector of integers from a data file and then displays a histogram of those numbers, divided into the ranges 0–9, 10–19, 20–29, and so forth, up to the range containing only the value 100. Your program should generate output that looks as much like the sample run as possible.

5. Extend the flexibility of the previous exercise by defining a `hist.h` interface that gives clients more control over the format of the histogram. At a minimum, your interface should allow clients to specify the minimum and maximum values along with the size of each histogram range, but you should feel free to provide other capabilities as well. Use your imagination!

6. In the third century B.C.E., the Greek astronomer Eratosthenes developed an algorithm for finding all the prime numbers up to some upper limit N. To apply the algorithm, you start by writing down a list of the integers between 2 and N. For example, if N is 20, you begin by writing the following list:

    2   3   4   5   6   7   8   9   10 11 12 13 14 15 16 17 18 19 20

    You then circle the first number in the list, indicating that you have found a prime. Whenever you mark a number as a prime, you go through the rest of the list and cross off every multiple of that number, since none of those multiples can itself be prime. Thus, after executing the first cycle of the algorithm, you will have circled the number 2 and crossed off every multiple of 2, as follows:

    ② 3 4̸ 5 6̸ 7 8̸ 9 1̸0̸ 11 1̸2̸ 13 1̸4̸ 15 1̸6̸ 17 1̸8̸ 19 2̸0̸

    To complete the algorithm, you simply repeat the process by circling the first number in the list that is neither crossed off nor circled, and then crossing off its multiples. In this example, you would circle 3 as a prime and cross off all multiples of 3 in the rest of the list, which would result in the following state:

    ②③ 4̸ 5 6̸ 7 8̸ 9̸ 1̸0̸ 11 1̸2̸ 13 1̸4̸ 1̸5̸ 1̸6̸ 17 1̸8̸ 19 2̸0̸

    Eventually, every number in the list will either be circled or crossed out, as shown in this diagram:

    ②③ 4̸ ⑤ 6̸ ⑦ 8̸ 9̸ 1̸0̸ ⑪ 1̸2̸ ⑬ 1̸4̸ 1̸5̸ 1̸6̸ ⑰ 1̸8̸ ⑲ 2̸0̸

    The circled numbers are the primes; the crossed-out numbers are composites. This algorithm is called the *sieve of Eratosthenes.*

    Write a program that uses the sieve of Eratosthenes to generate a list of the primes between 2 and 1000.

7. One of the problems in using the `Grid` class is that it isn't as easy to set up a particular set of initial values as it is with the `Vector` class, which allows you

to add the elements you want with the **+=** operator. One way to streamline the process of initializing a grid is to define a function

```
void fillGrid(Grid<int> & grid, Vector<int> & values);
```

that fills the elements of the grid from the values in the vector. For example, the code

```
Grid<int> matrix(3, 3);
Vector<int> values;
values += 1, 2, 3;
values += 4, 5, 6;
values += 7, 8, 9;
fillGrid(matrix, values);
```

initializes the variable **matrix** to be a 3×3 grid containing the values

1	2	3
4	5	6
7	8	9

8. A *magic square* is a two-dimensional grid of integers in which the rows, columns, and diagonals all add up to the same value. One of the most famous magic squares appears in the 1514 engraving *Melencolia I* by Albrecht Dürer shown in Figure 5-12, in which a 4×4 magic square appears at the upper right, just under the bell. In Dürer's square, which can be read more easily in the magnified inset shown at the right of the figure, all four rows, all four columns, and both diagonals add up to 34. A more familiar example is the following 3×3 magic square in which each of the rows, columns, and diagonals add up to 15, as shown:

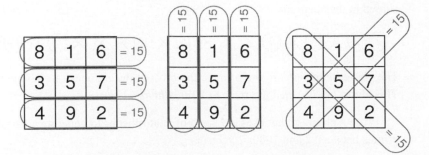

Implement a function

```
bool isMagicSquare(Grid<int> & square);
```

FIGURE 5-12 **Magic square in Albrecht Durer's** *Melencolia I* **(1514)**

that tests to see whether the grid contains a magic square. Your program should work for square grids of any size. If you call **isMagicSquare** with a grid in which the number of rows and columns are different, the function should simply return **false**.

9. In the last several years, a new logic puzzle called *Sudoku* has become quite popular throughout the world. In Sudoku, you start with a 9×9 grid of integers in which some of the cells have been filled with a digit between 1 and 9. Your job in the puzzle is to fill each of the empty spaces with a digit between 1 and 9 so that each digit appears exactly once in each row, each column, and each of the smaller 3×3 squares. Each Sudoku puzzle is carefully constructed so that there is only one solution. For example, Figure 5-13 shows a typical Sudoku puzzle on the left and its unique solution on the right.

FIGURE 5-13 Typical Sudoku puzzle and its solution

		2	4		5	8		
	4	1	8				2	
6			7				3	9
2			3				9	6
		9	6		7	1		
1	7			5				3
9	6			8				1
	2				9	5	6	
		8	3			6	9	

3	9	2	4	6	5	8	1	7
7	4	1	8	9	3	6	2	5
6	8	5	2	7	1	4	3	9
2	5	4	1	3	8	7	9	6
8	3	9	6	2	7	1	5	4
1	7	6	9	5	4	2	8	3
9	6	7	5	8	2	3	4	1
4	2	3	7	1	9	5	6	8
5	1	8	3	4	6	9	7	2

Although you won't discover the algorithmic strategies you need to solve Sudoku puzzles until Chapter 9, you can easily write a method that checks to see whether a proposed solution follows the Sudoku rules against duplicating values in a row, column, or outlined 3×3 square. Write a function

```
bool checkSudokuSolution(Grid<int> & puzzle);
```

that performs this check and returns **true** if the **puzzle** is a valid solution. Your program should check to make sure that **puzzle** contains a 9×9 grid of integers and report an error if this is not the case.

10. In the game of Minesweeper, a player searches for hidden mines on a rectangular grid that might—for a very small board—look like this:

One way to represent that grid in C++ is to use a grid of Boolean values marking mine locations, where **true** indicates the location of a mine. In Boolean form, the grid for this sample board therefore looks like this:

T	F	F	F	F	T
F	F	F	F	F	T
T	T	F	T	F	T
T	F	F	F	F	F
F	F	T	F	F	F
F	F	F	F	F	F

Given such a grid of mine locations, write a function

```
void fixCounts(Grid<bool> & mines, Grid<int> & counts);
```

that uses the reference parameter **counts** to return a grid of integers in which each element indicates the number of mines in the corresponding neighborhood of the **mines** grid, where the neighborhood of a location includes the location itself and any of the eight adjacent locations that are inside the boundaries of the grid. For example, if **mineLocations** contains the Boolean grid shown earlier on this page, the code

```
Grid<int> mineCounts;
fixCounts(mineLocations, mineCounts);
```

should initialize **mineCounts** as follows:

1	1	0	0	2	2
3	3	2	1	4	3
3	3	2	1	3	2
3	4	3	2	2	1
1	2	1	1	0	0
0	1	1	1	0	0

11. The **resize** method in the **Grid** class resets the dimensions of a grid but also initializes every element of the grid to its default value. Write a function

```
void reshape(Grid<int> & grid, int nRows, int nCols);
```

that resizes the grid but fills in the data from the original grid by copying elements in the standard row-major order (left-to-right/top-to-bottom). For example, if **myGrid** initially contains the values

1	2	3	4
5	6	7	8
9	10	11	12

calling the function

```
reshape(myGrid, 4, 3)
```

should change the dimensions and contents of **myGrid** as follows:

1	2	3
4	5	6
7	8	9
10	11	12

If the new grid does not include enough space for all of the original values, the values at the bottom of the grid are simply dropped. For example, if you call

```
reshape(myGrid, 2, 5)
```

there is no room for the last two elements, so the new grid looks like this:

1	2	3	4	5
6	7	8	9	10

Conversely, if there are not enough elements in the original grid to fill the available space, the entries at the end should simply retain their default values.

12. Write a program that uses a stack to reverse a sequence of integers read from the console one number per line, as shown in the following sample run:

```
ReverseList
Enter a list of integers, ending with 0:
? 10
? 20
? 30
? 40
? 0
Those integers in reverse order are:
   40
   30
   20
   10
```

13.   *And the first one now*
       Will later be last
       For the times they are a-changin'.
                              —Bob Dylan, "The Times They Are a-Changin'," 1963

Following the inspiration from Bob Dylan's song (which is itself inspired by
Matthew 19:30), write a function

```
void reverseQueue(Queue<string> & queue);
```

that reverses the elements in the queue. Remember that you have no access to
the internal representation of the queue and must therefore come up with an
algorithm—presumably involving other structures—that accomplishes the
task.

14.   Write a program that checks whether the bracketing operators (parentheses,
       brackets, and curly braces) in a string are properly matched. As an example of
       proper matching, consider the string

```
{ s = 2 * (a[2] + 3); x = (1 + (2)); }
```

If you go through the string carefully, you will discover that all the bracketing
operators are correctly nested, with each open parenthesis matched by a close
parenthesis, each open bracket matched by a close bracket, and so on. On the
other hand, the following strings are all unbalanced for the reasons indicated:

   `(([])`   *The line is missing a close parenthesis.*
   `)(`   *The close parenthesis comes before the open parenthesis.*
   `{(})`   *The bracketing operators are improperly nested.*

15.   The figures in this book are created using PostScript®, a powerful graphics
       language developed by the Adobe Corporation in the early 1980s. PostScript
       programs store their data on a stack. Many of the operators available in the
       PostScript language have the effect of manipulating the stack in some way.
       You can, for example, invoke the **pop** operator, which pops the top element
       off the stack, or the **exch** operator, which swaps the top two elements.

       One of the most interesting (and surprisingly useful) PostScript operators is
       the **roll** operator, which takes two arguments: n and k. The effect of
       applying **roll**(n, k) is to rotate the top n elements of a stack by k positions,
       where the general direction of the rotation is toward the top of the stack. More
       specifically, **roll**(n, k) has the effect of removing the top n elements,
       cycling the top element to the last position k times, and then replacing the
       reordered elements on the stack. Figure 5-14 shows before and after pictures
       for three different examples of **roll**.

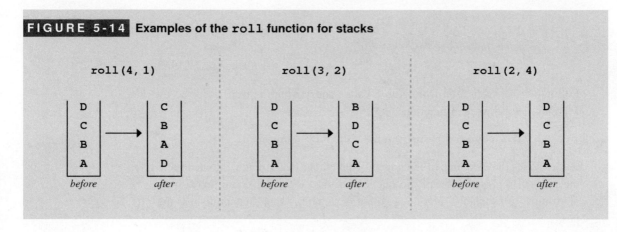

FIGURE 5-14 Examples of the `roll` function for stacks

Write a function

```
void roll(Stack<char> & stack, int n, int k)
```

that implements the `roll`(n, k) operation on the specified stack. Your implementation should check that **n** and **k** are both nonnegative and that **n** is not larger than the stack size; if either of these conditions is violated, your implementation should call **error** with the message

```
roll: argument out of range
```

Note, however, that **k** can be larger than **n**, in which case the **roll** operation continues through more than a complete cycle. This case is illustrated in the final example in Figure 5-14, in which the top two elements on the stack are rolled four times, leaving the stack exactly as it started.

16. You can extend checkout-line simulation in Figure 5-5 to investigate important practical questions about how waiting lines behave. As a first step, rewrite the simulation so that there are several independent queues, as is usually the case in supermarkets. A customer arriving at the checkout area finds the shortest checkout line and enters that queue. Your revised simulation should report the same results as the simulation in the chapter.

17. As a second extension to the checkout-line simulation, change the program from the preceding exercise so that there is a single waiting line served by multiple cashiers—a practice that has become more common in recent years. In each cycle of the simulation, any cashier who becomes idle serves the next customer in the queue. If you compare the data produced by this exercise and the preceding one, what can you say about the relative advantages of these two strategies for organizing a checkout line?

18. Write a program to simulate the following experiment, which was included in the 1957 Disney film *Our Friend the Atom,* to illustrate the chain reactions involved in nuclear fission. The setting for the experiment is a large cubical box, the bottom of which is completely covered with 625 mousetraps arranged to form a square grid with 25 mousetraps on a side. Each of the mousetraps is initially loaded with two ping-pong balls. At the beginning of the simulation, an additional ping-pong ball is released from the top of the box and falls on one of the mousetraps. That mousetrap springs and shoots its two ping-pong balls into the air. The ping-pong balls bounce around the sides of the box and eventually land on the floor, where they are likely to set off more mousetraps.

    In writing this simulation, you should make the following simplifying assumptions:

    • Every ping-pong ball that falls always lands on a mousetrap, chosen randomly by selecting a random row and column in the grid. If the trap is loaded, its balls are released into the air. If the trap has already been sprung, having a ball fall on it has no effect.

    • Once a ball falls on a mousetrap—whether or not the trap is sprung—that ball stops and takes no further role in the simulation.

    • Balls launched from a mousetrap bounce around the room and land again after a random number of simulation cycles have gone by. That random interval is chosen independently for each ball and is always between one and four cycles.

    Your simulation should run until there are no balls in the air. At that point, your program should report how many time units have elapsed since the beginning, what percentage of the traps have been sprung, and the maximum number of balls in the air at any time in the simulation.

19. In May of 1844, Samuel F. B. Morse sent the message "What hath God wrought!" by telegraph from Washington to Baltimore, heralding the beginning of the age of electronic communication. To make it possible to communicate information using only the presence or absence of a single tone, Morse designed a coding system in which letters and other symbols are represented as coded sequences of short and long tones, traditionally called *dots* and *dashes*. In Morse code, the 26 letters of the alphabet are represented by the codes shown in Figure 5-15.

    Write a program that reads in lines from the user and translates each line either to or from Morse code, depending on the first character of the line:

    • If the line starts with a letter, you want to translate it to Morse code. Any characters other than the 26 letters should simply be ignored.

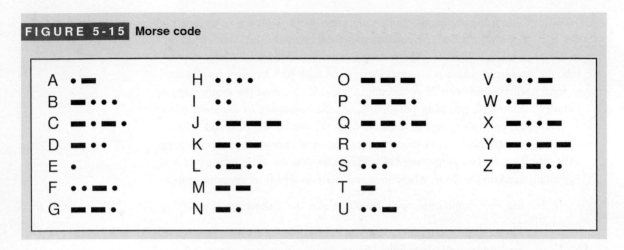

FIGURE 5-15 Morse code

- If the line starts with a period (dot) or a hyphen (dash), it should be read as a series of Morse code characters that you need to translate back to letters. You may assume that each sequence of dots and dashes in the input string will be separated by spaces, and you are free to ignore any other characters that appear. Because there is no encoding for the space between words, the characters of the translated message will be run together when your program translates in this direction.

The program should end when the user enters a blank line. A sample run of this program (taken from the messages between the Titanic and the Carpathia in 1912) might look like this:

```
● ● ●                    MorseCode
Morse code translator
> SOS TITANIC
... --- ... - .- -. .. -.-.
> WE ARE SINKING FAST
.-- . .- .-. . ... -. -.- .. -. --. ..-. .- ... -
> .... . .- -.. .. -. --. ..-. --- .-. -.-- --- ..-
HEADINGFORYOU
>
```

20. Telephone numbers in the United States and Canada are organized into various three-digit *area codes*. A single state or province will often have many area codes, but a single area code will not cross a state or provincial boundary. This rule makes it possible to list the geographical locations of each area code in a data file. For this problem, assume that you have access to the file **AreaCodes.txt**, which lists all the area codes paired with their locations, as illustrated by the first few lines of that file:

```
AreaCodes.txt
201-New Jersey
202-District of Columbia
203-Connecticut
204-Manitoba
205-Alabama
206-Washington
```

Using the **AirportCodes** program from Figure 5-7 as a model, write the code necessary to read this file into a **Map<int,string>**, where the key is the area code and the value is the location. Once you've read in the data, write a main program that repeatedly asks the user for an area code and then looks up the corresponding location, as illustrated in the following sample run:

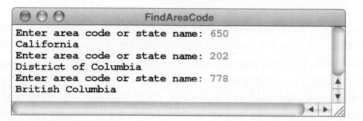

As the prompt suggests, however, your program should also allow users to enter the name of a state or province and have the program list all the area codes that serve that area, as illustrated by the following sample run:

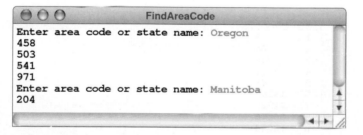

21. When you wrote the **FindAreaCode** program for the preceding exercise, it is likely that you generated the list of area codes for a state by looping through the entire map and printing any area codes that mapped to that state. Although this strategy is fine for small maps like the area code example, efficiency becomes an issue in working with much larger data maps.

An alternative approach is to *invert* the map so that you can perform lookup operations in either direction. You can't, however, declare the inverted map as a **Map<string,int>**, because there is often more than one area code associated with a state. What you need to do instead is to make the inverted map a **Map< string,Vector<int> >** that maps each state name to a vector of the area codes that serve that state. Rewrite the **FindAreaCode** program so that it creates an inverted map after reading in the data file and then uses that map to list the area codes for a state.

22. Section 3.6 defines the function **isPalindrome** that checks whether a word reads identically forward and backward. Use that function together with the English lexicon to display a list of all words that are palindromes.

23. In Scrabble, knowing the two-letter word list is important because those short words make it easy to "hook" a new word into tiles already on the board. Another list that Scrabble experts memorize is the list of three-letter words that can be formed by adding a letter to the front or back of a two-letter word. Write a program that generates this list.

24. One of the most important strategic principles in Scrabble is to conserve your **S** tiles, because the rules for English plurals mean that many words take an **S**-hook at the end. Some words, of course, allow an **S** tile to be added at the beginning, but it turns out that there are 680 words—including, for example, both the words *cold* and *hot*—that allow **S**-hooks on either end. Write a program that uses the English lexicon to make a list of all such words.

25. Write a program that displays a table showing the number of words that appear in the English lexicon, sorted by the length of the word. For the lexicon in **EnglishWords.dat**, the output of this program looks like this:

```
                    WordCountsByLength
 1       3
 2      94
 3     962
 4    3862
 5    8548
 6   14383
 7   21729
 8   26448
 9   18844
10   12308
11    7850
12    5194
13    3275
14    1775
15     954
16     495
17     251
18      89
19      48
20      21
21       6
22       3
24       1
28       1
29       1
```

Chapter 6
Designing Classes

You don't understand. I coulda had class. . . .

— Marlon Brando's character in
On the Waterfront, 1954

Although you have been using classes extensively throughout this book, you have not yet had the chance to define classes of your own. The purpose of this chapter is to fill that gap by giving you the tools you need to implement new classes. This chapter, however, only scratches the surface of what you need to know about classes. In later chapters, you will have a chance to learn other important aspects of class design, including memory management and inheritance.

6.1 Representing points

One of the useful properties of classes is that they make it possible to combine several related pieces of information into a composite value that can be manipulated as a unit. As a simple example, suppose that you are working with coordinates in an *x*-*y* grid in which the coordinates are always integers. Although it is possible to work with the *x* and *y* values independently, it is more convenient to define an abstract data type that combines an *x* and a *y* value together. Since in geometry, this unified pair of coordinate values is called a *point,* it makes sense to use the name **Point** for the corresponding type. C++ offers several strategies for defining a **Point** type, ranging in sophistication from the simple structure types that have always been available in the C family of languages to definitions that adopt a modern object-oriented style. The sections that follow explore these strategies, beginning with the structure-based model and then moving on to the class-based form.

Defining `Point` as a structure type

In your past experience with programming, you have almost certainly encountered types that are defined by combining values of simpler types that already exist. Such types are called *records* or *structures.* The first term is used more broadly in the computer science community, and the second is more common among C++ programmers. Given that C++ supports the facilities available in C, you can define the **Point** type as a structure type with the following C-style structure definition:

```
struct Point {
   int x;
   int y;
};
```

This code defines the type **Point** as a traditional structure with two components. In a structure, components are called *fields* or *members.* In this example, the **Point** structure contains a field named **x** and a field named **y**, both of type **int**.

When you work with structures or classes in C++, it is important to keep in mind that the definition introduces a new type and does not in itself declare any variables. Once you have the definition, you can then use the type name to declare variables, just as you would with any other type. For example, if you include the local variable declaration

```
Point p;
```

in a function, the compiler will reserve space in the stack frame for a variable of type **Point** named p, just as the declaration

```
int n;
```

reserves space for a variable of type **int** named **n**. The only difference is that the **Point** variable **p** includes internal fields that hold the values of its *x* and *y* components. If you were to draw a box diagram of the variable **p**, it would look something like this:

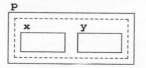

The variable **p** holds a compound value, which contains the internal fields **x** and **y**.

Given a structure, you can select the individual fields using the ***dot operator,*** which is written in the form

var . name

where *var* is the variable containing the structured value and *name* specifies the desired field. For example, you can use the expressions **p.x** and **p.y** to select the individual coordinate value of the **Point** structure stored in the variable **p**. Selection expressions are assignable, so you can initialize the components of **p** to represent the point (2, 3) using the following code:

```
p.x = 2;
p.y = 3;
```

which leads to the state shown in the following diagram:

The fundamental characteristic of a structure is that it is possible to view it both as a collection of individual fields and as a single value. At the lower levels of the implementation, the values stored in the individual fields are likely to be important. At higher levels of detail, it makes sense to focus on the value as an integral unit.

C++ makes it easier to maintain a high-level perspective by defining several important operations that work with the structure as a whole. Given a `Point` value, for example, you can assign that value to a variable, pass it as a parameter to a function, or return it as a result. You can also select the `x` and `y` fields if you need to look at the components individually, but it is often sufficient to work with the value as a whole. These design decisions mean that you can pass a structure up and down through the various levels of an application. At all but the lowest levels, the underlying details of that structure are unimportant.

Defining `Point` as a class

Although structure types are part of the history of C++ and the languages that came before it, they have largely been supplanted by classes, which offer greater power and flexibility. The `Point` structure from the preceding section is identical to the following class definition:

```
class Point {
public:
    int x;
    int y;
};
```

As you can see from this example, declarations for the fields of a class—which are also called *instance variables*—use the same syntax as declarations for fields in a structure. The only syntactic difference is that fields within a class are separated into public and private sections to control what parts of the program have access to those fields. The keyword `public` introduces the *public section,* which contains fields that are available to anyone who uses the defining class. A class definition, however, can also include a *private section* introduced by the keyword `private`. Fields that are declared in the private section are visible only to the defining class and not to any of its clients. In C++ today, structures and classes are implemented in the same way. The only difference is that entries in a structure are public by default, while entries in a class are private.

As the definition of the `Point` class now stands, the `x` and `y` fields are included as part of the public section, which makes them visible to clients. You can select a public field in an object by using the dot operator. For example, if you have a variable `pt` containing an object that is an instance of the `Point` class, you can select its `x` field by writing

```
pt.x
```

just as if it were still the `Point` structure from the preceding section.

Declaring public instance variables, however, is discouraged in modern object-oriented programming. These days, the common practice is to make all instance variables private, which means that clients have no direct access to the internal variables. Clients instead use methods exported by the class to obtain access to any information the class contains. Keeping implementation details away from the client is likely to foster simplicity, flexibility, and security, as described in the introduction to Chapter 5.

Making the instance variables private is easy enough. All you have to do is change the label that introduces that section of the class from **public** to **private**, as follows:

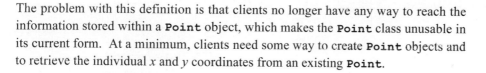

```
class Point {
private:
   int x;
   int y;
};
```

The problem with this definition is that clients no longer have any way to reach the information stored within a **Point** object, which makes the **Point** class unusable in its current form. At a minimum, clients need some way to create **Point** objects and to retrieve the individual *x* and *y* coordinates from an existing **Point**.

As you know from your experience with collection classes in Chapter 5, creating objects is the responsibility of a ***constructor,*** which always has the same name as the class. Classes often define more than one version of the constructor to take account of different initialization patterns. In particular, most classes define a constructor that takes no arguments, which is called the ***default constructor.*** The default constructor is used to initialize an object declared without specifying a parameter list. In the case of the **Point** class, it is useful to define a version of the constructor that takes a pair of coordinate values.

In computer science, methods that retrieve the values of instance variables are formally called ***accessors,*** but are more often known as ***getters.*** By convention, the name of a getter method begins with the prefix **get** followed by the name of the field after capitalizing the first letter in its name. The getters for the **Point** class are therefore **getX** and **getY**.

In keeping with the general strategy used in this book of showing examples before explaining each new concept in detail, Figure 6-1 offers a minimal definition of a **Point** class that defines two constructors, the methods **getX** and **getY**, and a **toString** method in its public section. I have omitted the comments that would ordinarily accompany the class and its methods to provide room for the annotations, which illustrate the structure of the class definition.

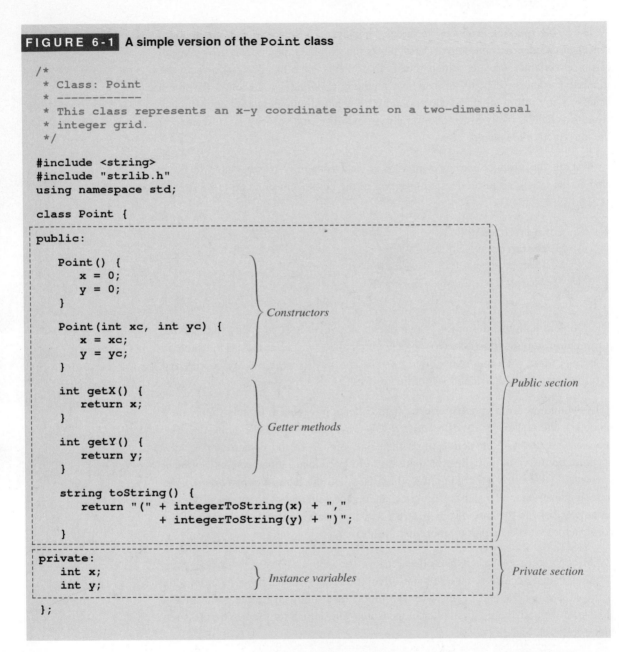

FIGURE 6-1 A simple version of the `Point` class

```
/*
 * Class: Point
 * ------------
 * This class represents an x-y coordinate point on a two-dimensional
 * integer grid.
 */

#include <string>
#include "strlib.h"
using namespace std;

class Point {
public:

    Point() {
        x = 0;
        y = 0;
    }                                        } Constructors

    Point(int xc, int yc) {
        x = xc;
        y = yc;
    }

    int getX() {
        return x;
    }                                        } Getter methods     } Public section

    int getY() {
        return y;
    }

    string toString() {
        return "(" + integerToString(x) + ","
                   + integerToString(y) + ")";
    }

private:
    int x;                                   } Instance variables  } Private section
    int y;

};
```

For the most part, the code in Figure 6-1 should be easy to understand. The only subtlety is the names of the parameters in the second form of the constructor. Logically, since the constructor takes an *x* and a *y* coordinate, it would therefore be reasonable to expect the parameter names to be **x** and **y** instead of **xc** and **yc** (where I've included the **c** to suggest the word *coordinate*). Unfortunately, using the names **x** and **y** as parameters to the constructor would result in confusion as to whether a reference to the variable **x** was intended to refer to the parameter or to the instance variable with that name.

Having one variable hide an identically named variable declared at some larger scope is called **shadowing.** In Chapter 11, you'll learn a simple technique to resolve this ambiguity; unfortunately, that technique depends on concepts that are as yet beyond your knowledge. For the moment, therefore, the examples in this text avoid the problem of shadowing altogether by choosing different names for parameters and instance variables.

The other question you may have after reading the code in Figure 6-1 is why certain methods *aren't* part of the class. Although the getter methods make it possible to get information out of a **Point** object, the current definition provides no means of changing the values of these fields. One approach that is useful in some situations is to export methods that set the values of specific instance variables. Such methods are called *mutators* or, more informally, *setters.* If the **Point** class were to export a **setX** and a **setY** method that allowed the client to change the values of these fields, you could easily replace any application that previously used the old structure type with a version that relies entirely on the new **Point** class. All you would need to do is replace every assignment of the form

```
pt.x = value;
```

with a call to

```
pt.setX(value);
```

Similarly, every reference to **pt.y** that isn't on the left side of an assignment statement would need to be rewritten as **pt.getY()**.

It is, however, a bit unsatisfying to think about adding setter methods to a class so soon after deciding that it was important to make its instance variables private. After all, part of the reason for making instance variables private is to ensure that clients don't have unrestricted access to them. Having every instance variable in a class come with a public setter method circumvents those restrictions and eliminates the advantages one might have obtained by making the variables private in the first place. In general, it is considerably safer to allow clients to *read* the values of the instance variables than it is to have clients *change* those values. As a result, setter methods are far less common than getters in object-oriented design.

In fact, many programmers take the recommendation against allowing change to an even higher level by making it impossible to change the values of any instance variables after an object has been created. Classes designed in this way are said to be *immutable.* The **Point** class is immutable, at least insofar as immutability tends to be defined in C++. Although it is still possible to change the contents of a **Point** object by assigning another **Point** to it, there is no way to change the individual fields in a point independently.

Separating the interface from the implementation

The **Point** class as it appears in Figure 6-1 is useful only if you plan to use that class entirely within the context of a single source file. It is generally more useful to export class definitions in a library, thereby making those definitions available to a broader set of applications. In this case, what you would like to do is create a **point.h** file that serves as the interface for the class and a separate **point.cpp** file that includes the corresponding implementation.

As you know from Chapter 2, an interface typically contains only the prototypes for its functions and not the full implementation. The same is true for the methods in a class. The class definition in the interface includes only the method prototypes, deferring the code for those methods to the implementation. The header files therefore look similar to header files for the other libraries you have seen, except for the fact that the prototypes appear inside a class definition. The structure of the implementation file, however, is somewhat different.

In C++, when you separate the interface for a class from its implementation, the class definition itself exists only in the **.h** file. The corresponding code appears in the **.cpp** file as independent method definitions that are not nested within a class definition the way prototypes are. For this reason, the method definitions need to specify the class to which they belong in a different way. In C++, this identification is accomplished by adding the class name as a *qualifier* before the method name, separating the two with a double colon. Thus, the fully qualified name of the **getX** method in the **Point** class is **Point::getX**.

Once that minor syntactic wrinkle is out of the way, the implementations are straightforward. Figure 6-2 provides a complete interface for the **Point** class, and the corresponding implementation appears in Figure 6-3.

6.2 Operator overloading

As you know from your experience with the library classes in several earlier chapters, C++ makes it possible to extend the standard operators so that they apply to new types. This technique is called *operator overloading.* For example, the **string** class overloads the **+** operator so that it behaves differently when applied to strings. When the C++ compiler sees the **+** operator, it decides how to evaluate it by looking at the types of the operand, just as it uses the argument signature to choose among various overloaded versions of a function. If the compiler sees **+** applied to two integers, it generates the instructions necessary to add those values to produce an integer result. If the operands are strings, the compiler instead generates a call to the method provided by the **string** class that implements concatenation.

FIGURE 6-2 Preliminary interface for the `Point` class

```
/*
 * File: point.h
 * --------------
 * This interface exports the Point class, which represents a point on
 * a two-dimensional integer grid.
 */

#ifndef _point_h
#define _point_h

#include <string>

class Point {

public:

/*
 * Constructor: Point
 * Usage: Point origin;
 *        Point pt(xc, yc);
 * --------------------------
 * Creates a Point object.  The default constructor sets the coordinates
 * to 0; the second form sets the coordinates to xc and yc.
 */

   Point();
   Point(int xc, int yc);

/*
 * Methods: getX, getY
 * Usage: int x = pt.getX();
 *        int y = pt.getY();
 * --------------------------
 * Return the x and y coordinates of the point, respectively.
 */

   int getX();
   int getY();

/*
 * Method: toString
 * Usage: string str = pt.toString();
 * ----------------------------------
 * Returns a string representation of the Point in the form "(x,y)".
 */

   std::string toString();

private:

   int x;                       /* The x-coordinate */
   int y;                       /* The y-coordinate */

};

#endif
```

FIGURE 6-3 Preliminary implementation of the Point class

```cpp
/*
 * File: point.cpp
 * ----------------
 * This file implements the point.h interface.
 */

#include <string>
#include "point.h"
#include "strlib.h"
using namespace std;

/*
 * Implementation notes: Constructors
 * ------------------------------------
 * The constructors initialize the instance variables x and y.  In the
 * second form of the constructor, the parameter names are xc and yc
 * to avoid the problem of shadowing the instance variables.
 */

Point::Point() {
   x = 0;
   y = 0;
}

Point::Point(int xc, int yc) {
   x = xc;
   y = yc;
}

/*
 * Implementation notes: Getters
 * ------------------------------
 * The getters return the value of the corresponding instance variable.
 * No setters are provided to ensure that Point objects are immutable.
 */

int Point::getX() {
   return x;
}

int Point::getY() {
   return y;
}

/*
 * Implementation notes: toString
 * --------------------------------
 * The implementation of toString uses the integerToString function
 * from the strlib.h interface.
 */

string Point::toString() {
   return "(" + integerToString(x) + "," + integerToString(y) + ")";
}
```

The ability to overload operators is a powerful feature of C++ that can make programs much easier to read, but only if the interpretation of each operator remains consistent across the types to which it is applied. The classes that overload the **+** operator, for example, use it for operations that are conceptually similar to addition, like concatenating strings. If you write an expression like

```
s1 + s2
```

for two variables of type **string**, it is easy to think about this operation as one of adding the strings together. If, however, you redefine an operator in such a way that readers have no clue what it means, operator overloading can make programs essentially unreadable. It is therefore important to exercise restraint by using this feature only when it enhances program readability.

The sections that follow illustrate how you can overload operators in your own type definitions, using the **Point** class from section 6.1 as the starting point for the examples and then moving on to add some useful operators to the **Direction** type introduced in Chapter 1.

Overloading the insertion operator

As you can see from the **point.h** interface in Figure 6-2, the **Point** class exports a method called **toString** that converts a **Point** object into a string containing the coordinate values enclosed in parentheses. The primary purpose for including this method is to make it easy to display the value of a **Point**. When you're debugging a program, it is often convenient to display the value of a variable. To display the value of a **Point** variable named **pt**, all you need to do is add a statement to your program that looks something like this:

```
cout << "pt = " << pt.toString() << endl;
```

Operator overloading makes it possible to simplify this process even further. C++ already overloads the stream insertion operator **<<** so that it can display strings along with the primitive types. If you overload this operator to support the **Point** class as well, you can simplify the preceding statement to

```
cout << "pt = " << pt << endl;
```

This is a minor change to be sure, but one that makes printing the value of a point require even less thought.

Each of the operators in C++ is associated with a function name used to define its overloaded behavior. In almost all cases, the function name consists of the keyword **operator** followed by the operator symbol. For example, if you want to redefine the **+** operator for some new type, you define a function named **operator+**

that takes arguments of that type. Similarly, you overload the insertion operator by supplying a new definition for the function `operator<<`.

The hardest part of coding the `operator<<` function is writing its prototype. The left operand of the `<<` operator is the output stream, but the `<iostream>` library defines an entire hierarchy of output streams. In most cases, it makes sense to choose the most general class that implements the necessary operations. In the hierarchy of output streams, the most general class is `ostream`. The right operand of `<<` is the `Point` object you want to insert into that stream. The overloaded definition of `<<` therefore takes two arguments: an `ostream` and a `Point`.

Completing the prototype, however, requires some care to take account of the fact that streams cannot be copied. This restriction implies that the `ostream` argument must be passed by reference. That same restriction, however, also comes up when the `<<` operator returns. As I describe on page 160, the insertion operator implements its incredibly useful chaining behavior by returning the output stream, which is then carried forward to the next `<<` operator in the chain. To avoid copying the stream on this end of the process, the definition of `operator<<` must also return its result by reference.

Returning results by reference is much less common than passing parameters by reference. For those applications where it comes up—such as the current example of overloading the `<<` operator—it is enough to know that you can specify return by reference using pretty much the same syntax that you use to indicate call by reference: you simply add an ampersand after the result type.

Putting all these observations together suggests that the prototype for the overloaded version of `operator<<` will look like this:

```
ostream & operator<<(ostream & os, Point pt);
```

The implementation must print the string representation of `pt` on the output stream and then return the stream by reference so that it can be used again in the surrounding context. If you implement these steps sequentially, you get the following code:

```
ostream & operator<<(ostream & os, Point pt) {
   os << pt.toString();
   return os;
}
```

You can, however, reduce this implementation to a single line, as follows:

```
ostream & operator<<(ostream & os, Point pt) {
   return os << pt.toString();
}
```

The classes in this text use this second form, which emphasizes the fact that the **<<** operator returns an output stream.

Testing points for equality

If you look at the final version of the **point.h** interface in the Stanford libraries, you will discover that the **Point** class supports other operators besides stream insertion. For example, given two points, **p1** and **p2**, you can test whether those points are equal by applying the **==** operator, just as you would with strings or primitive values.

C++ offers two strategies for overloading a built-in operator so that it works with objects of a newly defined class:

1. You can define the operator as a *method* within the class. When you use this style to overload a binary operator, the left operand is the receiver object and the right operand is passed as a parameter.

2. You can define the operator as a *free function* outside the class. If you use this style, the operands for a binary operator are both passed as parameters.

If you use the method-based style, the first step in extending the **==** operator is to add the prototypes for the **==** operator to the **point.h** interface, as follows:

```
bool operator==(Point rhs);
```

This method is part of the **Point** class and must therefore be defined as part of its public section. The corresponding implementation appears in the **point.cpp** file, where you would need to add the following code.

```
bool Point::operator==(Point rhs) {
    return x == rhs.x && y == rhs.y;
}
```

As with other methods that are part of a class exported through an interface, the implementation of **operator==** must specify that it is associated with the **Point** class by including the **Point::** prefix before the method name.

The client code that calls this method presumably looks something like this:

```
if (pt == origin) . . .
```

Assuming that both **pt** and **origin** are variables of type **Point**, the compiler will invoke the **==** operator from the **Point** class when it encounters this expression. Because **operator==** is a method, the compiler designates the variable **pt** as the receiver and then copies the value of **origin** to the parameter **rhs**. In the body of the **operator==** method, the unqualified references to **x** and **y** therefore refer to fields in the variable **pt**, while the expressions **rhs.x** and **rhs.y** refer to fields in the variable **origin**.

The code for the **operator==** method offers a useful illustration of an important property of object-oriented programming. The **operator==** method clearly has access to the **x** and **y** fields of the current object, because any method in a class has access to its own private variables. What is perhaps harder to understand is that the **operator==** method also has access to the private variables of **rhs**, even though that variable holds a completely different object. These references are legal in C++ because the definitions in the private section of a class are private to the *class* and not to the *object*. The code for the methods of a class can refer to the instance variables of any object of that class.

In my experience, students often find the method-based form of operator overloading confusing because the compiler treats the left and right operands differently, designating one as the receiver and passing the other as a parameter. The easiest way to restore symmetry is to use the alternative approach of defining the operators as free functions. If you use this strategy, the **point.h** interface needs to include the following prototype:

```
bool operator==(Point p1, Point p2);
```

This prototype declares a free function and must therefore appear outside the definition of the **Point** class. The corresponding implementation—which no longer includes the **Point::** prefix because the operator is no longer part of the class—looks like this:

```
bool operator==(Point p1, Point p2) {
   return p1.x == p2.x && p1.y == p2.y;
}
```

Although this implementation is easier to follow because it treats the parameters **p1** and **p2** symmetrically, this code has a significant problem: it doesn't actually work. In fact, if you add this definition to the **Point** class, your code won't even compile. The crux of the problem is that the **==** operator is now defined as a free function and therefore has no access to the private instance variables **x** and **y**.

I haven't included a bug icon here because the code for the **==** operator is going to end up looking exactly as it does in this example. What saves the day is that C++ makes it possible to solve the access problem in another way. Since the **==** operator appears in the **point.h** interface, it is conceptually associated with the **Point** class and therefore in some sense *deserves* to have access to the private variables of the class.

To make this design work, the **Point** class must let the C++ compiler know that it is appropriate for a particular function—in this case the overloaded version of the **==** operator—to see its private instance variables. To make such access legal, the **Point** class must designate the **operator==** function as a *friend.* In this context, friendship has much the same character as it does in social networks. In both cases, private information is typically not shared with the community at large, but is accessible only to those you have accepted as your friends.

In C++, the syntax for declaring a free function as a friend is

> **friend** *prototype;*

where *prototype* is the function prototype. In the current example, you need to specify that the free function **operator==** is a friend of the **Point** class by writing

> **friend bool operator==(Point p1, Point p2);**

This line is part of the class definition and must therefore be part of the **point.h** interface.

In C++, a class can declare that everything in some other class should gain the benefits of friendship by including the line

> **friend class** *name;*

where *name* is the name of the class. In C++, such declarations of friendship are not automatically reciprocal. If two classes each require access to the private variables of the other, each class must explicitly declare the other class as a friend.

Whenever you overload the **==** operator for a class, it is good practice to provide an overloaded definition for the **!=** operator as well. After all, clients will expect that they can test whether two points are different as easily as they can test whether those points are the same. C++ does not assume that **==** and **!=** return opposite values; if you want that behavior, you have to overload each of these operators separately. You can, however, make use of **operator==** when you implement **operator!=**, because **operator==** is a public member of the class. The most straightforward implementation of **!=** therefore looks like this:

```
bool operator!=(Point p1, Point p2) {
    return !(p1 == p2);
}
```

The final version of the **Point** class appears on the next few pages. Figure 6-4 presents the **point.h** interface; Figure 6-5 contains the corresponding **point.cpp** implementation.

FIGURE 6-4 Complete interface for the `Point` class

```
/*
 * File: point.h
 * --------------
 * This interface exports the Point class, which represents a point on
 * a two-dimensional integer grid.
 */

#ifndef _point_h
#define _point_h

#include <iostream>
#include <string>

class Point {

public:

/*
 * Constructor: Point
 * Usage: Point origin;
 *        Point pt(xc, yc);
 * -------------------------
 * Creates a Point object.  The default constructor sets the coordinates
 * to 0; the second form sets the coordinates to xc and yc.
 */

   Point();
   Point(int xc, int yc);

/*
 * Methods: getX, getY
 * Usage: int x = pt.getX();
 *        int y = pt.getY();
 * --------------------------
 * These methods return the x and y coordinates of the point.
 */

   int getX();
   int getY();

/*
 * Method: toString
 * Usage: string str = pt.toString();
 * ------------------------------------
 * Returns a string representation of the Point in the form "(x,y)".
 */

   std::string toString();
```

FIGURE 6-4 Complete interface for the `Point` class (continued)

```
/* Private section */

private:

/* Friend declaration */

   friend bool operator==(Point p1, Point p2);

/* Instance variables */

   int x;                       /* The x-coordinate */
   int y;                       /* The y-coordinate */

};

/*
 * Operator: <<
 * Usage: cout << pt;
 * -------------------
 * Overloads the << operator so that it is able to display Point values.
 */

std::ostream & operator<<(std::ostream & os, Point pt);

/*
 * Operator: ==
 * Usage: p1 == p2
 * ---------------
 * Implements the == operator for points.
 */

bool operator==(Point p1, Point p2);

/*
 * Operator: !=
 * Usage: p1 != p2
 * ---------------
 * Implements the != operator for points.  It is good practice to
 * overload this operator whenever you overload == to ensure that
 * clients can perform either test.
 */

bool operator!=(Point p1, Point p2);

#endif
```

FIGURE 6-5 Complete implementation of the `Point` class

```cpp
/*
 * File: point.cpp
 * ----------------
 * This file implements the point.h interface.  The comments have been
 * eliminated from this listing so that the implementation fits on a
 * single page.
 */

#include <string>
#include "point.h"
#include "strlib.h"
using namespace std;

Point::Point() {
   x = 0;
   y = 0;
}

Point::Point(int xc, int yc) {
   x = xc;
   y = yc;
}

int Point::getX() {
   return x;
}

int Point::getY() {
   return y;
}

string Point::toString() {
   return "(" + integerToString(x) + "," + integerToString(y) + ")";
}

bool operator==(Point p1, Point p2) {
   return p1.x == p2.x && p1.y == p2.y;
}

bool operator!=(Point p1, Point p2) {
   return !(p1 == p2);
}

ostream & operator<<(ostream & os, Point pt) {
   return os << pt.toString();
}
```

Adding operators to the `Direction` type

Although operator overloading is most commonly associated with classes, C++ also allows you to extend the definition of operators so that they work with enumerated types. This feature makes it possible to add two operators to the `direction.h` interface from Chapter 2 that make the enumerated `Direction` type considerably easier to use.

For exactly the same reasons that made it useful to overload the `<<` operator for the `Point` class, it makes sense to define that operator for the `Direction` type as well. Given that the `direction.h` interface exports the `directionToString` function, the extended implementation of `operator<<` is straightforward:

```
ostream & operator<<(ostream & os, Direction dir) {
    return os << directionToString(dir);
}
```

As with any function in a library interface, the body of this function belongs in `direction.cpp`, and its prototype must appear in `direction.h`.

Before introducing the second operator, which is both more important and more subtle, it is useful to take note of an unfortunate limitation in the capabilities provided by the `Direction` type. As you will discover in Chapter 9, it is often useful to iterate through the elements of the `Direction` type, cycling through the values `NORTH`, `EAST`, `SOUTH`, and `WEST` in order. To accomplish that goal, what you would like to do is use what seems to be the obvious `for` loop idiom, as follows:

```
for (Direction dir = NORTH; dir <= WEST; dir++) . . .
```

Unfortunately, that statement doesn't quite work for the `Direction` type as it is currently defined. The problem is that the `++` operator doesn't work for enumerated types. To achieve the effect of `dir++`, you have to write the much less elegant expression

```
dir = Direction(dir + 1)
```

Once again, operator overloading comes to the rescue. To make the standard `for` loop idiom work exactly as it should, all you have to do is overload the `++` operator for the `Direction` type. Doing so is, however, not quite as simple as it sounds. The `++` and `--` operators are special in C++ because they occur in two forms. When they are written in the prefix position, as in the expression `++x`, the operator is applied first and the value of the expression is the value at the end of the operation. When they are written in the suffix position, as in the expression `x++`, the value of the variable changes in exactly the same way, but the value of the expression is the value of the variable before the operation takes place.

When you overload the **++** or **--** operators in C++, you have to tell the compiler whether you want to redefine the prefix or suffix form of the operator. The designers of C++ chose to indicate the suffix form by passing an integer argument that has no purpose other than to differentiate it from its prefix counterpart. Thus, to overload the prefix form of the **++** operator for the **Direction** type, you would define the function

```
Direction operator++(Direction & dir) {
    dir = Direction(dir + 1);
    return dir;
}
```

To overload the suffix form, you would instead define the function

```
Direction operator++(Direction & dir, int) {
    Direction old = dir;
    dir = Direction(dir + 1);
    return old;
}
```

Note that the **dir** parameter must be passed by reference so that the function can change its value. This example also illustrates the fact that C++ doesn't require a parameter name if you aren't going to use the value.

Given that the only purpose in overloading this operator is to enable the standard **for** loop idiom, the library version of the **Direction** type overrides only the suffix form. This extension is useful for any enumerated type for which it makes sense to iterate through the elements.

Once you have made the extensions described in this section, the **Direction** type becomes much easier to use. For example, if you execute

```
for (Direction dir = NORTH; dir <= WEST; dir++)
    cout << dir << endl;
}
```

you get the following output:

Generating this output without these extensions would be much more difficult.

6.3 Rational numbers

Although the **Point** class from section 6.1 illustrates the basic mechanics used to define a new class, developing a solid understanding of the topic requires you to consider more sophisticated examples. This section walks you through the design of a class to represent *rational numbers,* which are those numbers that can be represented as the quotient of two integers. In elementary school, you probably called these numbers *fractions.*

In some respects, rational numbers are similar to the floating-point numbers you have been using since Chapter 1. Both types of numbers can represent fractional values, such as 1.5, which is the rational number 3/2. The difference is that rational numbers are exact, while floating-point numbers are approximations limited by the precision of the hardware.

To get a sense of why this distinction might be important, consider the arithmetic problem of adding together the following fractions:

$$\frac{1}{2} + \frac{1}{3} + \frac{1}{6}$$

Basic arithmetic—or even a little intuition—makes it clear that the mathematically precise answer is 1, but that answer is difficult to get if you use the type **double**. The following program, which uses double-precision arithmetic to compute the sum and then displays the result with 16 digits of precision, illustrates the problem:

```
int main() {
    double a = 1.0 / 2.0;
    double b = 1.0 / 3.0;
    double c = 1.0 / 6.0;
    double sum = a + b + c;
    cout << setprecision(16);
    cout << "1/2 + 1/3 + 1/6 = " << sum << endl;
    return 0;
}
```

If you run this program, you get the following result:

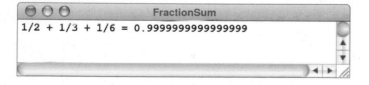

```
FractionSum
1/2 + 1/3 + 1/6 = 0.9999999999999999
```

The problem is that the memory cells used to store numbers inside a computer have a limited storage capacity, which in turn restricts the precision they can offer.

Within the limits of double-precision arithmetic, the sum of one-half plus one-third plus one-sixth is closer to 0.9999999999999999 than it is to 1.0. Worse still, the calculated value of the sum really is less than 1 and would show up as such if you were to test it in your program. At the end of the run, the value of the expression `sum < 1` would be `true`, and the value of `sum == 1` would be `false`. That result is all rather unsettling from a mathematical point of view.

By contrast, rational numbers are not subject to rounding errors because no approximations are involved. What's more, rational numbers obey well-defined arithmetic rules, which are summarized in Figure 6-6. C++, however, does not include rational numbers among its predefined types. If you want to use rational numbers in C++, you have to define a class to represent them.

A strategy for defining new classes

When you work in object-oriented languages, designing new classes is the most important skill you need to master. As with much of programming, designing a new class is as much an art as it is a science. Developing effective class designs requires a strong sense of aesthetics and considerable sensitivity to the needs and desires of clients who will use those classes as tools. Experience and practice are the best teachers, but following a general design framework can help get you started along this path.

From my own experience, I've found that the following step-by-step approach is often helpful:

1. *Think generally about how clients are likely to use the class.* From the very beginning of the process, it is essential to remember that library classes are designed to meet the needs of clients and not for the convenience of the implementer. In a professional context, the most effective way to ensure that a new class meets those needs is to involve clients in the design process. At a minimum, however, you need to put yourself in the client role as you sketch the outlines of the class design.

FIGURE 6-6 Rules for rational arithmetic

Addition

$$\frac{a}{b} + \frac{c}{d} = \frac{ad + bc}{bd}$$

Multiplication

$$\frac{a}{b} \times \frac{c}{d} = \frac{ac}{bd}$$

Subtraction

$$\frac{a}{b} - \frac{c}{d} = \frac{ad - bc}{bd}$$

Division

$$\frac{a}{b} \div \frac{c}{d} = \frac{ad}{bc}$$

2. *Determine what information belongs in the private state of each object.* Although the private section is conceptually part of the implementation of a class, it simplifies the later design phases if you have at least an intuitive sense of what information objects of this class contain. In many cases, you can write down the instance variables that go into the private section. Although such a precise level of detail is not essential at this point, having at least a feeling for the inner structure makes it easier to define the constructors and methods.

3. *Define a set of constructors to create new objects.* Since classes usually define more than one overloaded form of the constructor, it is useful to think from the client's point of view about the types of objects that will need to be created and what information the client will have on hand at that time. Typically, every class exports a default constructor, which makes it possible for clients to declare variables of that class and initialize them later on. During this phase, it is also useful to consider whether the constructors need to apply any restrictions to ensure that the resulting objects are valid.

4. *Enumerate the operations that will become the public methods of the class.* In this phase, the goal is to write the prototypes for the exported methods, thereby adding specificity to the general outline you developed at the beginning of the process. You can also use this phase to refine the overall design, following the principles of unity, simplicity, sufficiency, generality, and stability outlined in Chapter 2.

5. *Code and test the implementation.* Once you have the interface specification, you need to write the code that implements it. Writing the implementation is not only essential to having a working program but also offers validation for the design. As you write the implementation, it is sometimes necessary to revisit the interface design if, for example, you discover that a particular feature is difficult to implement at an acceptable level of efficiency. As the implementer, you also have a responsibility to test your implementation to ensure that the class delivers the functionality it advertises in the interface.

The sections that follow carry out these steps for the `Rational` class.

Adopting the client perspective

As a first step toward the design of the `Rational` class, you need to think about what features your clients are likely to need. In a large company, you might have various implementation teams that would need to use rational numbers and could give you a good sense of what they needed. In that setting, it would be useful to work together with those clients to agree on a set of design goals.

Since this example is a textbook scenario, however, it isn't possible for you to schedule meetings with prospective clients. The primary purpose of the example is to illustrate the structure of class definitions in C++. Given these limitations and the need to manage the complexity of the example, it makes sense to limit the design goals so that the **Rational** class implements only the arithmetic operations defined in Figure 6-6.

Specifying the private state of the Rational class

For the **Rational** class, the private state is easy to specify. A rational number is defined as the quotient of two integers. Each rational object must therefore keep track of these two integers. The declarations of the instance variables that will go into the private section will therefore look something like this:

```
int num;
int den;
```

The names for these variables are shortened versions of the mathematical terms **numerator** and **denominator,** which refer to the upper and lower parts of a fraction.

It is interesting to note that the instance variables of the **Point** class and the **Rational** class are the same except for the variable names. The values maintained by each of these classes consist of a pair of integers. What makes these classes different is the interpretation of those integers, which is reflected in the operations each class supports.

Defining constructors for the Rational class

Given that a rational number represents the quotient of two integers, one of the constructors will presumably take two integers representing the components of the fraction. Having such a constructor makes it possible, for example, to define the rational number one-third by calling **Rational(1, 3)**. The prototype for this form of the constructor—which is the only part of the definition that goes into the interface—looks like this:

```
Rational(int x, int y);
```

Although it isn't necessary to think about the implementation at this stage in the process, keeping implementation issues at least at the back of your mind can sometimes save you headaches later on. In this case, it is worth recognizing that it isn't appropriate to implement this constructor in the following form:

```
Rational(int x, int y) {
   num = x;
   den = y;
}
```

The problem with this implementation is that the rules of arithmetic place constraints on the values of the numerator and denominator—constraints that need to be incorporated into the constructor. The most obvious constraint is that the value of the denominator cannot be zero. The constructor should check for this case and signal an error if it occurs. There is, however, a more subtle issue. If the client is given unconstrained choice for the numerator and denominator, there will be many different ways to represent the same rational number. For example, the rational number one-third can be written as a fraction in any of the following ways:

$$\frac{1}{3} \qquad \frac{2}{6} \qquad \frac{100}{300} \qquad \frac{-1}{-3}$$

Given that these fractions all represent the same rational number, it is inelegant to allow arbitrary combinations of numerator and denominator values in a **Rational** object. It simplifies the implementation if every rational number has a consistent, unique representation.

Mathematicians achieve this goal by insisting on the following rules:

- The fraction is always expressed in lowest terms, which means that any common factors are eliminated from the numerator and the denominator. In practice, the easiest way to reduce a fraction to lowest terms is to divide both the numerator and the denominator by their greatest common divisor, which you already know how to compute using the **gcd** function presented on page 61.

- The denominator is always positive, which means that the sign of the value is stored with the numerator.

- The rational number 0 is always represented as the fraction 0/1.

Implementing these rules results in the following code for the constructor:

```
Rational(int x, int y) {
   if (y == 0) error("Rational: Division by zero");
   if (x == 0) {
      num = 0;
      den - 1;
   } else {
      int g = gcd(abs(x), abs(y));
      num = x / g;
      den = abs(y) / g;
      if (y < 0) num = -num;
   }
}
```

As a general rule, every class should have a default constructor, which is used when no parameters are provided in a declaration. The appropriate mathematical value for the default rational number is zero, which is represented as the fraction 0/1. The code for the default constructor therefore looks like this:

```
Rational() {
    num = 0;
    den = 1;
}
```

Finally, it is useful to define a third version of the constructor that allows clients to create a **Rational** object from an integer, in which case the denominator is always 1:

```
Rational(int n) {
    num = n;
    den = 1;
}
```

Defining methods for the Rational class

In light of the earlier decision to limit the functionality of the **Rational** class to the arithmetic operators, figuring out what methods to export is a relatively easy task, particularly in C++. In many object-oriented languages—including Java, for example—the only way to define arithmetic operations is to export methods, presumably called **add**, **subtract**, **multiply**, and **divide**, that implement the four arithmetic operations. What's worse is that you have to use the receiver syntax to apply those methods. Instead of writing the intuitively satisfying declaration

```
Rational sum = a + b + c;
```

languages like Java require you to write

```
Rational sum = a.add(b).add(c);
```

While it is not all that difficult to puzzle out what this expression means, it has none of the fluidity and expressiveness that redefining the arithmetic operators provides.

The situation is much better in C++. In C++, you implement rational arithmetic by overloading the operators **+**, **-**, *****, and **/** to work with **Rational** objects. As was true for the **Point** class in section 6.2, it is easier to define these operators as free functions than as methods, which means that the prototypes for the four operators look like this:

```
Rational operator+(Rational r1, Rational r2);
Rational operator-(Rational r1, Rational r2);
Rational operator*(Rational r1, Rational r2);
Rational operator/(Rational r1, Rational r2);
```

As with the == operator in the **Point** class, these arithmetic operators need to have access to the fields of **r1** and **r2**, which means that these operator methods must be declared as friends of the **Rational** class.

Although there are many other methods and operators that would make sense in a professional implementation of the **Rational** class, the only additional facilities included in this example are a **toString** method and an overloaded version of the << operator, mostly to get you in the habit of including these facilities in every class you design. Being able to display the values of your objects in a human-readable form is tremendously important for both testing and debugging, which are essential phases of the development process.

These design decisions make it possible to complete the definition of the **rational.h** interface, which appears in Figure 6-7.

Implementing the Rational class

The final step in the process is writing the code for the **Rational** class, as shown in Figure 6-8. Particularly given the fact that the only complex part of the implementation is the constructor for which you have already seen the necessary code, the contents of **rational.cpp** are reasonably straightforward.

Particularly when you implement the operators as free functions, the code for the operators follows directly from the mathematical definitions in Figure 6-6. For example, the implementation of **operator+**

```
Rational operator+(Rational r1, Rational r2) {
    return Rational(r1.num * r2.den + r2.num * r1.den,
                    r1.den * r2.den);
}
```

is a direct translation of the rules for adding the rational numbers **r1** and **r2**:

$$\texttt{r1} + \texttt{r2} = \frac{\texttt{r1}_{num}\,\texttt{r2}_{den} + \texttt{r2}_{num}\,\texttt{r1}_{den}}{\texttt{r1}_{den}\,\texttt{r2}_{den}}$$

The implementation of the **Rational** class includes a private method called **gcd** that implements Euclid's algorithm for finding the greatest common divisor, which was originally introduced on page 60. The implementation of this method appears in the **rational.cpp** file, as you would expect. The prototype for the private method, however, must appear as part of the private section of the class. That prototype must therefore be part of the **rational.h** file, even though clients cannot call it. If you are using a class only as a client, it makes sense to ignore the contents of the private section of a class, even though C++ requires that the private section be included in the interface.

FIGURE 6-7 Interface for the Rational class

```
/*
 * File: rational.h
 * ----------------
 * This interface exports a class for representing rational numbers.
 */

#ifndef _rational_h
#define _rational_h

#include <string>
#include <iostream>

/*
 * Class: Rational
 * ---------------
 * The Rational class is used to represent rational numbers, which
 * are defined to be the quotient of two integers.
 */

class Rational {

public:

/*
 * Constructor: Rational
 * Usage: Rational zero;
 *        Rational num(n);
 *        Rational r(x, y);
 * -------------------------
 * Creates a Rational object.  The default constructor creates the
 * rational number 0.  The single-argument form creates a rational
 * number equal to the specified integer, and the two-argument form
 * creates a rational number corresponding to the fraction x/y.
 */

   Rational();
   Rational(int n);
   Rational(int x, int y);

/*
 * Method: toString()
 * Usage: string str = r.toString();
 * ---------------------------------
 * Returns the string representation of this rational number.
 */

   std::string toString();

/* Declare the operator functions as friends */

   friend Rational operator+(Rational r1, Rational r2);
   friend Rational operator-(Rational r1, Rational r2);
   friend Rational operator*(Rational r1, Rational r2);
   friend Rational operator/(Rational r1, Rational r2);
```

☞

FIGURE 6-7 Interface for the `Rational` class (continued)

```
/* Private section */

private:

/* Instance variables */

    int num;      /* The numerator of this Rational object   */
    int den;      /* The denominator of this Rational object */

};

/*
 * Operator: <<
 * -------------
 * Overloads the << operator so that it is able to display Rational values.
 */

std::ostream & operator<<(std::ostream & os, Rational rat);

/*
 * Operator: +
 * Usage: r1 + r2
 * ---------------
 * Overloads the + operator so that it can add rational numbers.
 */

Rational operator+(Rational r1, Rational r2);

/*
 * Operator: -
 * Usage: r1 - r2
 * ---------------
 * Overloads the - operator so that it can subtract rational numbers.
 */

Rational operator-(Rational r1, Rational r2);

/*
 * Operator: *
 * Usage: r1 * r2
 * ---------------
 * Overloads the * operator so that it can multiply rational numbers.
 */

Rational operator*(Rational r1, Rational r2);

/*
 * Operator: /
 * Usage: r1 / r2
 * ---------------
 * Overloads the / operator so that it can divide rational numbers.
 */

Rational operator/(Rational r1, Rational r2);

#endif
```

FIGURE 6-8 Implementation of the `Rational` class

```cpp
/*
 * File: rational.cpp
 * -------------------
 * This file implements the Rational class.
 */

#include <string>
#include <cstdlib>
#include "error.h"
#include "rational.h"
#include "strlib.h"
using namespace std;

/* Function prototypes */

int gcd(int x, int y);

/*
 * Implementation notes: Constructors
 * ----------------------------------
 * There are three constructors for the Rational class.  The default
 * constructor creates a Rational with a zero value, the one-argument
 * form converts an integer to a Rational, and the two-argument form
 * allows you to specify a fraction.  The constructors ensure that
 * the following invariants are maintained:
 *
 * 1. The fraction is always reduced to lowest terms.
 * 2. The denominator is always positive.
 * 3. Zero is always represented as 0/1.
 */

Rational::Rational() {
   num = 0;
   den = 1;
}

Rational::Rational(int n) {
   num = n;
   den = 1;
}

Rational::Rational(int x, int y) {
   if (y == 0) error("Rational: Division by zero");
   if (x == 0) {
      num = 0;
      den = 1;
   } else {
      int g = gcd(abs(x), abs(y));
      num = x / g;
      den = abs(y) / g;
      if (y < 0) num = -num;
   }
}
```

☞

FIGURE 6-8 Implementation of the Rational class (continued)

```
/* Implementation of toString and the << operator */

string Rational::toString() {
   if (den == 1) {
      return integerToString(num);
   } else {
      return integerToString(num) + "/" + integerToString(den);
   }
}

ostream & operator<<(ostream & os, Rational rat) {
   return os << rat.toString();
}

/*
 * Implementation notes: arithmetic operators
 * -------------------------------------------
 * The implementation of the operators follows directly from the definitions.
 */

Rational operator+(Rational r1, Rational r2) {
   return Rational(r1.num * r2.den + r2.num * r1.den, r1.den * r2.den);
}

Rational operator-(Rational r1, Rational r2) {
   return Rational(r1.num * r2.den - r2.num * r1.den, r1.den * r2.den);
}

Rational operator*(Rational r1, Rational r2) {
   return Rational(r1.num * r2.num, r1.den * r2.den);
}

Rational operator/(Rational r1, Rational r2) {
   return Rational(r1.num * r2.den, r1.den * r2.num);
}

/*
 * Implementation notes: gcd
 * --------------------------
 * This implementation uses Euclid's algorithm to calculate the
 * greatest common divisor.
 */

int gcd(int x, int y) {
   int r = x % y;
   while (r != 0) {
      x = y;
      y = r;
      r = x % y;
   }
   return y;
}
```

6.4 Designing a token scanner class

In Chapter 3, the most sophisticated example of string processing is the Pig Latin translator. As it appears in Figure 3-2, the `PigLatin` program decomposes the problem into two phases: the `lineToPigLatin` function divides the input into words and then calls `wordToPigLatin` to convert each word to its Pig Latin form. The first phase of this decomposition, however, is not at all specific to the Pig Latin domain. Many applications need to divide a string into words, or more generally, into logical units that may be larger than a single character. In computer science, such units are typically called *tokens.*

Since the problem of dividing a string into individual tokens comes up so frequently in applications, it is useful to build a library package that takes care of that task. This section introduces a `TokenScanner` class designed for that purpose. The primary goal is to build a package that is both simple to use and flexible enough to meet the needs of a variety of clients.

What clients want from a token scanner

As always, the best way to begin the design of the `TokenScanner` class is to look at the problem from the client perspective. Every client that wants to use a scanner starts with a source of tokens, which might be a string but might also be an input stream for applications that read data from files. In either case, what the client needs is some way to retrieve individual tokens from that source.

There are several strategies for designing a `TokenScanner` class that offers the necessary functionality. You could, for example, have the token scanner return a vector containing the entire list of tokens. That strategy, however, isn't appropriate for applications that work with large input file, because the scanner has to create a single vector containing the entire list of tokens. A more space-efficient approach is to have the scanner deliver its tokens one at a time. When you use this design, the process of reading tokens from a scanner has the following pseudocode form:

> *Set the input for the token scanner to be some string or input stream.*
> `while` (*more tokens are available*) {
>   *Read the next token.*
> }

This pseudocode structure immediately suggests the sort of methods that the `TokenScanner` class will have to support. From this example, you would expect `TokenScanner` to export the following methods:

• A `setInput` method that allows clients to specify the token source. Ideally, this method should be overloaded to take either a string or an input stream.

- A **hasMoreTokens** method that tests whether the token scanner has any tokens left to process.

- A **nextToken** method that scans and returns the next token.

These methods define the operational structure of a token scanner and are largely independent of the specifics of the applications. Different applications, however, define tokens in all sorts of different ways, which means that the **TokenScanner** class must give the client some control over what types of tokens are recognized.

The need to recognize different types of tokens is easiest to illustrate by offering a few examples. As a starting point, it is instructive to revisit the problem of translating English into Pig Latin. If you rewrite the **PigLatin** program to use the token scanner, you can't ignore the spaces and punctuation marks, because those characters need to be part of the output. In the context of the Pig Latin problem, tokens fall into one of two categories:

1. A string of consecutive alphanumeric characters representing a word

2. A single-character string consisting of a space or punctuation mark

If you gave the token scanner the input

```
        this is "pig latin"
```

calling **nextToken** repeatedly would return the following sequence of nine tokens:

Other applications, however, are likely to define tokens in different ways. Your C++ compiler, for example, uses a token scanner to break programs into tokens that make sense in the programming context, including identifiers, constants, operators, and other symbols that define the syntactic structure of the language. For example, if you gave the compiler's token scanner the line

```
        cout << "hello, world" << endl;
```

you would like it to deliver up the following sequence of tokens:

cout << "hello, world" << endl ;

There are several differences between these two application domains in the definition of a token. In the Pig Latin translator, anything that's not a sequence of alphanumeric characters is returned as a single-character token. In the compiler example, the situation is more complicated. For one thing, programming languages often define multicharacter operators like **<<** that must be treated as single tokens.

Similarly, the string constant **"hello, world"** has the correct meaning only if the token scanner treats it as a single entity. Perhaps less obviously, the compiler's token scanner ignores spaces in the input entirely, unless they appear inside string constants.

As you will learn if you go on to take a course on compilers, it is possible to build a token scanner that allows the client to specify what constitutes a legal token, typically by supplying a precise set of rules. That design offers the greatest possible generality. Generality, however, sometimes comes at the expense of simplicity. If you force clients to specify the rules for token formation, they need to learn how to write those rules, which is similar in many respects to learning a new language. Worse still, the rules for token formation—particularly if you are trying to specify, for example, the rules that a compiler uses to recognize numbers—are complicated and difficult for clients to get right.

If your goal in the interface is to maximize simplicity, it is probably better to design the **TokenScanner** class so that clients can enable specific options that allow it to recognize the type of tokens used in specific application contexts. If all you want is a token scanner that collects consecutive alphanumeric characters into words, you use the **TokenScanner** class in its simplest possible configuration. If you instead want the **TokenScanner** to identify the units in a C++ program, you enable options that tell the scanner, for example, to ignore whitespace characters, to treat quoted strings as single units, and to recognize particular combinations of punctuation marks as multicharacter operators.

The tokenscanner.h interface

The Stanford C++ library includes a **TokenScanner** class that offers considerable flexibility without sacrificing simplicity. The methods exported by **TokenScanner** appear in Table 6-1. Many of the methods in the interface are used to enable options that change the default behavior of the scanner. For example, you can ignore all whitespace characters by initializing a token scanner as follows:

```
TokenScanner scanner;
scanner.ignoreWhitespace();
```

If you instead want to initialize a **TokenScanner** so that it adheres to the rules for tokens in C++, you can use the code

```
TokenScanner scanner;
scanCPlusPlusTokens(scanner);
```

where the **scanCPlusPlusTokens** method is defined as shown in Figure 6-9 on page 296.

TABLE 6-1 Methods exported by the library `TokenScanner` class

Constructors

`TokenScanner()` `TokenScanner(`*str*`)` `TokenScanner(`*infile*`)`	Initializes a scanner object. The source for the tokens is initialized from the specified string or input file. If no token source is provided, the client must call `setInput` before reading tokens from the scanner.

Methods for reading tokens

`hasMoreTokens()`	Returns `true` if there are more tokens to read from the input source.
`nextToken()`	Returns the next token from this scanner. If `nextToken` is called when no tokens are available, it returns the empty string.
`saveToken(token)`	Saves the specified token as part of this scanner's internal state so that it will be returned on the next call to `nextToken`. The library implementation allows clients to save any number of tokens, which are then delivered in a stack-like fashion.

Methods for controlling scanner options

`ignoreWhitespace()`	Tells the scanner to ignore whitespace characters.
`ignoreComments()`	Tells the scanner to ignore comments, which can be in either the slash-star or slash-slash form.
`scanNumbers()`	Tells the scanner to recognize any legal number as a single token. The syntax for numbers is the same as that used in C++.
`scanStrings()`	Tells the scanner to return a string enclosed in quotation marks as a single token. The quotation marks (which may be either single or double quotes) are included in the scanned token so that clients can differentiate strings from other token types.
`addWordCharacters(`*str*`)`	Adds the characters in `str` to the set of characters legal in a word.
`addOperator(`*op*`)`	Defines a new multicharacter operator. The scanner will return the longest defined operator, but will always return at least one character.

Miscellaneous methods

`setInput(`*str*`)` `setInput(`*infile*`)`	Sets the input source for this scanner to the specified string or input stream. Any tokens remaining in the previous source are lost.
`getPosition()`	Returns the current position of the scanner in the input stream.
`isWordCharacter(`*ch*`)`	Returns `true` if the character `ch` is valid in a word.
`verifyToken(`*expected*`)`	Reads the next token and makes sure it matches the string *expected*.
`getTokenType(`*token*`)`	Returns the type of the token, which must be one of the following constants: `EOF`, `SEPARATOR`, `WORD`, `NUMBER`, `STRING`, `OPERATOR`.

Initializing a TokenScanner to scan C++ tokens

```
/*
 * Function: scanCPlusPlusTokens
 * Usage: scanCPlusPlusTokens(scanner);
 * ----------------------------------------
 * Sets the necessary options for the scanner so that it can
 * read C++ source code.
 */

void scanCPlusPlusTokens(TokenScanner & scanner) {
   scanner.ignoreWhitespace();
   scanner.ignoreComments();
   scanner.scanNumbers();
   scanner.scanStrings();
   scanner.addWordCharacters("_");
   scanner.addOperator("++");
   scanner.addOperator("--");
   scanner.addOperator("==");
   scanner.addOperator("!=");
   scanner.addOperator("<=");
   scanner.addOperator(">=");
   scanner.addOperator("<<");
   scanner.addOperator(">>");
   scanner.addOperator("&&");
   scanner.addOperator("||");
   scanner.addOperator("+=");
   scanner.addOperator("-=");
   scanner.addOperator("*=");
   scanner.addOperator("%=");
   scanner.addOperator("^=");
   scanner.addOperator("&=");
   scanner.addOperator("|=");
   scanner.addOperator("<<=");
   scanner.addOperator(">>=");
   scanner.addOperator("->");
   scanner.addOperator("::");
}
```

The implementation of **scanCPlusPlusTokens** in Figure 6-9 tells the scanner that it should ignore whitespace characters and comments, that numbers and strings should be scanned as single tokens, that the underscore is a legal character in an identifier, and that it should recognize the multicharacter operators (many of which are likely to be unfamiliar but are nonetheless defined in C++) shown in the various calls to **addOperator**.

The **tokenscanner.h** interface makes it much easier to write a variety of applications, including several you have already seen in this book. You could, for example, use it to simplify the **PigLatin** program from Figure 3-2 by rewriting the **lineToPigLatin** function as follows:

```
string lineToPigLatin(string line) {
    TokenScanner scanner(line);
    string result = "";
    while (scanner.hasMoreTokens()) {
        string word = scanner.nextToken();
        if (isalpha(word[0])) word = wordToPigLatin(word);
        result += word;
    }
    return result;
}
```

While the new version of **lineToPigLatin** is shorter than the original implementation, the real simplification is conceptual. The original code had to operate at the level of individual characters; the new version gets to work with complete words, because the **TokenScanner** class takes care of the low-level details.

Implementing the TokenScanner class

Particularly given the number of options it supports, the complete implementation of the **TokenScanner** class is too complicated to serve as an effective example. Figures 6-10 and 6-11 therefore present a simplified version of the token scanner package that defines only the following methods:

- A constructor that takes a string argument, in addition to the default constructor

- The **setInput** method, which sets the scanner input to a string

- The **nextToken** method, which returns the next token from the string

- The **hasMoreTokens** method, which allows clients to see if tokens are available

- The **ignoreWhitespace** method, which tells the scanner to ignore spaces

FIGURE 6-10 Simplified interface for the TokenScanner class

```
/*
 * File: tokenscanner.h
 * ---------------------
 * This file exports a simple TokenScanner class that divides a string
 * into individual logical units called tokens.
 */

#ifndef _tokenscanner_h
#define _tokenscanner_h

#include <string>
```

FIGURE 6-10 Simplified interface for the TokenScanner class (continued)

```
/*
 * Class: TokenScanner
 * -------------------
 * This class is used to represent a single instance of a scanner.
 * In this simplified version of the class, tokens come in two forms:
 *
 * 1. Strings of consecutive letters and digits representing words
 * 2. One-character strings representing punctuation or separators
 *
 * The use of the TokenScanner class is illustrated by the following code
 * pattern, which reads the tokens in the string variable input:
 *
 *     TokenScanner scanner;
 *     scanner.setInput(input);
 *     while (scanner.hasMoreTokens()) {
 *         string token = scanner.nextToken();
 *         . . . process the token . . .
 *     }
 *
 * This version of the TokenScanner class includes the ignoreWhitespace
 * method.  The other options available in the library version of the
 * class are included as exercises in the text.
 */

class TokenScanner {

public:

/*
 * Constructor: TokenScanner
 * Usage: TokenScanner scanner;
 *        TokenScanner scanner(str);
 * -----------------------------------
 * Initializes a scanner object.  The initial token stream comes from
 * the string str, if it is specified.  The default constructor creates
 * a scanner with an empty token stream.
 */

   TokenScanner();
   TokenScanner(std::string str);

/*
 * Method: setInput
 * Usage: scanner.setInput(str);
 * -----------------------------
 * Sets the input for this scanner to the specified string.  Any
 * previous input string is discarded.
 */

   void setInput(std::string str);
```

FIGURE 6-10 Simplified interface for the `TokenScanner` class (continued)

```
/*
 * Method: hasMoreTokens
 * Usage: if (scanner.hasMoreTokens()) . . .
 * --------------------------------------------
 * Returns true if there are additional tokens for this scanner to read.
 */

   bool hasMoreTokens();

/*
 * Method: nextToken
 * Usage: token = scanner.nextToken();
 * ---------------------------------------
 * Returns the next token from this scanner.  If called when no tokens
 * are available, nextToken returns the empty string.
 */

   std::string nextToken();

/*
 * Method: ignoreWhitespace()
 * Usage: scanner.ignoreWhitespace();
 * ---------------------------------------
 * Tells the scanner to ignore whitespace characters.  By default, the
 * nextToken method treats whitespace characters (typically spaces and
 * tabs) just like any other punctuation mark and returns them as
 * single-character tokens.  Calling
 *
 *     scanner.ignoreWhitespace();
 *
 * changes this behavior so that the scanner ignores whitespace characters.
 */

   void ignoreWhitespace();

private:

/* Instance variables */

   std::string buffer;            /* The input string containing the tokens */
   int cp;                        /* The current position in the buffer     */
   bool ignoreWhitespaceFlag;     /* Flag set by a call to ignoreWhitespace */

/* Private methods */

   void skipWhitespace();

};

#endif
```

FIGURE 6-11 Implementation of the simplified `TokenScanner` class

```cpp
/*
 * File: tokenscanner.cpp
 * ----------------------
 * This file implements the TokenScanner class.  Most of the methods
 * are straightforward enough to require no additional documentation.
 */

#include <cctype>
#include <string>
#include "tokenscanner.h"
using namespace std;

TokenScanner::TokenScanner() {
   /* Empty */
}

TokenScanner::TokenScanner(string str) {
   setInput(str);
}

void TokenScanner::setInput(string str) {
   buffer = str;
   cp = 0;
}

bool TokenScanner::hasMoreTokens() {
   if (ignoreWhitespaceFlag) skipWhitespace();
   return cp < buffer.length();
}

/*
 * Implementation notes: nextToken
 * -------------------------------
 * This method starts by looking at the current character, which is
 * indicated by the index cp.  If the index is past the end of the string,
 * nextToken returns the empty string.  If the character is alphanumeric,
 * nextToken scans ahead until it finds the end of a word; if not,
 * nextToken returns the character as a one-character string.
 */

string TokenScanner::nextToken() {
   if (ignoreWhitespaceFlag) skipWhitespace();
   if (cp >= buffer.length()) {
      return "";
   } else if (isalnum(buffer[cp])) {
      int start = cp;
      while (cp < buffer.length() && isalnum(buffer[cp])) {
         cp++;
      }
      return buffer.substr(start, cp - start);
   } else {
      return string(1, buffer[cp++]);
   }
}
```

| FIGURE 6-11 | Implementation of the simplified `TokenScanner` class (continued) |

```
/*
 * Implementation notes: ignoreWhitespace and skipWhitespace
 * -----------------------------------------------------------
 * The ignoreWhitespace method simply sets a flag.  The private method
 * skipWhitespace is called only if that flag is true.
 */

void TokenScanner::ignoreWhitespace() {
   ignoreWhitespaceFlag = true;
}

void TokenScanner::skipWhitespace() {
   while (cp < buffer.length() && isspace(buffer[cp])) {
      cp++;
   }
}
```

The `ignoreWhitespace` method serves as a model for the other option settings that are available in this package, and you will have a chance to implement all of these options in the exercises. Adding the functionality to read tokens from data files, however, depends on concepts that won't be introduced until Chapter 11, so you will need to wait until then to complete the `TokenScanner` implementation.

6.5 Encapsulating programs as classes

Most of the class definitions you have seen in this chapter create new abstract types that you can use as if they were primitive objects. Once you have defined the `Rational` class, for example, you can then use `Rational` objects in much the same ways that you use the primitive types in C++. You can declare variables that hold `Rational` values, assign new values to those variables, combine them using operators, print them on `cout`, and store them in any of the collection classes. Programs that work with rational numbers typically create many `Rational` objects, all of which are instances of the same class.

Classes, however, can still be useful even if you never intend to have more than one object of a particular class. For example, it often makes sense to write a program as a class rather than as a collection of free functions. The primary advantage of doing so is that classes provide better encapsulation. The fact that access to any private data is limited to the class itself means that it is much safer to use private instance variables to share information than it is to use global variables, which offer no such security.

As an illustration of this technique, the program in Figure 6-12 shows how to redesign the checkout-line simulation from Figure 5-5 as a class. In the new design,

---

FIGURE 6-12   Class-based version of the checkout-line simulation

```cpp
/*
 * File: CheckoutLineClass.cpp
 * -----------------------------
 * This program duplicates the CheckoutLine program from Chapter 5,
 * but embeds the entire program in a class definition.
 */

#include <iostream>
#include <iomanip>
#include "queue.h"
#include "random.h"
using namespace std;

/* Constants */

const double ARRIVAL_PROBABILITY = 0.05;
const int MIN_SERVICE_TIME =   5;
const int MAX_SERVICE_TIME = 15;
const int SIMULATION_TIME = 2000;

/*
 * Class: CheckoutLineSimulation
 * ------------------------------
 * This class encapsulates the code and data for the simulation.
 */

class CheckoutLineSimulation {

public:

   void runSimulation() {
      ... same as in Figure 5-5 ...
   }

   void printReport() {
      ... same as in Figure 5-5 ...
   }

private:
   int nServed;          /* Number of customers served             */
   int totalWait;        /* Sum of all customer waiting times       */
   int totalLength;      /* Sum of the queue length at each time step */

};

/* Main program */

int main() {
   CheckoutLineSimulation simulation;
   simulation.runSimulation();
   simulation.printReport();
   return 0;
}
```

the free functions **runSimulation** and **printReport** become public methods in a new **CheckoutLineSimulation** class. Given that the bodies of those methods are exactly the same as they were before, this change alone has little impact on the complexity of the code. What has changed, however, is that the information shared between these methods can now be stored in instance variables and need not be passed as arguments. Being able to share access to such data among all the methods in the class substantially reduces the size and complexity of the parameter lists, which in this example shrink from three parameters to zero.

When you use this approach, the **main** function typically becomes considerably shorter. It declares an object of the class that encapsulates the program operation and then calls the public methods necessary to get the program going, as illustrated by the definition of **main** in Figure 6-12:

```
int main() {
    CheckoutLineSimulation simulation;
    simulation.runSimulation();
    simulation.printReport();
    return 0;
}
```

The advantage of using a class increases along with the complexity of the program. Programs in this book use this technique only if doing so simplifies the code.

Summary

The primary purpose of this chapter has been to give you the tools you need to design and implement classes on your own. The examples in this chapter have focused on classes that encapsulate data and operations into a coherent whole, deferring the more complex issue of inheritance to Chapter 19.

Important points covered in this chapter include:

- In many applications, it is useful to combine several independent data values into a single abstract data type. C++ offers several strategies for encapsulating data in this way. At the lowest level, C++ continues to support the definition of C-style structure types. In modern programming practice, however, this kind of encapsulation is more commonly accomplished using classes.

- In C++, a class is divided into sections that control the access clients have to the fields and methods in that section. The **public** section of a class is accessible to all clients; the **private** section is accessible only to the implementation. In modern object-oriented programming, instance variables are declared in the private section. One class can give other functions and classes access to its private data by declaring them as *friends*.

- Given a compound object that is either a structure or a class, you select the individual components using the *dot operator*. Clients can select a field from a compound object only if that field is in the public section. The implementation of a class, however, has access to the private members of all objects of that class.

- Class definitions typically export one or more *constructors* that are responsible for initializing objects of that class. In general, all class definitions include a *default constructor* that takes no arguments.

- Methods that give clients access to the values of the instance variables are called *getters;* methods that allow clients to change the value of an instance variable are called *setters*. A class that gives the client no opportunity to change the value of an object after it is created is said to be *immutable*.

- Class definitions exported by an interface typically separate the definition of class methods between the interface and the implementation. The `.h` file contains only method prototypes; the bodies of those methods go in the `.cpp` file. In C++, the implementation file must specify the class to which each method belongs by adding a `::` tag before the method name.

- Class definitions can overload the standard operators in either of two ways. Defining an operator as a class method means that the operator is part of the class and therefore has free access to the private methods. Defining an operator as a free function often produces code that is easier to read but means that the operator function must be designated as a friend so that the operator can refer to the private data of the class.

- One of the most useful operators to overload is the insertion operator `<<`, because doing so makes it easy to display values of that class on the console. In this text, most classes overload the `<<` operator and define a `toString` method that converts a value of that class to a string.

- Designing new classes is as much an art as a science. Although the chapter offers some general guidelines to guide you in this process, experience and practice are the best teachers.

- The Stanford libraries export a `TokenScanner` class that supports the process of breaking input text into individual units called *tokens*. The library version of the `TokenScanner` class supports a variety of options that make this package useful in a wide range of applications.

- For applications that are complex enough to require maintaining more than a modest amount of internal state, it often makes sense to encapsulate the entire program inside a class. When you use such a design, the main program creates a variable of that class and then invokes a method in that class to get the program running.

Review questions

1. Define each of the following terms: *object, structure, class, instance variable, method.*

2. In a C++ class definition, what do the keywords `public` and `private` mean?

3. True or false: In C++, the only difference between the keyword `struct` and the keyword `class` is that `struct` makes fields public by default.

4. What operator does C++ use to select an instance variable from an object?

5. What is the syntax for a C++ constructor?

6. How many arguments are passed to the *default constructor?*

7. What are *getters* and *setters?*

8. What does it mean for a class to be *immutable?*

9. When you separate the interface and implementation of a class, how does the implementation let the compiler know to which class a particular method definition belongs?

10. What strategy is used in the `.h` files in this chapter to prevent clients from seeing the contents of the private section?

11. In C++, what method name would you use to overload the `%` operator?

12. How does C++ differentiate between the prefix and suffix versions of the `++` and `--` operators?

13. Why does the overloaded implementation of the `<<` operator require the use of return by reference?

14. True or false: Return by reference is used as frequently in C++ programs as call by reference.

15. Describe the differences between the method-based and free-function-based approaches to overloading the operators for a class. What are the advantages and disadvantages of each style?

16. What does it mean for one class to declare a method or another class as a friend?

17. What reason does this chapter offer for overloading the **++** operator for the **Direction** type?

18. What are the five steps suggested in this chapter as guidelines for designing a class?

19. What is a *rational number?*

20. What restrictions does the **Rational** constructor place on the values of the **num** and **den** variables?

21. The code for the **Rational** constructor on page 290 includes an explicit check to see whether **x** is zero. Would the **Rational** class still work the same way if this check were eliminated?

22. In the **rational.h** file in Figure 6-7, why is it necessary to designate the operator methods for **+**, **-**, *****, and **/** as friends but not the operator method for the **<<** insertion operator?

23. What is a *token?*

24. What is the standard pattern for reading all tokens from a string?

25. How do you initialize a **TokenScanner** object so that it ignores spaces, tabs, and other whitespace characters in the input?

26. In your own words, explain the technique of embedding a program in a class.

Exercises

1. The game of *dominos* is played using pieces that are usually black rectangles with some number of white dots on each side. For example, the domino

   is called the 4-1 domino, with four dots on its left side and one on its right.

   Define a simple **Domino** class that represents a traditional domino. Your class should export the following entries:

   • A default constructor that creates the 0-0 domino

   • A constructor that takes the number of dots on each side

   • A **toString** method that creates a string representation of the domino

   • Two getter methods named **getLeftDots** and **getRightDots**

Write the `domino.h` interface and the `domino.cpp` implementation that export this class. As with the examples in the text, all instance variables should be private to the class, and the interface should overload the `<<` operator so that it is possible to print a string representation of a domino.

Test your implementation of the `Domino` class by writing a program that creates a full set of dominos from 0-0 to 6-6 and then displays those dominos on the console. A full set of dominos contains one copy of each possible domino in that range, disallowing duplicates that result from flipping a domino over. Thus, a domino set has a 4-1 domino but not a separate 1-4 domino.

2. Define a `Card` class suitable for representing a standard playing card, which is identified by two components: a *rank* and a *suit*. The rank is stored as an integer between 1 and 13 in which an ace is a 1, a jack is an 11, a queen is a 12, and a king is a 13. The suit is one of the four constants in the following enumeration type:

```
enum Suit = { CLUBS, DIAMONDS, HEARTS, SPADES };
```

The `Card` class should export the following methods:

-   A default constructor that creates a card that can later be assigned a value
-   A constructor that takes a short string name like `"10S"` or `"JD"`
-   A constructor that takes separate values for the rank and the suit
-   A `toString` method that returns the short string representation of the card
-   The getter methods `getRank` and `getSuit`

Write the `card.h` interface and the `card.cpp` implementation necessary to export the `Card` class. In addition to the `Card` class itself, the `card.h` interface should export the `Suit` type, constant names for the ranks that are usually named rather than numbered (`ACE`, `JACK`, `QUEEN`, `KING`), and any other definitions you need to run the following main program:

```
int main() {
   for (Suit suit = CLUBS; suit <= SPADES; suit++) {
      for (int rank = ACE; rank <= KING; rank++) {
         cout << " " << Card(rank, suit);
      }
      cout << endl;
   }
   return 0;
}
```

Your program should produce the following sample run:

```
⊖ ⊖ ⊖                 TestCardClass
AC 2C 3C 4C 5C 6C 7C 8C 9C 10C JC QC KC
AD 2D 3D 4D 5D 6D 7D 8D 9D 10D JD QD KD
AH 2H 3H 4H 5H 6H 7H 8H 9H 10H JH QH KH
AS 2S 3S 4S 5S 6S 7S 8S 9S 10S JS QS KS
```

3. The **gtypes.h** interface exports several useful classes designed to work together with the graphics library. The simplest of these classes is **GPoint**, which is identical to the **Point** class from this chapter except for the fact that it uses floating-point numbers for the coordinates instead of integers. Another useful class is **GRectangle**, which represents a rectangular region defined by the *x* and *y* coordinates of its upper left corner along with a *width* and a *height*. Using the description of the **GRectangle** class in the online documentation for reference, implement the **GRectangle** class.

4. The classes exported by the **gtypes.h** interface described in the preceding exercise make it simpler to create intricate graphical patterns, in part because they make it easy to store coordinate information inside collection classes and other abstract data types. In this exercise, for example, you get to have some fun with a vector of **GPoint** objects. Imagine that you start with a rectangular board and then arrange pegs around the edges so that they are evenly spaced along all four edges, with **N_ACROSS** pegs along the top and bottom and **N_DOWN** pegs along the left and right edges. To model this process using the graphics window, what you want to do is create a **Vector<GPoint>** that holds the coordinates of each of these pegs, which are inserted into the vector starting at the upper left and then proceeding clockwise around the edges of the rectangle, as follows:

```
      0   1   2   3   4   5   6   7   8   9
      •   •   •   •   •   •   •   •   •   •
  27 •                                      • 10
  26 •                                      • 11
  25 •                                      • 12
  24 •                                      • 13
      •   •   •   •   •   •   •   •   •   •
     23  22  21  20  19  18  17  16  15  14
```

From here, you create a figure by drawing lines between the pegs, starting at peg 0 and then moving ahead a fixed number of spaces on each cycle, as specified by the constant **DELTA**. For example, if **DELTA** is 11, the first line goes from peg 0 to peg 11, the second goes from peg 11 to peg 22, and the third—which has to count 11 pegs clockwise past the beginning—goes from peg 22 to peg 5. The process continues in this way until the line returns to peg 0. As usual, implementing the wrap-around feature is much easier if you make use of the **%** operator.

Write a program that simulates this process on the graphics window using larger values for **N_ACROSS** and **N_DOWN**. As an example, the output of the program with **N_ACROSS** equal to 50, **N_DOWN** equal to 30, and **DELTA** equal to 67 appears in Figure 6-13. By changing those constants, you can create other wonderful patterns composed entirely of straight lines.

5. Extend the **calendar.h** interface from Chapter 2, exercise 11 so that it also exports a **Date** class that exports the following methods:

- A default constructor that sets the date to January 1, 1900.

- A constructor that takes a month, day, and year and initializes the **Date** to contain those values. For example, the declaration

    ```
    Date moonLanding(JULY, 20, 1969);
    ```

    should initialize **moonLanding** so that it represents July 20, 1969.

FIGURE 6-13 **Sample run of the yarn-pattern program**

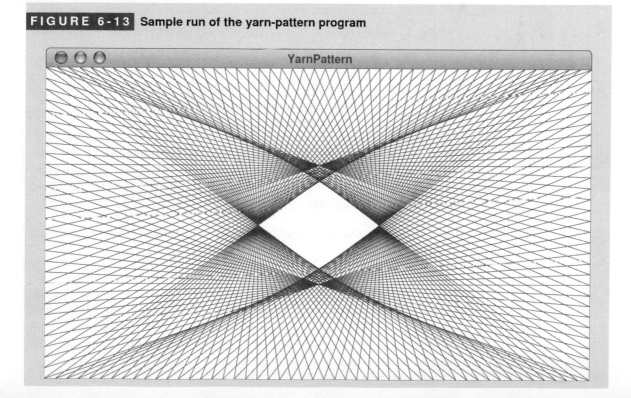

- An overloaded version of the constructor that takes the first two parameters in the opposite order, for the benefit of clients in other parts of the world. This change allows the declaration of **moonLanding** to be written as

  ```
  Date moonLanding(20, JULY, 1969);
  ```

- The getter methods **getDay**, **getMonth**, and **getYear**.

- A **toString** method that returns the date in the form *dd–mmm–yyyy*, where *dd* is a one- or two-digit date, *mmm* is the three-letter English abbreviation for the month, and *yyyy* is the four-digit year. Thus, calling **toString(moonLanding)** should return the string **"20-Jul-1969"**.

6. Extend the **calendar.h** interface still further by adding overloaded versions of the following operators:

    - The insertion operator **<<**

    - The relational operators **==**, **!=**, **<**, **<=**, **>**, and **>=**

    - The expression *date* **+** *n*, which returns the date *n* days after *date*

    - The expression *date* **–** *n*, which returns the date *n* days before *date*

    - The expression d_1 **–** d_2, which returns how many days separate d_1 and d_2

    - The shorthand assignment operators **+=** and **-=** with an integer on the right

    - The **++** and **--** operators in both their prefix and suffix forms

    Suppose, for example, that you have made the following definitions:

    ```
    Date electionDay(6, NOVEMBER, 2012);
    Date inaugurationDay(21, JANUARY, 2013);
    ```

    Given these values of the variables, **electionDay < inaugurationDay** is **true** because **electionDay** comes before **inaugurationDay**. Evaluating **inaugurationDay - electionDay** returns 76, which is the number of days between the two events. The definitions of these operators, moreover, allow you to write a **for** loop like

    ```
    for (Date d = electionDay; d <= inaugurationDay; d++)
    ```

    that cycles through each of these days, including both endpoints.

7. For certain applications, it is useful to be able to generate a series of names that form a sequential pattern. For example, if you were writing a program to number figures in a paper, having some mechanism to return the sequence of strings **"Figure 1"**, **"Figure 2"**, **"Figure 3"**, and so on, would be very handy. However, you might also need to label points in a geometric diagram,

in which case you would want a similar but independent set of labels for points such as "**P0**", "**P1**", "**P2**", and so forth.

If you think about this problem more generally, the tool you need is a label generator that allows the client to define arbitrary sequences of labels, each of which consists of a prefix string ("**Figure** " or "**P**" for the examples in the preceding paragraph) coupled with an integer used as a sequence number. Because the client may want different sequences to be active simultaneously, it makes sense to define the label generator as a **LabelGenerator** class. To initialize a new generator, the client provides the prefix string and the initial index as arguments to the **LabelGenerator** constructor. Once the generator has been created, the client can return new labels in the sequence by calling **nextLabel** on the **LabelGenerator**.

As an illustration of how the interface works, the main program shown in Figure 6-14 produces the following sample run:

```
○ ○ ○              TestLabelGenerator
Figure numbers: Figure 1, Figure 2, Figure 3
Point numbers:  P0, P1, P2, P3, P4
More figures:   Figure 4, Figure 5, Figure 6
```

Write the files **labelgen.h** and **labelgen.cpp** to support this class.

FIGURE 6-14 **Main program to test the label generator**

```cpp
int main() {
   LabelGenerator figureNumbers("Figure ", 1);
   LabelGenerator pointNumbers("P", 0);
   cout << "Figure numbers: ";
   for (int i = 0; i < 3; i++) {
      if (i > 0) cout << ", ";
      cout << figureNumbers.nextLabel();
   }
   cout << endl << "Point numbers:   ";
   for (int i = 0; i < 5; i++) {
      if (i > 0) cout << ", ";
      cout << pointNumbers.nextLabel();
   }
   cout << endl << "More figures:    ";
   for (int i = 0; i < 3; i++) {
      if (i > 0) cout << ", ";
      cout << figureNumbers.nextLabel();
   }
   cout << endl;
   return 0;
}
```

8. The **Rational** class presented in the text defines the operators **+**, **−**, *****, **/** but needs several other operators for completeness. Add the following operators to both the interface and implementation:

    -   The relational operators **==**, **!=**, **<**, **<=**, **>**, and **>=**

    -   The shorthand assignment operators **+=**, **−=**, ***=**, and **/=**

    -   The **++** and **−−** operators in both their prefix and suffix forms

9. Reimplement the RPN calculator from Figure 5-4 so that it performs its internal calculations using rational instead of floating-point numbers. For example, your program should be able to produce the following sample run (which demonstrates that rational arithmetic is always exact):

```
RationalRPNCalculator
RPN Calculator Simulation (type H for help)
> 1
> 2
> /
1/2
> 1
> 3
> /
1/3
> 1
> 6
> /
1/6
> +
1/2
> +
1
> Q
```

10. Write a program that checks the spelling of all words in a file. Your program should use the **TokenScanner** class to read tokens from an input file and then look up each word in the lexicon stored in the file **EnglishWords.dat** introduced in Chapter 5. If the word does not appear in the lexicon, your program should print a message to that effect. If, for example, you ran the program on a file containing the text of this paragraph, the **SpellCheck** program would produce the following output:

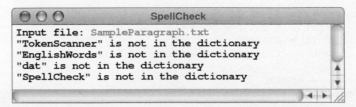

```
SpellCheck
Input file: SampleParagraph.txt
"TokenScanner" is not in the dictionary
"EnglishWords" is not in the dictionary
"dat" is not in the dictionary
"SpellCheck" is not in the dictionary
```

11. Write a program that implements a simple arithmetic calculator. Input to the calculator consists of lines composed of numbers (either integers or reals) combined together using the arithmetic operators +, -, *, and /. For each line of input, your program should display the result of applying the operators from left to right. You should use the token scanner to read the terms and operators and set up the scanner so that it ignores any whitespace characters. Your program should exit when the user enters a blank line. A sample run of your program might look like this:

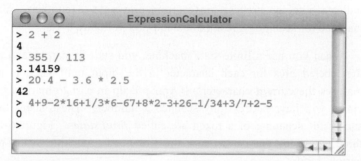

The last line in this sample run is the arithmetic problem the Mathemagician gives to Milo in Norton Juster's children's story, *The Phantom Tollbooth*.

12. Extend the program you wrote for the preceding exercise so that the terms in the expressions can also be variable names assigned earlier in the session by entering simple assignment statements as shown in the following sample run:

```
●  ○  ○             ExpressionCalculator
> pi = 3.1415926535
> r = 1.5
> area = pi * r * r
> area
7.06858
>
```

13. Implement the **saveToken** method for the **TokenScanner** class. This method saves the specified token so that subsequent calls to **nextToken** return the saved token without consuming any additional characters from the input. Your implementation should allow clients to save multiple tokens, which are then returned so that the last token saved is the first token returned.

14. Implement the **scanStrings** method for the **TokenScanner** class. When **scanStrings** is in effect, the token scanner should return quoted strings as single tokens. The strings may use either single or double quotation marks and should include the quotation marks in the string that **nextToken** returns.

15. Implement the **scanNumbers** method for the **TokenScanner** class, which causes the token scanner to read any valid C++ number as a single token. The difficult part of this extension lies in understanding the rules for what constitutes a valid numeric string and then finding a way to implement those rules efficiently. The easiest way to specify those rules is in a form that computer scientists call a *finite-state machine,* which is usually represented diagrammatically as a collection of circles representing the possible states of the machine. The circles are then connected by a set of labeled arcs that indicate how the process moves from one state to another. A finite-state machine for scanning a real number appears in Figure 6-15.

When you use a finite-state machine, you start in state s_0 and then follow the labeled arcs for each character in the input until there is no arc that matches the current character. If you end up in a state marked by a double circle, you have successfully scanned a number. These states that indicate successful scanning of a token are called *final states.* Figure 6-15 includes three examples that show how the finite-state machine scans numbers of various kinds.

The easiest way to write the code that scans a token when **scanNumbers** is in effect is to simulate the operation of the finite-state machine. Your code should keep track of the current state and then go through the input one character at a time. Each character will either signal the end of the number or send the machine into a new state.

FIGURE 6-15   Finite-state machine for scanning numbers

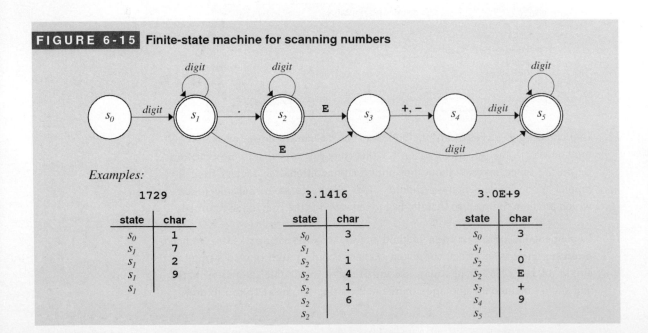

Examples:

1729			3.1416			3.0E+9	
state	char		state	char		state	char
s_0	1		s_0	3		s_0	3
s_1	7		s_1	.		s_1	.
s_1	2		s_2	1		s_2	0
s_1	9		s_2	4		s_2	E
s_1			s_2	1		s_3	+
			s_2	6		s_4	9
			s_2			s_5	

Chapter 7
Introduction to Recursion

And often enough, our faith beforehand in a certain result is the only thing that makes the result come true.

— William James, *The Will to Believe,* 1897

Most algorithmic strategies used to solve programming problems have counterparts outside the domain of computing. When you perform a task repeatedly, you are using iteration. When you make a decision, you exercise conditional control. Because these operations are familiar, most people learn to use the control statements `for`, `while`, and `if` with relatively little trouble.

Before you can solve many sophisticated programming tasks, however, you will have to learn to use a powerful problem-solving strategy that has few direct counterparts in the real world. That strategy, called *recursion,* is defined as any solution technique in which large problems are solved by reducing them to smaller problems *of the same form.* The italicized phrase is crucial to the definition, which otherwise describes the basic strategy of stepwise refinement. Both strategies involve decomposition. What makes recursion special is that the subproblems in a recursive solution have the same form as the original problem.

If you are like most beginning programmers, the idea of breaking a problem down into subproblems of the same form does not make much sense when you first hear it. Unlike repetition or conditional testing, recursion is not a concept that comes up in day-to-day life. Because it is unfamiliar, learning how to use recursion can be difficult. To do so, you must develop the intuition necessary to make recursion seem as natural as all the other control structures. For most students of programming, reaching that level of understanding takes considerable time and practice. Even so, learning to use recursion is definitely worth the effort. As a problem-solving tool, recursion is so powerful that it at times seems almost magical. In addition, using recursion often makes it possible to write complex programs in simple and profoundly elegant ways.

7.1 A simple example of recursion

To gain a better sense of what recursion is, let's imagine that you have been appointed as the funding coordinator for a large charitable organization that is long on volunteers and short on cash. Your job is to raise $1,000,000 in contributions so the organization can meet its expenses.

If you know someone who is willing to write a check for the entire $1,000,000, your job is easy. On the other hand, you may not be lucky enough to have friends who are generous millionaires. In that case, you must raise the $1,000,000 in smaller amounts. If the average contribution to your organization is $100, you might choose a different tack: call 10,000 friends and ask each of them for $100. But then again, you probably don't have 10,000 friends. So what can you do?

As is often the case when you are faced with a task that exceeds your own capacity, the answer lies in delegating part of the work to others. Your organization has a reasonable supply of volunteers. If you could find 10 dedicated supporters in different parts of the country and appoint them as regional coordinators, each of those 10 people could then take responsibility for raising $100,000.

Raising $100,000 is simpler than raising $1,000,000, but it hardly qualifies as easy. What should your regional coordinators do? If they adopt the same strategy, they will in turn delegate parts of the job. If they each recruit 10 fundraising volunteers, those people will only have to raise $10,000 each. The delegation process can continue until the volunteers are able to raise the money on their own; because the average contribution is $100, the volunteer fundraisers can probably raise $100 from a single donor, which eliminates the need for further delegation.

If you express this fundraising strategy in pseudocode, it has the following structure:

```
void collectContributions(int n) {
    if (n <= 100) {
        Collect the money from a single donor.
    } else {
        Find 10 volunteers.
        Get each volunteer to collect n/10 dollars.
        Combine the money raised by the volunteers.
    }
}
```

The most important thing to notice about this pseudocode translation is that the line

> Get each volunteer to collect **n/10** dollars.

is simply the original problem reproduced at a smaller scale. The basic character of the task—raise n dollars—remains exactly the same; the only difference is that n has a smaller value. Moreover, because the problem is the same, you can solve it by calling the original function. Thus, the preceding line of pseudocode would eventually be replaced with the following line:

```
collectContributions(n / 10);
```

It's important to note that the `collectContributions` function ends up calling itself if the contribution level is greater than $100. In the context of programming, having a function call itself is the defining characteristic of recursion.

The structure of the `collectContributions` function is typical of recursive functions. In general, the body of a recursive function has the following form:

```
if (test for simple case) {
    Compute a simple solution without using recursion.
} else {
    Break the problem down into subproblems of the same form.
    Solve each of the subproblems by calling this function recursively.
    Reassemble the subproblem solutions into a solution for the whole.
}
```

This structure provides a template for writing recursive functions and is therefore called the **recursive paradigm.**   You can apply this technique to programming problems as long as they meet the following conditions:

1. You must be able to identify **simple cases** for which the answer is easily determined.

2. You must be able to identify a **recursive decomposition** that allows you to break any complex instance of the problem into simpler problems of the same form.

The `collectContributions` example illustrates the power of recursion. As with any recursive technique, the original problem is solved by breaking it down into smaller subproblems that differ from the original only in their scale. Here, the original problem is to raise $1,000,000. At the first level of decomposition, each subproblem is to raise $100,000. These problems are then subdivided in turn to create smaller problems until the problems are simple enough to be solved immediately without recourse to further subdivision. Because the solution depends on dividing hard problems into simpler instances of the same problem, recursive solutions of this form are often called **divide-and-conquer** algorithms.

▉ 7.2 The factorial function

Although the `collectContributions` example illustrates the idea of recursion, it gives little insight into how recursion is used in practice, mostly because the steps that make up the solution, such as finding 10 volunteers and collecting money, are not easily represented in a C++ program. To get a practical sense of the nature of recursion, you need to consider problems that fit more easily into the programming domain.

For most people, the best way to understand recursion is to start with simple mathematical functions in which the recursive structure follows directly from the statement of the problem and is therefore easy to see. Of these, the most common is the factorial function—traditionally denoted in mathematics as $n!$—which is defined as the product of the integers between 1 and n. In C++, the equivalent problem is to write an implementation of a function with the prototype

```
int fact(int n);
```

that takes an integer **n** and returns its factorial.

As you probably know from your programming experience, it is easy to code the **fact** function using a **for** loop, as illustrated by the following implementation:

```
int fact(int n) {
    int result = 1;
    for (int i = 1; i <= n; i++) {
        result *= i;
    }
    return result;
}
```

This implementation uses a **for** loop to cycle through each of the integers between 1 and **n**. In the recursive implementation, this loop does not exist. The same effect is generated instead by the cascading recursive calls.

Implementations that use looping (typically by using **for** and **while** statements) are said to be *iterative.* Iterative and recursive strategies are often seen as opposites because they can be used to solve the same problem in rather different ways. These strategies, however, are not mutually exclusive. Recursive functions sometimes employ iteration internally. Although the examples in this chapter are purely recursive, you will see examples of this technique in Chapter 8.

The recursive formulation of fact

The iterative implementation of **fact**, however, does not take advantage of an important mathematical property of factorials. Each factorial is related to the factorial of the next smaller integer in the following way:

$$n! = n \times (n-1)!$$

Thus, 4! is $4 \times 3!$, 3! is $3 \times 2!$, and so on. To make sure that this process stops at some point, mathematicians define 0! to be 1. Thus, the conventional mathematical definition of the factorial function looks like this:

$$n! = \begin{cases} 1 & \text{if } n = 0 \\ n \times (n-1)! & \text{otherwise} \end{cases}$$

This definition is recursive, because it defines the factorial of n in terms of the factorial of $n - 1$. The new problem—finding the factorial of $n - 1$—has the same form as the original problem, which is the fundamental characteristic of recursion.

You can then use the same process to define $(n-1)!$ in terms of $(n-2)!$. Moreover, you can carry this process forward step by step until the solution is expressed in terms of 0!, which is equal to 1 by definition.

From your perspective as a programmer, the practical impact of the mathematical definition is that it provides a template for a recursive implementation. In C++, you can implement a function **fact** that computes the factorial of its argument as follows:

```
int fact(int n) {
   if (n == 0) {
      return 1;
   } else {
      return n * fact(n - 1);
   }
}
```

If **n** is 0, the result of **fact** is 1. If not, the implementation computes the result by calling **fact(n - 1)** and then multiplying the result by **n**. This implementation follows directly from the mathematical definition of the factorial function and has precisely the same recursive structure.

Tracing the recursive process

If you work from the mathematical definition, writing the recursive implementation of **fact** is straightforward. On the other hand, even though the definition is easy to write, the brevity of the solution may seem suspicious. When you are learning about recursion for the first time, the recursive implementation of **fact** seems to leave something out. Even though it clearly reflects the mathematical definition, the recursive formulation makes it hard to identify where the actual computational steps occur. When you call **fact**, for example, you want the computer to give you the answer. In the recursive implementation, all you see is a formula that transforms one call to **fact** into another one. Because the steps in that calculation are not explicit, it seems somewhat magical when the computer gets the right answer.

If you trace through the logic the computer uses to evaluate any function call, however, you discover that no magic is involved. When the computer evaluates a call to the recursive **fact** function, it goes through the same process it uses to evaluate any other function call. To visualize the process, suppose that you have executed the statement

```
cout << "fact(4) = " << fact(4) << endl;
```

as part of the function **main**. When **main** calls **fact**, the computer creates a new stack frame and copies the argument value into the formal parameter **n**. The frame for **fact** temporarily supersedes the frame for **main**, as shown in the following diagram:

```
int main() {
    int fact(int n) {
    ☞ if (n == 0) {
            return 1;
        } else {
            return n * fact(n - 1);
        }
    }                                    n
}                                        4
```

In the diagram, the code for the body of **fact** is shown inside the frame to make it easier to keep track of the current position in the program. In this diagram, the current position indicator appears at the beginning of the code because all function calls start at the first statement of the function body.

The computer now begins to evaluate the body of the function, starting with the **if** statement. Because **n** is not equal to 0, control proceeds to the **else** clause, where the program must evaluate and return the value of the expression

    n * fact(n - 1)

Evaluating this expression requires computing the value of **fact(n - 1)**, which introduces a recursive call. When that call returns, all the program has to do is to multiply the result by **n**. The current state of the computation can therefore be diagrammed as follows:

```
int main() {
    int fact(int n) {
        if (n == 0) {
            return 1;
        } else {
            return n * fact(n - 1);
        }                              n
    }                  ↳ ?            4
}
```

As soon as the call to **fact(n - 1)** returns, the result is substituted for the expression underlined in the diagram, which allows computation to proceed.

The next step in the computation is to evaluate the call to **fact(n - 1)**, beginning with the argument expression. Because the current value of **n** is 4, the argument expression **n - 1** has the value 3. The computer then creates a new frame for **fact** in which the formal parameter is initialized to this value. Thus, the next frame looks like this:

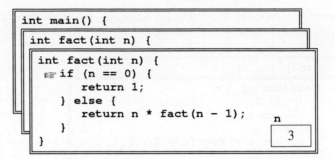

```
int main() {
  int fact(int n) {
    int fact(int n) {
    ☞ if (n == 0) {
          return 1;
        } else {
          return n * fact(n - 1);
        }                              n
    }
  }                                   3
}
```

There are now two frames labeled **fact**. In the most recent one, the computer is just starting to calculate **fact(3)**. This new frame hides the previous frame for **fact(4)**, which will not reappear until the **fact(3)** computation is complete.

Computing **fact(3)** again begins by testing the value of **n**. Since **n** is still not 0, the **else** clause instructs the computer to evaluate **fact(n - 1)**. As before, this process requires the creation of a new stack frame, as shown:

```
int main() {
  int fact(int n) {
    int fact(int n) {
      int fact(int n) {
      ☞ if (n == 0) {
            return 1;
          } else {
            return n * fact(n - 1);
          }                              n
      }
    }                                   2
  }
}
```

Following the same logic, the program must now call **fact(1)**, which in turn calls **fact(0)**, creating two new stack frames, as follows:

```
int main() {
  int fact(int n) {
    int fact(int n) {
      int fact(int n) {
        int fact(int n) {
          int fact(int n) {
          ☞ if (n == 0) {
                return 1;
              } else {
                return n * fact(n - 1);
              }                              n
          }
        }                                   0
}
```

At this point, however, the situation changes. Because the value of **n** is 0, the function can return its result immediately by executing the statement

```
return 1;
```

The value 1 is returned to the calling frame, which resumes its position on top of the stack, as shown:

```
int main() {
  int fact(int n) {
    int fact(int n) {
      int fact(int n) {
        int fact(int n) {
          if (n == 0) {
            return 1;
          } else {
            return n * fact(n - 1);       n
          }                          └─ 1      ┌───┐
        }                                      │ 1 │
      }                                        └───┘
```

From this point, the computation proceeds back through each of the recursive calls, completing the calculation of the return value at each level. In this frame, for example, the call to **fact(n - 1)** can be replaced by the value 1, as shown in the diagram for the stack frame. In this stack frame, **n** has the value 1, so the result of this call is simply 1. This result gets propagated back to its caller, which is represented by the top frame in the following diagram:

```
int main() {
  int fact(int n) {
    int fact(int n) {
      int fact(int n) {
        if (n == 0) {
          return 1;
        } else {
          return n * fact(n - 1);       n
        }                          └─ 1      ┌───┐
      }                                      │ 2 │
    }                                        └───┘
```

Because **n** is now 2, evaluating the **return** statement causes the value 2 to be passed back to the previous level, as follows:

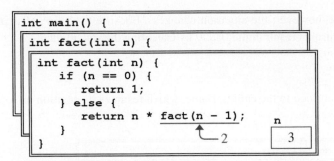

At this stage, the program returns 3×2 to the previous level, so that the frame for the initial call to **fact** looks like this:

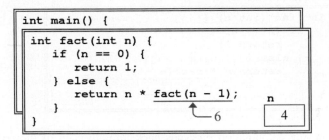

The final step in the calculation process consists of calculating 4×6 and returning the value 24 to the main program.

The recursive leap of faith

The point of including the complete trace of the **fact(4)** computation is to convince you that the computer treats recursive functions just like all other functions. When you are faced with a recursive function, you can—at least in theory—mimic the operation of the computer and figure out what it will do. By drawing all the frames and keeping track of all the variables, you can duplicate the entire operation and come up with the answer. If you do so, however, you will usually find that the complexity of the process ends up making the computation much harder to follow.

Whenever you try to understand a recursive program, it is useful to put the underlying details aside and focus instead on a single level of the operation. At that level, you are allowed to assume that any recursive call automatically gets the right answer as long as the arguments to that call are in some sense simpler than the original arguments. This psychological strategy—assuming that any simpler recursive call will work correctly—is called the ***recursive leap of faith.*** Learning to apply this strategy is essential to using recursion in practical applications.

As an example, consider what happens when this implementation is used to compute `fact(n)` with **n** equal to 4. To do so, the recursive implementation must compute the value of the expression

```
n * fact(n - 1)
```

By substituting the current value of **n** into the expression, you know that the result is

```
4 * fact(3)
```

Stop right there. Computing `fact(3)` is simpler than computing `fact(4)`. Because it is simpler, the recursive leap of faith allows you to assume that it works. Thus, you should assume that the call to `fact(3)` will correctly compute the value of 3!, which is 3 × 2 × 1, or 6. The result of calling `fact(4)` is therefore 4 × 6, or 24.

As you look at the examples in the rest of this chapter, try to focus on the big picture instead of the details. Once you have made the recursive decomposition and identified the simple cases, be satisfied that the computer can handle the rest.

7.3 The Fibonacci function

In a mathematical treatise entitled *Liber Abbaci* published in 1202, the Italian mathematician Leonardo Fibonacci proposed a problem that has had a wide influence on many fields, including computer science. The problem was phrased as an exercise in population biology—a field that has become increasingly important in recent years. Fibonacci's problem concerns how the population of rabbits would grow from generation to generation if the rabbits reproduced according to the following, admittedly fanciful, rules:

- Each pair of fertile rabbits produces a new pair of offspring each month.
- Rabbits become fertile in their second month of life.
- Old rabbits never die.

If a pair of newborn rabbits is introduced in January, how many pairs of rabbits are there at the end of the year?

You can solve Fibonacci's problem simply by keeping a count of the rabbits at each month during the year. At the beginning of January, there are no rabbits, since the first pair is introduced sometime in that month, which leaves one pair of rabbits on February 1st. Since the initial pair of rabbits is newborn, they are not yet fertile in February, which means that the only rabbits on March 1st are the original pair of rabbits. In March, however, the original pair is now of reproductive age, which means that a new pair of rabbits is born. The new pair increases the colony's population—counting by pairs—to two on April 1st. In April, the original pair goes right on reproducing, but the rabbits born in March are as yet too young. Thus, there are three pairs of rabbits at the beginning of May. From here on, with more and more rabbits becoming fertile each month, the rabbit population begins to grow more quickly.

Computing terms in the Fibonacci sequence

At this point, it is useful to record the population data so far as a sequence of terms, indicated by the subscripted value t_i, each of which shows the number of rabbit pairs at the beginning of the ith month from the start of the experiment on January 1st. The sequence itself is called the ***Fibonacci sequence*** and begins with the following terms, which represent the results of our calculation so far:

t_0	t_1	t_2	t_3	t_4
0	1	1	2	3

You can simplify the computation of further terms in this sequence by making an important observation. Because in this problem pairs of rabbits never die, all the rabbits that were around in the previous month are still around. Moreover, every pair of fertile rabbits has produced a new pair. The number of fertile rabbit pairs capable of reproduction is simply the number of rabbits that were alive in the month before the previous one. The net effect is that each new term in the sequence must simply be the sum of the preceding two. Thus, the next several terms in the Fibonacci sequence look like this:

t_0	t_1	t_2	t_3	t_4	t_5	t_6	t_7	t_8	t_9	t_{10}	t_{11}	t_{12}
0	1	1	2	3	5	8	13	21	34	55	89	144

The number of rabbit pairs at the end of the year is therefore 144.

From a programming perspective, it helps to express the rule for generating new terms in the following more mathematical form:

$$t_n = t_{n-1} + t_{n-2}$$

An expression of this type, in which each element of a sequence is defined in terms of earlier elements, is called a ***recurrence relation.***

The recurrence relation alone is not sufficient to define the Fibonacci sequence. Although the formula makes it easy to calculate new terms in the sequence, the process has to start somewhere. In order to apply the formula, you need to have at least two terms already available, which means that the first two terms in the sequence—t_0 and t_1—must be defined explicitly. The complete specification of the terms in the Fibonacci sequence is therefore

$$t_n = \begin{cases} n & \text{if } n \text{ is 0 or 1} \\ t_{n-1} + t_{n-2} & \text{otherwise} \end{cases}$$

This mathematical formulation is an ideal model for a recursive implementation of a function `fib(n)` that computes the nth term in the Fibonacci sequence. All you need to do is plug the simple cases and the recurrence relation into the standard recursive paradigm. The recursive implementation of `fib(n)` is shown in Figure 7-1, which also includes a test program that displays the terms in the Fibonacci sequence between two specified indices.

Gaining confidence in the recursive implementation

Now that you have a recursive implementation of the function `fib`, how can you go about convincing yourself that it works? You can always begin by tracing through the logic. Consider, for example, what happens if you call `fib(5)`. Because this is not one of the simple cases enumerated in the `if` statement, the implementation computes the result by evaluating the line

```
    return fib(n - 1) + fib(n - 2);
```

which in this case is equivalent to

```
    return fib(4) + fib(3);
```

At this point, the computer calculates the result of `fib(4)`, adds that to the result of calling `fib(3)`, and returns the sum as the value of `fib(5)`.

But how does the computer go about evaluating `fib(4)` and `fib(3)`? The answer, of course, is that it uses precisely the same strategy. The essence of recursion is to break problems down into simpler ones that can be solved by calls to exactly the same function. Those calls get broken down into simpler ones, which in turn get broken down into even simpler ones, until at last the simple cases are reached.

On the other hand, it is best to regard this entire mechanism as irrelevant detail. Instead, just remember the recursive leap of faith. Your job at this level is to understand how the call to `fib(5)` works. In the course of walking though the execution of that function, you have managed to transform the problem into computing the sum of `fib(4)` and `fib(3)`. Because the argument values are

FIGURE 7-1 Program to list the Fibonacci series

```cpp
/*
 * File: Fib.cpp
 * -------------
 * This program lists the terms in the Fibonacci sequence with
 * indices ranging from MIN_INDEX to MAX_INDEX.
 */

#include <iostream>
#include <iomanip>
using namespace std;

/* Constants */

const int MIN_INDEX  = 0;    /* Index of first term to generate */
const int MAX_INDEX = 20;    /* Index of last term to generate  */

/* Function prototypes */

int fib(int n);

/* Main program */

int main() {
   cout << "This program lists the Fibonacci sequence." << endl;
   for (int i = MIN_INDEX; i <= MAX_INDEX; i++) {
      if (i < 10) cout << " ";
      cout << "fib(" << i << ")";
      cout << " = " << setw(4) << fib(i) << endl;
   }
   return 0;
}

/*
 * Function: fib
 * Usage: int f = fib(n);
 * ----------------------
 * Returns the nth term in the Fibonacci sequence using the
 * following recursive formulation:
 *
 *    fib(0) = 0
 *    fib(1) = 1
 *    fib(n) = fib(n - 1) + fib(n - 2)
 */

int fib(int n) {
   if (n < 2) {
      return n;
   } else {
      return fib(n - 1) + fib(n - 2);
   }
}
```

smaller, each of these calls represents a simpler case. Applying the recursive leap of faith, you can assume that the program correctly computes each of these values, without going through all the steps yourself. For the purposes of validating the recursive strategy, you can just look the answers up in the table: `fib(4)` is 3 and `fib(3)` is 2. The result of calling `fib(5)` is therefore $3 + 2$, or 5, which is indeed the correct answer. Case closed. You don't need to see all the details, which are best left to the computer.

Efficiency of the recursive implementation

If you do decide to go through the details of the evaluation of the call to `fib(5)`, however, you will quickly discover that the calculation is extremely inefficient. The recursive decomposition makes many redundant calls, in which the computer ends up calculating the same term in the Fibonacci sequence several times. This situation is illustrated in Figure 7-2, which shows all the recursive calls required in the calculation of `fib(5)`. As you can see from the diagram, the program ends up making one call to `fib(4)`, two calls to `fib(3)`, three calls to `fib(2)`, five calls to `fib(1)`, and three calls to `fib(0)`. Given that the Fibonacci function can be implemented efficiently using iteration, the explosion of steps required by the recursive implementation is more than a little disturbing.

FIGURE 7-2 **Steps in the calculation of `fib(5)`**

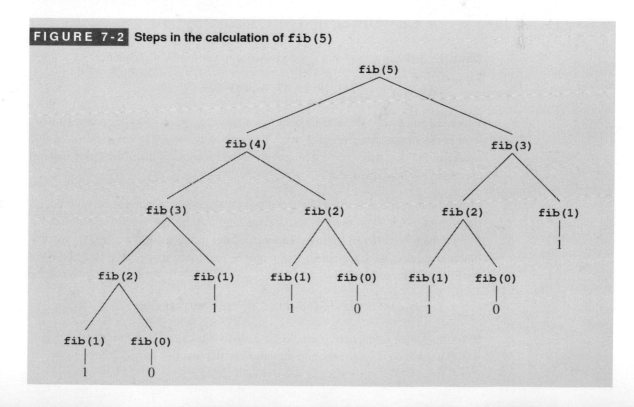

Recursion is not to blame

On discovering that the implementation of `fib(n)` given in Figure 7-1 is highly inefficient, many people are tempted to point their finger at recursion as the culprit. The problem in the Fibonacci example, however, has nothing to do with recursion *per se* but rather with the way in which recursion is used. By adopting a different strategy, it is possible to write a recursive implementation of the `fib` function in which the large-scale inefficiencies revealed in Figure 7-2 disappear completely.

As is often the case when using recursion, the key to finding a more efficient solution lies in adopting a more general approach. The Fibonacci sequence is not the only sequence whose terms are defined by the recurrence relation

$$t_n = t_{n-1} + t_{n-2}$$

Depending on how you choose the first two terms, you can generate many different sequences. The traditional Fibonacci sequence

$$0, 1, 1, 2, 3, 5, 8, 13, 21, 34, 55, 89, 144, \ldots$$

comes from defining $t_0 = 0$ and $t_1 = 1$. If, for example, you defined $t_0 = 3$ and $t_1 = 7$, you would get this sequence instead:

$$3, 7, 10, 17, 27, 44, 71, 115, 186, 301, 487, 788, 1275, \ldots$$

Similarly, defining $t_0 = -1$ and $t_1 = 2$ gives rise to the following sequence:

$$-1, 2, 1, 3, 4, 7, 11, 18, 29, 47, 76, 123, 199, \ldots$$

These sequences all use the same recurrence relation, which specifies that each new term is the sum of the preceding two. The only way the sequences differ is in the choice of the first two terms. As a general class, sequences that follow this pattern are called ***additive sequences.***

This concept of an additive sequence makes it possible to convert the problem of finding the nth term in the Fibonacci sequence into the more general problem of finding the nth term in an additive sequence whose initial terms are t_0 and t_1. Such a function requires three arguments and might be expressed in C++ as a function with the following prototype:

```
int additiveSequence(int n, int t0, int t1);
```

If you had such a function, it would be easy to implement `fib` using it. All you would need to do is supply the correct values of the first two terms, as follows:

```
int fib(int n) {
    return additiveSequence(n, 0, 1);
}
```

The body consists of a single line of code that does nothing but call another function, passing along a few extra arguments. Functions of this sort, which simply return the result of another function, often after transforming the arguments in some way, are called **wrapper** functions. Wrapper functions are extremely common in recursive programming. In most cases, a wrapper function is used—as it is here—to supply additional arguments to a subsidiary function that solves a more general problem.

From this point, the one remaining task is to implement **additiveSequence**. If you think about this more general problem for a few minutes, you will discover that additive sequences have an interesting recursive character of their own. The simple case for the recursion consists of the terms t_0 and t_1, whose values are part of the definition of the sequence. In the C++ implementation, the values of these terms are passed as arguments. If you need to compute t_0, for example, all you have to do is return the argument **t0**.

But what if you are asked to find a term further down in the sequence? Suppose, for example, that you want to find t_6 in the additive sequence whose initial terms are 3 and 7. By looking at the list of terms in the sequence

t_0	t_1	t_2	t_3	t_4	t_5	t_6	t_7	t_8	t_9	
3	7	10	17	27	44	71	115	186	301	...

you can see that the correct value is 71. The interesting question, however, is how you can use recursion to determine this result.

The key insight you need to discover is that the nth term in any additive sequence is simply the $n-1^{st}$ term in the additive sequence that begins one step further along. For example, t_6 in the sequence shown in the most recent example is simply t_5 in the additive sequence

t_0	t_1	t_2	t_3	t_4	t_5	t_6	t_7	t_8	
7	10	17	27	44	71	115	186	301	...

that begins with 7 and 10.

This insight makes it possible to implement the function **additiveSequence** as follows:

```
int additiveSequence(int n, int t0, int t1) {
    if (n == 0) return t0;
    if (n == 1) return t1;
    return additiveSequence(n - 1, t1, t0 + t1);
}
```

If you trace through the steps in the calculation of `fib(5)` using this technique, you will discover that the calculation involves none of the redundant computation that plagued the earlier recursive formulation. The steps lead directly to the solution, as shown in the following diagram:

```
fib(5)
  = additiveSequence(5, 0, 1)
    = additiveSequence(4, 1, 1)
      = additiveSequence(3, 1, 2)
        = additiveSequence(2, 2, 3)
          = additiveSequence(1, 3, 5)
            = 5
```

Even though the new implementation is entirely recursive, it is comparable in efficiency to the traditional iterative version of the Fibonacci function. In fact, it is possible to use more sophisticated mathematics to write an entirely recursive implementation of `fib(n)` that is considerably more efficient than the iterative strategy. You will have a chance to code this implementation on your own in the exercises for Chapter 10.

7.4 Checking palindromes

Although the factorial and Fibonacci functions provide excellent examples of how recursive functions work, they are mathematical in nature and may therefore convey the incorrect impression that recursion is applicable only to mathematical functions. In fact, you can apply recursion to any problem that can be decomposed into simpler problems of the same form. It is therefore useful to consider a few more examples of recursion, focusing on those that are less mathematical in nature. This section, for example, illustrates the use of recursion in a simple string application.

A *palindrome* is a string that reads identically backward and forward, such as `"level"` or `"noon"`. Although it is easy to check whether a string is a palindrome by iterating through its characters, palindromes can also be defined recursively. The insight you need is that any palindrome longer than a single character must contain a shorter palindrome in its interior. For example, the string `"level"` consists of the palindrome `"eve"` with an `"l"` at each end. Thus, to check whether a string is a palindrome—assuming the string is sufficiently long that it does not constitute a simple case—all you need to do is

1. Check to see that the first and last characters are the same.
2. Check to see whether the substring generated by removing the first and last characters is itself a palindrome.

If both conditions apply, the string is a palindrome.

The only other question you must consider before writing a recursive solution to the palindrome problem is what the simple cases are. Clearly, any single-character string is a palindrome because reversing a one-character string has no effect. The one-character string therefore represents a simple case, but it is not the only one. The empty string—which contains no characters at all—is also a palindrome, and any recursive solution must operate correctly in this case as well.

Figure 7-3 contains a recursive implementation of the `isPalindrome` function, which returns `true` if and only if its argument is a palindrome. The function begins by checking to see whether the length of the string is less than 2. If it is, the string is certainly a palindrome. If not, the function checks to make sure that the string meets both of the necessary criteria.

Unfortunately, the implementation shown in Figure 7-3 is inefficient, even though the recursive decomposition is easy to follow. You can improve the performance of `isPalindrome` by making the following changes:

FIGURE 7-3 Program to check for palindromes

```
/*
 * Function: isPalindrome
 * Usage: if (isPalindrome(str)) . . .
 * --------------------------------------
 * Returns true if str is a palindrome, which is a string that
 * reads the same backwards and forwards.  This implementation
 * uses the recursive insight that all strings of length 0 or 1
 * are palindromes and that longer strings are palindromes if
 * their first and last characters match and the remaining substring
 * is a palindrome.
 */

bool isPalindrome(string str) {
   int len = str.length();
   if (len <= 1) {
      return true;
   } else {
      return str[0] == str[len - 1] && isPalindrome(str.substr(1, len - 2));
   }
}
```

- *Calculate the length of the argument only once.* The original implementation of **isPalindrome** calculates the length of the string at every level of the recursive decomposition. It is more efficient to call the **length** method once and then pass that information down through the chain of recursive calls.

- *Don't make a substring on each call.* The other source of inefficiency in the first version of **isPalindrome** is the repeated **substr** calls that remove the first and last characters. You can avoid the calls to **substr** entirely by passing indices to keep track of the positions at which the desired substring begins and ends.

Each of these changes requires the recursive function to take additional arguments. Figure 7-4 shows a revised version of **isPalindrome** implemented as a wrapper function that calls the helper function **isSubstringPalindrome** to do the actual work. The **isSubstringPalindrome** function takes the additional arguments **p1** and **p2**, which specify the indices between which the checking occurs.

FIGURE 7-4 **More efficient implementation of isPalindrome**

```
/*
 * Function: isPalindrome
 * Usage: if (isPalindrome(str)) . . .
 * ------------------------------------
 * Returns true if str is a palindrome, which is a string that reads the
 * same backwards and forwards.  This level of the implementation is
 * simply a wrapper for isSubstringPalindrome, which does the real work.
 */

bool isPalindrome(string str) {
   return isSubstringPalindrome(str, 0, str.length() - 1);
}

/*
 * Function: isSubstringPalindrome
 * Usage: if (isSubstringPalindrome(str, p1, p2)) . . .
 * ----------------------------------------------------
 * Returns true if the characters in str from p1 to p2, inclusive, form
 * a palindrome.  This implementation uses the recursive insight that
 * all strings of length 0 or 1 are palindromes (the simple cases) and
 * that longer strings are palindromes only if their first and last
 * characters match and the remaining substring is a palindrome.
 */

bool isSubstringPalindrome(string str, int p1, int p2) {
   if (p1 >= p2) {
      return true;
   } else {
      return str[p1] == str[p2] && isSubstringPalindrome(str, p1 + 1, p2 - 1);
   }
}
```

7.5 The binary search algorithm

When you work with sequences of values stored in a vector, one of the common operations consists of searching that vector for a particular element. For example, if you work frequently with string vectors, it is useful to have a function

```
int findInVector(string key, Vector<string> & vec);
```

that searches through each of the elements of **vec**, looking for an element whose value is equal to **key**. If a matching value is found, **findInVector** returns the index at which it appears. If no such value exists, the function returns –1.

If you have no specific knowledge about the order of elements within the vector, the implementation of **findInVector** must simply check each of the elements in turn until it either finds a match or runs out of elements. This strategy is called the *linear-search algorithm,* which can be time-consuming if the vectors are large. On the other hand, if you know that the elements of the vector are arranged in alphabetical order, you can adopt a much more efficient approach. All you have to do is divide the vector in half and compare the key you're trying to find against the element closest to the middle of the vector, using the order defined by the ASCII character codes, which is called *lexicographic order.* If the key you're looking for precedes the middle element, then the key—if it exists at all—must be in the first half. Conversely, if the key follows the middle element in lexicographic order, you only need to look at the elements in the second half. This strategy is called the *binary-search algorithm.* Because binary search makes it possible for you to discard half the possible elements at each step in the process, it turns out to be much more efficient than linear search for sorted vectors.

The binary-search algorithm—which appears in Figure 7-5—is also a perfect example of the divide-and-conquer strategy. It should therefore not be particularly surprising that binary search has a natural recursive implementation. Note that the function **findInSortedVector** is implemented as a wrapper, leaving the real work to the recursive function **binarySearch**, which takes two additional arguments—the indices **p1** and **p2**—to limit the range of the search.

The simple cases for **binarySearch** are

1. *There are no elements in the active part of the vector.* This condition is marked by the fact that the index **p1** is greater than the index **p2**, which means that there are no elements left to search.

2. *The middle element matches the specified key.* Since the key has just been found, **findInSortedVector** can simply return the index of that value.

FIGURE 7-5 **Divide-and-conquer implementation of binary search**

```
/*
 * Function: findInSortedVector
 * Usage: int index = findInSortedVector(key, vec);
 * -----------------------------------------------------
 * Searches for the specified key in the Vector<string> vec, which
 * must be sorted in lexicographic (character code) order.  If the
 * key is found, the function returns the index in the vector at
 * which that key appears. (If the key appears more than once in
 * the vector, any of the matching indices may be returned).  If the
 * key does not exist in the vector, the function returns -1.  This
 * implementation is simply a wrapper function; all of the real work
 * is done by the more general binarySearch function.
 */

int findInSortedVector(string key, Vector<string> & vec) {
   return binarySearch(key, vec, 0, vec.size() - 1);
}

/*
 * Function: binarySearch
 * Usage: int index = binarySearch(key, vec, p1, p2);
 * -----------------------------------------------------
 * Searches for the specified key in the Vector<string> vec, looking
 * only at indices between p1 and p2, inclusive.  The function returns
 * the index of a matching element, or -1 if no match is found.
 */

int binarySearch(string key, Vector<string> & vec, int p1, int p2) {
   if (p1 > p2) return -1;
   int mid = (p1 + p2) / 2;
   if (key == vec[mid]) return mid;
   if (key < vec[mid]) {
      return binarySearch(key, vec, p1, mid - 1);
   } else {
      return binarySearch(key, vec, mid + 1, p2);
   }
}
```

If neither of these cases applies, the implementation can simplify the problem by choosing the appropriate half of the vector and calling itself recursively with an updated set of search limits.

7.6 Mutual recursion

In each of the examples considered so far, the recursive functions have called themselves directly, in the sense that the body of the function contains a call to itself. Although most of the recursive functions you encounter are likely to adhere to this style, the definition of recursion is actually somewhat broader. To be recursive, a function must call itself at some point during its evaluation. If a function is subdivided into subsidiary functions, the recursive call can occur at a deeper level of nesting. For example, if a function *f* calls a function *g*, which in turn calls *f*, those function calls are still considered to be recursive. Because the functions *f* and *g* call each other, this type of recursion is called ***mutual recursion.***

As a simple example, it turns out to be easy—although wildly inefficient—to use recursion to test whether a number is even or odd. The code in Figure 7-6, for example, implements the **isEven** and **isOdd** functions, by taking advantage of the following informal definition:

- A number is *even* if its predecessor is odd.
- A number is *odd* if is not even.
- The number 0 is even by definition.

Even though these rules seem simplistic, they form the basis of an effective strategy for distinguishing odd and even numbers, as long as the numbers are nonnegative.

FIGURE 7-6 **Mutually recursive definitions of isEven and isOdd**

```
/*
 * Function: isOdd
 * Usage: if (isOdd(n)) . . .
 * ---------------------------
 * Returns true if the unsigned number n is odd.  A number is odd
 * if it is not even.
 */

bool isOdd(unsigned int n) {
   return !isEven(n);
}

/*
 * Function: isEven
 * Usage: if (isEven(n)) . . .
 * ---------------------------
 * Returns true if the unsigned number n is even.  A number is even
 * either (1) if it is zero or (2) if its predecessor is odd.
 */

bool isEven(unsigned int n) {
   if (n == 0) {
      return true;
   } else {
      return isOdd(n - 1);
   }
}
```

The code in Figure 7-6 ensures that condition by having `isEven` and `isOdd` take arguments of type `unsigned`, which C++ uses to represent an integer that can never be less than zero.

7.7 Thinking recursively

For most people, recursion is not an easy concept to grasp. Learning to use it effectively requires considerable practice and forces you to approach problems in entirely new ways. The key to success lies in developing the right frame of mind—in learning how to think recursively. The remainder of this chapter is designed to help you achieve that goal.

Maintaining a holistic perspective

When you are learning to program, I think it helps enormously to keep in mind the philosophical concepts of holism and reductionism. Simply stated, **reductionism** is the belief that the whole of an object can be understood merely by understanding the parts that make it up. Its antithesis is **holism,** the position that the whole is often greater than the sum of its parts. As you learn about programming, it helps to be able to interleave these two perspectives, sometimes focusing on the behavior of a program as a whole, and at other times delving into the details of its execution. When you try to learn about recursion, however, this balance seems to change. Thinking recursively requires you to think holistically. In the recursive domain, reductionism is the enemy of understanding and almost always gets in the way.

To maintain the holistic perspective, you must become comfortable adopting the recursive leap of faith, which was introduced in its own section earlier in this chapter. Whenever you are writing a recursive program or trying to understand the behavior of one, you must get to the point where you ignore the details of the individual recursive calls. As long as you have chosen the right decomposition, identified the appropriate simple cases, and implemented your strategy correctly, those recursive calls will simply work. You don't need to think about them.

Unfortunately, until you have had extensive experience working with recursive functions, applying the recursive leap of faith does not come easily. The problem is that doing so requires to suspend your disbelief and make assumptions about the correctness of your programs that fly in the face of your experience. After all, when you write a program, the odds are good—even if you are an experienced programmer—that your program won't work the first time. In fact, it is quite likely that you have chosen the wrong decomposition, messed up the definition of the simple cases, or somehow gotten things muddled as you tried to implement your strategy. If you have done any of these things, your recursive calls won't work.

When things go wrong—as they inevitably will—you have to remember to look for the error in the right place. The problem lies somewhere in your recursive implementation, not in the recursive mechanism itself. If there is a problem, you should be able to find it by looking at a single level of the recursive hierarchy. Looking down through additional levels of recursive calls is not going to help. If the simple cases work and the recursive decomposition is correct, the subsidiary calls will work correctly. If they don't, the problem must lie in your formulation of the recursive decomposition.

Avoiding the common pitfalls

As you gain experience with recursion, the process of writing and debugging recursive programs will become more natural. At the beginning, however, finding out what you need to fix in a recursive program can be difficult. The following is a checklist that will help you identify the most common sources of error.

- *Does your recursive implementation begin by checking for simple cases?* Before you attempt to solve a problem by transforming it into a recursive subproblem, you must first check to see if the problem is so simple that such decomposition is unnecessary. In almost all cases, recursive functions begin with the keyword **if**. If your function doesn't, you should look carefully at your program and make sure that you know what you're doing.

- *Have you solved the simple cases correctly?* A surprising number of bugs in recursive programs arise from having incorrect solutions to the simple cases. If the simple cases are wrong, the recursive solutions to more complicated problems will inherit the same mistake. For example, if you had mistakenly defined **fact(0)** as 0 instead of 1, calling **fact** on any argument would end up returning 0.

- *Does your recursive decomposition make the problem simpler?* For recursion to work, the problems have to get simpler as you go along. More formally, there must be some *metric*—a standard of measurement that assigns a numeric difficulty rating to the problem—that gets smaller as the computation proceeds. For mathematical functions like **fact** and **fib**, the value of the integer argument serves as a metric. On each recursive call, the value of the argument gets smaller. For the **isPalindrome** function, the appropriate metric is the length of the argument string, because the string gets shorter on each recursive call. If the problem instances do not get simpler, the decomposition process will just keep making more and more calls, giving rise to the recursive analogue of the infinite loop, which is called *nonterminating recursion.*

- *Does the simplification process eventually reach the simple cases, or have you left out some of the possibilities?* A common source of error is failing to include simple case tests for all the cases that can arise as the result of the recursive decomposition. For example, in the `isPalindrome` implementation presented in Figure 7-3, it is critically important for the function to check the zero-character case as well as the one-character case, even if the client never intends to call `isPalindrome` on the empty string. As the recursive decomposition proceeds, the string arguments get shorter by two characters at each level of the recursive call. If the length of the original argument string is even, the recursive decomposition will never get to the one-character case.

- *Do the recursive calls in your function represent subproblems that are truly identical in form to the original?* When you use recursion to break down a problem, it is essential that the subproblems be of the same form. If the recursive calls change the nature of the problem or violate one of the initial assumptions, the entire process can break down. As several of the examples in this chapter illustrate, it is often useful to define the publicly exported function as a simple wrapper that calls a more general recursive function that is private to the implementation. Because the private function has a more general form, it is usually easier to decompose the original problem and still have it fit within the recursive structure.

- *When you apply the recursive leap of faith, do the solutions to the recursive subproblems provide a complete solution to the original problem?* Breaking a problem down into recursive subinstances is only part of the recursive process. Once you get the solutions, you must also be able to reassemble them to generate the complete solution. The way to check whether this process in fact generates the solution is to walk through the decomposition, religiously applying the recursive leap of faith. Work through all the steps in the current function call, but assume that every recursive call generates the correct answer. If following this process yields the right solution, your program should work.

Summary

This chapter has introduced the idea of *recursion,* a powerful programming strategy in which complex problems are broken down into simpler problems of the same form. The important points presented in this chapter include:

- Recursion is similar to stepwise refinement in that both strategies consist of breaking a problem down into simpler problems that are easier to solve. The distinguishing characteristic of recursion is that the simpler subproblems must have the same form as the original.

- To use recursion, you must be able to identify *simple cases* for which the answer is easily determined and a *recursive decomposition* that allows you to break any complex instance of the problem into simpler problems of the same type.

- In C++, recursive functions typically have the following paradigmatic form:

  ```
  if (test for simple case) {
      Compute a simple solution without using recursion.
  } else {
      Break the problem down into subproblems of the same form.
      Solve each of the subproblems by calling this function recursively.
      Reassemble the subproblem solutions into a solution for the whole.
  }
  ```

- Recursive functions are implemented using exactly the same mechanism as any other function call. Each call creates a new stack frame that contains the local variables for that call. Because the computer creates a separate stack frame for each function call, the local variables at each level of the recursive decomposition remain separate.

- Before you can use recursion effectively, you must learn to limit your analysis to a single level of the recursive decomposition and to rely on the correctness of all simpler recursive calls without tracing through the entire computation. Trusting these simpler calls to work correctly is called the *recursive leap of faith.*

- Mathematical functions often express their recursive nature in the form of a *recurrence relation,* in which each element of a sequence is defined in terms of earlier elements.

- Although some recursive functions may be less efficient than their iterative counterparts, recursion itself is not the problem. As is typical with all types of algorithms, some recursive strategies are more efficient than others.

- In order to ensure that a recursive decomposition produces subproblems that are identical in form to the original, it is often necessary to generalize the problem. As a result, it is often useful to implement the solution to a specific problem as a simple *wrapper* function whose only purpose is to call a subsidiary function that handles the more general case.

- Recursion need not consist of a single function that calls itself but may instead involve several functions that call each other in a cyclical pattern. Recursion that involves more than one function is called *mutual recursion.*

- You will be more successful at understanding recursive programs if you can maintain a holistic perspective rather than a reductionistic one.

Thinking about recursive problems in the right way does not come easily. Learning to use recursion effectively requires practice and more practice. For many students, mastering the concept takes years. But because recursion will turn out to be one of the most powerful techniques in your programming repertoire, that time will be well spent.

Review questions

1. Define the terms *recursive* and *iterative*. Is it possible for a function to employ both strategies?

2. What is the fundamental difference between recursion and traditional stepwise refinement?

3. In the pseudocode for the `collectContributions` function, the `if` statement looks like this:

    ```
    if (n <= 100)
    ```

    Why is it important to use the `<=` operator instead of simply checking whether `n` is exactly equal to 100?

4. What is the standard recursive paradigm?

5. What two properties must a problem have for recursion to make sense as a solution strategy?

6. Why is the term *divide and conquer* appropriate to recursive techniques?

7. What is meant by the *recursive leap of faith?* Why is this concept important to you as a programmer?

8. In the section entitled "Tracing the recursive process," the text goes through a long analysis of what happens internally when `fact(4)` is called. Using this section as a model, trace through the execution of `fib(3)`, sketching out each stack frame created in the process.

9. What is a *recurrence relation?*

10. Modify Fibonacci's rabbit problem by introducing the additional rule that rabbit pairs stop reproducing after giving birth to three litters. How does this assumption change the recurrence relation? What changes do you need to make in the simple cases?

11. How many times is `fib(1)` called when calculating `fib(n)` using the recursive implementation given in Figure 7-1?

12. What is a wrapper function? Why are they often useful in writing recursive functions?

13. What would happen if you eliminated the `if (n == 1)` check from the function `additiveSequence`, so that the implementation looked like this:

```
int additiveSequence(int n, int t0, int t1) {
    if (n == 0) return t0;
    return additiveSequence(n - 1, t1, t0 + t1);
}
```

Would the function still work? Why or why not?

14. Why is it important that the implementation of `isPalindrome` in Figure 7-3 checks for the empty string as well as the single character string? What would happen if the function didn't check for the single character case and instead checked only whether the length is 0? Would the function still work correctly?

15. Explain the effect of the function call

```
isPalindrome(str, p1 + 1, p2 - 1)
```

in the `isPalindrome` implementation given in Figure 7-4.

16. What is mutual recursion?

17. What would happen if you defined `isEven` and `isOdd` as follows:

```
bool isEven(unsigned int n) {
    return !isOdd(n);
}

bool isOdd(unsigned int n) {
    return !isEven(n);
}
```

Which of the errors explained in the section "Avoiding the common pitfalls" is illustrated by this example?

18. The following definitions of `isEven` and `isOdd` are also incorrect:

```
bool isEven(unsigned int n) {
    if (n == 0) {
        return true;
    } else {
        return isOdd(n - 1);
    }
}
```

```
bool isOdd(unsigned int n) {
   if (n == 1) {
      return true;
   } else {
      return isEven(n - 1);
   }
}
```

Give an example that shows how this implementation can fail. What common pitfall is illustrated here?

Exercises

1. Spherical objects, such as cannonballs, can be stacked to form a pyramid with one cannonball at the top, sitting on top of a square composed of four cannonballs, sitting on top of a square composed of nine cannonballs, and so forth. Write a recursive function **cannonball** that takes as its argument the height of the pyramid and returns the number of cannonballs it contains. Your function must operate recursively and must not use any iterative constructs, such as **while** or **for**.

2. Unlike many programming languages, C++ does not include a predefined operator that raises a number to a power. As a partial remedy for this deficiency, write a recursive implementation of a function

    ```
    int raiseToPower(int n, int k)
    ```

    that calculates n^k. The recursive insight that you need to solve this problem is the mathematical property that

    $$n^k = \begin{cases} 1 & \text{if } k \text{ is } 0 \\ n \times n^{k-1} & \text{otherwise} \end{cases}$$

3. In the 18th century, the astronomer Johann Daniel Titius proposed a rule, later recorded by Johann Elert Bode, for calculating the distance from the sun to each of the planets known at that time. To apply that rule, which is now known as the ***Titius-Bode Law,*** you begin by writing down the sequence

    $$b_1 = 1 \quad b_2 = 3 \quad b_3 = 6 \quad b_4 = 12 \quad b_5 = 24 \quad b_6 = 48 \quad \cdots$$

    where each subsequent element in the sequence is twice the preceding one. It turns out that an approximate distance to the ith planet can be computed from this series by applying the formula

$$d_i = \frac{4 + b_i}{10}$$

The distance d_i is expressed in ***astronomical units*** (AU), which correspond to the average distance from the earth to the sun (approximately 93,000,000 miles). Except for a disconcerting gap between Mars and Jupiter, the Titius-Bode law gives reasonable approximations for the distances to the seven planets known at the time:

Mercury	0.5 AU
Venus	0.7 AU
Earth	1.0 AU
Mars	1.6 AU
?	2.8 AU
Jupiter	5.2 AU
Saturn	10.0 AU
Uranus	19.6 AU

Concern about the gap in the sequence led astronomers to discover the asteroid belt, which they suggested might have been the remains of a planet that had once orbited the sun at the distance specified by the missing entry in the table.

Write a recursive function **getTitiusBodeDistance(k)** that calculates the expected distance between the sun and the kth planet, numbering outward from Mercury starting with 1. Test your function by writing a program that displays the distances to each of these planets in tabular form.

4. The ***greatest common divisor*** (often abbreviated to ***gcd***) of two nonnegative integers is the largest integer that divides evenly into both. In the third century BCE, the Greek mathematician Euclid discovered that the greatest common divisor of x and y can always be computed as follows:

- If x is evenly divisible by y, then y is the greatest common divisor.

- Otherwise, the greatest common divisor of x and y is always equal to the greatest common divisor of y and the remainder of x divided by y.

Use Euclid's insight to write a recursive function **gcd(x, y)** that computes the greatest common divisor of x and y.

5. Write an iterative implementation of the function **fib(n)**.

6. For each of the two recursive implementations of the function **fib(n)** presented in this chapter, write a recursive function (you can call the two functions **countFib1** and **countFib2**) that counts the number of function

calls made during the evaluation of the corresponding Fibonacci calculation. Write a main program that uses these functions to display a table showing the number of calls made by each algorithm for various values of **n**, as shown in the following sample run:

```
●○○                           CountFib
This program counts the number of calls made by the two
algorithms used to compute the Fibonacci sequence.

     n     fib1    fib2
    --     ----    ----
     0      1       2
     1      1       2
     2      3       3
     3      5       4
     4      9       5
     5     15       6
     6     25       7
     7     41       8
     8     67       9
     9    109      10
    10    177      11
    11    287      12
    12    465      13
```

7. Write a recursive function **digitSum(n)** that takes a nonnegative integer and returns the sum of its digits. For example, calling **digitSum(1729)** should return $1 + 7 + 2 + 9$, which is 19.

    The recursive implementation of **digitSum** depends on the fact that it is very easy to break an integer down into two components using division by 10. For example, given the integer 1729, you can divide it into two pieces as follows:

    Each of the resulting integers is strictly smaller than the original and thus represents a simpler case.

8. The **digital root** of an integer n is defined as the result of summing the digits repeatedly until only a single digit remains. For example, the digital root of 1729 can be calculated using the following steps:

Step 1:	$1 + 7 + 2 + 9$	→	19
Step 2:	$1 + 9$	→	10
Step 3:	$1 + 0$	→	1

Because the total at the end of step 3 is the single digit 1, that value is the digital root.

Write a function `digitalRoot(n)` that returns the digital root of its argument. Although it is easy to implement `digitalRoot` using the `digitSum` function from exercise 7 and a `while` loop, part of the challenge of this problem is to write the function recursively without using any explicit loop constructs.

9. As you know from Chapter 2, the mathematical combinations function $c(n, k)$ is usually defined in terms of factorials, as follows:

$$c(n, k) = \frac{n!}{k! \times (n - k)!}$$

The values of $c(n, k)$ can also be arranged geometrically to form a triangle in which n increases as you move down the triangle and k increases as you move from left to right. The resulting structure, which is called **Pascal's Triangle** after the French mathematician Blaise Pascal, is arranged like this:

$$c(0, 0)$$
$$c(1, 0) \quad c(1, 1)$$
$$c(2, 0) \quad c(2, 1) \quad c(2, 2)$$
$$c(3, 0) \quad c(3, 1) \quad c(3, 2) \quad c(3, 3)$$
$$c(4, 0) \quad c(4, 1) \quad c(4, 2) \quad c(4, 3) \quad c(4, 4)$$

Pascal's Triangle has the interesting property that every entry is the sum of the two entries above it, except along the left and right edges, where the values are always 1. Consider, for example, the circled entry in the following display of Pascal's Triangle:

```
                1
              1   1
            1   2   1
          1   3   3   1
        1   4   6   4   1
      1   5  10  10   5   1
    1   6  (15) 20  15   6   1
  1   7  21  35  35  21   7   1
```

This entry, which corresponds to $c(6, 2)$, is the sum of the two entries—5 and 10—that appear above it to either side. Use this relationship between entries in

Pascal's Triangle to write a recursive implementation of the `c(n, k)` function that uses no loops, no multiplication, and no calls to `fact`.

10. Write a recursive function that takes a string as argument and returns the reverse of that string. The prototype for this function should be

    ```
    string reverse(string str);
    ```

    and the statement

    ```
    cout << reverse("program") << endl;
    ```

    should display

    Your solution should be entirely recursive and should not use any iterative constructs such as `while` or `for`.

11. The `strlib.h` library contains a function `integerToString`. Reimplement this function without using streams by exploiting the recursive decomposition of an integer outlined in exercise 8.

Chapter 8
Recursive Strategies

Tactics without strategy is the noise before defeat.

— Sun Tzu, ~5th Century BCE

When a recursive decomposition follows directly from a mathematical definition, as it does in the case of the `fact` and `fib` functions in Chapter 7, applying recursion is not particularly hard. In most cases, you can translate the mathematical definition directly into a recursive implementation by plugging the appropriate expressions into the standard recursive paradigm. The situation changes, however, as you begin to solve more complex problems.

This chapter introduces several programming problems that seem—at least on the surface—much more difficult than those in Chapter 7. In fact, if you try to solve these problems without using recursion, relying instead on more familiar iterative techniques, you will find them quite difficult. By contrast, each of the problems has a recursive solution that is surprisingly short. If you exploit the power of recursion, a few lines of code are sufficient for each task.

The brevity of these solutions, however, endows them with a deceptive aura of simplicity. The hard part of solving these problems has nothing to do with the length of the code. What makes the programming difficult is finding the recursive decomposition in the first place. Doing so occasionally requires some cleverness, but what you really need is confidence. You have to take the recursive leap of faith.

■ 8.1 The Towers of Hanoi

The first example in this chapter is a simple puzzle that has come to be known as the *Towers of Hanoi.* Invented by French mathematician Édouard Lucas in the 1880s, the Towers of Hanoi puzzle quickly became popular in Europe. Its success was due in part to the legend that grew up around the puzzle, which was described as follows in *La Nature* by the French mathematician Henri de Parville (as translated by the mathematical historian W. W. R. Ball):

> In the great temple at Benares beneath the dome which marks the center of the world, rests a brass plate in which are fixed three diamond needles, each a cubit high and as thick as the body of a bee. On one of these needles, at the creation, God placed sixty-four disks of pure gold, the largest disk resting on the brass plate and the others getting smaller and smaller up to the top one. This is the Tower of Brahma. Day and night unceasingly, the priests transfer the disks from one diamond needle to another according to the fixed and immutable laws of Brahma, which require that the priest on duty must not move more than one disk at a time and that he must place this disk on a needle so that there is no smaller disk below it. When all the sixty-four disks shall have been thus transferred from the needle on which at the creation God placed them to one of the other needles, tower, temple and Brahmins alike will crumble into dust, and with a thunderclap the world will vanish.

Over the years, the setting has shifted from India to Vietnam, but the puzzle and its legend remain the same.

As far as I know, the Towers of Hanoi puzzle has no practical use except one: teaching recursion to computer science students. In that domain, it has tremendous value because the solution involves nothing other than recursion. In contrast to most recursive algorithms that arise in response to real-world problems, the Towers of Hanoi problem has no extraneous complications that might interfere with your understanding and keep you from seeing how the recursive solution works. Because it works so well as an example, the Towers of Hanoi is included in most textbooks that treat recursion and has become—much like the "hello, world" program in Chapter 1—part of the cultural heritage that computer scientists share.

In commercial versions of the puzzle, the 64 golden disks of legend are replaced with eight wooden or plastic ones, which makes the puzzle considerably easier to solve (not to mention less expensive). The initial state of the puzzle looks like this:

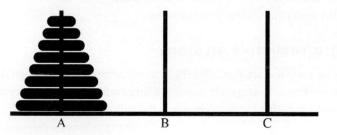

At the beginning, all eight disks are on spire A. Your goal is to move the eight disks from spire A to spire B, while adhering to the following rules:

- You can only move one disk at a time.

- You are not allowed to move a larger disk on top of a smaller one.

Framing the problem

In order to apply recursion to the Towers of Hanoi problem, you must first frame the problem in more general terms. Although the ultimate goal is to move eight disks from A to B, the recursive decomposition of the problem will involve moving smaller subtowers from spire to spire in various configurations. In the more general case, the problem you need to solve is moving a tower of a given height from one spire to another, using the third spire as a temporary repository. To ensure that all subproblems fit the original form, your recursive procedure must therefore take the following arguments:

1. The number of disks to move

2. The name of the spire where the disks start out

3. The name of the spire where the disks should finish

4. The name of the spire used for temporary storage

The number of disks to move is clearly an integer, and the fact that the spires are labeled with the letters *A, B,* and *C* suggests the use of type **char** to indicate which spire is involved. Knowing the types allows you to write a prototype for the operation that moves a tower, as follows:

```
void moveTower(int n, char start, char finish, char tmp);
```

To move the eight disks in the example, the initial call is

```
moveTower(8, 'A', 'B', 'C');
```

This function call corresponds to the English command "Move a tower of size 8 from spire A to spire B using spire C as a temporary." As the recursive decomposition proceeds, **moveTower** will be called with different arguments that move smaller towers in various configurations.

Finding a recursive strategy

Now that you have a more general definition of the problem, you can return to the problem of finding a strategy for moving a large tower. To apply recursion, you must first make sure that the problem meets the following conditions:

1. *There must be a simple case.* In this problem, the simple case occurs when **n** is equal to 1, which means that there is only a single disk to move. As long as you don't violate the rule of placing a larger disk on top of a smaller one, you can move a single disk in a single operation.

2. *There must be a recursive decomposition.* In order to implement a recursive solution, it must be possible to break the problem down into simpler problems in the same form as the original. This part of the problem is harder and will require closer examination.

To see how solving a simpler subproblem helps solve a larger problem, it helps to go back and consider the original example with eight disks.

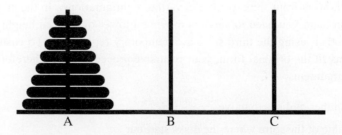

The goal here is to move eight disks from spire A to spire B. You need to ask yourself how it would help if you could solve the same problem for a smaller number of disks. In particular, you should think about how being able to move a stack of seven disks would help you to solve the eight-disk case.

If you think about the problem for a few moments, it becomes clear that you can solve the problem by dividing it into these three steps:

1.   Move the entire stack consisting of the top seven disks from spire A to spire C.

2.   Move the bottom disk from spire A to spire B.

3.   Move the stack of seven disks from spire C to spire B.

Executing the first step takes you to the following position:

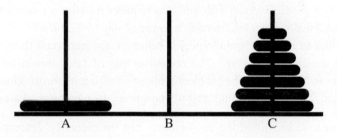

Once you have gotten rid of the seven disks on top of the largest disk, the second step is simply to move that disk from spire A to spire B, which results in the following configuration:

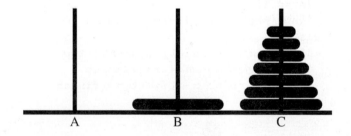

All that remains is to move the tower of seven disks back from spire C to spire B, which is again a smaller problem of the same form. This operation is the third step in the recursive strategy and leaves the puzzle in the desired final configuration:

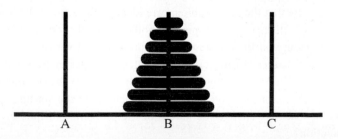

That's it! You're finished. You've reduced the problem of moving a tower of size eight to one of moving a tower of size seven. More importantly, this recursive strategy generalizes to towers of size *N,* as follows:

1. Move the top *N*–1 disks from the start spire to the temporary spire.
2. Move a single disk from the start spire to the finish spire.
3. Move the stack of *N*–1 disks from the temporary spire back to the finish spire.

At this point, it is hard to avoid saying to yourself, "Okay, I can reduce the problem to moving a tower of size *N*–1, but how do I accomplish that?" The answer, of course, is that you move a tower of size *N*–1 in precisely the same way. You break that problem down into one that requires moving a tower of size *N*–2, which further breaks down into moving a tower of size *N*–3, and so forth, until there is just one disk to move. Psychologically, however, the important thing is to avoid asking that question altogether. The recursive leap of faith should be sufficient. You've reduced the scale of the problem without changing its form. That's the hard work. All the rest is bookkeeping, and it's best to let the computer take care of that.

Once you have identified the simple cases and the recursive decomposition, all you need to do is plug them into the standard recursive paradigm, which results in the following pseudocode procedure:

```
void moveTower(int n, char start, char finish, char tmp) {
    if (n == 1) {
        Move a single disk from start to finish.
    } else {
        Move a tower of size n - 1 from start to tmp.
        Move a single disk from start to finish.
        Move a tower of size n - 1 from tmp to finish.
    }
}
```

Validating the strategy

Although the pseudocode strategy is in fact correct, the derivation up to this point has been a little careless. Whenever you use recursion to decompose a problem, you must make sure that the new problems are identical in form to the original. The task of moving *N*–1 disks from one spire to another certainly sounds like an instance of the same problem and fits the **moveTower** prototype. Even so, there is a subtle but important difference. In the original problem, the destination and temporary spires are empty. When you move a tower of size *N*–1 to the temporary spire as part of the recursive strategy, you've left a disk behind on the starting spire. Does the presence of that disk change the nature of the problem and thus invalidate the recursive solution?

To answer this question, you need to think about the subproblem in light of the rules of the game. If the recursive decomposition doesn't end up violating the rules, everything should be okay. The first rule—that only one disk can be moved at a time—is not an issue. If there is more than a single disk, the recursive decomposition breaks the problem down to generate a simpler case. The steps in the pseudocode that actually transfer disks move only one disk at a time. The second rule—that you are not allowed to place a larger disk on top of a smaller one—is the critical one. You need to convince yourself that you will not violate this rule in the recursive decomposition.

The important observation to make is that, as you move a subtower from one spire to the other, the disk you leave behind on the original spire—and indeed any disk left behind at any previous stage in the operation—must be larger than anything in the current subtower. Thus, as you move those disks among the spires, the only disks below them will be larger in size, which is consistent with the rules.

Coding the solution

To complete the Towers of Hanoi solution, the only remaining step is to substitute function calls for the remaining pseudocode. The task of moving a complete tower requires a recursive call to the **moveTower** function. The only other operation is moving a single disk from one spire to another. For the purposes of writing a test program that displays the steps in the solution, all you need is a function that records its operation on the console. For example, you can implement the function **moveSingleDisk** as follows:

```
void moveSingleDisk(char start, char finish) {
   cout << start << " -> " << finish << endl;
}
```

The **moveTower** code itself looks like this:

```
void moveTower(int n, char start, char finish, char tmp) {
   if (n == 1) {
      moveSingleDisk(start, finish);
   } else {
      moveTower(n - 1, start, tmp, finish);
      moveSingleDisk(start, finish);
      moveTower(n - 1, tmp, finish, start);
   }
}
```

The complete implementation appears in Figure 8-1.

FIGURE 8-1 Program to solve the Towers of Hanoi puzzle

```cpp
/*
 * File: Hanoi.cpp
 * ----------------
 * This program solves the Towers of Hanoi puzzle.
 */

#include <iostream>
#include "simpio.h"
using namespace std;

/* Function prototypes */

void moveTower(int n, char start, char finish, char tmp);
void moveSingleDisk(char start, char finish);

/* Main program */

int main() {
   int n = getInteger("Enter number of disks: ");
   moveTower(n, 'A', 'B', 'C');
   return 0;
}

/*
 * Function: moveTower
 * Usage: moveTower(n, start, finish, tmp);
 * ------------------------------------------
 * Moves a tower of size n from the start spire to the finish
 * spire using the tmp spire as the temporary repository.
 */

void moveTower(int n, char start, char finish, char tmp) {
   if (n == 1) {
      moveSingleDisk(start, finish);
   } else {
      moveTower(n - 1, start, tmp, finish);
      moveSingleDisk(start, finish);
      moveTower(n - 1, tmp, finish, start);
   }
}

/*
 * Function: moveSingleDisk
 * Usage: moveSingleDisk(start, finish);
 * ------------------------------------------
 * Executes the transfer of a single disk from the start spire to the
 * finish spire.  In this implementation, the move is simply displayed
 * on the console; in a graphical implementation, the code would update
 * the graphics window to show the new arrangement.
 */

void moveSingleDisk(char start, char finish) {
   cout << start << " -> " << finish << endl;
}
```

Tracing the recursive process

The only problem with this implementation of **moveTower** is that it seems like magic. If you're like most students learning about recursion for the first time, the solution seems so short that you feel sure there must be something missing. Where is the strategy? How can the computer know which disk to move first and where it should go?

The answer is that the recursive process—breaking a problem down into smaller subproblems of the same form and then providing solutions for the simple cases—is all you need to solve the problem. If you take the recursive leap of faith, you're done. You can skip this section of the book and go on to the next. If, on the other hand, you're still suspicious, it may be necessary for you to go through the steps in the complete process and watch what happens.

To make the problem more manageable, consider what happens if there are only three disks in the original tower. The main program call is therefore

```
moveTower(3, 'A', 'B', 'C');
```

To trace how this call computes the steps necessary to transfer a tower of size 3, all you need to do is keep track of the operation of the program, using precisely the same strategy as in the factorial example from Chapter 7. For each new function call, you introduce a stack frame that shows the values of the parameters for that call. The initial call to **moveTower**, for example, creates the following stack frame:

```
int main() {
    void moveTower(int n, char start, char finish, char tmp) {
☞      if (n == 1) {
            moveSingleDisk(start, finish);
        } else {
            moveTower(n - 1, start, tmp, finish);
            moveSingleDisk(start, finish);
            moveTower(n - 1, tmp, finish, start);
        }
    }
}
```

n	start	finish	tmp
3	'A'	'B'	'C'

As the arrow in the code indicates, the function has just been called, so execution begins with the first statement in the function body. The current value of **n** is not equal to 1, which means that the program skips ahead to the **else** clause and executes the statement

```
moveTower(n-1, start, tmp, finish);
```

As with any function call, you begin by evaluating the arguments. To do so, you need to determine the values of the variables **n**, **start**, **tmp**, and **finish**.

Whenever you need to find the value of a variable, you use the value as it is defined in the current stack frame. Thus, the `moveTower` call is equivalent to

```
moveTower(2, 'A', 'C', 'B');
```

This operation, however, requires making another function call, which means that the current operation is suspended until the new function call is complete. To trace the operation of the new function call, you need to generate a new stack frame and repeat the process. As always, the parameters in the new stack frame are copied from the calling arguments in the order in which they appear. Thus, the new stack frame looks like this:

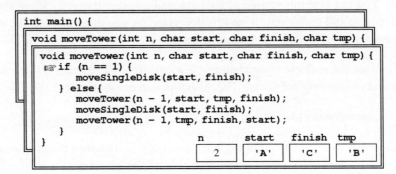

As the diagram illustrates, the new stack frame has its own set of variables, which temporarily supersede the variables in frames that are further down on the stack. Thus, as long as the program is executing in this stack frame, `n` will have the value 2, `start` will be `'A'`, `finish` will be `'C'`, and `tmp` will be `'B'`. The old values in the previous frame will not reappear until the subtask represented by this call to `moveTower` is complete.

The evaluation of the recursive call to `moveTower` proceeds exactly like that of the original one. Once again, `n` is not 1, which requires another call of the form

```
moveTower(n-1, start, tmp, finish);
```

Because this call comes from a different stack frame, however, the value of the individual variables are different from those in the original call. If you evaluate the arguments in the context of the current stack frame, you discover that this function call is equivalent to

```
moveTower(1, 'A', 'B', 'C');
```

The effect of making this call is to introduce yet another stack frame for the `moveTower` function, as follows:

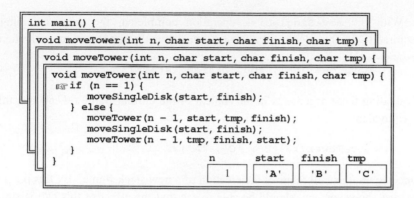

This call to **moveTower**, however, does represent the simple case. Since **n** is 1, the program calls the **moveSingleDisk** function to move a disk from A to B, leaving the puzzle in the following configuration:

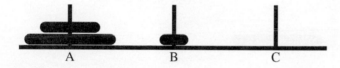

At this point, the most recent call to **moveTower** is complete, and the function returns. In the process, its stack frame is discarded, which brings the execution back to the preceding stack frame. Execution in that frame continues from the point after the just-completed call, as indicated in the following diagram:

```
int main() {
  void moveTower(int n, char start, char finish, char tmp) {
    void moveTower(int n, char start, char finish, char tmp) {
        if (n == 1) {
            moveSingleDisk(start, finish);
        } else {
            moveTower(n - 1, start, tmp, finish);
          ☞ moveSingleDisk(start, finish);
            moveTower(n - 1, tmp, finish, start);
        }
    }
}
```

n	start	finish	tmp
2	'A'	'C'	'B'

The call to **moveSingleDisk** again represents a simple operation, which leaves the puzzle in the following state:

With the `moveSingleDisk` operation completed, the only remaining step required to finish the current call to `moveTower` is the last statement in the function:

```
moveTower(n-1, tmp, finish, start);
```

Evaluating these arguments in the context of the current frame reveals that this call is equivalent to

```
moveTower(1, 'B', 'C', 'A');
```

Once again, this call requires the creation of a new stack frame. By this point in the process, however, you should be able to see that the effect of this call is simply to move a tower of size 1 from B to C, using A as a temporary repository. Internally, the function determines that `n` is 1 and then calls `moveSingleDisk` to reach the following configuration:

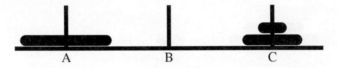

This operation again completes a call to `moveTower`, allowing it to return to its caller having completed the subtask of moving a tower of size 2 from A to C. Discarding the stack frame from the just-completed subtask reveals the stack frame for the original call to `moveTower`, which is now in the following state:

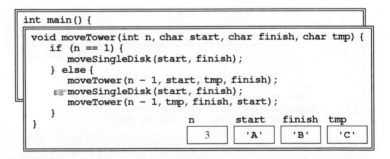

The next step is to call `moveSingleDisk` to move the largest disk from A to B, which results in the following position:

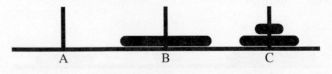

The only operation that remains is to call

```
        moveTower(n-1, tmp, finish, start);
```

with the arguments from the current stack frame, which are

```
        moveTower(2, 'C', 'B', 'A');
```

If you're still suspicious of the recursive process, you can draw the stack frame created by this function call and continue tracing the process to its ultimate conclusion. At some point, however, it is essential that you trust the recursive process enough to see that function call as a single operation that has the effect of the following command in English:

> *Move a tower of size 2 from C to B, using A as a temporary repository.*

If you think about the process in this holistic form, you can immediately see that completion of this step will move the tower of two disks back from C to B, leaving the desired final configuration:

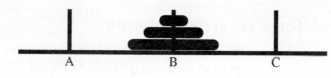

8.2 The subset-sum problem

Although the Towers of Hanoi problem offers a wonderful illustration of the power of recursion, its effectiveness as an example is compromised by its lack of any practical application. Many people are drawn to programming because it enables them to solve practical problems. If all examples of recursion were like the Towers of Hanoi, it would be easy to conclude that recursion is useful only for solving abstract puzzles. Nothing could be further from the truth. Recursive strategies give rise to extremely efficient solutions to practical problems—most notably the problem of sorting introduced in Chapter 10—that are hard to solve in other ways.

The problem covered in this section is the *subset-sum problem,* which can be defined as follows:

> Given a set of integers and a target value, determine whether it is possible to find a subset of those integers whose sum is equal to the specified target.

For example, given the set { −2, 1, 3, 8 } and the target value 7, the answer to the subset-sum question is yes, because the subset { −2, 1, 8 } adds up to 7. If the target value had been 5, however, the answer would be no, because there is no way to choose a subset of the integers in { −2, 1, 3, 8 } that adds up to 5.

It is easy to translate the idea of the subset-sum problem into C++. The concrete goal is to write a predicate function

```
bool subsetSumExists(Set<int> & set, int target);
```

that takes the required information and returns **true** if it is possible to generate the value **target** by adding together some combination of elements chosen from **set**.

Even though the subset-sum problem might at first seem just as esoteric as the Towers of Hanoi, it is important in both the theory and practice of computer science. As you will discover in Chapter 10, the subset-sum problem is an instance of an important class of computational problems that are hard to solve efficiently. That very fact, however, makes problems like subset-sum useful in applications where the goal is to keep information secret. The first implementation of public-key cryptography, for example, used a variant of the subset-sum problem as its mathematical foundation. Modern encryption strategies base their operation on problems that are provably hard, which makes such codes very difficult to break.

The search for a recursive solution

The subset-sum problem is difficult to solve using a traditional iterative approach. To make any headway, you need to think recursively. As always, you therefore need to identify a simple case and a recursive decomposition. In applications that work with sets, the simple case almost always occurs when the set is empty. If the set is empty, there is no way that you can add elements to produce a target value unless the target is zero. That discovery suggests that the code for **subsetSumExists** will start off like this:

```
bool subsetSumExists(Set<int> & set, int target) {
    if (set.isEmpty()) {
        return target == 0;
    } else {
        Find a recursive decomposition that simplifies the problem.
    }
}
```

In this problem, the hard part is finding that recursive decomposition.

When you are seeking a recursive decomposition, you need to be on the lookout for some value in the inputs—which are conveyed as arguments in the C++ formulation of the problem—that you can make smaller. In this case, you need to make the set smaller, because what you're trying to do is move toward the simple case that occurs when the set is empty. If you take an element out of the set, what's left over is smaller by one element. The operations exported by the **Set** class make

it easy to choose an element from a set and then determine what remains. All you
need is the following code:

```
int element = set.first();
Set<int> rest = set - element;
```

The **first** method returns the element of the set that appears first in its iteration
order, and the expression involving the overloaded - operator produces the set that
contains every element in **set** except the value of **element**. The fact that **element**
is first in iteration order is not important here. All you really need is some way to
choose an element and then create a smaller set by removing the element you
selected from the original set.

   Making the set smaller, however, is not enough to solve this problem. In terms
of structure, you know that **subsetSumExists** must call itself recursively on the
smaller set now stored in the variable **rest**. What you haven't yet determined is
how the solution to these recursive subproblems will help to solve the original. The
strategy you need to do so, which is described in the following section, illustrates a
general programming pattern that will prove useful in many applications.

The inclusion/exclusion pattern

The key insight you need to complete the implementation of **subsetSumExists** is
that there are two ways you might be able to produce the desired target sum after
you have identified a particular element. One possibility is that the subset you're
looking for *includes* that element. In that case, it must be possible to take the rest of
the set and produce the value **target - element**. The other possibility is that the
subset you're looking for *excludes* that element, in which case it must be possible to
generate the value **target** using only the leftover set of elements. This insight is
enough to complete the implementation of **subsetSumExists**, as follows:

```
bool subsetSumExists(Set<int> & set, int target) {
   if (set.isEmpty()) {
      return target == 0;
   } else {
      int element = set.first();
      Set<int> rest = set - element;
      return subsetSumExists(rest, target)
          || subsetSumExists(rest, target - element);
   }
}
```

   Because the recursive strategy subdivides the general case into one branch that
includes a particular element and another that excludes it, this strategy is sometimes
called the ***inclusion/exclusion pattern.*** As you work through the exercises in this

chapter as well as several subsequent ones, you will find that this same strategy, with slight variations, comes up in many different contexts. Although the pattern is easiest to recognize when you are working with sets, it also arises in applications involving vectors and strings, and you should be on the lookout for it in those situations as well.

8.3 Generating permutations

Many word games and puzzles require the ability to rearrange a set of letters to form a word. Thus, if you wanted to write a Scrabble program, it would be useful to have a facility for generating all possible arrangements of a particular set of tiles. In word games, such arrangements are generally called *anagrams*. In mathematics, they are known as *permutations.*

Let's suppose you want to write a function

```
Set<string> generatePermutations(string str);
```

that returns a set containing all permutations of the string. For example, if you call

```
generatePermutations("ABC")
```

the function should return a set containing the following elements:

```
{ "ABC", "ACB", "BAC", "BCA", "CAB", "CBA" }
```

How might you go about implementing the `generatePermutations` function? If you are limited to iterative control structures, finding a general solution that works for strings of any length is difficult. Thinking about the problem recursively, on the other hand, leads to a relatively straightforward solution.

As is usually the case with recursive programs, the hard part of the solution process is figuring out how to divide the original problem into simpler instances of the same problem. In this case, to generate all permutations of a string, you need to discover how being able to generate all permutations of a shorter string might contribute to the solution.

Before you look at the solution on the next page, stop and think about this problem for a few minutes. When you are first learning about recursion, it is easy to look at a recursive solution and believe that you could have generated it on your own. Without trying it first, however, it is hard to know whether you would have come up with the necessary recursive insight.

To give yourself more of a feel for the problem, it helps to consider a concrete case. Suppose you want to generate all permutations of a five-character string, such as `"ABCDE"`. In your solution, you can apply the recursive leap of faith to generate all permutations of any shorter string. Just assume that the recursive calls work and be done with it. Once again, the critical question is how being able to permute shorter strings helps you solve the problem of permuting the original five-character string.

If you focus on breaking the five-character permutation problem down into some number of instances of the permutation problem involving four-character strings, you will soon discover that the permutations of the five-character string `"ABCDE"` consist of the following strings:

- The character `'A'` followed by every possible permutation of `"BCDE"`
- The character `'B'` followed by every possible permutation of `"ACDE"`
- The character `'C'` followed by every possible permutation of `"ABDE"`
- The character `'D'` followed by every possible permutation of `"ABCE"`
- The character `'E'` followed by every possible permutation of `"ABCD"`

More generally, you can construct the set of all permutations of a string of length n by selecting each character in turn and then, for each of those n possible first characters, concatenating the selected character on to the front of every possible permutation of the remaining $n-1$ characters. The problem of generating all permutations of $n-1$ characters is a smaller instance of the same problem and can therefore be solved recursively.

As always, you also need to define a simple case. One possibility is to check whether the string contains a single character. Computing all the permutations of a single-character string is easy, because there is only one possible ordering. In string processing, however, the best choice for the simple case is rarely a one-character string, because there is in fact an even simpler alternative: the empty string containing no characters at all. Just as there is only one ordering for a single-character string, there is only one way to write the empty string. If you call `generatePermutations("")`, you should get back a set containing a single element, which is the empty string.

Once you have both the simple case and the recursive insight, writing the code for `generatePermutations` becomes reasonably straightforward. The code for `generatePermutations` appears in Figure 8-2, along with a simple test program that asks the user for a string and then prints every possible permutation of the characters in that string.

FIGURE 8-2   Program to generate all permutations of a string

```cpp
/*
 * File: Permutations.cpp
 * -----------------------
 * This file generates all permutations of an input string.
 */

#include <iostream>
#include "set.h"
#include "simpio.h"
using namespace std;

/* Function prototypes */

Set<string> generatePermutations(string str);

/* Main program */

int main() {
   string str = getLine("Enter a string: ");
   cout << "The permutations of \"" << str << "\" are:" << endl;
   for (string s : generatePermutations(str)) {
      cout << "   \"" << s << "\"" << endl;
   }
   return 0;
}

/*
 * Function: generatePermutations
 * Usage: Set<string> permutations = generatePermutations(str);
 * ----------------------------------------------------------------
 * Returns a set consisting of all permutations of the specified string.
 * This implementation uses the recursive insight that you can generate
 * all permutations of a string by selecting each character in turn,
 * generating all permutations of the string without that character,
 * and then concatenating the selected character on the front of each
 * string generated.
 */

Set<string> generatePermutations(string str) {
   Set<string> result;
   if (str == "") {
      result += "";
   } else {
      for (int i = 0; i < str.length(); i++) {
         char ch = str[i];
         string rest = str.substr(0, i) + str.substr(i + 1);
         for (string s : generatePermutations(rest)) {
            result += ch + s;
         }
      }
   }
   return result;
}
```

If you run the **Permutations** program and enter the string **"ABC"**, you see the following output:

```
┌─────────────────────────────────────────────────┐
│  ⊖ ⊜ ⊖              Permutations                  │
├─────────────────────────────────────────────────┤
│ Enter a string: ABC                               │
│ The permutations of "ABC" are:                    │
│    "ABC"                                           │
│    "ACB"                                           │
│    "BAC"                                           │
│    "BCA"                                           │
│    "CAB"                                           │
│    "CBA"                                           │
│                                                   │
└─────────────────────────────────────────────────┘
```

The use of sets in this application ensures that the program generates permutations in alphabetical order and that each distinct ordering of the characters appears exactly once, even if there are repeated letters in the input string. For example, if you enter the string **AABB** in response to the prompt, the program produces only six permutations, as follows:

```
┌─────────────────────────────────────────────────┐
│  ⊖ ⊜ ⊖              Permutations                  │
├─────────────────────────────────────────────────┤
│ Enter a string: AABB                              │
│ The permutations of "AABB" are:                   │
│    "AABB"                                          │
│    "ABAB"                                          │
│    "ABBA"                                          │
│    "BAAB"                                          │
│    "BABA"                                          │
│    "BBAA"                                          │
│                                                   │
└─────────────────────────────────────────────────┘
```

The recursive process calls the **add** method 24 (4!) times, but the implementation of the **Set** class ensures that no duplicate values appear.

You can use the **generatePermutations** function to generate all anagrams of a word by changing the main program from Figure 8-2 so that it checks each string against the English lexicon. If you enter the string **"aeinrst"**, you get the following output—a list that serious Scrabble players will recognize instantly:

```
┌─────────────────────────────────────────────────┐
│  ⊖ ⊜ ⊖               Anagrams                     │
├─────────────────────────────────────────────────┤
│ Enter the letters: aeinrst                        │
│ The anagrams of aeinrst are:                      │
│    anestri                                         │
│    nastier                                         │
│    ratines                                         │
│    retains                                         │
│    retinas                                         │
│    retsina                                         │
│    stainer                                         │
│    stearin                                         │
│                                                   │
└─────────────────────────────────────────────────┘
```

▮▮ 8.4 Graphical recursion

Some of the most exciting applications of recursion use graphics to create intricate pictures in which a particular motif is repeated at many different scales. The remainder of this chapter offers a few examples of graphical recursion that make use of the **GWindow** class introduced briefly at the end of Chapter 2. This material is not essential to learning about recursion, and you can skip it if you don't have ready access to the graphics library. On the other hand, working through these examples will make recursion seem a lot more powerful, not to mention more fun.

An example from computer art

In the early part of the twentieth century, a controversial artistic movement arose in Paris, largely under the influence of Pablo Picasso and Georges Braque. The Cubists—as they were called by their critics—rejected classical artistic notions of perspective and representationalism and instead produced highly fragmented works based on simple geometrical forms. Strongly influenced by Cubism, the Dutch painter Piet Mondrian (1872–1944) produced a series of compositions based on horizontal and vertical lines. The recursive structure of those paintings make them ideal candidates for computer simulation.

Suppose, for example, that you wanted to generate a Mondrian-like composition such as the following:

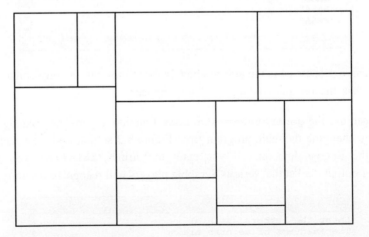

How would you go about designing a general strategy to create such a figure using the graphics library?

To understand how a program might produce such a figure, it helps to think about the process as one of successive decomposition. At the beginning, the canvas was simply an empty rectangle that looked like this:

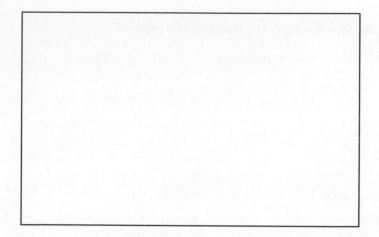

If you want to subdivide the canvas using a series of horizontal and vertical lines, the easiest way to start is by drawing a single line that divides the rectangle in two:

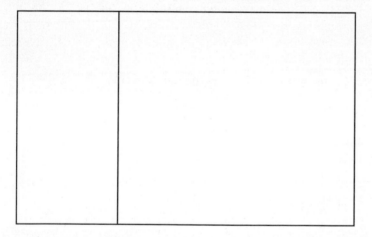

If you're thinking recursively, the thing to notice at this point is that you now have two empty rectangular canvases, each of which is smaller in size. The task of subdividing these rectangles is the same as before, so you can perform it by using a recursive implementation of the same procedure.

The only thing needed to complete the recursive strategy is a simple case. The process of dividing up rectangles can't go on indefinitely. As the rectangles get smaller and smaller, at some point the process has to stop. One approach is to look at the area of each rectangle before you start. Once the area of a rectangle falls below some threshold, you needn't bother to subdivide it any further.

The **Mondrian.cpp** program in Figure 8-3 implements the recursive algorithm, using the entire graphics window as the initial canvas. In **Mondrian.cpp**, the recursive function **subdivideCanvas** does all the work. The arguments give the

FIGURE 8-3 Program to subdivide the plane in a Mondrian-like style

```cpp
/*
 * File: Mondrian.cpp
 * --------------------
 * This program creates a line drawing in a style reminiscent of Mondrian.
 */

#include <iostream>
#include "gwindow.h"
#include "random.h"
using namespace std;

/* Constants */

const double MIN_AREA = 10000;    /* Smallest square that will be split */
const double MIN_EDGE = 20;       /* Smallest edge length allowed        */

/* Function prototypes */

void subdivideCanvas(GWindow & gw, double x, double y,
                                   double width, double height);

/* Main program */

int main() {
   GWindow gw;
   subdivideCanvas(gw, 0, 0, gw.getWidth(), gw.getHeight());
   return 0;
}

/*
 * Function: subdivideCanvas
 * Usage: subdivideCanvas(gw, x, y, width, height);
 * ----------------------------------------------------
 * Decomposes the specified rectangular region on the canvas recursively
 * by splitting that rectangle randomly along its larger dimension.  The
 * recursion continues until the area falls below the constant MIN_AREA.
 */

void subdivideCanvas(GWindow & gw, double x, double y,
                                   double width, double height) {
   if (width * height >= MIN_AREA) {
      if (width > height) {
         double mid = randomReal(MIN_EDGE, width - MIN_EDGE);
         subdivideCanvas(gw, x, y, mid, height);
         subdivideCanvas(gw, x + mid, y, width - mid, height);
         gw.drawLine(x + mid, y, x + mid, y + height);
      } else {
         double mid = randomReal(MIN_EDGE, height - MIN_EDGE);
         subdivideCanvas(gw, x, y, width, mid);
         subdivideCanvas(gw, x, y + mid, width, height - mid);
         gw.drawLine(x, y + mid, x + width, y + mid);
      }
   }
}
```

position and dimensions of the current rectangle on the canvas. At each step in the decomposition, the function simply checks to see whether the rectangle is large enough to split. If it is, the function checks to see which dimension—width or height—is larger and accordingly divides the rectangle with a vertical or horizontal line. In each case, the function draws only a single line; all remaining lines in the figure are drawn by subsequent recursive calls.

Fractals

In the late 1970s, a researcher at IBM named Benoit Mandelbrot (1924–2010) generated a great deal of excitement by publishing a book on *fractals,* which are geometrical structures in which the same pattern is repeated at many different scales. Although mathematicians have known about fractals for a long time, there was a resurgence of interest in the subject during the 1980s, partly because the development of computers made it possible to do so much more with fractals than had ever been possible before.

One of the earliest examples of fractal figures is called the ***Koch snowflake*** after its inventor, Helge von Koch (1870–1924). The Koch snowflake begins with an equilateral triangle like this:

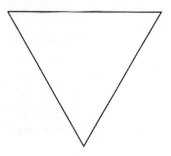

This triangle, in which the sides are straight lines, is called the Koch snowflake of order 0. The figure is then revised in stages to generate fractals of successively higher orders. At each stage, every straight-line segment in the figure is replaced by one in which the middle third consists of a triangular bump protruding outward from the figure. Thus, the first step is to replace each line segment in the triangle with a line that looks like this:

Applying this transformation to each of the three sides of the original triangle generates the Koch snowflake of order 1, as follows:

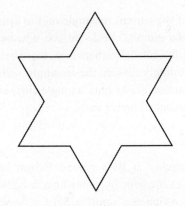

If you then replace each line segment in this figure with a new line that again includes a triangular wedge, you create the following order-2 Koch snowflake:

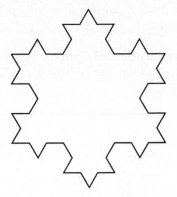

Replacing each of these line segments gives the order-3 fractal shown in the following diagram, which now looks even more like a snowflake:

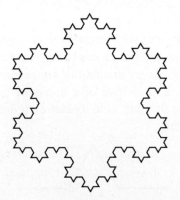

Because figures like the Koch snowflake are much easier to draw by computer than by hand, it makes sense to write a program that uses the facilities exported by the **graphics.h** interface to generate this design. Although it is possible to draw fractal snowflakes using only the **drawLine** method, it is usually easier to use the **drawPolarLine** method in the **GWindow** class, which lets you specify a line in terms of its length and a direction. In mathematics, the length and direction of a line segment are conventionally represented by the symbols r and θ, which are called its **polar coordinates.** The use of polar coordinates is illustrated by the following diagram, in which the solid line has length r and extends from its starting point at the angle θ measured in degrees counterclockwise from the x-axis:

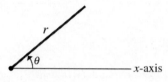

The **drawPolarLine** method takes the coordinates of the starting point (either as separate coordinates or as a **GPoint** object) and returns the coordinates of the other endpoint of the line segment, thereby making it easy to chain consecutive segments together. For example, the following code draws a downward-pointing equilateral triangle whose upper left corner is at the original value of **pt**:

```
pt = gw.drawPolarLine(pt, size, 0);
pt = gw.drawPolarLine(pt, size, -120);
pt = gw.drawPolarLine(pt, size, +120);
```

This code creates the snowflake fractal of order 0. To generalize it so that it creates higher-order fractals, all you need to do is replace the calls to **drawPolarLine** with a new function called **drawFractalLine** that takes—in addition to the graphics window—an additional parameter indicating the order of the fractal line, as follows:

```
pt = drawFractalLine(gw, pt, size, 0, order);
pt = drawFractalLine(gw, pt, size, -120, order);
pt = drawFractalLine(gw, pt, size, +120, order);
```

The only remaining task is to implement **drawFractalLine**, which is easy if you think about it recursively. The simple case for **drawFractalLine** occurs when **order** is 0, in which case the function simply draws a straight line with the specified length and direction. If **order** is greater than 0, the fractal line is broken down into four components, each of which is a fractal line of the next lower order. Like **drawPolarLine**, the **drawFractalLine** function returns the end point of the last segment it draws so that the next fractal line can begin where the last one left off. The complete implementation of the **Snowflake** program, which includes the finished code for **drawFractalLine**, appears in Figure 8-4.

FIGURE 8-4   Program to draw the Koch fractal snowflake

```cpp
/*
 * File: Snowflake.cpp
 * -------------------
 * This program draws a Koch fractal snowflake.
 */

#include <iostream>
#include <cmath>
#include "gwindow.h"
using namespace std;

/* Constants */

const double SIZE = 200;          /* Size of the order 0 fractal in pixels */
const int ORDER = 4;              /* Order of the fractal snowflake         */

/* Function prototypes */

GPoint drawFractalLine(GWindow & gw, GPoint pt,
                       double r, double theta, int order);

/* Main program */

int main() {
   GWindow gw;
   cout << "Program to draw a snowflake fractal." << endl;
   double cx = gw.getWidth() / 2;
   double cy = gw.getHeight() / 2;
   GPoint pt(cx - SIZE / 2, cy - sqrt(3.0) * SIZE / 6);
   pt = drawFractalLine(gw, pt, SIZE, 0, ORDER);
   pt = drawFractalLine(gw, pt, SIZE, -120, ORDER);
   pt = drawFractalLine(gw, pt, SIZE, +120, ORDER);
   return 0;
}

/*
 * Function: drawFractalLine
 * Usage: GPoint end = drawFractalLine(gw, pt, r, theta, order);
 * -------------------------------------------------------------
 * Draws a fractal edge starting from pt and extending r units in direction
 * theta.  If order > 0, the edge is divided into four fractal edges of the
 * next lower order.  The function returns the endpoint of the line.
 */

GPoint drawFractalLine(GWindow & gw, GPoint pt,
                       double r, double theta, int order) {
   if (order == 0) {
      return gw.drawPolarLine(pt, r, theta);
   } else {
      pt = drawFractalLine(gw, pt, r / 3, theta, order - 1);
      pt = drawFractalLine(gw, pt, r / 3, theta + 60, order - 1);
      pt = drawFractalLine(gw, pt, r / 3, theta - 60, order - 1);
      return drawFractalLine(gw, pt, r / 3, theta, order - 1);
   }
}
```

Summary

This chapter has introduced relatively few new concepts because the fundamental precepts of recursion were introduced in Chapter 7. The point of this chapter is to raise the sophistication of the recursive examples to the point at which the problems become difficult to solve in any other way. Given this increase in sophistication, beginning students often find these problems much harder to comprehend than those in the preceding chapter. They are indeed more difficult, but recursion is a tool for solving hard problems. To master it, you need to practice with problems at this level of complexity.

The important points in this chapter include:

- Whenever you want to apply recursion to a programming problem, you have to devise a strategy that transforms the problem into simpler instances of the same problem. Until you find an insight that leads to the recursive strategy, there is no way to apply recursive techniques.

- Once you identify a recursive approach, it is important for you to check your strategy to ensure that it does not violate any conditions imposed by the problem.

- When the problems you are trying to solve increase in complexity, the importance of accepting the recursive leap of faith increases.

- Recursion is not magical. If you need to do so, you can simulate the operation of the computer yourself by drawing the stack frames for every procedure that is called in the course of the solution. On the other hand, it is critical to get beyond the skepticism that forces you to look at all the underlying details.

Review questions

1. In your own words, describe the recursive insight necessary to solve the Towers of Hanoi puzzle.

2. The following strategy for solving the Towers of Hanoi puzzle is structurally similar to the strategy used in the text:

    a. Move the top disk from the start spire to the temporary spire.

    b. Move a stack of $N-1$ disks from the start spire to the finish spire.

    c. Move the top disk now on the temporary spire back to the finish spire.

    Why does this strategy fail?

3. If you call

    ```
    moveTower(16, 'A', 'B', 'C')
    ```

what line is displayed by **moveSingleDisk** as the first step in the solution? What is the last step in the solution?

4. What is a *permutation?*

5. In your own words, explain the recursive insight necessary to enumerate the permutations of the characters in a string.

6. How many permutations are there of the string **"WXYZ"**?

7. What simple case is used to terminate the recursion in **Mondrian.cpp**?

8. Draw a picture of the order-1 fractal snowflake.

9. How many line segments appear in the order-2 fractal snowflake?

Exercises

1. Following the logic of the **moveTower** function, write a recursive function **countHanoiMoves(n)** that computes the number of moves required to solve the Towers of Hanoi puzzle for **n** disks.

2. To make the operation of the program somewhat easier to explain, the implementation of **moveTower** in this chapter uses

   ```
   if (n == 1)
   ```

   as its simple case test. Whenever you see a recursive program use 1 as its simple case, it pays to be a little skeptical; in most applications, 0 is a more appropriate choice. Rewrite the Towers of Hanoi program so that the **moveTower** function checks whether **n** is 0 instead. What happens to the length of the **moveTower** implementation?

3. Rewrite the Towers of Hanoi program so that it uses an explicit stack of pending tasks instead of recursion. In this context, a task can be represented most easily as a structure containing the number of disks to move and the names of the spires used for the start, finish, and temporary repositories. At the beginning of the process, you push onto your stack a single task that describes the process of moving the entire tower. The program then repeatedly pops the stack and executes the task found there until no tasks are left. Except for the simple cases, the process of executing a task results in the creation of more tasks that get pushed onto the stack for later execution.

4. In the subset-sum problem introduced in section 8.2, there are often several ways to generate the desired target number. For example, given the set

{ 1, 3, 4, 5 }, there are two different ways to produce the target value 5:

- Select the 1 and the 4
- Select just the 5

By contrast, there is no way to partition the set { 1, 3, 4, 5 } to get 11.

Write a function

```
int countSubsetSumWays(Set<int> & set, int target);
```

that returns the number of ways in which you can produce the target value by choosing a subset of the specified set. For example, suppose that **sampleSet** has been initialized as follows:

```
Set<int> sampleSet;
sampleSet += 1, 3, 4, 5;
```

Given this definition of **sampleSet**, calling

```
countSubsetSumWays(sampleSet, 5);
```

should return 2 (there are two ways to make 5), and calling

```
countSubsetSumWays(sampleSet, 11)
```

should return 0 (there are no ways to make 11).

5. Write a program **EmbeddedWords** that finds all English words that can be formed by taking some subset of letters in order from a given starting word. For example, given the starting word *happy,* you can certainly produce the words *a, ha, hap,* and *happy,* in which the letters appear consecutively. You can also produce the words *hay* and *ay,* because those letters appear in *happy* in the correct left-to-right order. You cannot, however, produce the words *pa* or *pap* because the letters—even though they appear in the word—don't appear in the correct order. A sample run of the program might look like this:

```
● ● ●              EmbeddedWords
Enter starting word: happy
The embedded words are:
   a
   ay
   ha
   hap
   happy
   hay
```

6.   *I am the only child of parents who weighed, measured,*
and priced everything; for whom what could not be
weighed, measured, and priced had no existence.

—Charles Dickens, *Little Dorrit,* 1857

In Dickens's time, merchants measured many commodities using weights and a two-pan balance—a practice that continues in many parts of the world today. If you are using a limited set of weights, however, you can measure only certain quantities. For example, suppose that you have only two weights: a 1-ounce weight and a 3-ounce weight. With these weights you can easily measure out 4 ounces, as shown:

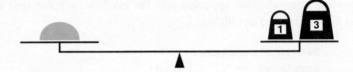

It is somewhat more interesting to discover that you can also measure out 2 ounces by shifting the 1-ounce weight to the other side, as follows:

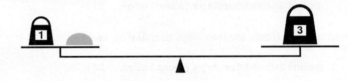

Write a recursive function

```
bool isMeasurable(int target, Vector<int> & weights)
```

that determines whether it is possible to measure out the desired target amount with a given set of weights, which is stored in the vector `weights`.

For example, suppose that `sampleWeights` has been initialized like this:

```
Vector<int> sampleWeights;
sampleWeights += 1, 3;
```

Given these values, the function call

```
isMeasurable(2, sampleWeights)
```

should return `true` because it is possible to measure out 2 ounces using the sample weight set as illustrated in the preceding diagram. On the other hand, calling

```
isMeasurable(5, sampleWeights)
```

should return **false** because it is impossible to use the 1- and 3-ounce weights to measure out 5 ounces.

7. In the card game called Cribbage, part of the game consists of adding up the score from a set of five playing cards. One of the components of the score is the number of distinct card combinations whose values add up to 15, with aces counting as 1 and all face cards (jacks, queens, and kings) counting as 10. Consider, for example, the following cards:

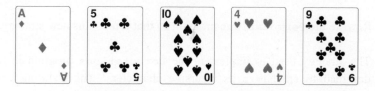

There are three different combinations that sum to 15, as follows:

AD + 10S + 4H   AD + 5C + 9C   5C + 10S

As a second example, the cards

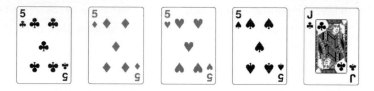

contain the following eight different combinations that add up to 15:

5C + JC   5D + JC   5H + JC   5S + JC
5C + 5D + 5H   5C + 5D + 5S   5C + 5H + 5S   5D + 5H + 5S

Write a function

```
int countFifteens(Vector<Card> & cards);
```

that takes a vector of **Card** values (as defined in Chapter 6, exercise 2) and returns the number of ways you can make 15 from that set of cards. You don't need to know much about the **Card** class to solve this problem. The only thing you need is the **getRank** method, which returns the rank of the card as an integer. You may assume that the **card.h** interface exports the constant names **ACE**, **JACK**, **QUEEN**, and **KING** with the values 1, 11, 12, and 13, respectively.

8. The recursive decomposition presented in section 8.3 to solve the problem of generating permutations is not the only effective strategy. Another way of implementing the recursive case looks like this:

    a) Remove the first character from the string and store it in the variable `ch`.

    b) Generate the set containing all permutations of the remaining characters.

    c) Form a new set by inserting `ch` in every possible position in each of those permutations.

    Rewrite the `Permutations` program so that it uses this new strategy.

9. The strategy used to implement the `Permutations` program in the text is designed to emphasize its recursive character. The resulting code is not particularly efficient, mostly because it ends up generating sets that are later discarded and because it applies methods like `substr` that require copying the characters in a string. It is possible to eliminate those inefficiencies using the following recursive formulation:

    a) At each level, pass the entire string along with an index that indicates where the permutation process starts. Characters in the string before this index stay where they are; characters at or after that position must go through all their permutations.

    b) The simple case occurs when the index reaches the end of the string.

    c) The recursive case operates by swapping the character at the index position with every other character in the string and then generating every permutation starting with the next higher index and then swapping the characters back to ensure that the original order is restored.

    Use this strategy to implement a function

    ```
    void listPermutations(string str);
    ```

    that lists on `cout` all permutations of the string `str` without generating any sets at all or applying any string methods other than `length` or selection. The `listPermutations` function itself must be a wrapper function for a second function that includes the index.

    This function is relatively easy to implement if you don't try to take account of duplicated letters in the string. The interesting challenge arises only when you change the structure of the algorithm so that it lists each unique permutation exactly once without using sets to accomplish that task. You should not, however, worry about the order in which `listPermutations` delivers its output.

10. On a telephone keypad, the digits are mapped onto the alphabet as shown in the following diagram:

In order to make their phone numbers more memorable, service providers like to find numbers that spell out some word (called a *mnemonic*) appropriate to their business that makes that phone number easier to remember.

Imagine that you have just been hired by a local telephone company to write a function `listMnemonics` that will generate all possible letter combinations that correspond to a given number, represented as a string of digits. For example, the call

```
listMnemonics("723")
```

should list the following 36 possible letter combinations that correspond to that prefix:

```
PAD PBD PCD QAD QBD QCD RAD RBD RCD SAD SBD SCD
PAE PBE PCE QAE QBE QCE RAE RBE RCE SAE SBE SCE
PAF PBF PCF QAF QBF QCF RAF RBF RCF SAF SBF SCF
```

11. Rewrite the program from exercise 10 so that it uses the `Lexicon` class and the `EnglishWords.dat` file so that the program only lists mnemonics that are valid English words.

12. These days, the letters on a telephone keypad are not used for mnemonics as much as they are for texting. Entering text using a keypad is problematic, because there are fewer keys than there are letters in the alphabet. Some cell phones use a "multi-tap" user interface, in which you tap the 2 key once for **a**, twice for **b**, and three times for **c**, which can get tedious. A streamlined alternative is to use a predictive strategy in which the cell phone guesses which of the possible letters you intended, based on the sequence so far and its possible completions.

For example, if you type the digit sequence 72, there are 12 possibilities: **pa**, **pb**, **pc**, **qa**, **qb**, **qc**, **ra**, **rb**, **rc**, **sa**, **sb**, and **sc**. Only four of these letter pairs—**pa**, **ra**, **sa**, and **sc**—seem promising because they are prefixes of common English words like **party**, **radio**, **sandwich**, and **scanner**. The others can be ignored because there are no common words that begin with those sequences of letters. If the user enters 9956, there are 144 (4 x 4 x 3 x 3) possible letter sequences, but you can be assured the user meant **xylo** since that is the only sequence that is a prefix of any English words.

Write a function

```
void listCompletions(string digits, Lexicon & lex);
```

that prints all words from the lexicon that can be formed by extending the given digit sequence. For example, calling

```
listCompletions("72547", english)
```

should generate the following sample run:

```
ListCompletions
palisade
palisaded
palisades
palisading
palish
rakis
rakish
rakishly
rakishness
sakis
```

If your only concern is getting the answer, the easiest way to solve this problem is to iterate through the words in the lexicon and print each word that matches the specified digit string. That solution requires no recursion and very little thinking. Your managers, however, believe that looking through every word in the dictionary is slow and insist that your code use the lexicon only to test whether a given string is a word or a prefix of an English word. With that restriction, you need to figure out how to generate all possible letter sequences from the string of digits. That task is easiest to solve recursively.

13. Many of Mondrian's geometrical paintings fill in the rectangular regions with some color. Extend the **Mondrian** program from the text so that it fills with randomly chosen colors some fraction of the rectangular regions it creates.

14. In countries like the United States that still use the traditional English system of measurement, each inch on a ruler is marked off into fractions using tick marks that look like this:

The longest tick mark falls at the half-inch position, two smaller tick marks indicate the quarter inches, and even smaller ones are used to mark the eighths and sixteenths. Write a recursive program that draws a 1-inch line at the center of the graphics window and then draws the tick marks shown in the diagram. Assume that the length of the tick mark indicating the half-inch position is given by the constant definition

```
const double HALF_INCH_TICK = 0.2;
```

and that each smaller tick mark is half the size of the next larger one.

15. One of the reasons that fractals have generated so much interest is that they turn out to be useful in some surprising practical contexts. For instance, the most successful techniques for drawing computer images of mountains and certain other landscape features involve using fractal geometry.

As a simple example of a situation in which this issue comes up, consider the problem of connecting two points A and B with a fractal that looks like a coastline on a map. The simplest possible strategy would be to draw a straight line between the two points:

A•━━━━━━━━━━━━━━━━━━━━━━━━━━━━•B

This is the order-0 coastline and represents the base case of the recursion.

Of course, an actual coastline will have small peninsulas or inlets somewhere along its length, so you would expect a more realistic drawing of a coastline to jut in or out occasionally. As a first approximation, you could replace the straight line with the same fractal line used to create the snowflake fractal, as follows:

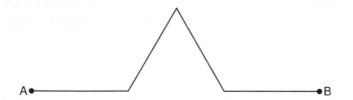

This process creates the order-1 coastline. The jags in coastlines, however, don't always point in the same direction. It is therefore important for the triangular wedge sometimes to point up and sometimes down, presumably with equal probability.

If you then replace each of the straight-line segments in the order-1 fractal with a fractal line in a random direction, you get the order-2 coastline, which might look like this:

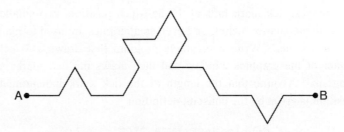

Continuing this process eventually results in a drawing that conveys a remarkably realistic sense, as in this order-5 coastline:

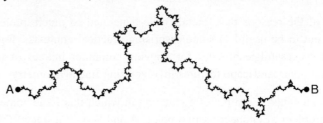

Write a program to draw a fractal coastline on the graphics window.

16. If you search the web for fractal designs, you will find many intricate wonders beyond the Koch snowflake illustrated in this chapter. One is the **H-*fractal,*** in which the repeated pattern is shaped like an elongated letter **H** that fits inside a square. Thus, the order-0 H-fractal looks like this:

To create the order-1 fractal, all you do is add four new H-fractals—each half the original size—at each open end of the order-0 fractal, like this:

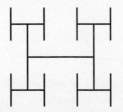

To create the order-2 fractal, you just add even smaller H-fractals (again half the size of the fractal to which they connect) to each of the open endpoints. This process gives rise to the following order-2 fractal:

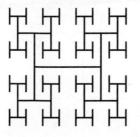

Write a recursive function

```
drawHFractal(GWindow & gw, double x, double y,
                           double size, int order);
```

where **x** and **y** are the coordinates of the center of the H-fractal, **size** specifies the width and the height, and **order** indicates the order of the fractal. As an example, the main program

```
int main() {
    GWindow gw;
    double xc = gw.getWidth() / 2;
    double yc = gw.getHeight() / 2;
    drawHFractal(gw, xc, yc, 100, 3);
    return 0;
}
```

would draw an order-3 H-fractal at the center of the graphics window, like this:

17. To celebrate its 550th anniversary in 2008, Magdalen College at Oxford University commissioned the English artist Mark Wallinger to create a sculpture called Y that has a decidedly recursive structure. A photograph of

---

Photograph and structure of Mark Wallinger's fractal tree

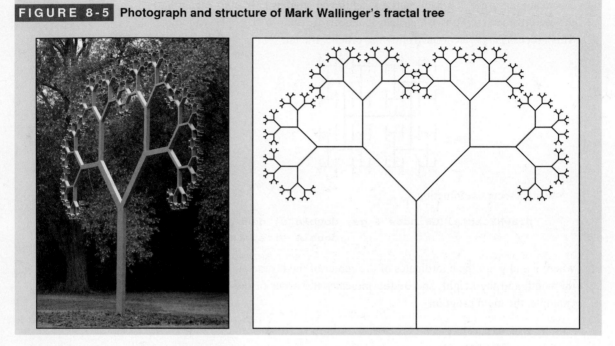

---

the sculpture appears at the left of Figure 8-5 and a diagram illustrating its fractal design appears at the right. Given its branching structure, the underlying pattern in Wallinger's sculpture is called a *fractal tree.* The tree begins as a simple trunk indicated by a straight vertical line, as follows:

The trunk branches at the top to form two lines that veer off at an angle, as shown:

These branches themselves split to form new branches, which split to form new ones, and so on.

Write a program that uses the graphics library to draw the fractal tree in Wallinger's sculpture. If you carry this process on to the eighth-order fractal, you get the image on the right of Figure 8-7.

18.   Another interesting fractal is the ***Sierpinski Triangle,*** named after its inventor, the Polish mathematician Wacław Sierpiński (1882–1969).   The order-0 Sierpinski Triangle is an equilateral triangle:

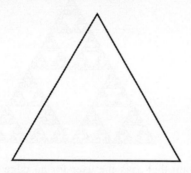

To create an order-N Sierpinski Triangle, you draw three Sierpinski Triangles of order $N-1$, each of which has half the edge length of the original.   Those three triangles are placed in the corners of the larger triangle, which means that the order-1 Sierpinski Triangle looks like this:

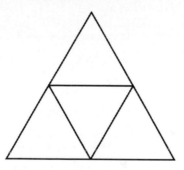

The downward-pointing triangle in the middle of this figure is not drawn explicitly, but is instead formed by the sides of the other three triangles.   That area, moreover, is not recursively subdivided and will remain unchanged at every level of the fractal decomposition.   Thus, the order-2 Sierpinski Triangle has the same open area in the middle:

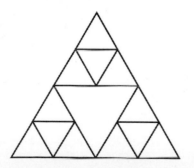

If you continue this process through three more recursive levels, you get the order-5 Sierpinski Triangle, which looks like this:

Write a program that asks the user for an edge length and a fractal order and draws the resulting Sierpinski Triangle in the center of the graphics window.

Chapter 9
Backtracking Algorithms

Truth is not discovered by proofs but by exploration. It is always experimental.

— Simone Weil, *The New York Notebook*, 1942

For many real-world problems, the solution process consists of working your way through a sequence of decision points in which each choice leads you further along some path. If you make the correct set of choices, you end up at the solution. On the other hand, if you reach a dead end or otherwise discover that you have made an incorrect choice somewhere along the way, you have to backtrack to a previous decision point and try a different path. Algorithms that take this approach are called *backtracking algorithms.*

If you think about a backtracking algorithm as the process of repeatedly exploring paths until you encounter the solution, the process appears to have an iterative character. As it happens, however, most problems of this form are easier to solve recursively. The fundamental recursive insight is simply this: a backtracking problem has a solution if and only if at least one of the smaller backtracking problems that result from making each possible initial choice has a solution. The examples in this chapter are designed to illustrate this process and demonstrate the power of recursion in this domain.

9.1 Recursive backtracking in a maze

Once upon a time, in the days of Greek mythology, the Mediterranean island of Crete was ruled by a tyrannical king named Minos. From time to time, Minos demanded tribute from the city of Athens in the form of young men and women, whom he would sacrifice to the Minotaur, a fearsome beast with the head of a bull and the body of a man. To house this deadly creature, Minos forced his servant Daedalus (the engineering genius who later escaped by constructing a set of wings) to build a vast underground labyrinth at Knossos. The young sacrifices from Athens would be led into the labyrinth, where they would be eaten by the Minotaur before they could find their way out. This tragedy continued until young Theseus of Athens volunteered to be one of the sacrifices. Following the advice of Minos's daughter Ariadne, Theseus entered the labyrinth with a sword and a ball of string. After slaying the monster, Theseus was able to find his way back to the exit by unwinding the string as he went along.

The right-hand rule

Ariadne's strategy is an algorithm for escaping from a maze, but not everyone trapped in a maze is lucky enough to have a ball of string. Fortunately, there are other strategies for solving a maze. Of these strategies, the best known is called the *right-hand rule,* which can be expressed in the following pseudocode form:

```
    Put your right hand against a wall.
    while (you have not yet escaped from the maze) {
        Walk forward keeping your right hand on a wall.
    }
```

To visualize the operation of the right-hand rule, imagine that Theseus has successfully dispatched the Minotaur and is now standing in the position marked by the first character in Theseus's name, the Greek letter theta (Θ):

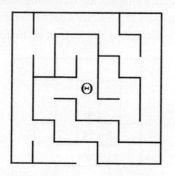

If Theseus puts his right hand on the wall and then follows the right-hand rule from there, he will trace out the path shown by the dashed line in this diagram:

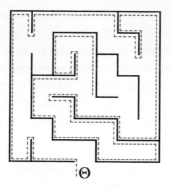

Unfortunately, the right-hand rule does not work in every maze. If there is a loop that surrounds the starting position, Theseus can get trapped in an infinite loop, as illustrated by the following simple maze:

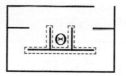

Finding a recursive approach

As the `while` loop in its pseudocode form makes clear, the right-hand rule is an *iterative* strategy. You can, however, also think about the process of solving a maze from a *recursive* perspective. To do so, you must adopt a different mental strategy. You can no longer think about the problem in terms of finding a complete path. Instead, your goal is to find a recursive insight that simplifies the problem, one step at a time. Once you have made the simplification, you use the same process to solve each of the resulting subproblems.

Let's go back to the initial configuration of the maze shown in the illustration of the right-hand rule. Put yourself in Theseus's place. From the initial configuration, you have three choices, as indicated by the arrows in the following diagram:

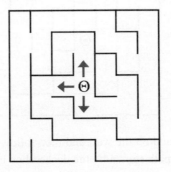

The exit, if any, must lie along one of those paths. Moreover, if you choose the correct direction, you will be one step closer to the solution. The maze has therefore become simpler along that path, which is the key to a recursive solution. This observation suggests the necessary recursive insight. The original maze has a solution if and only if it is possible to solve at least one of the new mazes shown in Figure 9-1. The × in each diagram marks the original starting square and is off-limits for any of the recursive solutions because the optimal solution will never have to backtrack through this square.

If you look at the mazes in Figure 9-1, it is easy to see—at least from your global vantage point—that the submazes labeled (a) and (c) represent dead-end paths and that the only solution begins in the direction shown in the submaze (b). If you are thinking recursively, however, you don't need to proceed with the analysis all the

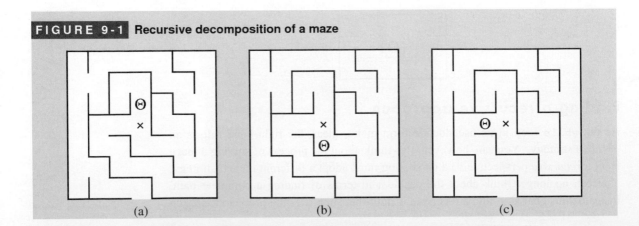

FIGURE 9-1   Recursive decomposition of a maze

(a)   (b)   (c)

way to the solution. You have already decomposed the problem into simpler instances. All you need to do is rely on the power of recursion to solve the individual subproblems, and you're home free. You still have to identify a set of simple cases so that the recursion can terminate, but the hard work has been done.

Identifying the simple cases

What constitutes the simple case for a maze? One possibility is that you might already be standing outside the maze. If so, you're finished. Clearly, this situation represents one simple case. There is, however, another possibility. You might also reach a blind alley where you've run out of places to move. For example, if you try to solve the sample maze by moving north and then continue to make recursive calls along that path, you will eventually be in the position of trying to solve the following maze:

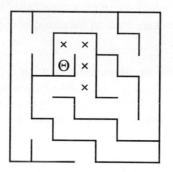

At this point, you've run out of room to maneuver. Every path from the new position is either marked or blocked by a wall, which makes it clear that the maze has no solution from this point. Thus, the maze problem has a second simple case in which every direction from the current square is blocked, either by a wall or a marked square.

It is easier to code the recursive algorithm if, instead of checking for marked squares as you consider the possible directions of motion, you go ahead and make the recursive calls on those squares. If you check at the beginning of the procedure to see whether the current square is marked, you can terminate the recursion at that point. After all, if you find yourself positioned on a marked square, you must be retracing your path, which means that the optimal solution must lie in some other direction.

Thus, the two simple cases for this problem are as follows:

1. If the current square is outside the maze, the maze is solved.

2. If the current square is marked, the maze is unsolvable, at least along the path you've chosen so far.

Coding the maze solution algorithm

Although the recursive insight and the simple cases are all you need to solve the problem on a conceptual level, writing a complete program to navigate a maze requires you to consider a number of implementation details as well. For example, you need to decide on a representation for the maze itself that allows you to figure out where the walls are, keep track of the current position, indicate that a particular square is marked, and determine whether you have escaped from the maze. While designing an appropriate data structure for the maze is an interesting programming challenge in its own right, it has very little to do with understanding the recursive algorithm, which is the focus of this discussion. If anything, the details of the data structure are likely to get in the way and make it more difficult for you to understand the algorithmic strategy as a whole. Fortunately, it is possible to set those details aside by introducing a new interface that hides some of the complexity. The `maze.h` interface in Figure 9-2 exports a class called `Maze` that encapsulates all the information necessary to keep track of the passages in a maze and to display that maze in the graphics window.

Once you have access to the `Maze` class, writing a program to solve a maze becomes much simpler. The goal of this exercise is to write a function

```
bool solveMaze(Maze & maze, Point pt);
```

The arguments to `solveMaze` are (1) the `Maze` object that holds the data structure and (2) the starting position, which changes for each of the recursive subproblems. To ensure that the recursion can terminate when a solution is found, the `solveMaze` function returns `true` if a solution has been found, and `false` otherwise.

Given this definition of `solveMaze`, the main program looks like this:

```
int main() {
   initGraphics();
   Maze maze("SampleMaze.txt");
   maze.showInGraphicsWindow();
   if (solveMaze(maze, maze.getStartPosition())) {
      cout << "The marked path is a solution." << endl;
   } else {
      cout << "No solution exists." << endl;
   }
   return 0;
}
```

```
FIGURE 9-2   The maze.h interface

/*
 * File: maze.h
 * ------------
 * This interface exports the Maze class.
 */

#ifndef _maze_h
#define _maze_h

#include <string>
#include "grid.h"
#include "gwindow.h"
#include "point.h"

/*
 * Class: Maze
 * -----------
 * This class represents a two-dimensional maze contained in a rectangular
 * grid of squares.  The maze is read from a data file in which the
 * characters '+', '-', and '|' represent corners, horizontal walls, and
 * vertical walls, respectively; spaces represent open passageway squares.
 * The starting position is indicated by the character 'S'.  For example,
 * the following data file defines a simple maze:
 *
 *       +-+-+-+-+-+
 *       |     |
 *       + +-+ + +-+
 *       |S |     |
 *       +-+-+-+-+-+
 */

class Maze {

public:

/*
 * Constructor: Maze
 * Usage: Maze maze(filename);
 *        Maze maze(filename, gw);
 * ----------------------------------
 * Constructs a new maze by reading the specified data file.  If the
 * second argument is supplied, the maze is displayed in the center
 * of the graphics window.
 */

   Maze(std::string filename);
   Maze(std::string filename, GWindow & gw);
```

FIGURE 9-2 The `maze.h` interface (continued)

```
/*
 * Method: getStartPosition
 * Usage: Point start = maze.getStartPosition();
 * -------------------------------------------------
 * Returns a Point indicating the coordinates of the start square.
 */

  Point getStartPosition();

/*
 * Method: isOutside
 * Usage: if (maze.isOutside(pt)) . . .
 * ---------------------------------------
 * Returns true if the specified point is outside the boundary of the maze.
 */

  bool isOutside(Point pt);

/*
 * Method: wallExists
 * Usage: if (maze.wallExists(pt, dir)) . . .
 * ---------------------------------------------
 * Returns true if there is a wall in direction dir from the square at pt.
 */

  bool wallExists(Point pt, Direction dir);

/*
 * Method: markSquare
 * Usage: maze.markSquare(pt);
 * ---------------------------
 * Marks the specified square in the maze.
 */

  void markSquare(Point pt);

/*
 * Method: unmarkSquare
 * Usage: maze.unmarkSquare(pt);
 * -----------------------------
 * Unmarks the specified square in the maze.
 */

  void unmarkSquare(Point pt);

/*
 * Method: isMarked
 * Usage: if (maze.isMarked(pt)) . . .
 * ------------------------------------
 * Returns true if the specified square is marked.
 */

  bool isMarked(Point pt);

};

#endif
```

The code for the `solveMaze` function appears in Figure 9-3, along with the function `adjacentPoint(start, dir)`, which returns the point you reach if you move in the specified direction from the starting point.

FIGURE 9-3 Implementation of the `solveMaze` function

```
/*
 * Function: solveMaze
 * Usage: solveMaze(maze, start);
 * -------------------------------
 * Attempts to generate a solution to the current maze from the specified
 * start point.  The solveMaze function returns true if the maze has a
 * solution and false otherwise.  The implementation uses recursion
 * to solve the submazes that result from marking the current square
 * and moving one step along each open passage.
 */

bool solveMaze(Maze & maze, Point start) {
   if (maze.isOutside(start)) return true;
   if (maze.isMarked(start)) return false;
   maze.markSquare(start);
   for (Direction dir = NORTH; dir <= WEST; dir++) {
      if (!maze.wallExists(start, dir)) {
         if (solveMaze(maze, adjacentPoint(start, dir))) {
            return true;
         }
      }
   }
   maze.unmarkSquare(start);
   return false;
}

/*
 * Function: adjacentPoint
 * Usage: Point finish = adjacentPoint(start, dir);
 * -------------------------------------------------
 * Returns the point that results from moving one square from start
 * in the direction specified by dir.  For example, if pt is the
 * point (1, 1), calling adjacentPoint(pt, EAST) returns the
 * point (2, 1).  To maintain consistency with the graphics package,
 * the y coordinates increase as you move downward on the screen.  Thus,
 * moving NORTH decreases the y component, and moving SOUTH increases it.
 */

Point adjacentPoint(Point start, Direction dir) {
   switch (dir) {
    case NORTH: return Point(start.getX(), start.getY() - 1);
    case EAST:  return Point(start.getX() + 1, start.getY());
    case SOUTH: return Point(start.getX(), start.getY() + 1);
    case WEST:  return Point(start.getX() - 1, start.getY());
   }
   return start;
}
```

Convincing yourself that the solution works

In order to use recursion effectively, at some point you must be able to look at a recursive function like the **solveMaze** example in Figure 9-3 and say to yourself something like this: "I understand how this works. The problem is getting simpler because more squares are marked each time. The simple cases are clearly correct. This code must do the job." For most of you, however, that confidence in the power of recursion will not come easily. Your natural skepticism makes you want to see the steps in the solution. The problem is that, even for a maze as simple as the one shown earlier in this chapter, the complete history of the steps involved in the solution is far too large to think about comfortably. Solving that maze, for example, requires 66 calls to **solveMaze** that are nested 27 levels deep when the solution is finally discovered. If you attempt to trace the code in detail, you will almost certainly get lost.

If you are not yet ready to adopt the recursive leap of faith, the best you can do is track the operation of the code in a more general sense. You know that the program first tries to solve the maze by moving one square to the north, because the **for** loop goes through the directions in the order defined by the **Direction** enumeration. Thus, the first step in the solution process is to make a recursive call that starts in the following position:

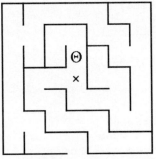

At this point, the same process occurs again. The program again tries to move north and makes a new recursive call in this position:

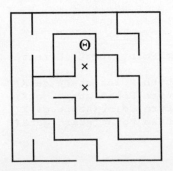

At this level of the recursion, moving north is no longer possible, so the `for` loop cycles through the other directions. After a brief excursion southward, upon which the program encounters a marked square, the program finds the opening to the west and proceeds to generate a new recursive call. The same process occurs in this new square, which in turn leads to the following configuration:

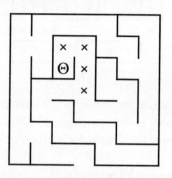

In this position, none of the directions in the `for` loop do any good; every square is either blocked by a wall or already marked. Thus, when the `for` loop at this level exits at the bottom, it unmarks the current square and returns to the previous level. It turns out that all the paths have been explored in this position as well, so the program once again unmarks the square and returns to the next higher level in the recursion. Eventually, the program backtracks all the way to the initial call, having completely exhausted the possibilities that begin by moving north. The `for` loop then tries the eastward direction, finds it blocked, and continues on to explore the southern corridor, beginning with a recursive call from this configuration:

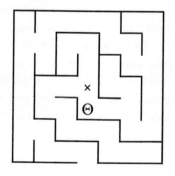

From here on, the same process ensues. The recursion systematically explores every corridor along this path, backing up through the stack of recursive calls whenever it reaches a dead end. The only difference along this route is that eventually—after descending through an additional recursive level for every step on the path—the program makes a recursive call in the following position:

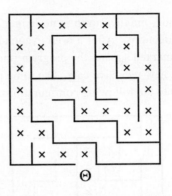

At this point, Theseus is outside the maze, so the simple case kicks in and returns **true** to its caller. This value is then propagated back through all 27 levels of the recursion, eventually returning back to the main program.

9.2 Backtracking and games

Although backtracking is easiest to illustrate in the context of a maze, the strategy is considerably more general. For example, you can apply backtracking to most two-player strategy games. Initially, the first player has several choices for a move. Depending on which move is chosen, the second player then has a particular set of responses. Each of these responses leads in turn to new options for the first player, and this process continues until the end of the game. The different possible positions at each turn in the game form a branching structure in which each option opens up more and more possibilities.

If you want to program a computer to take one side of a two-player game, one approach is to have the computer follow all the branches in the list of possibilities. Before making its first move, the computer would try every possible choice. For each of these choices, it would then try to determine what its opponent's response would be. To do so, it would follow the same logic: try every possibility and evaluate the possible counterplays. If the computer can look far enough ahead to discover that some move would leave its opponent in a hopeless position, it should make that move.

In theory, this strategy can be applied to any two-player strategy game. In practice, the process of looking at all the possible moves, potential responses, responses to those responses, and so on requires too much time and memory, even for modern computers. There are several games, however, that are simple enough to solve by looking at all the possibilities, yet complex enough so that the solution is not immediately obvious to the human player.

The game of Nim

To see how recursive backtracking applies to two-player games, it helps to consider a simple example such as the game of *Nim,* which is the generic name for an entire class of games in which players take turns removing objects from some initial configuration. In this particular version, the game begins with a pile of 13 coins. On each turn, a player takes either one, two, or three coins from the pile and puts them aside. The object of the game is to avoid being forced to take the last coin. Figure 9-4 shows a sample game between the computer and a human player.

How would you go about writing a program to play a winning game of Nim? The mechanical aspects of the game—keeping track of the number of coins, asking the player for a move, determining the end of the game, and so forth—constitute a straightforward programming task. The interesting part of the program consists of figuring out how to give the computer a strategy for playing the best possible game.

Finding a successful strategy for Nim is not particularly hard, especially if you work backward from the end of the game. The rules of Nim indicate that the loser is the player who takes the last coin. Thus, if you ever find yourself with just one coin on the table, you're in a bad position: you have to take that coin and lose. On the other hand, things look good if you find yourself with two, three, or four coins. In any of these cases, you can always take all but one of the remaining coins, leaving your opponent in the unenviable position of being stuck with just one coin.

FIGURE 9-4 Sample run of the Nim game

```
⊙ ⊙ ⊙                        Nim
Welcome to the game of Nim!
In this game, we will start with a pile of
13 coins on the table.  On each turn, you
and I will alternately take between 1 and
3 coins from the table.  The player who
takes the last coin loses.

There are 13 coins in the pile.
How many would you like? 2
There are 11 coins in the pile.
I'll take 2.
There are 9 coins in the pile.
How many would you like? 3
There are 6 coins in the pile.
I'll take 1.
There are 5 coins in the pile.
How many would you like? 1
There are 4 coins in the pile.
I'll take 3.
There is only one coin left.
I win.
```

But what if there are five coins on the table? What can you do then? After a bit of thought, it's easy to see that you're also doomed if you're left with five coins. No matter what you do, you have to leave your opponent with two, three, or four coins—situations that you've just discovered represent good positions from your opponent's perspective. If your opponent is playing intelligently, you will surely be left with a single coin on your next turn. Since you have no good moves, being left with five coins is clearly a bad position.

This informal analysis reveals an important insight about the game of Nim. On each turn, you are looking for a good move. A good move is one that leaves your opponent in a bad position. But what is a bad position? A bad position is one in which there is no good move.

Even though these definitions of *good move* and *bad position* are circular, they nonetheless constitute a complete strategy for playing a perfect game of Nim. You just have to rely on the power of recursion. If you have a function **findGoodMove** that takes the number of coins as its argument, all it has to do is try every possibility, looking for one that leaves a bad position for the opponent. You can then assign the job of determining whether a particular position is bad to the predicate function **isBadPosition**, which calls **findGoodMove** to see if there is one. The two functions call each other back and forth, evaluating all possible branches as the game proceeds.

The mutually recursive functions **findGoodMove** and **isBadPosition** provide all the strategy that the Nim program needs to play a perfect game. To complete the program, all you need to do is write the code that takes care of the mechanics of playing Nim with a human player. This code is responsible for setting up the game, printing instructions, keeping track of whose turn it is, asking the user for a move, checking whether that move is legal, updating the number of coins, figuring out when the game is over, and letting the user know who won.

Although none of these tasks is conceptually difficult, the **Nim** application is large enough that it makes sense to adopt the implementation strategy described in section 6.5, in which the program is defined as a class rather than as a collection of free functions. Figure 9-5 shows an implementation of the Nim game that adopts this design. The code for the game is encapsulated in a class called **SimpleNim**, along with two instance variables that keep track of the progress of play:

- An integer variable **nCoins** that records the number of coins in the pile.

- A variable **whoseTurn** that indicates which player is about to move. This value is stored using the enumerated type **Player**, which defines the constants **HUMAN** and **COMPUTER**. At the end of each turn, the code for the **play** method passes the turn to the next player by setting **whoseTurn** to **opponent(whoseTurn)**.

FIGURE 9-5 The `Nim.cpp` implementation

```cpp
/*
 * File: Nim.cpp
 * -------------
 * This program simulates a simple variant of the game of Nim.  In this
 * version, the game starts with a pile of 13 coins on a table.  Players
 * then take turns removing 1, 2, or 3 coins from the pile.  The player
 * who takes the last coin loses.
 */

#include <iostream>
#include <string>
#include "error.h"
#include "simpio.h"
#include "strlib.h"
using namespace std;

/* Constants */

const int N_COINS = 13;        /* Initial number of coins            */
const int MAX_MOVE =  3;       /* Number of coins a player may take  */
const int NO_GOOD_MOVE = -1;   /* Marker indicating there is no good move */

/*
 * Type: Player
 * ------------
 * This enumerated type differentiates the human and computer players.
 */

enum Player { HUMAN, COMPUTER };

/*
 * Method: opponent
 * Usage: Player other = opponent(player);
 * ------------------------------------------
 * Returns the opponent of the player.  The opponent of the computer
 * is the human player and vice versa.
 */

Player opponent(Player player) {
   return (player == HUMAN) ? COMPUTER : HUMAN;
}

/*
 * Constant: STARTING_PLAYER
 * -------------------------
 * Indicates which player should start the game.
 */

const Player STARTING_PLAYER = HUMAN;
```

FIGURE 9-5 The `Nim.cpp` implementation (continued)

```cpp
/*
 * Class: SimpleNim
 * ----------------
 * The SimpleNim class implements the simple version of Nim.
 */

class SimpleNim {

public:

/*
 * Method: play
 * Usage: game.play();
 * --------------------
 * Plays one game of Nim with the human player.
 */

   void play() {
      nCoins = N_COINS;
      whoseTurn = STARTING_PLAYER;
      while (nCoins > 1) {
         cout << "There are " << nCoins << " coins in the pile." << endl;
         if (whoseTurn == HUMAN) {
            nCoins -= getUserMove();
         } else {
            int nTaken = getComputerMove();
            cout << "I'll take " << nTaken << "." << endl;
            nCoins -= nTaken;
         }
         whoseTurn = opponent(whoseTurn);
      }
      announceResult();
   }

/*
 * Method: printInstructions
 * Usage: game.printInstructions();
 * --------------------------------
 * Explains the rules of the game to the user.
 */

   void printInstructions() {
      cout << "Welcome to the game of Nim!"  << endl;
      cout << "In this game, we will start with a pile of" << endl;
      cout << N_COINS << " coins on the table.  On each turn, you" << endl;
      cout << "and I will alternately take between 1 and" << endl;
      cout << MAX_MOVE << " coins from the table.  The player who" << endl;
      cout << "takes the last coin loses." << endl << endl;
   }
```

FIGURE 9-5 The `Nim.cpp` implementation (continued)

```cpp
private:

/*
 * Method: getComputerMove
 * Usage: int nTaken = getComputerMove();
 * -----------------------------------------
 * Figures out what move is best for the computer player and returns
 * the number of coins taken.  The method first calls findGoodMove
 * to see if a winning move exists.  If none does, the program takes
 * only one coin to give the human player more chances to make a mistake.
 */

   int getComputerMove() {
      int nTaken = findGoodMove(nCoins);
      return (nTaken == NO_GOOD_MOVE) ? 1 : nTaken;
   }

/*
 * Method: findGoodMove
 * Usage: int nTaken = findGoodMove(nCoins);
 * ---------------------------------------------
 * Looks for a winning move, given the specified number of coins.
 * If there is a winning move in the current position, the method
 * returns that value; if not, the method returns the constant
 * NO_GOOD_MOVE.  This method depends on the recursive insight that
 * a good move is one that leaves your opponent in a bad position and
 * a bad position is one that offers no good moves.
 */

   int findGoodMove(int nCoins) {
      int limit = (nCoins < MAX_MOVE) ? nCoins : MAX_MOVE;
      for (int nTaken = 1; nTaken <= limit; nTaken++) {
         if (isBadPosition(nCoins - nTaken)) return nTaken;
      }
      return NO_GOOD_MOVE;
   }

/*
 * Method: isBadPosition
 * Usage: if (isBadPosition(nCoins)) . . .
 * ---------------------------------------------
 * Returns true if nCoins represents a bad position.
 * A bad position is one in which there is no good move.
 * Being left with a single coin is clearly a bad position
 * and represents the simple case of the recursion.
 */

   bool isBadPosition(int nCoins) {
      if (nCoins == 1) return true;
      return findGoodMove(nCoins) == NO_GOOD_MOVE;
   }
```

FIGURE 9-5 The `Nim.cpp` implementation (continued)

```cpp
/*
 * Method: getUserMove
 * Usage: int nTaken = getUserMove();
 * ----------------------------------------
 * Asks the user to enter a move and returns the number of coins taken.
 * If the move is not legal, the user is asked to reenter a valid move.
 */

   int getUserMove() {
      while (true) {
         int nTaken = getInteger("How many would you like? ");
         int limit = (nCoins < MAX_MOVE) ? nCoins : MAX_MOVE;
         if (nTaken > 0 && nTaken <= limit) return nTaken;
         cout << "That's cheating!  Please choose a number";
         cout << " between 1 and " << limit << "." << endl;
         cout << "There are " << nCoins << " coins in the pile." << endl;
      }
   }

/*
 * Method: announceResult
 * Usage: announceResult();
 * ----------------------------
 * Announces the final result of the game.
 */

   void announceResult() {
      if (nCoins == 0) {
         cout << "You took the last coin.  You lose." << endl;
      } else {
         cout << "There is only one coin left." << endl;
         if (whoseTurn == HUMAN) {
            cout << "I win." << endl;
         } else {
            cout << "I lose." << endl;
         }
      }
   }

/* Instance variables */

   int nCoins;                  /* Number of coins left on the table */
   Player whoseTurn;            /* Marker showing whose turn it is   */

};

/* Main program */

int main() {
   SimpleNim game;
   game.printInstructions();
   game.play();
   return 0;
}
```

A generalized program for two-player games

The code in Figure 9-5 is highly specific to Nim. The **play** method, for example, is directly responsible for setting up the **nCoins** variable and updating it after each player moves. The general structure of a two-player game, however, is more widely applicable. Many games can be solved using the same overall strategy, even though different games will require different implementations to get the details right.

One of the key concepts in this text is the notion of *abstraction,* which is the process of separating out the general aspects of a problem so that they are no longer obscured by the details of a specific domain. You may not be terribly interested in a program that plays Nim; after all, Nim is rather boring once you figure it out. What you would probably enjoy more is a program that is general enough to be adapted to play Nim, tic-tac-toe, or any other two-player strategy game you choose.

The possibility of creating such a generalization arises from the fact that most games share a few fundamental concepts. The first such concept is that of *state.* For any game, there are data values that define exactly what is happening at any point. In the Nim game, for example, the state consists of the values of its two instance variables, **nCoins** and **whoseTurn**. For a game like chess, the state would need to include what pieces are currently placed on which squares, although it would presumably also include the **whoseTurn** variable, or something that fulfills the same function. For any two-player game, however, it should be possible to store the relevant data in the instance variables of the class that implements the game.

The second important concept is that of a *move.* In Nim, a move consists of an integer representing the number of coins taken away. In chess, a move might consist of a pair indicating the starting and ending coordinates of the piece that is moving, although this approach is in fact complicated by the need to represent such esoteric moves as castling or the promotion of a pawn. For any game, however, it is possible to define a **Move** type that encapsulates whatever information is necessary to represent a move in that game.

Although it might at first seem that **Move** should be defined as a class, doing so introduces additional overhead that can reduce the readability of the code. The essence of the problem is that the default visibility for entries in a class is private, which means that the class implementing the game has no access to those entries.

There are several strategies you can adopt to fix this problem. One strategy is to define **Move** as a class but to make its instance variables public. That strategy, however, violates the rule used in this book that no instance variables appear in the public section. A second approach is to define getter and setter methods in the style of the classes introduced in Chapter 6. That strategy is consistent with modern object-oriented programming but makes the **Move** class harder to use. The extra complexity is unwarranted for a class whose only client is likely to be the class that implements the game. A third strategy is to have the **Move** class declare the game class as a friend. A fourth strategy is to declare **Move** not as a class but as a structure type. In a sense, doing so has the effect of making its instance variables public, but the fact that **Move** is declared as a **struct** serves as a warning that it should be used only within the context of the game with which it is associated.

This text adopts the last strategy, which means that the **Move** type looks like this:

```
struct Move {
   int nTaken;
};
```

Once you have a **Move** type, it is possible to define a few additional helper methods that allow you to rewrite the **play** method as follows:

```
void play() {
   initGame();
   while (!gameIsOver()) {
      displayGame();
      if (getCurrentPlayer() == HUMAN) {
         makeMove(getUserMove());
      } else {
         Move move = getComputerMove();
         displayMove(move);
         makeMove(move);
      }
      switchTurn();
   }
   announceResult();
}
```

The most important thing to notice about the implementation of the **play** method is that the code gives no indication of what game is being played. It might be Nim, but it could just as easily be some other game. Every game requires its own definition for the **Move** type, along with specialized implementations of the various game-specific methods such as **initGame** and **makeMove**. Even so, the structure of the **play** method is general enough to work for many different two-player games.

If you compare the generalized implementation of **play** with the code in Figure 9-5, you will also notice that the code to switch turns has been incorporated into the general structure through the helper methods **getCurrentPlayer** and **switchTurn**. Making this change means that the **play** method no longer refers directly to the instance variables but instead calls methods to do the job. This strategy allows more flexibility in the underlying implementation.

The **play** method and the mechanics of taking turns, however, are not the most exciting aspects of writing a program for a two-player game. The algorithmically interesting part is embedded inside the method **getComputerMove**, which is responsible for choosing the best move for the computer. The version of Nim in Figure 9-5 implements this strategy using the mutually recursive methods **findGoodMove** and **isBadPosition**, which search through all possible choices to find a winning move in the current position. Since that strategy is also independent of the details of any particular game, it therefore ought to be possible to write these methods in a more general way. Before going further down that path, however, it helps to generalize the problem further, which will make it suitable for a wider variety of games.

9.3 The minimax algorithm

The techniques described in the preceding section work well for simple, completely solvable games like Nim. As games become more complex, though, it quickly becomes impossible to examine every possible outcome. If you tried to go through every possible game of chess, for example, the process could take billions of years, even at the speed of modern computers. Yet, somehow, in spite of this limitation, computers are very good at chess. In 1997, IBM's "Deep Blue" supercomputer beat the reigning world champion at that time, Garry Kasparov. Deep Blue did not win by conducting an exhaustive analysis of all possible games; it instead looked ahead only for a restricted number of moves, in much the same way that humans do.

Even with games for which it is computationally infeasible to work through every possible sequence of moves, the recursive concepts of good moves and bad positions from the Nim game still come in handy. Although it may not be possible to identify a move as a surefire winner, it is still true that the best move in any position is the one that leaves your opponent in the worst position. Similarly, the worst position is the one that offers your opponent the weakest best move. This strategy—which consists of finding the position that leaves your opponent with the worst possible best move—is called the *minimax* algorithm because the goal is to find the move that minimizes your opponent's maximum opportunity.

Game trees

The best way to visualize the operation of the minimax strategy is to think about the possible future moves in a game as forming a branching diagram that expands at each turn. Because of this branching structure, such diagrams are called *game trees.* The initial state is represented by a dot at the top of the game tree. If there are, for example, three possible moves from this position, there will be three lines emanating downward from the current state to three new states that represent the results of these moves, as shown in the following diagram:

From each of the new positions, your opponent also has options. If each position again has three options, the next generation of the game tree looks like this:

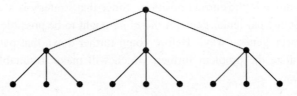

Which move do you choose in the initial position? Clearly, your goal is to achieve the best outcome. Unfortunately, you only get to control half of the game. If you were able to select your opponent's move as well as your own, you could select the path to the state two turns away that left you in the best position. Given that your opponent is also trying to win, the best thing you can do is choose the initial move that leaves your opponent with as few winning chances as possible.

Rating positions and moves

In order to get a sense of how you can find the optimal move from a particular position, it helps to add some quantitative data to the analysis. Deciding whether one move is better than another is much easier if you assign a numeric score to each possible move. The higher the numeric score, the better the move. Thus, a move that has a score of +7, for example, is better than a move with a rating of −4. In addition to rating each possible move, it makes sense to assign a similar numeric rating to each position in the game. Thus, one position might have a rating of +9 and would therefore be better than a position with a score of only +2.

Both positions and moves are rated from the perspective of the player making the move. Moreover, the rating system is designed to be symmetric around 0, in the sense that a position that has a score of +9 for the current player would have a score of −9 from the opponent's point of view. This interpretation of rating numbers captures the idea that a position that is good for one player is bad for the other, as was true in the case of the game of Nim. More importantly, defining the rating system in this way makes it easy to express the relationship between the scores for moves and positions. The rating for any move is simply the negative of the rating for the resulting position when evaluated by your opponent. Similarly, the rating of any position can be defined as the rating of its best move.

To make this discussion more concrete, it helps to consider a simple example. Suppose that you have looked two steps ahead in the game, anticipating one move by you and the possible responses from your opponent. In computer science, a single move for a single player is called a ***ply*** to avoid the ambiguity associated with the words *move* and *turn,* which sometimes suggest that both players have a chance to play. If you rated the positions at the conclusion of your two-ply analysis, the game tree might look like this:

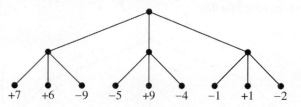

Because the positions at the bottom of this tree are again positions in which—as at the top of the tree—you have to move, the rating numbers in those positions are assigned from your perspective. Given these ratings of the potential positions, what move should you make from the original configuration?

   At first glance, you might be attracted by the fact that the center branch contains a path that leads to a +9, which is an excellent outcome for you. Unfortunately, the fact that the center branch offers such a wonderful outcome doesn't really matter. If your opponent is playing rationally, there is no way that the game can reach the +9 position. Suppose, for example, that you do choose the center branch. Given the options available, your opponent will select the leftmost branch, as illustrated by the highlighted path in the following game tree:

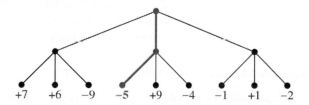

Your initial choice thus leaves you in a position that—from your point of view—has a rating of −5. You would do better to choose the rightmost branch, from which your opponent's best strategy leaves you in a position with a −2 rating:

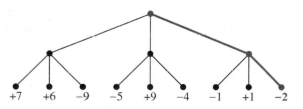

   As noted earlier in this section, the rating of a move is the negative of the rating of the resulting position when evaluated from the opponent's perspective. The rating of the last move in the highlighted line of the game tree is +2 because it leads to a position with a −2 rating. The negative sign indicates the shift in perspective. Moves that lead to positions that are bad for your opponent are good for you, and vice versa. The rating of each position is simply the rating of the best move it offers. The ratings for the positions and moves along the highlighted path in the game tree therefore look like this:

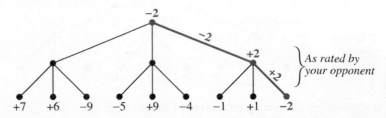

The rating of the starting position is therefore −2. While this position is hardly ideal, it is better for you than the other possible outcomes, assuming that your opponent is playing rationally.

In the implementation of the minimax application outlined later in this chapter, the values used as ratings are integers that must fall between the limits defined by the following constants:

```
const int WINNING_POSITION  = 1000;
const int LOSING_POSITION   = -WINNING_POSITION;
```

At the end of a game, the rating of a position can be determined by checking to see who has won. The rating of any position for which the outcome is not yet determined must be an integer somewhere between these extremes.

Limiting the depth of the recursive search

If you could search an entire game tree from the beginning of a game through to every possible conclusion, you could implement the minimax algorithm using pretty much the same structure as in the earlier Nim example. All you would need are two mutually recursive functions, one that finds the best move and one that evaluates positions. For games that involve a significant level of complexity, it is impossible to search the entire game tree in a reasonable amount of time. A practical implementation of the minimax algorithm must therefore include a provision for cutting off the search at a certain point.

The usual strategy for limiting the search is to set some maximum value for the depth of the recursion. You could, for example, allow the recursion to continue until each player has made five moves, for a total of ten ply. If the game ends before that limit is reached, you can evaluate the final position by checking to see who won the game and then returning **WINNING_POSITION** or **LOSING_POSITION**, as appropriate.

But what happens if you hit the recursion limit before the outcome of the game is decided? At that point, you need to evaluate the position in some other way that does not involve making additional recursive calls. Given that this kind of analysis depends only on the state of the game as it stands, it is usually called ***static analysis.*** In chess-playing programs, for example, static analysis usually performs some simple calculation based on the values of the pieces each side has on the board. If the player to move is ahead in that calculation, the position has a positive rating; if not, the rating is negative.

Although any simple calculation is sure to overlook some important factor, it is important to remember that static analysis applies only after the recursion limit is reached. If, for example, there is some line of play that will force a win in the game in the next few moves, the quality of the static analysis is irrelevant, because the recursive evaluation will find that winning line of play before getting to the static-analysis phase.

The easiest way to add a depth limit to the minimax implementation is to have each of the recursive methods take a parameter named **depth** that records how many levels have already been analyzed and add one to that value before trying to rate the next position. If that parameter exceeds a defined constant **MAX_DEPTH**, any further evaluations must be performed using static analysis.

Implementing the minimax algorithm

The minimax algorithm can be implemented using two mutually recursive methods: **findBestMove** and **evaluatePosition**, which appear in Figure 9-6 on the next page. The **findBestMove** method considers every possible move and then calls **evaluatePosition** on the resulting positions, looking for the one with the lowest rating when evaluated from the opponent's perspective. The **evaluatePosition** method uses **findBestMove** to determine the best move and then return the rating of that move, unless the recursion limit or state of the game require static analysis.

As you can see from the code in Figure 9-6, the **findBestMove** function exists in two forms. The first form takes no arguments and is called by the client to find the best move from the current position. Recursive invocations of **findBestMove** call the second form, which takes two parameters. The first is the depth of the recursion, which allows the algorithm to cut off computation after a certain number of moves as described in the preceding section. The second is the reference parameter **rating**, which allows **findMove** to pass its evaluation of the optimal move back to the **evaluatePosition** function.

FIGURE 9-6 Generalized implementation of the minimax algorithm

```
/*
 * Method: findBestMove
 * Usage: Move move = findBestMove();
 *        Move move = findBestMove(depth, rating);
 * -----------------------------------------------------
 * Finds the best move for the current player and returns that move as the
 * value of the function.  The second form is used for later recursive calls
 * and includes two parameters.  The depth parameter is used to limit the
 * depth of the search for games that are too difficult to analyze.  The
 * reference parameter rating is used to store the rating of the best move.
 */

   Move findBestMove() {
      int rating;
      return findBestMove(0, rating);
   }

   Move findBestMove(int depth, int & rating) {
      Vector<Move> moveList;
      Move bestMove;
      int minRating = WINNING_POSITION + 1;
      generateMoveList(moveList);
      if (moveList.isEmpty()) error("No moves available");
      for (Move move : moveList) {
         makeMove(move);
         int moveRating = evaluatePosition(depth + 1);
         if (moveRating < minRating) {
            bestMove = move;
            minRating = moveRating;
         }
         retractMove(move);
      }
      rating = -minRating;
      return bestMove;
   }

/*
 * Method: evaluatePosition
 * Usage: int rating = evaluatePosition(depth);
 * -----------------------------------------------
 * Evaluates a position by finding the rating of the best move starting at
 * that point.  The depth parameter is used to limit the search depth.
 */

   int evaluatePosition(int depth) {
      if (gameIsOver() || depth >= MAX_DEPTH) {
         return evaluateStaticPosition();
      }
      int rating;
      findBestMove(depth, rating);
      return rating;
   }
```

The code in Figure 9-6 calls several methods—each of which is coded independently for a particular game—that are worth some further explanation:

- The **generateMoveList** method fills the **moveList** vector with the legal moves available in the current state.

- The methods **makeMove** and **retractMove** have the effect of making and taking back a particular move. These methods allow the program to try out a potential move, evaluate the resulting position, and then go back to the original state.

- The **isGameOver** method checks to see if the game has reached a final state in which no further analysis is possible.

- The **evaluateStaticPosition** method evaluates a particular state in the game without making any further recursive calls.

Summary

In this chapter, you have learned to solve problems that require making a sequence of choices as you search for a goal, as illustrated by finding a path through a maze or a winning strategy in a two-player game. The basic strategy is to write programs that can backtrack to previous decision points if the choices lead to dead ends. By exploiting the power of recursion, however, you can avoid coding the details of the backtracking process and develop general solution strategies that apply to a wide variety of problem domains.

Important points in this chapter include:

- You can solve most problems that require backtracking by adopting the following recursive approach:

    If you are already at a solution, report success.
    for (*every possible choice in the current position*) {
        Make that choice and take one step along the path.
        Use recursion to solve the problem from the new position.
        If the recursive call succeeds, report the success to the next higher level.
        If not, back out of the current choice to restore the previous state.
    }
    Report failure.

- The complete history of recursive calls in a backtracking problem—even for relatively simple applications—is usually too complex to understand in detail. For problems that involve any significant amount of backtracking, it is essential to accept the recursive leap of faith.

- You can often find a winning strategy for two-player games by adopting a recursive-backtracking approach. Because the goal in such games involves minimizing the winning chances for your opponent, the conventional strategic approach is called the *minimax algorithm*.

Review questions

1.   What is the principal characteristic of a backtracking algorithm?

2.   Using your own words, state the right-hand rule for escaping from a maze. Would a left-hand rule work equally well?

3.   What is the insight that makes it possible to solve a maze by recursive backtracking?

4.   What are the simple cases that apply in the recursive implementation of `solveMaze`?

5.   Why is important to mark squares as you proceed through the maze? What would happen in the `solveMaze` function if you never marked any squares?

6.   What is the purpose of the `unmarkSquare` call at the end of the `for` loop in the `solveMaze` implementation? Is this statement essential to the algorithm?

7.   What is the purpose of the Boolean result returned by `solveMaze`?

8.   In your own words, explain how the backtracking process actually takes place in the recursive implementation of `solveMaze`.

9.   In the simple Nim game, the human player plays first and begins with a pile of 13 coins. Is this a good or a bad position? Why?

10.   Write a simple C++ expression based on the value of `nCoins` that has the value `true` if the position is good for the current player and `false` otherwise.

11.   What is the minimax algorithm? What does its name signify?

12.   Why is it useful to develop an abstract implementation of the minimax algorithm that does not depend on the details of a particular game?

13.   What is the role of the `depth` argument in the functions `findBestMove` and `evaluatePosition`?

14. Explain the role of the **evaluateStaticPosition** function in the minimax implementation.

15. Suppose you are in a position in which the analysis for the next two moves shows the following rated outcomes from your original player's point-of-view:

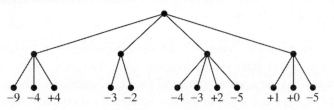

-9 -4 +4   -3 -2   -4 -3 +2 -5   +1 +0 -5

If you adopt the minimax strategy, what is the best move to make in this position? What is the rating of that move from your perspective?

Exercises

1. In many mazes, there are multiple paths. For example, Figure 9-7 shows three solutions for the same maze. None of these solutions, however, is optimal. The shortest path through the maze has a path length of 11:

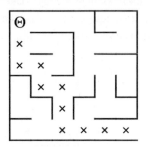

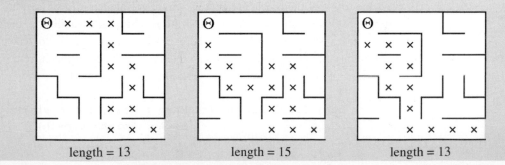

FIGURE 9-7 Multiple paths through a maze

length = 13   length = 15   length = 13

Write a function

```
int shortestPathLength(Maze & maze, Point start);
```

that returns the length of the shortest path in the maze from the specified position to any exit. If there is no solution, **shortestPathLength** should return −1.

2. As implemented in Figure 9-3, the **solveMaze** function unmarks each square as it discovers there are no solutions from that point. Although this design strategy has the advantage that the final configuration of the maze shows the solution path as a series of marked squares, the decision to unmark squares as you backtrack has a cost in terms of the overall efficiency of the algorithm. If you've marked a square and then backtracked through it, you've already explored the possibilities leading from that square. If you come back to it by some other path, you might as well rely on your earlier analysis instead of exploring the same options again.

    To give yourself a sense of how much these unmarking operations cost in terms of efficiency, extend the **solveMaze** program so that it records the number of recursive calls as it proceeds. Use this program to calculate how many recursive calls are required to solve the following maze if the call to **unmarkSquare** remains part of the program:

    Run your program again, this time without the call to **unmarkSquare**. What happens to the number of recursive calls?

3. As the result of the preceding exercise makes clear, the idea of keeping track of the path through a maze by using the **markSquare** facility in the **Maze** class has a substantial cost. A more practical approach is to change the definition of the recursive function so that it keeps track of the current path as it goes. Following the logic of **solveMaze**, write a function

```
bool findSolutionPath(Maze & maze, Point start,
                      Vector<Point> & path);
```

that takes, in addition to the coordinates of the starting position, a vector of **Point** values called **path**. Like **solveMaze**, **findSolutionPath** returns a Boolean value indicating whether the maze is solvable. In addition, the **findSolutionPath** function initializes the elements of the **path** vector to a sequence of coordinates beginning with the starting position and ending with the coordinates of the first square that lies outside the maze. For this exercise, it is sufficient for **findPath** to find any solution path. It need not find the shortest one.

4. Most drawing programs for personal computers make it possible to fill an enclosed region on the screen with a solid color. Typically, you invoke this operation by selecting a "paint bucket" tool and then clicking the mouse, with the cursor somewhere in your drawing. When you do, the paint spreads to every part of the picture it can reach without going through a line.

    For example, suppose you have just drawn the following picture of a house:

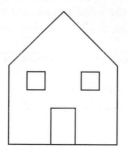

If you select the paint bucket and click inside the door, the drawing program fills the area bounded by the door frame as shown at the left side of the following diagram. If you instead click somewhere on the front wall of the house, the program fills the entire wall space except for the windows and doors, as shown on the right:

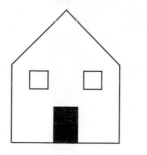 

In order to understand how this process works, it is important to understand that the screen of the computer is broken down into an array of tiny dots called

pixels. On a monochrome display, pixels can be either white or black. The paint-fill operation consists of painting black the starting pixel (i.e., the pixel you click while using the paint-bucket tool) along with any pixels connected to that starting point by an unbroken chain of white pixels. Thus, the patterns of pixels on the screen representing the preceding two diagrams would look like this:

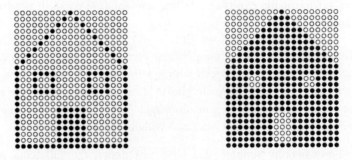

It is easy to represent a pixel grid using the type **Grid<bool>**. White pixels in the grid have the value **false**, and black pixels have the value **true**. Given this representation, write a function

```
void fillRegion(Grid<bool> & pixels, int row, int col)
```

that simulates the operation of the paint-bucket tool by painting in black all white pixels reachable from the specified row and column without crossing an existing black pixel.

5. The most powerful piece in the game of chess is the queen, which can move any number of squares in any direction, horizontally, vertically, or diagonally. For example, the queen shown in this chessboard can move to any of the marked squares:

Even though the queen can cover a large number of squares, it is possible to place eight queens on an 8×8 chessboard so that none of them attacks any of the others, as shown in the following diagram:

Write a program that solves the more general problem of whether it is possible to place N queens on an $N \times N$ chessboard so that none of them can move to a square occupied by any of the others in a single turn. Your program should either display a solution if it finds one or report that no solutions exist.

6. In chess, a knight moves in an L-shaped pattern: two squares in one direction horizontally or vertically, and then one square at right angles to that motion. For example, the white knight in the following diagram can move to any of the eight squares marked with an ✕:

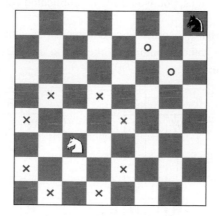

The mobility of a knight decreases near the edge of the board, as illustrated by the black knight in the corner, which can reach only the two squares marked with an **o**.

It turns out that a knight can visit all 64 squares on a chessboard without ever moving to the same square twice. A path for the knight that moves through all the squares without repeating a square is called a ***knight's tour***. One such tour is shown in the following diagram, in which the numbers in the squares indicate the order in which they were visited:

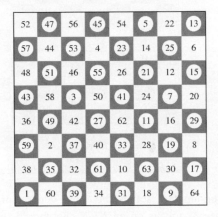

Write a program that uses backtracking recursion to find a knight's tour.

7.   In the 1960s, a puzzle called *Instant Insanity* was popular for some years before it faded from view. The puzzle consisted of four cubes whose faces were each painted with one of the colors red, blue, green, and white, represented in the rest of this problem by their initial letter. The goal of the puzzle was to arrange the cubes into a line so that if you looked at the line from any of its edges, you would see no duplicated colors.

Cubes are hard to draw in two dimensions, but the following diagram shows what the cubes would look like if you unfolded them and placed them flat on the page:

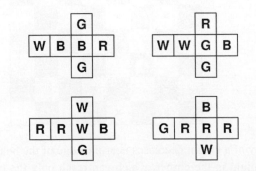

Write a program that uses backtracking to solve the Instant Insanity puzzle.

8.   In theory, the recursive backtracking strategy described in this chapter should be sufficient to solve puzzles that involve performing a sequence of moves until the puzzle reaches some goal state. In practice, however, many of those puzzles are too complex to solve in a reasonable amount of time. One puzzle that is just at the limit of what recursive backtracking can accomplish without some additional cleverness is the *peg solitaire* puzzle, which dates from the 17th century. Peg solitaire is usually played on a board that looks like this:

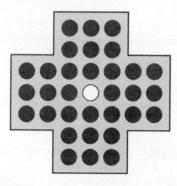

The black dots in the diagram are pegs, which fill the board except for the center hole. On a turn, you are allowed to jump over and remove a peg, as illustrated in the following diagram, in which the colored peg jumps into the vacant center hole and the peg in the middle is removed:

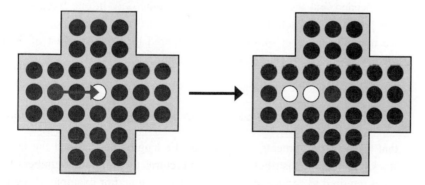

The object of the game is to perform a series of jumps that leaves only one peg in the center hole. Write a program to solve this puzzle.

9.   The game of dominos is played with rectangular pieces composed of two connected squares, each of which is marked with a certain number of dots. For example, each of the following four rectangles represents a domino:

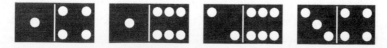

Dominos can be connected end-to-end to form chains, subject to the condition that two dominos can be linked together only if the numbers match where the dominos touch. For example, you can form a chain consisting of these four dominos by connecting them in the following order:

In the traditional game, dominos can be rotated by 180° so that their numbers are reversed. In this chain, for example, the 1–6 and 3–4 dominos have been "turned around" so that they fit into the chain.

Suppose that you have access to a **Domino** class (see Chapter 6, exercise 1) that exports the methods **getLeftDots** and **getRightDots**. Given this class, write a recursive function

```
bool formsDominoChain(Vector<Domino> & dominos);
```

that returns **true** if it is possible to build a chain consisting of every domino in the vector.

10. Suppose that you have been assigned the job of buying the plumbing pipes for a construction project. Your foreman gives you a list of the varying lengths of pipe needed, but the distributor sells stock pipe only in one fixed size. You can, however, cut each stock pipe in any way needed. Your job is to figure out the minimum number of stock pipes required to satisfy the list of requests, thereby saving money and minimizing waste.

Write a recursive function

```
int cutStock(Vector<int> & requests, int stockLength);
```

that takes two arguments—a vector of the lengths needed and the length of stock pipe that the distributor sells—and returns the minimum number of stock pipes required to service all requests in the vector. For example, if the vector contains [4, 3, 4, 1, 7, 8] and the stock pipe length is 10, you can purchase three stock pipes and divide them as follows:

         Pipe 1: 4, 4, 1
         Pipe 2: 3, 7
         Pipe 3: 8

Doing so leaves you with two small remnants left over. There are other possible arrangements that also fit into three stock pipes, but the task cannot be done with fewer.

11. Most operating systems and many applications that allow users to work with files support *wildcard patterns,* in which special characters are used to create filename patterns that can match many different files. The most common special characters used in wildcard matching are `?`, which matches any single character, and `*`, which matches any sequence of characters. Other characters in a filename pattern must match the corresponding character in a filename. For example, the pattern `*.*` matches any filename that contains a period, such as **EnglishWords.dat** or **HelloWorld.cpp**, but does not match filenames that do not contain a period. Similarly, the pattern **test.?** matches any filename that consists of the name **test**, a period, and a single character; thus, **test.?** matches **test.h** but not **test.cpp**. These patterns can be combined in any way you like. For example, the pattern **??*** matches any filename containing at least two characters.

    Write a function

    ```
    bool wildcardMatch(string filename, string pattern);
    ```

    that takes two strings, representing a filename and a wildcard pattern, and returns **true** if that filename matches the pattern. Thus,

wildcardMatch("US.txt", "*.*")	*returns*	**true**
wildcardMatch("test", "*.*")	*returns*	**false**
wildcardMatch("test.h", "test.?")	*returns*	**true**
wildcardMatch("test.cpp", "test.?")	*returns*	**false**
wildcardMatch("x", "??*")	*returns*	**false**
wildcardMatch("yy", "??*")	*returns*	**true**
wildcardMatch("zzz", "??*")	*returns*	**true**

12. Rewrite the simple Nim game so that it uses the generalized minimax algorithm presented in Figure 9-6. Your program should not change the code for **findBestMove** or **evaluatePosition**. Your job is to come up with an appropriate definition of the **Move** type and the various game-specific methods so that the program still plays a perfect game of Nim.

13. Modify the code for the simple Nim game you wrote for exercise 12 so that it plays a different variant of Nim. In this version, the pile begins with 17 coins. On each turn, players alternate taking one, two, three, or four coins from the pile. In the simple Nim game, the coins the players took away were simply ignored; in this game, the coins go into a pile for each player. The player whose pile contains an even number of coins after the last coin is taken wins the game.

14.   In the most common variant of Nim, the coins are not combined into a single pile but are instead arranged in three rows like this:

Row 0:

Row 1:

Row 2:

A move in this game consists of taking any number of coins, subject to the condition that all the coins must come from the same row. The player who takes the last coin loses.

Write a program that uses the minimax algorithm to play a perfect game of three-pile Nim. The starting configuration shown here is a typical one, but your program should be general enough so that you can easily change either the number of rows or the number of coins in each row.

15.   The game of *tic-tac-toe* (or ***naughts and crosses***) is played by two players who take turns placing **X**s and **O**s in a 3×3 grid that looks like this:

The object of the game is to line up three of your own symbols in a row, horizontally, vertically, or diagonally. In the following game, for example, **X** has won the game by completing three in a row across the top:

If the board fills up without anyone completing a row, the game is a draw, which is called a ***cat's game*** in tic-tac-toe.

Write a program that uses the minimax algorithm to play a perfect game of tic-tac-toe. Figure 9-8 shows a sample run against a particularly inept player.

FIGURE 9-8 Sample run of the tic-tac-toe game

```
 ○ ○ ○                          TicTacToe
Welcome to TicTacToe, the game of three in a row.
I'll be X, and you'll be O.
The squares are numbered like this:

 1 | 2 | 3
---+---+---
 4 | 5 | 6
---+---+---
 7 | 8 | 9

I'll move to 1.
The game now looks like this:

 X |   |
---+---+---
   |   |
---+---+---
   |   |

Your move.
What square? 5
The game now looks like this:

 X |   |
---+---+---
   | O |
---+---+---
   |   |

I'll move to 2.
The game now looks like this:

 X | X |
---+---+---
   | O |
---+---+---
   |   |

Your move.
What square? 7
The game now looks like this:

 X | X |
---+---+---
   | O |
---+---+---
 O |   |

I'll move to 3.
The final position looks like this:

 X | X | X
---+---+---
   | O |
---+---+---
 O |   |

I win.
```

FIGURE 9-9 Sample configuration in the Boggle® game and the words it contains

	X C E R			
	I M G A			
	N O M L			
	G Z R P			

ager	agog	agon	agonic	algor
ammino	ammo	ammonic	among	argon
cion	egal	emic	ergo	gammer
gamming	gammon	gamp	gear	gemma
glamor	glare	gnome	gnomic	going
gomeral	gong	gorp	gram	gramme
gramp	lager	lamming	lamp	large
largo	mage	malgre	mare	marge
meal	mice	minor	mome	momi
nice	nicer	noma	nome	norm
normal	ogam	ogre	omega	omer
plage	prog	program	programming	prom
prong	rage	ramming	ramp	real
realm	ream	regal	regma	remix
roger	romp	zoic		

16. The game of Boggle is played with a 4×4 grid of cubes, each of which shows a letter on its face. The goal is to form as many words of four or more letters as possible, moving only between letter cubes that are adjacent—horizontally, vertically, or diagonally—and never using any cube more than once. Figure 9-9 shows a possible Boggle layout and the words in the **EnglishWords.dat** lexicon that you can find in that layout. As an example, you can form the word *programming* using the following sequence of cubes:

Write a function

```
void findBoggleWords(const Grid<char> & board,
                     const Lexicon & english,
                     Vector<string> & wordsFound);
```

that finds all the legal words on the board that appear in the **english** lexicon and adds those words to the vector **wordsFound**.

Chapter 10
Algorithmic Analysis

Without analysis, no synthesis.

— Friedrich Engels, *Herr Eugen Dühring's Revolution in Science,* 1878

In Chapter 7, you were introduced to two different recursive implementations of the function **fib(n)**, which computes the nth Fibonacci number. The first, which is based directly on the mathematical definition

$$\texttt{fib(n)} = \begin{cases} \texttt{n} & \textit{if } \textbf{n} \textit{ is 0 or 1} \\ \texttt{fib(n - 1) + fib(n - 2)} & \textit{otherwise} \end{cases}$$

turns out to be wildly inefficient. The second implementation, which uses the notion of additive sequences to produce a version of **fib(n)** that is comparable in efficiency to traditional iterative approaches, demonstrates that recursion itself is not the cause of the problem. Even so, examples like the first version of the Fibonacci function have such high execution costs that recursion sometimes gets a bad name as a result.

As you will see in this chapter, the ability to think recursively about a problem often leads to new strategies that are considerably *more* efficient than anything that would come out of an iterative design process. The enormous power of divide-and-conquer algorithms has a profound impact on many problems that arise in practice. By using recursive algorithms of this form, it is possible to achieve dramatic increases in efficiency that can cut the solution times, not by factors of two or three, but by factors of a thousand or more.

Before looking at these algorithms, however, it is important to ask a few questions. What does the term *efficiency* mean in an algorithmic context? How would you go about measuring that efficiency? These questions form the foundation for the subfield of computer science known as ***analysis of algorithms.*** Although a detailed understanding of algorithmic analysis requires a reasonable facility with mathematics and a lot of careful thought, you can get a sense of how it works by investigating the performance of a few simple algorithms.

10.1 The sorting problem

The best way to appreciate the importance of algorithmic analysis is to consider a problem domain in which different algorithms vary widely in their performance. Of these, one of the most interesting problems is that of *sorting,* which consists of rearranging the elements in an array or vector so that they appear in some defined order. For example, suppose you have stored the following integers in the variable **vec**, which is a **Vector<int>**:

vec

56	25	37	58	95	19	73	30
0	1	2	3	4	5	6	7

Your mission is to write a function `sort(vec)` that rearranges the elements into ascending order, like this:

19	25	30	37	56	58	73	95
0	1	2	3	4	5	6	7

The selection sort algorithm

There are many algorithms you could choose to sort a vector of integers into ascending order. One of the simplest is called **selection sort.** Given a vector of size *N*, the selection sort algorithm goes through each element position and finds the value that should occupy that position in the sorted vector. When it finds the appropriate element, the algorithm exchanges it with the value that previously occupied the desired position to ensure that no elements are lost. Thus, on the first cycle, the algorithm finds the smallest element and swaps it with the first element, which appears at index position 0 in C++. On the second cycle, it finds the smallest remaining element and swaps it with the second element. Thereafter, the algorithm continues this strategy until all positions in the vector are correctly ordered. An implementation of `sort` that uses selection sort is shown in Figure 10-1.

FIGURE 10-1 Implementation of the selection sort algorithm

```
/*
 * Implementation notes: sort
 * --------------------------
 * This implementation uses an algorithm called selection sort, which can
 * be described as follows.  With your left hand (lh), point at each element
 * in the vector in turn, starting at index 0.  At each step in the cycle:
 *
 * 1. Find the smallest element in the range between your left hand and the
 *    end of the vector, and point at that element with your right hand (rh).
 *
 * 2. Move that element into its correct position by exchanging the elements
 *    indicated by your left and right hands.
 */

void sort(Vector<int> & vec) {
   int n = vec.size();
   for (int lh = 0; lh < n; lh++) {
      int rh = lh;
      for (int i = lh + 1; i < n; i++) {
         if (vec[i] < vec[rh]) rh = i;
      }
      int tmp = vec[lh];
      vec[lh] = vec[rh];
      vec[rh] = tmp;
   }
}
```

For example, if the initial contents of the vector are

56	25	37	58	95	19	73	30
0	1	2	3	4	5	6	7

the first cycle through the outer **for** loop identifies the 19 in index position 5 as the smallest value in the entire vector and then swaps it with the 56 in index position 0 to leave the following configuration:

19	25	37	58	95	56	73	30
0	1	2	3	4	5	6	7

On the second cycle, the algorithm finds the smallest element between positions 1 and 7, which turns out to be the 25 in position 1. The program goes ahead and performs the exchange operation, leaving the vector unchanged from the preceding diagram. On each subsequent cycle, the algorithm performs a swap operation to move the next smallest value into its appropriate final position. When the **for** loop is complete, the entire vector is sorted.

Empirical measurement of performance

How efficient is the selection sort algorithm as a strategy for sorting? To answer questions of this kind, it helps to collect empirical data about how long it takes the computer to complete a task for problems of varying size. When I ran the selection sort algorithm on my MacBook Pro laptop, for example, I observed the following running times, where N represents the number of elements in the vector:

N	Running time
10	0.0000024 sec
50	0.0000448 sec
100	0.000169 sec
500	0.00402 sec
1000	0.0159 sec
5000	0.395 sec
10,000	1.58 sec
50,000	39.6 sec
100,000	158.7 sec

For a vector of 10 integers, the selection sort algorithm completes its work in a couple of microseconds. Even for 5000 integers, this implementation of **sort** takes less than a second, which certainly seems fast enough in terms of our human sense of time. As the vector sizes get larger, however, the performance of selection sort begins to go downhill. For a vector of 100,000 integers, the algorithm requires more than two and a half minutes. If you're sitting in front of your computer waiting for it to reply, that seems an awfully long time.

Even more disturbing is the fact that the performance of selection sort rapidly gets worse as the vector size increases. As you can see from the timing data, every time you multiply the number of values by 10, the time required to sort the vector goes up a hundredfold. Sorting a list of a million numbers would therefore take about four and a half hours. If your business required sorting vectors on this scale, you would have no choice but to find a more efficient approach.

Analyzing the performance of selection sort

What makes selection sort perform so badly as the number of values to be sorted becomes large? To understand the answer this question, it helps to think about what the algorithm has to do on each cycle of the outer loop. To correctly determine the first value in the vector, the selection sort algorithm must consider all N elements as it searches for the smallest value. Thus, the time required on the first cycle of the loop is presumably proportional to N. For each of the other elements in the vector, the algorithm performs the same basic steps but looks at a smaller number of elements each time. It looks at $N-1$ elements on the second cycle, $N-2$ on the third, and so on, so the total running time is roughly proportional to

$$N + N-1 + N-2 + \ldots + 3 + 2 + 1$$

Because it is difficult to work with an expression in this expanded form, it is useful to simplify it by applying a bit of mathematics. As you may have learned in an algebra course, the sum of the first N integers is given by the formula

$$\frac{N \times (N+1)}{2}$$

or, multiplying out the numerator,

$$\frac{N^2 + N}{2}$$

You will learn how to prove that this formula is correct in the section on "Mathematical induction" later in this chapter. For the moment, all you need to know is that the sum of the first N integers can be expressed in this more compact form.

If you write out the values of the function

$$\frac{N^2 + N}{2}$$

for various values of N, you get a table that looks like this:

N	$\dfrac{N^2 + N}{2}$
10	55
50	1275
100	5050
500	125,250
1000	500,500
5000	12,502,500
10,000	50,005,000
50,000	1,250,025,000
100,000	5,000,050,000

Because the running time of the selection sort algorithm is presumably related to the amount of work the algorithm needs to do, the values in this table should be roughly proportional to the observed execution time of the algorithm, which turns out to be true. If you look at the measured timing data for selection sort in Figure 10-2, for example, you discover that the algorithm requires 1.58 seconds to sort 10,000 numbers. In that time, the selection sort algorithm has to perform 50,005,000 operations in its innermost loop. Assuming that there is indeed a proportionality relationship between these two values, dividing the time by the number of operations gives the following estimate of the proportionality constant:

$$\frac{1.58 \text{ seconds}}{50,005,000} = 3.16 \times 10^{-8} \text{ seconds}$$

If you apply this same proportionality constant to the other entries in the table, you discover that the formula

FIGURE 10-2 Observed and estimated times for selection sort

N	Observed time	Estimated time	Error
10	0.0000024 sec	0.0000017 sec	28%
50	0.0000448 sec	0.0000403 sec	10%
100	0.000169 sec	0.000159 sec	6%
500	0.00402 sec	0.00395 sec	2%
1000	0.0159 sec	0.0159 sec	< 1%
5000	0.395 sec	0.395 sec	< 1%
10,000	1.58 sec	1.58 sec	< 1%
50,000	39.6 sec	39.5 sec	< 1%
100,000	158.7 sec	158.0 sec	< 1%

$$3.16 \times 10^{-8} \text{ seconds } \times \frac{N^2 + N}{2}$$

offers a reasonable approximation of the running time, at least for large values of N. The observed times and the estimates calculated using this formula appear in Figure 10-2, along with the relative error between the two.

10.2 Computational complexity

The problem with carrying out a detailed analysis like the one shown in Figure 10-2 is that you end up with too much information. Although it is occasionally useful to have a formula for predicting exactly how long a program will take, you can usually get away with more qualitative measures. The reason that selection sort is impractical for large values of N has little to do with the precise timing characteristics of a particular implementation running on the laptop I happen to own at the moment. The problem is simpler and more fundamental. At its essence, the problem with selection sort is that doubling the size of the input vector increases the running time of the selection sort algorithm by a factor of four, which means that the running time grows more quickly than the number of elements in the vector.

The most valuable qualitative insights you can obtain about algorithmic efficiency are usually those that help you understand how the performance of an algorithm responds to changes in problem size. Problem size is usually easy to quantify. For algorithms that operate on numbers, it generally makes sense to let the numbers themselves represent the problem size. For most algorithms that operate on arrays or vectors, you can use the number of elements. When evaluating algorithmic efficiency, computer scientists traditionally use the letter N to indicate the size of the problem, no matter how it is calculated. The relationship between N and the performance of an algorithm as N becomes large is called the *computational complexity* of that algorithm. In general, the most important measure of performance is execution time, although it is also possible to apply complexity analysis to other concerns, such as the amount of memory space required. Unless otherwise stated, all assessments of complexity used in this text refer to execution time.

Big-O notation

Computer scientists use a special shorthand called *big-O notation* to denote the computational complexity of algorithms. Big-O notation was introduced by the German mathematician Paul Bachmann in 1892—long before the development of computers. The notation itself is very simple and consists of the letter O, followed by a formula enclosed in parentheses. When it is used to specify computational complexity, the formula is usually a simple function involving the problem size N. For example, in this chapter you will soon encounter the big-O expression

$$O(N^2)$$

which reads aloud as "big-oh of N squared."

Big-O notation is used to specify qualitative approximations and is therefore ideal for expressing the computational complexity of an algorithm. Coming as it does from mathematics, big-O notation has a precise definition, which appears later in this chapter in the section entitled "A formal definition of big-O." At this point, however, it is far more important for you—no matter whether you think of yourself as a programmer or a computer scientist—to understand what big-O means from a more intuitive point of view.

Standard simplifications of big-O

When you use big-O notation to estimate the computational complexity of an algorithm, the goal is to provide a *qualitative* insight as to how changes in N affect the algorithmic performance as N becomes large. Because big-O notation is not intended to be a quantitative measure, it is not only appropriate but desirable to reduce the formula inside the parentheses so that it captures the qualitative behavior of the algorithm in the simplest possible form. The most common simplifications that you can make when using big-O notation are as follows:

1. *Eliminate any term whose contribution to the total ceases to be significant as N becomes large.* When a formula involves several terms added together, one of the terms often grows much faster than the others and ends up dominating the entire expression as N becomes large. For large values of N, this term alone will control the running time of the algorithm, and you can ignore the other terms in the formula entirely.

2. *Eliminate any constant factors.* When you calculate computational complexity, your main concern is how running time changes as a function of the problem size N. Constant factors have no effect on the overall pattern. If you bought a machine that was twice as fast as your old one, any algorithm that you executed on your machine would run twice as fast as before for every value of N. The growth pattern, however, would remain exactly the same. Thus, you can ignore constant factors when you use big-O notation.

The computational complexity of selection sort

You can apply the simplification rules from the preceding section to derive a big-O expression for the computational complexity of selection sort. From the analysis in the section "Analyzing the performance of selection sort" earlier in the chapter, you know that the running time of the selection sort algorithm for a vector of N elements is proportional to

$$\frac{N^2 + N}{2}$$

Although it would be mathematically correct to use this formula directly in the big-O expression

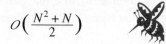

$$O\left(\frac{N^2 + N}{2}\right)$$

you would never do so in practice because the formula inside the parentheses is not expressed in the simplest form.

The first step toward simplifying this relationship is to recognize that the formula is actually the sum of two terms, as follows:

$$\frac{N^2}{2} \ + \ \frac{N}{2}$$

You then need to consider the contribution of each of these terms to the total formula as N increases in size, which is illustrated by the following table:

N	$\dfrac{N^2}{2}$	$\dfrac{N}{2}$	$\dfrac{N^2 + N}{2}$
10	50	5	55
100	5000	50	5050
1000	500,000	500	500,500
10,000	50,000,000	5000	50,005,000
100,000	5,000,000,000	50,000	5,000,050,000

As N increases, the term involving N^2 quickly dominates the term involving N. As a result, the simplification rule allows you to eliminate the smaller term from the expression. Even so, you would not write that the computational complexity of selection sort is

$$O\left(\frac{N^2}{2}\right)$$

because you can eliminate the constant factor. The simplest expression you can use to indicate the complexity of selection sort is

$$O(N^2)$$

This expression captures the essence of the performance of selection sort. As the size of the problem increases, the running time tends to grow by the square of that increase. Thus, if you double the size of the vector, the running time goes up by a factor of four. If you instead multiply the number of input values by 10, the running time explodes by a factor of 100.

Deducing computational complexity from code

It is often possible to determine the computational complexity of a function simply by looking at the code, as in the following function that computes the average of the elements in a vector:

```
double average(Vector<double> & vec) {
    int n = vec.size();
    double total = 0;
    for (int i = 0; i < n; i++) {
        total += vec[i];
    }
    return total / n;
}
```

When you call this function, some parts of the code are executed only once, such as the initialization of **total** to 0 and the division operation in the **return** statement. These computations take a certain amount of time, but that time is constant in the sense that it doesn't depend on the size of the vector. Code whose execution time does not depend on the problem size is said to run in ***constant time***, which is expressed in big-O notation as $O(1)$.

The designation $O(1)$ can seem confusing, because the expression inside the parentheses does not depend on N. In fact, this lack of any dependency on N is the whole point of the $O(1)$ notation. As you increase the size of the problem, the time required to execute code whose running time is $O(1)$ increases in exactly the same way that 1 increases; in other words, the running time does not increase at all.

There are, however, other parts of the **average** function that are executed exactly **n** times, once for each cycle of the **for** loop. These components include the expression **i++** in the **for** loop and the statement

```
total += vec[i];
```

that constitutes the loop body. Although any single execution of this part of the computation takes a fixed amount of time, the fact that these statements are executed **n** times means that their total execution time is directly proportional to the vector size. The computational complexity of this part of the **average** function is $O(N)$, which is commonly called ***linear time.***

The total running time for **average** is therefore the sum of the times required for the constant parts and the linear parts of the algorithm. As the size of the problem increases, however, the constant term becomes less and less relevant. By exploiting the simplification rule that allows you to ignore terms that become insignificant as N gets large, you can assert that the **average** function as a whole runs in $O(N)$ time.

You could, however, predict this result just by looking at the loop structure of the code. For the most part, the individual expressions and statements—unless they involve function calls that must be accounted separately—run in constant time. What matters in terms of computational complexity is how often those statements are executed. For many programs, you can determine the computational complexity simply by finding the piece of the code that is executed most often and determining how many times it runs as a function of N. In the case of the **average** function, the body of the loop is executed **n** times. Because no part of the code is executed more often than this, you can predict that the computational complexity will be $O(N)$.

The selection sort function can be analyzed in a similar way. The most frequently executed part of the code is the comparison in the statement

```
if (vec[i] < vec[rh]) rh = i;
```

That statement is nested inside two **for** loops whose limits depend on the value of N. The inner loop runs N times as often as the outer loop, which implies that the inner loop body is executed $O(N^2)$ times. Algorithms like selection sort that exhibit $O(N^2)$ performance are said to run in **quadratic time.**

Worst-case versus average-case complexity

In some cases, the running time of an algorithm depends not only on the size of the problem but also on the specific characteristics of the data. For example, consider the function

```
int linearSearch(int key, Vector<int> & vec) {
   int n = vec.size();
   for (int i = 0; i < n; i++) {
      if (key == vec[i]) return i;
   }
   return -1;
}
```

which returns the first index position in **vec** at which the value **key** appears, or -1 if the value **key** does not appear anywhere in the vector. Because the **for** loop in the implementation executes **n** times, you expect the performance of **linearSearch**, as its name implies, to be $O(N)$.

On the other hand, some calls to `linearSearch` can be executed very quickly. Suppose, for example, that the key element you are searching for happens to be in the first position in the vector. In that case, the body of the `for` loop will run only once. If you're lucky enough to search for a value that always occurs at the beginning of the vector, `linearSearch` will run in constant time.

When you analyze the computational complexity of a program, you're usually not interested in the minimum possible time. In general, computer scientists tend to be concerned about the following two types of complexity analysis:

- *Worst-case complexity.* The most common type of complexity analysis consists of determining the performance of an algorithm in the worst possible case. Such an analysis is useful because it allows you to set an upper bound on the computational complexity. If you analyze for the worst case, you can guarantee that the performance of the algorithm will be at least as good as your analysis indicates. You might sometimes get lucky, but you can be confident that the performance will not get any worse.

- *Average-case complexity.* From a practical point of view, it is often useful to consider how well an algorithm performs if you average its behavior over all possible sets of input data. Particularly if you have no reason to assume that the specific input to your problem is in any way atypical, the average-case analysis provides the best statistical estimate of actual performance. The problem, however, is that average-case analysis is usually much more difficult to carry out and typically requires considerable mathematical sophistication.

The worst case for the `linearSearch` function occurs when the key is not in the vector at all. When the key is not there, the function must complete all **n** cycles of the `for` loop, which means that its performance is $O(N)$. If the key is known to be in the vector, the `for` loop will be executed about half as many times on average, which implies that average-case performance is also $O(N)$. As you will discover in the section on "The Quicksort algorithm" later in this chapter, the average-case and worst-case performances of an algorithm sometimes differ in qualitative ways, which means that in practice it is often important to take both performance characteristics into consideration.

A formal definition of big-O

Because understanding big-O notation is critical to modern computer science, it is important to offer a more formal definition to help you understand why the intuitive model of big-O works and why the suggested simplifications of big-O formulas are in fact justified. Doing so, however, inevitably requires some mathematics. If mathematics scares you, try not to worry. It is much more important for you to understand what big-O means in practice than it is to follow all the steps presented in this section.

In computer science, big-O notation is used to express the relationship between two functions, typically in an expression like this:

$$t(N) = O(f(N))$$

The formal meaning of this expression is that $f(N)$ is an approximation of $t(N)$ with the following characteristic: it must be possible to find a constant N_0 and a positive constant C so that for every value of $N \geq N_0$, the following condition holds:

$$t(N) \leq C \times f(N)$$

In other words, as long as N is sufficiently large, the function $t(N)$ is always bounded by a constant multiple of the function $f(N)$.

When it is used to express computational complexity, the function $t(N)$ represents the actual running time of the algorithm, which is usually difficult to compute. The function $f(N)$ is a much simpler formula that nonetheless provides a reasonable qualitative estimate for how the running time changes as a function of N, because the condition expressed in the mathematical definition of big-O ensures that the actual running time cannot grow faster than $f(N)$.

To see how the formal definition applies, it is useful to go back to the selection sort example. Analyzing the loop structure of selection sort showed that the operations in the innermost loop were executed

$$\frac{N^2 + N}{2}$$

times and that the running time was presumably roughly proportional to this formula. When this complexity was expressed in terms of big-O notation, the constants and low-order terms were eliminated, leaving only the assertion that the execution time was $O(N^2)$, which is in fact an assertion that

$$\frac{N^2 + N}{2} = O(N^2)$$

To show that this expression is indeed true under the formal definition of big-O, all you need to do is come up with values for the constants C and N_0 such that

$$\frac{N^2 + N}{2} \leq C \times N^2$$

for all values of $N \geq N_0$. This particular example is extremely simple, since the inequality always holds if you set the constants C and N_0 both to 1. After all, as long as N is no smaller than 1, you know that $N^2 \geq N$. It must therefore be the case that

$$\frac{N^2 + N}{2} \leq \frac{N^2 + N^2}{2}$$

But the right side of this inequality is simply N^2, which means that

$$\frac{N^2 + N}{2} \leq N^2$$

for all values of $N \geq 1$, as required by the definition.

You can use a similar argument to show that any polynomial of degree k, which can be expressed in general terms as

$$a_k N^k + a_{k-1} N^{k-1} + a_{k-2} N^{k-2} + \ldots + a_2 N^2 + a_1 N + a_0$$

is $O(N^k)$. Once again, your goal is to find constants C and N_0 such that

$$a_k N^k + a_{k-1} N^{k-1} + a_{k-2} N^{k-2} + \ldots + a_2 N^2 + a_1 N + a_0 \leq C \times N^k$$

for all values of $N \geq N_0$. As in the preceding example, you can start by choosing 1 for the value of the constant N_0. For all values of $N \geq 1$, each successive power of N is at least as large as its predecessor, so

$$N^k \geq N^{k-1} \geq N^{k-2} \geq \ldots \geq N \geq 1$$

This property in turn implies that

$$a_k N^k + a_{k-1} N^{k-1} + a_{k-2} N^{k-2} + \ldots + a_1 N + a_0$$
$$\leq |a_k| N^k + |a_{k-1}| N^k + |a_{k-2}| N^k + \ldots + |a_1| N^k + |a_0| N^k$$

where the vertical bars surrounding the coefficients on the right side of the equation indicate absolute value. By factoring out N^k, you can simplify the right side of this inequality to

$$(|a_k| + |a_{k-1}| + |a_{k-2}| + \ldots + |a_1| + |a_0|) N^k$$

Thus, if you define the constant C to be

$$|a_k| + |a_{k-1}| + |a_{k-2}| + \ldots + |a_1| + |a_0|$$

you have established that

$$a_k\,N^k\,+\,a_{k-1}\,N^{k-1}\,+\,a_{k-2}\,N^{k-2}\,+\,.\,.\,.\,+\,a_2\,N^2\,+\,a_1\,N\,+\,a_0\,\leq\,C\times N^k$$

This result proves that the entire polynomial is $O(N^k)$.

10.3 Recursion to the rescue

At this point, you know considerably more about complexity analysis than you did when you started the chapter. However, you are no closer to solving the practical problem of how to write a sorting algorithm that is more efficient for large vectors. The selection sort algorithm is clearly not up to the task, because the running time increases in proportion to the square of the input size. The same is true for most sorting algorithms that process the elements of the vector in a linear order. To develop a better sorting algorithm, you need to adopt a qualitatively different approach.

The power of divide-and-conquer strategies

Oddly enough, the key to finding a better sorting strategy lies in recognizing that the quadratic behavior of algorithms like selection sort has a hidden virtue. The basic characteristic of quadratic complexity is that, as the size of a problem doubles, the running time increases by a factor of four. The reverse, however, is also true. If you divide the size of a quadratic problem by two, you decrease the running time by that same factor of four. This fact suggests that dividing a vector in half and then applying a recursive divide-and-conquer approach might reduce the required sorting time.

To make this idea more concrete, suppose you have a large vector that you need to sort. What happens if you divide the vector into two halves and then use the selection sort algorithm to sort each of those pieces? Because selection sort is quadratic, each of the smaller vectors requires one quarter of the original time. You need to sort both halves, of course, but the total time required to sort the two smaller vectors is still only half the time that would have been required to sort the original vector. If it turns out that sorting two halves of a vector simplifies the problem of sorting the complete vector, you will be able to reduce the total time substantially. More importantly, once you discover how to improve performance at one level, you can use the same algorithm recursively to sort each half.

To determine whether a divide-and-conquer strategy is applicable to the sorting problem, you need to answer the question of whether dividing a vector into two smaller vectors and then sorting each one helps to solve the general problem. As a way to gain some insight into this question, suppose that you start with a vector containing the following eight elements:

vec

56	25	37	58	95	19	73	30
0	1	2	3	4	5	6	7

If you divide the vector of eight elements into two vectors of length four and then sort each of those smaller vectors—remember that the recursive leap of faith means you can assume that the recursive calls work correctly—you get the following situation in which each of the smaller vectors is sorted:

v1

25	37	56	58
0	1	2	3

v2

19	30	73	95
0	1	2	3

How useful is this decomposition? Remember that your goal is to take the values out of these smaller vectors and put them back into the original vector in the correct order. How does having these smaller sorted vectors help you accomplish that goal?

Merging two vectors

As it happens, reconstructing the complete vector from the smaller sorted vectors is a much simpler problem than sorting itself. The required technique, called **merging,** depends on the fact that the first element in the complete ordering must be either the first element in **v1** or the first element in **v2**, whichever is smaller. In this example, the first element you want in the new vector is the 19 in **v2**. If you add that element to an empty vector **vec** and, in effect, cross it out of **v2**, you get the following configuration:

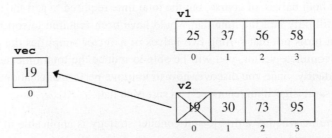

Once again, the next element can only be the first unused element in one of the two smaller vectors. This time, you compare the 25 from **v1** against the 30 in **v2** and choose the former:

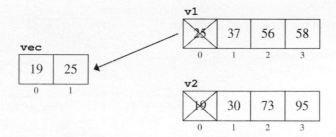

You can easily continue this process of choosing the smaller value from **v1** or **v2** until you have reconstructed the entire vector.

The merge sort algorithm

The merge operation, combined with recursive decomposition, gives rise to a sorting algorithm called **merge sort**, which turns out to be much more efficient than selection sort. The basic outline of the merge sort algorithm looks like this:

1. Check to see if the vector is empty or has only one element. If so, it must already be sorted. This condition defines the simple case for the recursion.

2. Divide the vector into two smaller vectors, each of which is half the size.

3. Sort each of the smaller vectors recursively.

4. Clear the original vector so that it is again empty.

5. Merge the two sorted vectors back into the original one.

The code for the merge sort algorithm, shown in Figure 10-3, divides neatly into two functions: **sort** and **merge**. The code for **sort** follows directly from the outline of the algorithm. After checking for the special case, the algorithm divides the original vector into two smaller ones, **v1** and **v2**. As soon as the code for **sort** has copied all the elements into either **v1** or **v2**, the rest of the function sorts these vectors recursively, clears the original vector, and then calls **merge** to reassemble the complete solution.

Most of the work is done by the **merge** function, which takes the destination vector, along with the smaller vectors **v1** and **v2**. The indices **p1** and **p2** mark the progress through each of the subsidiary vectors. On each cycle of the loop, the function selects an element from **v1** or **v2**—whichever is smaller—and adds that value to the end of **vec**. As soon as the elements in either of the two smaller vectors are exhausted, the function can simply copy the elements from the other vector without bothering to test them. In fact, because one of these vectors is already exhausted when the first **while** loop exits, the function can simply copy the rest of each vector to the destination. One of these vectors will be empty, and the corresponding **while** loop will therefore not be executed at all.

FIGURE 10-3 Implementation of the merge sort algorithm

```
/*
 * Implementation notes: sort
 * ---------------------------
 * This function sorts the elements of the vector into increasing order
 * using the merge sort algorithm, which consists of the following steps:
 *
 * 1. Divide the vector into two halves.
 * 2. Sort each of these smaller vectors recursively.
 * 3. Merge the two vectors back into the original one.
 */

void sort(Vector<int> & vec) {
    int n = vec.size();
    if (n <= 1) return;
    Vector<int> v1;
    Vector<int> v2;
    for (int i = 0; i < n; i++) {
        if (i < n / 2) {
            v1.add(vec[i]);
        } else {
            v2.add(vec[i]);
        }
    }
    sort(v1);
    sort(v2);
    vec.clear();
    merge(vec, v1, v2);
}

/*
 * Implementation notes: merge
 * ---------------------------
 * This function merges two sorted vectors, v1 and v2, into the vector
 * vec, which should be empty before this operation.  Because the input
 * vectors are sorted, the implementation can always select the first
 * unused element in one of the input vectors to fill the next position.
 */

void merge(Vector<int> & vec, Vector<int> & v1, Vector<int> & v2) {
    int n1 = v1.size();
    int n2 = v2.size();
    int p1 = 0;
    int p2 = 0;
    while (p1 < n1 && p2 < n2) {
        if (v1[p1] < v2[p2]) {
            vec.add(v1[p1++]);
        } else {
            vec.add(v2[p2++]);
        }
    }
    while (p1 < n1) vec.add(v1[p1++]);
    while (p2 < n2) vec.add(v2[p2++]);
}
```

The computational complexity of merge sort

You now have an implementation of the **sort** function based on the strategy of divide-and-conquer. How efficient is it? You can measure its efficiency by sorting vectors of numbers and timing the result, but it is helpful to start by thinking about the algorithm in terms of its computational complexity.

When you call the merge sort implementation of **sort** on a list of N numbers, the running time can be divided into two components:

1.   The amount of time required to execute the operations at the current level of the recursive decomposition

2.   The time required to execute the recursive calls

At the top level of the recursive decomposition, the cost of performing the nonrecursive operations is proportional to N. The loop to fill the subsidiary vectors accounts for N cycles, and the call to **merge** has the effect of refilling the original N positions in the vector. If you add these operations and ignore the constant factor, you discover that the complexity of any single call to **sort**—not counting the recursive calls within it—requires $O(N)$ operations.

But what about the cost of the recursive operations? To sort a vector of size N, you must recursively sort two vectors of size $N/2$. Each of these operations requires some amount of time. If you apply the same logic, you quickly determine that sorting each of these smaller vectors requires time proportional to $N/2$ at that level of the recursive decomposition, plus whatever time is required by any further recursive calls. The same process then continues until you reach the simple case in which the vectors consist of a single element or no elements at all.

The total time required to solve the problem is the sum of the time required at each level of the recursive decomposition. In general, the decomposition has the structure shown in Figure 10-4. As you move down through the recursive hierarchy, the vectors get smaller, but more numerous. The amount of work done at each level, however, is always directly proportional to N. Determining the total amount of work is thus a question of finding out how many levels there will be.

At each level of the hierarchy, the value of N is divided by 2. The total number of levels is therefore equal to the number of times you can divide N by 2 before you get down to 1. Rephrasing this problem in mathematical terms, you need to find a value of k such that

$$N = 2^k$$

FIGURE 10-4 Recursive decomposition of merge sort

Sorting a vector of size N

N operations

requires sorting two vectors of size N / 2

$2 \times N/2$ operations

requires sorting four vectors of size N / 4

$4 \times N/4$ operations

requires sorting eight vectors of size N / 8

$8 \times N/8$ operations

and so on.

Solving the equation for *k* gives you

$$k = \log_2 N$$

Because the number of levels is $\log_2 N$ and the amount of work done at each level is proportional to *N,* the total amount of work is proportional to $N \log_2 N$.

Unlike other scientific disciplines, in which logarithms are expressed in terms of powers of 10 (common logarithms) or the mathematical constant *e* (natural logarithms), computer science tends to use **binary logarithms,** which are based on powers of 2. Logarithms computed using different bases differ only by a constant factor, and it is therefore traditional to omit the logarithmic base when you talk about computational complexity. Thus, the computational complexity of merge sort is usually written as

$$O(N \log N)$$

Comparing N² and N log N performance

But how much better is an algorithm that runs in $O(N \log N)$ time than one that requires $O(N^2)$? One way to assess the level of improvement is to look at empirical data to get a sense of how the running times of the selection and merge sort algorithms compare. That timing information appears in Figure 10-5. For 10 items, this implementation of merge sort is more than five times slower than selection sort. At 100 items, selection sort is still faster, but not by very much. By the time you get up to 100,000 items, merge sort is almost 500 times faster than selection sort. On

FIGURE 10-5 Empirical comparison of selection and merge sorts

N	Selection sort	Merge sort
10	0.0000024 sec	0.0000128 sec
50	0.0000448 sec	0.0000887 sec
100	0.000169 sec	0.000196 sec
500	0.00402 sec	0.00110 sec
1000	0.0159 sec	0.00236 sec
5000	0.395 sec	0.0129 sec
10,000	1.58 sec	0.027 sec
50,000	39.6 sec	0.156 sec
100,000	158.7 sec	0.324 sec

my computer, the selection sort algorithm requires more than two and a half minutes to sort 100,000 items while merge sort completes the job in less than half a second. For large vectors, merge sort clearly represents a significant improvement.

You can get much the same information by comparing the computational complexity formulas for the two algorithms, as follows:

N	N^2	$N \log N$
10	100	33
100	10,000	664
1000	1,000,000	9965
10,000	100,000,000	132,877

The numbers in both columns grow as N becomes larger, but the N^2 column grows much faster than the $N \log N$ column. Sorting algorithms based on an $N \log N$ algorithm will therefore be useful over a much larger range of vector sizes.

10.4 Standard complexity classes

In programming, most algorithms fall into one of several common complexity classes. The most important complexity classes are shown in Figure 10-6, which gives the common name of the class along with the corresponding big-O expression and a representative algorithm in that class.

The classes in Figure 10-6 are presented in strictly increasing order of complexity. If you have a choice between one algorithm that requires $O(\log N)$ time and another that requires $O(N)$ time, the first will always outperform the second as N grows large. For small values of N, terms that are discounted in the big-O calculation may allow a theoretically less efficient algorithm to outperform

FIGURE 10-6 **Standard complexity classes**

Constant	$O(1)$	Returning the first element in a vector
Logarithmic	$O(\log N)$	Binary search in a sorted vector
Linear	$O(N)$	Linear search in a vector
$N \log N$	$O(N \log N)$	Merge sort
Quadratic	$O(N^2)$	Selection sort
Cubic	$O(N^3)$	Conventional algorithms for matrix multiplication
Exponential	$O(2^N)$	Tower of Hanoi

one that has a lower computational complexity. On the other hand, as N grows larger, there will always be a point at which the theoretical difference in efficiency becomes the deciding factor.

The differences in efficiency between these classes are in fact profound. You can begin to get a sense of how the different complexity functions stand in relation to one another by looking at the graph in Figure 10-7, which plots these complexity

FIGURE 10-7 **Growth characteristics of the standard complexity classes: linear plot**

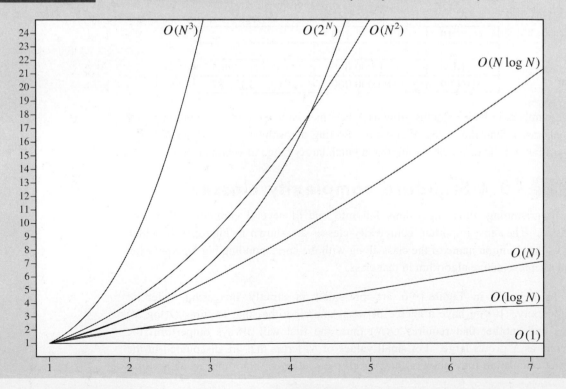

functions on a traditional linear scale. Unfortunately, this graph tells an incomplete and somewhat misleading part of the story, because the values of N are all very small. Complexity analysis, after all, is primarily relevant as the values of N become large. Figure 10-8 shows the same data plotted on a logarithmic scale, which gives you a better sense of how these functions grow over a more extensive range of values.

Algorithms that fall into the constant, linear, quadratic, and cubic complexity classes are all part of a more general family called *polynomial algorithms* that execute in time N^k for some constant k. One of the useful properties of the logarithmic plot shown in Figure 10-8 is that the graph of any function N^k always comes out as a straight line whose slope is proportional to k. If you look at the figure, it is clear that the function N^k—no matter how big k happens to be—will invariably grow more slowly than the exponential function represented by 2^N, which continues to curve upward as the value of N increases. This property has important implications in terms of finding practical algorithms for real-world problems. Even though the selection sort example demonstrates that quadratic algorithms have substantial performance problems for large values of N, algorithms whose

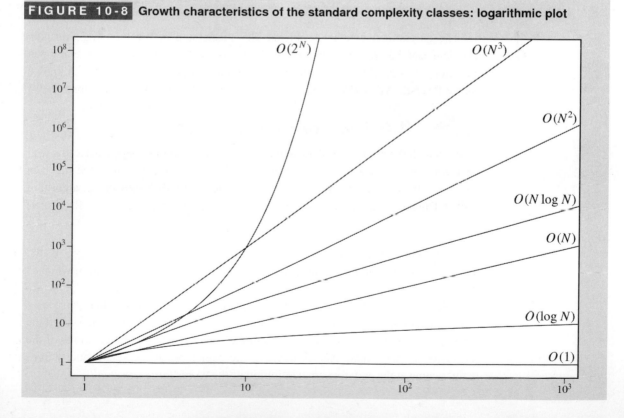

FIGURE 10-8 Growth characteristics of the standard complexity classes: logarithmic plot

complexity is $O(2^N)$ are considerably less efficient. As a general rule of thumb, computer scientists classify problems that can be solved using algorithms that run in polynomial time as *tractable,* in the sense that they are amenable to implementation on a computer. Problems for which no polynomial time algorithm exists are regarded as *intractable.*

Unfortunately, there are many commercially important problems for which all known algorithms require exponential time. One of those is the subset-sum problem introduced in Chapter 8, which arises in several practical contexts. Another is the *traveling salesman problem,* which consists of finding the shortest route by which one can visit a set of N cities connected by some transportation system and then return to the starting point. As far as anyone knows, it is not possible to solve either the subset-sum problem or the traveling salesman problem in polynomial time. The best-known approaches all have exponential performance in the worst case and are equivalent in efficiency to generating all possible routings and comparing the cost. At least for the moment, the optimal solution to each of these problems is to try every possibility, which requires exponential time. On the other hand, no one has been able to prove conclusively that no polynomial-time algorithm for this problem exists. There might be some clever algorithm that would make these problems tractable. If so, many problems currently believed to be difficult would move into the tractable range as well.

The question of whether problems like subset-sum or the traveling salesman problem can be solved in polynomial time is one of the most important open questions in computer science and indeed in mathematics. This question is known as the *P versus NP problem* and carries a million dollar prize for its solution.

10.5 The Quicksort algorithm

Even though the merge sort algorithm presented earlier in this chapter performs well in theory and has a worst-case complexity of $O(N \log N)$, it is not used much in practice. Instead, most sorting programs in use today are based on an algorithm called Quicksort, developed by the British computer scientist C. A. R. (Tony) Hoare.

Both Quicksort and merge sort employ a divide-and-conquer strategy. In the merge sort algorithm, the original vector is divided into two halves, each of which is sorted independently. The resulting sorted vectors are then merged together to complete the sort operation for the entire vector. Suppose, however, that you took a different approach to dividing up the vector. What would happen if you started the process by making an initial pass through the vector, changing the positions of the elements so that "small" values come at the beginning of the vector and "large" values come at the end, for some definition of the words *large* and *small?*

For example, suppose that the original vector you wanted to sort was the following one, presented earlier in the discussion of merge sort:

vec

56	25	37	58	95	19	73	30
0	1	2	3	4	5	6	7

Since half of these elements are larger than 50 and half are smaller, it might make sense to define *small* in this case as being less than 50 and *large* as being 50 or more. If you could then find a way to rearrange the elements so that all the small elements came at the beginning and all the large ones at the end, you would wind up with a vector that looks something like the following diagram, which shows one of many possible orderings in which the small and large elements appear on opposite sides of the boundary:

19	25	37	30	56	95	73	58
0	1	2	3	4	5	6	7

small elements   *large elements*

When the elements are divided into parts in this fashion, all that remains to be done is to sort each of the parts, using a recursive call to the function that does the sorting. Since all the elements on the left side of the boundary line are smaller than all those on the right, the final result will be a completely sorted vector:

19	25	37	30	56	95	73	58
0	1	2	3	4	5	6	7

small elements   *large elements*

If you could always choose the optimal boundary between the small and large elements on each cycle, this algorithm would divide the vector in half each time and end up demonstrating the same qualitative characteristics as merge sort. In practice, the Quicksort algorithm selects some existing element in the vector and uses that value to represent the dividing line between the small and large elements. Although you will have a chance to explore more effective strategies in the exercises, one strategy is to pick the first element (56 in the original vector) and use that to represent the boundary value. When the vector is reordered, the boundary will fall at a particular index position rather than between two positions, as follows:

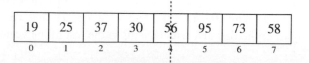

19	25	37	30	56	95	73	58
0	1	2	3	4	5	6	7

From this point, the recursive calls must sort the vector between positions 0 and 3 and the vector between positions 5 and 7, leaving index position 4 right where it is.

As in merge sort, the simple case of the Quicksort algorithm is a vector of size 0 or 1, which must already be sorted. The recursive part of the Quicksort algorithm consists of the following steps:

1. *Choose an element to serve as the boundary between the small and large elements.* This element is traditionally called the ***pivot.*** For the moment, it is sufficient to choose any element for this purpose, and the simplest strategy is to select the first element in the vector.

2. *Rearrange the elements in the vector so that large elements are moved toward the end of the vector and small elements toward the beginning.* More formally, the goal of this step is to divide the elements around a boundary position so that all elements to the left of the boundary are less than the pivot and all elements to the right are greater than or possibly equal to the pivot. This processing is called ***partitioning*** the vector and is discussed in detail in the next section.

3. *Sort the elements in each of the partial vectors.* Because all elements to the left of the pivot boundary are strictly less than all those to the right, sorting each of the vectors must leave the entire vector in sorted order. Moreover, since the algorithm uses a divide-and-conquer strategy, these smaller vectors can be sorted using a recursive application of Quicksort.

Partitioning the vector

In the partition step of the Quicksort algorithm, the goal is to rearrange the elements so that they are divided into three classes: those that are smaller than the pivot; the pivot element itself, which is situated at the boundary position; and those elements that are at least as large as the pivot. The tricky part about partitioning is to rearrange the elements without using any extra storage, which is typically done by swapping pairs of elements.

Tony Hoare's original approach to partitioning is fairly easy to explain in English. As in the preceding section, the discussion that follows assumes that the pivot is stored in the initial element position. Because the pivot value has already been selected when you start the partitioning phase of the algorithm, you can tell immediately whether a value is large or small relative to that pivot. Hoare's partitioning algorithm then proceeds as follows:

1. For the moment, ignore the pivot element at index position 0 and concentrate on the remaining elements. Use two index values, `lh` and `rh`, to record the index positions of the first and last elements in the rest of the vector, as shown:

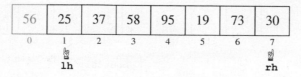

2. Move the `rh` index to the left until it either coincides with `lh` or points to an element containing a value that is small with respect to the pivot. In this example, the value 30 in position 7 is already a small value, so the `rh` index does not need to move.

3. Move the `lh` index to the right until it coincides with `rh` or points to an element containing a value that is larger than or equal to the pivot. In this example, the `lh` index must move to the right until it points to an element larger than 56, which leads to the following configuration:

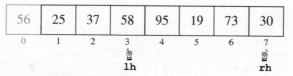

4. If the `lh` and `rh` index values have not yet reached the same position, exchange the elements in the `lh` and `rh` positions, which leaves the vector looking like this:

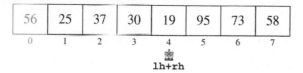

5. Repeat steps 2 through 4 until the `lh` and `rh` positions coincide. On the next pass, for example, the exchange operation in step 4 swaps the 19 and the 95. As soon as that happens, the next execution of step 2 moves the `rh` index to the left, where it ends up matching the `lh`, as follows:

56	25	37	30	19	95	73	58
0	1	2	3	4	5	6	7

lh+rh

6. Unless the chosen pivot just happened to be the smallest element in the entire vector (and the code includes a special check for this case), the point at which the `lh` and `rh` index positions coincide will be the small value that is furthest to the right in the vector. The only remaining step is to exchange that value with the pivot element at the beginning of the vector, as shown:

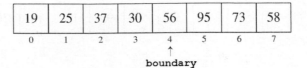

Note that this configuration meets the requirements of the partitioning step. The pivot value is at the marked boundary position, with every element to the left being smaller and every element to the right being at least as large.

An implementation of **sort** using the Quicksort algorithm is shown in Figure 10-9.

FIGURE 10-9 Implementation of the Quicksort algorithm

```
/*
 * Implementation notes: sort
 * --------------------------
 * This function sorts the elements of the vector into
 * increasing numerical order using the Quicksort algorithm.
 * In this implementation, sort is a wrapper function that
 * calls quicksort to do all the work.
 */

void sort(Vector<int> & vec) {
   quicksort(vec, 0, vec.size() - 1);
}

/*
 * Implementation notes: quicksort
 * -------------------------------
 * This function sorts the elements in the vector between index
 * positions start and finish, inclusive.  The Quicksort algorithm
 * begins by "partitioning" the vector so that all elements smaller
 * than a designated pivot element appear to the left of a
 * boundary and all equal or larger values appear to the right.
 * Sorting the subsidiary vectors to the left and right of the
 * boundary ensures that the entire vector is sorted.
 */

void quicksort(Vector<int> & vec, int start, int finish) {
   if (start >= finish) return;
   int boundary = partition(vec, start, finish);
   quicksort(vec, start, boundary - 1);
   quicksort(vec, boundary + 1, finish);
}
```

FIGURE 10-9   Implementation of the Quicksort algorithm (continued)

```
/*
 * Implementation notes: partition
 * --------------------------------
 * This function rearranges the elements of the vector so that the
 * small elements are grouped at the left end of the vector and the
 * large elements are grouped at the right end.  The distinction
 * between small and large is made by comparing each element to the
 * pivot value, which is initially taken from vec[start].  When the
 * partitioning is done, the function returns a boundary index such
 * that vec[i] < pivot for all i < boundary, vec[i] == pivot
 * for i == boundary, and vec[i] >= pivot for all i > boundary.
 */

int partition(Vector<int> & vec, int start, int finish) {
   int pivot = vec[start];
   int lh = start + 1;
   int rh = finish;
   while (true) {
      while (lh < rh && vec[rh] >= pivot) rh--;
      while (lh < rh && vec[lh] < pivot) lh++;
      if (lh == rh) break;
      int tmp = vec[lh];
      vec[lh] = vec[rh];
      vec[rh] = tmp;
   }
   if (vec[lh] >= pivot) return start;
   vec[start] = vec[lh];
   vec[lh] = pivot;
   return lh;
}
```

Analyzing the performance of Quicksort

A head-to-head comparison of the actual running times for the merge sort and Quicksort algorithms appears in Figure 10-10. As you can see, this implementation of Quicksort tends to run several times faster than the implementation of merge sort given in Figure 10-3, which is one of the reasons why programmers use it more frequently in practice. Moreover, the running times for both algorithms appear to grow in roughly the same way.

The empirical results presented in Figure 10-10, however, obscure an important point. As long as the Quicksort algorithm chooses a pivot that is close to the median value in the vector, the partition step will divide the vector into roughly equal parts. If the pivot value does not actually fall near the middle of the range of values, one of the two partial vectors may be much larger than the other, which defeats the purpose of the divide-and-conquer strategy. In a vector with randomly chosen elements, Quicksort tends to perform well, with an average-case complexity

Empirical comparison of merge sort and Quicksort

N	Merge sort	Quicksort
10	0.0000128 sec	0.0000014 sec
50	0.0000887 sec	0.0000120 sec
100	0.000196 sec	0.0000288 sec
500	0.00110 sec	0.000200 sec
1000	0.00236 sec	0.000456 sec
5000	0.0129 sec	0.00284 sec
10,000	0.027 sec	0.00608 sec
50,000	0.156 sec	0.0365 sec
100,000	0.324 sec	0.0774 sec

of $O(N \log N)$. In the worst case—which paradoxically consists of a vector that is already sorted—the performance degenerates to $O(N^2)$. Despite this inferior behavior in the worst case, Quicksort is so much faster in practice than most other algorithms that it has become the standard choice for general sorting procedures.

There are several strategies you can use to increase the likelihood that the pivot is in fact close to the median value in the vector. One simple approach is to have the Quicksort implementation choose the pivot element at random. Although it is still possible that the random process will choose a poor pivot value, it is unlikely that it would make the same mistake repeatedly at each level of the recursive decomposition. Moreover, there is no distribution of the original vector that is always bad. Given any input, choosing the pivot randomly ensures that the average-case performance for that vector would be $O(N \log N)$. Another possibility, which you can explore in more detail in exercise 6, is to select a few values, typically three or five, from the vector and choose the median of those values as the pivot.

You do have to be somewhat careful as you try to improve the algorithm in this way. Picking a good pivot improves performance, but also costs some time. If the algorithm spends more time choosing the pivot than it gets back from making a good choice, you will end up slowing down the implementation rather than speeding it up.

10.6 Mathematical induction

Earlier in the chapter, I asked you to rely on the fact that the sum

$$N + N{-}1 + N{-}2 + \ldots + 3 + 2 + 1$$

could be simplified to the more manageable formula

$$\frac{N^2 + N}{2}$$

If you were skeptical about this simplification, how would you go about proving that the simplified formula is indeed correct?

There are, in fact, several different proof techniques you could try. One possibility is to represent the original extended sum in a geometric form. Suppose, for example, that N is 5. If you then represent each term in the summation with a row of dots, those dots form the following triangle:

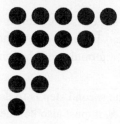

If you make a copy of this triangle and flip it upside down, the two triangles fit together to form a rectangle, shown here with the lower triangle in gray:

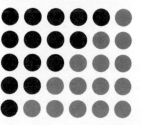

Since the pattern is now rectangular, the total number of dots—both black and gray—is easy to compute. In this picture, there are five rows of six dots each, so the total collection of dots, counting both colors, is 5×6, or 30. Since the two triangles are identical, exactly half of these dots are black; thus the number of black dots is 30 / 2, or 15. In the more general case, there are N rows containing $N+1$ dots each, and the number of black dots from the original triangle is therefore

$$\frac{N \times (N+1)}{2}$$

Proving that a formula is correct in this fashion, however, has some potential drawbacks. For one thing, geometrical arguments presented in this style are not as formal as many computer scientists would like. More to the point, constructing this type of argument requires that you come up with the right geometrical insight, which is different for each problem. It would be better to adopt a more general proof strategy that would apply to many different problems.

The technique that computer scientists generally use to prove propositions like

$$N + N{-}1 + N{-}2 + \cdots + 3 + 2 + 1 = \frac{N \times (N+1)}{2}$$

is called ***mathematical induction.*** Mathematical induction applies when you want to show that a proposition is true for all values of an integer N beginning at some initial starting point. This starting point is called the ***basis*** of the induction and is typically 0 or 1. The process consists of the following steps:

- *Prove the base case.* The first step is to establish that the proposition holds true when N has the basis value. In most cases, this step is a simple matter of plugging the basis value into a formula and showing that the desired relationship holds.

- *Prove the inductive case.* The second step is to demonstrate that, if you assume the proposition to be true for N, it must also be true for $N{+}1$.

As an example, here is how you can use mathematical induction to prove the proposition that

$$N + N{-}1 + N{-}2 + \cdots + 3 + 2 + 1 = \frac{N \times (N+1)}{2}$$

is indeed true for all N greater than or equal to 1. The first step is to prove the base case, in which N is equal to 1. That part is easy. All you have to do is substitute 1 for N in both halves of the formula to determine that

$$1 = \frac{1 \times (1+1)}{2} = \frac{2}{2} = 1$$

To prove the inductive case, you begin by assuming that the proposition

$$N + N{-}1 + N{-}2 + \cdots + 3 + 2 + 1 = \frac{N \times (N+1)}{2}$$

is indeed true for N. This assumption is called the ***inductive hypothesis.*** Your goal is now to verify that the same relationship holds for $N{+}1$. In other words, what you need to do to establish the truth of the current formula is to show that

$$N{+}1 + N + N{-}1 + N{-}2 + \cdots + 3 + 2 + 1 = \frac{(N+1) \times (N+2)}{2}$$

If you look at the left side of the equation, you should notice that the sequence of terms beginning with N is exactly the same as the left side of your inductive hypothesis. Since you have assumed that the inductive hypothesis is true, you can substitute the equivalent closed-form expression, so that the left side of the proposition you're trying to prove looks like this:

$$N+1 \ + \ \frac{N \times (N + 1)}{2}$$

From here on, the rest of the proof is simple algebra:

$$N+1 \ + \ \frac{N \times (N + 1)}{2}$$

$$= \ \frac{2N + 2}{2} \ + \ \frac{N^2 + N}{2}$$

$$= \ \frac{N^2 + 3N + 2}{2}$$

$$= \ \frac{(N + 1) \times (N + 2)}{2}$$

The last line in this derivation is precisely the result you were looking for and therefore completes the proof.

Many students need time to get used to the idea of mathematical induction. At first glance, the inductive hypothesis seems to be "cheating" in some sense; after all, you get to assume precisely the proposition that you are trying to prove. In fact, the process of mathematical induction is nothing more than an infinite family of proofs, each of which proceeds by the same logic. The base case in a typical example establishes that the proposition is true for $N = 1$. Once you have proved the base case, you can adopt the following chain of reasoning:

> Now that I know the proposition is true for $N = 1$, I can prove it is true for $N = 2$.
> Now that I know the proposition is true for $N = 2$, I can prove it is true for $N = 3$.
> Now that I know the proposition is true for $N = 3$, I can prove it is true for $N = 4$.
> Now that I know the proposition is true for $N = 4$, I can prove it is true for $N = 5$.
> And so on. . . .

At each step in this process, you could write out a complete proof by applying the logic you used to establish the inductive case. The power of mathematical induction comes from the fact that you don't actually need to write out the details of each step individually.

In a way, the process of mathematical induction is like the process of recursion viewed from the opposite direction. If you try to explain a typical recursive decomposition in detail, the process usually sounds something like this:

> To calculate this function for $N = 5$, I need to know its value for $N = 4$.
> To calculate this function for $N = 4$, I need to know its value for $N = 3$.
> To calculate this function for $N = 3$, I need to know its value for $N = 2$.
> To calculate this function for $N = 2$, I need to know its value for $N = 1$.
> The value $N = 1$ represents a simple case, so I can return the result immediately.

Both induction and recursion require you to make a leap of faith. When you write a recursive function, this leap consists of believing that all simpler instances of the function call will work without your paying any attention to the details. Making the inductive hypothesis requires much the same mental discipline. In both cases, you have to restrict your thinking to one level of the solution and not get sidetracked trying to follow the details all the way to the end.

Summary

The most valuable concept to take with you from this chapter is that algorithms for solving a problem can vary widely in their performance characteristics. Choosing an algorithm that has better computational properties can often reduce the time required to solve a problem by many orders of magnitude. The difference in behavior is illustrated dramatically by the tables presented in this chapter that give the actual running times for various sorting algorithms. When sorting a vector of 10,000 integers, for example, the Quicksort algorithm outperforms selection sort by a factor of almost 250; as the vector sizes get larger, the difference in efficiency between these algorithms will become even more pronounced.

Other important points in this chapter include:

- Most algorithmic problems can be characterized by an integer N that represents the size of the problem. For algorithms that operate on large integers, the size of the integer provides an effective measure of problem size; for algorithms that operate on arrays or vectors, it usually makes sense to define the problem size as the number of elements.

- The most useful qualitative measure of efficiency is *computational complexity,* which is defined as the relationship between problem size and algorithmic performance as the problem size becomes large.

- *Big-O notation* provides an intuitive way of expressing computational complexity because it allows you to highlight the most important aspects of the complexity relationship in the simplest possible form.

- When you use big-O notation, you can simplify the formula by eliminating any term in the formula that becomes insignificant as N becomes large, along with any constant factors.

- You can often predict the computational complexity of a program by looking at the nesting structure of the loops it contains.

- Two useful measures of complexity are *worst-case* and *average-case* analysis. Average-case analysis is usually much more difficult to conduct.

- Divide-and-conquer strategies make it possible to reduce the complexity of sorting algorithms from $O(N^2)$ to $O(N \log N)$, which is a significant reduction.

- Most algorithms fall into one of several common *complexity classes*, which include the *constant, logarithmic, linear, N log N, quadratic, cubic,* and *exponential* classes. Algorithms whose complexity class appears earlier in this list are more efficient than those that come later, at least when the problems being considered are sufficiently large.

- Problems that can be solved in *polynomial time*, which is defined to be $O(N^k)$ for some constant value k, are considered to be *tractable*. Problems for which no polynomial-time algorithm exists are considered *intractable* because solving such problems requires prohibitive amounts of time, even for problems of relatively modest size.

- Because it tends to perform extremely well in practice, most sorting programs are based on the *Quicksort algorithm,* developed by Tony Hoare, even though its worst-case complexity is $O(N^2)$.

- Mathematical induction provides a general technique for proving that a property holds for all values of N greater than or equal to some *base* value. To apply this technique, your first step is to demonstrate that the property holds in the base case. In the second step, you must prove that, if the formula holds for a specific value N, then it must also hold for $N+1$.

Review questions

1. The simplest recursive implementation of the Fibonacci function is considerably less efficient than the iterative version. Does this fact allow you to make any general conclusions about the relative efficiency of recursive and iterative solutions?

2. What is the sorting problem?

3. The implementation of **sort** shown in Figure 10-1 runs through the code to exchange the values at positions **lh** and **rh** even if these values happen to be the same. If you change the program so that it checks to make sure **lh** and **rh**

are different before making the exchange, it is likely to run more slowly than the original algorithm. Why might this be so?

4. Suppose that you are using the selection sort algorithm to sort a vector of 250 values and find that it takes 50 milliseconds to complete the operation. What would you expect the running time to be if you used the same algorithm to sort a vector of 1000 values on the same machine?

5. What is the closed-form expression that computes the sum of the series

$$N + N{-}1 + N{-}2 + \cdots + 3 + 2 + 1$$

6. In your own words, define the concept of computational complexity.

7. True or false: Big-O notation was invented as a means of expressing computational complexity.

8. What are the two rules presented in this chapter for simplifying big-O notation?

9. Is it technically correct to say that selection sort runs in

$$O\left(\frac{N^2 + N}{2}\right)$$

time? What, if anything, is wrong with expressing computational complexity in this form?

10. Is it technically correct to say that selection sort runs in $O(N^3)$ time? Again, what, if anything, is wrong with characterizing selection sort in this way?

11. Why is it customary to omit the base of the logarithm in big-O expressions such as $O(N \log N)$?

12. What is the computational complexity of the following function:

```
int mystery1(int n) {
    int sum = 0;
    for (int i = 0; i < n; i++) {
        for (int j = 0; j < i; j++) {
            sum += i * j;
        }
    }
    return sum;
}
```

13. What is the computational complexity of this function:

```
int mystery2(int n) {
    int sum = 0;
    for (int i = 0; i < 10; i++) {
        for (int j = 0; j < i; j++) {
            sum += j * n;
        }
    }
    return sum;
}
```

14. Explain the difference between worst-case and average-case complexity. In general, which of these measures is harder to compute?

15. Explain the roles of the constants C and N_0 in the formal definition of big-O.

16. In your own words, explain why the **merge** function runs in linear time.

17. The last two lines of the **merge** function are

```
while (p1 < n1) vec.add(v1[p1++]);
while (p2 < n2) vec.add(v2[p2++]);
```

Would it matter if these two lines were reversed? Why or why not?

18. What are the seven complexity classes identified in this chapter as the most common classes encountered in practice?

19. What does the term *polynomial algorithm* mean?

20. What criterion do computer scientists use to differentiate tractable and intractable problems?

21. In the Quicksort algorithm, what conditions must be true at the conclusion of the partitioning step?

22. What are the worst- and average-case complexities for Quicksort?

23. Describe the two steps involved in a proof by mathematical induction.

24. In your own words, describe the relationship between recursion and mathematical induction.

Exercises

1. It is easy to write a recursive function

    ```
    double raiseToPower(double x, int n)
    ```

    that calculates x^n, by relying on the recursive insight that

    $$x^n = x \times x^{n-1}$$

    Such a strategy leads to an implementation that runs in linear time. You can, however, adopt a recursive divide-and-conquer strategy which takes advantage of the fact that

    $$x^{2n} = x^n \times x^n$$

    Use this fact to write a recursive version of **raiseToPower** that runs in $O(\log N)$ time.

2. There are several other sorting algorithms that exhibit the $O(N^2)$ behavior of selection sort. Of these, one of the most important is **_insertion sort,_** which operates as follows. You go through each element in the vector in turn, as with the selection sort algorithm. At each step in the process, however, the goal is not to find the smallest remaining value and switch it into its correct position, but rather to ensure that the values considered so far are correctly ordered with respect to each other. Although those values may shift as more elements are processed, they form an ordered sequence in and of themselves.

    For example, if you consider again the data used in the sorting examples from this chapter, the first cycle of the insertion sort algorithm requires no work, because a vector of one element is always sorted:

    in order

56	25	37	58	95	19	73	30
0	1	2	3	4	5	6	7

    On the next cycle, you need to put 25 into the correct position with respect to the elements you have already seen, which means that you need to exchange the 56 and 25 to reach the following configuration:

    in order

25	56	37	58	95	19	73	30
0	1	2	3	4	5	6	7

    On the third cycle, you need to find where the value 37 should go. To do so, you need to move backward through the earlier elements—which you know are in order with respect to each other—looking for the position where 37 belongs. As you go, you need to shift each of the larger elements one position to the right, which eventually makes room for the value you're trying to insert. In this case, the 56 gets shifted by one position, and the 37 winds up in position 1. Thus, the configuration after the third cycle looks like this:

in order

25	37	56	58	95	19	73	30
0	1	2	3	4	5	6	7

After each cycle, the initial portion of the vector is always sorted, which implies that cycling through all the positions in this way will sort the entire vector.

The insertion sort algorithm is important in practice because it runs in linear time if the vector is already more or less in the correct order. It therefore makes sense to use insertion sort to restore order to a large vector in which only a few elements are out of sequence.

Write an implementation of **sort** that uses the insertion sort algorithm. Construct an informal argument to show that the worst-case behavior of insertion sort is $O(N^2)$.

3.   Write a function that keeps track of the elapsed time as it executes the **sort** procedure on a randomly chosen vector. Use that function to write a program that produces a table of the observed running times for a predefined set of sizes, as shown in the following sample run:

```
                    SortTimer
    N    |  Time (msec)
---------+--------------------
      10 |     0.00080
      50 |     0.00701
     100 |     0.01714
     500 |     0.11578
    1000 |     0.26476
    5000 |     1.62524
   10000 |     3.45750
   50000 |    20.63560
  100000 |    43.91070
```

The best way to measure elapsed system time for programs of this sort is to use the ANSI **clock** function, which is exported by the **ctime** interface. The **clock** function takes no arguments and returns the amount of time the processing unit of the computer has used in the execution of the current program. The unit of measurement and even the type used to store the result of `clock` differ depending on the type of machine, but you can always convert the system-dependent clock units into seconds using the following expression:

```
double(clock()) / CLOCKS_PER_SEC
```

If you record the starting and finishing times in the variables `start` and `finish`, you can use the following code to compute the time required by a calculation:

```
double start = double(clock()) / CLOCKS_PER_SEC;
. . . Perform some calculation . . .
double finish = double(clock()) / CLOCKS_PER_SEC;
double elapsed = finish - start;
```

Unfortunately, calculating the time requirements for a program that runs quickly requires some subtlety because there is no guarantee that the system clock unit is precise enough to measure the elapsed time. For example, if you used this strategy to time the process of sorting 10 integers, the odds are good that the time value of `elapsed` at the end of the code fragment would be 0. The reason is that the processing unit on most machines can execute many instructions in the space of a single clock tick—almost certainly enough to get the entire sorting process done for a vector of 10 elements. Because the system's internal clock may not tick in the interim, the values recorded for `start` and `finish` are likely to be the same.

The best way to get around this problem is to repeat the calculation many times between the two calls to the `clock` function. For example, if you want to determine how long it takes to sort 10 numbers, you can perform the sort-10-numbers experiment 1000 times in a row and then divide the total elapsed time by 1000. This strategy gives you a timing measurement that is much more accurate.

4. Suppose you know that all the values in an integer array fall into the range 0 to 9999. Show that it is possible to write a $O(N)$ algorithm to sort arrays with this restriction. Implement your algorithm and evaluate its performance by taking empirical measurements using the strategy outlined in exercise 3. Explain why the algorithm is less efficient than selection sort for small values of N.

5. Write a program that generates a table comparing the performance of two algorithms—linear and binary search—when used to find a randomly chosen integer key in a sorted `Vector<int>`. The linear search algorithm simply goes through each element of the vector in turn until it finds the desired one or determines that the key does not appear. The binary search algorithm, which

is implemented for string vectors in Figure 7-5, uses a divide-and-conquer strategy by checking the middle element of the vector and then deciding which half of the remaining elements to search.

The table you generate in this problem, rather than computing the time as in exercise 3, should instead calculate the number of comparisons made against elements of the vector. To ensure that the results are not completely random, your program should average the results over several independent trials. A sample run of the program might look like this:

```
┌─────────────────────────────────────────────────┐
│ ● ○ ○              SearchComparison              │
│    N    |   Linear  |   Binary                   │
│  -------+-----------+---------                    │
│      10 |      6.4  |    2.8                      │
│      50 |     29.4  |    4.4                      │
│     100 |     78.6  |    6.0                      │
│     500 |    390.6  |    9.0                      │
│    1000 |    827.2  |    8.8                      │
│    5000 |   2520.8  |   12.0                      │
│   10000 |   6585.2  |   13.4                      │
│   50000 |  43003.8  |   15.4                      │
│  100000 |  54166.6  |   16.4                      │
└─────────────────────────────────────────────────┘
```

6. Change the implementation of the Quicksort algorithm so that, instead of picking the first element in the vector as the pivot, the **partition** function chooses the median of the first, middle, and last elements.

7. Although $O(N \log N)$ sorting algorithms are clearly more efficient than $O(N^2)$ algorithms for large vectors, the simplicity of quadratic algorithms like selection sort often means that they perform better for small values of N. This fact raises the possibility of developing a strategy that combines the two algorithms, using Quicksort for large vectors but selection sort whenever the vectors become less than some threshold called the ***crossover point.*** Approaches that combine two different algorithms to exploit the best features of each are called ***hybrid strategies.***

    Reimplement **sort** using a hybrid of the Quicksort and selection sort strategies. Experiment with different values of the crossover point below which the implementation chooses to use selection sort, and determine what value gives the best performance. The value of the crossover point depends on the specific timing characteristics of your computer and will change from system to system.

8. Another interesting hybrid strategy for the sorting problem is to start with a recursive implementation of Quicksort that simply returns when the size of the vector falls below a certain threshold. When this function returns, the vector is

not sorted, but all the elements are relatively close to their final positions. At this point, you can use the insertion sort algorithm presented in exercise 2 on the entire vector to fix any remaining problems. Because insertion sort runs in linear time on vectors that are mostly sorted, this two-step process may run more quickly than either algorithm alone. Write an implementation of the **sort** function that uses this hybrid approach.

9. Suppose you have two functions, f and g, for which $f(N)$ is less than $g(N)$ for all values of N. Use the formal definition of big-O to prove that

$$15f(N) + 6g(N)$$

is $O(g(N))$.

10. Use the formal definition of big-O to prove that N^2 is $O(2^N)$.

11. Use mathematical induction to prove that the following properties hold for all positive values of N.

a) $1 + 3 + 5 + 7 + \cdots + 2N{-}1 = N^2$

b) $1_2 + 2_2 + 3_2 + 4_2 + \cdots + N_2 = \dfrac{N \times (N+1) \times (2N+1)}{6}$

c) $1^3 + 2^3 + 3^3 + 4^3 + \ldots + N^3 = (1 + 2 + 3 + 4 + \ldots + N)^2$

d) $2^0 + 2^1 + 2^2 + 2^3 + \ldots + 2^N = 2^{N+1} - 1$

12. Exercise 1 shows that it is possible to compute x^n in $O(\log N)$ time. This fact in turn makes it possible to write an implementation of the function **fib(n)** that also runs in $O(\log N)$ time, which is much faster than the traditional iterative version. To do so, you need to rely on the somewhat surprising fact that the Fibonacci function is closely related to a value called the **golden ratio,** which has been known since the days of Greek mathematics. The golden ratio, which is usually designated by the Greek letter phi (φ), is defined to be the value that satisfies the equation

$$\varphi^2 - \varphi - 1 = 0$$

Because this is a quadratic equation, it actually has two roots. If you apply the quadratic formula, you will discover that these roots are

$$\varphi = \frac{1 + \sqrt{5}}{2}$$

$$\hat{\varphi} = \frac{1 - \sqrt{5}}{2}$$

In 1718, the French mathematician Abraham de Moivre discovered that the nth Fibonacci number can be represented in closed form as

$$\frac{\varphi^n - \phi^n}{\sqrt{5}}$$

Moreover, because ϕ^n is always very small, the formula can be simplified to

$$\frac{\varphi^n}{\sqrt{5}}$$

rounded to the nearest integer.

Use this formula and the **raiseToPower** function from exercise 1 to write an implementation of **fib(n)** that runs in $O(\log N)$ time. Once you have verified empirically that the formula seems to work for the first several terms in the sequence, use mathematical induction to prove that the formula

$$\frac{\varphi^n - \phi^n}{\sqrt{5}}$$

actually computes the nth Fibonacci number.

13. If you're ready for a real algorithmic challenge, write the function

```
int findMajorityElement(Vector<int> & vec);
```

that takes a vector of nonnegative integers and returns the ***majority element,*** which is defined to be a value that occurs in an absolute majority (at least 50 percent plus one) of the element positions. If no majority element exists, the function should return −1 to signal that fact. Your function must also meet the following conditions:

- It must run in $O(N)$ time.

- It must use $O(1)$ additional space. In other words, it may use individual temporary variables but may not allocate any additional array or vector storage. Moreover, this condition rules out recursive solutions, because the space required to store the stack frames would grow with the depth of the recursion.

- It may not change any of the values in the vector.

The hard part about this problem is coming up with the algorithm, not implementing it. Play with some sample vectors and see if you can come up with an effective strategy that satisfies the conditions.

14. If you enjoyed the previous problem, here's an even more challenging one that used to be an interview question at Microsoft. Suppose that you have a vector of N elements, in which each element has a value in the inclusive range 1 to

$N-1$. Given that there are N elements in the vector and only $N-1$ possible values to store in each slot, there must be at least one value that is duplicated in the vector. There may, of course, be many duplicated values, but you know that there must be at least one by virtue of what mathematicians call the ***pigeonhole principle:*** if you have more items to put into a set of pigeonholes than the number of pigeonholes, there must be some pigeonhole that ends up with more than one item.

Your task in this problem is to write a function

```
int findDuplicate(Vector<int> vec);
```

that takes a vector whose values are constrained to be in the 1 to $N-1$ range and returns one of the duplicated values. The hard part of this problem is to design an algorithm so that your implementation adheres to the same set of conditions as the solution to the preceding exercise:

- It must run in $O(N)$ time.

- It must use $O(1)$ additional space. In other words, it may use individual temporary variables but may not allocate any additional array or vector storage. Moreover, this condition rules out recursive solutions, because the space required to store the stack frames would grow with the depth of the recursion.

- It may not change any of the values in the vector.

It's easy, for example, to write a quadratic-time solution to this problem, which looks like this:

```
int findDuplicate(Vector<int> & vec) {
    for (int i = 0; i < vec.size(); i++) {
        for (int j = 0; j < i; j++) {
            if (vec[i] == vec[j]) return vec[i];
        }
    }
    error("Vector has no duplicates");
    return -1;
}
```

The hard part is optimizing it so that it runs in linear time.

Chapter 11
Pointers and Arrays

*Orlando ran her eyes through it and then, using the first finger of
her right hand as pointer, read out the following facts as being
most germane to the matter.*

— Virginia Woolf, *Orlando,* 1928

For the most part, the programs in this book have relied on abstract data types to represent compound objects. From a practical point of view, this strategy is clearly correct. When you write programs in an object-oriented language like C++, you should take as much advantage as you can of the abstract types provided by the libraries and stay as far away as possible from the complexity of the low-level details. At the same time, it is useful to know a bit more about how C++ represents data. Having that knowledge gives you a better sense of how those abstract types work and helps you understand why C++ behaves as it does.

At this point in the text, there is another compelling reason to learn how memory works in C++. In Chapter 5, you learned about the wonderful collection classes in C++ that make programming so much easier. In the chapters that follow, the primary goal is to understand how those structures can be implemented efficiently. Evaluating the efficiency of different possible algorithms requires you to know what costs are involved in the various options. Without a detailed understanding of the low-level structures that C++ uses to implement those algorithms—most notably pointers and arrays—those costs are impossible to evaluate.

11.1 The structure of memory

Before you can understand C++'s memory model in any detail, you need to know how information is stored inside a computer. Every modern computer contains some amount of high-speed internal memory that is its principal repository for information. In a typical machine, that memory is built out of special integrated-circuit chips called ***RAM,*** which stands for ***random-access memory.*** Random-access memory allows the program to use the contents of any memory cell at any time. The technical details of how the RAM chip operates are not important to most programmers. What is important is how the memory is organized.

Bits, bytes, and words

Inside the computer, all data values—no matter how complex—are stored as combinations of the fundamental unit of information, which is called a ***bit.*** Each bit can be in one of two possible states. If you think of the circuitry inside the machine as if it were a tiny light switch, you might label those states as *off* and *on*. If you think of each bit as a Boolean value, you might instead use the labels *false* and *true*. However, because the word *bit* comes originally from a contraction of *binary digit,* it is more common to label those states as **0** and **1**, which are the two digits used in the binary number system on which computer arithmetic is based.

Since a single bit holds so little information, individual bits are not the most convenient mechanism for storing data. To make it easier to store such traditional types of information as numbers or characters, individual bits are collected together into larger units that are then treated as integral units of storage. The smallest such combined unit is called a ***byte,*** which consists of eight bits and is large enough to hold a value of type `char`. On most machines, bytes are assembled into larger structures called ***words,*** where a word is usually defined to be the size required to hold a value of type `int`. Today, most machines use words that are either four or eight bytes long (32 or 64 bits).

The amount of memory available to a particular computer varies over a wide range. Early machines supported memories whose size was measured in kilobytes (KB), the machines of the 1980s and '90s had memory sizes measured in megabytes (MB), and today's machines typically have memories measured in gigabytes (GB). In most sciences, the prefixes *kilo, mega,* and *giga* stand for one thousand, one million, and one billion, respectively. In the world of computers, however, those base-10 values do not fit well into the internal structure of the machine. By tradition, therefore, these prefixes are taken to represent the power of two closest to their traditional interpretations. Thus, in programming, the prefixes *kilo, mega,* and *giga* have the following meanings:

$$\begin{aligned}
\text{kilo (K)} \quad &= \quad 2^{10} \quad = \quad 1{,}024 \\
\text{mega (M)} \quad &= \quad 2^{20} \quad = \quad 1{,}048{,}576 \\
\text{giga (G)} \quad &= \quad 2^{30} \quad = \quad 1{,}073{,}741{,}824
\end{aligned}$$

A 64KB computer from the early 1970s would have had 64×1024 or 65,536 bytes of memory. Similarly, a modern 4GB machine would have 4×1,037,741,824 or 4,294,967,296 bytes of memory.

Binary and hexadecimal representations

Each of the bytes inside a machine holds data whose meaning depends on how the system interprets the individual bits. Depending on the hardware instructions that are used to manipulate it, a particular sequence of bits can represent an integer, a character, or a floating-point value, each of which requires some kind of encoding scheme. The easiest encoding scheme to describe is that for unsigned integers. The bits in an unsigned integer are represented using ***binary notation,*** in which the only legal values are **0** and **1**, just as is true for the underlying bits. Binary notation is similar in structure to our more familiar decimal notation, but uses 2 rather than 10 as its base. The contribution that a binary digit makes to the entire number depends on its position within the number as a whole. The rightmost digit represents the units field, and each of the other positions counts for twice as much as the digit to its right.

Consider, for example, the eight-bit byte containing the following binary digits:

That sequence of bits represents the number forty-two, which you can verify by calculating the contribution for each of the individual bits, as follows:

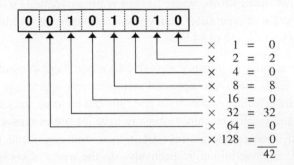

This diagram illustrates how to map an integer into bits using binary notation, but also helps to demonstrate the fact that writing numbers in binary form is terribly inconvenient. Binary numbers are cumbersome, mostly because they tend to be so long. Decimal representations are intuitive and familiar but make it harder to understand how the number translates into bits.

For applications in which it is useful to understand how a number translates into its binary representation without having to work with binary numbers that stretch all the way across the page, computer scientists tend to use *hexadecimal* (base 16) representation instead. In hexadecimal notation, there are sixteen digits, representing values from 0 to 15. The decimal digits 0 through 9 are perfectly adequate for the first ten digits, but classical arithmetic does not define the extra symbols you need to represent the remaining six digits. Computer science traditionally uses the letters **A** through **F** for this purpose, where the letters have the following values:

$$\begin{aligned}
\textbf{A} &= 10 \\
\textbf{B} &= 11 \\
\textbf{C} &= 12 \\
\textbf{D} &= 13 \\
\textbf{E} &= 14 \\
\textbf{F} &= 15
\end{aligned}$$

What makes hexadecimal notation so attractive is that you can instantly convert between hexadecimal values and the underlying binary representation. All you need to do is combine the bits into groups of four. For example, the number forty-two can be converted from binary to hexadecimal like this:

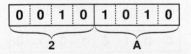

The first four bits represent the number 2, and the next four represent the number 10. Converting each of these to the corresponding hexadecimal digit gives **2A** as the hexadecimal form. You can then verify that this number still has the value 42 by adding up the digit values, as follows:

$$
\begin{array}{c}
\textbf{2 A} \\
\downarrow\,\downarrow \\
\end{array}
\begin{array}{rcl}
\times\ \ 1 &=& 10 \\
\times\ 16 &=& \underline{32} \\
 & & 42
\end{array}
$$

For the most part, numeric representations in this book use decimal notation for readability. If the base is not clear from the context, the text follows the usual strategy of using a subscript to denote the base. Thus, the three most common representations for the number forty-two—decimal, binary, and hexadecimal—look like this:

$$42_{10} = 00101010_2 = 2A_{16}$$

The key point is that the number itself is always the same; the numeric base affects only the representation. Forty-two has a real-world interpretation that is independent of the base. That real-world interpretation is perhaps easiest to see in the representation an elementary school student might use, which is after all just another way of writing the number down:

$$\cancel{||||}\ \cancel{||||}\ \cancel{||||}\ \cancel{||||}\ \cancel{||||}\ \cancel{||||}\ \cancel{||||}\ \cancel{||||}\ ||$$

The number of line segments in this representation is forty-two. The fact that a number is written in binary, decimal, or any other base is a property of the representation and not of the number itself.

Representing other data types

In many ways, the fundamental idea behind modern computing is that any data value can be represented as a collection of bits. It is easy to see, for example, how to represent a Boolean value in a single bit. All you have to do is assign each of the possible states of a bit to one of the two Boolean values. Conventionally, **0** is interpreted as **false**, and **1** is interpreted as **true**. As the last section makes clear, you can store unsigned integers by interpreting a sequence of bits as a number in binary notation, so that the eight-bit sequence **00101010** represents the number 42. With eight bits, it is possible to represent numbers between 0 and 2^8-1, or 255. Sixteen bits are sufficient to represent numbers between 0 and $2^{16}-1$, or 65,535. Thirty-two bits allow for numbers up to $2^{32}-1$, or 4,294,967,295.

The fact that each byte of memory can store a numeric value between 0 and 255 means that a byte is a perfect size to store an ASCII character. For historical reasons dating back to its predecessor languages, C++ defines the data type **char** to be exactly one byte in size. This design decision makes it more difficult for C++ programs to work with expanded character sets needed to encode languages that don't fit easily into the ASCII model. The C++ standard libraries define a type called **wchar_t** to represent "wide characters" that extend outside the ASCII range. Those facilities, however, are beyond the scope of this book.

Signed integers can also be stored as bit sequences by making a minor change to the encoding. Primarily because doing so simplifies the hardware design, most computers use a representation called **two's complement arithmetic** to represent signed integers. If you want to express a nonnegative value in two's complement arithmetic, you simply use its traditional binary expansion. To represent a negative value, you subtract its absolute value from 2^N, where N is the number of bits used in the representation. For example, the two's complement representation of −1 in a 32-bit word is calculated by performing the following binary subtraction:

$$
\begin{array}{r}
1\,0\,0\,0\,0\,0\,0\,0\,0\,0\,0\,0\,0\,0\,0\,0\,0\,0\,0\,0\,0\,0\,0\,0\,0\,0\,0\,0\,0\,0\,0\,0 \\
-\,0\,0\,0\,0\,0\,0\,0\,0\,0\,0\,0\,0\,0\,0\,0\,0\,0\,0\,0\,0\,0\,0\,0\,0\,0\,0\,0\,0\,0\,0\,0\,1 \\
\hline
1\,1\,1\,1\,1\,1\,1\,1\,1\,1\,1\,1\,1\,1\,1\,1\,1\,1\,1\,1\,1\,1\,1\,1\,1\,1\,1\,1\,1\,1\,1\,1
\end{array}
$$

Floating-point numbers are also represented as fixed-length bit sequences in C++. Although the details of floating-point representation are beyond the scope of this text, it isn't too hard to imagine building hardware that would use some subset of the bits in a word to represent the digits in the floating-point value and some other subset to represent the exponent by which that value is scaled. The important thing to remember is simply that, internally, every data value is stored in the form of bits.

In C++, different data types require different amounts of memory. For the primitive types, the following values are typical (although the C++ standard gives compiler-writers some flexibility to choose different sizes that are more convenient for a particular type of hardware):

char	1 byte (by definition)
bool	1 byte
short	2 bytes
int	4 bytes
float	4 bytes
long	8 bytes
double	8 bytes
long double	16 bytes

In C++, the size of an object is usually just the sum of the sizes of the instance variables it contains. If, for example, you define the **Point** class as it appears in Chapter 6, its private section contains the following instance variables:

```
int x;
int y;
```

Each of these instance variables typically requires four bytes, so the total space required to store the data for the object is eight bytes on most machines. Compilers, however, are allowed to add memory space to the underlying representation of an object, mostly because doing so sometimes allows them to generate more efficient machine language code. Thus, the size of a **Point** object must be at least the eight bytes necessary to hold the instance variable **x** and **y**, but it might be larger.

In a C++ program, you can determine how much memory will be assigned to a variable using the **sizeof** operator. The **sizeof** operator takes a single operand, which must be either a type name enclosed in parentheses or an expression. If the operand is a type, the **sizeof** operator returns the number of bytes required to store a value of that type; if the operand is an expression, **sizeof** returns the number of bytes required to store the value of that expression. For example, the expression

```
sizeof(int)
```

returns the number of bytes required to store a value of type **int**. The expression

```
sizeof x
```

returns the number of bytes required to store the variable **x**.

Memory addresses

Within the memory system of a typical computer, every byte is identified by a numeric *address*. The first byte in the computer is numbered 0, the second is numbered 1, and so on, up to the number of bytes in the machine minus one. As an example, the memory addresses in a tiny 64KB computer would begin with a byte numbered 0 and end with a byte numbered 65,535. Those numbers, however, are represented as decimal values, which is not how most programmers think about addresses. Given that addresses are closely tied to the internal structure of the hardware, it is more common to think about addresses as beginning at address **0000** and ending with **FFFF**, using the hexadecimal notation introduced in the preceding section. It is important, however, to remember that addresses are simply numbers and that the base determines only how those numbers are written down.

Although it is possible to work with decimal addresses, this book uses hexadecimal notation for the following reasons:

- Address numbers are conventionally written in hexadecimal, and C++ debuggers and runtime environments tend to display addresses in this form.

- Writing address numbers in their hexadecimal form using a sans-serif font makes it easier to recognize that a particular number represents an address rather than some unidentified integer. In this text, if you see the number 65,536, you can assume that it represents an integer. If you see instead the number **FFFF**, you can be confident that number represents an address.

- Using hexadecimal notation makes it easier to see why particular limits are chosen. If you write it as a decimal value, the number 65,535 seems like a rather random value. If you express that same number in hexadecimal as **FFFF**, it becomes easier to recognize that this value is the largest that can be represented in 16 bits.

Although addresses in memory are usually specified in terms of bytes, most computers support operations on larger units such as words. In a typical machine, a word consists of four bytes, and it is therefore possible to group four bytes together to refer to an individual word. In that case, however, the addresses of consecutive words increase by four. The difference between byte and word addressing is illustrated in Figure 11-1.

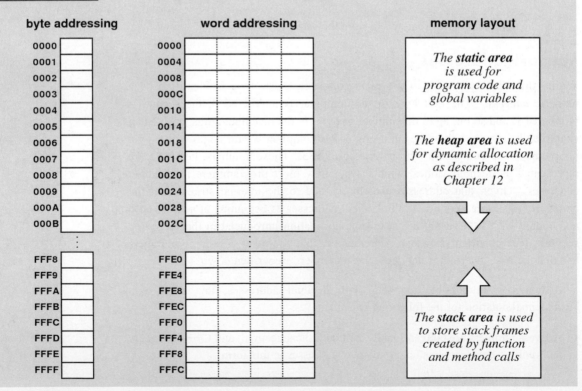

FIGURE 11-1 Typical memory layout for C++ programs

The right side of Figure 11-1 provides a rough sketch of how memory is organized in a typical C++ program. The instructions in the program—which are represented internally as bit patterns stored in memory words—and global variables tend to be stored in the *static area,* which typically appears near the beginning of the address space. The amount of memory allocated in this region typically does not change as the program runs.

The highest addresses in memory represent the *stack area.* Each time your program calls a function or a method, the computer creates a new stack frame in this memory region. When that function returns, the stack frame is discarded, which leaves the memory free to be used for the stack frames of subsequent calls. The structure of these stack frames is described in more detail in the next section.

The region of memory between the end of the program data and the stack is called the *heap area.* This region is available to the program if it needs to acquire more memory as it runs. This technique is extremely important in the design and implementation of abstract data types and is described in Chapter 12.

Assigning memory to variables

When you declare a variable in a C++ program, the compiler must make sure that the variable is assigned enough memory to hold a value of that type. The source from which that memory is taken depends on how the variable is declared. Global variables—of which the only kind used in this book are constants—are typically allocated in the same region of memory as the program, which in most architectures today appears at relatively small addresses in memory. Thus, if the compiler sees the declaration

```
const double PI = 3.14159;
```

it will reserve eight bytes of memory somewhere in the low-address region of memory and store the value 3.14159 in that variable. As a programmer, you have no idea what memory address the compiler will choose, but it often helps you to visualize what is happening inside the machine if you make up an address and use that in a diagram. Here, for example, you might imagine that the constant `PI` is stored in the address **0200**, as shown in the following diagram:

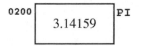

Most variables, however, are local variables. Local variables are allocated in the stack region at the high end of memory in a contiguous block of addresses called a *stack frame.* You've already seen stack frames beginning in Chapter 2, but those frames have been represented abstractly as boxes. Internally, these variables are assigned space in a block that is pushed onto the top of the stack at the time of each function call.

To make this discussion concrete, it makes sense to walk through the execution of the **PowersOfTwo** program from Chapter 1 to show exactly what happens on the stack. So that you don't have to keep flipping back to the original figure, the code for the program—without the comments and prototype lines—is reprinted as Figure 11-2 at the bottom of this page.

When you run the **PowersOfTwo** program, the first thing that happens is that the operating system generates a call to the **main** function. The **main** function takes no arguments but does have two local variables, **limit** and **i**. The stack frame must therefore allocate space for these integer variables, as follows:

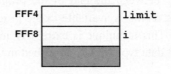

FIGURE 11-2 Code for the **PowersOfTwo** program

```
/*
 * File: PowersOfTwo.cpp
 * -----------------------
 * This figure contains only the function definitions from the
 * PowersOfTwo program from Chapter 1.
 */

int main() {
   int limit;
   cout << "This program lists powers of two." << endl;
   cout << "Enter exponent limit: ";
   cin >> limit;
   for (int i = 0; i <= limit; i++) {
      cout << "2 to the " << i << " = "
           << raiseToPower(2, i) << endl;
   }
   return 0;
}

int raiseToPower(int n, int k) {
   int result = 1;
   for (int i = 0; i < k; i++) {
      result *= n;
   }
   return result;
}
```

In this diagram, the variable **limit** has been assigned to address **FFF4**, and the variable **i** appears at **FFF8**. These addresses are in some sense arbitrary in that there is no way to predict exactly what addresses the compiler will assign or whether **limit** will come before **i** or the other way around. What you can count on is that both of these variables will be allocated in the region assigned to that stack frame. The gray rectangle at the bottom of the diagram indicates that the computer will need to keep track of additional information about each function call beyond the values of the local variables. If nothing else, each stack frame needs to keep track of the location in the program to which it should return. The format of that information depends on the architecture of the machine and is not at all essential to understanding the data model. The stack diagrams in this book include a gray rectangle in each stack frame both to remind you that this extra information exists and to make it easier to see the extent of each frame visually.

When the program runs, each function has access to its own stack frame and updates the values of the local variables as they change. Assuming that the user has entered 8 as the value of **limit**, the situation immediately before the first call to **raiseToPower** looks like this:

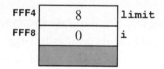

Calling **raiseToPower(2, i)** creates a new stack frame on top of the existing one. The frame contains entries for the parameter variables **n** and **k**, as well as the local variables **result** and **i**. The parameter variables are initialized to the values of the arguments, which means that the stack now looks like this:

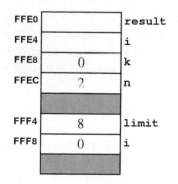

When **raiseToPower** returns, its stack frame is discarded, restoring the state before the call.

This example is quite simple and includes none of the complexity involved in creating more accurate memory diagrams. The example does, however, give you enough of a sense of how variables are assigned to memory for you to understand the topic of *pointers,* which are introduced in the following section. In Chapter 12, you'll have a chance to get back to memory diagrams and learn more about strategies for memory allocation.

11.2 Pointers

One of the principles behind the design of C++ is that programmers should have as much access as possible to the facilities provided by the underlying hardware. For this reason, C++ makes the fact that memory locations have addresses visible to the programmer. A data item whose value is an address in memory is called a ***pointer.*** In many high-level programming languages, pointers are used sparingly because those languages provide other mechanisms that eliminate much of the need for pointers. The Java programming language, for example, hides pointers from the programmer altogether. In C++, pointers are pervasive, and it is impossible to understand most professional C++ programs without knowing how pointers work.

In C++, pointers serve several purposes, of which the following are the most important:

- *Pointers allow you to refer to a large data structure in a compact way.* Data structures in a program can become arbitrarily large. No matter how large they grow, however, the data structures still reside somewhere in the computer's memory and therefore have an address. Pointers allow you to use the address as a shorthand for the complete value. Because a memory address typically fits in four bytes of memory, this strategy offers considerable space savings when the data structures themselves are large.

- *Pointers make it possible to reserve new memory during program execution.* Up to now, the only memory you could use in your programs was the memory assigned to variables that you have declared explicitly. In many applications, it is convenient to acquire new memory as the program runs and to refer to that memory using pointers. This strategy is discussed in the section on "Dynamic allocation" in Chapter 12.

- *Pointers can be used to record relationships among data items.* In advanced programming applications, pointers are used extensively to model connections between individual data values. For example, programmers often indicate that one data item follows another in a conceptual sequence by including a pointer to the second item in the internal representation of the first. Data structures that use pointers to create connections between individual components are called ***linked structures.*** Linked structures play a critical role in implementing many of the abstract data types you will encounter later in this book.

Using addresses as data values

In C++, any expression that refers to an internal memory location capable of storing data is called an *lvalue* (pronounced "ell-value"). The *l* at the beginning of *lvalue* comes from the observation that lvalues can appear on the left side of an assignment statement in C++. For example, simple variables are lvalues because you can write a statement like

```
x = 1.0;
```

Many values in C++, however, are not lvalues. For example, constants are not lvalues because a constant cannot be changed. Similarly, although the result of an arithmetic expression is a value, it is not an lvalue, because you cannot assign a new value to the result of an arithmetic expression.

The following properties apply to lvalues in C++:

- Every lvalue is stored somewhere in memory and therefore has an address.

- Once it has been declared, the address of an lvalue never changes, even though the contents of those memory locations may change.

- The address of an lvalue is a pointer value, which can be stored in memory and manipulated as data.

Declaring pointer variables

As with all other variables in C++, you must declare pointer variables before you use them. To declare a variable as a pointer, all you need to do is add an asterisk (*) before the variable name in the declaration. For example, the line

```
int *p;
```

declares **p** to be of the conceptual type pointer-to-**int**. Similarly, the line

```
char *cptr;
```

declares **cptr** to be of type pointer-to-**char**. These two types—pointer-to-**int** and pointer-to-**char**—are distinct in C++, even though each of them is represented internally as an address. To use the value at that address, the compiler needs to know how to interpret it and therefore requires that its type be specified explicitly. The value at the address specified by a pointer is called its *target*. The type of that target value is called the *base type* for the pointer. Thus, the type pointer-to-**int** has **int** as its base type.

It is important to note that the asterisk symbol used to indicate that a variable is a pointer belongs syntactically with the variable name and not with the base type. If you use the same declaration to declare two pointers of the same type, you need to mark each of the variables with an asterisk, as in

```
int *p1, *p2;
```

The declaration

```
int *p1, p2;
```

declares **p1** as a pointer to an integer, but declares **p2** as an integer variable.

The fundamental pointer operations

C++ defines two operators that allow you to move back and forth between a pointer and its target value:

        &   Address-of
        *   Value-pointed-to

The **&** operator takes an lvalue as its operand and returns the memory address in which that lvalue is stored. The ***** operator takes a value of any pointer type and returns the lvalue to which it points. This operation is called **_dereferencing_** the pointer. The ***** operation produces an lvalue, which means that you can assign a value to a dereferenced pointer.

    The easiest way to illustrate these operators is by example. Consider the declarations

```
int x, y;
int *p1, *p2;
```

These declarations allocate memory for four words, two of type **int** and two of type pointer-to-**int**. For concreteness, let's suppose that these values are stored on the stack at the machine addresses indicated by the following diagram:

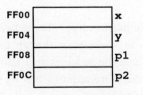

Given these declarations, you can assign values to **x** and **y** just as you always have. For example, executing the assignment statements

```
x = 42;
y = 163;
```

results in the following memory state:

FF00	42	x
FF04	163	y
FF08		p1
FF0C		p2

To initialize the pointer variables **p1** and **p2**, you need to assign values that represent the addresses of some integer objects. In C++, the operator that produces addresses is the **&** operator. You can use assignment and the **&** operator to make **p1** point to **y** and **p2** point to **x**, like this:

```
p1 = &y;
p2 = &x;
```

These assignments leave memory in the following state:

FF00	42	x
FF04	163	y
FF08	FF04	p1
FF0C	FF00	p2

The variable **p1** contains the value **FF04**, which is the address of the variable **y**. Similarly, **p2** contains the value **FF00**, which is the address of the variable **x**.

Using explicit addresses to represent pointers emphasizes the fact that addresses are stored internally as numbers. It does not, however, give you an intuitive sense of what pointers mean. To accomplish that goal, it is better to use arrows to indicate the target of each pointer. If you eliminate the address values entirely and use arrows to represent the pointers, the diagram looks like this:

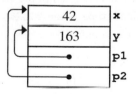

Using arrows in the diagram makes it clear that the variables **p1** and **p2** point to the cells indicated by the arrowheads. Arrows makes it easier to understand how pointers work and therefore appear in most of the memory diagrams in this text. At the same time, it is important to remember that pointers are simply numeric addresses and that there are no arrows inside the machine.

To move from a pointer to the value it points to, you use the `*` operator. For example, the expression

```
*p1
```

indicates the value in the memory location to which `p1` points. Moreover, since `p1` is declared as a pointer to an integer, the compiler knows that the expression `*p1` must refer to an integer. Thus, given the configuration of memory illustrated in the diagram, `*p1` turns out to be another name for the variable `y`.

Like the simple variable name `y`, the expression `*p1` is an lvalue, and you can assign new values to it. Executing the assignment statement

```
*p1 = 17;
```

changes the value in the variable `y` because that is the target of the pointer `p1`. After you make this assignment, the memory configuration is

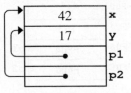

You can see that the value of `p1` itself is unaffected by this assignment. It continues to point to the variable `y`.

It is also possible to assign new values to the pointer variables themselves. For instance, the statement

```
p1 = p2;
```

tells the computer to take the value contained in the variable `p2` and copy it into the variable `p1`. The value contained in `p2` is the pointer value `FF00`. If you copy this value into `p1`, both `p1` and `p2` contain the same pointer, as illustrated by the following diagram:

42	x
17	y
FF00	p1
FF00	p2

As long as you remember the fact that a pointer has an underlying representation as an integer, the idea of copying a pointer is not at all mysterious. The value of the pointer is simply copied unchanged to the destination. If you draw your memory diagrams using arrows, you have to keep in mind that copying a pointer replaces the destination pointer with a new arrow that points to the same location as the old one. Thus, the effect of the assignment

```
p1 = p2;
```

is to change the arrow leading from **p1** so that it points to the same location as the arrow originating at **p2**, like this:

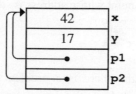

It is important to distinguish the assignment of a pointer from that of a value. *Pointer assignment,* such as

```
p1 = p2;
```

makes **p1** and **p2** point to the same location. By contrast, *value assignment,* which is represented by the statement

```
*p1 = *p2;
```

copies the value from the memory location addressed by **p2** into the location addressed by **p1**.

Pointers to structures and objects

The examples in the preceding sections declare pointers only to the primitive types. In C++, it is much more common to use pointers in conjunction with structures or objects. For example, the declarations

```
Point pt(3, 4);
Point *pp = &pt;
```

declare two local variables. The variable **pt** contains a **Point** object with the coordinate values 3 and 4. The variable **pp** contains a pointer to that same **Point** object. Using the pointer-based format, the memory diagram that results from these declarations looks like this:

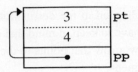

From the pointer **pp**, you can move to the object using the * operator, so that ***pp** and **pt** are effectively synonyms.

You do, however, need to exercise a bit of caution if you have a pointer to an object and need to refer to the fields and methods of that object. You cannot, for example, invoke **getX** on the point whose address is stored in **pp** by writing

      *pp.getX()

Although the code looks right, there is a problem with the precedence of the operators in this expression. In C++, the dot operator has higher precedence than the star operator, which means that the compiler tries to interpret this expression as

      *(pp.getX())

which is meaningless. What you want to do is dereference the pointer first and then invoke the method, which means that the statement needs to be parenthesized as follows:

      (*pp).getX()

This expression has the desired effect but is too cumbersome for everyday use. As you write more sophisticated applications, you'll find yourself using pointers to objects all the time. Forcing programmers to include these parentheses in every selection operation would make pointers to objects considerably less convenient. To eliminate some of the inconvenience, C++ defines the operator **->** (usually read aloud as "arrow"), which combines the operations of dereference and selection into a single operator. The conventional syntax used to invoke the **getX** method on the value to which **pp** points is therefore

      pp->getX()

The keyword this

When you are writing the implementation of a class, C++ defines the keyword **this** as a pointer to the current object. That definition has several important applications that you will discover in examples throughout the rest of the book. Of these, one of the most common is that you can use the keyword **this** to select the instance variables of an object even if those names are shadowed by a parameter or local variable.

The problem of shadowing was introduced in Chapter 6 in the context of the constructor for the **Point** class, which at the time looked like this:

```
Point(int cx, int cy) {
    x = cx;
    y = cy;
}
```

The parameters in this constructor had to be named something other than **x** and **y** to avoid name conflicts with the instance variables. Clients, however, are likely to find the new names at least a bit confusing. From the client's point of view, **x** and **y** are precisely the right names for the constructor parameters. From the perspective of the implementer, however, **x** and **y** are the perfect names for the instance variables.

Using the keyword **this** to select the instance variables makes it possible to satisfy both the client and the implementer, as follows:

```
Point(int x, int y) {
    this->x = x;
    this->y = y;
}
```

Some programmers argue that using **this** with *every* reference to a member of the current object makes the code easier to read. The JavaScript language goes so far as to require the keyword **this** for all such references. This text, however, follows the common C++ convention of using **this** only when doing so helps to resolve an ambiguity.

The special pointer NULL

In many pointer applications, it is useful to have a special pointer value that indicates that the pointer does not in fact refer to any valid memory address, at least for the present. That special value is called the ***null pointer*** and is represented internally as the value 0. In C++, the best way to indicate the null pointer is to use the constant **NULL**, which is defined in the **<cstddef>** interface.

It is illegal to use the * operator on a null pointer. The popular programming environments in use today typically detect that error and terminate the program, but that response is not guaranteed. On some machines, trying to read the target value of a null pointer simply gives you back the contents of address **0000** in the machine. The situation is much the same in the case of uninitialized pointers. If you declare a pointer but fail to initialize it, the computer will try to interpret the contents of that pointer as an address and try to read that region of memory. In such cases, programs can fail in ways that are extremely difficult to detect.

The uses of the null pointer will be introduced in this text as they become relevant to a particular application. For now, the important thing to remember is that this constant exists.

Pointers and call by reference

Pointers are used internally by C++ to implement call by reference. When a parameter is passed by reference, the stack frame stores a pointer to the location in the caller at which that value resides. Any changes to that value are made to the target of the pointer, which means that those changes remain in effect after the function returns.

The program in Figure 11-3 offers a simple illustration of how C++ implements call by reference. The program reads two integers from the user and then checks to see that they are in ascending order. If not, the program calls the function **swap**, which exchanges the values of its arguments.

Suppose that you run this program and enter the values 20 and 10, as follows:

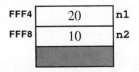

Those values are out of order, so the main program will call **swap**. The contents of the stack immediately before that call look like this:

FFF4	20	n1
FFF8	10	n2

The function **swap** takes its parameters by reference, which means that the stack frame for **swap** is given the *addresses* of the calling arguments rather than the *values*. Immediately after the call, the contents of the stack look like this:

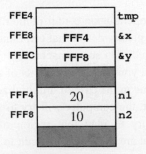

FIGURE 11-3 Program to ensure two integers are in sequence

```cpp
/*
 * File: SwapIntegers.cpp
 * ------------------------
 * This program illustrates the use of call by reference to exchange
 * the values of two integers.
 */

#include <iostream>
#include "simpio.h"
using namespace std;

/* Function prototype */

void swap(int & x, int & y);

/* Main program */

int main() {
    int n1 = getInteger("Enter n1: ");
    int n2 = getInteger("Enter n2: ");
    if (n1 > n2) swap(n1, n2);
    cout << "The range is " << n1 << " to " << n2 << "." << endl;
    return 0;
}

/*
 * Function: swap
 * Usage: swap(x, y);
 * -------------------
 * Exchanges the values of x and y.  The arguments are passed by
 * reference and can therefore be modified.
 */

void swap(int & x, int & y) {
    int tmp = x;
    x = y;
    y = tmp;
}
```

All references to **x** and **y** inside **swap** are passed along to the variables **n1** and **n2**, which are the targets of the pointers. Exchanging those values means that the effect of this function persists after the call to **swap** returns, as follows:

FFF4	10	n1
FFF8	20	n2

The program continues with the updated values, which leads to the following output:

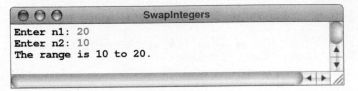

Although call by reference is extremely convenient, it is not an essential feature of the C++ language. You can simulate the effect of call by reference by making the pointers explicit. In this program, all you would have to do is change the implementation of **swap** to

```
void swap(int *px, int *py) {
    int tmp = *px;
    *px = *py;
    *py = tmp;
}
```

and the call in the main program to

```
swap(&n1, &n2);
```

In the exercises, you'll have a chance to practice converting programs that use call by reference into their pointer-based equivalents.

11.3 Arrays

When the **Vector** class first appeared in Chapter 5, the introduction to that section described vectors in terms of arrays, noting that you were likely to have some idea about arrays from your previous programming experience. C++ offers a built-in array type, which is based on the language model that C++ inherits from C. Given that the **Vector** collection class is uniformly more flexible and convenient, there are few reasons to use arrays in new code, although you will certainly encounter arrays in existing applications.

In C++, an *array* is a low-level collection of individual data values with two distinguishing characteristics:

1. *An array is ordered.* You must be able to count off the individual components of an array in order: here is the first, here is the second, and so on.

2. *An array is homogeneous.* Every value stored in an array must be of the same type. Thus, you can define an array of integers or an array of floating-point numbers but not an array in which the two types are mixed.

Since you are already familiar with the **Vector** class, it's probably easiest to think of arrays as a primitive implementation of the vector idea. As with vectors, arrays are composed of individual *elements* of some *base type* selected by an integer *index*. The pictures one draws to represent a vector almost certainly work for arrays as well. There are a few small differences in syntax, but they are easily mastered. The real difference is that arrays have the following limitations that make them less useful in practice than the more powerful vector type:

• Arrays are allocated with a fixed size that you can't subsequently change.

• Even though arrays have a fixed size, C++ does not make that size available to the programmer. As a result, programs that work with arrays typically need an additional variable to keep track of the number of elements.

• Arrays offer no support for inserting and deleting elements.

• C++ performs no bounds-checking to ensure that the elements you select are actually present in the array.

Despite these clear disadvantages, arrays are the framework from which the more powerful collection classes are built. To understand the implementation of those classes, you need to have some familiarity with the mechanics of arrays.

Array declaration

Like any other variable in C++, an array must be declared before it is used. The general form for an array declaration is

    type   name[*size*] ;

where *type* is the type of each element in the array, *name* is the name of the array variable, and *size* is an integer value indicating the number of elements allocated to the array. For example, the declaration

    int intArray[10];

declares an array named **intArray** with 10 elements, each of which is of type **int**. In most cases, however, you should specify the size as a symbolic constant rather than an explicit integer so that the array size is easier to change. Thus, a more conventional declaration would look like this:

    const int N_ELEMENTS = 10;

    int intArray[N_ELEMENTS];

You can represent this declaration pictorially as follows:

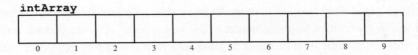

As with the elements in a vector, the index numbers for an array always begin with 0 and run up to the array size minus one. Thus, in an array with 10 elements, the index numbers are 0, 1, 2, 3, 4, 5, 6, 7, 8, and 9.

Array selection

To refer to a specific element within an array, you specify both the array name and the index corresponding to the position of that element within the array. The process of identifying a particular element within an array is called *selection,* and is indicated in C++ by writing the name of the array and following it with the index written in square brackets, just as if you are selecting an element from a vector.

The result of a selection expression is an lvalue, which means that you can assign new values to it. For example, if you execute the **for** loop

```
for (int i = 0; i < N_ELEMENTS; i++) {
    intArray[i] = 10 * i;
}
```

the variable **intArray** will be initialized as follows:

intArray

0	10	20	30	40	50	60	70	80	90
0	1	2	3	4	5	6	7	8	9

When you select an element from an array, C++ performs no bounds checking. If the index is out of range, C++ simply figures out where that element would be in memory and uses that value, which leads to unpredictable results. Worse still, if you assign a new value to that element, you may overwrite the contents of memory used by some other part of the program. Writing beyond the end of an array is one of the primary vulnerabilities used by hackers to attack computer systems.

Static initialization of arrays

Array variables can be given initial values at the time they are declared. In this case, the equal sign specifying the initial value is followed by a list of initializers enclosed in curly braces. For example, the declaration

```
const int DIGITS[] = { 0, 1, 2, 3, 4, 5, 6, 7, 8, 9 };
```

declares a constant array called **DIGITS** in which each of the 10 elements is initialized to its own index number. As you can see from this example, specifying explicit initializers allows you to omit the array size, which is then taken from the number of values.

In the **DIGITS** example, you know that there are 10 digits in the list. In many cases, however, the program will need to determine the number of elements in a statically initialized array in order to free the programmer from having to count the number of elements each time the program is changed. As an example, imagine you're writing a program that requires an array containing the names of all U.S. cities with populations of over 1,000,000. Taking data from the 2010 census, you could declare and initialize **BIG_CITIES** as a constant global array using the following declaration:

```
const string BIG_CITIES[] = {
    "New York",
    "Los Angeles",
    "Chicago",
    "Houston",
    "Philadelphia",
    "Phoenix",
    "San Antonio",
    "San Diego",
    "Dallas",
};
```

This list, however, is not static over time. Between the census results of 1990 and 2000, Detroit dropped off this list while Phoenix and San Antonio joined it. When the results are in from the 2020 census, it is likely that San Jose will join the list of cities with more than 1,000,000 people. If you are responsible for maintaining the program that contains this code, the last thing you want to do is to have to count how many cities there are in the list just so the program can determine how many elements there are. What you would like to do instead is update the list of cities and have the compiler figure out how many there are.

Fortunately, C++ offers a standard idiom for determining the allocated size of an array that uses static initialization to set the number of elements. Given a statically initialized array named **MY_ARRAY**, the number of elements in **MY_ARRAY** can be computed using the idiomatic pattern

```
sizeof MY_ARRAY / sizeof MY_ARRAY[0]
```

This expression takes the size of the entire array and divides it by the size of the initial element in the array. Because all elements of an array are the same size, the result is the number of elements in the array, regardless of the element type. Thus you could initialize a variable **N_BIG_CITIES** to hold the number of cities in the **bigCities** array by writing

```
const int N_BIG_CITIES = sizeof BIG_CITIES /
                         sizeof BIG_CITIES[0];
```

Effective and allocated sizes

Although the **sizeof** technique allows you to determine the size of a statically allocated array, there are many applications in which you have no way of knowing how large an array should be when you write the code, because the actual number of elements depends on the user's data. One strategy for solving the problem of choosing an appropriate array size is to declare an array that you know is larger than you need and then use only part of it. Thus, instead of declaring the array so that it holds the *actual* number of elements, you define a constant indicating the *maximum* number of elements and use that constant in the declaration of the array. On any given use of the program, the actual number of elements is less than or equal to this bound. When you use this strategy, you need to maintain a separate integer variable that keeps track of the number of values that are actually in use. The size of the array specified in the declaration is called the ***allocated size.*** The number of elements actively in use is called the ***effective size.***

Suppose, for example, that you want to define an array that holds the scores for competitors in a sport like gymnastics, where judges rate each entrant on a numeric scale, which might run—as Olympic gymnastics did until 2005—from 0.0 to 10.0. If you wanted your program to allow for a maximum of 100 judges even though the actual number is usually smaller, you might declare the array like this:

```
const int MAX_JUDGES = 100;

double scores[MAX_JUDGES];
```

To keep track of the effective size, you need to declare an additional variable, which you might call **nJudges**, and make sure that it keeps track of how many judges there actually are.

The relationship between pointers and arrays

In C++, the name of an array is synonymous with a pointer to its initial element. This identity is most easily illustrated by example. The declaration

```
int list[5];
```

allocates space for an array of five integers, which is assigned storage in the current stack frame, as illustrated in the following diagram:

```
  FF60  |_____|  list[0]
  FF64  |_____|  list[1]
  FF68  |_____|  list[2]
  FF6C  |_____|  list[3]
  FF70  |_____|  list[4]
```

The name **list** represents an array but can also be used as a pointer value. When it is used as a pointer, **list** is defined to be the address of the initial element in the array. Thus, if the compiler encounters the variable name **list** on its own, without any subscript after it, it translates the array name into the pointer value at which the array begins in memory.

One of the most important implications of the way C++ treats arrays as pointers is that array parameters appear to be shared with the calling argument even though no explicit call by reference is involved. You can, for example, implement an array-based version of the selection sort algorithm as follows:

```
void sort(int array[], int n) {
   for (int lh = 0; lh < n; lh++) {
      int rh = lh;
      for (int i = lh + 1; i < n; i++) {
         if (array[i] < array[rh]) rh = i;
      }
      swap(array[lh], array[rh]);
   }
}
```

This function correctly sorts the array passed by the caller, because the function initializes the **array** parameter by copying the address of the calling argument. The function then selects elements from the array using that address, which means that the elements are the ones in the calling argument.

The **sort** function would work exactly the same way if you had written its prototype like this:

```
void sort(int *array, int n)
```

In this case, the first argument is declared as a pointer, but the effect is the same as in the original implementation, which declared this parameter as an array. In either case, the value stored in the stack frame under the name **array** is the address of the initial element of the calling argument. Inside the machine, the declarations are equivalent. No matter which of these forms you use in the declaration, you can apply the same operations to the variable **array**.

As a general rule, you should declare parameters in the way that reflects their use. If you intend to use a parameter as an array and select elements from it, you should declare that parameter as an array. If you intend to use the parameter as a pointer and dereference it, you should declare it as a pointer.

The crucial difference between arrays and pointers in C++ comes into play when variables are originally declared, not when those values are passed as parameters. The fundamental distinction between the declaration

```
int array[5];
```

and the declaration

```
int *p;
```

is one of memory allocation. The first declaration reserves five consecutive words of memory capable of holding the array elements. The second declaration reserves only a single word, which is large enough to hold a machine address. The implication of this distinction is important for you to keep in mind. If you declare an array, you have storage to work with; if you declare a pointer variable, that variable is not associated with any storage until you initialize it.

The simplest way to initialize a pointer to an array is to copy the base address of an existing array into the pointer variable. As an example, if, after making the preceding declarations, you were to write the statement

```
p = array;
```

the pointer variable **p** would point to the same address used for **array**, and you could use the two names interchangeably.

The technique of setting a pointer to the address of an existing array is rather limited. After all, if you already have an array name, you might as well use it. Assigning that name to a pointer does not really do much good. The real advantage of using a pointer as an array comes from the fact that you can initialize that pointer to new memory that has not previously been allocated, which allows you to create new arrays as the program runs. This technique is described in Chapter 12.

▐▬▬ 11.4 Pointer arithmetic

In C++, you can apply the operators + and – to pointers. The results are similar to the familiar arithmetic operations in certain respects but different in others. The process of applying these operators to pointer values is called *pointer arithmetic.*

Pointer arithmetic is defined by a simple rule. If **p** is a pointer to the initial element in an array named **array**, and **k** is an integer, the following identity always holds:

> **p + k**   *is defined to be*   **&array[k]**

In other words, if you add an integer **k** to a pointer value, the result is the address of the array element at index **k** for an array beginning at the original pointer address.

Array indexing and memory addresses

To get a better sense of how pointer arithmetic operates, it is useful to consider an example that takes into account how array storage is allocated in memory. Suppose, for example, that a function includes the following declarations:

```
double list[3] = { 1.61803, 2.71828, 3.14159 };
double *p = list;
```

Each of these variables is given space in the frame for that function. For the array variable **list**, the compiler allocates space for the three elements in the array, each of which is large enough to hold a **double**. For **p**, the compiler allocates enough space for a pointer, which will be used to hold the address of some lvalue of type **double**.

The declarations in this example also specify initial values for the array. The elements of the array **list** are initialized to the values 1.61803, 2.71828, and 3.14159. The declaration

```
double *p = list;
```

initializes the pointer variable **p** so that it holds the address of the beginning of the array. If the stack frame begins at location **FFA0**, the memory looks like this:

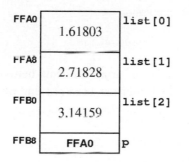

In this diagram, **p** now points to the initial address in the array **list**. If you add an integer **k** to the pointer **p**, the result is the address corresponding to the array element at index position **k**. For example, if a program contained the expression

```
p + 2
```

the result of evaluating this expression would be a new pointer value that contains the address of **list[2]**. Thus, in the preceding diagram, in which **p** contains the address **FFA0**, **p + 2** points to the address of the element that appears two elements later in the array, which is at address **FFB0**.

It's important to note that pointer addition is not equivalent to traditional addition because the calculation must take into account the size of the base type. In this example, for each unit that is added to a pointer value in the current example, the internal numeric value must be increased by eight to take account of the fact that a **double** requires eight bytes.

The C++ compiler interprets subtraction of an integer from a pointer in a similar way. If **p** is a pointer variable and **k** is an integer, the expression

```
p - k
```

computes the address of an array element located **k** elements before the address currently indicated by **p**. Thus, if you had set **p** to the address of **list[1]** using

```
p = &list[1];
```

the addresses corresponding to **p - 1** and **p + 1** would be the addresses of **list[0]** and **list[2]**, respectively.

The arithmetic operations *****, **/**, and **%** make no sense for pointers and cannot be used with pointer operands. Moreover, the uses of **+** and **−** with pointers are limited. In C, you can add or subtract an integer from a pointer, but you cannot, for example, add two pointers together.

The only other arithmetic operation defined for pointers is subtracting one pointer from another. The expression

```
p1 - p2
```

is defined to return the number of array elements between the current values of **p1** and **p2**. For example, if **p1** points at **list[2]** and **p2** points at **list[0]**, the expression

```
p1 - p2
```

has the value 2, since there are two elements between the current pointer values.

Incrementing and decrementing pointers

Knowing the rules for pointer arithmetic makes it possible to understand one of the most common idiomatic constructions in C++, which is the expression

    `*p++`

In this expression, the `*` operator and the `++` operator compete for the operand `p`. Because unary operators in C++ are evaluated in right-to-left order, the `++` takes precedence over the `*`, so the compiler interprets this expression as if it had been written like this:

    `*(p++)`

As you learned in Chapter 1, the suffix `++` operator increments the value of `p` and then returns the value that `p` had prior to the increment operation. Since `p` is a pointer, the increment operation uses pointer arithmetic. Thus, adding 1 to the value of `p` creates a pointer to the next element in the array. If `p` originally pointed to `arr[0]`, for example, the increment operation would cause it to point to `arr[1]`. Thus, the expression

    `*p++`

has the following meaning in English:

> Dereference the pointer `p` and return as an lvalue the object to which it currently points. As a side effect, increment the value of `p` so that, if the original lvalue was an element in an array, the new value of `p` points to the next element in that array.

C-style strings

The easiest way to illustrate the `*p++` idiom is to introduce it in the context in which you are most likely to see it used, which is in code that works with C-style strings. As you know from Chapter 3, C++ uses two different string types. By far the easiest one to use is the **string** class exported by the **<string>** interface, which defines a set of high-level operations that make string manipulation relatively easy. For historical reasons, however, C++ supports a more primitive string model that it inherited from the earlier language C. In C, strings are represented as arrays of characters terminated by a character whose ASCII value is zero, which is called the **null character** and is written in programs using the two-character escape sequence `\0`. If, for example, you use the string constant `"hello, world"` in a C++ program, the compiler generates an array of characters in memory containing the characters in the string plus an extra null character at the end, as follows:

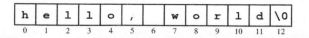

As the diagram makes clear, the length of a C-style string is not stored explicitly as part of the data structure, but is instead indicated by the null character that serves as a sentinel to mark the end. If you need to find the length of a C-style string, you have to count characters until you reach the end. In the standard C libraries (which remain available in C++), this operation is accomplished by the **strlen** function, which can be implemented in many different ways. The following implementation, for example, declares the argument as an array of characters and uses array selection to look at each character in turn:

```
int strlen(char str[]) {
    int n = 0;
    while (str[n] != '\0') {
        n++;
    }
    return n;
}
```

That implementation, however, can be replaced by the following code, which treats the argument as a character pointer:

```
int strlen(char *cp) {
    int n = 0;
    while (*cp++ != '\0') {
        n++;
    }
    return n;
}
```

In this version, the **while** test checks each character in turn to see if it matches the null character. At the same time, the ***cp++** expression automatically advances the character pointer so that each subsequent cycle checks the next character in the string. It is, however, even more efficient to advance the pointer until it reaches the end and then to use pointer subtraction to determine the number of characters, as in the following code:

```
int strlen(char *str) {
    char *cp;
    for (cp = str; *cp != '\0'; cp++);
    return cp - str;
}
```

Note that the **for** loop ends with a semicolon, which indicates that the body is empty; the necessary work happens in the initialization, test, and step expressions.

If you encounter code that performs similar string manipulation operations in an existing application, the odds are good that the implementer will leave out the explicit comparison that checks to see that the character is not equal to the null character. In both C and C++, an integral value is taken to be **true** if it has a nonzero value. One implication of this rule is that the expression ***cp++** is **true** exactly when it is not equal to the null character, which has the ASCII value of 0.

Code involving pointer arithmetic is often even more cryptic than the examples on the preceding page. The implementation of the **strcpy** function from the standard C libraries, which copies a C-style string from **src** to the character array indicated by **dst**, typically looks something like this:

```
void strcpy(char *dst, char *src) {
    while (*dst++ = *src++);
}
```

The body of the **while** loop is empty in this example; all of the work occurs in the extremely streamlined test expression

```
*dst++ = *src++
```

The effect of this expression is to copy the character currently addressed by **src** into the address indicated by **dst**, incrementing each of the pointers along the way. The result, moreover, is zero—and therefore **false**—only when the code copies the null character at the end of the string.

As you can see, the definition of **strcpy** is marked with a bug icon, even though the code is not technically incorrect. This implementation of **strcpy** does precisely what its C++ specification says it should do. The problem—and the reason for the bug symbol—is that the specification of **strcpy**, which C++ inherits from the older C language, makes the function extremely dangerous to use. The danger lies in the fact that **strcpy** doesn't check whether the destination has enough room to hold a copy of the source string. If there isn't enough memory to hold the complete string, **strcpy** goes ahead and copies the extra characters into memory allocated for other purposes. Problems of this form are called *buffer overflow errors.*

Buffer overflow errors often cause programs to crash in mysterious ways that are extremely difficult to debug. The problems such errors cause, however, can be significantly more serious than that. Applications that fail to check for buffer overflow errors—and programs that call **strcpy** are likely to fall into this category—typically present serious security risks. By allowing **strcpy** to copy carefully chosen strings into memory areas that are too small to hold those values, attackers can gain control of a machine by overwriting parts of an existing application with malicious code.

Pointer arithmetic and programming style

For reasons of history and habit, many C++ programmers use pointer arithmetic in places where array notation makes the intent much clearer. Except for the code in this chapter used to illustrate the concept, the examples in this text avoid pointer arithmetic, relying instead on array indexing to improve readability. In general, you would be well-advised to adopt the same rule in your own code.

If you are ever in the position of having to maintain existing code, you will certainly encounter the ***p++** idiom, along with even more esoteric examples of pointer arithmetic. Since maintaining existing code is an essential part of the programming process, you need to know how pointer arithmetic works. The ***p++** syntactic pattern, moreover, is used by the Standard Template Library to implement *iterators,* which are introduced in Chapter 20. In that context, it is useful to remember that ***p++** is C++ shorthand for retrieving the current element of an array and then advancing to the next one.

Summary

One of the goals of this book is to encourage you to use high-level structures that allow you to think about data in an abstract way that is independent of the underlying representation. Abstract data types and classes help make it possible to maintain this holistic viewpoint. At the same time, using C++ effectively requires you to have a mental model of how data structures are represented in memory. In this chapter, you have had a chance to see how those structures are stored and to get a sense of what goes on "under the hood" as you write your programs.

The important points introduced in this chapter include:

- The fundamental unit of information in a modern computer is a *bit,* which can be in one of two possible states. The state of a bit is usually represented in memory diagrams using the binary digits 0 and 1, but it is equally appropriate to think of these values as *off* and *on* or *false* and *true,* depending on the application.

- Sequences of bits are combined inside the hardware to form larger structures, including *bytes,* which are eight bits long, and *words,* which contain either four bytes (32 bits) or eight bytes (64 bits), depending on the machine architecture.

- The internal memory of a computer is arranged into a sequence of bytes in which each byte is identified by its index position in that sequence, which is called its *address.*

- Computer scientists tend to write address values and the contents of memory locations in *hexadecimal* notation (base 16) because doing so makes it easy to identify the individual bits.

- The primitive types in C++ require different amounts of memory. A value of type **char** requires one byte, a value of type **int** typically requires four, and a value of type **double** requires eight.

- Addresses of data in memory are themselves data values and can be manipulated as such by a program. A data value that is the address of some other piece of data is called a *pointer*. Pointer variables are declared in C++ by writing an asterisk in front of the variable name in its declaration line.

- The fundamental operations on pointers are **&** and *****, which indicate the address of a stored value and the value stored at a particular address, respectively.

- Data values that you create in a C++ program are allocated in different regions of memory. Static variables and constants are allocated in a region of memory devoted to the program code and static data. Local variables are allocated in a region called the *stack,* which is apportioned into structures called *frames* that contain all the local variables for a function or method. As you will discover in Chapter 12, programs can also allocate additional memory as they run.

- The keyword **this** indicates a pointer to the current object.

- C++ uses the **->** operator to select a member of a structure or an object when the left operand is a pointer to that value.

- The constant **NULL** is used to indicate that a pointer does not refer to anything.

- Reference parameters are implemented in C++ by storing a pointer to the calling argument in the stack frame.

- Like most languages, C++ includes a built-in *array* type for storing an ordered, homogeneous collection of elements. As in a vector, each element in an array has an integer index that begins with 0.

- Arrays are declared by specifying the size in square brackets after the array name. The size specified in the declaration is the *allocated size* of the array and is typically larger than the *effective size,* which is the number of elements in use.

- Arrays in C++ are interpreted internally as a pointer to their first element. An important implication of this design is that passing an array as a parameter does not copy the elements. Instead, the function stores the address of the array in the caller. As a result, if a function changes the values of any elements of an array passed as a parameter, those changes will be visible to the caller.

- C++ defines arithmetic on pointers so that adding an integer to a pointer generates the address of an array element that number of index positions further down in the array. Thus, if the pointer **p** points to **array[0]**, the expression **p + 2** points to **array[2]**.

- The idiomatic pattern ***p++** returns the value to which **p** currently points and then increments **p** so that it points to the next element in an array of that type.

Review questions

1.   Define the following terms: *bit, byte,* and *word.*

2.   What is the etymology of the word *bit?*

3.   How many bytes of memory are there in a 2GB machine?

4.   Convert each of the following decimal numbers to its hexadecimal equivalent:

   a) 17   c) 1729
   b) 256   d) 2766

5.   Convert each of the following hexadecimal numbers to decimal:

   a) **17**   c) **CC**
   b) **64**   d) **FADE**

6.   How many bytes does C++ assign to a value of type **char**? How many bytes are typically required for a **double**?

7.   True or false: In C++, values of type **char** always require one byte of memory.

8.   True or false: In C++, values of type **int** always require four bytes of memory.

9.   If a machine uses two's complement arithmetic to represent negative numbers, what is the internal representation of −7 in a 32-bit integer format?

10.   What are the three areas of memory in which values can be stored in a C++ program?

11.   What is the purpose of the **sizeof** operator? How do you use it?

12.   What is an *address?*

13.   What is an *lvalue?*

14.   What reasons for using pointers are cited in this chapter?

15.   What are the types of the variables introduced by the following declaration:

```
int * p1, p2;
```

16.   What are the two fundamental pointer operations? Which one corresponds to the term *dereferencing?*

17.   Explain the difference between *pointer assignment* and *value assignment.*

18. Assuming that variables of type `int` and all pointers require four bytes of memory, draw a diagram showing a portion of the stack frame that contains the following declarations:

    ```
    int v1 = 10;
    int v2 = 25;
    int *p1 = &v1;
    int *p2 = &v2;
    ```

    In your diagram, trace through the operation of these statements:

    ```
    *p1 += *p2;
    p2 = p1;
    *p2 = *p1 + *p2;
    ```

19. True or false: For any variable `x`, the expression `*&x` is essentially a synonym for `x`.

20. True or false: For any variable `p`, the expression `&*p` is essentially a synonym for `p`.

21. How are pointers used in the implementation of call by reference?

22. Write array declarations for the following array variables:

    a) An array `realArray` consisting of 100 floating-point values
    b) An array `inUse` consisting of 16 Boolean values
    c) An array `lines` that can hold up to 1000 strings

    Remember to declare constants to specify the allocated size for these arrays.

23. Write the variable declaration and `for` loop necessary to create and initialize the following integer array:

    squares

0	1	4	9	16	25	36	49	64	81	100
0	1	2	3	4	5	6	7	8	9	10

24. What is the difference between the *allocated size* and the *effective size* of an array?

25. Assuming that `intArray` is declared as

    ```
    int intArray[10];
    ```

and that **j** is an integer variable, describe the steps the computer would take to determine the value of the following expression:

```
&intArray[j + 3];
```

26. If **array** is declared to be an array, describe the distinction between the expressions

```
array[2]
```

and

```
array + 2
```

27. Assume that variables of type **double** take up eight bytes on the computer system you are using. If the base address of the array **doubleArray** is **FF00**, what is the address value of **doubleArray + 5**?

28. True or false: If **p** is a pointer variable, the expression **p++** adds 1 to the internal representation of **p**.

29. Describe the effect of the idiomatic C++ expression

```
*p++
```

30. In the expression ***p++**, which operator (***** or **++**) is applied first? In general, what rule does C use to determine the precedence of unary operators?

▮▮ Exercises

1. As you know from the chapter, integers are represented inside the computer as a sequence of bits, each of which is a single digit in the binary number system and can therefore have only the value 0 or 1. With N bits, you can represent 2^N distinct integers. For example, three bits are sufficient to represent the eight (2^3) integers between 0 and 7, as follows:

$$
\begin{aligned}
000 &\rightarrow 0\\
001 &\rightarrow 1\\
010 &\rightarrow 2\\
011 &\rightarrow 3\\
100 &\rightarrow 4\\
101 &\rightarrow 5\\
110 &\rightarrow 6\\
111 &\rightarrow 7
\end{aligned}
$$

The bit patterns for these integers follow a recursive pattern. The binary numbers with N bits consist of the following two sets in order:

- All binary numbers with $N - 1$ bits preceded by a **0**
- All binary numbers with $N - 1$ bits preceded by a **1**

Write a recursive function

```
void generateBinaryCode(int nBits);
```

that generates the bit patterns for the binary representation of all integers that can be represented using the specified number of bits. For example, calling **generateBinaryCode(3)** should produce the following output:

```
GenerateBinaryCode
000
001
010
011
100
101
110
111
```

2. Although the binary coding used in exercise 1 is ideal for most applications, it has certain drawbacks. As you count in standard binary notation, there are some points in the sequence at which several bits change at the same time. For example, in the three-bit binary code, the value of every bit changes as you move from 3 (**011**) to 4 (**100**).

In some applications, this instability in the bit patterns used to represent adjacent numbers can lead to problems. Imagine for the moment that you are using some hardware measurement device that produces a three-bit value from some real-world phenomenon that happens to be varying between 3 and 4. Sometimes, the device will register **011** to indicate the value 3; at other times, it will register **100** to indicate 4. For this device to work correctly, the transitions for each of the individual bits must occur simultaneously. If the first bit changes more quickly than the others, for example, there may be an intermediate state in which the device reads **111**, which would be a highly inaccurate reading.

It turns out that you can avoid this problem simply by changing the numbering system. If instead of using binary representation in the traditional way, you can assign three-bit values to each of the numbers 0 through 7 with the highly useful property that only one bit changes in the representation between every pair of adjacent integers. Such an encoding is called a *Gray code* (after its inventor, the mathematician Frank Gray) and looks like this:

$$
\begin{aligned}
000 &\rightarrow 0 \\
001 &\rightarrow 1 \\
011 &\rightarrow 2 \\
010 &\rightarrow 3 \\
110 &\rightarrow 4 \\
111 &\rightarrow 5 \\
101 &\rightarrow 6 \\
100 &\rightarrow 7
\end{aligned}
$$

In the Gray code representation, the bit patterns for 3 and 4 differ only in their leftmost bit. If the hardware measurement device used Gray codes, a value oscillating between 3 and 4 would simply turn that bit on and off, eliminating any problems with synchronization.

The recursive insight that you need to create a Gray code of N bits is summarized in the following informal procedure:

1. Write down the Gray code for $N - 1$ bits.

2. Copy that same list *in reverse order* below the original one.

3. Add a **0** bit in front of the encodings in the original half of the list and a **1** bit in front of those in the reversed copy.

This procedure is illustrated in the following derivation of the Gray code for three bits:

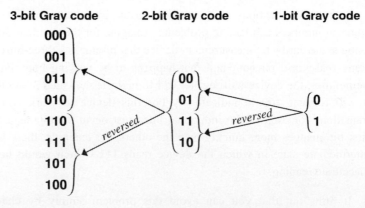

Write a recursive function **generateGrayCode(nBits)** that generates the Gray code patterns for the specified number of bits. For example, if you call the function

```
generateGrayCode(3)
```

the program should produce the following output:

```
000
001
011
010
110
111
101
100
```

3. Write overloaded versions of the **integerToString** and **stringToInteger** functions that take a second argument indicating the numeric base, which can be any integer in the range 2 through 36 (the 10 digits plus the 26 letters). For example, calling

```
integerToString(42, 16)
```

should return the string **"2A"**. Similarly, calling

```
stringToInteger("111111", 2)
```

should return the integer 63. Your functions should allow for negative numbers and should generate an error if any of the digits in the first argument to **stringToInteger** is out of range for the specified base.

4   Rewrite the simple expression calculator from Chapter 6, exercise 11, so that both the input and output values are represented in hexadecimal. A sample run of this program might look like this:

```
> 2 + 2
4
> 9 + 3
C
> 10000 - 1
FFFF
> 6 * 7
2A
> FEED - CAFE
33EF
>
```

In writing this program, the easiest approach is to scan all tokens as words rather than numbers and then call the functions you wrote for exercise 3 to perform the conversions.

5.   Rewrite the **Quadratic** program from Figure 2-3 so that it uses explicit pointers instead of call by reference to return values from the functions **getCoefficients** and **solveQuadratic**.

6.   Using the definitions of **MAX_JUDGES** and **scores** on page 498 as a starting point, write a program that reads in gymnastics scores between 0 and 10 from a set of judges and then computes the average of the scores after eliminating both the highest and lowest scores from consideration. Your program should accept input values until the maximum number of judges is reached or the user enters a blank line. A sample run of this program might look like this:

```
                         GymnasticsJudge
Enter a score for each judge in the range 0 to 10.
Enter a blank line to signal the end of the list.
Judge #1:  9.0
Judge #2:  9.1
Judge #3:  9.3
Judge #4:  9.0
Judge #5:  8.8
Judge #6:  9.0
Judge #7:
The average after eliminating 8.80 and 9.30 is 9.03.
```

7.   Rewrite the implementation of the merge sort algorithm from Figure 10-3 so that it sorts an array rather than a vector. As in the reimplementation of the selection sort algorithm on page 499, your function should use the prototype

```
void sort(int array[], int n)
```

8.   Even though it is illegal to copy stream objects in C++, you can store a pointer to a stream in a data structure. This technique, for example, makes it possible to implement the method

```
void setInput(istream & infile)
```

from the **TokenScanner** class introduced in section 6.4. All you need to do is store the address of **infile** in a pointer variable and then dereference the pointer to read from the stream.

Extend the simplified **TokenScanner** class presented in Figures 6-10 and 6-11 so that it can read tokens from input streams as well as strings.

Chapter 12
Dynamic Memory Management

You have burdened your memory with exploded systems and useless names.

— Mary Shelley, *Frankenstein*, 1818

Up to this point in the text, you have seen two mechanisms for assigning memory to variables. When you declare a global constant, the compiler allocates memory space that persists throughout the entire program. This style of allocation is called ***static allocation*** because the variables are assigned to locations in memory that remain unchanged throughout the lifetime of the program. When you declare a local variable inside a function, the space for that variable is allocated on the stack. Calling the function assigns memory to the variable; that memory is freed when the function returns. This style of allocation is called ***automatic allocation.*** There is, however, a third way of allocating memory that permits you to acquire new memory as the program runs. The process of acquiring new storage while the program is running is called ***dynamic allocation.***

Dynamic allocation is one of the most important techniques that you need to learn before you can consider yourself fluent in C++. In part, the importance comes from the fact that dynamic allocation makes it possible for data structures to expand as needed while a program is running. The collection classes introduced in Chapter 5, for example, depend on this ability. There is no arbitrary limit on the size of a **Vector** or a **Map**. If these classes need more memory, they simply request it from the system.

In C++, dynamic allocation takes on special importance because the language assigns much more responsibility to the programmer than most modern languages do. In C++, it is not enough to know how to *allocate* memory. You also have to learn how to *free* memory when it is no longer needed. The process of allocating and freeing memory in a disciplined way is called ***memory management.***

12.1 Dynamic allocation and the heap

When a program is loaded into memory, it usually occupies only a fraction of the available storage. Like most programming languages, C++ allows you to allocate some of the unused storage to the program whenever your application needs more memory. For example, if you need space for an array while the program is running, you can reserve part of the unallocated memory, leaving the rest for subsequent allocations. The pool of unallocated memory available to a program is called the ***heap.***

In most modern architectures, memory is arranged so that the heap and the stack grow in opposite directions toward each other, as illustrated in the following diagram:

| *heap* | *stack* |
| (grows toward higher addresses) | (grows toward lower addresses) |

The advantage of this strategy is that either region can grow as needed until all of the available memory is filled.

The ability to allocate memory from the heap when you need it is an extremely useful technique that has widespread application to programming. For example, all the collection classes use the heap to store their elements, because dynamic allocation is essential to creating data structures that can expand as needed. Later in this chapter, you'll have a chance to build a simplified version of one of those collection classes. Before doing so, however, it is important to learn the underlying mechanics of dynamic allocation and how the process works.

The new operator

C++ uses the **new** operator to allocate memory from the heap. In its simplest form, the **new** operator takes a type and allocates space for a variable of that type located in the heap. For example, if you want to allocate an integer in the heap, you call

```
int *ip = new int;
```

The call to the **new** operator returns the address of a storage location in the heap that has been set aside to hold an integer. If the first free word in the heap is located at address **1000**, the variable **ip** in the current stack frame will be assigned the address of that memory word, as follows:

Conceptually, the local variable **ip** on the stack points to the newly allocated word on the heap. That relationship becomes clearer if you indicate the relationship with an arrow rather than an address, as follows:

The contents of the memory locations are the same. The only change is in how you draw the picture.

Once you have allocated the space for the integer value in heap memory, you can refer to that integer by dereferencing the pointer. For example, you can store the integer 42 into the newly allocated word by executing the statement

```
*ip = 42;
```

which leaves memory looking like this:

Dynamic arrays

The **new** operator also makes it possible to allocate space for an array in the heap, which is called a *dynamic array.* To allocate space for a dynamic array, you follow the type name with the desired number of elements enclosed in square brackets. Thus, the declaration

```
double *array = new double[3];
```

initializes **array** so that it points to a contiguous block of memory large enough to hold three **double**s, like this:

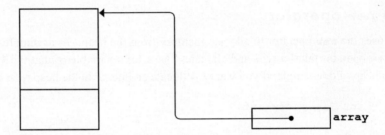

The variable **array** is now a fully functioning array whose storage is located in the heap rather than on the stack. You can assign values to the elements of **array**, which are then stored in the appropriate memory locations in the heap.

Although dynamic arrays are useful in the low-level implementation of a variety of data structures, you won't have much occasion to use them in applications. The **Vector** class introduced in Chapter 5 is almost always a better choice in practice, primarily because the **Vector** class performs its own memory management, thereby relieving you of that responsibility.

Dynamic objects

The **new** operator is also used to allocate objects or structures on the heap. If you supply only the class name, as in

```
Rational *rp = new Rational;
```

C++ allocates space for a **Rational** object on the heap and invokes the default constructor, creating the following state in memory:

If you supply arguments after the type name, C++ will call the matching version of the constructor. The declaration

```
Rational *rp = new Rational(2, 3);
```

therefore creates the following state:

12.2 Linked lists

Pointers make it possible to record connections among different values in a larger data structure. When one data structure contains the address of another, those structures are said to be *linked*. In the chapters to come, you will see many examples of linked structures. To give you a preview of those coming attractions and to provide more examples of the use of pointers to structures in the heap, the sections that follow introduce a fundamental data structure called a *linked list* in which the pointers connect individual data values in a single linear chain.

The Beacons of Gondor

My favorite example of a linked list takes its inspiration from the following passage in *The Return of the King* by J. R. R. Tolkien:

> For answer Gandalf cried aloud to his horse. "On, Shadowfax! We must hasten. Time is short. See! The beacons of Gondor are alight, calling for aid. War is kindled. See, there is the fire on Amon Dîn, and flame on Eilenach; and there they go speeding west: Nardol, Erelas, Min-Rimmon, Calenhad, and the Halifirien on the borders of Rohan."

In adapting this scene for the concluding episode in his *Lord of the Rings* trilogy, Peter Jackson produced an evocative interpretation of this scene. After the first beacon is lit in the towers of Minas Tirith, we see the signal pass from mountaintop to mountaintop as the keepers of each signal tower, ever vigilant, light their own fires when they see the triggering fire at the preceding station. The message of Gondor's danger thus passes quickly over the many leagues that separate it from Rohan, as illustrated in Figure 12-1.

FIGURE 12-1 Schematic diagram of Tolkien's Beacons of Gondor

To simulate the Beacons of Gondor in C++, you need to define a structure type to represent each of the towers in the chain. That structure must contain the name of the tower along with a pointer to the next tower in the chain. Thus, the structure representing Minas Tirith contains a pointer to the one used for Amon Dîn, which in turn contains a pointer to the structure for Eilenach, and so on, up to a **NULL** pointer that marks the end of the chain.

If you adopt this approach, the definition of the **Tower** structure looks like this:

```
struct Tower {
    string name;
    Tower *link;
};
```

The **name** field records the name of the tower, and the **link** field points to the next signal tower in the chain. Figure 12-2 illustrates how these structures appear in memory. Each of the individual **Tower** structures represents a *cell* in the linked list, and the internal pointers are called *links.* The cells may appear anywhere in memory; the order is determined by the links that connect each cell to its successor.

The program in Figure 12-3 simulates the process of lighting the Beacons of Gondor. The program begins by calling the function **createBeaconsOfGondor**, which assembles the linked list and returns a pointer to the first tower in the chain. The individual towers are created by the **createTower** function, which allocates space for a new **Tower** value and then fills in the **name** and **link** fields from the arguments. The implementation of **createBeaconsOfGondor** assembles the list in reverse order, starting with Rohan at the end of the chain and continuing on, one tower at a time, until it reaches Minas Tirith at the beginning of the chain. In a more general application, it would be preferable to read the values for the individual cells from a data file; you will have a chance to implement this extension in exercise 3.

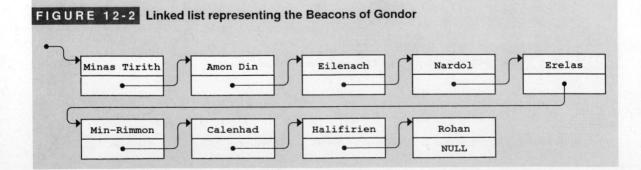

FIGURE 12-2 Linked list representing the Beacons of Gondor

FIGURE 12-3 Program to simulate the Beacons of Gondor

```cpp
/*
 * File: BeaconsOfGondor.cpp
 * ---------------------------
 * This program illustrates the concept of a linked list by simulating the
 * Beacons of Gondor story from J. R. R. Tolkien's Return of the King.
 */

#include <iostream>
#include <string>
using namespace std;

/*
 * Type: Tower
 * -----------
 * This structure contains the name of the tower and a link to the next one.
 */

struct Tower {
   string name;              /* The name of this tower                */
   Tower *link;              /* Pointer to the next tower in the chain */
};

/* Function prototypes */

Tower *createBeaconsOfGondor();
Tower *createTower(string name, Tower *link);
void signal(Tower *start);

/* Main program */

int main() {
   Tower *list = createBeaconsOfGondor();
   signal(list);
   return 0;
}

/*
 * Function: createBeaconsOfGondor
 * Usage: Tower *list = createBeaconsOfGondor();
 * ------------------------------------------------
 * Creates a linked list of the towers described by Tolkien.  The function
 * builds the list backwards and returns a pointer to the first tower.
 */

Tower *createBeaconsOfGondor() {
   Tower *tp = createTower("Rohan", NULL);
   tp = createTower("Halifirien", tp);
   tp = createTower("Calenhad", tp);
   tp = createTower("Min-Rimmon", tp);
   tp = createTower("Erelas", tp);
   tp = createTower("Nardol", tp);
   tp = createTower("Eilenach", tp);
   tp = createTower("Amon Din", tp);
   return createTower("Minas Tirith", tp);
}
```

FIGURE 12-3   **Program to simulate the Beacons of Gondor (continued)**

```
/*
 * Function: createTower
 * Usage: Tower *chain = createTower(name, link);
 * -------------------------------------------------
 * Creates a new Tower structure with the specified components.
 */

Tower *createTower(string name, Tower *link) {
   Tower *tp = new Tower;
   tp->name = name;
   tp->link = link;
   return tp;
}

/*
 * Function: signal
 * Usage: signal(start);
 * ---------------------
 * Generates a signal starting at the current tower and proceeding
 * through the end of the chain.
 */

void signal(Tower *start) {
   for (Tower *tp = start; tp != NULL; tp = tp->link) {
      cout << "Lighting " << tp->name << endl;
   }
}
```

After the linked list has been initialized, the main program calls **signal** to display the names of the towers. If you start with the linked list from Figure 12-2, the output of the program looks like this:

```
○ ○ ○                    BeaconsOfGondor
Lighting Minas Tirith
Lighting Amon Din
Lighting Eilenach
Lighting Nardol
Lighting Erelas
Lighting Min-Rimmon
Lighting Calenhad
Lighting Halifirien
Lighting Rohan
```

Although this result is less exciting than the scene from Jackson's Oscar-winning movie, you could extend the **BeaconsOfGondor** program so that it used the graphics library to show the flames as they pass from tower to tower along the chain.

Iteration in linked lists

The code for **signal** illustrates one of the fundamental programming patterns for linked lists, which is embodied in the **for** loop

```
for (Tower *tp = start; tp != NULL; tp = tp->link)
```

The effect of the **for** loop pattern in the **signal** function is to cycle through each element in the linked list in much the same way as the classic **for** loop pattern cycles through the elements in an array. The initialization expression declares the pointer variable **tp** and initializes it so that it points to the first pointer in the list. The test expression ensures that the loop continues as long as the **tp** variable is not **NULL**, which is the value that marks the end. The step expression in the **for** loop is

```
tp = tp->link;
```

which changes the value of **tp** to the value of the link pointer in the current **Tower** structure, thereby advancing **tp** to the next tower in the list.

Recursion and lists

Although most code used to process linked lists proceeds iteratively in the manner described in the preceding section, linked lists have a recursive character that often turns out to be useful in practice. The simple case is that of the *empty list,* which is represented in C++ using the pointer value **NULL**. In the general case, a linked list consists of a cell followed by a linked list. This formulation leads to a natural recursive decomposition in which you first check whether the list is empty and, if not, perform some operation on the first cell and then make a recursive call whose argument is the rest of the list. For example, you can implement the **signal** function recursively as follows:

```
void signal(Tower *start) {
   if (start != NULL) {
      cout << "Lighting " << start->name << endl;
      signal(start->link);
   }
}
```

12.3 Freeing memory

Although they are getting larger all the time, computer memory systems are finite. As a result, the heap will eventually run out of space. When this occurs, the **new** operator will be unable to allocate a block of the requested size. Failure to fulfill an allocation request is such a serious error that there is usually nothing the program can do to recover.

The `delete` operator

The best strategy to ensure that you don't run out of memory is to free any heap storage when you are finished using it. To make this strategy possible, C++ includes the operator **delete**, which takes a pointer previously allocated by **new** and frees the memory associated with that pointer.

As an illustration, suppose that you have declared a pointer to an **int** as follows:

```
int *ip = new int;
```

At some later point in the program, you discover that you no longer need this variable. At that point, the right thing to do is to free that storage by calling

```
delete ip;
```

If the heap memory is an array, you need to add square brackets after the **delete** keyword. Thus, if you allocate a dynamic array by writing

```
double *array = new double[3];
```

you can free the allocated memory by executing the statement

```
delete[] array;
```

If you need to free a linked list, you have to cycle through the individual cells, freeing each one as you go. Doing so, however, requires a bit of care because you can't refer to the **link** field of an object after you've freed it. Your loop structure must therefore store the pointer to the next cell before it frees the cell in which that pointer appears, as illustrated by the following **while** loop:

```
while (list != null) {
   Tower *next = list->link;
   delete list;
   list = next;
}
```

Deleting every pointer in a linked list is easier if you use the following recursive formulation:

```
void freeList(Tower *list) {
   if (list != NULL) {
      freeList(list->link);
      delete list;
   }
}
```

Strategies for freeing memory

Knowing when to free a piece of memory is not easy, particularly as programs become large. If several parts of a program share some data structure that has been allocated in the heap, it may not be possible for any single part to recognize that the memory is no longer needed. For simple programs that run only until they produce the desired results, it is often a reasonable strategy to allocate whatever memory you need without bothering to free it again. Doing so, however, is likely to create a dangerous habit. If another programmer tries to use your code in a long-running application, the fact that you were careless with memory will become a serious problem. It is therefore good practice to make sure that at some point you free any heap storage that you allocate. When a program fails to free its unused heap storage, that program is said to contain a *memory leak.*

Some languages, including Java along with most scripting languages, support a strategy for dynamic allocation that actively goes through memory freeing any storage that is no longer in use. This strategy is called *garbage collection.* Garbage collection makes memory management extremely easy for programmers, although it also imposes some costs. Scanning through the entire heap to figure out what parts of it are in use takes some time. Worse still, garbage collection often makes it impossible to predict how long it will take to execute a specific task. A function that usually runs very quickly can suddenly take a significant amount of time if that particular call ends up running the garbage collector. If that function is responsible for some time-critical task, the application may fail to respond in time.

Nonetheless, most new programming languages adopt garbage collection as their strategy for memory management. As a general principle, it is worth sacrificing a small amount of processing time to save a lot of programming time. Processors, after all, are cheap, and programmers are expensive. C++, however, dates from an earlier era. For better or worse, the designers of C++ decided to leave the responsibility for freeing heap memory in the hands of the programmers instead of delegating that task to an automatic process.

Fortunately, those designers made up for the lack of garbage collection by offering programmers a different strategy for memory management that simplifies the problem enormously. In C++, each class is allowed to specify what happens when an object of that class disappears. In well-designed C++ applications, each class takes responsibility for its own heap storage, thereby freeing clients from the nearly impossible task of remembering exactly what heap storage is currently active. Learning to use this strategy effectively is one of the most important techniques you need to master as a C++ programmer, so it is worth paying particular attention to the following section, which describes this approach in detail.

Destructors

As you know from the examples you have already seen, C++ classes typically define one or more constructors that initialize an object. Each class can also define a *destructor,* which is called automatically when an object of that class disappears. This destructor can perform a variety of cleanup operations. It can, for example, close any files the object has opened. The most important role for a destructor, however, is freeing any heap memory created by that object.

In C++, the name of the destructor is simply the name of the class preceded by the character ~, which is called a *tilde.* Thus, if you needed to define a destructor for a class named `MyClass`, the prototype in the interface would look like this:

```
~MyClass();
```

As with the constructors, the destructor does not include a result type. Unlike constructors, the destructor cannot be overloaded. Each class has only one destructor, which takes no arguments.

In C++, objects disappear in several different ways. In most cases, objects are declared as local variables within some function, which means that they are allocated on the stack. Those objects disappear when the function returns. That means that their destructor is automatically called at the same time, which gives the class definition the chance to free any heap memory that it allocated during that object's lifetime. In most C++ documentation, local variables that disappear when a function returns are said to *go out of scope.*

Objects can also be created as temporaries in the evaluation of expressions, even if their value is never stored in a local variable. As an example, the test program for the `Rational` class from Chapter 6 includes the following code:

```
Rational a(1, 2);
Rational b(1, 3);
Rational c(1, 6);
Rational sum = a + b + c;
```

The local variables `a`, `b`, `c`, and `sum` will disappear when the function returns. The final line, however, ends up computing the `Rational` value 5/6 as an intermediate result before going on to compute the final value. Temporary values of this sort go out of scope as soon as the evaluation is complete for the expression that generated them. If the `Rational` class had a destructor, it would be called at that point to free the storage associated with the temporary object.

▰ 12.4 Defining a `CharStack` class

The easiest way to get a more detailed sense of how to write classes that use dynamic allocation is to implement one of the container classes from Chapter 5. The easiest container class to implement is the `Stack` class, mostly because it exports the fewest methods. To make the implementation even simpler, however, it makes sense to restrict the elements in the stack to a single data type—in this case a stack of characters that will turn out to be useful in Chapter 13. You will have a chance to write the polymorphic version of the `Stack` class when you learn about the template facility described in Chapter 14. At the moment, the goal is to see how classes like `Stack` use dynamic allocation to manage memory. For that purpose, the base type of the stack is not important, and the character stack will be sufficient to illustrate the general principles.

The `charstack.h` interface

The contents of the `charstack.h` interface appear in Figure 12-4. The entries exported by the interface include the default constructor, a destructor, and the various methods—`size`, `isEmpty`, `clear`, `push`, `pop`, and `peek`—that define the behavior of the stack abstraction. The only unfamiliar feature is the destructor, which has the following prototype:

```
~CharStack();
```

The destructor for the `CharStack` class is never invoked explicitly. The prototype appears in the interface to let the compiler know that the `CharStack` class defines a destructor that needs to be called whenever a `CharStack` object goes out of scope. The destructor takes care of freeing any heap memory that the class has allocated, thereby hiding the details of memory management from the client.

If you read to the end of Figure 12-4, you'll discover that the private section of the `CharStack` class does not actually appear in the program listing. In its place is a blue box whose contents will be filled in later. Conceptually, the private section of a class is not part of the public interface. Unfortunately, the syntactic rules of C++ require that the private section be defined within the body of the class. The implementation of any private methods is usually relegated to the `.cpp` file, but the prototypes for those methods and the declaration of any instance variables must appear in the `.h` file. When you are using a class as a client, you should get in the habit of ignoring the details of the private section. Those details only get in the way of understanding the public features of the class. Leaving the private section out of the interface listings in the book makes it easier to keep those details hidden.

FIGURE 12-4 Array-based interface for the `CharStack` class

```
/*
 * File: charstack.h
 * ------------------
 * This interface defines the CharStack class, which implements
 * the stack abstraction for characters.
 */

#ifndef _charstack_h
#define _charstack_h

/*
 * Class: CharStack
 * ----------------
 * This class models a stack of characters.  The fundamental operations
 * are the same as those for the Stack<char> class.
 */

class CharStack {

public:

/*
 * Constructor: CharStack
 * Usage: CharStack cstk;
 * ----------------------
 * Initializes a new empty stack that can contain characters.
 */

   CharStack();

/*
 * Destructor: ~CharStack
 * Usage: (usually implicit)
 * -------------------------
 * Frees any heap storage associated with this character stack.
 */

   ~CharStack();

/*
 * Method: size
 * Usage: int nElems = cstk.size();
 * --------------------------------
 * Returns the number of characters in this stack.
 */

   int size();
```

FIGURE 12-4 Array-based interface for the `CharStack` class (continued)

```
/*
 * Method: isEmpty
 * Usage: if (cstk.isEmpty()) . . .
 * ---------------------------------
 * Returns true if this stack contains no characters.
 */

   bool isEmpty();

/*
 * Method: clear
 * Usage: cstk.clear();
 * ---------------------
 * Removes all characters from this stack.
 */

   void clear();

/*
 * Method: push
 * Usage: cstk.push(ch);
 * ----------------------
 * Pushes the character ch onto this stack.
 */

   void push(char ch);

/*
 * Method: pop
 * Usage: char ch = cstk.pop();
 * -----------------------------
 * Removes the top character from this stack and returns it.
 */

   char pop();

/*
 * Method: peek
 * Usage: char ch = cstk.peek();
 * ------------------------------
 * Returns the value of the top character from this stack without
 * removing it.  Raises an error if called on an empty stack.
 */

   char peek();
```

```
   The private section of the class goes here.
```

```
};

#endif
```

There is, however, another important reason to keep the details of the private section out of the interface listings. A central focus of the next few chapters is the relationship between efficiency and implementation strategy. Understanding that relationship typically requires being able to compare several implementations of the same class. Even though those implementations use different data structures, the public part of the class stays exactly the same. In the next few sections, you'll have a chance to explore several possible representations for the character stack, each of which requires you to replace the box in Figure 12-4 with a different piece of code appropriate for that representation.

Choosing a representation for the character stack

When you set out to design the underlying data structure for a class, the first question you should ask yourself is what information needs to be stored inside each object. A character stack must keep track of the characters that have been pushed in the order in which they appear. As with any collection class, there is no reason to put an arbitrary limit on the number of characters the stack can contain. As the implementer, you therefore need to choose a data structure that can expand dynamically as the program runs.

As you think about what such a structure might look like, one idea you will probably consider is to use a `Vector<char>` to hold the elements of the stack. Vectors grow dynamically, which is just what you need for this application. In fact, using `Vector<char>` as the underlying representation makes the implementation extremely easy, as shown in Figures 12-5 and 12-6.

FIGURE 12-5 Private section for `CharStack` using `Vector`

```
/* Private section */

/*
 * Implementation notes
 * --------------------
 * This version of the CharStack class uses a Vector<char> as its
 * underlying representation.  Characters are always added and
 * removed from the end, which gives rise to the last-in/first-out
 * behavior that is characteristic of stacks.
 */

private:

/* Instance variables */

   Vector<char> elements;      /* Data structure to hold the stack elements */

};
```

FIGURE 12-6 Implementation of CharStack using Vector

```cpp
/*
 * File: charstack.cpp
 * --------------------
 * This file implements the CharStack class using a Vector<char> as the
 * underlying representation.  The Vector class already implements most
 * of the essential operations for the CharStack class, which can simply
 * forward the request to the underlying structure.  The methods are
 * short enough to require no detailed documentation.
 */

#include "charstack.h"
#include "error.h"
#include "vector.h"
using namespace std;

CharStack::CharStack() {
   /* Empty */
}

CharStack::~CharStack() {
   /* Empty */
}

int CharStack::size() {
   return elements.size();
}

bool CharStack::isEmpty() {
   return elements.isEmpty();
}

void CharStack::clear() {
   elements.clear();
}

void CharStack::push(char ch) {
   elements.add(ch);
}

char CharStack::pop() {
   if (isEmpty()) error("pop: Attempting to pop an empty stack");
   char result = elements[elements.size() - 1];
   elements.remove(elements.size() - 1);
   return result;
}

char CharStack::peek() {
   if (isEmpty()) error("peek: Attempting to peek at an empty stack");
   return elements[elements.size() - 1];
}
```

Choosing **Vector<char>** as the underlying representation shows just the right instincts. You should always be on the lookout for ways that you can reframe each new problem in terms of other problems that you have already solved. Moreover, as a software-engineering strategy, there is absolutely nothing wrong with using vectors to implement stacks. The library version of the **Stack** class does just that. The only problem is that using **Vector** compromises the instructional value of the example. Implementing vectors turns out to be considerably more complicated than implementing stacks. Using **Vector** as the underlying representation does nothing to demystify the operation of the **CharStack** class, but merely hides the mystery under a somewhat larger stone.

Perhaps more importantly, relying on the **Vector** class makes it harder to analyze the performance of the **CharStack** class because the **Vector** class hides so much complexity. Because you don't yet know how the **Vector** class works in detail, you have no idea how much work is involved in adding or deleting an element, as the **push** and **pop** methods require. The primary purpose of the next several chapters is to analyze how data representation affects the efficiency of algorithms. That analysis is much easier to carry out if all the costs are visible.

One way to ensure that there are no hidden costs is to limit the implementation so that it relies only on the most primitive operations supported by the language. In the case of the character stack, using the built-in array type to store the elements has the advantage that an array hides nothing. Selecting an element from an array requires a couple of machine-language instructions and therefore takes very little time on a modern computer. Allocating array storage on the heap or reclaiming that storage when it is no longer needed generally takes more time than selection, but these operations still run in constant time. In a typical memory-management system, it takes the same amount of time to allocate a block of 1000 bytes as it does to allocate a block of 10.

Despite the fact that they offer constant-time performance, it isn't immediately clear that arrays can serve as the underlying representation for a collection class. As noted at the beginning of this section, whatever representation you use to store the characters in the stack must allow for expansion. Arrays don't. Once you've allocated space for an array, there is no way to change its size.

What you *can* do, however, is allocate an array of some fixed initial size and then replace it with a larger array whenever the old one runs out of space. In the process, you will have to copy all the elements from the old array to the new one and then make sure that the memory used by the old array gets recycled back to the heap. Once you've done all that, the new array will have the space you need.

To store the stack elements, the new version of the private section needs to keep track of several variables. Most importantly, it needs a pointer to a dynamic array that contains all the characters in the **CharStack**. It also needs to keep track of how many elements have been allocated to that array so that the implementation can tell when the stack runs out of space and needs to reallocate its internal storage. Since that value indicates how many characters the array can store in its current configuration, it is usually called the *capacity* of the dynamic array. Finally, it is important to remember that the array will typically contain fewer characters than its capacity allows. The data structure therefore needs to include a variable that keeps track of the effective size. Including these three instance variables in the private section makes it possible to implement the stack operations using nothing more complicated than array operations. The contents of the updated private section are shown in Figure 12-7, and the associated implementation appears in Figure 12-8.

Although much of the code in **charstack.cpp** is similar to classes you've seen earlier in this text, a few of the methods bear special mention. The constructor, for example, must initialize the internal data structure to represent an empty stack. The **count** variable must be zero, but there is no reason not to provide the stack with some initial capacity. In this implementation, the constructor reserves space for 10 characters, which is the value of **INITIAL_CAPACITY**. There is nothing magical about that value. Any number would work. Choosing a large value reduces the chance that the stack will have to expand and therefore saves execution time; choosing a small one conserves memory. Determining the right value is an example of a *time-space tradeoff,* which will be covered in more detail in Chapter 13.

FIGURE 12-7 Private section for the **CharStack** class implemented using a dynamic array

```
/* Private section */

/*
 * Implementation notes
 * ---------------------
 * In this version of CharStack, the characters are stored in a dynamic
 * array that doubles in size whenever the stack runs out of space.
 */

private:

/* Private constants */

   static const int INITIAL_CAPACITY = 10;

/* Instance variables */

   char *array;            /* Dynamic array of characters   */
   int capacity;           /* Allocated size of that array  */
   int count;              /* Current count of chars pushed */

/* Private function prototype */

   void expandCapacity();
```

FIGURE 12-8   Array-based implementation of the `CharStack` class

```cpp
/*
 * File: charstack.cpp
 * --------------------
 * This file implements the CharStack class.
 */

#include "charstack.h"
#include "error.h"
using namespace std;

/*
 * Implementation notes: constructor and destructor
 * -------------------------------------------------
 * The constructor allocates the array storage for the stack elements and
 * initializes the fields of the object.  The destructor frees any heap
 * memory allocated by the class, which is just the array of elements.
 */

CharStack::CharStack() {
   capacity = INITIAL_CAPACITY;
   array = new char[capacity];
   count = 0;
}

/*
 * Implementation notes: ~CharStack
 * --------------------------------
 * The destructor frees any heap memory allocated by the class, which
 * is just the dynamic array of elements.
 */

CharStack::~CharStack() {
   delete[] array;
}

/*
 * Implementation notes: size, isEmpty, clear
 * -------------------------------------------
 * These methods are each a single line and need no detailed documentation.
 */

int CharStack::size() {
   return count;
}

bool CharStack::isEmpty() {
   return count == 0;
}

void CharStack::clear() {
   count = 0;
}
```

FIGURE 12-8 Array-based implementation of the `CharStack` class (continued)

```
/*
 * Implementation notes: push
 * --------------------------
 * This function first checks to see whether there is enough room for
 * the character and then expands the array storage if necessary.
 */

void CharStack::push(char ch) {
   if (count == capacity) expandCapacity();
   array[count++] = ch;
}

/*
 * Implementation notes: pop, peek
 * -------------------------------
 * These functions check for an empty stack and report an error if
 * there is no top element.
 */

char CharStack::pop() {
   if (isEmpty()) error("pop: Attempting to pop an empty stack");
   return array[--count];
}

char CharStack::peek() {
   if (isEmpty()) error("peek: Attempting to peek at an empty stack");
   return array[count - 1];
}

/*
 * Implementation notes: expandCapacity
 * ------------------------------------
 * This method doubles the capacity of the elements array whenever it runs
 * out of space.  To do so, the method must copy the pointer to the old
 * array, allocate a new array with twice the capacity, copy the characters
 * from the old array to the new one, and finally free the old storage.
 */

void CharStack::expandCapacity() {
   char *oldArray = array;
   capacity *= 2;
   array = new char[capacity];
   for (int i = 0; i < count; i++) {
      array[i] = oldArray[i];
   }
   delete[] oldArray;
}
```

The next method that bears at least some mention is the destructor, if for no other reason than the fact that it's the first destructor you've seen. The primary responsibility that most destructors have is freeing any heap memory allocated by the class. When the **CharStack** is ready to be reclaimed, the only pointer to heap storage is the dynamic array whose address is stored in the instance variable **array**. The implementation of the destructor is therefore

```
CharStack::~CharStack() {
    delete[] array;
}
```

where the empty brackets are required because the target of the **delete** keyword is a dynamic array.

The most significant change from the vector-based implementation occurs in the **push** method, which adds a new character to the top of the stack. As long as there is room for the character, the method simply stores the character in the first unused array position and increments the **count** field. Things get tricky only if there is no space left in the array. At that point, the implementation has to allocate a new array with extra capacity and then copy the characters from the old array into the new one. Rather than include that code directly in the **push** method itself, the code in Figure 12-8 delegates that task to a private helper method called **expandCapacity**. Like all helper methods, the prototype for **expandCapacity** appears in the private section of the class definition even though the code appears in the **.cpp** file. As you can see from the code, the **expandCapacity** method begins by saving a pointer to the old array. It then allocates a new array with twice the capacity of the existing one, copies all the characters from the old array into the new one, and finally frees the old array storage.

The use of destructors in C++ is not a magical solution to the problem of memory allocation. As the **charstack.cpp** implementation makes clear, you still have to pay close attention to memory management and make sure that the implementation frees any heap memory it allocates. The advantage of using destructors is that the complexity of memory management is then hidden from the client. A client can declare a **CharStack**, use it for a time, and then forget about it. The implementation of the **CharStack** class takes care of freeing the heap memory used by a character stack as soon as it goes out of scope.

12.5 Heap-stack diagrams

It is difficult to understand how memory allocation works without drawing lots of pictures. In my experience, the single best tool for visualizing the allocation process is the *heap-stack diagram,* in which you diagram the state of memory on both the heap and the stack. Dynamically allocated memory created using the **new** operator appears on the left side of the diagram, which represents the heap. The stack frames for each function call appear on the right.

Unlike the process of writing code, which invariably requires creativity, drawing heap-stack diagrams is essentially a mechanical activity. That fact, however, does not mean that the process is trivial or that the insights you get from making these diagrams are unimportant. When I'm helping students debug their code, I've found that drawing these diagrams is the best way to help students get past those sticking points that can make coding so frustrating. If spending a few minutes drawing a few pictures saves hours of frustration as a result, that time is certainly well spent.

The best way to understand how to create heap-stack diagrams is to go through an example. Suppose that you have defined the **CharStack** class as it appears in Figure 12-8 and that you want to test it by running the following main program, which pushes each letter of the alphabet onto a newly declared **CharStack**:

```
int main() {
   CharStack cstk;
   for (int i = 0; i < 26; i++) {
      cstk.push(char('A' + i));
   }
   return 0;
}
```

You should ignore for the moment the fact that the program doesn't actually generate any output. The focus of this example is not on what the program does, but rather on how it allocates memory on the stack and the heap. The rest of this section traces the execution of the program in the form of a series of heap-stack diagrams constructed according to the process outlined in Figure 12-9. I'm convinced that it helps to work through this process a few times until you understand the rules the compiler uses to allocate memory. Once you've mastered that idea, there is no need to carry out the entire process each time.

As with any C++ program, the first thing that happens is that the operating system issues a call to the **main** function. In this example, the **main** function declares two local variables: the variable **cstk** of type **CharStack** and the index variable **i** used in the **for** loop. The **CharStack** object requires three words of memory, one for the address of the dynamic array and one for each of the integer fields **capacity** and **count**. Before any initialization, the stack frame therefore looks like this (nothing has yet been allocated on the heap, so that side of the diagram is empty):

FIGURE 12-9 **Steps to follow in creating heap-stack diagrams**

1. *Start with an empty diagram.* Before you begin, draw a vertical line on the page to separate the heap space from the stack space. Both sides of the diagram are empty at the beginning. In a typical machine, the heap expands towards larger memory addresses and thus grows downward on the page; the stack, by contrast grows in the opposite direction and therefore grows upward on the page. The diagrams in this book make **1000** the first address in the heap and **FFFF** the last byte in the stack, but these choices are simply a convention.

2. *Hand-simulate the program, allocating memory as you go.* The allocation of memory is a dynamic process that happens as the program runs. To figure out what memory looks like at a particular point, you need to trace through the program from the beginning. As you do so, the rest of the rules will apply at the appropriate time.

3. *Add a new stack frame for each function or method call.* Every time the program begins a function call (including the initial call to **main**), new memory is allocated on the stack side of the diagram to store the stack frame for that call. Drawing a stack frame is worth describing in a step-by-step process of its own.

   3a) *Add an overhead word represented as a rectangle filled in gray.* As noted in the chapter, the contents of this gray area are machine-dependent, but drawing the gray rectangle helps to separate the frames visually.

   3b) *Include space in the stack frame for all local variables declared by the function.* The size of the stack frame you create depends on the number of variables it declares. Go through the code and find all the local variable declarations in the function, including the parameters. For each variable you find, allocate as much space in the stack frame as that variable requires, and then label the space with the variable name. Parameters passed by reference use only the space of a pointer rather than the actual value. If the call is a method call, the stack frame should also include a cell labeled **this** pointing to the current object. The order of variables within a stack frame is arbitrary, so you can arrange them in any order you want.

   3c) *Initialize the parameters by copying the values of the actual arguments.* After you have drawn the variables in the stack frame, you need to copy the argument values into the parameter variables, keeping in mind that the association is determined by the order of the arguments and not by their names. Arguments in C++ are passed by value unless the declaration of the parameter variable includes an **&** to indicate call by reference. When a parameter uses call by reference, you don't copy the value of the argument but instead assign its address to the pointer variable stored in the frame.

   3d) *Continue the hand-simulation through the body of the function.* Once you've initialized the parameters, you are ready to execute the steps in the function body. This process will likely involve assignments (rule 4), dynamic allocation (rule 5), and nested function calls (recursive invocations of rule 3).

   3e) *Pop the entire stack frame when the function returns.* When you finish executing a function, the stack frame that it was using is automatically reclaimed. On a diagram, you can simply cross out that space. The next function call will reuse the same memory.

4. *Execute each assignment statement by copying values from right to left.* The nature of the copy depends on the type of value. If you assign a primitive value or an enumerated type, you simply copy the value. If you assign a pointer value to a pointer variable, the *pointer* is copied, but not the underlying value. Moreover, because C++ treats array names as being synonymous with a pointer to their initial element, assigning an array name to a variable copies only the pointer and not the underlying elements. If you assign one object to another, the behavior depends on how that class defines assignment.

5. *Allocate new heap memory when the program explicitly asks for it.* The only time that a C++ program creates new memory in the heap is when the **new** operator appears explicitly in an expression. Whenever you see the keyword **new**, you need to draw space in the heap that is large enough to hold the value being allocated. The value of the **new** operator is a pointer to the heap space, which you then treat just like any other pointer value.

heap   *stack*

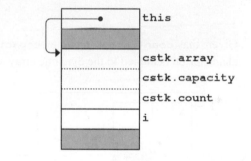

Declaring an object in C++ automatically invokes its constructor, so the first thing that happens is a call to the **CharStack** constructor. Even though the constructor takes no arguments and declares no local variables, the stack frame still contains an entry named **this** that points to the current object, since every method call includes this entry as an implicit parameter. In this case, **this** points to the **cstk** object in the main program, as follows:

The steps in the constructor are quite straightforward. Every variable mentioned in the constructor is a field in the current object. The first line sets the capacity to the constant **INITIAL_CAPACITY**, which is defined to be 10. The second line allocates a dynamic array of 10 characters. As with any value allocated using the operator **new**, the space for that array is allocated on the heap. In C++, the type **char** takes up one byte, so the array requires 10 bytes of heap memory, although that number is typically rounded up so that it fills an integral number of words. The last line initializes the **count** to zero to indicate that the stack is empty. The contents of the heap and stack now look like this:

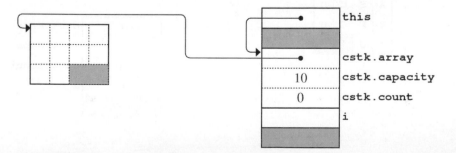

The constructor then returns, leaving the object initialized as shown.

The next method call occurs during the first cycle of the **for** loop, when **i** has the value 0. This cycle generates a call to **cstk.push** with an argument equal to the character **'A'**. Once again, **push** is a method call, so the frame includes the pointer variable **this** along with the parameter **ch**, as follows:

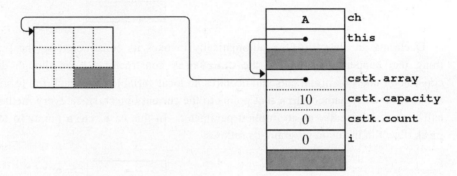

Given that **count** is not equal to **capacity**, this call is straightforward. The character **ch** is copied to the dynamic array and the **count** is incremented, like this:

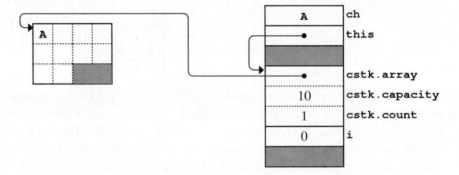

The next nine cycles of the **for** loop proceed in the same way, filling up the available capacity in the stack:

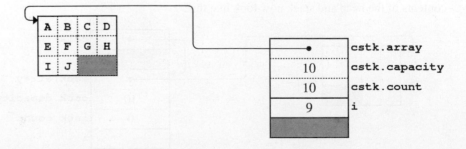

At this point, the next call to **cstk.push** creates a new frame as it prepares to push
the character **'K'** on the stack:

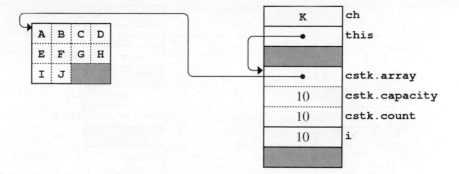

The difference this time around is that **count** is equal to **capacity**, which
indicates that the existing array of characters is full. This condition triggers a call to
the private method **expandCapacity**, which leads to the creation of another stack
frame. The **expandCapacity** method declares the local variables **oldArray** and
i, which means that these variables appear in the stack frame, along with the pointer
to the current object. The resulting stack frame appears at the top of the following
diagram:

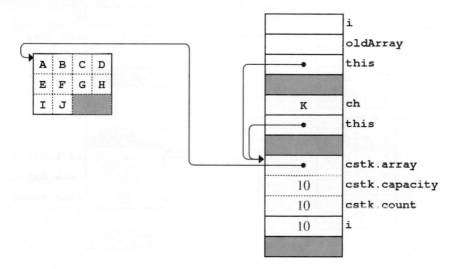

The operation of **expandCapacity** is sufficiently interesting that it makes sense
to go through the process in more detail. The lines

```
char *oldArray = array;
capacity *= 2;
char *array = new char[capacity];
```

copy the old array pointer and then allocate a new dynamic array with twice the original capacity:

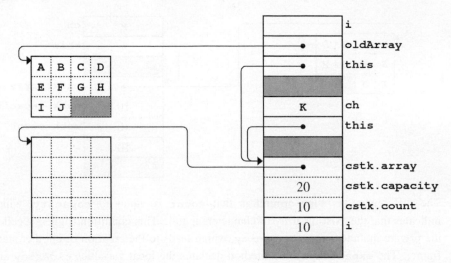

The **for** loop then copies the characters from the old array into the new one, leaving the following configuration:

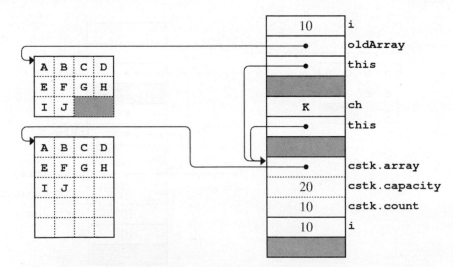

The last statement in the body of **expandCapacity** is

```
delete[] oldArray;
```

This statement frees the old array storage so that the memory looks like this after **expandCapacity** returns:

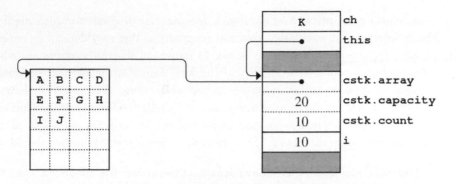

Now that there is room in the array, the **push** method can operate just as it did before. The state after **push** returns looks like this:

The main program then continues through the rest of the alphabet, doubling the capacity once more when the count hits 20.

The only other noteworthy event in this example occurs when the function **main** returns. At that point, the variable **cstk** goes out of scope, which triggers a call to the **~CharStack** destructor. The destructor ensures that the dynamic array storage allocated during the lifetime of the character stack is returned to the heap.

12.6 Unit testing

The main program in the preceding section is useful as an illustration of heap-stack diagrams but does not really constitute an adequate test of the **CharStack** class, even if you were to display the contents of the stack by popping the letters and printing them in reverse order. When you define a new class for clients to use, it is essential to test your implementation as thoroughly as you can. Untested code is almost always buggy, and it is your responsibility as an implementer to put classes like **CharStack** through their paces, checking every method exported by the interface under conditions that approximate the expected patterns of use. In the case of the **CharStack** class, for example, it is important to push a large enough number of characters to ensure that **expandCapacity** gets called, ideally more than once.

It is also good practice to develop a separate test program for each class or library interface. If you design your test programs so that they depend on several classes functioning correctly, it is harder to figure out where the errors are when something goes wrong. The strategy of checking each class or interface separately in isolation from any other module is called ***unit testing.*** Figure 12-10 shows a possible unit test for the `CharStack` class. It includes code to push the letters of the alphabet and then make sure they are popped in reverse order, but it also checks the other methods in the class to see whether they are functioning as they should.

The individual tests in the `CharStackUnitTest.cpp` file are coded using the `assert` facility exported by the `<cassert>` library. The call to `assert` (which is implemented using the C++ macro facility that is beyond the scope of this text) has the following form:

> `assert(`*test*`);`

As long as the *test* expression evaluates to `true`, the `assert` macro has no effect. If, however, *test* evaluates to `false`, the `assert` macro generates an error message and exits from the program with a status code indicating failure. The format of the `assert` message is system-dependent, but typically looks something like this:

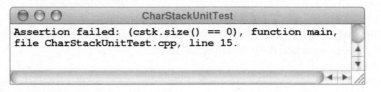

The message includes the text of the test that fails, which makes it easier to find the source of the error.

Although testing is essential to software development, it does not eliminate the need for careful implementation. The number of ways clients will find to use a library package is just too large. The late Edsger W. Dijkstra defined the essential problem of testing in a 1972 monograph entitled *Notes on Structured Programming:*

> Program testing can be used to show the presence of bugs, but never to show their absence!

As an implementer, you need to employ many different techniques to reduce the number of errors. Careful design helps to simplify the overall structure, making it much easier to find where things go awry. Tracing your code by hand—using heap-stack diagrams or whatever strategies seem most helpful—can often reveal bugs before the formal testing phase even begins. In many cases, having other programmers look over your code is one of the best ways to find problems you have managed to overlook. In the industry, this process is often formalized in a series of ***code reviews*** scheduled during the software development cycle.

FIGURE 12-10 Unit test for the `CharStack` class

```cpp
/*
 * File: CharStackUnitTest.cpp
 * ---------------------------
 * This file contains a unit test of the CharStack class that uses the
 * C++ assert macro to check that each operation performs as it should.
 */

#include <iostream>
#include <cassert>
#include "charstack.h"
using namespace std;

int main() {
   CharStack cstk;                             /* Declare an empty CharStack */
   assert(cstk.size() == 0);                   /* Make sure its size is 0    */
   assert(cstk.isEmpty());                     /* And that isEmpty is true   */
   cstk.push('A');                             /* Push the character 'A'     */
   assert(!cstk.isEmpty());                    /* The stack is now not empty */
   assert(cstk.size() == 1);                   /* And has size 1             */
   assert(cstk.peek() == 'A');                 /* Check that peek returns 'A'*/
   cstk.push('B');                             /* Push the character 'B'     */
   assert(cstk.peek() == 'B');                 /* Make sure peek returns it  */
   assert(cstk.size() == 2);                   /* And that the size is now 2 */
   assert(cstk.pop() == 'B');                  /* Pop and test for the 'B'   */
   assert(cstk.size() == 1);                   /* Recheck the size           */
   assert(cstk.peek() == 'A');                 /* And make sure 'A' is on top*/
   cstk.push('C');                             /* Test a push after a pop    */
   assert(cstk.size() == 2);                   /* Make sure size is correct  */
   assert(cstk.pop() == 'C');                  /* And that pop returns a 'C' */
   assert(cstk.peek() == 'A');                 /* The 'A' is now back on top */
   assert(cstk.pop() == 'A');                  /* Pop and test for the 'A'   */
   assert(cstk.size() == 0);                   /* And make sure size is 0    */
   for (char ch = 'A'; ch <= 'Z'; ch++) {      /* Push the entire alphabet   */
      cstk.push(ch);                           /*   one character at a time  */
   }                                           /*   to test stack expansion  */
   assert(cstk.size() == 26);                  /* Make sure the size is 26   */
   for (char ch = 'Z'; ch >= 'A'; ch--) {      /* Pop the characters in      */
      assert(cstk.pop() == ch);                /*   reverse order to make    */
   }                                           /*   sure they're all there   */
   assert(cstk.isEmpty());                     /* Ensure the stack is empty  */
   for (char ch = 'A'; ch <= 'Z'; ch++) {      /* Push the alphabet again to */
      cstk.push(ch);                           /*   test that it works after */
   }                                           /*   expansion                */
   assert(cstk.size() == 26);                  /* Check that size is again 26*/
   cstk.clear();                               /* Check the clear method     */
   assert(cstk.size() == 0);                   /* And check if stack is empty*/
   cstk.clear();                               /* Test clear with empty stack*/
   assert(cstk.size() == 0);
   cout << "CharStack unit test succeeded" << endl;
   return 0;
}
```

▌ 12.7 Copying objects

As it appears in Figures 12-7 and 12-8, the definition of the **CharStack** class is not quite finished. As long as you pass every **CharStack** object by reference and never assign one **CharStack** value to another, everything will work just fine. If, however, your code ends up passing a **CharStack** by value or tries to make a copy of an existing **CharStack**, your program will almost certainly crash in some unpredictable way.

Shallow versus deep copying

The crux of the problem in the current implementation of the **CharStack** class is that C++ interprets assignment of one object to another in a way that often makes sense, but which fails miserably if that object contains any dynamically allocated memory. By default, C++ assigns one object to another by copying the value of each of its instance variables. If those values are the usual kinds of data values—numbers, characters, and the like—the copy operation does exactly what you want. If the value is a pointer, however, copying the pointer does not actually copy the underlying values. C++'s default behavior is called *shallow copying* because it doesn't extend beneath the surface. When you copy an object that contains dynamic memory, you usually want to copy the underlying data as well. That process is called *deep copying.*

To get more of a sense of the importance of this problem, think about what happens if you call the following code:

```
CharStack s1, s2;
s1.push('A');
s2 = s1;
```

What you want this program to do is initialize **s2** to be a copy of **s1**, which means that both stacks would contain the character **A** at the top of an independent stack. That is exactly what would happen if C++ used deep copying to initialize **s2**. If you allow C++ to use its default technique of shallow copying, however, executing these statements will almost certainly cause problems at some point in the program.

The easiest way to see how this code works is to draw a heap-stack diagram showing the state of memory at the end of this sequence of statements. That diagram looks like this:

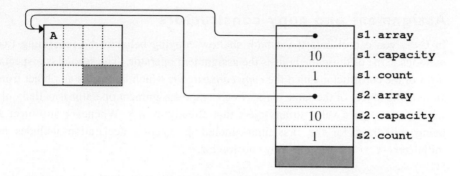

The shallow copy has copied the **count** and **capacity** fields correctly but leaves the **array** field in each structure pointing to the same dynamic array. If you were to pop the top character off stack **s2** and then push some other character, that operation would change the contents of **s1** as well, which is not what you want if the stacks are supposed to be independent copies.

Worse still, the entire program is likely to crash when the function declaring the variables **s1** and **s2** returns. When that happens, both variables go out of scope, which in each case triggers a call to the **CharStack** destructor. The first destructor call will free the array, and the second one will try to do the same thing. Freeing the same memory twice is illegal, but there is no guarantee that C++ will detect and report the error. On some machines, the second call to **free** will compromise the internal structure of the heap, which will at some point cause the program to fail.

If you want to copy a **CharStack** so that the copy is independent of the original, you need to make a deep copy, which looks like this:

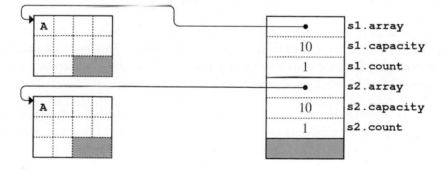

Writing the code to make a deep copy isn't hard. The challenge is getting C++ to invoke that code when you assign one **CharStack** to another. The programming patterns that accomplish this task are described in the following section.

Assignment and copy constructors

In C++, you can change the default shallow-copying behavior by redefining two methods. One of those methods is the assignment operator. The second is a special form of the constructor called the *copy constructor,* which initializes an object from an existing object of the same class. In C++, the assignment operator is called only when you assign a value to an object that already exists. Whenever an object is being initialized for the first time—including when a declaration includes an initializer—C++ invokes the copy constructor.

By default, the assignment operator and the copy constructor create a shallow copy as described in the preceding section. If you want your classes to support deep copying, all you have to do is supply new definitions for these two methods that copy the dynamically allocated data as well.

In C++, the definitions required to override the copy constructor and the assignment operator are full of details that are easy to get wrong if you try to write these definitions from scratch. In most cases, the best approach is to copy these methods from a standard pattern and then make whatever changes are necessary to support your class. Figure 12-11 illustrates the standard technique in the context of the `CharStack` class. The code redefines the copy constructor and the assignment operator, delegating most of the work to a private method called `deepCopy`.

When you look at the code in Figure 12-11, one of the first things you're likely to notice is that the parameter declarations for all three methods include the keyword `const`, as illustrated by the header line for the `deepCopy` method:

```
void deepCopy(const CharStack & src);
```

In this context, the `const` keyword guarantees that `deepCopy` will not change the value of `src` even though it is passed by reference. This style of parameter transmission is called *constant call by reference.* The details of constant call by reference are described later in this chapter.

The copy constructor simply calls the `deepCopy` method to copy the internal data from the original `CharStack` into the current one. The more interesting method is the overloaded assignment operator, which looks like this:

```
CharStack & operator=(const CharStack & src) {
   if (this != &src) {
      delete[] array;
      deepCopy(src);
   }
   return *this;
}
```

FIGURE 12-11 Implementation of deep copying for the `CharStack` class

```
/*
 * Implementation notes: copy constructor and assignment operator
 * --------------------------------------------------------------
 * These methods make it possible to pass a CharStack by value or
 * assign one CharStack to another.  The actual work is done by the
 * private deepCopy method, which represents a useful pattern
 * for designing other classes that need to implement deep copying.
 */

CharStack::CharStack(const CharStack & src) {
   deepCopy(src);
}

CharStack & CharStack::operator=(const CharStack & src) {
   if (this != &src) {
      delete[] array;
      deepCopy(src);
   }
   return *this;
}

/*
 * Implementation notes: deepCopy
 * ------------------------------
 * This method copies the data from the src parameter into the current
 * object.  All dynamic memory is reallocated to create a "deep copy"
 * in which the current object and the source object are independent.
 */

void CharStack::deepCopy(const CharStack & src) {
   array = new char[src.count];
   for (int i = 0; i < src.count; i++) {
      array[i] = src.array[i];
   }
   count = src.count;
   capacity = src.capacity;
}
```

The `if` statement at the beginning of the code for the assignment operator checks to see whether the left and right sides of the assignment are in fact the same object. This test is an essential part of the standard pattern for overloaded assignment operators. The purpose of this test is not simply to eliminate an unnecessary copy operation. Without this test, assigning a **CharStack** object to itself would end up freeing the array before calling **deepCopy** to copy the data into the destination stack. The last line in the redefined assignment operator is probably also worth a note. In C++, the assignment operator is defined so that it returns the value on its left-hand side. The keyword **this** is a pointer to that object, so the expression ***this** represents the object itself.

If the process of overriding the copy constructor and the assignment operator gets too confusing, you do have another option. The much simpler pattern in Figure 12-12 defines private versions of the copy constructor and the assignment operator. These definitions override the defaults that C++ provides. At the same time, the fact that these methods appear in the private section makes them unavailable to clients. The net effect is to prevent clients from copying a **CharStack** under any circumstances. The standard C++ libraries, for example, use this approach to make it illegal to copy streams.

Understanding these intricacies, however, is not as important as knowing how to integrate these patterns into the design of your own classes. If you allocate dynamic memory as part of a class, you have a responsibility to redefine the copy constructor and the assignment operator. Unless you tell it otherwise by defining overloaded versions of the copy constructor and the assignment operator, the compiler will automatically define versions of these methods that do the wrong thing. It therefore makes sense to pick one of these strategies—either implementing deep copying or forbidding copying altogether—for each class you design. You can then use the code in Figure 12-11 or 12-12 as a model, making whatever substitutions are necessary for your own class.

12.8 The uses of const

Up until this chapter, the only place you encountered the **const** keyword was in the definition of constant values, such as the following example from Chapter 1:

```
const double PI = 3.14159265358979323846;
```

The preceding section introduced a new application of **const** in the examples of constant call by reference. Professional C++ programmers, however, use **const** in several other contexts as well. Unfortunately, using **const** correctly is difficult, particularly for novices. If you intend to become a serious C++ programmer, you

FIGURE 12-12 Definitions necessary to make copying illegal

```
private:

/*
 * Standard methods: copy constructor and assignment operator
 * ------------------------------------------------------------
 * The following lines make it illegal to copy a CharStack, by defining
 * private versions of the copy constructor and assignment operator.
 */

   CharStack(const CharStack & src) { }
   CharStack & operator=(const CharStack & src) { return *this; }
```

have to master the many subtleties of the **const** keyword. To help support you in reaching that goal, the sections that follow outline the most common uses of **const** and describe some of the pitfalls you are likely to encounter.

Constant definitions

You have been using the **const** keyword to give names to constant values ever since Chapter 1. In Chapter 2, you learned how to export constants from a library interface by adding the **extern** keyword to the declaration in both the .**h** and .**cpp** files. The only other subtlety you need to understand about defining constant values is that you need to add the keyword **static** to any constants declared as part of a class. In the **charstack.h** file, for example, the constant **INITIAL_CAPACITY** is declared in the private section like this:

```
static const int INITIAL_CAPACITY = 10;
```

Including **static** in this declaration ensures that there is only one copy of the **INITIAL_CAPACITY** constant and not one in every **CharStack** object.

Constant call by reference

Prior to this chapter, it has made sense to simplify the mechanics of parameter passing by using only the basic forms of call by value and call by reference. To implement deep copying, however, the C++ compiler requires you to use constant call by reference for the overloaded copy constructor and assignment operator, as illustrated in section 12.6. Constant call by reference, however, is by no means limited to those methods. In fact, constant call by reference is usually preferable to both traditional call by reference and call by value if the parameter you are passing is an object. In many ways, constant call by reference combines the best aspects of each of the more traditional modes of parameter passing. It offers the efficiency of call by reference along with the safety of call by value.

Although the syntax for specifying constant call by reference seems simple enough in the examples you have already seen, it does get tricky if you try to apply it to a pointer-valued parameter. Consider, for example, the function prototype

```
int strlen(const char *cptr);
```

which is essentially the prototype used for the library function that returns the length of a C-style string. If you reason by analogy to the earlier examples of constant call by reference, you might imagine that this prototype declares **cptr** as an immutable pointer to a character. The C++ interpretation, however, is slightly different. The **const** attaches to the type name, which means that the declaration actually makes **cptr** a pointer to a **const char**. Given that interpretation, it is perfectly fine to change the value of **cptr** inside the **strlen** function, but not the values of the characters to which it points. In the unlikely event that you wanted to prevent changes to the **cptr** variable itself, you would need to place the **const** keyword after the asterisk instead.

The only problem with using constant call by reference as a general replacement for call by value is that adding the **const** keyword to a parameter forces the C++ compiler to ensure that the value is not modified by the function that receives that argument. In general, having the compiler perform that check is a good thing. To do so, however, the compiler must be able to determine which methods of a class modify an object and which do not. In C++, the responsibility for providing that information rests squarely on the programmer. The cost of using constant call by reference is therefore that class designers must specify more information about the methods defined by a class, as described in the next section.

Const methods

In a typical class definition, some methods change the value of the object and others do not. In the case of the **CharStack** class for example, the **push**, **pop**, and **clear** methods all change the contents of the stack. By contrast, the **size**, **isEmpty**, and **peek** methods all return information without affecting the underlying contents. C++ allows the programmer to specify that a method does not change the state of the associated object, by adding the keyword **const** after the parameter list. For example, the prototype for the **size** method in the **charstack.h** file should be written using the keyword **const** to let the compiler know that it leaves the stack unchanged, as follows:

```
int size() const;
```

The **const** keyword must also appear in the implementation, which looks like this:

```
int CharStack::size() const {
   return count;
}
```

If a class uses the **const** keyword to indicate which parameters are subject to change and which methods are capable of changing the underlying structure, that class is said to be *const correct*. The classes in both the STL and the Stanford libraries are **const** correct. Writing **const** correct classes requires more effort, but allows you to write code that is more efficient and easier to read. A **const** correct version of the **CharStack** class appears in Figures 12-13 and 12-14.

FIGURE 12-13   Const-correct version of the `charstack.h` interface

```
/*
 * File: charstack.h
 * -------------------
 * This interface defines the CharStack class, which implements
 * the stack abstraction for characters.
 */

#ifndef _charstack_h
#define _charstack_h

/*
 * Class: CharStack
 * ----------------
 * This class models a stack of characters.  The fundamental operations
 * are the same as those for the Stack<char> class.
 */

class CharStack {

public:

/*
 * Constructor: CharStack
 * Usage: CharStack cstk;
 * -----------------------
 * Initializes a new empty stack that can contain characters.
 */

   CharStack();

/*
 * Destructor: ~CharStack
 * Usage: (usually implicit)
 * ---------------------------
 * Frees any heap storage associated with this character stack.
 */

   ~CharStack();

/*
 * Method: size
 * Usage: int nElems = cstk.size();
 * ---------------------------------
 * Returns the number of characters in this stack.
 */

   int size() const;
```

FIGURE 12-13 Const-correct version of the `charstack.h` interface (continued)

```
/*
 * Method: isEmpty
 * Usage: if (cstk.isEmpty()) . . .
 * --------------------------------
 * Returns true if this stack contains no characters.
 */

   bool isEmpty() const;

/*
 * Method: clear
 * Usage: cstk.clear();
 * ----------------------
 * Removes all characters from this stack.
 */

   void clear();

/*
 * Method: push
 * Usage: cstk.push(ch);
 * ----------------------
 * Pushes the character ch onto this stack.
 */

   void push(char ch);

/*
 * Method: pop
 * Usage: char ch = cstk.pop();
 * --------------------------------
 * Removes the top character from this stack and returns it.
 */

   char pop();

/*
 * Method: peek
 * Usage: char ch = cstk.peek();
 * --------------------------------
 * Returns the value of the top character from this stack without
 * removing it.  Raises an error if called on an empty stack.
 */

   char peek() const;
```

FIGURE 12-13 Const-correct version of the `charstack.h` interface (continued)

```
/*
 * Copy constructor: CharStack
 * Usage: (usually implicit)
 * ---------------------------
 * Initializes the current object to be a deep copy of the specified source.
 */

   CharStack(const CharStack & src);

/*
 * Operator: =
 * Usage: dst = src;
 * -----------------
 * Assigns src to dst so that the two stacks are independent copies.
 */

   CharStack & operator=(const CharStack & src);

/* Private section */

private:

/* Private constants */

   static const int INITIAL_CAPACITY = 10;

/* Instance variables */

   char *array;             /* Dynamic array of characters   */
   int capacity;            /* Allocated size of that array  */
   int count;               /* Current count of chars pushed */

/* Private method prototypes */

   void deepCopy(const CharStack & src);
   void expandCapacity();

};

#endif
```

FIGURE 12-14 Const-correct version of the `charstack.cpp` implementation

```cpp
/*
 * File: charstack.cpp
 * --------------------
 * This file implements the CharStack class.
 */

#include "charstack.h"
#include "error.h"
using namespace std;

/*
 * Implementation notes: constructor and destructor
 * -------------------------------------------------
 * The constructor allocates the array storage for the stack elements and
 * initializes the fields of the object.  The destructor frees any heap
 * memory allocated by the class, which is just the array of elements.
 */

CharStack::CharStack() {
   capacity = INITIAL_CAPACITY;
   array = new char[capacity];
   count = 0;
}

CharStack::~CharStack() {
   delete[] array;
}

/*
 * Implementation notes: size, isEmpty, clear
 * -------------------------------------------
 * These methods are each a single line and need no detailed documentation.
 * Note that size and isEmpty leave the stack unchanged and are therefore
 * marked as const.
 */

int CharStack::size() const {
   return count;
}

bool CharStack::isEmpty() const {
   return count == 0;
}

void CharStack::clear() {
   count = 0;
}
```

FIGURE 12-14 Const-correct version of the `charstack.cpp` implementation (continued)

```
/*
 * Implementation notes: push
 * --------------------------
 * This function first checks to see whether there is enough room for
 * the character and then expands the array storage if necessary.
 */

void CharStack::push(char ch) {
   if (count == capacity) expandCapacity();
   array[count++] = ch;
}

/*
 * Implementation notes: pop, peek
 * -------------------------------
 * These functions check for an empty stack and report an error if
 * there is no top element.
 */

char CharStack::pop() {
   if (isEmpty()) error("pop: Attempting to pop an empty stack");
   return array[--count];
}

char CharStack::peek() const {
   if (isEmpty()) error("peek: Attempting to peek at an empty stack");
   return array[count - 1];
}

/*
 * Implementation notes: copy constructor and assignment operator
 * --------------------------------------------------------------
 * These methods make it possible to pass a CharStack by value or
 * assign one CharStack to another.  The actual work is done by the
 * private deepCopy method, which represents a useful pattern
 * for designing other classes that need to implement deep copying.
 */

CharStack::CharStack(const CharStack & src) {
   deepCopy(src);
}

CharStack & CharStack::operator=(const CharStack & src) {
   if (this != &src) {
      delete[] array;
      deepCopy(src);
   }
   return *this;
}
```

FIGURE 12-14 **Const-correct version of the `charstack.cpp` implementation (continued)**

```
/*
 * Implementation notes: deepCopy
 * -----------------------------------
 * This method copies the data from the src parameter into the current
 * object.  All dynamic memory is reallocated to create a "deep copy"
 * in which the current object and the source object are independent.
 */

void CharStack::deepCopy(const CharStack & src) {
   array = new char[src.count];
   for (int i = 0; i < src.count; i++) {
      array[i] = src.array[i];
   }
   count = src.count;
   capacity = src.capacity;
}

/*
 * Implementation notes: expandCapacity
 * -------------------------------------
 * This method doubles the capacity of the elements array whenever it runs
 * out of space.  To do so, the method must copy the pointer to the old
 * array, allocate a new array with twice the capacity, copy the characters
 * from the old array to the new one, and finally free the old storage.
 */

void CharStack::expandCapacity() {
   char *oldArray = array;
   capacity *= 2;
   array = new char[capacity];
   for (int i = 0; i < count; i++) {
      array[i] = oldArray[i];
   }
   delete[] oldArray;
}
```

12.9 Efficiency of the `CharStack` class

Chapter 13 uses the **CharStack** class as one of several possible implementation strategies for creating a text editor. Since the primary goal of the next chapter is to evaluate the relative efficiency of these different strategies, you need to have some understanding of the efficiency of the **CharStack** class itself. As you know from Chapter 10, the efficiency of an algorithm is traditionally expressed in terms of its computational complexity, which examines how running time varies as a function of the size of the problem.

For the **CharStack** class, most of the methods run in constant time as a function of the current size of the stack. In fact, there is only one method for which the size of the stack makes any difference at all. Ordinarily, the **push** method simply adds a character to the next free slot in an array, which requires only constant time. If, however, the array is full, the **expandCapacity** method has to copy the contents of that array into newly allocated memory, which will run more slowly as the stack grows larger. Calling **expandCapacity** requires linear time, which indicates that the computational complexity of the **push** method is $O(N)$ in the worst case.

Up to this point in the book, complexity analysis has focused on how a particular algorithm performs in the worst case. There is, however, an important characteristic that makes the **push** operation different from the other operations that arise in traditional complexity analysis: the worst case can't possibly happen every time. In particular, if pushing one item on the stack triggers an expansion that makes that particular call run in $O(N)$ time, the cost of pushing the next item is guaranteed to be $O(1)$ because the capacity has already been expanded. It therefore makes sense to distribute the cost of the expansion over all the **push** operations that benefit from it. This style of complexity measurement is called *amortized analysis.*

To make this process easier to understand, it is useful to compute the total cost of the **push** operation if it is repeated N times, where N is some large number. Every **push** operation incurs some cost whether or not the stack is expanded. If you represent that fixed cost using the Greek letter alpha (α), the total fixed cost of pushing N items is αN. Every so often, however, the implementation needs to expand the capacity of the internal array, which is a linear-time operation that costs some constant—indicated by the Greek letter beta (β)—times the number of characters on the stack.

In terms of the total running time across all N **push** operations, the worst-case situation arises when expansion is required on the very last cycle. In that case, the final **push** operation incurs an additional cost of βN. Given that **expandCapacity** always doubles the size of the array, the capacity also had to be expanded when the stack was half as large as N, a quarter as large as N, and so on. The total cost of pushing N items is therefore given by the following formula:

$$\textit{total time} = \alpha N + \beta\left(N + \frac{N}{2} + \frac{N}{4} + \frac{N}{8} + \cdots\right)$$

The average time is simply this total divided by N, as follows:

$$\textit{average time} = \alpha + \beta\left(1 + \frac{1}{2} + \frac{1}{4} + \frac{1}{8} + \cdots\right)$$

Although the sum inside the parentheses depends on N, the total can never be larger than 2, which means that the average time is bounded by the constant value $\alpha + 2\beta$ and is therefore $O(1)$.

▇ Summary

One of the goals of this book is to encourage you to use high-level structures that allow you to think about data in an abstract way that is independent of the underlying representation. Abstract data types and classes help make it possible to maintain this holistic viewpoint. At the same time, using C++ effectively requires that you have a mental model of how data structures are represented in memory. In this chapter, you have had a chance to see how those structures are stored and to get a sense of what goes on "under the hood" as you write your programs.

The important points introduced in this chapter include:

- C++ allocates memory from the heap using the **new** operator, which takes a type name and returns a pointer to a block of memory large enough to hold a value of that type.

- Primitive types, objects, and structures can be allocated on the heap by writing the **new** operator before the type name, as in the following example:

```
int *ip = new int;
```

In the case of a dynamically allocated object, you can also specify constructor parameters after the type name, as follows:

```
Rational *pointerToOneHalf = new Rational(1, 2);
```

- Pointers are often used to specify connections among individual elements in a data structure. One particularly important application of this technique is the *linked list* in which the pointers form a linear chain. Each element in a linked list is called a *cell,* and the pointers that define the order of the elements are called *links*. The last cell in a linked list contains a **NULL** link pointer, which serves as a sentinel marking the end of the list.

- Storage for dynamic arrays is allocated by specifying the desired size in square brackets after the type name, as in the following declaration, which allocates a dynamic array of 10 characters:

```
char *cp = new char[10];
```

- Unlike many modern languages, C++ makes the programmer responsible for memory management. The most significant challenge that programmers face is to free any heap memory that the program allocates. At the lowest level, C++ uses the **delete** operator to free individual heap values and the **delete[]** operator to free dynamically allocated arrays.

- The task of memory management in C++ is simplified considerably by the existence of *destructors,* which are called automatically when the stack frame containing an object disappears at the end of a method call. The primary role of the destructor is to free any heap memory allocated by the object.

- The name of the destructor is the class name preceded by the tilde character ~. Each class can have only one destructor, which never takes any arguments.

- As the **CharStack** class presented in this chapter illustrates, it is possible to use arrays to implement abstract data types that expand their capacity dynamically.

- Heap-stack diagrams are useful in understanding how C++ allocates memory. Each function or method call creates a new stack frame with space for the local variables declared by that function. Memory is allocated on the heap only when the program executes the **new** operator. That heap memory is reclaimed only when the program executes the **delete** operator. Stack memory is reclaimed automatically when a function returns.

- Whenever you implement a class for others to use, you have a responsibility to test that package as thoroughly as possible. One useful technique is to write a program that automatically tests every method in that class independently of any other modules in an application. Such test programs are called *unit tests* and are an essential part of good software engineering practice.

- When you assign one object to another or pass an object by value, the default rule in C++ is to make a *shallow copy* in which the instance variables are copied but not any structures to which those instance variables point. When objects contain dynamically allocated memory, it is usually necessary to make a *deep copy* in which the targets of the pointers are copied as well.

- You can change the way C++ copies objects of a specific class by overriding the *assignment operator* and the *copy constructor.* The rules for defining these methods correctly are sufficiently subtle that you should copy the basic structure from an existing class and then modify the code as necessary.

- You can prohibit copying altogether by defining the assignment operator and the copy constructor in the private section of the class.

- The **const** keyword has many different applications in C++ programs. In addition to defining constant values, you can use **const** to specify that a method will not change the value of a particular parameter or the value of the underlying object.

- Even though the **push** method in the **CharStack** class sometimes requires $O(N)$ time to expand the capacity of the dynamic array, this cost cannot be incurred many times in succession. The fact that this cost is paid infrequently makes it legitimate to distribute the cost over a series of calls. Using this style of amortized analysis, every method in the **CharStack** class runs in $O(1)$ time.

Review questions

1.   What are the three allocation mechanisms described in this chapter?

2.   What is the *heap?*

3.   Why does it make sense to start the heap and the stack at opposite ends of memory and have them grow toward each other?

4.   What declaration would you use to create and initialize each of the following variables:

     a)   A pointer **bp** that points to a Boolean value

     b)   A pointer named **pp** that points to a **Point** with the coordinates (3, 4)

     c)   A dynamic array called **names** capable of holding 100 C++ strings?

5.   What statements would you use to free the storage allocated in the preceding exercise?

6.   Define the terms *cell* and *link* as they are used in the context of the linked list data structure.

7.   What is the standard technique for marking the end of a linked list?

8.   What structure definition would you use to define the cell type for a linked list of integers?

9.   Given your definition in the preceding exercise, how would you write a **for** loop to step through every element of a linked list stored in the variable **list**?

10.   What is a *memory leak?*

11.   True or false: C++ uses garbage collection to manage memory.

12.   What is a *destructor?* What is its most important role?

13.   If you create a class named **IntArray**, how would you write the prototype for its destructor?

14.   What does it mean for a variable to *go out of scope?*

15.   True or false: Destructors can be invoked even on temporary values that are never assigned to local variables.

16.   How is it possible for the **CharStack** class to expand its capacity dynamically even though it uses arrays whose size is fixed at the time they are allocated?

17. Describe the purpose of each of the instance variables in the **CharStack** class.

18. Explain each of the statements in the implementation of **expandCapacity** in Figure 12-8.

19. Suppose that, instead of doubling the capacity of the array, **expandCapacity** simply added one more element to the array. Would the **push** method still have an average computational complexity of $O(1)$? Why or why not?

20. When is new memory added to the stack side of a heap-stack diagram? When does that memory get reclaimed?

21. When is new memory added to the heap side of a heap-stack diagram and when is it reclaimed?

22. What reason does the chapter give for including the *overhead word* in heap-stack diagrams?

23. How do you represent a reference parameter in a heap-stack diagram?

24. What additional local variable gets added to a stack frame when you call a method as opposed to a function?

25. What is the implication of the word *unit* in the phrase *unit test?*

26. What is the difference between a *shallow copy* and a *deep copy?* Which of these two strategies does C++ use by default?

27. What methods must you override to change how C++ copies an object?

28. How does *constant call by reference* differ from the more familiar parameter passing paradigms of *call by value* and *call by reference?*

29. What does it mean for a class to be **const** correct?

30. The argument that the amortized complexity of the **push** operation is $O(1)$ depends on the claim that the sum of the series

$$1 + \frac{1}{2} + \frac{1}{4} + \frac{1}{8} + \cdots$$

can never exceed 2 no matter how many terms you include. In your own words, try to explain why. (If you have trouble, you might try looking up *Zeno's Paradox* on the web and then giving it another go.)

Exercises

1. Write a function **createIndexArray(n)** that allocates a dynamic array of **n** integers in which each integer is initialized to its own index. For example, calling **createIndexArray(8)** should return a pointer to the following array on the heap:

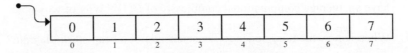

2. The definition of **strcpy** on page 505 is marked with a skull-and-crossbones icon to remind you how dangerous this function can be. The danger stems from the fact that **strcpy** fails to check that there is sufficient space in the character array that receives the copy, which thereby increases the chance of a buffer-overflow error. It is possible, however, to eliminate much of the danger by using dynamic allocation to create memory space for the copied string.

    Write a function

    ```
    char *copyCString(char *str);
    ```

    that allocates enough memory for the C-style string **str** and then copies the characters—along with the terminating null character—into the newly allocated memory.

3. The names of the towers in the **BeaconsOfGondor** program from Figure 12-3 are listed explicitly in the **createBeaconsOfGondor** function. One way to provide more flexibility would be to read the names of the beacons from a data file instead. Modify the **BeaconsOfGondor** program so that the first statement in the main program calls a function

    ```
    Tower *readBeaconsFromFile(string filename);
    ```

    that reads in the list of towers from the specified file. For example, if the file **BeaconsOfGondor.txt** contains

    ```
    Minas Tirith
    Amon Din
    Eilenach
    Nardol
    Erelas
    Min-Rimmon
    Calenhad
    Halifirien
    Rohan
    ```

    the program should run exactly as it does in the chapter.

4. Design and implement a class called **IntArray** that implements the following methods:

    -   A constructor **IntArray(n)** that creates an **IntArray** object with **n** elements, each of which is initialized to 0.

    -   A destructor that frees any heap storage allocated by the **IntArray**.

    -   A method **size()** that returns the number of elements in the **IntArray**.

    -   A method **get(k)** that returns the element at position **k**. If **k** is outside the vector bounds, **get** should call **error** with an appropriate message.

    -   A method **put(k, value)** that assigns **value** to the element at position **k**. As with **get**, the **put** method should call **error** if **k** is out of bounds.

    Your solution should be split into separate interface and implementation files in a manner similar to the **CharStack** example from this chapter. In the initial version of the code, you should add the necessary definitions to the **intarray.h** file to prevent clients from copying **IntArray** objects. Design and implement a unit test to check the methods exported by the class.

    By keeping track of the array size and checking that index values are inside the array bounds, this simple **IntArray** class already fixes two of the most serious shortcomings of the built-in array type.

5. You can make the **IntArray** class from the preceding exercise look a little more like traditional arrays by overriding the bracket-selection operator, which has the following prototype:

    ```
    int & operator[](int k);
    ```

    Like the **get** and **put** methods, your implementation of **operator[]** should check to make sure that the index **k** is valid. If it is, the **operator[]** method should return the element by reference so that clients can assign a new value to a selection expression.

6. Implement deep copying for the **IntArray** class from exercises 4 and 5.

7. Suppose that you have a file containing the code in Figure 12-15. Draw a heap-stack diagram showing the contents of memory just before the function **initPair** returns. For extra practice, draw two versions of this diagram: one that uses explicit addresses and one that uses arrows to indicate the pointers.

8. As in the preceding exercise, draw a heap-stack diagram showing the state of memory at the indicated point in Figure 12-16, which asks you to diagram memory during the *second* call to the constructor.

FIGURE 12-15 Code for the domino program used in exercise 7

```
struct Domino {
   int leftDots;
   int rightDots;
};

void initPair(Domino list[], Domino & dom);

int main() {
   Domino onetwo;
   onetwo.leftDots = 1;
   onetwo.rightDots = 2;
   Domino *array = new Domino[2];
   initPair(array, onetwo);
   return 0;
}

void initPair(Domino list[], Domino & dom) {
   list[0] = dom;
   list[1].leftDots = dom.rightDots;
   list[1].rightDots = dom.leftDots;
   dom = list[1];    ← Diagram memory at this point in the execution
}
```

FIGURE 12-16 Code for the Student class used in exercise 8

```
class Student {
public:

   Student() {
      id = 0;
      gpa = 4.0;
   }

   Student(int id, double gpa) {
      this->id = id;
      this->gpa = gpa;    ← Diagram at this point on the second call to the constructor
   }

private:

   int id;
   double gpa;

};

int main() {
   Student *advisees = new Student[2];
   advisees[0] = Student(2718281, 3.61);
   advisees[1] = Student(3141592, 4.2);
   return 0;
}
```

9.   Even though programmers tend to think of strings as relatively simple entities, their implementation involves the full range of techniques you have seen in this chapter. In this exercise, your mission is to define a class called **MyString** that approximates the behavior of the **string** class from the Standard C++ libraries. Your class should export the following methods:

- A constructor **MyString(str)** that creates a **MyString** object from a C++ **string**.

- A destructor that frees any heap storage allocated by the **MyString**.

- A **toString()** method that converts a **MyString** to a C++ **string**.

- A method **length()** that returns the number of characters in the string.

- A method **substr(start, n)** that returns a substring of the current string object. As in the library version of the **string** class, the substring should begin at the index position **start** and continue for **n** characters or through the end of the string, whichever comes first. The parameter **n** should be optional; if it is missing, the substring should always extend through the end of the original string.

- A redefinition of the operator **+** that concatenates two **MyString** objects. It also makes sense to overload the operator **+=** so that it appends a character or a string to the end of an existing one.

- A redefinition of the operator **<<** so that **MyString** objects can be written to output streams.

- A redefinition of the bracket-selection operator (as described in exercise 5) so that **str[i]** returns by reference the character at index position **i** in **str**. As an improvement over the **string** class in the C++ libraries, your implementation of the bracket operator should call **error** if the index is outside the bounds of the string.

- A redefinition of the relational operators **==**, **!=**, **<**, **<=**, **>**, and **>=** that compares strings lexicographically.

- A redefinition of the assignment operator and the copy constructor for the **MyString** class so that any copying operations make a deep copy that creates a new character array.

Your code should work directly with your underlying representation and should make no calls to any of the methods in the C++ **string** class. Your interface and implementation should also be **const** correct so that both clients and the C++ compiler know exactly what methods can change the value of the string.

10. As a preliminary test of the **MyString** class from exercise 9, rewrite the Pig Latin program from Figure 3-2 on page 143 so that it uses **MyString** instead of **string**.

11. The Pig Latin program from the preceding exercise is not an adequate test of the **MyString** class. Design and implement a more comprehensive unit test of the **MyString** package.

12. Write a unit test for the **Rational** class introduced in section 6.3. If you have implemented the extensions to the **Rational** class described in exercise 8 from Chapter 6, you should include those extensions in your unit test as well.

13. Rewrite the **rational.h** and **rational.cpp** files so that the **Rational** class is **const** correct.

Chapter 13
Efficiency and Representation

Time granted does not necessarily coincide with time that can be most fully used.
— Tillie Olsen, *Silences,* 1965

This chapter brings together two ideas that might at first seem to have little to do with each other: the design of data structures and the concept of algorithmic efficiency. Up to now, discussions of efficiency have focused on the algorithms. If you choose a more efficient algorithm, you can reduce the running time of a program substantially, particularly if the new algorithm is in a different complexity class. In some cases, however, choosing a different underlying representation for a class can have an equally dramatic effect. To illustrate this idea, this chapter looks at a specific class that can be represented in several different ways and contrasts the efficiency of those representations.

13.1 Software patterns for editing text

In this age in which most people carry cell phones, texting has become one of the most popular forms of communication. You create a message on the keypad of your phone and send it off to one or more friends who then read it on their own phones. Modern cell phones require an enormous amount of software, typically involving several million lines of code. To manage that level of complexity, it is essential to decompose the implementation into separate modules that can be developed and managed independently. It is helpful, moreover, to make use of well-established software patterns to simplify the implementation process.

To get a sense of what patterns might be useful, it helps to think about what happens when you compose a text message on your phone. You enter the characters on a keypad, which also includes keys for editing. Depending on the type of phone, that keypad might take different forms. On older phones, it typically consists of a numeric keypad in which you use a series of clicks to generate each letter. A smart phone might not have a physical keypad at all but might rely instead on images of keys displayed on a touch-sensitive screen. In either case, there is a conceptual keypad that allows you to compose and edit the message. A cell phone also has a display that lets you see the message as you write it. In any modern design, however, there is a third component that is invisible to you as a user. Between the keypad and the display is an abstract data structure that records the current contents of the message. The keypad updates the contents of that data structure, which in turn provides the information you see on the display.

The tripartite decomposition described in the preceding paragraph is an example of an important design strategy called the ***model-view-controller pattern,*** or ***MVC*** for short. In the case of the cell phone, the keypad represents the controller, the display represents the view, and the underlying data structure represents the model. The application of this pattern to the cell phone example is illustrated in Figure 13-1, which traces the flow of information among the different modules.

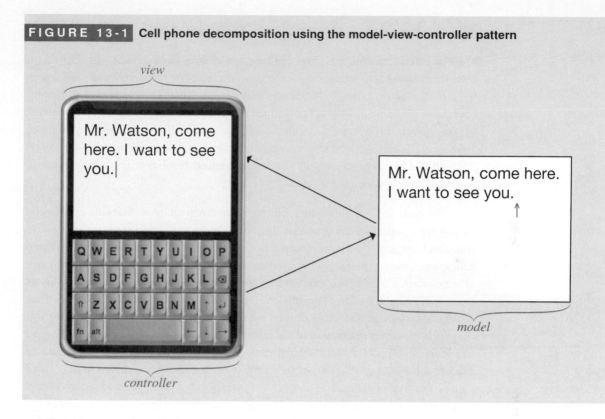

FIGURE 13-1 **Cell phone decomposition using the model-view-controller pattern**

When you use your cell phone to send a text message as pictured in Figure 13-1, you are using an ***editor,*** which is a software module that supports the creation and manipulation of text data. Editors show up in many different applications. When you enter information on a web-based form or compose a C++ program in your development environment, you are using an editor. Most editors today are designed using the model-view-controller pattern. Inside the model, an editor maintains a sequence of characters, which is usually called a ***buffer.*** The controller allows users to perform various operations on the contents of the buffer, many of which are limited to the current location in the buffer. This location is marked on the screen by a symbol called a ***cursor,*** which typically appears in the view as a vertical line between two characters.

Although the controller and the view components of the editor application present interesting programming challenges, the focus of this chapter is on the editor buffer that constitutes the model. The efficiency of the editor application as a whole is extremely sensitive to the data structures you choose to represent the buffer. This chapter implements the editor buffer abstraction using three different underlying representations—a character array, a pair of character stacks, and a linked list of characters—and evaluates their advantages and disadvantages.

13.2 Designing a simple text editor

Modern editors provide a highly sophisticated editing environment, complete with such fancy features as using a mouse to position the cursor or commands that search for a particular text string. Moreover, they tend to show the results of all editing operations precisely as they are performed. Editors that display the current contents of the buffer throughout the editing process are called *wysiwyg* (pronounced "wizzy-wig") editors, which is an acronym for "what you see is what you get." Such editors are easy to use, but all those advanced features make it harder to see how an editor works on the inside.

In the early days of computing, editors were much simpler. Lacking access to a mouse or a sophisticated graphics display, editors were designed to respond to commands entered on the keyboard. For example, with a typical keyboard-based editor, you insert new text by typing the command letter **I**, followed by a sequence of characters. Additional commands perform other editing functions, such as moving the cursor around in the buffer. By entering the right combinations of these commands, you can make any desired set of changes. Given that the focus of this chapter is on the representation of the editor buffer and not on the advanced features necessary to support a more sophisticated editing environment, it makes sense to explore the buffer abstraction in the context of this command-driven style. Once you've finished implementing the editor buffer, you can go back and incorporate it into a more sophisticated application based on the model-view-controller pattern.

Editor commands

The next few sections walk through the development of an extremely simple editor that can execute the commands shown in Table 13-1. Except for the **I** command,

TABLE 13-1 Commands available in a simple command-based editor

F	Moves the editing cursor forward one character position.
B	Moves the editing cursor backward one character position.
J	Jumps to the beginning of the buffer.
E	Moves the cursor to the end of the buffer.
I*xxx*	Inserts the characters *xxx* at the current cursor position.
D	Deletes the character just after the current cursor position.
H	Prints a help message listing the commands.
Q	Quits the editor program.

which also takes the characters to be inserted, every editor command consists of a single letter read in on a line.

The following sample run illustrates the operation of the command-based editor, along with annotations that describe each action. In this session, the user first inserts the characters **axc** and then corrects the contents of the buffer to **abc**.

The editor program displays the state of the buffer after each command. As you can see in the sample run, the program marks the position of the cursor with a caret symbol (**^**) on the next line. That behavior is not what you would expect in a real editor, but will make it easy to see exactly what is going on.

In an object-oriented language like C++, it makes sense to define a class to represent an editor buffer. The advantage of using a class in this context is that doing so allows you to separate the specification of behavior and representation. Because you understand the operations to which it must respond, you already know how an editor buffer behaves. In the **buffer.h** interface, you define the **EditorBuffer** class whose public interface provides the required set of operations, while the data representation is kept private. Clients work entirely with **EditorBuffer** objects through their public interface without any access to the underlying data representation. That fact, in turn, leaves you free to change that representation without requiring your clients to make any changes in their programs.

The public interface of the EditorBuffer class

The public interface consists of prototypes for the methods that implement the primitive operations on an editor buffer. What operations do you need to define? If nothing else, you need to define methods for each of the six editor commands. As with any class, however, you also need to define a constructor that initializes a new buffer. Given the class name of **EditorBuffer**, the prototype for the constructor is

```
EditorBuffer();
```

The class must also provide a destructor

```
~EditorBuffer();
```

that relinquishes any heap storage allocated by the **EditorBuffer** object.

Once these details are out of the way, the next step is to define the prototypes for the methods that correspond to the editor commands. To move the cursor forward, for example, you could define a method like

```
void moveCursorForward();
```

As you design the interface, it is important to keep in mind that you are not concerned with how such an operation is performed or with how the buffer and its cursor are represented. The **moveCursorForward** method is defined entirely in terms of its abstract effect.

In addition to the methods that implement the editor commands, the editor application program must be able to display the contents of the buffer, including the position of the cursor. To make these operations possible, the **EditorBuffer** class exports the methods

```
string toString() const;
```

which returns the contents of the entire buffer as a C++ **string**, and

```
int getCursor() const;
```

which returns the position of the cursor as an integer between 0 and the length of the buffer. These methods leave the contents of the buffer unchanged, and it is therefore good practice to mark them with the keyword **const**.

The contents of the **editorbuffer.h** interface appear in Figure 13-2. As in the interface listings from Chapter 12, the private section of the **EditorBuffer** class appears as an empty blue box that will be filled in with different definitions depending on what strategy is chosen to represent the buffer data.

FIGURE 13-2 Interface for the editor buffer abstraction

```
/*
 * File: buffer.h
 * --------------
 * This file defines the interface for the EditorBuffer class.
 */

#ifndef _buffer_h
#define _buffer_h

/*
 * Class: EditorBuffer
 * -------------------
 * This class represents an editor buffer, which maintains an ordered
 * sequence of characters along with an insertion point called the cursor.
 */

class EditorBuffer {

public:

/*
 * Constructor: EditorBuffer
 * Usage: EditorBuffer buffer;
 * ---------------------------
 * Creates an empty editor buffer.
 */

   EditorBuffer();

/*
 * Destructor: ~EditorBuffer
 * -------------------------
 * Frees any heap storage associated with this buffer.
 */

   ~EditorBuffer();

/*
 * Methods: moveCursorForward, moveCursorBackward
 * Usage: buffer.moveCursorForward();
 *        buffer.moveCursorBackward();
 * ----------------------------------------------
 * Moves the cursor forward or backward one character.  If the command
 * would shift the cursor beyond either end of the buffer, this method
 * has no effect.
 */

   void moveCursorForward();
   void moveCursorBackward();
```

FIGURE 13-2 Interface for the editor buffer abstraction (continued)

```
/*
 * Methods: moveCursorToStart, moveCursorToEnd
 * Usage: buffer.moveCursorToStart();
 *        buffer.moveCursorToEnd();
 * --------------------------------------
 * Moves the cursor to the start or the end of this buffer.
 */

   void moveCursorToStart();
   void moveCursorToEnd();

/*
 * Method: insertCharacter
 * Usage: buffer.insertCharacter(ch);
 * --------------------------------------
 * Inserts the character ch into this buffer at the cursor position,
 * leaving the cursor after the inserted character.
 */

   void insertCharacter(char ch);

/*
 * Method: deleteCharacter
 * Usage: buffer.deleteCharacter();
 * --------------------------------------
 * Deletes the character immediately after the cursor, if any.
 */

   void deleteCharacter();

/*
 * Method: getText
 * Usage: string str = buffer.getText();
 * --------------------------------------
 * Returns the contents of the buffer as a string.
 */

   std::string getText() const;

/*
 * Method: getCursor
 * Usage: int cursor = buffer.getCursor();
 * --------------------------------------
 * Returns the index of the cursor.
 */

   int getCursor() const;
```

The private section of the class goes here.

```
};
```

The implementation of the class goes here.

```
#endif
```

Choosing an underlying representation

Even at this early stage, you probably have some ideas about what internal data structures might be appropriate. Because the buffer contains an ordered sequence of characters, one seemingly obvious choice is to use a **string** or a **Vector<char>** as the underlying representation. As long as these classes are available, either would be an appropriate choice. The goal of this chapter, however, is to investigate how the choice of representation affects the efficiency of applications. That point is harder to understand if the program uses higher-level structures like **string** and **Vector**, because the inner workings of those classes are not visible to clients. If you choose instead to limit your implementation to the built-in data structures, every operation becomes visible, and it is therefore easier to determine the relative efficiency of various competing designs. That logic suggests using a character array as the underlying representation, because array operations have no hidden costs.

Although using an array to represent the buffer is certainly a reasonable approach, there are other representations that offer interesting possibilities. The fundamental lesson in this chapter—and indeed in much of this book—is that you should not choose a particular representation hastily. In the case of the editor buffer, arrays are only one of several options, each of which has certain advantages and disadvantages. After evaluating the tradeoffs, you might decide to use one strategy in a certain set of circumstances and a different strategy in another. At the same time, it is important to note that, no matter what representation you choose, the editor must always be able to perform the same set of commands. Thus, the external behavior of an editor buffer must remain the same, even if the underlying representation changes.

Coding the editor application

Once you have defined the public interface, you are free to go back and write the editor application, even though you have not yet implemented the buffer class or settled on an appropriate internal representation. When you're writing the editor application, the only important consideration is what each of the operations does. At this level, the details of the implementation are unimportant.

As long as you limit yourself to the commands in Table 13-1, writing the editor program is relatively simple. The program simply creates a new **EditorBuffer** object and then enters a loop in which it reads a series of editor commands. Whenever the user enters a command, the program looks at the first character in the command name and performs the requested operation by calling the appropriate method from the buffer interface. The code for the command-based editor appears in Figure 13-3.

FIGURE 13-3   Simple text editor to test the `EditorBuffer` class

```cpp
/*
 * File: SimpleTextEditor.cpp
 * ----------------------------
 * This program implements a simple command-driven text editor, which is
 * used to test the EditorBuffer class.
 */

#include <cctype>
#include <iostream>
#include "buffer.h"
#include "foreach.h"
#include "simpio.h"
using namespace std;

/* Function prototypes */

void executeCommand(EditorBuffer & buffer, string line);
void displayBuffer(EditorBuffer & buffer);
void printHelpText();

int main() {
    EditorBuffer buffer;
    while (true) {
        string cmd = getLine("*");
        if (cmd != "") executeCommand(buffer, cmd);
    }
    return 0;
}

/*
 * Function: executeCommand
 * Usage: executeCommand(buffer, line);
 * ----------------------------------------
 * Executes the command specified by line on the editor buffer.
 */

void executeCommand(EditorBuffer & buffer, string line) {
    switch (toupper(line[0])) {
      case 'I': for (int i = 1; i < line.length(); i++) {
                    buffer.insertCharacter(line[i]);
                }
                displayBuffer(buffer);
                break;
      case 'D': buffer.deleteCharacter(); displayBuffer(buffer); break;
      case 'F': buffer.moveCursorForward(); displayBuffer(buffer); break;
      case 'B': buffer.moveCursorBackward(); displayBuffer(buffer); break;
      case 'J': buffer.moveCursorToStart(); displayBuffer(buffer); break;
      case 'E': buffer.moveCursorToEnd(); displayBuffer(buffer); break;
      case 'H': printHelpText(); break;
      case 'Q': exit(0);
      default:  cout << "Illegal command" << endl; break;
    }
}
```

FIGURE 13-3 Simple text editor to test the `EditorBuffer` class (continued)

```
/*
 * Function: displayBuffer
 * Usage: displayBuffer(buffer);
 * --------------------------------
 * Displays the state of the buffer including the position of the cursor.
 */

void displayBuffer(EditorBuffer & buffer) {
   string str = buffer.getText();
   for (int i = 0; i < str.length(); i++) {
      cout << " " << str[i];
   }
   cout << endl;
   cout << string(2 * buffer.getCursor(), ' ') << "^" << endl;
}

/*
 * Function: printHelpText
 * Usage: printHelpText();
 * -------------------------
 * Displays a message showing the legal commands.
 */

void printHelpText() {
   cout << "Editor commands:" << endl;
   cout << "  Iabc   Inserts the characters abc at the cursor position" << endl;
   cout << "  F      Moves the cursor forward one character" << endl;
   cout << "  B      Moves the cursor backward one character" << endl;
   cout << "  D      Deletes the character after the cursor" << endl;
   cout << "  J      Jumps to the beginning of the buffer" << endl;
   cout << "  E      Jumps to the end of the buffer" << endl;
   cout << "  H      Prints this message" << endl;
   cout << "  Q      Exits from the editor program" << endl;
}
```

13.3 An array-based implementation

As noted earlier in the section on "Choosing an underlying representation," one of the possible representations for the buffer is an array of characters. Although this design is not the only option for representing the editor buffer, it is nonetheless a useful starting point. After all, the characters in the buffer form an ordered, homogeneous sequence, which is precisely the context in which one traditionally uses arrays. The array used to implement the buffer, however, must be allocated dynamically so that it can expand as the number of characters in the buffer grows.

Defining the private data structure

In many respects, the underlying representation for the array-based editor buffer looks like the one used for the **CharStack** class in Chapter 12. The **CharStack** class defines three instance variables: a pointer to the dynamic array containing the elements, the capacity of that array, and the number of characters. For the array-based buffer, you need the same instance variables, although it probably makes sense to change the name of the **count** variable to **length** simply because it is conventional to talk about the length of a buffer. In addition to those variables, the private data for the **EditorBuffer** class must also contain an integer indicating the current location of the cursor. These instance variables, along with the prototypes for the private methods and the standard definitions to disable copying for the **EditorBuffer** class, appear in Figure 13-4.

FIGURE 13-4   Private section for the array-based editor

```
/* Private section */

private:

/*
 * Implementation notes: Buffer data structure
 * --------------------------------------------
 * In the array-based implementation of the buffer, the characters in the
 * buffer are stored in a dynamic array.  In addition to the array, the
 * structure keeps track of the capacity of the buffer, the length of the
 * buffer, and the cursor position.  The cursor position is the index of
 * the character that follows the cursor on the screen.
 */

/* Constants */

   static const int INITIAL_CAPACITY = 10;

/* Instance variables */

   char *array;          /* Dynamic array of characters    */
   int capacity;         /* Allocated size of that array   */
   int length;           /* Number of character in buffer  */
   int cursor;           /* Index of character after cursor */

/* Make it illegal to copy editor buffers */

   EditorBuffer(const EditorBuffer & value) { }
   const EditorBuffer & operator=(const EditorBuffer & rhs) { return *this; }

/* Private method prototype */

   void expandCapacity();
```

Given this data-structure design, a buffer containing

$$H \; E \; L \; L \; O$$
$$_\wedge$$

would look like this:

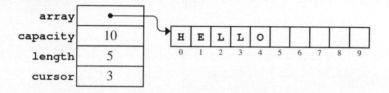

Implementing the buffer operations

Most of the editor operations for the array-based editor are very easy to implement. Each of the four operations that move the cursor can be implemented by assigning a new value to the contents of the **cursor** field. Moving to the beginning of the buffer, for example, requires nothing more than assigning the value 0 to **cursor**; moving to the end is simply a matter of copying the **length** field into the **cursor** field. Similarly, moving forward and backward is a simple matter of incrementing or decrementing the **cursor** field, although it is important to make sure that the value of **cursor** doesn't go outside the legal range. You can see the code for these simple methods in the implementation of the **EditorBuffer** class shown in Figure 13-5.

The only operations in Figure 13-5 that require any additional discussion are the constructor, the destructor, and the **insertCharacter** and **deleteCharacter** methods. Because these methods might seem a little tricky, particularly to someone encountering these implementations for the first time, it is worth including comments in the code that document their operation. The code in Figure 13-5, for example, offers additional documentation for these particular methods in comments labeled "Implementation notes"; the simple methods that implement cursor motion are not documented individually.

The constructor has the responsibility for initializing the instance variables that represent an empty buffer, so the comments for the constructor are a good place to describe those instance variables and what they represent. The destructor is charged with freeing any dynamically allocated storage that was acquired by an object during its lifetime. For the array-based implementation of the **EditorBuffer**, the only dynamically allocated memory is the array used to hold the text. Thus, the code for the destructor consists of the line

```
delete[] array;
```

which deletes the dynamic array storage assigned to **array**.

FIGURE 13-5   Array-based implementation of the editor buffer

```cpp
/*
 * File: buffer.cpp (array version)
 * ---------------------------------
 * This file implements the buffer.h interface using an array representation.
 */

#include <iostream>
#include "buffer.h"
using namespace std;

/*
 * Implementation notes: Constructor and destructor
 * -------------------------------------------------
 * The constructor initializes the private fields.  The destructor
 * frees the heap-allocated memory, which is the dynamic array.
 */

EditorBuffer::EditorBuffer() {
   capacity = INITIAL_CAPACITY;
   array = new char[capacity];
   length = 0;
   cursor = 0;
}

EditorBuffer::~EditorBuffer() {
   delete[] array;
}

/*
 * Implementation notes: moveCursor methods
 * -----------------------------------------
 * The four moveCursor methods simply adjust the value of cursor.
 */

void EditorBuffer::moveCursorForward() {
   if (cursor < length) cursor++;
}

void EditorBuffer::moveCursorBackward() {
   if (cursor > 0) cursor--;
}

void EditorBuffer::moveCursorToStart() {
   cursor = 0;
}

void EditorBuffer::moveCursorToEnd() {
   cursor = length;
}
```

FIGURE 13-5   Array-based implementation of the editor buffer (continued)

```cpp
/*
 * Implementation notes: character insertion and deletion
 * -------------------------------------------------------
 * Each of the functions that inserts or deletes characters must shift
 * all subsequent characters in the array, either to make room for new
 * insertions or to close up space left by deletions.
 */

void EditorBuffer::insertCharacter(char ch) {
   if (length == capacity) expandCapacity();
   for (int i = length; i > cursor; i--) {
      array[i] = array[i - 1];
   }
   array[cursor] = ch;
   length++;
   cursor++;
}

void EditorBuffer::deleteCharacter() {
   if (cursor < length) {
      for (int i = cursor+1; i < length; i++) {
         array[i - 1] = array[i];
      }
      length--;
   }
}

/* Simple getter methods: getText, getCursor */

string EditorBuffer::getText() const {
   return string(array, length);
}

int EditorBuffer::getCursor() const {
   return cursor;
}

/*
 * Implementation notes: expandCapacity
 * -------------------------------------
 * This private method doubles the size of the array whenever the old one
 * runs out of space.  To do so, expandCapacity allocates a new array,
 * copies the old characters to the new array, and then frees the old array.
 */

void EditorBuffer::expandCapacity() {
   char *oldArray = array;
   capacity *= 2;
   array = new char[capacity];
   for (int i = 0; i < length; i++) {
      array[i] = oldArray[i];
   }
   delete[] oldArray;
}
```

The `insertCharacter` and `deleteCharacter` methods are interesting because each of them requires shifting characters in the array, either to make room for a character you want to insert or to close up space left by a deleted character. Suppose, for example, that you want to insert the character **X** at the cursor position in the buffer containing

H E L̬ L O

To do so in the array representation of the buffer, you first need to make sure that there is room in the array. If the `length` field is equal to the `capacity` field, there is no more room in the currently allocated array to accommodate the new character. In that case, it is necessary to expand the array capacity in precisely the same way that the `CharStack` implementation does in Chapter 12.

The extra space in the array, however, is entirely at the end. To insert a character in the middle, you need to make room for that character at the current position of the cursor. The only way to get that space is to shift the remaining characters one position to the right, leaving the buffer structure in the following state:

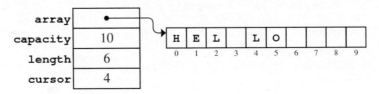

The resulting gap in the array gives you the space you need to insert the **X**, after which the cursor advances so that it follows the newly inserted character, leaving the following configuration:

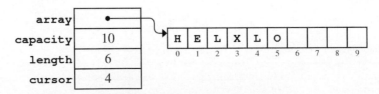

The `deleteCharacter` operation is similar in that it requires a loop to close the gap left by the deleted character.

Computational complexity of the array-based editor

In order to establish a baseline for comparison with other representations, it is useful to determine the computational complexity of the array-based implementation of the editor. As usual, the goal of the complexity analysis is to understand how the execution time required for the editing operations varies qualitatively as a function of the problem size. In the editor example, the number of characters in the buffer is the best measure of problem size. For the editor buffer, you therefore need to determine how the size of the buffer affects the running time of each of the editing operations.

For the array-based implementation, the easiest operations to understand are the ones that move the cursor. As an example, the method `moveCursorForward` has the following implementation:

```
void EditorBuffer::moveCursorForward() {
    if (cursor < length) cursor++;
}
```

Even though the method checks the length of the buffer, it doesn't take long to realize that the execution time of the method is independent of the buffer length. This method executes precisely the same operations no matter how long the buffer is: there is one test and, in almost all cases, one increment operation. Because the execution time is independent of N, the `moveCursorForward` operation runs in $O(1)$ time. The same analysis holds for the other operations that move the cursor, none of which involve any operations that depend on the length of the buffer.

But what about `insertCharacter`? In the array-based implementation of the `EditorBuffer` class, the `insertCharacter` method contains the following `for` loop:

```
for (int i = length; i > cursor; i--) {
    array[i] = array[i - 1];
}
```

If you insert a character at the end of the buffer, this method runs pretty quickly, because there is no need to shift characters to make room for the new one. On the other hand, if you insert a character at the beginning of the buffer, every character in the buffer must be shifted one position rightward in the array. Thus, in the worst case, the running time for `insertCharacter` is proportional to the number of characters in the buffer and is therefore $O(N)$. Because the `deleteCharacter` operation has a similar structure, its complexity is also $O(N)$. The computational complexities for each of the editor operations appear in Table 13-2.

The fact that the last two operations in the table require linear time has important performance implications for the editor program. If an editor uses arrays to represent its internal buffer, it will start to run more slowly as the number of characters in the buffer becomes large. Because this problem seems serious, it makes sense to explore other representational possibilities.

TABLE 13-2 Computational complexity of the array-based buffer

Operation	Array
moveCursorForward	$O(1)$
moveCursorBackward	$O(1)$
moveCursorToStart	$O(1)$
moveCursorToEnd	$O(1)$
insertCharacter	$O(N)$
deleteCharacter	$O(N)$

13.4 A stack-based implementation

The problem with the array implementation of the editor buffer is that insertions and deletions run slowly when they occur near the beginning of the buffer. When those same operations are applied at the end of the buffer, they run relatively quickly because there is no need to shift the characters in the internal array. This property suggests an approach to making things faster: force all insertions and deletions to occur at the end of the buffer. While this approach is completely impractical from the user's point of view, it does contain the seed of a workable idea.

The key insight necessary to make insertions and deletions faster is that you can divide the buffer at the cursor boundary and store the characters before and after the cursor in separate structures. Because all changes to the buffer occur at the cursor position, each of those structures behaves like a stack and can be represented using the **CharStack** class introduced in Chapter 12. The characters that precede the cursor are pushed on one stack so that the beginning of the buffer is at the base and the character just before the pointer is at the top. The characters after the cursor are stored in the opposite direction, with the end of the buffer at the base of the stack and the character just after the pointer at the top.

The best way to illustrate this structure is with a diagram. If the buffer contains

$$H\ E\ L\underset{\wedge}{\ }L\ O$$

the two-stack representation of the buffer looks like this:

```
L
E        L
H        O
─────   ─────
before   after
```

To read the contents of the buffer, it is necessary to read up through the characters in the **before** stack and then down the **after** stack, as indicated by the arrow.

Defining the private data structure

Using this strategy, the instance variables for a buffer object are a pair of stacks, one to hold the characters before the cursor and another to hold the ones that come after it. For the stack-based buffer, the private section of the class declares only the two instance variables shown in Figure 13-6. Note that the cursor is not explicitly represented in this model but is instead simply the boundary between the two stacks.

Implementing the buffer operations

In the stack model, implementing most of the operations for the editor is surprisingly easy. For example, moving backward consists of popping a character from the **before** stack and pushing it back on the **after** stack. Moving forward is entirely symmetrical. Inserting a character consists of pushing that character on the **before** stack. Deleting a character consists of popping a character from the **after** stack and throwing it away.

This conceptual outline makes it easy to write the code for the stack-based editor, which appears in Figure 13-7. Four of the commands—**insertCharacter**, **deleteCharacter**, **moveCursorForward**, and **moveCursorBackward**—run in constant time because the stack operations they call are themselves $O(1)$ operations.

FIGURE 13-6 **Private section for the stack-based editor**

```
/* Private section */

private:

/*
 * Implementation notes: Buffer data structure
 * --------------------------------------------
 * In the stack-based buffer model, the characters are stored in two
 * stacks.  Characters before the cursor are stored in a stack named
 * "before"; characters after the cursor are stored in a stack named
 * "after".  In each case, the characters closest to the cursor are
 * closer to the top of the stack.  The advantage of this
 * representation is that insertion and deletion at the current
 * cursor position occurs in constant time.
 */

/* Instance variables */

   CharStack before;      /* Stack of characters before the cursor */
   CharStack after;       /* Stack of characters after the cursor  */

/* Make it illegal to copy editor buffers */

   EditorBuffer(const EditorBuffer & value) { }
   const EditorBuffer & operator=(const EditorBuffer & rhs) { return *this; }
```

FIGURE 13-7   Stack-based implementation of the editor buffer

```cpp
/*
 * File: buffer.cpp (stack version)
 * ----------------------------------
 * This file implements the EditorBuffer class using a pair of character
 * stacks to represent the buffer.
 */

#include <iostream>
#include "buffer.h"
#include "charstack.h"
using namespace std;

/*
 * Implementation notes: Constructor and destructor
 * -------------------------------------------------
 * In this implementation, all dynamic allocation is managed by the
 * CharStack class, which means there is no work for EditorBuffer to do.
 */

EditorBuffer::EditorBuffer() { }
EditorBuffer::~EditorBuffer() { }

/*
 * Implementation notes: moveCursor methods
 * -----------------------------------------
 * The four moveCursor methods use push and pop to transfer values
 * between the two stacks.
 */

void EditorBuffer::moveCursorForward() {
   if (!after.isEmpty()) {
      before.push(after.pop());
   }
}

void EditorBuffer::moveCursorBackward() {
   if (!before.isEmpty()) {
      after.push(before.pop());
   }
}

void EditorBuffer::moveCursorToStart() {
   while (!before.isEmpty()) {
      after.push(before.pop());
   }
}

void EditorBuffer::moveCursorToEnd() {
   while (!after.isEmpty()) {
      before.push(after.pop());
   }
}
```

FIGURE 13-7 Stack-based implementation of the editor buffer (continued)

```
/*
 * Implementation notes: character insertion and deletion
 * -------------------------------------------------------
 * Each of the functions that inserts or deletes characters can do so
 * with a single push or pop operation.
 */

void EditorBuffer::insertCharacter(char ch) {
   before.push(ch);
}

void EditorBuffer::deleteCharacter() {
   if (!after.isEmpty()) {
      after.pop();
   }
}

/*
 * Implementation notes: getText and getCursor
 * -------------------------------------------------
 * The only difficult part of implementing these operators is making
 * sure that the state of the buffer is restored after copying the
 * characters from the two stacks.
 */

string EditorBuffer::getText() const {
   CharStack beforeCopy = before;
   CharStack afterCopy = after;
   string str = "";
   while (!beforeCopy.isEmpty()) {
      str = beforeCopy.pop() + str;
   }
   while (!afterCopy.isEmpty()) {
      str += afterCopy.pop();
   }
   return str;
}

int EditorBuffer::getCursor() const {
   return before.size();
}
```

But what about the two remaining operations? The **moveCursorToStart** and **moveCursorToEnd** methods each require the program to transfer the entire contents of one of the stacks to the other. Given the operations provided by the **CharStack** class, the only way to accomplish this operation is to pop values from one stack and push them back on the other stack, one value at a time, until the original stack is empty. For example, the **moveCursorToEnd** operation has the following implementation:

```
void EditorBuffer::moveCursorToEnd() {
    while (!after.isEmpty()) {
        before.push(after.pop());
    }
}
```

These implementations have the desired effect, but require $O(N)$ time in the worst case.

Comparing computational complexities

Table 13-3 shows the computational complexity of the editor operations for both the array- and the stack-based implementations of the editor. Which implementation is better? Without some knowledge of the usage pattern, it is impossible to answer this question. Knowing a little about the way people use editors, however, suggests that the stack-based strategy is likely to be more efficient because the slow operations for the array implementation (insertion and deletion) are used much more frequently than the slow operations for the stack implementation (moving the cursor a long distance).

While this tradeoff seems reasonable given the relative frequency of the operations involved, it makes sense to ask whether it is possible to do even better. After all, it is now true that each of the six fundamental editing operations runs in constant time in at least one of the two editor implementations. Insertion is slow in

TABLE 13-3 Computational complexity of the array- and stack-based buffers

Operation	Array	Stack
moveCursorForward	$O(1)$	$O(1)$
moveCursorBackward	$O(1)$	$O(1)$
moveCursorToStart	$O(1)$	$O(N)$
moveCursorToEnd	$O(1)$	$O(N)$
insertCharacter	$O(N)$	$O(1)$
deleteCharacter	$O(N)$	$O(1)$

the array implementation but fast when the implementation uses the stack approach. By contrast, moving to the front of the buffer is fast in the array case but slow in the stack case. None of the operations, however, seems to be *fundamentally* slow, since there is always some implementation that makes that operation fast. Is it possible to develop an implementation in which all the operations are fast? The answer to this question turns out to be "yes," but discovering the key to the puzzle will require you to learn a new approach to representing ordering relationships in a data structure.

13.5 A list-based implementation

As an initial step toward finding a more efficient representation for the editor buffer, it makes sense to examine why the previous approaches have failed to provide efficient service for certain operations. In the case of the array implementation, the answer is obvious: the problem comes from the fact that you have to move a large number of characters whenever you need to insert some new text near the beginning of the buffer. For example, suppose that you were trying to enter the alphabet and instead typed

A C D E F G H I J K L M N O P Q R S T U V W X Y Z

When you discovered that you'd left out the letter **B**, you would have to shift each of the next 24 characters one position to the right in order to make room for the missing letter. A modern computer could handle this shifting operation relatively quickly as long as the buffer did not grow too large; even so, the delay would eventually become noticeable for such an operation if the number of characters in the buffer became sufficiently large.

Let's suppose, however, that you were writing before the invention of modern computers. Imagine for the moment that you are Thomas Jefferson, busily at work drafting the Declaration of Independence. In the list of grievances against King George, you carefully pen the following text:

Our repeated Petitions have been answered by repeated injury.

Unfortunately, just at the last minute, someone decides that this sentence needs the word *only* before the phrase *by repeated injury*. After perhaps contesting the issue for a while, you might decide—as someone clearly did in the actual text of the Declaration—to take out your pen and add the missing word like this:

Our repeated Petitions have been answered by repeated injury.

If you applied the same strategy to the alphabet with the missing letter, you might simply make the following edit:

B
A C D E F G H I J K L M N O P Q R S T U V W X Y Z
^

The result is perhaps a trifle inelegant, but nonetheless acceptable in such desperate circumstances.

The advantage of this age-old editing strategy is that it allows you to suspend the rule that says all letters are arranged in sequence in precisely the form in which they appear on the printed page. The caret symbol below the line tells your eyes that, after reading the **A**, you have to then move up, read the **B**, come back down, read the **C**, and then continue with the sequence. It is also important to notice another advantage of using this insertion strategy. No matter how long the line is, all you have to draw is the new character and the caret symbol. When you use pencil and paper, insertion runs in constant time.

A linked list allows you to achieve much the same effect. If the characters are stored in a linked list rather than a character array, all you need to do to insert a missing character is change a couple of pointers. If the original contents of the buffer were stored as the linked list

A→C→D→E→F→G→H→I→J→K→L→M→N→O→P→Q→R→S→T→U→V→W→X→Y→Z

all you would need to do is (1) write the **B** down somewhere, (2) draw an arrow from **B** to the letter to which **A** is pointing (which is currently the **C**), and (3) change the arrow pointing from the **A** so that it now points to the **B**, like this:

A→C→D→E→F→G→H→I→J→K→L→M→N→O→P→Q→R→S→T→U→V→W→X→Y→Z

This structure has the same form as the linked-list example from Chapter 12. To represent the chain of characters, all you need to do is store the characters in the cells of a linked list. The list for the characters **ABC**, for example, looks like this:

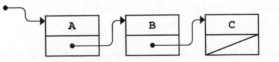

In list structure diagrams, however, it is common to indicate the **NULL** value with a diagonal line across the box, as shown in the preceding example.

At first glance, it might seem that the linked list is all you need to represent the contents of the buffer. The only problem is that you also need to represent the cursor. If you store the cursor as an integer, finding the current position will require counting through the cells in the list until you reach the desired index. That strategy requires linear time. A better approach is to define the **EditorBuffer** class so that it maintains two pointers to **Cell** objects: a **start** pointer that shows where the list begins and a **cursor** pointer that marks the current cursor position.

This design seems reasonable until you try to figure out how the cursor pointer works in detail. If you have a buffer containing three characters, your first reaction is almost certain to be that you using a linked list with three cells. Unfortunately, there's a bit of a problem. Given a buffer containing three characters, there are *four* possible positions for the cursor, as follows:

A B C   A B C   A B C   A B C

If there are only three cells to which the **cursor** field can point, it is not clear how you could represent each of the possible cursor locations.

There are many tactical approaches to solving this problem, but the one that usually turns out to be the best is to allocate an extra cell so that the list contains one cell for each possible insertion point. Typically, this cell goes at the beginning of the list and is called a ***dummy cell.*** The value of the **ch** field in the dummy cell is irrelevant and is indicated in diagrams by filling that field with a gray background.

When you use the dummy cell approach, the **cursor** field points to the cell immediately before the logical insertion point. For example, a buffer containing **ABC** with the cursor at the beginning of the buffer would look like this:

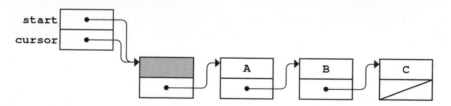

Both **start** and **cursor** point to the dummy cell, and insertions occur immediately after this cell. If the **cursor** field instead indicates the end of the buffer, the diagram looks like this:

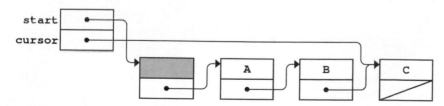

The only instance variables that appear in the private section are the **start** and **cursor** pointers. Even though the rest of this structure is not formally a part of the object, it will help programmers who later have to work with this structure if you document the data structure design in the private section of the **buffer.h** file, as shown in Figure 13-8.

FIGURE 13-8 Private section for the list-based editor

```
/* Private section */

private:

/*
 * Implementation notes: Buffer data structure
 * --------------------------------------------
 * In the linked-list implementation of the buffer, the characters
 * in the buffer are stored in a list of Cell structures, each of
 * which contains a character and a pointer to the next cell in the
 * chain.  To simplify the code used to maintain the cursor, this
 * implementation adds an extra "dummy" cell at the beginning of the
 * list.  The character in this cell is not used, but having it in
 * the data structure provides a cell for the cursor to point to
 * when the cursor is at the beginning of the buffer.
 *
 * The following diagram shows the structure of the list-based buffer
 * containing "ABC" with the cursor at the beginning:
 *
 *         +-----+         +-----+         +-----+         +-----+         +-----+
 *   start | o--+--==>|     |   -->| A  |   -->| B  |   -->| C  |
 *         +-----+  /  +-----+  /  +-----+  /  +-----+  /  +-----+
 *  cursor | o--+--   | o--+--   | o--+--   | o--+--   |  / |
 *         +-----+       +-----+       +-----+       +-----+       +-----+
 */

/*
 * Type: Cell
 * ----------
 * This structure type is used locally within the implementation to
 * store each cell in the linked-list representation.  Each cell
 * contains one character and a pointer to the next cell in the chain.
 */

    struct Cell {
      char ch;
      Cell *link;
    };

/* Instance variables */

    Cell *start;            /* Pointer to the dummy cell      */
    Cell *cursor;           /* Pointer to cell before cursor  */

/* Make it illegal to copy editor buffers */

    EditorBuffer(const EditorBuffer & value) { }
    const EditorBuffer & operator=(const EditorBuffer & rhs) { return *this; }
```

Insertion into a linked-list buffer

No matter where the cursor is positioned, the insertion operation for a linked list consists of the following steps:

1. Allocate space for a new cell, and store the pointer to this cell in the temporary variable **cp**.

2. Copy the character to be inserted into the **ch** field of the new cell.

3. Go to the cell indicated by the **cursor** field of the buffer and copy its link field to the **link** field of the new cell. This operation makes sure that you don't lose the characters that lie beyond the current cursor position.

4. Change the **link** field in the cell addressed by the cursor so that it points to the new cell.

5. Change the **cursor** field in the buffer so that it also points to the new cell. This operation ensures that the next character will be inserted after this one in repeated insertion operations.

To illustrate this process, suppose that you want to insert the letter **B** into a buffer that currently contains

$$\text{A } \underset{\wedge}{\text{ }} \text{C D}$$

with the cursor between the **A** and the **C** as shown. The situation prior to the insertion looks like this:

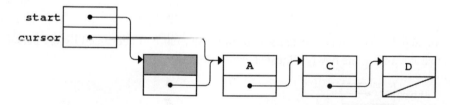

Step 1 in the insertion strategy consists of allocating a new cell and storing a pointer to it in the variable **cp**, as shown:

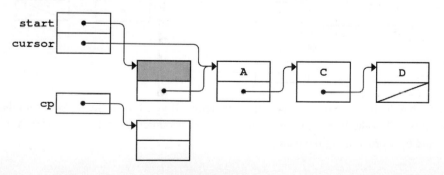

In step 2, you store the character **B** into the **ch** field of the new cell, which leaves the following configuration:

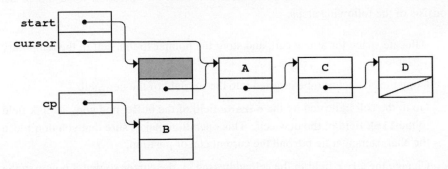

In step 3, you copy the **link** field from the cell whose address appears in the **cursor** field into the **link** field of the new cell. That **link** field points to the cell containing **C**, so the resulting diagram looks like this:

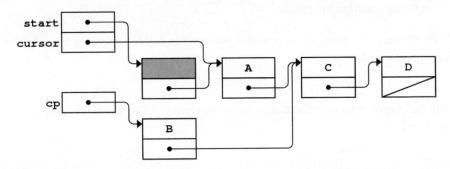

In step 4, you change the **link** field in the current cell addressed by the cursor so that it points to the newly allocated cell, as follows:

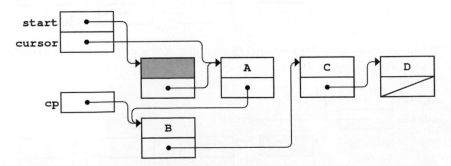

Note that the buffer now has the correct contents. If you follow the arrows from the dummy cell at the beginning of the buffer, you encounter the cells containing **A**, **B**, **C**, and **D**, in order along the path.

The final step consists of changing the **cursor** field in the buffer structure so that it also points to the new cell, which results in this configuration:

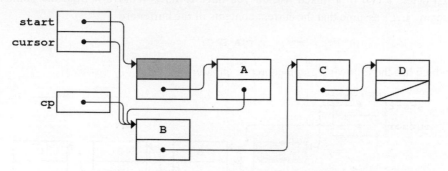

When the program returns from the **insertCharacter** method, the temporary variable **cp** is released, which results in the following final buffer state:

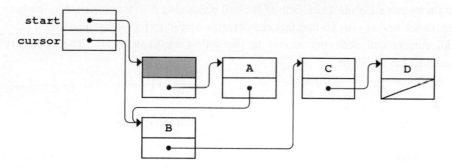

which represents the buffer contents

A B C D

The following implementation of the **insertCharacter** method is a simple translation into C++ code of the informal steps illustrated in the preceding several diagrams:

```
void EditorBuffer::insertCharacter(char ch) {
    Cell *cp = new Cell;
    cp->ch = ch;
    cp->link = cursor->link;
    cursor->link = cp;
    cursor = cp;
}
```

Because there are no loops inside this method, the **insertCharacter** method now runs in constant time.

Deletion in a linked-list buffer

To delete a cell in a linked list, all you have to do is remove it from the pointer chain. Let's assume that the current contents of the buffer are

A B C
  ^

which has the following graphical representation:

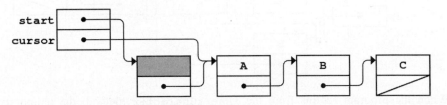

Deleting the character after the cursor requires you to eliminate the cell containing the **B** by changing the **link** field of the cell containing **A** so that it points to the next character further on. To find that character, you need to follow the **link** field from the current cell and continue on to the following **link** field. The necessary statement is therefore

```
cursor->link = cursor->link->link;
```

Executing this statement leaves the buffer in the following state:

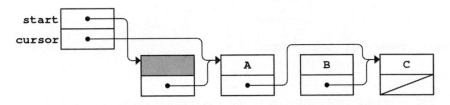

Because the cell containing **B** is no longer accessible through the linked-list structure, it is good policy to free its storage by calling **delete**, as shown in the following implementation of **deleteCharacter**:

```
void EditorBuffer::deleteCharacter() {
    if (cursor->link != NULL) {
        Cell *oldCell = cursor->link;
        cursor->link = cursor->link->link;
        delete oldCell;
    }
}
```

Note that you need a variable like `oldCell` to hold a copy of the pointer to the cell about to be freed while you adjust the chain pointers. If you do not save this value, there will be no way to refer to that cell when you call `delete`.

Cursor motion in the linked-list representation

The remaining operations in the `EditorBuffer` class simply move the cursor. How would you go about implementing these operations in the linked-list buffer? Two of these operations—`moveCursorForward` and `moveCursorToStart`—are easy to perform in the linked-list model. To move the cursor forward, for example, all you have to do is pick up the `link` field from the current cell and make that pointer be the new current cell by storing it in the `cursor` field of the buffer. The statement necessary to accomplish this operation is simply

```
cursor = cursor->link;
```

As an example, suppose that the editor buffer contains

A B C
^

with the cursor at the beginning as shown. The list structure diagram for the buffer is then

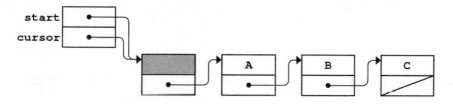

and the result of executing the `moveCursorForward` operation is

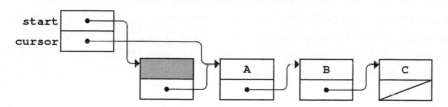

Of course, when you reach the end of the buffer, you can no longer move forward. The implementation of `moveCursorForward` must check for this case, so the complete method definition looks like this:

```
void EditorBuffer::moveCursorForward() {
    if (cursor->link != NULL) {
        cursor = cursor->link;
    }
}
```

Moving the cursor to the beginning of the buffer is equally easy. No matter where the cursor is, you can always restore it to the beginning of the buffer by copying the **start** field into the **cursor** field. Thus, the implementation of **moveCursorToStart** is simply

```
void EditorBuffer::moveCursorToStart() {
    cursor = start;
}
```

The operations **moveCursorBackward** and **moveCursorToEnd**, however, are more complicated. Suppose, for example, that the cursor is sitting at the end of a buffer containing the characters **ABC** and that you want to move back one position. In its graphical representation, the buffer looks like this:

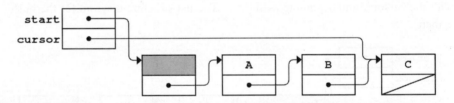

Given the structure of the **EditorBuffer**, there is no constant time strategy for backing up the pointer. The problem is that you have no easy way—given the information you can see—to find out what cell precedes the current one. Pointers allow you to follow a chain from the pointer to the object to which it points, but there is no way to reverse the direction. Given only the address of a cell, it is impossible to find out what cells point to it. With respect to the pointer diagrams, the effect of this restriction is that you can move from the dot at the base of an arrow to the cell to which the arrow points, but you can never go from an arrowhead back to its base.

In the list-structure representation of the buffer, you have to implement every operation in terms of the data that you can see from the buffer structure itself, which contains the **start** and the **cursor** pointers. Looking at just the **cursor** field and following the links that are accessible from that position does not seem promising, because the only cell reachable on that chain is the very last cell in the buffer. The **start** pointer, however, gives you access to the entire linked-list chain. At the same time, you clearly need to consider the value of the **cursor** field, because you need to back up from that position.

Before abandoning hope, you need to recognize that it is possible to find the cell that precedes the current cell. It is just not possible to do so in constant time. If you start at the beginning of the buffer and follow the links through all its cells, you will eventually find a cell whose `link` field points to the same cell as the `cursor` field in the `EditorBuffer` itself. This cell must be the preceding cell in the list. Once you find it, you can simply change the `cursor` field in the `EditorBuffer` to point to that cell, which has the effect of moving the cursor backward.

You can write the code to find the cursor pointer using the traditional `for` loop idiom for linked lists introduced in Chapter 12. There are, however, two problems with this approach. First, you need to use the value of the pointer variable after the loop is finished, which means that you need to declare it outside the loop. Second, if you do use the standard `for` loop idiom, you'll discover that there is absolutely nothing to do in the body, since all you care about is the final value of the pointer. Control structures with empty bodies give readers the impression that there is something missing and can make the code harder to read.

For these reasons, it is easier to code this loop using a `while` statement, like this:

```
Cell *cp = start;
while (cp->link != cursor) {
   cp = cp->link;
}
```

When the `while` loop exits, `cp` is set to the cell prior to the cursor. As with moving forward, you need to protect this loop against trying to move past the limits of the buffer, so the complete code for **moveCursorBackward** would be

```
void EditorBuffer::moveCursorBackward() {
   if (cursor != start) {
      Cell *cp = start;
      while (cp->link != cursor) {
         cp = cp->link;
      }
      cursor = cp;
   }
}
```

For the same reasons, you can implement **moveCursorToEnd** only by moving the cursor forward until it finds the **NULL** in the last cell in the chain, as follows:

```
void EditorBuffer::moveCursorToEnd() {
   while (cursor->link != NULL) {
      cursor = cursor->link;
   }
}
```

Completing the buffer implementation

The complete **EditorBuffer** class contains several methods that have yet to be implemented: the constructor, the destructor, and the getter methods **getText** and **getCursor**. In the constructor, the only wrinkle is that you need to remember the existence of the dummy cell. The code must allocate the dummy cell that is present even in the empty buffer. Once you remember this detail, however, the code is fairly straightforward:

```
EditorBuffer::EditorBuffer() {
    start = cursor = new Cell;
    start->link = NULL;
}
```

The implementation of the destructor is a bit more subtle. When the destructor is called, it is responsible for freeing any memory allocated by the class, which includes every cell in the linked-list chain. Given the earlier discussion of the **for** loop idiom, you might be tempted to code that loop as follows:

```
for (Cell *cp = start; cp != NULL; cp = cp->link) {
    delete cp;
}
```

The problem here is that the code tries to use the **link** pointer inside each block after that block has been freed. Once you call **delete** on a pointer to a record, you are no longer allowed to look inside that record. Doing so is likely to cause errors. To avoid this problem, you need to maintain your position in the list in a separate variable as you free each cell; in essence, you need a place to stand. Thus, the correct code for **~EditorBuffer** is slightly more convoluted and has the following form:

```
EditorBuffer::~EditorBuffer() {
    Cell *cp = start;
    while (cp != NULL) {
        Cell *next = cp->link;
        delete cp;
        cp = next;
    }
}
```

The complete code for the linked-list implementation of the buffer class appears in Figure 13-9.

FIGURE 13-9 List-based implementation of the editor buffer

```cpp
/*
 * File: buffer.cpp (list version)
 * --------------------------------
 * This file implements the EditorBuffer class using a linked
 * list to represent the buffer.
 */

#include <iostream>
#include "buffer.h"
using namespace std;

/*
 * Implementation notes: EditorBuffer constructor
 * -----------------------------------------------
 * The constructor initializes an empty editor buffer represented as
 * a linked list.  In this representation, the empty buffer contains
 * a "dummy" cell whose ch field is never used.  The constructor
 * allocates this dummy cell and then sets the internal pointers.
 */

EditorBuffer::EditorBuffer() {
   start = cursor = new Cell;
   start->link = NULL;
}

/*
 * Implementation notes: EditorBuffer destructor
 * ----------------------------------------------
 * The destructor deletes every cell in the buffer.  Note that the loop
 * structure is not exactly the standard for loop pattern for processing
 * every cell within a linked list.  The complication that forces this
 * change is that the body of the loop can't free the current cell and
 * later have the for loop use the link field of that cell to move to
 * the next one.  To avoid this problem, this implementation copies the
 * link pointer before calling delete.
 */

EditorBuffer::~EditorBuffer() {
   Cell *cp = start;
   while (cp != NULL) {
      Cell *next = cp->link;
      delete cp;
      cp = next;
   }
}
```

FIGURE 13-9   List-based implementation of the editor buffer (continued)

```
/*
 * Implementation notes: moveCursor methods
 * ---------------------------------------------
 * The four methods that move the cursor have different time complexities
 * because the structure of a linked list is asymmetrical with respect to
 * moving backward and forward.  The moveCursorForward and moveCursorToStart
 * methods operate in constant time.  By contrast, the moveCursorBackward
 * and moveCursorToEnd methods each require a loop that runs in linear time.
 */

void EditorBuffer::moveCursorForward() {
   if (cursor->link != NULL) {
      cursor = cursor->link;
   }
}

void EditorBuffer::moveCursorBackward() {
   if (cursor != start) {
      Cell *cp = start;
      while (cp->link != cursor) {
         cp = cp->link;
      }
      cursor = cp;
   }
}

void EditorBuffer::moveCursorToStart() {
   cursor = start;
}

void EditorBuffer::moveCursorToEnd() {
   while (cursor->link != NULL) {
      cursor = cursor->link;
   }
}

/*
 * Implementation notes: insertCharacter
 * ---------------------------------------
 * The steps required to insert a new character are:
 *
 * 1. Allocate a new cell and put the new character in it.
 * 2. Copy the pointer indicating the rest of the list into the link.
 * 3. Update the link in the current cell to point to the new one.
 * 4. Move the cursor forward over the inserted character.
 */

void EditorBuffer::insertCharacter(char ch) {
   Cell *cp = new Cell;
   cp->ch = ch;
   cp->link = cursor->link;
   cursor->link = cp;
   cursor = cp;
}
```

FIGURE 13-9 **List-based implementation of the editor buffer (continued)**

```
/*
 * Implementation notes: deleteCharacter
 * --------------------------------------
 * The steps necessary to delete the character after the cursor are:
 *
 * 1. Remove the current cell by pointing to its successor.
 * 2. Free the cell to reclaim the memory.
 */

void EditorBuffer::deleteCharacter() {
    if (cursor->link != NULL) {
        Cell *oldCell = cursor->link;
        cursor->link = cursor->link->link;
        delete oldCell;
    }
}

/*
 * Implementation notes: getText and getCursor
 * --------------------------------------------
 * The getText method uses the standard linked-list pattern to loop
 * through the cells in the linked list.  The getCursor method counts
 * the characters in the list until it reaches the cursor.
 */

string EditorBuffer::getText() const {
    string str = "";
    for (Cell *cp = start->link; cp != NULL; cp = cp->link) {
        str += cp->ch;
    }
    return str;
}

int EditorBuffer::getCursor() const {
    int nChars = 0;
    for (Cell *cp = start; cp != cursor; cp = cp->link) {
        nChars++;
    }
    return nChars;
}
```

Computational complexity of the linked-list buffer

From the discussion in the preceding section, it is easy to add another column to the complexity table showing the cost of the fundamental editing operations as a method of the number of characters in the buffer. The new table, which includes the data for all three implementations, appears in Table 13-4.

TABLE 13-4 Computational complexity of the three buffer models

Operation	Array	Stack	List
moveCursorForward	$O(1)$	$O(1)$	$O(1)$
moveCursorBackward	$O(1)$	$O(1)$	$O(N)$
moveCursorToStart	$O(1)$	$O(N)$	$O(1)$
moveCursorToEnd	$O(1)$	$O(N)$	$O(N)$
insertCharacter	$O(N)$	$O(1)$	$O(1)$
deleteCharacter	$O(N)$	$O(1)$	$O(1)$

Unfortunately, the table for the list structure representation still contains two $O(N)$ operations, **moveCursorBackward** and **moveCursorToEnd**. The problem with this representation is that the link pointers impose a preferred direction on the implementation: moving forward is easy because the pointers move in the forward direction.

Doubly linked lists

The good news is that this problem is easy to solve. To get around the problem that the links run only in one direction, all you need to do is make the pointers symmetrical. In addition to having a pointer from each cell that indicates the next one, you can also include a pointer to the previous cell. The resulting structure is called a *doubly linked list.*

Each cell in the doubly linked list has two link fields, a **prev** field that points to the previous cell and a **next** field that points to the next one. For reasons that will become clear when you implement the primitive operations, it simplifies the manipulation of the structure if the **prev** field of the dummy cell points to the end of the buffer and the **next** field of the last cell points back to the dummy cell.

If you use this design, the doubly linked representation of the buffer containing

$$A \ B \ C$$

looks like this:

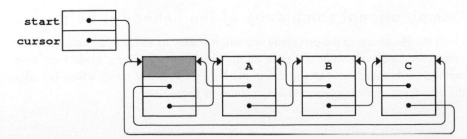

There are quite a few pointers in this diagram, which makes it is easy to get confused. On the other hand, the structure has all the information you need to implement each of the fundamental editing operations in constant time. The actual implementation, however, is left as an exercise so that you can refine your understanding of linked lists.

Time-space tradeoffs

The fact that you can implement the **EditorBuffer** class so that the standard editing operations all run in constant time is an important theoretical result. Unfortunately, that result may not in fact be so useful in practice, at least in the context of the editor application. By the time you get around to adding the **prev** field to each cell for the doubly linked list, you will end up using at least nine bytes of memory to represent each character. You may be able to perform editing operations very quickly, but you will use up memory at an extravagant rate. At this point, you face what computer scientists call a *time-space tradeoff.* You can improve the computational efficiency of your algorithm, but waste space in doing so. Wasting this space could matter a lot, if, for example, it meant that the maximum size of the file you could edit on your machine were only a tenth what it would have been if you had chosen the array representation.

When such situations arise in practice, it is usually possible to develop a hybrid strategy that allows you to select a point somewhere in the middle of the time-space tradeoff curve. For example, you could combine the array and linked-list strategies by representing the buffer as a doubly linked list of lines, where each line was represented using the array form. In this case, insertion at the beginning of a line would be a little slower, but only in proportion to the length of the line and not to the length of the entire buffer. On the other hand, this strategy requires link pointers for each line rather than for each character. Since a line typically contains many characters, using this representation would reduce the storage overhead considerably. Getting the details right on hybrid strategies can be a challenge, but it is important to know that such strategies exist and that there are ways to take advantage of algorithmic time improvements that are not prohibitively expensive in terms of their storage requirements.

Summary

Even though this chapter has focused on implementing a class representing an editor buffer, the buffer itself is not the main point. Text buffers that maintain a cursor position are useful in a relatively small number of application domains. The individual techniques used to improve the buffer representation are fundamental ideas that you will use over and over again.

Important points in this chapter include:

- The strategy used to represent a class can have a significant effect on the computational complexity of its operations.

- Although an array provides a workable representation for an editor buffer, you can improve its performance by using other representation strategies. Using a pair of stacks, for example, reduces the cost of insertion and deletion at the cost of making it harder to move the cursor a long distance.

- You can indicate the order of elements in a sequence by storing a pointer with each value linking it to the one that follows it. In programming, structures designed in this way are called *linked lists*. The pointers that connect one value to the next are called *links,* and the individual records used to store the values and link fields together are called *cells.*

- The conventional way to mark the end of a linked list is to store the pointer constant **NULL** in the link field of the last cell.

- If you are inserting and deleting values from a linked list, it is often convenient to allocate an extra dummy cell at the beginning of the list. The advantage of this technique is that the existence of the dummy cell reduces the number of special cases you need to consider in your code.

- Insertions and deletions at specified points in a linked list are constant-time operations.

- You can iterate through the cells of a linked list by using the following idiom:

```
for (Cell *cp = list; cp != NULL; cp = cp->link) {
    . . . code using cp . . .
}
```

- Doubly linked lists make it possible to traverse a list efficiently in both directions.

- Linked lists tend to be efficient in execution time but inefficient in their use of memory. In some cases, you may be able to design a hybrid strategy that allows you to combine the execution efficiency of linked lists with the space advantages of arrays.

Review questions

1. True or false: The computational complexity of a program depends only on its algorithmic structure, not on the structures used to represent the data.

2. What does *wysiwyg* stand for?

3. In your own words, describe the purpose of the buffer abstraction used in this chapter.

4. What are the six commands implemented by the editor application? What are the corresponding public methods in the **EditorBuffer** class?

5. In addition to the methods that correspond to the editor commands, what other public operations are exported by the **EditorBuffer** class?

6. Which editor operations require linear time in the array representation of the editor buffer? What makes those operations slow?

7. Draw a diagram showing the contents of the **before** and **after** stack in the two-stack representation of a buffer that contains the following text, with the cursor positioned as shown:

    A B C D E F G H I J
             ^

8. How is the cursor position indicated in the two-stack representation of the editor buffer?

9. Which editor operations require linear time in the two-stack representation?

10. What is the purpose of the dummy cell in a linked list used to represent the editor buffer?

11. Does the dummy cell go at the beginning or the end of a linked list? Why?

12. What are the five steps required to insert a new character into the linked-list buffer?

13. Draw a diagram showing all the cells in the linked-list representation of a buffer that contains the following text, with the cursor positioned as shown:

    H E L L O
           ^

14. Modify the diagram you drew in the preceding exercise to show what happens if you insert the character **X** at the cursor position.

15. What is meant by the phrase *traversing a list?*

16. What is the standard idiomatic pattern used in C++ to traverse a linked list?

17. Which editor operations require linear time in the linked-list representation of the editor buffer? What makes those operations slow?

18. What is a *time-space tradeoff?*

19. What modification can you make to the linked-list structure so that all six of the editor operations run in constant time?

20. What is the major drawback to the solution you offered in your answer to question 19? What might you do to improve the situation?

▮▮ Exercises

1. Although the **SimpleTextEditor** application is useful for demonstrating the workings of the editor, it is not ideal as a test program, mostly because it relies on explicit input from the user. Design and implement a unit test for the **EditorBuffer** class that exercises the methods in the class comprehensively enough to uncover likely errors in the implementation.

2. Even though the stacks in the two-stack implementation of the **EditorBuffer** class (see Figures 13-6 and 13-7) expand dynamically, the amount of character space required in the stacks is likely to be twice as large as that required in the corresponding array implementation. The problem is that each stack must be able to accommodate all the characters in the buffer. Suppose, for example, that you are working with a buffer containing N characters. If you're at the beginning of the buffer, those N characters are in the **after** stack; if you move to the end of the buffer, those N characters move to the **before** stack. As a result, each of the stacks must have a capacity of N characters.

   You can reduce the storage requirement in the two-stack implementation of the buffer by storing the two stacks at opposite ends of the same internal array. The **before** stack starts at the beginning of the array, while the **after** stack starts at the end. The two stacks then grow toward each other as indicated by the arrows in the following diagram:

   Reimplement the **EditorBuffer** class using this representation (which is, in fact, the design strategy used in many editors today). Make sure that your program continues to have the same computational efficiency as the two-stack implementation in the text and that the buffer space expands dynamically as needed.

3. If you were using a real editor application, you would probably want the program to display the contents of the buffer on request rather than after every command. Change the implementation of the **SimpleTextEditor** application so that it no longer displays the buffer after every command and instead offers a **T** command that prints the contents. In contrast to the **displayBuffer**

method included in Figure 13-3, the **T** command should simply print the contents of the buffer as a string, without showing the cursor position. A sample run of your new editor might look like this:

```
 ⊖ ⊖ ⊖           SimpleTextEditor
*I world
*T
 world
*J
*Ihello,
*T
hello, world
*
```

4. One of the serious limitations of the **SimpleTextEditor** application is that it offers no way to insert a newline character into the buffer, making it impossible to enter more than one line of data. Starting with the editor application from exercise 3, add an **A** command that reads text on subsequent lines, and ends when the user enters a line consisting of a single period (as in the **ed** editor on Unix systems). A sample run of this version of the editor might look like this:

```
 ⊖ ⊖ ⊖           SimpleTextEditor
*A
'Twas brillig, and the slithy toves
Did gyre and gimble in the wabe:
All mimsy were the borogoves,
And the mome raths outgrabe.
.
*J
*A
        JABBERWOCKY
                -- Lewis Carroll


.
*T
        JABBERWOCKY
                -- Lewis Carroll

'Twas brillig, and the slithy toves
Did gyre and gimble in the wabe:
All mimsy were the borogoves,
And the mome raths outgrabe.
*
```

5. Rewrite the editor application given in Figure 13-3 so that the **F**, **B**, and **D** commands take a repetition count specified by a string of digits before the command letter. Thus, the command **17F** would move the cursor forward 17 character positions.

6. Extend the editor application so that the **F**, **B**, and **D** commands can be preceded with the letter **W** to indicate word motion. Thus, the command **WF** should move

forward to the end of the next word, **WB** should move backward to the beginning of the preceding word, and **WD** should delete characters through the end of the next word. For the purposes of this exercise, a word consists of a consecutive sequence of alphanumeric characters (i.e., letters or digits) and includes any adjacent nonalphanumeric characters between the cursor and the word. This interpretation is easiest to see in the context of an example:

The most straightforward way to implement these commands is to extend the **EditorBuffer** class so that it exports methods that perform word-based operations, which are up to you to design. Implement these extensions for all three of the buffer representations introduced in this chapter.

7. Most modern editors provide a facility that allows the user to copy a section of the buffer text into an internal storage area and then paste it back at some other position. For each of the three representations of the buffer given in this chapter, implement the method

```
void EditorBuffer::copy(int count);
```

which stores a copy of the next **count** characters somewhere in the internal structure of the buffer, and the method

```
void EditorBuffer::paste();
```

which inserts those saved characters back into the buffer at the current cursor position. Calling **paste** does not affect the saved text, which means that you can insert multiple copies of the same text by calling **paste** more than once. Test your implementation by adding the commands **C** and **P** to the editor application for the copy and paste operations, respectively. The **C** command should take a numeric argument to specify the number of characters using the technique described in exercise 5.

8. Editors that support the copy/paste facility described in the preceding exercise usually provide a third operation called *cut* that copies the text from the buffer and then deletes it. Implement a new editor command called **X** that implements the cut operation without making any changes to the **EditorBuffer** class interface beyond those you needed to solve exercise 7.

9. For each of the three representations of the buffer given in this chapter, implement the method

```
bool EditorBuffer::search(string str);
```

When this method is called, it should start searching from the current cursor position, looking for the next occurrence of the string **str**. If it finds it, **search** should leave the cursor after the last character in **str** and return the value **true**. If **str** does not occur between the cursor and the end of the buffer, then **search** should leave the cursor unchanged and return **false**.

To illustrate the operation of **search**, suppose that you have added the **S** command to the **editor.cpp** program so that it calls the **search** method, passing it the rest of the input line. Your program should then be able to match the following sample run:

10. Without making any changes to the **EditorBuffer** class interface beyond those required for exercise 9, add an **R** command to the editor application that replaces the next occurrence of one string with another, where the two strings are specified after the **R** command separated by a slash, as shown:

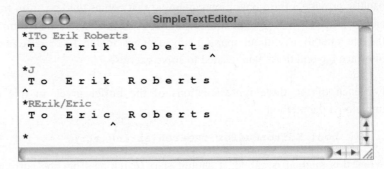

11. The dummy cell strategy described in the text is useful because it reduces the number of special cases in the code, but it is not strictly necessary. Write a new implementation of the linked-list version of **buffer.cpp** in which you make the following changes:

   • The linked list contains no dummy cell—just a cell for every character.

   • A buffer in which the cursor occurs before the first character is indicated by storing **NULL** in the **cursor** field.

   • Every method that checks the position of the cursor makes a special test for **NULL** and performs whatever special actions are necessary in that case.

12. Implement the **EditorBuffer** class using the strategy described in the section entitled "Doubly linked lists" on page 606. Be sure to test your implementation as thoroughly as you can. In particular, make sure that you can move the cursor in both directions across parts of the buffer where you have recently made insertions and deletions.

Chapter 14
Linear Structures

It does not come to me in quite so direct a line as that; it takes a bend or two, but nothing of consequence.

— Jane Austen, *Persuasion,* 1818

The **Stack**, **Queue**, and **Vector** classes introduced in Chapter 5 are examples of a general category of abstract data types called *linear structures,* in which the elements are arranged in a linear order. This chapter looks at several possible representations for these types and considers how the choice of representation affects efficiency.

Because the elements in a linear structure are arranged in an array-like order, using arrays to represent them seems like an obvious choice. Indeed, the **CharStack** class presented in Chapter 12 is implemented using an array as the underlying representation. Arrays, however, are not the only option. Stacks, queues, and vectors can also be implemented using a linked list much like the one used to implement the editor buffer in Chapter 13. By studying the linked-list implementation of these structures, you will increase your understanding not only of how linked lists work but also of how you can apply them in practical programming contexts.

This chapter has another purpose as well. As you know from Chapter 5, the collection classes—unlike the **CharStack** class from Chapter 12—aren't limited to a single data type. The actual **Stack** class allows the client to specify the type of value by providing a type parameter, as in **Stack<int>** or **Stack<Point>**. So far, however, you have only had a chance to use parameterized types as a client. In this chapter, you will learn how to implement them.

14.1 Templates

In computer science, being able to use the same code for more than one data type is called *polymorphism.* Programming languages implement polymorphism in a variety of ways. C++ uses an approach called *templates,* in which the programmer defines a common code pattern that can then be used for many different types. The collection classes from Chapter 5 depend on the C++ template facility, which means that you need to understand how templates work before you can appreciate the underlying implementation of the collection classes.

Before you try to understand templates in detail, it helps to go back and review the concept of *overloading,* which was introduced in Chapter 2. Overloading allows you to define several functions with the same name as long as those functions can be distinguished by their arguments. Given a particular function call, the compiler can then look at the number and types of the arguments and choose the version of the function that matches that signature.

As an example, you can use the following code to define two versions of a function named **max**—one for integers and one for floating-point values—that returns the larger of two arguments:

```
int max(int x, int y) {
    return (x > y) ? x : y;
}

double max(double x, double y) {
    return (x > y) ? x : y;
}
```

The body of each of these functions is exactly the same. The only thing that changes is the argument signature. If a client writes

```
max(17, 42)
```

the compiler notes that both arguments are integers and therefore issues a call to the integer version of the **max** method, which returns an **int** as its result. By contrast, calling

```
max(3.14159, 2.71828)
```

generates a call to the floating-point version, which returns a **double**.

Templates make it possible to automate the overloading process in situations where the code is identical except for the types involved. In C++, you can combine the earlier definitions of the **max** function into a single template definition, as follows:

```
template <typename ValueType>
ValueType max(ValueType x, ValueType y) {
    return (x > y) ? x : y;
}
```

In this definition, the identifier **ValueType** is a placeholder for the argument type used in the call to **max**. The **typename** keyword tells the C++ compiler that this placeholder represents the name of a type, which enables the compiler to interpret that identifier correctly.

Once you have defined this template function, you can use it with any of the primitive types. For example, if the compiler encounters the function call

```
max('A', 'Z')
```

it automatically generates a character version of **max** that looks like this:

```
char max(char x, char y) {
    return (x > y) ? x : y;
}
```

The compiler can then insert a call to this newly created version of **max**, which will correctly return the character **'Z'** as the value of the expression **max('A', 'Z')**.

The template version of the **max** function works with any data type that defines the **>** operator. For example, if you extended the **Rational** class as described in exercise 7 from Chapter 6 so that it includes the comparison operator, you could immediately use **max** to choose the larger of two **Rational** objects. The template facility means that making **max** work for new types essentially comes for free.

There is, however, some need for caution. Given the compiler that runs on my machine, calling

```
max("cat", "dog")
```

happens to return **"cat"**, which seems contrary to logic. The problem here is that the literals **"cat"** and **"dog"** are C strings rather than C++ strings, which means that they are pointers to characters. The C++ compiler therefore generates the more-or-less useless function

```
char *max(char *x, char *y) {
    return (x > y) ? x : y;
}
```

which returns the address of the C string stored at the higher address in memory. If the compiler stores the characters in **"cat"** at higher addresses than the characters in **"dog"**, then **"cat"** will be returned as the maximum. To use the string comparison operators defined for C++ strings, you would need to write this call as

```
max(string("cat"), string("dog"))
```

which correctly returns the C++ string **"dog"**.

It is interesting to note that using the template facility doesn't actually save any space in the compiled program over that required by the alternative strategy of defining individual overloaded versions of the functions. Whenever the compiler encounters an application of a template function to a type that it hasn't yet seen, it generates an entirely new copy of the function body that works for that type. Thus, if you use the **max** function on **int**s, **double**s, **char**s, **string**s, and **Rational**s all in the same program, the compiler will generate five copies of the code, one for each type. This implementation strategy underscores why the word *template* is so appropriate. In C++, you are not defining a single function that works with more than one type, but are instead providing a pattern from which the compiler can generate specially tailored versions whenever it needs them.

The fact that the compiler needs to create multiple copies of the template code has an important implication for you as a programmer. In C++, the compiler must have access to the template implementation when it encounters a call to a template function. The prototype by itself is not enough. This restriction means that one cannot separate the interface and implementation of a template function in the way that the programs in this book ordinarily put prototypes in the `.h` file and the corresponding implementations in the `.cpp` file. If you want to export a template function as part of a library, the implementation must be available to the compiler when the `.h` file is read.

14.2 Implementing stacks

The `CharStack` class in Chapter 12 defines the relevant operations that all stacks require, but is limited because it can only store elements of type `char`. To gain the flexibility of the library version of the `Stack` class, it is necessary to reimplement `Stack` as a *template class,* which is a class that uses the C++ template facility so that it works with any data type.

Creating the template form of an existing class involves some simple syntactic changes. For example, if you want to update the `CharStack` class from Chapter 12 with a general `Stack` template, you begin by replacing the name `CharStack` with `Stack` and then add the following line before the class definition:

```
template <typename ValueType>
```

The `template` keyword indicates that the entire syntactic unit that follows this line—in this case the class definition—is part of a template pattern that can be used for many different values of the `ValueType` parameter. In the code for the `Stack` class, for example, you need to use the placeholder name `ValueType` wherever you refer to the type of element being stored. Thus, as you convert the `CharStack` class definition to its more general template form, you have to replace every occurrence of the specific type `char` with the generic placeholder `ValueType`.

The updated version of the `stack.h` interface appears in Figure 14-1, which includes only those public definitions that are independent of the implementation strategy. These definitions, after all, are the only parts of the interface file that are of any interest to the client. As with the listing of the `buffer.h` interface in Chapter 13, the private section of the `Stack` class appears as a box that will later be replaced by the definitions appropriate to a particular representation. The fact that `Stack` is a template class, however, also means that the compiler must have access to the implementation along with the class definition itself. Figure 14-1 therefore ends with a second box that will eventually be replaced by the implementation that corresponds to the chosen representation. In the sections that follow, these boxes are replaced by two different underlying representations for the stack class: one that uses a dynamic array to store the values and a second that uses a linked list.

FIGURE 14-1 Interface for the polymorphic stack abstraction

```
/*
 * File: stack.h
 * -------------
 * This interface exports a template version of the Stack class.
 */

#ifndef _stack_h
#define _stack_h

#include "error.h"

/*
 * Class: Stack<ValueType>
 * -----------------------
 * This class implements a stack of the specified value type.
 */

template <typename ValueType>
class Stack {

public:

/*
 * Constructor: Stack
 * Usage: Stack<ValueType> stack;
 * ------------------------------
 * Initializes a new empty stack.
 */

   Stack();

/*
 * Destructor: ~Stack
 * Usage: (usually implicit)
 * -------------------------
 * Frees any heap storage associated with this stack.
 */

   ~Stack();

/*
 * Method: size
 * Usage: int n = stack.size();
 * ----------------------------
 * Returns the number of values in this stack.
 */

   int size() const;

/*
 * Method: isEmpty
 * Usage: if (stack.isEmpty()) . . .
 * ---------------------------------
 * Returns true if this stack contains no elements.
 */

   bool isEmpty() const;
```

☞

FIGURE 14-1 Interface for the polymorphic stack abstraction (continued)

```
/*
 * Method: clear
 * Usage: stack.clear();
 * ------------------------
 * Removes all elements from this stack.
 */

   void clear();

/*
 * Method: push
 * Usage: stack.push(value);
 * ---------------------------
 * Pushes the specified value onto this stack.
 */

   void push(ValueType value);

/*
 * Method: pop
 * Usage: ValueType top = stack.pop();
 * ------------------------------------
 * Removes the top element from this stack and returns it.  This
 * method signals an error if called on an empty stack.
 */

   ValueType pop();

/*
 * Method: peek
 * Usage: ValueType top = stack.peek();
 * -------------------------------------
 * Returns the value of top element from this stack without removing
 * it.  This method signals an error if called on an empty stack.
 */

   ValueType peek() const;

/*
 * Copy constructor and assignment operator
 * -----------------------------------------
 * These methods implement deep copying for stacks.
 */

   Stack(const Stack<ValueType> & src);
   Stack<ValueType> & operator=(const Stack<ValueType> & src);
```

> *The private section of the class goes here.*

```
};
```

> *The implementation of the class goes here.*

```
#endif
```

Implementing stacks using a dynamic array

The most straightforward strategy for implementing the template version of the stack class is simply to adopt the dynamic-array model used for the **CharStack** class in Chapter 12. As in the earlier example, the underlying representation of the **Stack** must keep track of a dynamic array of values, the capacity of that array, and the current count of the number of elements. The private section includes the declarations of these variables, along with a private constant to specify the initial capacity and the prototypes for the private methods. The private section for the array-based stack appears in Figure 14-2.

The conversion process for the implementation section is largely a matter of replacing instances of **char** with **ValueType** and changing variable names so that they are more appropriate to the generic type supported by the template class. For example, where the **CharStack** implementation uses the variable name **ch**, it makes more sense to use a name like **value**. The only substantive change is that the template version of the **Stack** class implements overloaded versions of the copy constructor and the assignment operator to ensure that clients can copy values of type **Stack**. The implementation section of **stack.h** appears in Figure 14-3.

FIGURE 14-2 **Private section for the array-based stack**

```
/* Private section */

/*
 * Implementation notes
 * --------------------
 * This version of the stack.h interface uses a dynamic array to store
 * the elements of the stack.  The array begins with INITIAL_CAPACITY
 * elements and doubles the size whenever it runs out of space.  This
 * discipline guarantees that the push method has O(1) amortized cost.
 */

private:

    static const int INITIAL_CAPACITY = 10;

/* Instance variables */

    ValueType *array;                    /* A dynamic array of the elements */
    int capacity;                        /* The allocated size of the array */
    int count;                           /* The number of stack elements    */

/* Private method prototypes */

    void deepCopy(const Stack<ValueType> & src);
    void expandCapacity();
```

FIGURE 14-3 Implementation of the array-based stack

```
/*
 * Implementation section
 * ----------------------
 * C++ requires that the implementation for a template class be available
 * to the compiler whenever that type is used.  The effect of this
 * restriction is that header files must include the implementation.
 * Clients should not need to look at any of the code beyond this point.
 */

/*
 * Implementation notes: Stack constructor
 * ---------------------------------------
 * The constructor allocates the array storage for the stack elements
 * and initializes the fields of the object.
 */

template <typename ValueType>
Stack<ValueType>::Stack() {
   capacity = INITIAL_CAPACITY;
   array = new ValueType[capacity];
   count = 0;
}

/*
 * Implementation notes: ~Stack
 * ----------------------------
 * The destructor frees any heap memory allocated by the class, which
 * is just the dynamic array of elements.
 */

template <typename ValueType>
Stack<ValueType>::~Stack() {
   delete[] array;
}

template <typename ValueType>
int Stack<ValueType>::size() const {
   return count;
}

template <typename ValueType>
bool Stack<ValueType>::isEmpty() const {
   return count == 0;
}

template <typename ValueType>
void Stack<ValueType>::clear() {
   count = 0;
}
```

FIGURE 14-3 Implementation of the array-based stack (continued)

```
/*
 * Implementation notes: push
 * ---------------------------
 * This function first checks to see whether there is enough room for
 * the value and then expands the array storage if necessary.
 */

template <typename ValueType>
void Stack<ValueType>::push(ValueType ch) {
   if (count == capacity) expandCapacity();
   array[count++] = ch;
}

/*
 * Implementation notes: pop, peek
 * -------------------------------
 * These functions checks for an empty stack and reports an error
 * if there is no top element.
 */

template <typename ValueType>
ValueType Stack<ValueType>::pop() {
   if (isEmpty()) error("pop: Attempting to pop an empty stack");
   return array[--count];
}

template <typename ValueType>
ValueType Stack<ValueType>::peek() const {
   if (isEmpty()) error("peek: Attempting to peek at an empty stack");
   return array[count - 1];
}

/*
 * Implementation notes: copy constructor and assignment operator
 * --------------------------------------------------------------
 * These methods follow the standard template, leaving the work to deepCopy.
 */

template <typename ValueType>
Stack<ValueType>::Stack(const Stack<ValueType> & src) {
   deepCopy(src);
}

template <typename ValueType>
Stack<ValueType> & Stack<ValueType>::operator=(const Stack<ValueType> & src) {
   if (this != &src) {
      delete[] array;
      deepCopy(src);
   }
   return *this;
}
```

FIGURE 14-3 Implementation of the array-based stack (continued)

```
/*
 * Implementation notes: deepCopy
 * ------------------------------
 * This function copies the data from the src parameter into the current
 * object.  All dynamic memory is reallocated to create a "deep copy" in
 * which the current object and the source object are independent.
 * The capacity is set so that the stack has some room to expand.
 */

template <typename ValueType>
void Stack<ValueType>::deepCopy(const Stack<ValueType> & src) {
   capacity = src.count + INITIAL_CAPACITY;
   this->array = new ValueType[capacity];
   for (int i = 0; i < src.count; i++) {
      array[i] = src.array[i];
   }
   count = src.count;
}

/*
 * Implementation notes: expandCapacity
 * -------------------------------------
 * This private method doubles the capacity of the elements array whenever
 * it runs out of space.  To do so, it copies the pointer to the old array,
 * allocates a new array with twice the capacity, copies the values from
 * the old array to the new one, and finally frees the old storage.
 */

template <typename ValueType>
void Stack<ValueType>::expandCapacity() {
   ValueType *oldArray = array;
   capacity *= 2;
   array = new ValueType[capacity];
   for (int i = 0; i < count; i++) {
      array[i] = oldArray[i];
   }
   delete[] oldArray;
}
```

Implementing stacks as linked lists

Although arrays are the most common underlying representation for stacks, it is also possible to implement the **Stack** class using linked lists. If you do so, the conceptual representation for the empty stack is simply the **NULL** pointer:

When you push a new element onto the stack, the element is simply added to the front of the linked-list chain. Thus, if you push the element e_1 onto an empty stack, that element is stored in a new cell that becomes the only link in the chain:

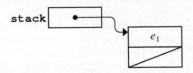

Pushing a new element onto the stack adds that element at the beginning of the chain. The steps involved are the same as those required to insert a character into a linked-list buffer. You first allocate a new cell, then enter the data, and, finally, update the link pointers so that the new cell becomes the first element in the chain. Thus, if you push the element e_2 on the stack, you get the following configuration:

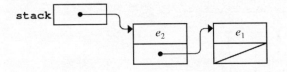

In the linked-list representation, the **pop** operation consists of removing the first cell in the chain and returning the value stored there. Thus, a **pop** operation from the stack shown in the preceding diagram returns e_2 and restores the previous state of the stack, as follows:

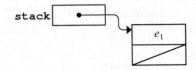

Although it is possible to store only the pointer to the start of the linked list in the underlying representation, doing so has an unfortunate consequence for the efficiency of the **size** method. If the class stores only the linked list, the only way to determine the length of that list is to walk through the elements of the list until you find the **NULL** pointer at the end. That process requires $O(N)$ time. To ensure that the **size** method runs in constant time, the simplest approach is to keep track of the number of values in a separate instance variable. Adopting this design means that the private section declares two instance variables: a pointer to the start of the list and the count of the number of items. A more complete picture of a stack containing two items therefore looks like this:

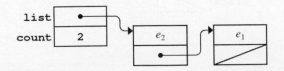

FIGURE 14-4 **Private section for the list-based stack**

```
/* Private section */

private:

/*
 * Implementation notes
 * --------------------
 * This version of the stack.h interface uses a linked list to store
 * the elements of the stack.  The top item is always at the front of
 * the linked list and is therefore always accessible without searching.
 * The instance variable count keeps track of the number of elements so
 * that the size method runs in constant time.
 */

/* Type for linked list cell */

   struct Cell {
      ValueType data;                    /* The data value             */
      Cell *link;                        /* Link to the next cell      */
   };

/* Instance variables */

   Cell *list;                           /* Initial pointer in the list */
   int count;                            /* Number of elements          */

/* Private method prototypes */

   void deepCopy(const Stack<ValueType> & src);
```

The contents of the revised private section of the **stack.h** interface for the list-based stack appear in Figure 14-4. Once you have defined the data structure, you can then move on to rewrite the **Stack** class methods so that they operate on the new data representation. The complete listing of the implementation section for the list-based version of **stack.h** appears in Figure 14-5.

There are several aspects of the implementation that are worth special mention. The constructor, as always, is responsible for setting up the initial state of the object, which consists of an empty linked list and an element count of zero. The constructor in Figure 14-5 initializes these fields explicitly, as follows:

```
template <typename ValueType>
Stack<ValueType>::Stack() {
   list = NULL;
   count = 0;
}
```

FIGURE 14-5 Implementation of the list-based stack

```
/*
 * Implementation section
 * ----------------------
 * C++ requires that the implementation for a template class be available
 * to the compiler whenever that type is used.  Clients should not need
 * to look at any of the code beyond this point.
 */

/*
 * Implementation notes: Stack constructor
 * ----------------------------------------
 * The constructor creates an empty linked list and initializes the count.
 */

template <typename ValueType>
Stack<ValueType>::Stack() {
   list = NULL;
   count = 0;
}

/*
 * Implementation notes: Stack destructor
 * ---------------------------------------
 * The destructor frees any heap memory that is allocated by the
 * implementation.  Because clear frees each element it processes,
 * this implementation of the destructor simply calls that method.
 */

template <typename ValueType>
Stack<ValueType>::~Stack() {
   clear();
}

/*
 * Implementation notes: size, isEmpty
 * ------------------------------------
 * These methods use the count variable and therefore run in constant time.
 */

template <typename ValueType>
int Stack<ValueType>::size() const {
   return count;
}

template <typename ValueType>
bool Stack<ValueType>::isEmpty() const {
   return count == 0;
}
```

FIGURE 14-5 Implementation of the list-based stack (continued)

```
/*
 * Implementation notes: clear
 * ----------------------------
 * This method pops the stack until it is empty, thereby freeing each cell.
 */

template <typename ValueType>
void Stack<ValueType>::clear() {
   while (count > 0) {
      pop();
   }
}

/*
 * Implementation notes: push
 * ---------------------------
 * This method chains a new element onto the front of the list where it
 * becomes the top of the stack.
 */

template <typename ValueType>
void Stack<ValueType>::push(ValueType value) {
   Cell *cp = new Cell;
   cp->data = value;
   cp->link = list;
   list = cp;
   count++;
}

/*
 * Implementation notes: pop, peek
 * -------------------------------
 * These methods check for an empty stack and report an error if
 * there is no top element.  The pop method frees the cell to ensure
 * that the implementation does not leak memory as it executes.
 */

template <typename ValueType>
ValueType Stack<ValueType>::pop() {
   if (isEmpty()) error("pop: Attempting to pop an empty stack");
   Cell *cp = list;
   ValueType result = cp->data;
   list = list->link;
   count--;
   delete cp;
   return result;
}

template <typename ValueType>
ValueType Stack<ValueType>::peek() const {
   if (isEmpty()) error("peek: Attempting to peek at an empty stack");
   return list->data;
}
```

FIGURE 14-5   Implementation of the list-based stack (continued)

```
/*
 * Implementation notes: copy constructor and assignment operator
 * ------------------------------------------------------------------
 * These methods follow the standard template, leaving the work to deepCopy.
 */

template <typename ValueType>
Stack<ValueType>::Stack(const Stack<ValueType> & src) {
   deepCopy(src);
}

template <typename ValueType>
Stack<ValueType> & Stack<ValueType>::operator=(const Stack<ValueType> & src) {
   if (this != &src) {
      clear();
      deepCopy(src);
   }
   return *this;
}

/*
 * Implementation notes: deepCopy
 * ----------------------------------
 * The deepCopy method creates a copy of the cells in the linked list.
 * The variable tail keeps track of the last cell in the chain.
 */

template <typename ValueType>
void Stack<ValueType>::deepCopy(const Stack<ValueType> & src) {
   count = src.count;
   Cell *tail = NULL;
   for (Cell *cp = src.list; cp != NULL; cp = cp->link) {
      Cell *ncp = new Cell;
      ncp->data = cp->data;
      if (tail == NULL) {
         list = ncp;
      } else {
         tail->link = ncp;
      }
      tail = ncp;
   }
   if (tail != NULL) tail->link = NULL;
}
```

The **push** method illustrates the standard pattern for adding a new cell to the beginning of a linked list:

```
template <typename ValueType>
void Stack<ValueType>::push(ValueType value) {
    Cell *cp = new Cell;
    cp->data = value;
    cp->link = list;
    list = cp;
    count++;
}
```

This pattern is sufficiently important that it is worth going through the steps using a heap-stack diagram. Suppose that you are executing the following main program:

```
int main() {
    Stack<int> myStack;
    myStack.push(42);
    cout << myStack.pop() << endl;
    return 0;
}
```

When execution reaches the call to **push**, no memory has yet been allocated on the heap, and the heap-stack diagram looks like this:

Calling **myStack.push(42)** creates a new stack frame, with space for the pointer to the current object accessible through the keyword **this**, the parameter variable **value**, and the local variable **cp**. After the parameters have been initialized, the diagram looks like this:

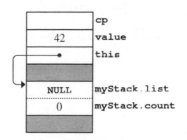

Once the new stack frame is ready to go, the **push** method has to allocate a new cell in which to store the value. The first line of the **push** method creates a new

`Cell` structure on the heap and assigns its address to the variable `cp`, which leads to the following diagram:

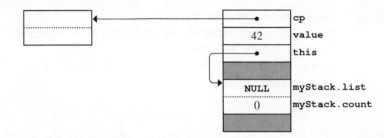

The next two lines fill in the contents of this newly allocated cell. The **value** field is simply the value supplied by the caller. The **link** field is the initial pointer in the chain of cells that follow this one. In this example, that chain is empty, but it always has the value that used to be in the **list** field of the **Stack** object to which **push** is applied. Thus, the statement

```
cp->link = list;
```

makes sure that this cell appears at the beginning of the existing list. These two statements leave the diagram in the following state:

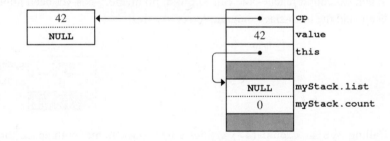

The next step in the process consists of updating the **list** field in the **Stack** object so that the list begins with the newly allocated cell. The statement

```
list = cp;
```

leaves memory looking like this:

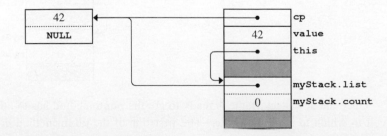

From there, the **push** method increments the **count** field and then returns to the main program, which results in the following memory diagram:

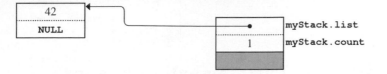

The **pop** method has to reverse this process. Calling **myStack.pop()** in the current configuration creates a new stack frame that is essentially identical to the one for **push**, except that **value** is now a local variable rather than a parameter:

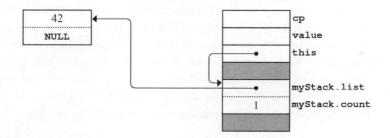

After making sure the stack is not empty, the first two assignment statements in **pop** copy the pointer to the top stack cell and the value from that cell into local variables in the frame, as follows:

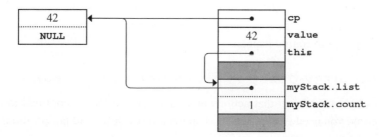

The need to make a local copy of the value stems from the fact that **pop** has to free the cell so that the **Stack** implementation does not consume more and more memory as it runs. Because it is illegal to look inside the cell after it's been freed, the value has to be stored in the frame so that the method can return it.

The heart of the **pop** implementation is the line

```
list = list->link;
```

which replaces the linked list in the **Stack** object with the sublist that follows the current cell, which is **NULL** in the current example. Assigning this value to the **list** component of the stack, decrementing the count, freeing the cell, and returning from the method results in the following final state, which corresponds to an empty stack:

14.3 Implementing queues

As you know from Chapter 5, stacks and queues are very similar structures. The only difference between them is in the order in which elements are processed. A stack uses a last-in/first-out (LIFO) discipline in which the last item pushed is always the first item popped. A queue adopts a first-in/first-out (FIFO) model that more closely resembles a waiting line. The interfaces for stacks and queues are also extremely similar. The only changes in the public section of the two interfaces are the names of the two methods that define the behavior of the class. The **push** method from the **Stack** class is now called **enqueue**, and the **pop** method is **dequeue**. The behavior of those methods is also different, which is reflected in the comments in the **queue.h** interface, which appears in Figure 14-6.

Given the conceptual similarity of these structures and their interfaces, it is not surprising that both stacks and queues can be implemented using either array-based or list-based strategies. With each of these models, however, the implementation of a queue has subtleties that don't arise in the case of a stack. These differences stem from the fact that all the operations on a stack occur at the same end of the internal data structure. In a queue, the **enqueue** operation happens at one end, and the **dequeue** operation happens at the other.

An array-based implementation of queues

In light of the fact that actions in a queue are no longer confined to one end of an array, you need two indices to keep track of the head and tail positions in the queue. The private instance variables therefore look like this:

```
ValueType *array;
int capacity;
int head;
int tail;
```

In this representation, the **head** field holds the index of the next element to come out of the queue, and the **tail** field holds the index of the next free slot. In an empty queue, it is clear that the **tail** field should be 0 to indicate the initial position in the array, but what about the **head** field? For convenience, the usual strategy is to set the **head** field to 0 as well. When queues are defined in this way, having the **head** and **tail** fields be equal indicates that the queue is empty.

FIGURE 14-6 Interface for the polymorphic queue abstraction

```
/*
 * File: queue.h
 * -------------
 * This interface exports a template version of the Queue class.
 */

#ifndef _queue_h
#define _queue_h

#include "error.h"

/*
 * Class: Queue<ValueType>
 * -----------------------
 * This class implements a queue of the specified value type.
 */

template <typename ValueType>
class Queue {

public:

/*
 * Constructor: Queue
 * Usage: Queue<ValueType> queue;
 * ------------------------------
 * Initializes a new empty queue.
 */

   Queue();

/*
 * Destructor: ~Queue
 * Usage: (usually implicit)
 * -------------------------
 * Frees any heap storage associated with this queue.
 */

   ~Queue();

/*
 * Method: size
 * Usage: int n = queue.size();
 * ----------------------------
 * Returns the number of values in the queue.
 */

   int size() const;

/*
 * Method: isEmpty
 * Usage: if (queue.isEmpty()) . . .
 * ---------------------------------
 * Returns true if the queue contains no elements.
 */

   bool isEmpty() const;
```

FIGURE 14-6 Interface for the polymorphic queue abstraction (continued)

```
/*
 * Method: clear
 * Usage: queue.clear();
 * -----------------------
 * Removes all elements from this queue.
 */

   void clear();

/*
 * Method: enqueue
 * Usage: queue.enqueue(value);
 * ------------------------------
 * Adds value to the end of the queue.
 */

   void enqueue(ValueType value);

/*
 * Method: dequeue
 * Usage: ValueType first = queue.dequeue();
 * ----------------------------------------------
 * Removes and returns the first item in the queue.  This method
 * signals an error if called on an empty queue.
 */

   ValueType dequeue();

/*
 * Method: peek
 * Usage: ValueType first = queue.peek();
 * ----------------------------------------
 * Returns the first value in the queue without removing it.  This
 * method signals an error if called on an empty queue.
 */

   ValueType peek() const;

/*
 * Copy constructor and assignment operator
 * ------------------------------------------
 * These methods implement deep copying for queues.
 */

   Queue(const Queue<ValueType> & src);
   Queue<ValueType> & operator=(const Queue<ValueType> & src);
```

```
   The private section of the class goes here.
```

```
};
```

```
   The implementation of the class goes here.
```

```
#endif
```

If you use this representation strategy, the `Queue` constructor looks like this:

```
template <typename ValueType>
Queue<ValueType>::Queue() {
    head = tail = 0;
}
```

Although it is tempting to think that the **enqueue** and **dequeue** methods will look almost exactly like their **push** and **pop** counterparts in the **Stack** class, you'll run into several problems if you try to copy the existing code. As is often the case in programming, it makes more sense to begin by drawing diagrams to make sure you understand exactly how the queue should operate before you turn to the implementation.

To get a sense of how this representation of a queue works, imagine that the queue represents a waiting line, similar to one in the simulation from Chapter 5. From time to time, a new customer arrives and is added to the queue. Customers waiting in line are periodically served at the head end of the queue, after which they leave the waiting line entirely. How does the queue data structure respond to each of these operations?

Assuming that the queue is empty at the beginning, its internal structure looks like this:

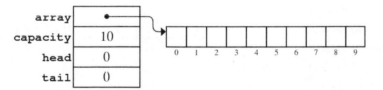

Suppose now that five customers arrive, indicated by the letters *A* through *E*. Those customers are enqueued in order, which gives rise to the following configuration:

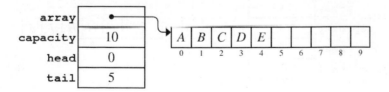

The value 0 in the **head** field indicates that the first customer in the queue is stored in position 0 of the array; the value 5 in **tail** indicates that the next customer will be placed in position 5. So far, so good. At this point, suppose that you alternately serve a customer at the beginning of the queue and then add a new customer to the end. For example, customer *A* is dequeued and customer *F* arrives, which leads to the following situation:

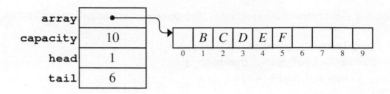

Imagine that you continue to serve one customer just before the next customer arrives and that this trend continues until customer *J* arrives. The internal structure of the queue then looks like this:

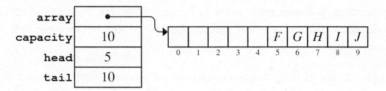

At this point, you've got a bit of a problem. There are only five customers in the queue, but you have used up all the available space. The `tail` field is pointing beyond the end of the array. On the other hand, you now have unused space at the beginning of the array. Thus, instead of incrementing `tail` so that it indicates the nonexistent position 10, you can "wrap around" from the end of the array back to position 0, as follows:

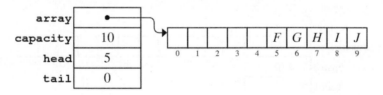

From this position, you have space to enqueue customer *K* in position 0, which leads to the following configuration:

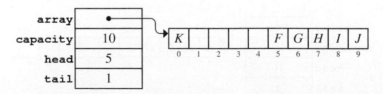

If you allow the elements in the queue to wrap around from the end of the array to the beginning, the active elements always extend from the `head` index up to the position immediately preceding the `tail` index, as illustrated in this diagram:

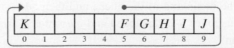

Because the ends of the array act as if they were joined together, programmers call this representation a ***ring buffer.***

The only remaining issue you need to consider before you can write the code for **enqueue** and **dequeue** is how to check whether the queue is completely full. Testing for a full queue is trickier than you might expect. To get a sense of where complications might arise, suppose that three more customers arrive before any additional customers are served. If you enqueue the customers *L, M,* and *N,* the data structure looks like this:

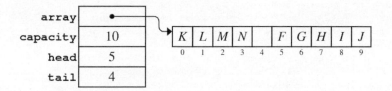

At this point, it appears as if there is one extra space. What happens, though, if customer *O* arrives at this moment? If you follow the logic of the earlier enqueue operations, you end up with the following configuration:

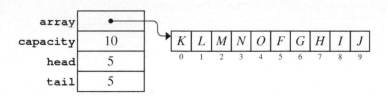

The queue array is now completely full. Unfortunately, whenever the **head** and **tail** fields have the same value, as they do in this diagram, the queue is considered to be empty. There is no way to tell from the contents of the queue structure itself which of the two conditions—empty or full—actually applies, because the data values look the same in each case. Although you can fix this problem by adopting a different definition for the empty queue and writing some special-case code, the simplest approach is to limit the number of elements in the queue to one less than the capacity and to expand the array whenever that limit is reached.

The code for the ring-buffer implementation of the **Queue** class template appears in Figures 14-7 and 14-8. It is important to observe that the code does not explicitly test the array indices to see whether they wrap around from the end of the array to the beginning. Instead, the code makes use of the **%** operator to compute the correct index automatically. The technique of using remainders to reduce the result of a computation to a small, cyclical range of integers is an important mathematical technique called ***modular arithmetic.***

FIGURE 14-7   Private section for the array-based queue

```
/* Private section */

/*
 * Implementation notes
 * --------------------
 * The array-based queue stores the elements in successive index
 * positions in an array, just as a stack does.  What makes the
 * queue structure more complex is the need to avoid shifting
 * elements as the queue expands and contracts.  In the array
 * model, this goal is achieved by keeping track of both the
 * head and tail indices.  The tail index increases by one each
 * time an element is enqueued, and the head index increases by
 * one each time an element is dequeued.  Each index therefore
 * marches toward the end of the allocated array and will
 * eventually reach the end.  Rather than allocate new memory,
 * this implementation lets each index wrap around back to the
 * beginning as if the ends of the array of elements were joined
 * to form a circle.  This representation is called a ring buffer.
 *
 * The elements of the queue are stored in a dynamic array of
 * the specified element type.  If the space in the array is ever
 * exhausted, the implementation doubles the array capacity.
 * Note that the queue capacity is reached when there is still
 * one unused element in the array.  If the queue is allowed to
 * fill completely, the head and tail indices have the same
 * value, and the queue appears empty.
 */

private:

   static const int INITIAL_CAPACITY = 10;

/* Instance variables */

   ValueType *array;                  /* A dynamic array of the elements */
   int capacity;                      /* The allocated size of the array */
   int head;                          /* The index of the head element   */
   int tail;                          /* The index of the tail element   */

/* Private method prototypes */

   void deepCopy(const Queue<ValueType> & src);
   void expandCapacity();
```

FIGURE 14-8 Implementation of the array-based queue

```
/*
 * Implementation section
 * ----------------------
 * Clients should not need to look at any of the code beyond this point.
 */

/*
 * Implementation notes: Queue constructor
 * ----------------------------------------
 * The constructor allocates the array storage and initializes the fields.
 */

template <typename ValueType>
Queue<ValueType>::Queue() {
   capacity = INITIAL_CAPACITY;
   array = new ValueType[capacity];
   head = 0;
   tail = 0;
}

/*
 * Implementation notes: ~Queue
 * ----------------------------
 * The destructor frees any memory that is allocated by the implementation.
 */

template <typename ValueType>
Queue<ValueType>::~Queue() {
   delete[] array;
}

/*
 * Implementation notes: size
 * ---------------------------
 * The size is calculated from head and tail using modular arithmetic.
 */

template <typename ValueType>
int Queue<ValueType>::size() const {
   return (tail + capacity - head) % capacity;
}

/*
 * Implementation notes: isEmpty
 * ------------------------------
 * The queue is empty whenever the head and tail pointers are equal.  This
 * interpretation means that the queue must always leave one unused space.
 */

template <typename ValueType>
bool Queue<ValueType>::isEmpty() const {
   return head == tail;
}
```

FIGURE 14-8 Implementation of the array-based queue (continued)

```
/*
 * Implementation notes: clear
 * ---------------------------
 * The clear method need not take account of where in the ring buffer the
 * existing values are stored and can simply reset the head and tail indices.
 */

template <typename ValueType>
void Queue<ValueType>::clear() {
   head = tail = 0;
}

/*
 * Implementation notes: enqueue
 * -----------------------------
 * This method first checks to see whether there is enough room for the
 * element and then expands the array storage if necessary.  Because it
 * is otherwise impossible to differentiate the case when a queue is
 * empty from when it is completely full, this implementation expands
 * the queue when the size is one less than the capacity.
 */

template <typename ValueType>
void Queue<ValueType>::enqueue(ValueType value) {
   if (size() == capacity - 1) expandCapacity();
   array[tail] = value;
   tail = (tail + 1) % capacity;
}

/*
 * Implementation notes: dequeue, peek
 * -----------------------------------
 * These methods check for an empty queue and report an error if
 * there is no first element.
 */

template <typename ValueType>
ValueType Queue<ValueType>::dequeue() {
   if (isEmpty()) error("dequeue: Attempting to dequeue an empty queue");
   ValueType result = array[head];
   head = (head + 1) % capacity;
   return result;
}

template <typename ValueType>
ValueType Queue<ValueType>::peek() const {
   if (isEmpty()) error("peek: Attempting to peek at an empty queue");
   return array[head];
}
```

FIGURE 14-8   Implementation of the array-based queue (continued)

```
/*
 * Implementation notes: Deep copying support
 * -------------------------------------------
 * These methods implement deep copying for queues.
 */

template <typename ValueType>
Queue<ValueType>::Queue(const Queue<ValueType> & src) {
   deepCopy(src);
}

template <typename ValueType>
Queue<ValueType> & Queue<ValueType>::operator=(const Queue<ValueType> & src) {
   if (this != &src) {
      delete[] array;
      deepCopy(src);
   }
   return *this;
}

template <typename ValueType>
void Queue<ValueType>::deepCopy(const Queue<ValueType> & src) {
   int count = src.size();
   capacity = count + INITIAL_CAPACITY;
   array = new ValueType[capacity];
   for (int i = 0; i < count; i++) {
      array[i] = src.array[(src.head + i) % src.capacity];
   }
   head = 0;
   tail = count;
}

/*
 * Implementation notes: expandCapacity
 * -------------------------------------
 * This private method doubles the capacity of the dynamic array whenever
 * it runs out of space.  For simplicity, this implementation also shifts
 * all the elements back to the beginning of the array.
 */

template <typename ValueType>
void Queue<ValueType>::expandCapacity() {
   int count = size();
   ValueType *oldArray = array;
   array = new ValueType[2 * capacity];
   for (int i = 0; i < count; i++) {
      array[i] = oldArray[(head + i) % capacity];
   }
   capacity *= 2;
   head = 0;
   tail = count;
   delete[] oldArray;
}
```

Linked-list representation of queues

The queue class also has a simple representation using list structure. If you adopt this approach, the elements of the queue are stored in a list beginning at the head of the queue and ending at the tail. To allow both **enqueue** and **dequeue** to run in constant time, the **Queue** object must keep a pointer to both ends of the queue. The private instance variables are therefore defined as shown in the revised version of the private section that appears in Figure 14-9. The ASCII data diagram in the comments is likely to convey more information to the implementer than the surrounding text. Such diagrams are sometimes tedious to produce, but they offer enormous value to the reader.

Given a modern word processor and a drawing program, it is possible to produce much more detailed diagrams than you can make using ASCII characters alone. If you are designing data structures for a large and complex system, it probably makes sense to create these diagrams and include them as part of the extended documentation of a package, ideally on a web page. Here, for example, is a somewhat more readable picture of a queue containing the customers *A, B,* and *C:*

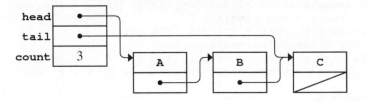

The code for the linked-list implementation of queues appears in Figure 14-10. On the whole, the code is reasonably straightforward, particularly if you use the linked-list implementation of stacks as a model. The diagram of the internal structure provides the essential insights you need to understand how to implement each of the queue operations. The **enqueue** operation, for example, adds a new cell after the one marked by the **tail** pointer and then updates the **tail** pointer so that it continues to indicate the end of the list. The **dequeue** operation consists of removing the cell addressed by the **head** pointer and returning the value in that cell.

The only place where the implementation gets tricky is in the representation of the empty queue. The most straightforward approach is to indicate an empty queue by storing **NULL** in the **head** pointer, as follows:

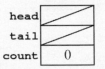

```
FIGURE 14-9   Private section for the list-based queue
```

```
/* Private section */

/*
 * Implementation notes: Queue data structure
 * -------------------------------------------
 * The list-based queue uses a linked list to store the elements
 * of the queue.  To ensure that adding a new element to the tail
 * of the queue is fast, the data structure maintains a pointer to
 * the last cell in the queue as well as the first.  If the queue is
 * empty, both the head pointer and the tail pointer are set to NULL.
 *
 * The following diagram illustrates the structure of a queue
 * containing two elements, A and B.
 *
 *         +--------+           +--------+           +--------+
 *  head | o---+-------->| A | +--==>| B |
 *         +--------+           +--------+  |  |    +--------+
 *  tail | o---+---+      | o---+--+  |  | NULL |
 *         +--------+  |    +--------+  |  |    +--------+
 *                       |                     |
 *                       +---------------------+
 */

private:

/* Type for linked list cell */

   struct Cell {
      ValueType data;                      /* The data value               */
      Cell *link;                          /* Link to the next cell        */
   };

/* Instance variables */

   Cell *head;                             /* Pointer to the cell at the head */
   Cell *tail;                             /* Pointer to the cell at the tail */
   int count;                              /* Number of elements in the queue */

/* Private method prototypes */

   void deepCopy(const Queue<ValueType> & src);
```

FIGURE 14-10   Implementation of the list-based queue

```
/*
 * Implementation section
 * ----------------------
 * C++ requires that the implementation for a template class be available
 * to the compiler whenever that type is used.  The effect of this
 * restriction is that header files must include the implementation.
 * Clients should not need to look at any of the code beyond this point.
 */

/*
 * Implementation notes: Queue constructor
 * ----------------------------------------
 * The constructor creates an empty linked list and sets the count to 0.
 */

template <typename ValueType>
Queue<ValueType>::Queue() {
   head = tail = NULL;
   count = 0;
}

/*
 * Implementation notes: ~Queue destructor
 * ----------------------------------------
 * The destructor frees any heap memory allocated by the queue.
 */

template <typename ValueType>
Queue<ValueType>::~Queue() {
   clear();
}

/*
 * Implementation notes: size, isEmpty, clear
 * -------------------------------------------
 * These methods use the count variable and therefore run in constant time.
 */

template <typename ValueType>
int Queue<ValueType>::size() const {
   return count;
}

template <typename ValueType>
bool Queue<ValueType>::isEmpty() const {
   return count == 0;
}

template <typename ValueType>
void Queue<ValueType>::clear() {
   while (count > 0) {
      dequeue();
   }
}
```

FIGURE 14-10   Implementation of the list-based queue (continued)

```
/*
 * Implementation notes: enqueue
 * ------------------------------
 * This method allocates a new list cell and chains it in at the tail of
 * the queue.  If the queue is currently empty, the new cell also becomes
 * the head pointer in the queue.
 */

template <typename ValueType>
void Queue<ValueType>::enqueue(ValueType value) {
   Cell *cp = new Cell;
   cp->data = value;
   cp->link = NULL;
   if (head == NULL) {
      head = cp;
   } else {
      tail->link = cp;
   }
   tail = cp;
   count++;
}

/*
 * Implementation notes: dequeue, peek
 * -----------------------------------
 * These methods check for an empty queue and report an error if
 * there is no first element.  The dequeue method also checks for
 * the case in which the queue becomes empty and sets both the head
 * and tail pointers to NULL.
 */

template <typename ValueType>
ValueType Queue<ValueType>::dequeue() {
   if (isEmpty()) error("dequeue: Attempting to dequeue an empty queue");
   Cell *cp = head;
   ValueType result = cp->data;
   head = cp->link;
   if (head == NULL) tail = NULL;
   delete cp;
   count--;
   return result;
}

template <typename ValueType>
ValueType Queue<ValueType>::peek() const {
   if (isEmpty()) error("peek: Attempting to peek at an empty queue");
   return head->data;
}
```

FIGURE 14-10 Implementation of the list-based queue (continued)

```
/*
 * Implementation notes: copy constructor and assignment operator
 * -----------------------------------------------------------------
 * These methods follow the standard template, leaving the work to deepCopy.
 */

template <typename ValueType>
Queue<ValueType>::Queue(const Queue<ValueType> & src) {
   deepCopy(src);
}

template <typename ValueType>
Queue<ValueType> & Queue<ValueType>::operator=(const Queue<ValueType> & src) {
   if (this != &src) {
      clear();
      deepCopy(src);
   }
   return *this;
}

/*
 * Implementation notes: deepCopy
 * --------------------------------
 * This function copies the data from the src parameter into the current
 * object.  This implementation simply walks down the linked list in the
 * source object and enqueues each value in the destination.
 */

template <typename ValueType>
void Queue<ValueType>::deepCopy(const Queue<ValueType> & src) {
   head = NULL;
   tail = NULL;
   count = 0;
   for (Cell *cp = src.head; cp != NULL; cp = cp->link) {
      enqueue(cp->data);
   }
}
```

The **enqueue** implementation must check for the empty queue as a special case. If the **head** pointer is **NULL**, **enqueue** must set both the **head** and **tail** pointers so that they point to the cell containing the new element. Thus, if you were to enqueue customer *A* into an empty queue, the internal structure of the pointers at the end of the **enqueue** operation would look like this:

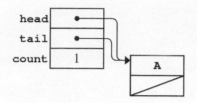

If you make another call to **enqueue**, the **head** pointer is no longer **NULL**, which means that the implementation no longer has to perform the special-case action for the empty queue. Instead, the **enqueue** implementation uses the **tail** pointer to find the end of the linked-list chain and adds the new cell at that point. For example, if you enqueue customer *B* after customer *A,* the resulting structure looks like this:

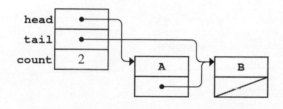

14.4 Implementing vectors

The **Vector** class introduced in Chapter 5 is another example of a linear structure. In many respects, the implementation of the **Vector** class is a combination of the editor buffer from Chapter 13 and the stack and queue abstractions you have seen in this chapter. The **Vector** class resembles the **EditorBuffer** class in that it allows clients to insert and remove elements at any point in the sequence of values. At the same time, **Vector** resembles the **Stack** and **Queue** classes because it implements deep copying and uses templates to support polymorphism.

The fact that **Vector** resembles classes you have already seen means that the code requires less in the way of explanation. The only method in the **Vector** class that doesn't appear in the earlier models is the use of square brackets for selection. As you know from several earlier chapters, C++ makes it possible to extend the standard operators so that they apply to new types. In much the same way, C++ allows classes to redefine the selection by overriding the definition of **operator[]**, which has the following prototype:

```
ValueType & operator[](int index);
```

As was true for the insertion operator, the selection operator must use return by reference so that it is possible to assign a new value to an element position.

The complete text of the polymorphic **vector.h** interface, including the private section and the implementation section, appears in Figure 14-11.

FIGURE 14-11 The `vector.h` interface

```
/*
 * File: vector.h
 * --------------
 * This interface exports the Vector template class, which provides an
 * efficient, safe, convenient replacement for the array type in C++.
 */

#ifndef _vector_h
#define _vector_h

#include "error.h"

/*
 * Class: Vector<ValueType>
 * ------------------------
 * This class stores an ordered list of values similar to an array.  It
 * supports traditional array selection using square brackets, but also
 * supports the insertion and deletion of elements.
 */

template <typename ValueType>
class Vector {

public:

/*
 * Constructor: Vector
 * Usage: Vector<ValueType> vec;
 *        Vector<ValueType> vec(n, value);
 * ------------------------------------------
 * Initializes a new Vector object.  The first form creates an empty vector;
 * the second creates a vector of size n in which each element is initialized
 * to the specified value or the default value for the element type.
 */

   Vector();
   Vector(int n, ValueType value = ValueType());

/*
 * Destructor: ~Vector
 * Usage: (usually implicit)
 * -------------------------
 * Frees any heap storage allocated by this vector.
 */

   ~Vector();

/*
 * Method: size
 * Usage: int n = vec.size();
 * --------------------------
 * Returns the number of values in this vector.
 */

   int size() const;
```

☞

FIGURE 14-11   The `vector.h` interface (continued)

```
/*
 * Method: isEmpty
 * Usage: if (vec.isEmpty()) . . .
 * -------------------------------
 * Returns true if this vector contains no elements.
 */

   bool isEmpty() const;

/*
 * Method: clear
 * Usage: vec.clear();
 * ---------------------
 * Removes all elements from this vector.
 */

   void clear();

/*
 * Method: get
 * Usage: ValueType value = vec.get(index);
 * ----------------------------------------
 * Returns the element at the specified index in this vector.  This method
 * signals an error if the index is not in the array range.
 */

   ValueType get(int index) const;

/*
 * Method: set
 * Usage: vec.set(index, value);
 * -------------------------------
 * Replaces the element at the specified index in this vector with a new
 * value.  The previous value at that index is overwritten.  This method
 * signals an error if the index is not in the array range.
 */

   void set(int index, ValueType value);

/*
 * Method: insert
 * Usage: vec.insert(0, value);
 * ------------------------------
 * Inserts the element into this vector before the specified index.  All
 * subsequent elements are shifted one position to the right.  This method
 * signals an error if the index is outside the range from 0 up to and
 * including the length of the vector.
 */

   void insert(int index, ValueType value);
```

FIGURE 14-11 The `vector.h` interface (continued)

```
/*
 * Method: remove
 * Usage: vec.remove(index);
 * ---------------------------
 * Removes the element at the specified index from this vector.  All
 * subsequent elements are shifted one position to the left.  This method
 * signals an error if the index is outside the array range.
 */

   void remove(int index);

/*
 * Method: add
 * Usage: vec.add(value);
 * ------------------------
 * Adds a new value to the end of this vector.
 */

   void add(ValueType value);

/*
 * Operator: []
 * Usage: vec[index]
 * ------------------
 * Overloads [] to select elements from this vector.  This extension
 * enables the use of traditional array notation to get or set individual
 * elements.  This method signals an error if the index is outside the
 * array range.
 */

   ValueType & operator[](int index);

/*
 * Copy constructor and assignment operator
 * ------------------------------------------
 * These methods implement deep copying for vectors.
 */

   Vector(const Vector<ValueType> & src);
   Vector<ValueType> & operator=(const Vector<ValueType> & src);
```

FIGURE 14-11   The vector.h interface (continued)

```cpp
/* Private section */

/*
 * Notes on the representation
 * ---------------------------
 * This version of the vector.h interface stores the elements in a
 * dynamic array of the specified element type.  If the space in the
 * array is ever exhausted, the implementation doubles the array capacity.
 */

private:

   static const int INITIAL_CAPACITY = 10;

/* Instance variables */

   ValueType *array;                   /* A dynamic array of the elements */
   int capacity;                       /* The allocated size of the array */
   int count;                          /* The number of elements in use   */

/* Private method prototypes */

   void deepCopy(const Vector<ValueType> & src);
   void expandCapacity();

};

/*
 * Implementation notes: Vector constructor and destructor
 * -------------------------------------------------------
 * The two implementations of the constructor each allocate storage for
 * the dynamic array and then initialize the other fields of the object.
 * The destructor frees the heap memory used by the dynamic array.
 */

template <typename ValueType>
Vector<ValueType>::Vector() {
   capacity = INITIAL_CAPACITY;
   count = 0;
   array = new ValueType[capacity];
}

template <typename ValueType>
Vector<ValueType>::Vector(int n, ValueType value) {
   capacity = (n > INITIAL_CAPACITY) ? n : INITIAL_CAPACITY;
   array = new ValueType[capacity];
   count = n;
   for (int i = 0; i < n; i++) {
      array[i] = value;
   }
}

template <typename ValueType>
Vector<ValueType>::~Vector() {
   delete[] array;
}
```

FIGURE 14-11   The vector.h interface (continued)

```
/*
 * Implementation notes: size, isEmpty, clear
 * --------------------------------------------
 * These methods require only the count field and do not look at the data.
 */

template <typename ValueType>
int Vector<ValueType>::size() const {
   return count;
}

template <typename ValueType>
bool Vector<ValueType>::isEmpty() const {
   return count == 0;
}

template <typename ValueType>
void Vector<ValueType>::clear() {
   count = 0;
}

/*
 * Implementation notes: get, set
 * --------------------------------
 * These methods first check that the index is in range and then get or set
 * the appropriate index position in the dynamic array.
 */

template <typename ValueType>
ValueType Vector<ValueType>::get(int index) const {
   if (index < 0 || index >= count) error("get: index out of range");
   return array[index];
}

template <typename ValueType>
void Vector<ValueType>::set(int index, ValueType value) {
   if (index < 0 || index >= count) error("set: index out of range");
   array[index] = value;
}

/*
 * Implementation notes: Vector selection
 * ----------------------------------------
 * The following code implements traditional array selection using square
 * brackets for the index.  To ensure that clients can assign to array
 * elements, this method uses an & to return the result by reference.
 */

template <typename ValueType>
ValueType & Vector<ValueType>::operator[](int index) {
   if (index < 0 || index >= count) error("Vector index out of range");
   return array[index];
}
```

FIGURE 14-11 The `vector.h` interface (continued)

```
/*
 * Implementation notes: add, insert, remove
 * ------------------------------------------
 * These methods shifts the existing elements in the array to make room
 * for a new element or to close up the space left by a deleted one.
 */

template <typename ValueType>
void Vector<ValueType>::add(ValueType value) {
   insert(count, value);
}

template <typename ValueType>
void Vector<ValueType>::insert(int index, ValueType value) {
   if (count == capacity) expandCapacity();
   if (index < 0 || index > count) error("insert: index out of range");
   for (int i = count; i > index; i--) {
      array[i] = array[i - 1];
   }
   array[index] = value;
   count++;
}

template <typename ValueType>
void Vector<ValueType>::remove(int index) {
   if (index < 0 || index >= count) error("remove: index out of range");
   for (int i = index; i < count - 1; i++) {
      array[i] = array[i + 1];
   }
   count--;
}

/*
 * Implementation notes: copy constructor and assignment operator
 * --------------------------------------------------------------
 * These methods follow the standard template, leaving the work to deepCopy.
 */

template <typename ValueType>
Vector<ValueType>::Vector(const Vector<ValueType> & src) {
   deepCopy(src);
}

template <typename ValueType>
Vector<ValueType> & Vector<ValueType>::operator=(const Vector<ValueType> & src)
   if (this != &src) {
      delete[] array;
      deepCopy(src);
   }
   return *this;
}
```

FIGURE 14-11 The `vector.h` interface (continued)

```
/*
 * Implementation notes: deepCopy
 * ---------------------------------
 * This function copies the data from the src parameter into the current
 * object.  All dynamic memory is reallocated to create a "deep copy" in
 * which the current object and the source object are independent.
 * The capacity is set so that the vector has some room to expand.
 */

template <typename ValueType>
void Vector<ValueType>::deepCopy(const Vector<ValueType> & src) {
   capacity = src.count + INITIAL_CAPACITY;
   this->array = new ValueType[capacity];
   for (int i = 0; i < src.count; i++) {
      array[i] = src.array[i];
   }
   count = src.count;
}

/*
 * Implementation notes: expandCapacity
 * ---------------------------------------
 * This method doubles the array capacity whenever it runs out of space.
 */

template <typename ValueType>
void Vector<ValueType>::expandCapacity() {
   ValueType *oldArray = array;
   capacity *= 2;
   array = new ValueType[capacity];
   for (int i = 0; i < count; i++) {
      array[i] = oldArray[i];
   }
   delete[] oldArray;
}

#endif
```

14.5 Integrating prototypes and code

One of the primary reasons for using interfaces is to hide the complexity of the implementation from the eyes of the client. For simple interfaces of the sort you saw in Chapter 2, the division between interface and implementation is achieved by putting them in separate files. Everything the client needs to see goes into the `.h` file that defines the interface; the messy details of the implementation are relegated to the corresponding `.cpp` file.

Unfortunately, C++ makes it difficult to maintain that level of separation as the interfaces become more sophisticated. The requirement that the private section of a class must be included in the body of the class definition means that those details must be part of the `.h` file. For template classes, the situation is even worse because C++ requires that the entire implementation be available whenever it expands a template. The effect of this restriction is that the interfaces for template classes must contain all the code as well as the definitions.

Given that the implementation for a template class is going to be part of the `.h` file anyway, some professional C++ programmers give up on the notion of physical separation altogether and include the bodies of the methods directly within the class. Adopting this strategy simplifies the syntactic structure of the class significantly. The **template** keyword appears only once at the beginning of the class and need not be repeated for each method implementation. The fact that each implementation is inside the scope of its class means you can eliminate the `::` tags.

However, despite the advantages in terms of syntactic simplicity, the examples in this text continue to put the prototypes and implementations in different parts of the `.h` file. The public version of the class contains only the prototypes. The corresponding implementations come at the end of the file, after a comment warning the client that everything else in the `.h` file is intended only for the implementer. Maintaining at least some separation means that it is still possible for clients to see a section of the interface file that is uncluttered with implementation details. More importantly, including both a prototype and an implementation in different parts of the `.h` file means that the comments associated with each part of the full definition can address the appropriate audience. The prototypes at the beginning of the `.h` file are written for the client and contain no implementation details. By contrast, the comments associated with the actual code are intended for the implementer. Putting these two parts together forces the comments to address both audiences, which makes them less useful to the client.

Summary

In this chapter, you have learned how to use the C++ template mechanism for generic container classes. A template allows you to define the class in terms of a type placeholder that can be specialized to a particular client data type. You have also had the chance to see array- and list-based implementations of the **Stack** and **Queue** classes, along with the public interface for a polymorphic **Vector** class.

Important points in this chapter include:

- Templates are used to define generic container classes.

- Stacks can be implemented using a linked-list structure in addition to the more traditional array-based representation.

- The array-based implementation of queues is somewhat more complex than its stack counterpart. The traditional implementation uses a structure called a *ring buffer,* in which the elements logically wrap around from the end of the array to the beginning. Modular arithmetic makes it easy to implement the ring buffer concept.

- In the ring-buffer implementation used in this chapter, a queue is considered empty when its head and tail indices are the same. This representation strategy means that the maximum capacity of the queue is one element less than the allocated size of the array. Attempting to fill all the elements in the array makes a full queue indistinguishable from an empty one.

- Queues can also be represented using a linked list marked by two pointers, one to the head of the queue and another to the tail.

- Vectors can easily be represented using dynamic arrays. Inserting new elements and removing existing ones requires shifting data in the array, which means that these operations typically require $O(N)$ time.

- You can redefine operators for a class by defining methods whose name consists of the keyword **operator** followed by the operator symbol. In particular, you can redefine selection by defining the **operator[]** method.

Review questions

1. What advantages do C++ templates offer designers of generic containers?

2. When specializing a class template for use as a client, how do you specify what type should be used to fill in the template placeholder?

3. Using the linked-list implementation, draw a diagram of the cells used to represent **myStack** after the following operations have been performed:

```
Stack<char> myStack;
myStack.push('A');
myStack.push('B');
myStack.push('C');
```

4. If you use an array to store the underlying elements in a queue, what private instance variables are needed for the **Queue** class?

5. What is a *ring buffer?* How does the ring-buffer concept apply to queues?

6. How can you tell whether an array-based queue is empty? How can you tell whether it has reached its capacity?

7. Assuming that **INITIAL_CAPACITY** has the artificially small value of 3, draw a diagram showing the underlying representation of the array-based queue **myQueue** after the following sequence of operations:

```
Queue<char> myQueue;
myQueue.enqueue('A');
myQueue.enqueue('B');
myQueue.enqueue('C');
myQueue.dequeue();
myQueue.dequeue();
myQueue.enqueue('D');
myQueue.enqueue('E');
myQueue.dequeue();
myQueue.enqueue('F');
```

8. Explain how modular arithmetic is useful in the array-based implementation of queues.

9. Describe what is wrong with the following implementation of **size** for the array-based representation of queues:

```
template <typename ValueType>
int Queue<ValueType>::size() const {
    return (tail - head) % capacity;
}
```

10. Draw a diagram showing the internal structure of a linked-list queue after the computer finishes the set of operations in question 7.

11. How can you tell whether a linked-list queue is empty?

12. What method do you need to override to redefine bracket selection for a class?

Exercises

1. The standard C++ header file **<algorithm>** (which you will learn more about in Chapter 20) includes a template function **swap(x, y)** that interchanges the values of **x** and **y**. Write and test your own implementation of the **swap** function.

2.   Write a `sort.h` interface that exports a polymorphic version of the `sort` function which works with any base type that implements the standard relational operators. Your function should use the following prototype:

```
template <typename ValueType>
void sort(Vector<ValueType> & vec);
```

Implement the `sort` function using the Quicksort algorithm as it appears in Figure 10-9.

3.   Design and implement a template class `Pair<T1,T2>` that represents a pair of values, the first of type `T1` and the second of type `T2`. The `Pair` class should export the following methods:

- A default constructor that generates a pair whose values are the default values for the types `T1` and `T2`.

- A constructor `Pair(v1, v2)` that takes explicit values of the two types.

- Getter methods `first` and `second` that return copies of the stored values.

4.   Develop a reasonably comprehensive unit test for the `stack.h` interface that tests the operations exported by the `Stack` class using stacks with several different base types. Use your unit test program to validate both the array- and list-based implementations of the `Stack` class.

5.   Devise a similar unit test for the `queue.h` interface.

6.   Because the ring-buffer implementation of queues makes it impossible to tell the difference between an empty queue and one that is completely full, the implementation must increase the capacity when there is still one unused cell in the dynamic array. You can avoid this restriction by changing the internal representation so that the concrete structure of the queue keeps track of the number of elements in the queue instead of the index of the tail element. Given the index of the head element and the number of data values in the queue, you can easily calculate the tail index, which means that you don't need to store this value explicitly. Rewrite the array-based queue representation so that it uses this representation.

7.   In exercise 13 from Chapter 5, you had the opportunity to write a function

```
void reverseQueue(Queue<string> & queue);
```

that reverses the elements in the queue, working entirely from the client side. If you are the designer of a class, however, you could add this facility to the `queue.h` interface and export it as one of its methods. For both the array- and list-based implementations of the queue, make all the changes necessary to export the method

```
void reverse();
```

that reverses the elements in the queue. In both cases, write the functions so that they use the original memory cells and do not allocate any additional storage.

8. In the queue abstraction presented in this chapter, new items are always added at the end of the queue and wait their turn in line. For some programming applications, it is useful to extend the simple queue abstraction into a *priority queue,* in which the order of the items is determined by a numeric priority value. When an item is enqueued in a priority queue, it is inserted in the list ahead of any lower priority items. If two items in a queue have the same priority, they are processed in the standard first-in/first-out order.

   Using the linked-list implementation of queues as a model, design and implement a `pqueue.h` interface that exports a class called `PriorityQueue`, which exports the same methods as the traditional `Queue` class with the exception of the `enqueue` method, which now takes an additional argument as follows:

```
void enqueue(ValueType value, double priority);
```

   The parameter `value` is the same as for the traditional versions of `enqueue`; the `priority` argument is a numeric value representing the priority. As in conventional English usage, smaller integers correspond to higher priorities, so that priority 1 comes before priority 2, and so forth.

9. Design a unit test for the `Vector` class that tests it with several different value types.

10. Rewrite `vector.h` so that it uses a linked list as its underlying representation. Make sure it passes the unit test you designed for the preceding exercise.

11. Use the techniques from the `Vector` implementation in section 12.4 to implement the `Grid` class, with the exception of bracket selection, which is much trickier to code for a two-dimensional structure.

12. In exercise 9 from Chapter 12, you were asked to implement a class called `MyString` that duplicated as closely as possible the behavior of the `string` class in the C++ libraries. For this exercise, reimplement `MyString` so that it uses a linked list of characters instead of a dynamic array as its underlying representation.

13. On newer machines, the data type **long** is stored using 64 bits, which means that the largest positive value of type **long** is 9,223,372,036,854,775,807 or $2^{63} - 1$. While this number seems enormous, there are applications that require even larger integers. For example, if you were asked to compute the number of possible arrangements for a deck of 52 cards, you would need to calculate 52!, which works out to be

> 80658175170943878571660636856403766975289505440883277824000000000000

If you are solving problems involving integer values on this scale (which come up often in cryptography, for example), you need a software package that provides *extended-precision arithmetic,* in which integers are represented in a form that allows them to grow dynamically.

Although there are more efficient techniques for doing so, one strategy for implementing extended-precision arithmetic is to store the individual digits in a linked list. In such representations, it is conventional—mostly because doing so makes the arithmetic operators easier to implement—to arrange the list so that the units digit comes first, followed by the tens digit, then the hundreds digit, and so on. Thus, to represent the number 1729 as a linked list, you would arrange the cells in the following order:

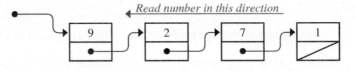

Design and implement a class called **BigInt** that uses this representation to implement extended-precision arithmetic, at least for nonnegative values. At a minimum, your **BigInt** class should support the following operations:

- A constructor that creates a **BigInt** from an **int** or from a string of digits

- A **toString** method that converts a **BigInt** to a string

- The operators **+** and ***** for addition and multiplication, respectively

You can implement the arithmetic operators by simulating what you do if you perform these calculations by hand. Addition, for example, requires you to keep track of the carries from one digit position to the next. Multiplication is a bit more challenging, but is still straightforward to implement if you find the right recursive decomposition.

Use your **BigInt** class to generate a table showing the value of *n*! for all values of *n* between 0 to 52, inclusive.

Chapter 15
Maps

A map was a fine thing to study when you were disposed to think of something else . . .

— George Eliot, *Middlemarch,* 1874

One of the most useful data structures you have encountered in this book is the *map,* which implements an association between keys and values. Chapter 5 introduces two classes—`Map` and `HashMap`—that implement the map idea. These two classes implement the same methods and can often be used interchangeably. The primary difference between these classes is the order in which keys are processed when you iterate over the elements. The `HashMap` class offers greater efficiency but iterates through the keys in a seemingly random order. The `Map` class is slightly less efficient but has the advantage of iterating through the keys in their natural order.

The goal of the next two chapters is to look at how these two classes are implemented. This chapter focuses on the `HashMap` class, which makes it possible to find the value associated with a key in constant time. Chapter 16 then introduces the concept of a tree. Although trees have many other applications as well, they provide the underlying framework for the `Map` class, which offers logarithmic-time operation while retaining the capability of processing the keys in order.

As you presumably discovered as you read through the long code examples in Chapter 14, using templates to define generic collection classes introduces a fair amount of complexity. Although templates are essential in the library versions of the collection classes, the additional complexity they require can easily get in the way of understanding the structure of the algorithms used to implement the map idea. For this reason, the next few sections implement a simpler class called a `StringMap` in which both the keys and the values are always strings. As a further simplification, the public section of the `StringMap` class exports only those methods that are essential to the map abstraction, `put` and `get`. The public interface for the `StringMap` class appears in Figure 15-1.

15.1 Implementing maps using vectors

Before moving on to consider more efficient strategies, it is useful to start with a simple vector-based implementation just to make sure that you understand how the `StringMap` class works. One particularly straightforward approach is to keep track of the key-value pairs in a vector, each of whose elements is a structure with the following definition:

```
struct KeyValuePair {
   string key;
   string value;
};
```

Given that this type is part of the `StringMap` class, both the `key` and the `value` field have type `string`. A template-based implementation would use a similar structure in which the two instances of `string` are replaced by the template parameters `KeyType` and `ValueType`, as you will see later in the chapter.

FIGURE 15-1 Simplified interface for the map abstraction

```
/*
 * File: stringmap.h
 * -------------------
 * This interface exports a simplified version of the Map class in which
 * the keys and values are always strings.
 */

#ifndef _stringmap_h
#define _stringmap_h

#include <string>

#include "vector.h"
class StringMap {

public:

/*
 * Constructor: StringMap
 * Usage: StringMap map;
 * ----------------------
 * Initializes a new empty map that uses strings as both keys and values.
 */

   StringMap();

/*
 * Destructor: ~StringMap
 * -----------------------
 * Frees any heap storage associated with this map.
 */

   ~StringMap();

/*
 * Method: get
 * Usage: string value = map.get(key);
 * ------------------------------------
 * Returns the value for key or the empty string, if key is unbound.
 */

   std::string get(const std::string & key) const;

/*
 * Method: put
 * Usage: map.put(key, value);
 * ----------------------------
 * Associates key with value in this map.
 */

   void put(const std::string & key, const std::string & value);
```

The private section of the class goes here.

```
#endif
```

The private section for the vector-based version of the **StringMap** class appears in Figure 15-2. The bindings for the keys are kept in a vector of **KeyValuePair**s called **bindings**, which is stored as an instance variable for the class.

The implementation of the vector-based version of **StringMap** appears in Figure 15-3. For the most part, the implementation is entirely straightforward. The constructor and destructor contain no code because the **Vector** class performs its own storage management. Given that both the **get** and **put** methods must search for an existing key, it makes sense for those methods to delegate the process of searching the vector to a private method called **findKey**, which looks like this:

```
int findKey(string key) {
    for (int i = 0; i < bindings.size(); i++) {
        if (bindings.get(i).key == key) return i;
    }
    return -1;
}
```

This method returns the index at which a particular key appears in the list of keys already included in the **bindings** vector; if the key does not appear, **findKey** returns −1. The use of the linear-search algorithm means that the **get** and **put** methods both require $O(N)$ time.

FIGURE 15-2 **Private section for the vector-based implementation of StringMap**

```
/*
 * Notes on the representation
 * ---------------------------
 * This version of the StringMap class stores key-value pairs in a Vector.
 */

private:

/*
 * Type: KeyValuePair
 * ------------------
 * This type combines a key and a value into a single structure.
 */

   struct KeyValuePair {
      std::string key;
      std::string value;
   };

/* Instance variables */

   Vector<KeyValuePair> bindings;

/* Private function prototypes */

   int findKey(const std::string & key) const;
```

FIGURE 15-3 Code for the vector-based implementation of `StringMap`

```
/*
 * File: stringmap.cpp
 * --------------------
 * This file implements the stringmap.h interface.
 */

#include <string>
#include "stringmap.h"
using namespace std;

/*
 * Implementation notes: StringMap constructor and destructor
 * ----------------------------------------------------------
 * All dynamic allocation is handled by the Vector class.
 */

StringMap::StringMap() { }
StringMap::~StringMap() { }

/*
 * Implementation notes: put, get
 * ------------------------------
 * These methods use findKey to search for the specified key.
 */

string StringMap::get(const string & key) const {
   int index = findKey(key);
   return (index == -1) ? "" : bindings.get(index).value;
}

void StringMap::put(const string & key, const string & value) {
   int index = findKey(key);
   if (index == -1) {
      KeyValuePair entry;
      entry.key = key;
      index = bindings.size();
      bindings.add(entry);
   }
   bindings[index].value = value;
}

/*
 * Private method: findKey
 * -----------------------
 * Returns the index at which the key appears, or -1 if the key is not found.
 */

int StringMap::findKey(const string & key) const {
   for (int i = 0; i < bindings.size(); i++) {
      if (bindings.get(i).key == key) return i;
   }
   return -1;
}
```

It is possible to improve the performance of the `get` method by keeping the keys in sorted order and applying the binary-search algorithm, which was introduced in section 7.5. Binary search reduces the search time to $O(\log N)$, which represents a dramatic improvement over the $O(N)$ time required by linear search. Unfortunately, there is no obvious way to apply that same optimization to the `put` method. Although it is certainly possible to check whether the key already exists in the map—and even to determine exactly where a new key needs to be added—in $O(\log N)$ time, inserting the new key-value pair at that position requires shifting every subsequent entry forward. Thus, `put` requires $O(N)$ time even in a sorted list.

15.2 Lookup tables

The map abstraction comes up so frequently in programming that it is worth investing significant effort into improving its performance. The implementation strategy described in the preceding section—storing the key-value pairs in sorted order in a vector—offers $O(\log N)$ performance for the `get` operation and $O(N)$ performance for the `put` operation. It is possible to do much better.

When you are trying to optimize the performance of a data structure, it is often helpful to identify performance enhancements that apply to some special case and then look for ways to apply those algorithmic improvements more generally. This section introduces a specific problem for which it is easy to find constant-time implementations of the `get` and `put` operations. It then goes on to explore how a similar technique might help in a more general context.

In 1963, the United States Postal Service introduced a set of two-letter codes for the individual states, districts, and territories of the United States. The codes for the 50 states appear in Figure 15-4. Although you might also want to translate in the opposite direction as well, this section considers only the problem of translating two-letter codes into state names. The data structure that you choose must therefore be able to represent a map from two-letter abbreviations to state names.

FIGURE 15-4	USPS abbreviations for the 50 states

AK	Alaska	HI	Hawaii	ME	Maine	NJ	New Jersey	SD	South Dakota
AL	Alabama	IA	Iowa	MI	Michigan	NM	New Mexico	TN	Tennessee
AR	Arkansas	ID	Idaho	MN	Minnesota	NV	Nevada	TX	Texas
AZ	Arizona	IL	Illinois	MO	Missouri	NY	New York	UT	Utah
CA	California	IN	Indiana	MS	Mississippi	OH	Ohio	VA	Virginia
CO	Colorado	KS	Kansas	MT	Montana	OK	Oklahoma	VT	Vermont
CT	Connecticut	KY	Kentucky	NC	North Carolina	OR	Oregon	WA	Washington
DE	Delaware	LA	Louisiana	ND	North Dakota	PA	Pennsylvania	WI	Wisconsin
FL	Florida	MA	Massachusetts	NE	Nebraska	RI	Rhode Island	WV	West Virginia
GA	Georgia	MD	Maryland	NH	New Hampshire	SC	South Carolina	WY	Wyoming

You could, of course, encode the translation table in a **StringMap** or, more generally, a **Map<string,string>**. If you look at this problem strictly from the client's point of view, however, the details of the implementation aren't particularly important. In this chapter, the goal is to identify new implementation strategies that allow maps to operate more efficiently. In this example, the important question to ask is whether the fact that the keys are two-letter strings makes it possible to design a more efficient implementation than was possible using the vector-based strategy.

As it turns out, the two-character restriction on the keys makes it easy to reduce the complexity of the lookup operation to constant time. All you need to do is store the state names in a two-dimensional grid in which the letters in the state abbreviation are used to compute the row and column indices. To select a particular element from the grid, you simply break the state abbreviation down into the two characters it contains, subtract the ASCII value of **'A'** from each character to get an index between 0 and 25, and then use these two indices to select a row and column. Thus, given a grid that has already been initialized to contain the state abbreviations as shown in Figure 15-5, you can use the following function to convert an abbreviation to the corresponding state name:

```
string getStateName(string key, Grid<string> & grid) {
    char row = key[0] - 'A';
    char col = key[1] - 'A';
    if (!grid.inBounds(row, col) || grid[row][col] == "") {
        error("No state name for " + abbr);
    }
    return grid[row][col];
}
```

This function contains nothing that looks like the traditional process of searching an array. What happens instead is that the function performs simple arithmetic on the character codes and then looks up the answer in a grid. There are no loops in the implementation nor any code that depends at all on the number of keys in the map. Looking up an abbreviation in the table must therefore run in $O(1)$ time.

The grid used in the **getStateName** function is an example of a *lookup table,* which is a programming structure that makes it possible to obtain a desired value simply by computing the appropriate index in a table, which is typically a vector or a grid. The reason that lookup tables are so efficient is that the key tells you immediately where to look for the answer. In the current application, however, the organization of the table depends on the fact that the keys always consist of two uppercase letters. If the keys could be arbitrary strings—as they are in the library version of the **Map** class—the lookup-table strategy would no longer apply, at least in its current form. The critical question is whether it is possible to generalize this strategy so that it applies to the more general case.

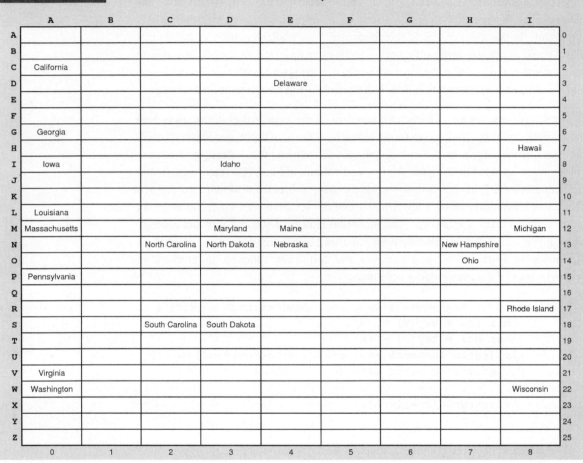

FIGURE 15-5 First nine columns of the state lookup table

If you think about how this question applies to real-life applications, you may discover that you in fact use something akin to the lookup-table strategy when you search for words in a dictionary. If you were to apply the vector-based map strategy to the dictionary-lookup problem, you would start at the first entry, go on to the second, and then the third, until you found the word. No one, of course, would apply this algorithm in a real dictionary of any significant size. But it is also unlikely that you would apply the $O(\log N)$ binary search algorithm, which consists of opening the dictionary exactly at the middle, deciding whether the word you're searching for appears in the first or second half, and then repeatedly applying this algorithm to smaller and smaller parts of the dictionary. In all likelihood, you would take advantage of the fact that many dictionaries have thumb tabs along the side that indicate where the entries for each letter appear. You look for words starting with A in the A section, words starting with B in the B section, and so on.

These thumb tabs represent a lookup-table that gets you to the right section, thereby reducing the number of words through which you need to search.

At least for maps like **StringMap** that use strings as their key type, it is possible to apply the same strategy. In this type of map, each key begins with some character value, although that character is not necessarily a letter. If you want to simulate the strategy of using thumb tabs for every possible first character, you can divide the map into 256 independent lists of key-value pairs—one for each starting character. Whenever the client calls **put** or **get** with some key, the code can choose the appropriate list on the basis of the first character. If the characters used to form keys were uniformly distributed, this strategy would reduce the average search time by a factor of 256.

Unfortunately, keys in a map—like words in a dictionary—are not uniformly distributed. In the dictionary case, for example, many more words begin with *C* than with *X*. If you use a map in an application, it is likely that most of the 256 possible first characters never appear at all. As a result, some of the lists will remain empty, while others become quite long. The increase in efficiency you get by applying the first-character strategy therefore depends on how common the first character in the key happens to be.

On the other hand, there is no reason that you have to use only the first character of the key as you try to optimize the performance of the map. The first-character strategy is simply the closest analogue to what you do with a physical dictionary. What you need is a strategy in which the value of the key tells you where to find the location of the value, as it does in a lookup table. That idea is most elegantly implemented using a technique called *hashing,* which is described in the following section.

15.3 Hashing

The best way to improve the efficiency of the map implementation is to come up with a way of using the key to determine, at least fairly closely, where to look for the corresponding value. Choosing any obvious property of the key, such as its first character or even its first two characters, runs into the problem that keys are not equally distributed with respect to that property.

Given that you are using a computer, however, there is no reason that the property you use to locate the key has to be something easy for a *human* to figure out. To maintain the efficiency of the implementation, the only thing that matters is whether the property is easy for a *computer* to determine. Since computers are better at computation than humans are, allowing for algorithmic computation opens a much wider range of possibilities.

The computational strategy called *hashing* operates as follows:

1. Select a function *f* that transforms a key into an integer value, which is called the *hash code* of that key. The function that computes the hash code is called, naturally enough, a *hash function.* An implementation of the map abstraction that uses this strategy is conventionally called a *hash table.*

2. Use the hash code for a key as the starting point as you search for a matching key in the table.

Designing the data structure

The first step in implementing the **StringMap** class as a hash table is to design the data structure. Although other representations are possible, a common strategy is to use the hash code to compute an index into an array of linked lists, each of which holds all the key-value pairs corresponding to that hash code. Each of those linked lists is traditionally called a *bucket.* To find the key you're looking for, all you need to do is search through the list of key-value pairs in that bucket.

In most implementations of hashing, the number of possible hash codes is larger than the number of buckets. You can, however, convert an arbitrarily large nonnegative hash code into a bucket number by computing the remainder of the hash code divided by the number of buckets. Thus, if the number of buckets is stored in the instance variable **nBuckets** and the function **hashCode** returns the hash code for a given key, you can compute the bucket number as follows:

```
int bucket = hashCode(key) % nBuckets;
```

A bucket number represents an index into an array, each of whose elements is a pointer to the first cell in a list of key-value pairs. Colloquially, computer scientists say that a key *hashes to a bucket* if the hash function applied to the key returns that bucket number after applying the remainder operation. Thus, the common property that links all the keys in a single linked list is that they all hash to the same bucket. Having two or more different keys hash to the same bucket is called *collision.*

The reason that hashing works is that the hash function always returns the same value for any particular key. If a key hashes to bucket #17 when you call **put** to enter it into the hash table, that key will still hash to bucket #17 when you call **get** to find its value.

Defining a hash function for strings

The next step in the implementation is to define the **hashCode** function. In the case of the **StringMap** class, **hashCode** must take a key of type **string** and return a nonnegative integer. To achieve the high level of efficiency that hash tables offer, the **hashCode** function must have the following two properties:

1. *The function must be inexpensive to compute.* If you make a hash function too complicated, it ends up taking too much time to calculate. The operations involved in the hash function should therefore be relatively easy to implement.

2. *The function should distribute keys as uniformly as possible across the integer range.* Hash functions are most effective if they minimize the number of collisions. If commonly used keys return the same hash code, the linked lists for those buckets will become longer and take more time to search.

Even though they are typically short, hash functions are extremely subtle and often depend on sophisticated mathematics. In general, writing hash functions is best left for experts. The Stanford implementation of the **HashMap** class uses the hash function for strings shown in Figure 15-6, which was developed by Daniel J. Bernstein, Professor of Mathematics at the University of Illinois at Chicago.

The hash function used for strings in any particular library may not look exactly like this one, but most implementations will have much the same structure. In this implementation, the code iterates through each character in the key, updating a value stored in the local variable **hash**, which is declared as an **unsigned** integer

FIGURE 15-6 Implementation of the hashCode function for strings

```
/*
 * Implementation notes: hashCode
 * -------------------------------
 * This function takes a string key and uses it to derive a hash code,
 * which is nonnegative integer related to the key by a deterministic
 * function that distributes keys well across the space of integers.
 * The specific algorithm used here is called djb2 after the initials
 * of its inventor, Daniel J. Bernstein, Professor of Mathematics at
 * the University of Illinois at Chicago.
 */

const int HASH_SEED = 5381;                /* Starting point for first cycle */
const int HASH_MULTIPLIER = 33;            /* Multiplier for each cycle      */
const int HASH_MASK = unsigned(-1) >> 1;   /* The largest positive integer   */

int hashCode(const string & str) {
   unsigned hash = HASH_SEED;
   int n = str.length();
   for (int i = 0; i < n; i++) {
      hash = HASH_MULTIPLIER * hash + str[i];
   }
   return int(hash & HASH_MASK);
}
```

and initialized to the seemingly random constant 5381. On each loop cycle, the **hashCode** function multiplies the previous value of **hash** by a constant called **HASH_MULTIPLIER** and then adds the ASCII value of the current character. At the end of the loop, the result is not simply the value of **hash** but is instead computed by means of the rather odd-looking expression

```
int(hash & HASH_MASK)
```

Given the amount of confusing code present in such a short function, you should feel perfectly justified in deciding that the intricacies of the **hashCode** function are not worth understanding in detail. The point of all the complexity is to ensure that the results of the **hashCode** function are distributed across the set of nonnegative integers. The details as to how the function achieves this goal, while interesting in their own right as a theoretical question, are not of immediate concern to clients.

Which **hashCode** function you choose can, however, have a significant effect on the efficiency of the implementation. Consider, for example, what might happen if you used the following, much simpler implementation:

```
int hashCode(const string & str) {
    int hash = 0;
    int n = str.length();
    for (int i = 0; i < n; i++) {
        hash += str[i];
    }
    return hash;
}
```

This code is far more understandable. All it does is add up the ASCII codes for the characters in the string, which will be a nonnegative integer unless the string is hugely long. Unfortunately, beyond the fact that long strings might cause integer overflow and result in negative results (which justifies the inclusion of the bug symbol), writing **hashCode** in this way would likely cause collisions in the table if the keys happened to fall into certain patterns. The strategy of adding the ASCII values means that any keys whose letters are permutations of each other would collide. Thus, **cat** and **act** would hash to the same bucket. So would the keys **a3**, **b2**, and **c1**. If you were using this hash table in the context of a compiler, variable names that fit such patterns would all end up hashing to the same bucket.

At the cost of making the code for the **hashCode** function more obscure, you can reduce the likelihood that similar keys will collide. Figuring out how to design such a function, however, requires a reasonably advanced knowledge of computer science theory. Most implementations of the **hashCode** function use techniques similar to those for generating pseudorandom numbers, as discussed in Chapter 2.

In both domains, it is important that the results are hard to predict. In the hash table, the consequence of this unpredictability is that keys chosen by a programmer are unlikely to exhibit any higher level of collision than one would expect by chance.

Even though careful design of the hash function can reduce the number of collisions and thereby improve performance, it is important to recognize that the *correctness* of the algorithm is not affected by the collision rate. Implementations that use poorly designed hash functions run more slowly but nonetheless continue to give correct results.

Implementing the hash table

Once you have the code for the hash function, the rest of the implementation is relatively easy to write. The private section of the **StringMap** class appears in Figure 15-7 and the corresponding implementation in Figure 15-8.

FIGURE 15-7 Private section for the hash table implementation of **StringMap**

```
/*
 * Notes on the representation
 * -------------------------------
 * This version of the StringMap class uses a hash table that keeps the
 * key-value pairs in an array of buckets, each of which is a linked list
 * of keys that hash to that bucket.
 */

private:

/* Type definition for cells in the bucket chain */

   struct Cell {
      std::string key;
      std::string value;
      Cell *link;
   };

/* Constant definitions */

   static const int INITIAL_BUCKET_COUNT = 13;

/* Instance variables */

   Cell **buckets;                    /* Dynamic array of pointers to cells */
   int nBuckets;                      /* The number of buckets in the array */

/* Private methods */

   Cell *findCell(int bucket, const std::string & key) const;

/* Make copying illegal */

   StringMap(const StringMap & src) { }
   StringMap & operator=(const StringMap & src) { return *this; }
```

FIGURE 15-8 Code for the hash table implementation of `StringMap`

```cpp
/*
 * File: stringmap.cpp
 * ----------------------
 * This file implements the stringmap.h interface using a hash table
 * as the underlying representation.
 */

#include <string>
#include "stringmap.h"
using namespace std;

/*
 * Implementation notes: HashMap constructor and destructor
 * --------------------------------------------------------------
 * The constructor allocates the array of buckets and initializes each
 * bucket to the empty list.  The destructor frees the allocated cells.
 */

StringMap::StringMap() {
   nBuckets = INITIAL_BUCKET_COUNT;
   buckets = new Cell*[nBuckets];
   for (int i = 0; i < nBuckets; i++) {
      buckets[i] = NULL;
   }
}

StringMap::~StringMap() {
   for (int i = 0; i < nBuckets; i++) {
      Cell *cp = buckets[i];
      while (cp != NULL) {
         Cell *oldCell = cp;
         cp = cp->link;
         delete oldCell;
      }
   }
}

/*
 * Implementation notes: get
 * ---------------------------
 * The get method calls findCell to search the linked list for the
 * matching key.  If no key is found, get returns the empty string.
 */

string StringMap::get(const string & key) const {
   int bucket = hashCode(key) % nBuckets;
   Cell *cp = findCell(bucket, key);
   return (cp == NULL) ? "" : cp->value;
}
```

FIGURE 15-8 Code for the hash table implementation of `StringMap` (continued)

```
/*
 * Implementation notes: put
 * --------------------------
 * The put method calls findCell to search the linked list for the
 * matching key.  If a cell already exists, put simply resets the
 * value field.  If no matching key is found, put adds a new cell
 * to the beginning of the list for that chain.
 */

void StringMap::put(const string & key, const string & value) {
   int bucket = hashCode(key) % nBuckets;
   Cell *cp = findCell(bucket, key);
   if (cp == NULL) {
      cp = new Cell;
      cp->key = key;
      cp->link = buckets[bucket];
      buckets[bucket] = cp;
   }
   cp->value = value;
}

/*
 * Private method: findCell
 * Usage: Cell *cp = findCell(bucket, key);
 * ---------------------------------------------
 * Finds a cell in the chain for the specified bucket that matches key.
 * If a match is found, the return value is a pointer to the cell
 * containing the matching key.  If no match is found, findCell
 * returns NULL.
 */

StringMap::Cell *StringMap::findCell(int bucket, const string & key) const {
   Cell *cp = buckets[bucket];
   while (cp != NULL && key != cp->key) {
      cp = cp->link;
   }
   return cp;
}
```

The private section of the **StringMap** class defines two instance variables: a dynamic array named **buckets** and an integer named **nBuckets** that stores the size of that array. Each of the elements in **buckets** is a linked list of the key-value pairs that hash to the bucket at that index. The cells in each chain are similar to those you have seen in the earlier examples of linked lists except for the fact that each cell contains both a key and a value. In this version, the number of buckets is constant, but that will change in later implementations.

If you look at the declaration of the instance variable **buckets** in Figure 15-7, the syntax may initially seem confusing. Up to now, the dynamic arrays you've created for the various collection classes have been declared as pointers to the base type. In this case, the declaration reads

```
Cell **buckets;
```

As in the earlier examples, **buckets** is a dynamic array and is represented in C++ as a pointer to the initial element in the array. Each element, moreover, is a pointer to the first cell in the linked-list chain of key-value pairs. The **buckets** variable is therefore a pointer to a pointer to a cell, which accounts for the double star.

Tracing the hash table implementation

The easiest way to understand the implementation of the hash table in Figure 15-8 is to go through a simple example. The constructor creates a dynamic array and sets each element of the **buckets** array to **NULL**, which indicates an empty list. This structure can therefore be diagrammed as follows:

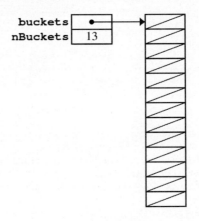

Suppose that the program then executes the call

```
stateMap.put("AK", "Alaska");
```

The first step in the code for **put** is to compute the bucket number for the key **"AK"**, which requires computing the value of **hashCode("AK")**. Even though the code for **hashCode** is intricate, it's worth running through the steps at least once. If you trace through the execution of the **for** loop inside the **hashCode** function as it appears in Figure 15-6, you will see that the execution involves the following steps:

• Before the first cycle of the **for** loop, the variable **hash** is set to the value of the constant **HASH_SEED**, which has the value 5381.

- The first cycle of the loop updates the value of **hash** by multiplying the initial value by 33 and then adding in the ASCII value of the character **'A'**, which is 65. The new value of **hash** is therefore $33 \times 5381 + 65$, which is 177638.

- The final cycle of the loop again multiplies **hash** by 33 and then adds in the ASCII value of **'K'**, which is 75. The value returned by the **hashCode** function is therefore $33 \times 177638 + 75$, or 5862129.

The bucket number is the remainder of 5862129 divided by 13, which happens to be 0. The **put** method therefore links the key **"AK"** into the list in bucket #0, which was initially empty. The result is therefore a linked list containing only the cell for Alaska, which looks like this:

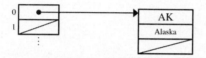

By much the same process, you can figure out that **"AL"** goes in bucket #1.

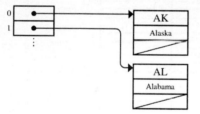

Eventually—particularly in a hash table with 13 buckets—a collision will occur. As an example, the key **"KS"** also hashes to bucket #0. The code for **put** must then search through the chain beginning at index 0 for a matching key. Since **"KS"** does not appear, **put** adds a new cell at the beginning of the chain, as follows:

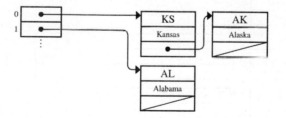

Figure 15-9 shows how the abbreviations for the 50 states fit into a table with 13 buckets. The abbreviations **AK, KS, ME, RI,** and **VT** all hash to bucket #0; **AL, MS, NY, OR, SC,** and **WA** all hash to bucket #1; and so on. By distributing the keys among the buckets, the **get** and **put** functions have a much shorter list to search. At the same time, arranging keys by their bucket number rather than the natural ordering of the key makes it hard to iterate through the keys in ascending order. Accomplishing that goal requires a new data structure called a *tree,* as described in Chapter 16.

FIGURE 15-9 Hash table containing the state abbreviations

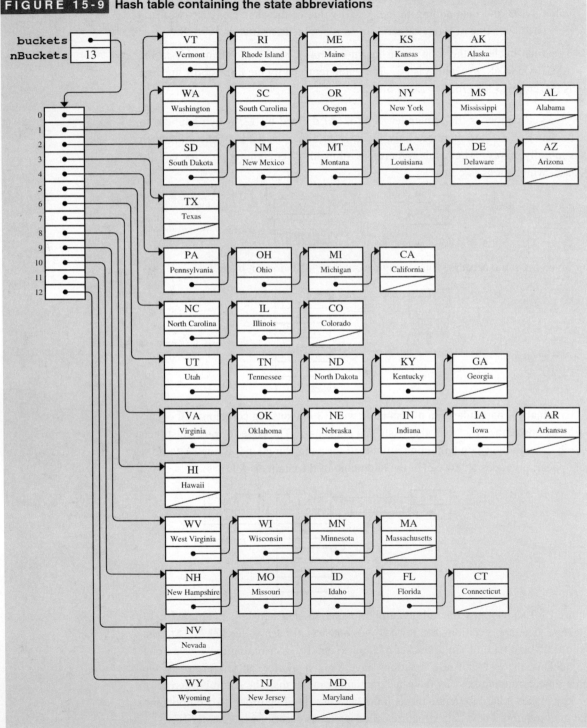

Adjusting the number of buckets

Although the design of the hash function is important, it is clear that the likelihood of collision also depends on the number of buckets. If the number is small, collisions occur more frequently. In particular, if there are more entries in the hash table than buckets, collisions are inevitable. Collisions affect the efficiency of the hash table because **put** and **get** have to search through longer chains. As the hash table fills up, the number of collisions rises, which in turn reduces performance.

It is important to remember that the goal of using a hash table is to optimize the **put** and **get** methods so that they run in constant time, at least in the average case. Achieving this goal requires that the linked-list chains emerging from each bucket remain short, which in turn implies that the number of buckets must always be large in comparison to the number of entries. Assuming that the hash function does a good job of distributing the keys evenly among the buckets, the average length of each bucket chain is given by the formula

$$\lambda = \frac{N_{entries}}{N_{buckets}}$$

For example, if the total number of entries in the table is three times the number of buckets, the average chain will contain three entries, which in turn means that three string comparisons will be required, on average, to find a key. This ratio, usually indicated by the Greek letter lambda (λ), is called the ***load factor*** of the hash table.

For good performance, you want to make sure that the value of λ remains small. Although the mathematical details are beyond the scope of this text, maintaining a load factor of 0.7 or less means that the average cost of looking up a key in a map is $O(1)$. Smaller load factors imply that there will be lots of empty buckets in the hash table array, which wastes a certain amount of space. Hash tables represent a good example of a time-space tradeoff, a concept introduced in Chapter 13. By increasing the amount of space used by the hash table, you can improve performance, but there is little advantage in reducing the load factor below the 0.7 threshold.

Unless the hashing algorithm is engineered for a particular application in which the number of keys is known in advance, it is impossible to choose a fixed value for **nBuckets** that works well for all clients. If a client keeps entering more and more entries into a map, the performance will eventually decline. If you want to maintain good performance, the best approach is to allow the implementation to increase the number of buckets dynamically. For example, you can design the implementation so that it allocates a larger hash table if the load factor in the table ever reaches a certain threshold. Unfortunately, if you increase the number of buckets, the bucket numbers all change, which means that the code to expand the table must reenter every key from the old table into the new one. This process is called ***rehashing***. Although rehashing can be time-consuming, it is performed infrequently and therefore has minimal impact on the overall running time of the application. You will have a chance to implement the rehashing strategy in exercise 5.

15.4 Implementing the HashMap class

Up to now, the code examples in this chapter have implemented the `StringMap` interface rather than the more general `HashMap` interface introduced in Chapter 5. Completing the implementation of the `HashMap` class requires making the following changes in the code:

- *Adding the missing methods.* In addition to the `put` and `get` methods supported by the minimal `StringMap` class, the `HashMap` class exports the methods `size`, `isEmpty`, `containsKey`, `remove`, and `clear`, along with bracket selection that makes it possible to use maps as associative arrays and the necessary definitions for the copy constructor and assignment operator to support deep copying.

- *Generalizing the key and value types.* The `HashMap` class uses the template parameters `KeyType` and `ValueType` to give clients more flexibility.

For the most part, these changes are straightforward. The only change that requires some subtlety is using the template facility to support client-specified key types.

The algorithm for implementing hash tables imposes several requirements on the type used to represent keys, as follows:

- The key type must be assignable so that the code can store copies of the keys in the cells.

- The key type must support the `==` comparison operator so that the code can tell whether two keys are identical.

- At the time the template for the `HashMap` class is expanded, the compiler must have access to a version of the `hashCode` function that produces a nonnegative integer for every value of the key type. For built-in types like `string` and `int`, these functions are defined in the `hashmap.h` interface itself. For types that are specific to an application, this function must be provided by the client.

In many cases, `hashCode` functions for other types can be extremely simple. For example, the `hashCode` function for integers is simply

```
int hashCode(int key) {
   return key & HASH_MASK;
}
```

The **HASH_MASK** constant is the same as the one defined in the section on "Defining a hash function for strings" and consists of a word whose internal representation contains a **1** in every bit position except the sign bit, which is **0**. The **&** operator, which is discussed in more detail in Chapter 18, has the effect of removing the sign bit from **key**, which ensures that the value of **hashCode** cannot be negative.

Writing good hash functions for compound types usually requires a degree of mathematical sophistication to ensure that the hash codes are distributed uniformly across the space of nonnegative integers. There is, however, a simple expedient that you can use to produce a reasonable hash function for any type that exports a **toString** method. All you have to do is convert the value to a string and then use the string version of **hashCode** to deliver the result. Using this approach, you could write a **hashCode** function for the **Rational** class like this:

```
int hashCode(const Rational & r) {
   return hashCode(r.toString());
}
```

Computing this function requires more execution time than performing arithmetic operations on the numerator and denominator, but the code is much easier to write.

Summary

This chapter has focused on a variety of strategies for implementing the basic operations provided by the library version of the **HashMap** class. The **Map** class itself—which makes it possible to iterate through the keys in ascending order—requires a more complex data structure called a *tree,* which is the subject of Chapter 16.

Important points in this chapter include:

- It is possible to implement the basic map operations by storing key-value pairs in a vector. Keeping the vector in sorted order makes it possible for **get** to run in $O(\log N)$ time, even though **put** remains $O(N)$.

- Specific applications may make it possible to implement map operations using a lookup table in which both **get** and **put** run in $O(1)$ time.

- Maps can be implemented very efficiently using a strategy called *hashing,* in which keys are converted to an integer that determines where the implementation should look for the result.

- A common implementation of the hashing algorithm is to allocate a dynamic array of *buckets,* each of which contains a linked list of the keys that hash to that bucket. As long as the ratio of the number of entries to the number of buckets does not exceed about 0.7, the **get** and **put** methods operate in $O(1)$ time on average. Maintaining this performance as the number of entries grows requires periodic *rehashing* to increase the number of buckets.

- The detailed design of a hash function is subtle and requires mathematical analysis to achieve optimum performance. Even so, any hash function that delivers nonnegative integer values will produce correct results.

Review questions

1. For the vector-based implementation of maps, what algorithmic strategy does the chapter suggest for reducing the cost of the **get** method to $O(\log N)$ time?

2. If you implement the strategy suggested in the preceding question, why does the **put** method still require $O(N)$ time?

3. What is a *lookup table?* In what cases is the use of lookup tables appropriate?

4. What disadvantages would you expect from using the ASCII value of the first character in a key as its hash code?

5. What is meant by the term *bucket* in the implementation of a hash table?

6. What is a *collision?*

7. The private section of the **stringmap.h** interface shown in Figure 15-7 includes definitions for the copy constructor and assignment operator that make it impossible to copy **StringMap** objects. Those definitions are missing from the earlier version of **stringmap.h** that uses a vector as its underlying representation. What happens if you copy a vector-based **StringMap**?

8. Explain the operation of the **findCell** method in the implementation of the hash-table version of the **StringMap** class shown in Figure 15-8.

9. The **hashCode** function for strings presented in the text has a structure similar to that of a random-number generator. If you took that similarity too literally, however, you might be tempted to write the following **hash** function:

```
int hashCode(const string & str) {
    return randomInteger(0, HASH_MASK);
}
```

Why would this approach fail?

10. Would the **HashMap** class still operate correctly if you supplied the following **hashCode** function:

```
int hashCode(const string & str) {
    return 42;
}
```

11. In tracing through the code that enters state abbreviations into a map with 13 buckets, the text notes that the entries for "**AK**" and "**KS**" collide in bucket #0. Assuming that new entries are added in alphabetical order by the state abbreviation, what is the first collision that occurs? You should be able to figure out the answer simply by looking over the diagram in Figure 15-9.

12. What time-space tradeoffs arise in the implementation of a hash table?

13. What is meant by the term *load factor?*

14. What is the approximate threshold for the load factor that ensures that the average performance of the **HashMap** class will remain $O(1)$?

15. What is meant by the term *rehashing?*

16. What operations must every key type implement?

17. Suppose that you want to use the **Point** class from Chapter 6 as a key type in a **HashMap**. What simple strategy does this chapter offer for implementing the necessary **hashCode** function?

Exercises

1. Modify the code in Figure 15-3 so that **put** always keeps the keys in sorted order in the array. Change the implementation of the private **findKey** method so that it uses binary search to find the key in $O(\log N)$ time.

2. Rewrite the vector-based implementation of the **StringMap** class so that it uses a dynamic array of **KeyValuePairs**, thereby ensuring that **StringMap** no longer depends on the **Vector** class from the Stanford libraries.

3. Starting with the array-based implementation of **StringMap** described in the preceding exercise, add the methods **size**, **isEmpty**, **containsKey**, and **clear** to the **stringmap.h** interface and the corresponding implementation.

4. Although it presumably made mathematics more difficult, the Romans wrote numbers using letters to stand for various multiples of 5 and 10. The characters used to encode Roman numerals have the following values:

$$
\begin{array}{ccc}
\text{I} & \rightarrow & 1 \\
\text{V} & \rightarrow & 5 \\
\text{X} & \rightarrow & 10 \\
\text{L} & \rightarrow & 50 \\
\text{C} & \rightarrow & 100 \\
\text{D} & \rightarrow & 500 \\
\text{M} & \rightarrow & 1000 \\
\end{array}
$$

Design a lookup table that makes it possible to determine the value of each letter in a single array selection. Use this table to implement a function

```
int romanToDecimal(const string & str);
```

that translates a string containing a Roman numeral into its numeric form.

To compute the value of a Roman numeral, you ordinarily add the values corresponding to each letter to a running total. There is, however, one exception to this rule: If the value of a letter is less than that of the following one, its value should be subtracted from the total instead of added. For example, the Roman numeral string

MCMLXIX

corresponds to

$$1000 - 100 + 1000 + 50 + 10 - 1 + 10$$

or 1969. The **C** and the **I** are subtracted rather than added because those letters precede a letter with a larger value.

5. Extend the implementation of the **StringMap** class from Figures 15-7 and 15-8 so that the array of buckets expands dynamically. Your implementation should keep track of the load factor for the hash table and perform a rehashing operation if the load factor exceeds the limit indicated by a constant defined as follows:

```
static const double REHASH_THRESHOLD = 0.7;
```

6. In certain applications, it is useful to extend the **HashMap** class so that you can insert a temporary definition for a particular key, hiding away any previous value associated with that key. Later in the program, you can delete the temporary definition, restoring the next most recent one. For example, you could use such a mechanism to capture the effect of local variables, which come into existence when a function is called and disappear again when the function returns.

Implement such a facility by adding the method

```
void add(const string & key, const string & value);
```

to the implementation of **StringMap** that uses a hash table to store the entries. Because the **get** and **put** methods always find the first entry in the linked list, you can ensure that **add** hides the previous definitions simply by adding each new entry at the beginning of the list for a particular hash bucket. Moreover, as long as the implementation of **remove** deletes only the first occurrence of a symbol from its hash chain, you can use **remove** to delete the most recently inserted definition for a key, restoring the definition of that key that appears next in the chain.

7. Follow the strategy described in section 15.4 to implement the **HashMap** class, as you know it from Chapter 5.

8. Write **hashCode** functions for each of the primitive types.

9. Although the bucket-chaining approach described in the text works well in practice, other strategies exist for resolving collisions in hash tables. In the early days of computing—when memories were small enough that the cost of introducing extra pointers was taken seriously—hash tables often used a more memory-efficient strategy called *open addressing,* in which the key-value pairs are stored directly in the array, like this:

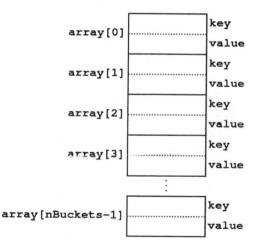

For example, if a key hashes to bucket #2, the open-addressing strategy tries to put that key and its value directly into the entry at **array[2]**.

The problem with this approach is that **array[3]** may already be assigned to another key that hashes to the same bucket. The simplest approach to dealing with collisions of this sort is to store each new key in the first free cell at or after its expected hash position. Thus, if a key hashes to bucket #2, the **put** and **get** functions first try to find or insert that key in **array[2]**. If that entry is filled with a different key, however, these functions move on to try **array[3]**, continuing the process until they find an empty entry or an entry with a matching key. As in the ring-buffer implementation of queues in Chapter 14, if the index advances past the end of the array, it should wrap around back to the beginning. This strategy for resolving collisions is called *linear probing.*

Reimplement the **StringMap** class so that it uses open addressing with linear probing. For this exercise, your implementation should simply signal an error if the client tries to add a key to a hash table that is already full.

10. Extend your solution to exercise 9 so that it expands the array dynamically whenever the load factor exceeds the constant **REHASH_THRESHOLD**, as defined in exercise 5. As in that exercise, you will need to rebuild the entire table because the bucket numbers for the keys change when you assign a new value to **nBuckets**.

Chapter 16
Trees

I like trees because they seem more resigned to the way they have to live than other things do.

— Willa Cather, *O Pioneers!*, 1913

As you have seen in several earlier chapters, linked lists make it possible to represent an ordered collection of values without using arrays. The link pointers associated with each cell form a linear chain that defines the underlying order. Although linked lists require more memory space than arrays and are less efficient for operations such as selecting a value at a particular index position, they have the advantage that insertion and deletion operations can be performed in constant time.

The use of pointers to define the ordering relationship among a set of values is considerably more powerful than the earlier linked-list examples suggest and is by no means limited to creating linear structures. In this chapter, you will learn about a data structure that uses pointers to model hierarchical relationships. That structure is called a *tree,* which is defined to be a collection of individual entries called ***nodes*** for which the following properties hold:

- As long as the tree contains any nodes at all, there is a specific node called the ***root*** that forms the top of a hierarchy.

- Every other node is connected to the root by a unique line of descent.

Tree-structured hierarchies occur in many contexts outside of computer science. The most familiar example is the family tree, which appears in the next section. Other examples include

- *Game trees.*   The game trees introduced in the section on "The minimax algorithm" in Chapter 9 have a branching pattern that is typical of trees. The current position is the root of the tree; the branches lead to positions that might occur later in the game.

- *Biological classifications.*   The classification system for living organisms, which was developed in the eighteenth century by the Swedish botanist Carl Linnaeus, is structured as a tree. The root of the tree is all living things. The classification system then branches to form separate kingdoms, of which animals and plants are the most familiar. From there, the hierarchy continues down through several additional levels until it defines an individual species.

- *Organizational charts.*   Many businesses are structured so that each employee reports to a single supervisor, thereby forming a tree that extends up to the company president, who represents the root.

- *Directory hierarchies.*   On most modern computers, files are stored in directories that form a tree. There is a top-level directory that represents the root, which can contain files along with other directories. Those directories may contain subdirectories, which gives rise to the hierarchical structure representative of trees.

■ 16.1 Family trees

Family trees provide a convenient way to represent the lines of descent from a single individual through a series of generations. For example, the diagram in Figure 16-1 shows the family tree of the House of Normandy, which ruled England after the accession of William I at the Battle of Hastings in 1066. The structure of the diagram fits the definition of a tree from the preceding section. William I is the root of the tree, and all other individuals in the chart are connected to William I through a unique line of descent.

Terminology used to describe trees

The family tree in Figure 16-1 makes it easy to introduce the terminology computer scientists use to describe tree structures. Each node in a tree may have several *children,* but only a single *parent* in the tree. For trees, the words *ancestor* and *descendant* have the same meaning as they do in English. The line of descent through Henry I and Matilda shows that Henry II is a descendant of William I, which in turn implies that William I is an ancestor of Henry II. Similarly, two nodes that share the same parent, such as Robert and Adela, are called *siblings.*

Although most of the terms used to describe trees come directly from the family-tree analogue, others—like the word *root*—come from the botanical metaphor instead. At the opposite end of the tree from the root, there are nodes that have no children, which are called *leaves.* Nodes that are neither the root nor a leaf are called *interior* nodes. For example, in Figure 16-1, Robert, William II, Stephen, William, and Henry II represent leaf nodes; Adela, Henry I, and Matilda represent interior nodes. The *height* of a nonempty tree is defined to be the length of the longest path from the root to a leaf. Thus, the height of the tree shown in Figure 16-1 is 3, because that is the length of the path from William I to Henry II, which is longer than any other path from the root. By convention, the height of an empty tree is defined to be -1.

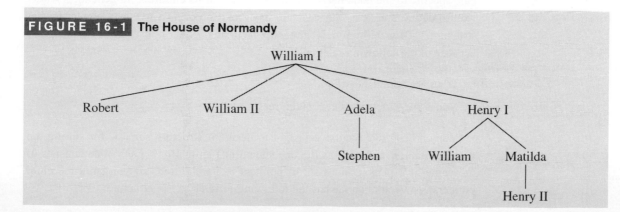

FIGURE 16-1   **The House of Normandy**

The recursive nature of a tree

One of the most important things to notice about any tree is that the same branching pattern occurs at every level of the decomposition. If you take any node in a tree together with all its descendants, the result fits the definition of a tree. For example, if you extract the portion of Figure 16-1 descending from Henry I, you get the following tree:

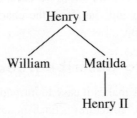

A tree formed by extracting a node and its descendants from an existing tree is called a *subtree* of the original one. The tree in this diagram, for example, is the subtree rooted at Henry I.

The fact that each node in a tree can be considered the root of its own subtree underscores the recursive nature of tree structures. If you think about trees from a recursive perspective, a tree is simply a node and a set—possibly empty, as in the case of a leaf node—of attached subtrees. The recursive character of trees is fundamental to their underlying representation as well as to most algorithms that operate on trees.

Representing family trees in C++

In order to represent a tree in C++, you need some way to model the hierarchical relationships among the data values. In most cases, the easiest way to represent the parent/child relationship is to include a pointer in the parent that points to the child. If you use this strategy, each node is a structure that contains—in addition to other data specific to the node itself—pointers to each of its children. In general, it works well to define a node as the structure itself and to define a tree as a pointer to that structure. This definition is mutually recursive even in its English conception because of the following relationship:

• Trees are pointers to nodes.

• Nodes are structures that contain trees.

You can use this recursive insight to design a structure suitable for storing the data in a family tree such as the one shown in Figure 16-1. Each node consists of the name of a person and a set of pointers to its children. If you store the child pointers in a vector, a node has the following form as a C++ structure:

```
struct FamilyTreeNode {
    string name;
    Vector<FamilyTreeNode *> children;
};
```

A family tree is simply a pointer to one of these nodes.

A diagram showing the internal representation of the royal family tree appears in Figure 16-2. To keep the figure neat and orderly, Figure 16-2 represents the children as if they were stored in a five-element array; in fact, the **children** field is a vector that grows to accommodate any number of children. You will have a chance to explore other strategies for storing the children, such as keeping them in a linked list rather than a vector, in the exercises at the end of this chapter.

16.2 Binary search trees

Although it is possible to illustrate tree algorithms using family trees, it is more effective to do so in a simpler environment that applies more directly to programming. Although the family-tree example provides a framework for introducing the terminology used to describe trees, it suffers in practice from the complication that each node can have an arbitrary number of children. In many

FIGURE 16-2 Pointer-based tree representation for the House of Normandy

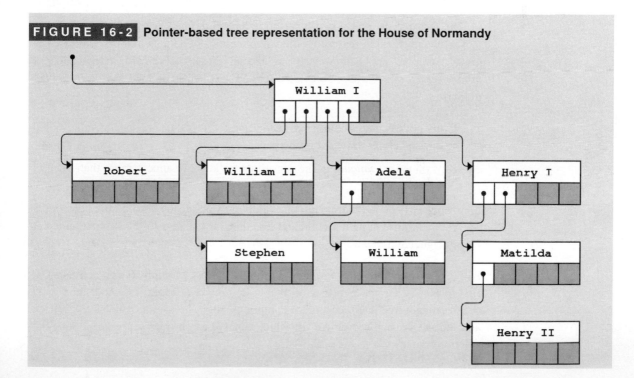

programming contexts, it is reasonable to restrict the number of children to make the resulting trees easier to implement.

One of the most important subclasses of trees—which has many practical applications—is a ***binary tree,*** which is defined to be a tree in which the following additional properties hold:

- Each node in the tree has at most two children.

- Every node except the root is designated as either a ***left child*** or a ***right child*** of its parent.

The second condition emphasizes the fact that child nodes in a binary tree are ordered with respect to their parents. For example, the binary trees

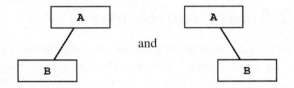

and

are different trees, even though they consist of the same nodes. In both cases, the node labeled **B** is a child of the root node labeled **A**, but it is a left child in the first tree and a right child in the second.

The fact that the nodes in a binary tree have a defined geometrical relationship makes it convenient to represent ordered collections of data using binary trees. The most common application uses a special class of binary tree called a ***binary search tree***—often abbreviated to ***BST***—which is defined by the following properties:

1.   Every node contains—possibly in addition to other data—a special value called a *key* that defines the order of the nodes.

2.   Key values are *unique,* in the sense that no key can appear more than once in the tree.

3.   At every node in the tree, the key value must be greater than all the keys in the subtree rooted at its left child and less than all the keys in the subtree rooted at its right child.

Although this definition is formally correct, it almost certainly seems confusing at first glance. To make sense of the definition and begin to understand why constructing a tree that meets these conditions might be useful, it helps to go back and look at a specific problem for which binary search trees represent a potential solution strategy.

The motivation behind binary search trees

In Chapter 15, one of the strategies proposed for representing maps—before the hashing algorithm made other options seem far less attractive—was to store the key-value pairs in a vector. This strategy has a useful computational property: if you keep the keys in sorted order, you can write an implementation of `get` that runs in $O(\log N)$ time. All you need to do is employ the binary search algorithm, which was introduced in Chapter 7. Unfortunately, the array representation does not offer any equally efficient way to code the `put` function. Although `put` can use binary search to determine where any new key fits into the array, maintaining the sorted order requires $O(N)$ time because each subsequent array element must be shifted to make room for the new entry.

This problem brings to mind a similar situation that arose in Chapter 13. When arrays were used to represent the editor buffer, inserting a new character was a linear-time operation. In that case, the solution was to replace the array with a linked list. Is it possible that a similar strategy would improve the performance of `put` for the map? After all, inserting a new element into a linked list—as long as you have a pointer to the cell prior to the insertion point—is a constant-time operation.

The trouble with linked lists is that they do not support the binary search algorithm in any efficient way. Binary search depends on being able to find the middle element in constant time. In an array, finding the middle element is easy. In a linked list, the only way to do so is to iterate through all the link pointers in the first half of the list.

To get a more concrete sense of why linked lists have this limitation, suppose that you have a linked list containing the names of Walt Disney's seven dwarves:

Bashful → Doc → Dopey → Grumpy → Happy → Sleepy → Sneezy

The elements in this list appear in lexicographic order, which is the order imposed by their internal character codes.

Given a linked list of this sort, you can easily find the first element, because the initial pointer gives you its address. From there, you can follow the link pointer to find the second element. On the other hand, there is no easy way to locate the element that occurs halfway through the sequence. To do so, you have to walk through each chain pointer, counting up to $N/2$. This operation requires linear time, which completely negates the efficiency advantage of binary search. If binary search is to offer any improvement in efficiency, the data structure must enable you to find the middle element quickly.

Although doing so might at first seem silly, it is useful to consider what happens if you simply point at the middle of the list instead of the beginning:

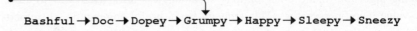

In this diagram, you have no problem at all finding the middle element. It's immediately accessible through the list pointer. The problem, however, is that you've thrown away the first half of the list. The pointers in the structure provide access to **Grumpy** and any name that follows it in the chain, but there is no longer any way to reach **Bashful**, **Doc**, and **Dopey**.

If you think about the situation from **Grumpy**'s point of view, the general outline of the solution becomes clear. What you need is to have two chains emanating from the **Grumpy** cell: one that consists of cells whose names precede **Grumpy** and another for cells whose names follow **Grumpy** in the alphabet. In the conceptual diagram, all you need to do is reverse the arrows:

Bashful ← Doc ← Dopey ← Grumpy → Happy → Sleepy → Sneezy

Each of the strings is now accessible, and you can easily divide the entire list in half.

At this point, you need to apply the same strategy recursively. The binary search algorithm requires you to find the middle of not only the original list but its sublists as well. You therefore need to restructure the lists that precede and follow **Grumpy**, using the same decomposition strategy. Every cell points in two directions: to the midpoint of the list that precedes it and to the midpoint of the list that follows it. Applying this process transforms the original list into the following binary tree:

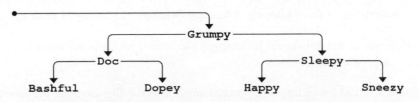

The most important feature about this particular style of binary tree is that it is ordered. For any particular node in the tree, the string it contains must follow all the strings in the subtree descending to the left and precede all strings in the subtree to the right. In this example, **Grumpy** comes after **Doc**, **Bashful**, and **Dopey** but before **Sleepy**, **Happy**, and **Sneezy**. The same rule applies at each level, so the node containing **Doc** comes after the **Bashful** node but before the **Dopey** node.

The formal definition of a binary search tree, which appears at the end of the preceding section, ensures that every node in the tree obeys this ordering rule.

Finding nodes in a binary search tree

The fundamental advantage of a binary search tree is that you can use the binary search algorithm to find a particular node. Suppose, for example, that you are looking for the node containing the string **Happy** in the tree diagram shown at the end of the preceding section. The first step is to compare **Happy** with **Grumpy**, which appears at the root of the tree. Since **Happy** comes after **Grumpy** in lexicographic order, you know that the **Happy** node, if it exists, must be in the right subtree. The next step, therefore, is to compare **Happy** and **Sleepy**. In this case, **Happy** comes before **Sleepy** and must therefore be in the left subtree of this node. That subtree consists of a single node, which contains the correct name.

Because trees are recursive structures, it is easy to code the search algorithm in its recursive form. For concreteness, let's suppose that the type definition for **BSTNode** looks like this:

```
struct BSTNode {
    string key;
    BSTNode *left, *right;
};
```

Given this definition, you can easily write a function **findNode** that implements the binary search algorithm, as follows:

```
BSTNode *findNode(BSTNode *t, const string & key) {
    if (t == NULL) return NULL;
    if (key == t->key) return t;
    if (key < t->key) {
        return findNode(t->left, key);
    } else {
        return findNode(t->right, key);
    }
}
```

If the tree is empty, the desired node is clearly not there, and **findNode** returns the value **NULL** as a sentinel indicating that the key cannot be found. If the tree is not equal to **NULL**, the implementation checks to see whether the desired key matches the one in the current node. If so, **findNode** returns a pointer to the current node. If the keys do not match, **findNode** proceeds recursively, looking in either the left or the right subtree depending on the result of the key comparison.

Inserting new nodes in a binary search tree

The next question to consider is how to create a binary search tree in the first place. The simplest approach is to begin with an empty tree and then call an `insertNode` function to insert new keys into the tree, one at a time. As each new key is inserted, it is important to maintain the ordering relationship among the nodes of the tree. To make sure the `findNode` function continues to work, the code for `insertNode` must use binary search to identify the correct insertion point.

As with `findNode`, the code for `insertNode` can proceed recursively beginning at the root of the tree. At each node, `insertNode` must compare the new key to the key in the current node. If the new key precedes the existing one, the new key belongs in the left subtree. Conversely, if the new key follows the one in the current node, it belongs in the right subtree. Eventually, the process will encounter a `NULL` subtree that represents the point in the tree where the new node needs to be added. At this point, the `insertNode` implementation must replace the `NULL` pointer with a new node initialized to contain a copy of the key.

The code for `insertNode`, however, is a bit tricky. The difficulty comes from the fact that `insertNode` must be able to change the value of the binary search tree by adding a new node. Since the function needs to change the values of the argument, it must be passed by reference. Instead of taking a `BSTNode *` as its argument the way `findNode` does, `insertNode` must instead take that node pointer by reference. The prototype for `insertNode` therefore looks like this:

```
void insertNode(BSTNode * & t, const string & key);
```

Once you understand the prototype for the `insertNode` function, writing the code is not particularly hard. The implementation has the following form:

```
void insertNode(BSTNode * & t, const string & key) {
   if (t == NULL) {
      t = new BSTNode;
      t->key = key;
      t->left = t->right = NULL;
   } else {
      if (key != t->key) {
         if (key < t->key) {
            insertNode(t->left, key);
         } else {
            insertNode(t->right, key);
         }
      }
   }
}
```

If **t** is **NULL**, **insertNode** creates a new node, initializes its fields, and then replaces the **NULL** pointer in the existing structure with a pointer to the new node. If **t** is not **NULL**, **insertNode** compares the new key with the one stored at the root of the tree **t**. If the keys match, the key is already in the tree and no further operations are required. If not, **insertNode** uses the result of the comparison to determine whether to insert the key in the left or the right subtree and then makes the appropriate recursive call.

Because the code for **insertNode** seems complicated until you've seen it work, it makes sense to go through the process of inserting a few keys in some detail. Suppose, for example, that you have declared and initialized an empty tree as follows:

```
BSTNode *dwarfTree = NULL;
```

These statements create a local variable **dwarfTree** that lives in the stack frame of the function that contains its declaration, as illustrated by the following diagram:

What happens if you then call

```
insertNode(dwarfTree, "Grumpy");
```

starting with this initial configuration in which **dwarfTree** is empty? In the frame for **insertNode**, the variable **t** is a reference parameter bound to the variable **dwarfTree** in the caller. The stack at the beginning of this call therefore looks like this:

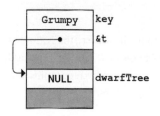

The code first checks to see whether **t** is **NULL**, which is true in this case. Execution therefore proceeds with the body of the **if** statement, which begins with the line

```
t = new BSTNode;
```

This line allocates a new node on the heap and assigns it to the reference parameter **t**, therefore changing the pointer cell in the caller, as follows:

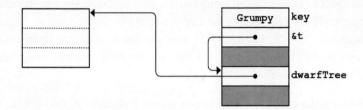

The remaining statements initialize the fields in the new node, copying the key **Grumpy** and initializing each of the subtree pointers to **NULL**. When **insertNode** returns, the tree looks like this:

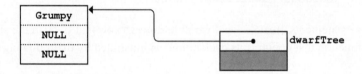

This structure correctly represents the binary search tree containing the single node **Grumpy**.

What happens if you then use **insertNode** to insert **Sleepy** into the tree? As before, the initial call generates a stack frame in which the reference parameter **t** is aliased to **dwarfTree**:

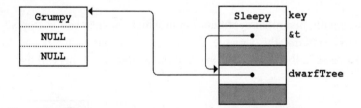

This time, however, the value of the tree **t** is no longer **NULL**, since the variable **dwarfTree** now contains the address of the **Grumpy** node. Because **Sleepy** comes after **Grumpy** in lexicographical order, the code for **insertNode** continues with the following recursive call:

```
insertNode(t->right, key);
```

At this point, the recursive call looks much like the insertion of **Grumpy** into the original empty tree. The only difference is that the reference parameter **t** now refers to a field within an existing node, as follows:

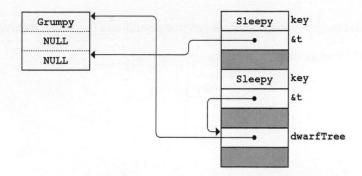

The new node allocated by **insertNode** replaces the right child of the **Grumpy** node, like this:

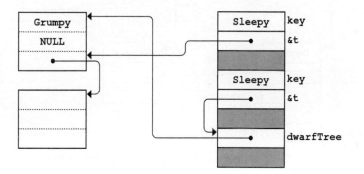

When this call to **insertNode** returns after filling in the contents of the new node, the tree looks like this:

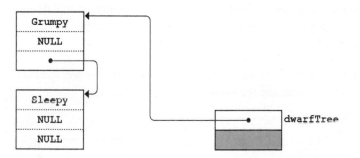

Additional calls to **insertNode** will create additional nodes and insert them into the structure in a way that preserves the ordering constraint required for binary search trees. For example, if you insert the names of the five remaining dwarves in the order **Doc**, **Bashful**, **Dopey**, **Happy**, and **Sneezy**, you end up with the binary search tree shown in Figure 16-3.

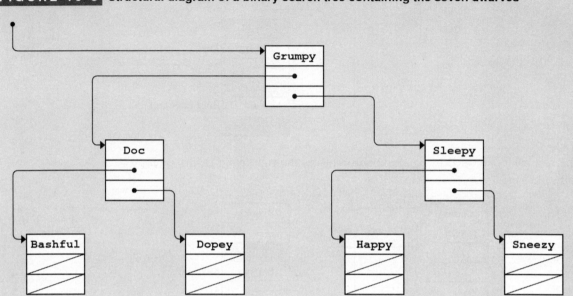

FIGURE 16-3 Structural diagram of a binary search tree containing the seven dwarves

Removing nodes

The operation of removing a node from a binary search tree is more complicated than that of inserting a new node. Finding the node to be removed is the easy part. All you need to do is use the same binary-search strategy that you use to locate a particular key. Once you find the matching node, however, you have to remove it from the tree without violating the ordering relationship that defines a binary search tree. Depending on where the node to be removed appears in the tree, removing it can get rather tricky.

To get a sense of the problem, suppose that you are working with the binary search tree containing the names of the seven dwarves:

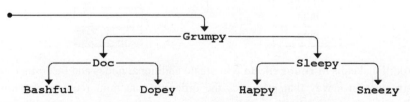

Removing **Sneezy** (presumably for creating an unhealthy work environment) is easy. All you have to do is replace the pointer to the **Sneezy** node with a **NULL** pointer, which produces the following tree:

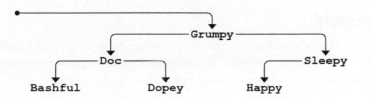

Starting from this configuration, it is also relatively easy to remove **Sleepy** (who has trouble staying awake on the job). If either child of the node you want to remove is **NULL**, all you have to do is replace it with its non-**NULL** child, like this:

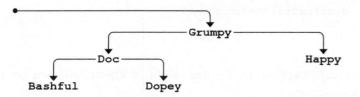

A problem arises, however, if you try to remove a node with both a left and a right child. Suppose, for example, that you instead want to remove **Grumpy** (for failure to whistle while working) from the original tree containing all seven dwarves. If you simply remove the **Grumpy** node, you're left with two partial search trees, one rooted at **Doc** and one rooted at **Sleepy**, as follows:

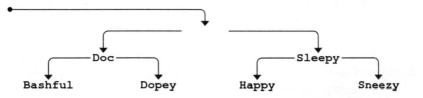

At this point, what you would like to do is find a node that can be inserted into the empty space left behind by the removal of the **Grumpy** node. To ensure that the resulting tree remains a binary search tree, there are only two nodes you can use: the rightmost node in the left subtree or the leftmost node in the right subtree. These two nodes work equally well. For example, if you choose the rightmost node in the left subtree, you get the **Dopey** node, which is guaranteed to be larger than anything else in the left subtree but smaller than the values in the right subtree. To complete the removal, all you have to do is replace the **Dopey** node with its left child—which may be **NULL**, as it is in this example—and then move the **Dopey** node into the deleted spot. The resulting picture looks like this:

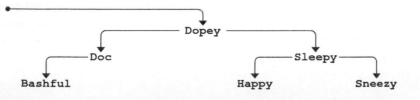

Tree traversals

The structure of a binary search tree makes it easy to go through the nodes of the tree in the order specified by the keys. For example, you can use the following function to display the keys in a binary search tree in lexicographic order:

```
void displayTree(BSTNode *t) {
   if (t != NULL) {
      displayTree(t->left);
      cout << t->key << endl;
      displayTree(t->right);
   }
}
```

Thus, if you call **displayTree** on the tree shown in Figure 16-3, you get the following output:

```
○ ○ ○                    DwarfTree
Bashful
Doc
Dopey
Grumpy
Happy
Sleepy
Sneezy
```

At each recursive level, **displayTree** checks to see whether the tree is empty. If it is, **displayTree** has no work to do. If not, the ordering of the recursive calls ensures that the output appears in the correct order. The first recursive call displays the keys that precede the current node, all of which must appear in the left subtree. Displaying the nodes in the left subtree before the current one therefore maintains the correct order. Similarly, it is important to display the key from the current node before making the last recursive call, which displays the keys that occur later in the ASCII sequence and therefore appear in the right subtree.

The process of going through the nodes of a tree and performing some operation at each node is called *traversing* or *walking* the tree. In many cases, you will want to traverse a tree in the order imposed by the keys, as in the **displayTree** example. This approach, which consists of processing the current node between the recursive calls to the left and right subtrees, is called an *inorder traversal.* There are, however, two other types of tree traversals that occur frequently in the context of binary trees, which are called *preorder* and *postorder* traversals. In the preorder traversal, the current node is processed before traversing either of its subtrees, as illustrated by the following code:

```
void preorderTraversal(BSTNode *t) {
    if (t != NULL) {
        cout << t->key << endl;
        preorderTraversal(t->left);
        preorderTraversal(t->right);
    }
}
```

Given the tree from Figure 16-3, the preorder traversal prints the nodes in the order shown in the following sample run:

```
○ ○ ○              PreorderTraversal
Grumpy
Doc
Bashful
Dopey
Sleepy
Happy
Sneezy
```

In the postorder traversal, the subtrees are processed first, followed by the current node. The code to display nodes in a postorder traversal is

```
void postorderTraversal(BSTNode *t) {
    if (t != NULL) {
        postorderTraversal(t->left);
        postorderTraversal(t->right);
        cout << t->key << endl;
    }
}
```

Running this function on the binary search tree containing the seven dwarves produces the following output:

```
○ ○ ○              PostorderTraversal
Bashful
Dopey
Doc
Happy
Sneezy
Sleepy
Crumpy
```

16.3 Balanced trees

Although the recursive strategy used to implement `insertNode` guarantees that the nodes are organized as a legal binary search tree, the structure of the tree depends on the order in which the nodes are inserted. The tree in Figure 16-3, for example, was generated by inserting the names of the dwarves in this order:

Grumpy, Sleepy, Doc, Bashful, Dopey, Happy, Sneezy

Suppose that you had instead entered the names of the dwarves in alphabetical order. The first call to `insertNode` would insert `Bashful` at the root of the tree. Subsequent calls would insert `Doc` after `Bashful`, `Dopey` after `Doc`, and so on, appending each new node to the `right` chain of the previously one.

The resulting figure, which is shown in Figure 16-4, looks more like a linked list than a tree. Nonetheless, the tree in Figure 16-4 maintains the property that the key field in any node follows all the keys in its left subtree and precedes all the keys in its right subtree. It therefore fits the definition of a binary search tree, so the `findNode` function will operate correctly. The running time of the `findNode` algorithm, however, is proportional to the height of the tree, which means that the structure of the tree can have a significant impact on the algorithmic performance. If a binary search tree is shaped like the one shown in Figure 16-3, the time required to find a key in the tree will be $O(\log N)$. On the other hand, if the tree is shaped like the one in Figure 16-4, the running time will deteriorate to $O(N)$.

The binary search algorithm used to implement `findNode` achieves its ideal performance only if the left and right subtrees have roughly the same height at each level of the tree. Trees in which this property holds—such as the tree in Figure 16-3—are said to be **balanced.** More formally, a binary tree is defined to be

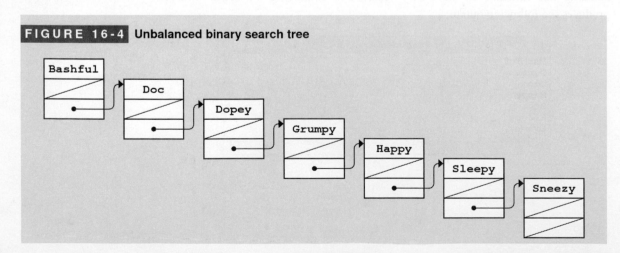

FIGURE 16-4 Unbalanced binary search tree

balanced if, at each node, the heights of the left and right subtrees differ by at most one. To illustrate this definition of a balanced binary tree, each of the tree diagrams in the top row of Figure 16-5 shows a balanced arrangement of a tree with seven nodes. The diagrams in the bottom row represent unbalanced arrangements. In each diagram, the nodes at which the balanced-tree definition fails are shown as open circles. In the leftmost unbalanced tree, for example, the left subtree of the root node has height 2 while the right subtree has height 0. In the remaining two examples, the root node is unbalanced because it has an unbalanced child.

The first diagram in Figure 16-5 is optimally balanced in the sense that the heights of the two subtrees at each node are equal. Such an arrangement is possible, however, only if the number of nodes is one less than a power of two. If the number of nodes does not meet this condition, there will be some point in the tree where the heights of the subtrees differ to some extent. By allowing the heights of the subtrees to differ by one, the definition of a balanced tree provides some flexibility in the structure of a tree without adversely affecting its computational performance.

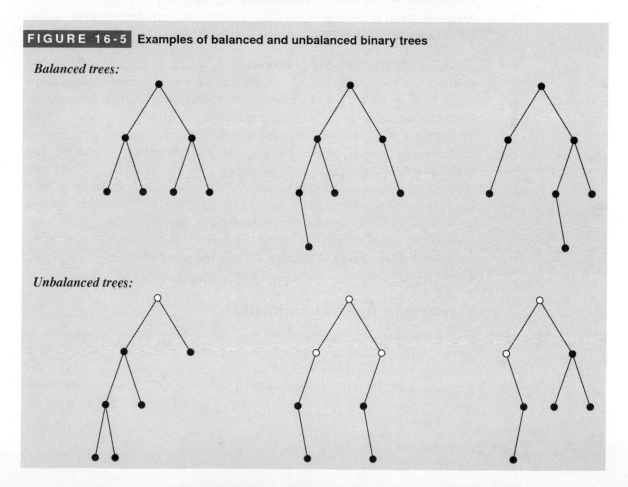

FIGURE 16-5 **Examples of balanced and unbalanced binary trees**

Balanced trees:

Unbalanced trees:

Tree-balancing strategies

Binary search trees are useful in practice only if it is possible to avoid the worst-case behavior associated with unbalanced trees. As trees become unbalanced, the `findNode` and `insertNode` operations become linear in their running time. If the performance of binary trees deteriorates to $O(N)$, you might as well use a sorted array to store the values. With a sorted array, it requires $O(\log N)$ time to implement `findNode` and $O(N)$ time to implement `insertNode`. From a computational perspective, an array-based representation is likely to outperform one based on unbalanced trees, as well as being considerably easier to write.

What makes binary search trees useful as a programming tool is the fact that you can keep them balanced as you build them. The basic idea is to extend the implementation of `insertNode` so that it keeps track of whether the tree is balanced while inserting new nodes. If the tree ever gets out of balance, `insertNode` must rearrange the nodes in the tree so that the balance is restored without disturbing the ordering relationships that make the tree a binary search tree. Assuming that it is possible to rearrange a tree in time proportional to its height, both `findNode` and `insertNode` can be implemented in $O(\log N)$ time.

Algorithms for maintaining balance in a binary tree have been studied extensively in computer science. The algorithms used today to implement balanced binary trees are the product of extensive theoretical research in computer science. Most of these algorithms, however, are difficult to explain without reviewing mathematical results beyond the scope of this text. To demonstrate that such algorithms are indeed possible, the next few sections present one of the first tree-balancing algorithms, which was published in 1962 by the Russian mathematicians Georgii Adelson-Velskii and Evgenii Landis and has since been known by the initials AVL. Although the AVL algorithm has been largely replaced in practice by more sophisticated techniques, it has the advantage of being considerably easier to explain than most current algorithms are. Moreover, the operations used to implement the basic strategy reappear in many other algorithms, which makes the AVL algorithm a good model for more modern techniques.

Visualizing the AVL algorithm

Before you attempt to understand the implementation of the AVL algorithm in detail, it helps to follow through the process of inserting nodes into a binary search tree to see what can go wrong and, if possible, what steps you can take to fix any problems that arise. Let's imagine that you want to create a binary search tree in which the nodes contain the symbols for the chemical elements. For example, the first six elements are

H   (Hydrogen)
He (Helium)
Li (Lithium)
Be (Beryllium)
B   (Boron)
C   (Carbon)

What happens if you insert the chemical symbols for these elements in the indicated order, which is how these elements appear in the periodic table? The first insertion is easy because the tree is initially empty. The node containing the symbol H becomes the root of the tree. If you call **insertNode** on the symbol He, the new node will be added after the node containing H, because He comes after H in lexicographic order. Thus, the first two nodes in the tree are arranged like this:

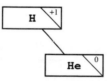

To keep track of whether the tree is balanced, the AVL algorithm associates an integer with each node, which is simply the height of the right subtree minus the height of the left subtree. This value is called the ***balance factor*** of the node. In the simple tree that contains the symbols for the first two elements, the balance factors, which are shown here in the upper right corner of each node, look like this:

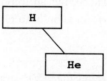

So far, the tree is balanced because none of the nodes has a balance factor whose absolute value is greater than 1. That situation changes, however, when you add the next element. If you follow the standard insertion algorithm, adding Li results in the following configuration:

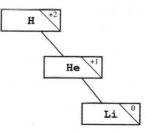

Here, the root node is out of balance because its right subtree has height 1 and its empty left subtree has (by definition) height −1, which differ by more than one.

To fix the imbalance, you need to restructure the tree. For this set of nodes, there is only one balanced configuration in which the nodes are correctly ordered with respect to each other. That tree has **He** at the root, with **H** and **Li** in the left and right subtrees, as follows:

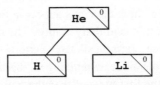

This tree is once again balanced, but an important question remains: how do you know what operations to perform in order to restore the balance in a tree?

Single rotations

The fundamental insight behind the AVL strategy is that you can always restore balance to a tree by a simple rearrangement of the nodes. If you think about what steps were necessary to correct the imbalance in the preceding example, it is clear that the **He** node moves upward to become the root while **H** moves downward to become its child. To a certain extent, the transformation has the characteristic of rotating the **H** and **He** nodes one position to the left, like this:

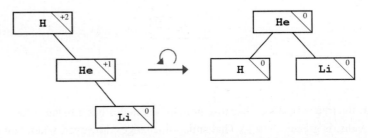

The two nodes involved in the rotation operation are called the *axis* of the rotation. In the example consisting of the elements **H**, **He**, and **Li**, the rotation was performed around the **H-He** axis. Because this operation moves nodes to the left, the operation illustrated by this diagram is called a *left rotation.* If a tree is out of balance in the opposite direction, you can apply a symmetric operation called a *right rotation,* in which all the operations are simply reversed. For example, the symbols for the next two elements—**Be** and **B**—each get added at the left edge of the tree. To rebalance the tree, you must perform a right rotation around the **Be-H** axis, as illustrated in the following diagram:

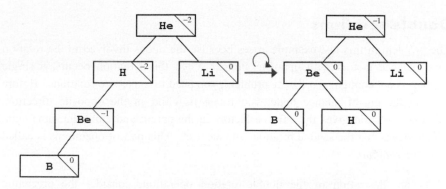

Unfortunately, simple rotation operations are not always sufficient to restore balance to a tree. Consider, for example, what happens when you add **c** to the tree. Before you perform any balancing operations, the tree looks like this:

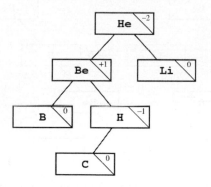

The **He** node at the root of the tree is out of balance. If you try to correct the imbalance by rotating the tree to the right around the **Be-He** axis, you get the following tree:

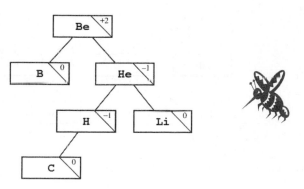

After the rotation, the tree is just as unbalanced as it was before. The only difference is that the root node is now unbalanced in the opposite direction.

Double rotations

The problem in this last example arises because the nodes involved in the rotation have balance factors with opposite signs. When this situation occurs, a single rotation is not enough. To fix the problem, you need to make two rotations. Before rotating the out-of-balance node, you rotate its child in the opposite direction. Rotating the child gives the balance factors in the parent and child the same sign, which means that the second rotation will succeed. This pair of operations is called a *double rotation.*

As an illustration of the double-rotation operation, consider the preceding unbalanced tree of elements just after the symbol C has been added. The first step is to rotate the tree to the left around the **Be-H** axis, like this:

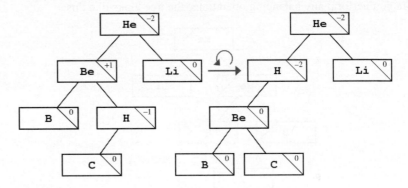

The resulting tree is still out of balance at the root node, but the **H** and **He** nodes now have balance factors that share the same sign. In this configuration, a single rotation to the right around the **H-He** axis restores balance to the tree, as follows:

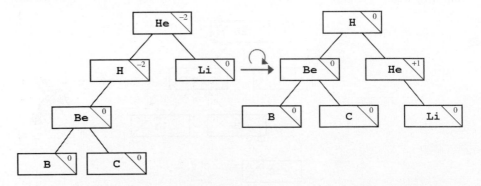

In their paper describing these trees, Adelson-Velskii and Landis demonstrated the following properties of their tree-balancing algorithm:

- If you insert a new node into an AVL tree, you can always restore its balance by performing at most one operation, which is either a single or a double rotation.

- After you complete the rotation operation, the height of the subtree at the axis of rotation is always the same as it was before inserting the new node. This property ensures that none of the balance factors change at any higher levels of the tree.

Implementing the AVL algorithm

Although the process involves quite a few details, implementing `insertNode` for AVL trees is not as difficult as you might imagine. The first change you need to make is to include a new field in the node structure that allows you to keep track of the balance factor, as follows:

```
struct BSTNode {
    string key;
    BSTNode *left, *right;
    int bf;
};
```

The code for `insertNode` itself appears in Figure 16-6. As you can see from the code, `insertNode` is implemented as a wrapper to a function `insertAVL`, which at first glance seems to have the same prototype. The parameters to the two functions are indeed the same. The only difference is that `insertAVL` returns an integer value that represents the change in the height of the tree after inserting the node. This return value, which will always be 0 or 1, makes it easy to fix the structure of the tree as the code makes its way back through the levels of recursive calls. The simple cases are

1. Adding a node in place of a **NULL** tree, which increases the height by one

2. Encountering the key in an existing node, which leaves the height unchanged

In the recursive cases, the code first adds the new node to the appropriate subtree, keeping track of the change in height in the local variable **delta**. If the height of the subtree to which the insertion was made has not changed, then the balance factor in the current node must also remain the same. If, however, the subtree has increased in height, there are three possibilities:

1. *That subtree was previously shorter than the other subtree in this node.* In this case, inserting the new node actually makes the tree more balanced than it was previously. The balance factor of the current node becomes 0, and the height of the subtree rooted there remains the same as before.

FIGURE 16-6 Code to insert a node into an AVL tree

```
/*
 * Function: insertNode
 * Usage: insertNode(t, key);
 * -----------------------------
 * Inserts a node with the specified key into the correct position in the
 * binary search tree.  If key already exists in the tree, this call has
 * no effect.
 */

void insertNode(BSTNode * & t, const string & key) {
   insertAVL(t, key);
}

/*
 * Function: insertAVL
 * Usage: delta = insertAVL(t, key);
 * ------------------------------------
 * Enters the key into the tree that is passed by reference as the first
 * argument.  The return value is the change in depth in the tree, which
 * is used to correct the balance factors in ancestor nodes.
 */

int insertAVL(BSTNode * & t, const string & key) {
   if (t == NULL) {
      t = new BSTNode;
      t->key = key;
      t->bf = 0;
      t->left = t->right = NULL;
      return +1;
   }
   if (key == t->key) return 0;
   if (key < t->key) {
      int delta = insertAVL(t->left, key);
      if (delta == 0) return 0;
      switch (t->bf) {
       case +1: t->bf =  0; return 0;
       case  0: t->bf = -1; return +1;
       case -1: fixLeftImbalance(t); return 0;
      }
   } else {
      int delta = insertAVL(t->right, key);
      if (delta == 0) return 0;
      switch (t->bf) {
       case -1: t->bf =  0; return 0;
       case  0: t->bf = +1; return +1;
       case +1: fixRightImbalance(t); return 0;
      }
   }
}
```

FIGURE 16-6 Code to insert a node into an AVL tree (continued)

```
/*
 * Function: fixLeftImbalance
 * Usage: fixLeftImbalance(t);
 * ----------------------------
 * This function is called when a node has been found that is out of
 * balance with the longer subtree on the left.  Depending on the balance
 * factor of the left child, the code performs a single or double rotation.
 */

void fixLeftImbalance(BSTNode * & t) {
   BSTNode *child = t->left;
   if (child->bf != t->bf) {
      int oldBF = child->right->bf;
      rotateLeft(t->left);
      rotateRight(t);
      t->bf = 0;
      switch (oldBF) {
        case -1: t->left->bf = 0; t->right->bf = +1; break;
        case  0: t->left->bf = t->right->bf = 0; break;
        case +1: t->left->bf = -1; t->right->bf = 0; break;
      }
   } else {
      rotateRight(t);
      t->right->bf = t->bf = 0;
   }
}

/*
 * Function: rotateLeft
 * Usage: rotateLeft(t);
 * ----------------------
 * Performs a single left rotation of the tree passed by reference as the
 * argument t.  The balance factors are unchanged by this function and must
 * be corrected at a higher level of the algorithm.
 */

void rotateLeft(BSTNode * & t) {
   BSTNode *child = t->right;
   if (DEBUG) {
      cout << "rotateLeft(" << t->key << "-" << child->key << ")" << endl;
   }
   t->right = child->left;
   child->left = t;
   t = child;
}
```

FIGURE 16-6 Code to insert a node into an AVL tree (continued)

```
/*
 * Function: fixRightImbalance
 * Usage: fixRightImbalance(t);
 * ----------------------------
 * This function is called when a node has been found that is out of
 * balance with the longer subtree on the right.  Depending on the balance
 * factor of the right child, the code performs a single or double rotation.
 */

void fixRightImbalance(BSTNode * & t) {
   BSTNode *child = t->right;
   if (child->bf != t->bf) {
      int oldBF = child->left->bf;
      rotateRight(t->right);
      rotateLeft(t);
      t->bf = 0;
      switch (oldBF) {
        case -1: t->left->bf = 0; t->right->bf = +1; break;
        case  0: t->left->bf = t->right->bf = 0; break;
        case +1: t->left->bf = -1; t->right->bf = 0; break;
      }
   } else {
      rotateLeft(t);
      t->left->bf = t->bf = 0;
   }
}

/*
 * Function: rotateRight
 * Usage: rotateRight(t);
 * ----------------------
 * Performs a single right rotation of the tree passed by reference as the
 * argument t.  The balance factors are unchanged by this function and must
 * be corrected at a higher level of the algorithm.
 */

void rotateRight(BSTNode * & t) {
   BSTNode *child = t->left;
   if (DEBUG) {
      cout << "rotateRight(" << t->key << "-" << child->key << ")" << endl;
   }
   t->left = child->right;
   child->right = t;
   t = child;
}
```

2. *The two subtrees in the current node were previously the same size.* In this case, increasing the size of one of the subtrees makes the current node slightly out of balance, but not to the point that any corrective action is required. The balance factor becomes −1 or +1, as appropriate, and the function returns 1 to show that the height of the subtree rooted at this node has increased.

3. *The subtree that grew taller was already taller than the other subtree.* When this situation occurs, the tree is now out of balance, because one subtree is two nodes taller than the other. At this point, the code must execute the appropriate rotation operations to correct the imbalance. If the balance factors in the current node and the root of the expanding subtree have the same sign, a single rotation is sufficient. If not, the code must perform a double rotation. After performing the rotation, the code must correct the balance factors in the nodes whose positions have changed. The effect of the single and double rotation operations on the balance factors in the node is shown in Figure 16-7.

Using the code for the AVL algorithm shown in Figure 16-6 ensures that the binary search tree remains in balance as new nodes are added. As a result, both **findNode** and **insertNode** will run in $O(\log N)$ time. Even without the AVL extension, however, the code will continue to work. The advantage of the AVL strategy is that it guarantees $O(\log N)$ performance, at some cost in the complexity of the code.

16.4 Implementing maps using BSTs

As noted in Chapter 15, the Standard Template Library uses binary search trees to implement the map abstraction. This implementation strategy means that the **get** and **put** methods run in $O(\log N)$ time, which is slightly less efficient than the $O(1)$ average running time offered by the hash table strategy. In practice, that difference is not all that important. The graph of $O(\log N)$ grows extremely slowly and is much closer to $O(1)$ than it is to $O(N)$. The designers of C++ felt that the ability to process keys in order more than compensated for the modest additional cost.

The hard parts of implementing the map abstraction using binary search trees are almost entirely in the code for binary search trees themselves, which you have already seen in this chapter. To apply this idea to the **Map** class, there are just a few tasks left to perform:

*   The node structure must include a value field along with the key.

*   The code must use templates to parameterize the key and value types.

*   The code for manipulating the tree must be embedded in the **Map** class.

Each of these changes makes a wonderful exercise that will reinforce your understanding of classes.

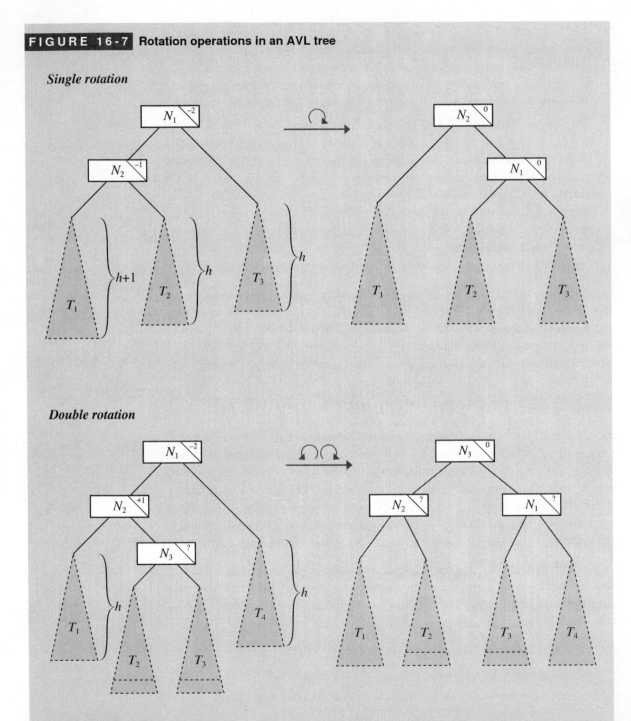

FIGURE 16-7 Rotation operations in an AVL tree

Single rotation

Double rotation

Note: At least one of the subtrees T_2 and T_3 must have height h; the other can have height h or $h-1$. The balance factors in the final nodes will need to be adjusted to take account of any difference in height.

16.5 Partially ordered trees

Trees come up in many other programming contexts. One particularly useful application arises in the implementation of *priority queues,* where the order in which elements are dequeued depends on a numeric priority. The Stanford C++ libraries implement this concept through the **pqueue.h** interface, which exports a class called **PriorityQueue**. This class operates identically to the standard **Queue** class with the exception of the **enqueue** method, which takes a second argument indicating the priority, as follows:

```
void enqueue(ValueType element, double priority);
```

As in conventional English usage, smaller priority numbers come first in the queue, so that elements entered with priority 1 are processed before any elements with priority 2.

Priority queues made a brief appearance earlier in this book in exercise 8 from Chapter 14. If you use the strategy suggested in that exercise, the **enqueue** method requires $O(N)$ time. You can improve the performance of the priority queue package to $O(\log N)$ by using a data structure called a *partially ordered tree,* in which the following properties hold:

1. The tree is a binary tree in that each node has at most two children. It is not, however, a binary search tree, which has different ordering rules.

2. The nodes of the tree are arranged in a pattern as close to that of a completely symmetrical tree as possible. Thus, the number of nodes along any path in the tree can never differ by more than one. Moreover, the bottom level must be filled in a strictly left-to-right order.

3. Each node contains a key that is always less than or equal to the key in its children. Thus, the smallest key in the tree is always at the root.

As an example, the following diagram shows a partially ordered tree with four nodes, each of which contains a numeric key:

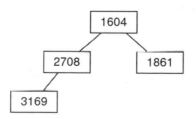

The second level of the tree is completely filled, and the third level is in the process of being filled from left to right, as required by the second property of partially ordered trees. The third property holds because the key in each node is always less than the keys in its children.

Suppose that you want to add a node with the key 2193. It is clear where the new node goes. The requirement that the lowest level of the tree be filled from left to right dictates that the new node be added at the following position:

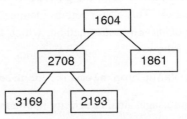

This diagram, however, violates the third property of partially ordered trees, because the key 2193 is smaller than the 2708 in its parent. To fix the problem, you begin by exchanging the keys in those nodes, like this:

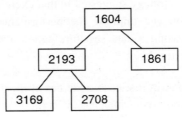

In general, it is possible that the newly inserted key would have to be exchanged with its parent in a cascading sequence of changes proceeding up through the levels of the tree. In this specific case, the process of exchanging keys stops here because 2193 is greater than 1604. In any event, the structure of the tree guarantees that these exchanges will never require more than $O(\log N)$ time.

The structure of the partially ordered tree means that the smallest value in the tree is always at the root. Removing the root node, however, takes a little more work because you have to arrange for the node that actually disappears to be the rightmost node in the bottom level. The standard approach is to replace the key in the root with the key in the node to be deleted and then swap keys down the tree until the ordering property is restored. If you wanted, for example, to delete the root node from the preceding tree diagram, the first step would be to replace the key in the root node with the 2708 in the rightmost node from the lowest level, as follows:

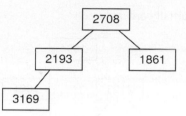

Then, because the nodes of the tree no longer have correctly ordered keys, you would need to exchange the key 2708 with the smaller of the two keys in its children, like this:

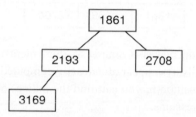

Although a single interchange is enough to restore the ordering property of the tree in this example, the general process of finding the correct position for the key that was moved into the root position may require you to swap that element through each of the levels in the tree. As with insertion, deleting the smallest key requires $O(\log N)$ time.

The operations that define the partially ordered tree are precisely the ones you need to implement priority queues. The **enqueue** operation consists of inserting a new node into the partially ordered tree. The **dequeue** operation consists of removing the lowest value. Thus, if you use partially ordered trees as the underlying representation, you can implement the priority queue package so that it runs in $O(\log N)$ time.

Although you can implement partially ordered trees using a pointer-based structure, most implementations of priority queues employ an array-based structure called a **heap,** which simulates the operation of a partially ordered tree. (The terminology is confusing at first, because the heap data structure bears no relationship to the pool of unused memory available for dynamic allocation, which is also referred to by the word *heap.*) The implementation strategy used in a heap depends on the property that you can store the nodes in a partially ordered tree of size N in the first N elements of an array simply by numbering the nodes, level by level, from left to right.

As an example, the partially ordered tree

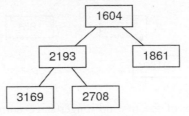

can be represented as the following heap:

1604	2193	1861	3169	2708			. . .
0	1	2	3	4	5	6	

The heap organization makes it simple to implement tree operations, because parent and child nodes always appear at an easily computed position. For example, given a node at index position **n**, you can find the indices of its parent and children using the following expressions:

parentIndex(n)	*is always given by*	**(n - 1) / 2**
leftChildIndex(n)	*is always given by*	**2 * n + 1**
rightChildIndex(n)	*is always given by*	**2 * n + 2**

The division operator in the calculation of **parentIndex** is the standard integer division operator from C++. Thus, the parent of the node at index position 4 in the array appears at position 1 in the array, because the result of evaluating the expression **(4 - 1) / 2** is 1.

Implementing the heap-based priority queue is an excellent exercise that will sharpen your programming skills and give you more experience working with many of the data structures you have seen in this text. You will have the opportunity to do so in exercise 13 at the end of this chapter.

▰ Summary

In this chapter, you have been introduced to the concept of *trees,* which are hierarchical collections of nodes that have the following properties:

- There is a single node at the top that forms the root of the hierarchy.

- Every node in the tree is connected to the root by a unique line of descent.

Important points in this chapter include:

- Many of the terms used to describe trees, such as *parent, child, ancestor, descendant,* and *sibling,* come directly from family trees. Other terms, including *root* and *leaf,* are derived from trees in nature. These metaphors make the terminology used for trees easy to understand because the words have the same interpretation in computer science that they do in more familiar contexts.

- Trees have a well-defined recursive structure because every node in a tree is the root of a subtree. Thus, a tree consists of a node together with its set of children, each of which is a tree. This recursive structure is reflected in the underlying representation for a tree, which is defined as a pointer to a node; a node, in turn, is a structure that contains trees.

- Binary trees are a subclass of trees in which nodes have at most two children and every node except the root is designated as either a left child or a right child of its parent.

- If a binary tree is organized so that every node in the tree contains a key field that follows all the keys in its left subtree and precedes all the keys in its right subtree, that tree is called a *binary search tree.* As its name implies, the structure of a binary search tree permits the use of the binary search algorithm, which makes it possible to find individual keys more efficiently. Because the keys are ordered, it is always possible to determine whether the key you're searching for appears in the left or right subtree of any particular node.

- Using recursion makes it easy to step through the nodes in a binary search tree, which is called *traversing* or *walking* the tree. There are several types of traversals, depending on the order in which the nodes are processed. If the key in each node is processed before the recursive calls to process the subtrees, the result is a *preorder* traversal. Processing each node after both recursive calls gives rise to a *postorder* traversal. Processing the current node between the two recursive calls represents an *inorder* traversal. In a binary search tree, the inorder traversal has the useful property that the keys are processed in order.

- Depending on the order in which nodes are inserted, given the same set of keys, binary search trees can have radically different structures. If the branches of the tree differ substantially in height, the tree is said to be unbalanced, which reduces its efficiency. By using techniques such as the AVL algorithm described in this chapter, you can keep a tree in balance as new nodes are added.

- Priority queues can be implemented efficiently using a data structure called a *heap,* which is based on a special class of binary tree called a *partially ordered tree.* If you use this representation, both the `enqueue` and `dequeue` operations run in $O(\log N)$ time.

Review questions

1. What two conditions must be satisfied for a collection of nodes to be a tree?

2. Give at least four real-world examples that involve tree structures.

3. Define the terms *parent, child, ancestor, descendant,* and *sibling* as they apply to trees.

4. The family tree for the House of Tudor, which ruled England in Shakespeare's time, is shown in Figure 16-8. Identify the root, leaf, and interior nodes. What is the height of this tree?

5. What is it about trees that makes them recursive?

6. Diagram the internal structure of the tree shown in Figure 16-8 when it is represented using the type **FamilyTreeNode**.

7. What is the defining property of a binary search tree?

8. Why are different type declarations used for the first argument in **findNode** and **insertNode**?

9. In *The Hobbit* by J. R. R. Tolkien, 13 dwarves arrive at the house of Bilbo Baggins in the following order: **Dwalin, Balin, Kili, Fili, Dori, Nori, Ori, Oin, Gloin, Bifur, Bofur, Bombur,** and **Thorin.** Diagram the binary search tree that results from inserting these names into an empty tree.

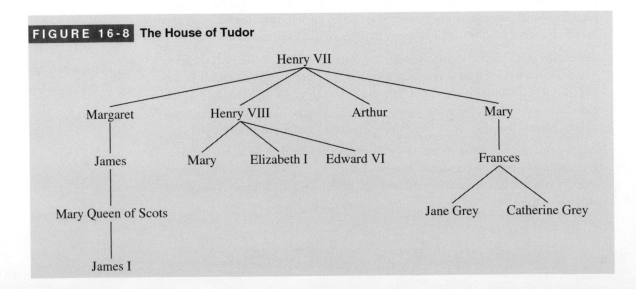

FIGURE 16-8 **The House of Tudor**

10. Given the tree you created to answer the preceding question, what key comparisons are made if you call **findNode** on the name **Bombur**?

11. Write down the preorder, inorder, and postorder traversals of the binary search tree you created for question 9.

12. One of the three standard traversal orders—preorder, inorder, or postorder—does not depend on the order in which the nodes are inserted into the tree. Which one is it?

13. What does it mean for a binary tree to be balanced?

14. For each of the following tree structures, indicate whether the tree is balanced:

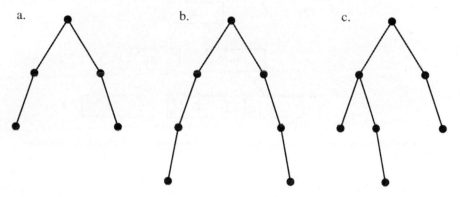

   a.   b.   c.

For any tree structure that is out of balance, indicate which nodes are out of balance.

15. True or false: If a binary search tree becomes unbalanced, the algorithms used in the functions **findNode** and **insertNode** will fail to work correctly.

16. How do you calculate the balance factor of a node?

17. Fill in the balance factors for each node in the following binary search tree:

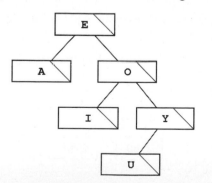

18. If you use the AVL balancing strategy, what rotation operation must you apply to the tree in the preceding question to restore its balanced configuration? What is the structure of the resulting tree, including the updated balance factors?

19. True or false: When you insert a new node into a balanced binary tree, you can always correct any resulting imbalance by performing one operation, which will be either a single or a double rotation.

20. As shown in the section on "Visualizing the AVL idea," inserting the symbols for the first six elements into an AVL tree results in the following configuration:

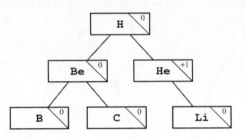

Show what happens to the tree as you add the next six element symbols:

N	(Nitrogen)
O	(Oxygen)
F	(Fluorine)
Ne	(Neon)
Na	(Sodium)
Mg	(Magnesium)

21. Describe in detail what happens during a call to `insertNode`.

22. What strategy does the text suggest to avoid having a binary search tree become disconnected if you remove an interior node?

23. Suppose that you are working with a partially ordered tree that contains the following data:

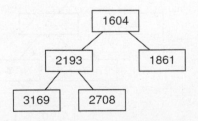

Show the state of the partially ordered tree after inserting a node with the key 1521.

24. What is the relationship between heaps and partially ordered trees?

Exercises

1. Working from the definition of **FamilyTreeNode** given in the section entitled "Representing family trees in C++," write a function

   FamilyTreeNode *readFamilyTree(string filename);

   that reads in a family tree from a data file whose name is supplied as the argument to the call. The first line of the file should contain a name corresponding to the root of the tree. All subsequent lines in the data file should have the following form:

   child:*parent*

   where *child* is the name of the new individual being entered and *parent* is the name of that child's parent, which must appear earlier in the data file. For example, if the file **Normandy.txt** contains the lines

   Normandy.txt
   ```
   William I
   Robert:William I
   William II:William I
   Adela:William I
   Henry I:William I
   Stephen:Adela
   William:Henry I
   Matilda:Henry I
   Henry II:Matilda
   ```

   calling **readFamilyTree("Normandy.txt")** should return the family-tree structure shown in Figure 16-2.

2. Write a function

   void displayFamilyTree(FamilyTreeNode *tree);

   that displays all the individuals in a family tree. To record the hierarchy of the tree, the output of your program should indent each generation so that the name of each child appears two spaces to the right of the corresponding parent, as shown in the following sample run:

```
 ○ ○ ○                    FamilyTree
William I
   Robert
   William II
   Adela
      Stephen
   Henry I
      William
      Matilda
         Henry II
```

3. As defined in the chapter, the **FamilyTreeNode** structure uses a vector to store the children. Another possibility is to include an extra pointer in these nodes that will allow them to form a linked list of the children. Thus, in this design, each node in the tree needs to contain only two pointers: one to its eldest child and one to its next younger sibling. Using this representation, the House of Normandy appears as shown in Figure 16-9. In each node, the pointer on the left always points down to a child; the pointer on the right indicates the next sibling in the same generation. Thus, the eldest child of William I is Robert, which you obtain by following the link at the left of the diagram. The remaining children are linked together through the link cells shown at the right of the node diagram. The chain of children ends at Henry I, which has the value **NULL** in its next-sibling link.

   Using the linked design illustrated in this diagram, write new definitions of **FamilyTreeNode**, **readFamilyTree**, and **displayFamilyTree**.

FIGURE 16-9 The House of Normandy using a list of siblings

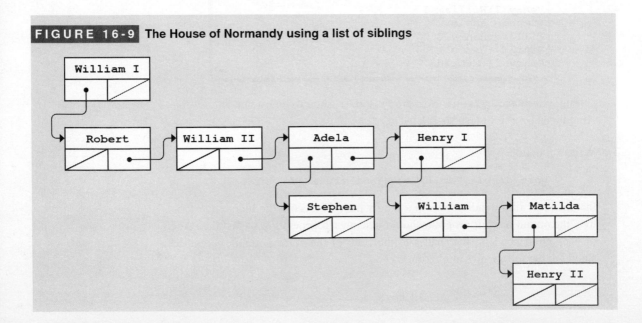

4. In exercise 3, the changes you made to the **FamilyTreeNode** structure forced
    you to rewrite the functions **readFamilyTree** and **displayFamilyTree**
    because those functions depend on the internal representation. If the family
    tree were instead represented as a class that maintains its interface despite any
    changes in representation, you could avoid much of this recoding. Such an
    interface appears in Figure 16-10. Write the corresponding implementation
    using a vector to store the list of children.

FIGURE 16-10 Interface for the **FamilyTreeNode** class

```
/*
 * File: familytree.h
 * --------------------
 * This file is an interface to a simple class that represents an individual
 * person in a family tree.
 */

#ifndef _familytree_h
#define _familytree_h

#include <string>
#include "vector.h"

/*
 * Class: FamilyTreeNode
 * ---------------------
 * This class defines the structure of an individual in the family
 * tree, which consists of a name and a vector of children.
 */

class FamilyTreeNode {

public:

/*
 * Constructor: FamilyTreeNode
 * Usage: FamilyTreeNode *person = new FamilyTreeNode(name);
 * ---------------------------------------------------------------
 * Constructs a new FamilyTreeNode with the specified name.  The
 * newly constructed entry has no children, but clients can add
 * children by calling the addChild method.
 */

   FamilyTreeNode(const std::string & name);

/*
 * Method: getName
 * Usage: string name = person->getName();
 * ------------------------------------------
 * Returns the name of the person.
 */

   string getName() const;
```

FIGURE 16-10 Interface for the `FamilyTreeNode` class (continued)

```
/*
 * Method: addChild
 * Usage: person->addChild(child);
 * ---------------------------------
 * Adds child to the end of the list of children for person, and
 * makes person the parent of child.
 */

   void addChild(FamilyTreeNode *child);

/*
 * Method: getParent
 * Usage: FamilyTreeNode *parent = person->getParent();
 * ----------------------------------------------------------
 * Returns the parent of the specified person.
 */

   FamilyTreeNode *getParent() const;

/*
 * Method: getChildren
 * Usage: Vector<FamilyTreeNode *> children = person->getChildren();
 * ----------------------------------------------------------------
 * Returns a vector of the children of the specified person.
 * Note that this vector is a copy of the one in the node, so
 * that the client cannot change the tree by adding or removing
 * children from this vector.
 */

   Vector<FamilyTreeNode *> getChildren() const;
```

┌───┐
│ *The private section of the class goes here.*   │
└───┘

```
};

#endif
```

---

5. Using the `familytree.h` interface defined in Figure 16-10, write a function

   ```
   FamilyTreeNode *commonAncestor(FamilyTreeNode *p1,
                                  FamilyTreeNode *p2);
   ```

   that returns the closest ancestor shared by `p1` and `p2`.

6. Using the definition of `BSTNode` from section 16.2, write a function

   ```
   int height(BSTNode *tree);
   ```

   that takes a binary search tree and returns its height.

7. Write a function

    bool isBalanced(BSTNode *tree);

    that determines whether a given tree is balanced according to the definition in the section on "Balanced trees." To solve this problem, all you really need to do is translate the definition of a balanced tree more or less directly into code. If you do so, however, the resulting implementation is likely to be relatively inefficient because it has to make several passes over the tree. The real challenge in this problem is to implement the **isBalanced** function so that it determines the result without looking at any node more than once.

8. Write a function

    bool hasBinarySearchProperty(BSTNode *tree);

    that takes a tree and determines whether it maintains the fundamental property that defines a binary search tree: that the key in each node follows every key in its left subtree and precedes every key in its right subtree.

9. The discussion of the AVL algorithm in the text offers a strategy for inserting a node but does not cover the symmetric process of removing a node, which also requires rebalancing the tree. As it turns out, these two algorithms are quite similar. Removing a node either may have no effect on the height of a tree or may shorten it by one. If a tree gets shorter, the balance factor in its parent node changes. If the parent node is then unbalanced, it is possible to rebalance the tree at that point by performing either a single or a double rotation.

    Implement a function

    void removeNode(BSTNode * & t, const string & key);

    that removes the node containing **key** from the tree while keeping the underlying AVL tree balanced. Think carefully about the various cases that can arise and make sure that your implementation handles these cases correctly.

10. Using the discussion in section 16.4 as a guide, implement the **map.h** interface using binary search trees as the underlying representation. Start with the simplified **StringMap** version of the interface presented in Figure 15-1 on page 665. Once you have that working, implement the missing operations.

11. In exercise 19 from Chapter 5, you had the opportunity to write a program that translated messages from Morse code to the equivalent English letters. That exercise encouraged you to use a map to store the translation tables, but there are other ways to approach the problem. You can, for example, think of the Morse encodings as a binary tree in which dots take you to the left and dashes take you to the right. In this formulation, the letters in the Morse code table

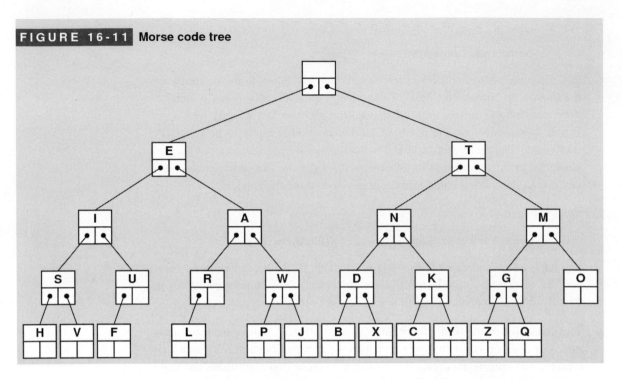

FIGURE 16-11 Morse code tree

have the structure shown in Figure 16-11. As an example, you can reach the letter **L** by starting at the root and then following a sequence of links in the order left-right-left-left, which tells you that the Morse code for **L** is •▬••.

Design a data structure to store the tree from Figure 16-11 and then write a function **getMorseCodeLetter**(*code*) that uses the tree to find the letter that corresponds to the Morse code string given by *code*.

12. From a practical standpoint, the AVL algorithm is too aggressive. Because it requires that the heights of the subtrees at each node never differ by more than one, the AVL algorithm spends quite a bit of time performing rotation operations to correct imbalances that occur as new nodes are inserted. If you allow trees to become somewhat more unbalanced—but still keep the subtrees relatively similar—you can reduce the balancing overhead significantly.

One data structure for binary search trees that provides better performance is called ***red-black trees.*** The name comes from the fact that every node in the tree is assigned a color, either red or black. A binary search tree is a legal red-black tree if all three of the following properties hold:

1. The root node is black.
2. The parent of every red node is black.
3. All paths from the root to a leaf contain the same number of black nodes.

These properties ensure that the longest path from the root to a leaf can never be more than twice the length of the shortest path. Given the rules, you know that every such path has the same number of black nodes, which means that the shortest possible path is composed entirely of black nodes, and the longest has black and red nodes alternating down the chain. Although this condition is less strict than the definition of a balanced tree used in the AVL algorithm, it is sufficient to guarantee that the operations of finding and inserting new nodes both run in logarithmic time.

The key to making red-black trees work is finding an insertion algorithm that allows you to add new nodes while maintaining the conditions that define red-black trees. The algorithm has much in common with the AVL algorithm and uses the same rotation operations. The first step is to insert the new node using the standard insertion algorithm with no balancing. The new node always replaces a **NULL** entry at some point in the tree. If the node is the first node entered into the tree, it becomes the root and is therefore colored black. In all other cases, the new node must initially be colored red to avoid violating the rule that every path from the root to a leaf must contain the same number of black nodes.

As long as the parent of the new node is black, the tree as a whole remains a legal red-black tree. The problem arises if the parent node is also red, which means that the tree violates the second condition, which requires that every red node have a black parent. In this case, you need to restructure the tree to restore the red-black condition. Depending on the relationship of the red-red pair to the remaining nodes in the tree, you can eliminate the problem by performing one of the following operations, each of which is illustrated in Figure 16-12:

1. A single rotation followed by a recoloring that leaves the top node black

2. A double rotation followed by a recoloring that leaves the top node black

3. A simple change in node colors that leaves the top node red and may therefore require further restructuring at a higher level in the tree

The diagram in Figure 16-12 shows only the cases in which the imbalance occurs on the left side. Imbalances on the right side are treated symmetrically.

Reimplement the **Map** class so that it uses a red-black tree as its underlying representation. When you are debugging your program, you will find it helpful to implement a method that displays the structure of the tree, including the colors of the nodes, which are not revealed to the client. This method should also check to see that the rules for forming red-black trees are maintained as the tree changes.

FIGURE 16-12   Rotation operations in a red-black tree

Case 1: N_4 is black (or nonexistent); N_1 and N_2 are out of balance in the same direction

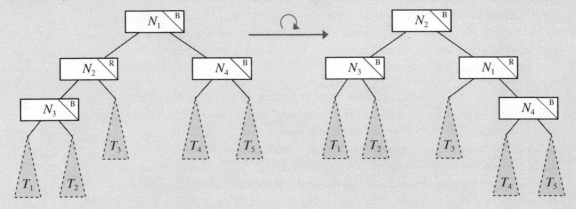

Case 2: N_4 is black (or nonexistent); N_1 and N_2 are out of balance in opposite directions

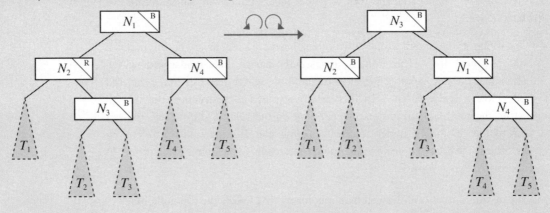

Case 3: N_4 is red; the relative balance of N_1 and N_2 doesn't matter

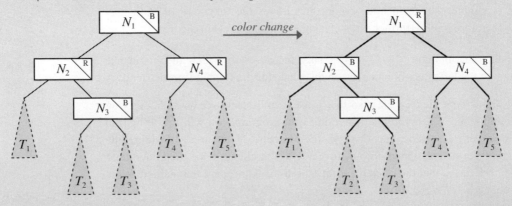

13. Use the algorithm from section 16.5 to implement the `PriorityQueue` class so that it uses a heap as its underlying representation. To eliminate some of the complexity, feel free to use a vector instead of a dynamic array.

14. The heap data structure forms a natural basis for a sorting algorithm that always runs in $O(N \log N)$ time. In this algorithm, which is called **heapsort,** all you do is enter each value into a heap and then take the items out of the heap from smallest to largest. Use this strategy to write a heapsort implementation of the template function

```
template <typename ValueType>
void sort(Vector<ValueType> & vec);
```

15. Trees have many applications beyond those listed in this chapter. For example, trees can be used to implement a lexicon, which was introduced in Chapter 5. The resulting structure, first developed by Edward Fredkin in 1960, is called a **trie.** (Over time, the pronunciation of this word has evolved to the point that it is now pronounced like *try,* even though the name comes from the central letters of *retrieval.*) The trie-based implementation of a lexicon, while somewhat inefficient in its use of space, makes it possible for you to determine whether a word is in the lexicon much more quickly than you can using a hash table.

At one level, a trie is simply a tree in which each node branches in as many as 26 ways, one for each possible letter of the alphabet. When you use a trie to represent a lexicon, the words are stored implicitly in the structure of the tree and represented as a succession of links moving downward from the root. The root of the tree corresponds to the empty string, and each successive level of the tree corresponds to the subset of the entire word list formed by adding one more letter to the string represented by its parent. For example, the *A* link descending from the root leads to the subtree containing all the words beginning with *A,* the *B* link from that node leads to the subtree containing all the words beginning with *AB,* and so forth. Each node is also marked with a flag indicating whether the substring that ends at that particular point is a legitimate word.

The structure of a trie is much easier to understand by example than by definition. Figure 16-13 shows a trie containing the symbols for the first six elements—**H**, **He**, **Li**, **Be**, **B**, and **C**. The root of the tree corresponds to the empty string, which is not a legal symbol, as indicated by the designation **no** in the field at the extreme right end of the structure. The link labeled **B** from the node at the root of the trie descends to a node corresponding to the string **"B"**. The rightmost field of this node contains **yes**, which indicates that the string

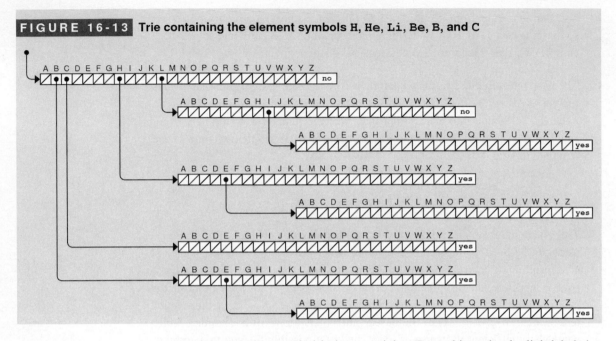

FIGURE 16-13   Trie containing the element symbols H, He, Li, Be, B, and C

"B" is a complete symbol in its own right. From this node, the link labeled E leads to a new node, which indicates that the string "BE" is a legal symbol as well. The NULL pointers in the trie indicate that no legal symbols appear in the subtree beginning with that substring and therefore make it possible to terminate the search process.

Reimplement the Lexicon class so that it uses a trie as its internal representation. Your implementation should be able to read text files but not binary data files such as EnglishWords.dat.

Chapter 17
Sets

We are an ambitious set, aren't we?

— Louisa May Alcott, *Little Women,* 1868

The **Set** and **HashSet** classes both made their appearance in Chapter 5. As with the rest of the chapters in this part of the text, one of the objectives in Chapter 17 is to learn how to implement those classes. As it happens, that discussion will take much less than a full chapter. Given the implementations of **Map** and **HashMap**, the corresponding **Set** classes turn out to be relatively easy to write. This chapter therefore takes on the additional challenge of defining sets in a more theoretically precise way. Sets are central to both the theory and practice of computer science. Understanding the theory makes it much easier for you to use sets effectively in your programs.

17.1 Sets as a mathematical abstraction

In all likelihood, you have already encountered sets at some point in your study of mathematics. Although the definition is not entirely precise, it is best to think of a *set* as an unordered collection of distinct elements. For example, the days of the week form a set of seven elements that can be written down as follows:

{ Sunday, Monday, Tuesday, Wednesday, Thursday, Friday, Saturday }

The individual elements are written in this order only because it is conventional. If you wrote these same names down in some other order, you would still have the same set. A set, however, never contains multiple copies of the same element.

The set of weekdays is a *finite set* because it contains a finite number of elements. In mathematics, there are also *infinite sets,* such as the set of all integers. In a computer system, sets are usually finite, even if they correspond to infinite sets in mathematics. For example, the set of integers that a computer can represent in a variable of type **int** is finite because the hardware imposes a limit on the range of integer values.

To illustrate the fundamental operations on sets, it is important to have a few sets to use as a foundation. In keeping with mathematical convention, this text uses the following symbols to refer to the indicated sets:

∅   The *empty set,* which contains no elements
Z   The set of all integers
N   The set of *natural numbers,* ordinarily defined in computer science as 0, 1, 2, 3, . . .
R   The set of all real numbers

Following mathematical convention, this text uses uppercase letters to refer to sets. Sets whose membership is defined—like **N, Z,** and **R**—are denoted using boldface letters. Names that refer to some unspecified set are written using italic letters, such as *S* and *T.*

Membership

The fundamental property that defines a set is that of ***membership,*** which has the same intuitive meaning in mathematics that it does in English. Mathematicians indicate membership symbolically using the notation $x \in S$, which indicates that the value x is an element of the set S. For example, given the sets defined in the preceding section, the following statements are true:

$$17 \in \mathbf{N} \qquad\qquad -4 \in \mathbf{Z} \qquad\qquad \pi \in \mathbf{R}$$

Conversely, the notation $x \notin S$ indicates that x is *not* an element of S. For example, $-4 \notin \mathbf{N}$, because the set of natural numbers does not include the negative integers.

The membership of a set is typically specified in one of the two following ways:

- *Enumeration.* Defining a set by enumeration is simply a matter of listing its elements. By convention, the elements in the list are enclosed in curly braces and separated by commas. For example, the set **D** of single-digit natural numbers can be defined by enumeration as follows:

    $$\mathbf{D} = \{0, 1, 2, 3, 4, 5, 6, 7, 8, 9\}$$

- *Rule.* You can also define a set by specifying a rule that distinguishes the members of that set. In most cases, the rule is expressed in two parts: a larger set that provides the potential candidates and some conditional expression that identifies the elements that should be selected for inclusion. For example, the set **D** from the preceding example can also be defined this way:

    $$\mathbf{D} = \{x \mid x \in \mathbf{N} \text{ and } x < 10\}$$

    If you read this definition aloud, it comes out sounding like this: "**D** is defined to be the set of all elements x such that x is a natural number and x is less than 10."

Set operations

Mathematical set theory defines several operations on sets, of which the following are the most important:

- ***Union.*** The union of two sets is written as $A \cup B$ and consists of all elements belonging to the set A, the set B, or both.

    $$
    \begin{aligned}
    \{1, 3, 5, 7, 9\} \cup \{2, 4, 6, 8\} &= \{1, 2, 3, 4, 5, 6, 7, 8, 9\} \\
    \{1, 2, 4, 8\} \cup \{2, 3, 5, 7\} &= \{1, 2, 3, 4, 5, 7, 8\} \\
    \{2, 3\} \cup \{1, 2, 3, 4\} &= \{1, 2, 3, 4\}
    \end{aligned}
    $$

- ***Intersection.*** The intersection of two sets is written as $A \cap B$ and consists of the elements belonging to both A and B.

$$\{1, 3, 5, 7, 9\} \cap \{2, 4, 6, 8\} = \varnothing$$
$$\{1, 2, 4, 8\} \cap \{2, 3, 5, 7\} = \{2\}$$
$$\{2, 3\} \cap \{1, 2, 3, 4\} = \{2, 3\}$$

- ***Set difference.*** The difference of two sets is written as $A - B$ and consists of the elements belonging to A except for those that are also contained in B.

$$\{1, 3, 5, 7, 9\} - \{2, 4, 6, 8\} = \{1, 3, 5, 7, 9\}$$
$$\{1, 2, 4, 8\} - \{2, 3, 5, 7\} = \{1, 4, 8\}$$
$$\{2, 3\} - \{1, 2, 3, 4\} = \varnothing$$

In addition to set-producing operations like union and intersection, the mathematical theory of sets also defines several operations that determine whether some property holds between two sets. Operations that test a particular property are the mathematical equivalent of predicate functions and are usually called ***relations.*** The most important relations on sets are the following:

- ***Equality.*** The sets A and B are equal if they have the same elements. The equality relation for sets is indicated by the standard equal sign used to denote equality in other mathematical contexts. Thus, the notation $A = B$ indicates that the sets A and B contain the same elements.

- ***Subset.*** The subset relation is written as $A \subseteq B$ and is true if all the elements of A are also elements of B. For example, the set $\{2, 3, 5, 7\}$ is a subset of the set $\{1, 2, 3, 4, 5, 6, 7, 8, 9\}$. Similarly, the set **N** of natural numbers is a subset of the set **Z** of integers. From the definition, it is clear that every set is a subset of itself. Mathematicians use the notation $A \subset B$ to indicate that A is a ***proper subset*** of B, which means that the subset relation holds but that the sets are not equal.

Set operations are often illustrated by drawing ***Venn diagrams,*** which are named for the British logician John Venn (1834–1923). In a Venn diagram, the individual sets are represented as geometric figures that overlap to indicate regions in which they share elements. For example, the results of the set operations union, intersection, and set difference are indicated by the shaded regions in the following Venn diagrams:

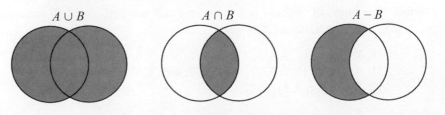

$A \cup B$ $A \cap B$ $A - B$

Set identities

One of the useful bits of knowledge you can derive from mathematical set theory is that the union, intersection, and difference operations are related to each other in various ways. These relationships are usually expressed as *identities,* which are rules indicating that two expressions are invariably equal. In this text, identities are written in the form

$$lhs \equiv rhs$$

which means that the set expressions *lhs* and *rhs* are equal by definition and can therefore be substituted for one another. The most common set identities are shown in Table 17-1.

You can get a sense of how these identities work by drawing Venn diagrams to represent individual stages in the computation. Figure 17-1, for example, verifies the first of De Morgan's laws listed in Table 17-1, which are named after the British mathematician Augustus De Morgan, who first formalized these identities. The shaded areas represent the value of each subexpression in the identity. The fact that the Venn diagrams along the right edge of Figure 17-1 have the same shaded region demonstrates that the set $A - (B \cup C)$ is the same as the set $(A - B) \cap (A - C)$.

What may still be unclear is why you as a programmer might ever need to learn rules that at first seem so complex and arcane. Mathematical techniques are important to computer science for several reasons. For one thing, theoretical knowledge is useful in its own right because it deepens your understanding of the foundations of computing. Moreover, this type of theoretical knowledge often has direct application to programming practice. By relying on data structures whose

TABLE 17-1 **Fundamental set identities**

$S \cup S \equiv S$ $S \cap S \equiv S$	Idempotence
$A \cup (A \cap B) \equiv A$ $A \cap (A \cup B) \equiv A$	Absorption
$A \cup B \equiv B \cup A$ $A \cap B \equiv B \cap A$	Commutative laws
$A \cup (B \cup C) \equiv (A \cup B) \cup C$ $A \cap (B \cap C) \equiv (A \cap B) \cap C$	Associative laws
$A \cup (B \cap C) \equiv (A \cup B) \cap (A \cup C)$ $A \cap (B \cup C) \equiv (A \cap B) \cup (A \cap C)$	Distributive laws
$A - (B \cap C) \equiv (A - B) \cup (A - C)$ $A - (B \cup C) \equiv (A - B) \cap (A - C)$	De Morgan's laws

Illustration of the first of De Morgan's laws using Venn diagrams

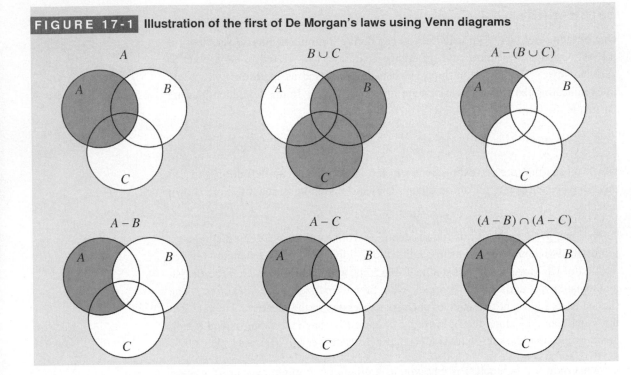

mathematical properties are well established, you can use the theoretical underpinnings of those structures to your advantage. For example, if you write a program that uses sets as an abstract type, you may be able to simplify your code by applying one of the standard set identities shown in Table 17-1. The justification for making that simplification comes from the abstract theory of sets. Choosing to use sets as a programming abstraction, as opposed to designing some less formal structure of your own, makes it easier for you to apply theory to practice.

17.2 Expanding the set interface

Although you have already encountered the **Set** class in the discussion of collection classes, the **set.h** interface in the Stanford libraries exports a richer set of methods and operators extending beyond the description in Chapter 5. Perhaps more importantly, the Stanford library implementation of the **Set** class includes several methods—which are not available in the Standard Template Library—that implement such high-level set operations as subset, equality, union, intersection, and set difference. The expanded version of the interface appears in Figure 17-2.

FIGURE 17-2 Interface for the Set class

```
/*
 * File: set.h
 * -----------
 * This interface exports the Set class, a collection for storing a set
 * of distinct elements.
 */

#ifndef _set_h
#define _set_h

#include "map.h"
#include "vector.h"

/*
 * Class: Set<ValueType>
 * ---------------------
 * This template class stores a collection of distinct elements.
 */

template <typename ValueType>
class Set {

public:

/*
 * Constructor: Set
 * Usage: Set<ValueType> set;
 * --------------------------
 * Initializes an empty set of the specified value type.
 */

   Set();

/*
 * Destructor: ~Set
 * ----------------
 * Frees any heap storage associated with set.
 */

   ~Set();

/*
 * Method: size
 * Usage: int count = set.size();
 * ------------------------------
 * Returns the number of elements in this set.
 */

   int size() const;
```

FIGURE 17-2 Interface for the Set class (continued)

```
/*
 * Method: isEmpty
 * Usage: if (set.isEmpty()) . . .
 * ------------------------------------
 * Returns true if this set contains no elements.
 */

   bool isEmpty() const;

/*
 * Method: add
 * Usage: set.add(value);
 * ------------------------
 * Adds an element to this set if it is not already there.
 */

   void add(const ValueType & value);

/*
 * Method: remove
 * Usage: set.remove(value);
 * ---------------------------
 * Removes an element from this set.  If the value was not contained in the
 * set, the set remains unchanged.
 */

   void remove(const ValueType & value);

/*
 * Method: contains
 * Usage: if (set.contains(value)) . . .
 * ---------------------------------------
 * Returns true if the specified value is in this set.
 */

   bool contains(const ValueType & value) const;

/*
 * Method: clear
 * Usage: set.clear();
 * ---------------------
 * Removes all elements from this set.
 */

   void clear();

/*
 * Method: isSubsetOf
 * Usage: if (set.isSubsetOf(set2)) . . .
 * ----------------------------------------
 * Implements the subset relation for sets.  This method returns true
 * if every element of this set is contained in set2.
 */

   bool isSubsetOf(const Set & set2) const;
```

```
┌────────────────────────────────────────────────────────────────┐
│ FIGURE 17-2  Interface for the Set class (continued)             │
```

```
/*
 * Operator: ==
 * Usage: set1 == set2
 * --------------------
 * Returns true if set1 and set2 contain the same elements.
 */

   bool operator==(const Set & set2) const;

/*
 * Operator: !=
 * Usage: set1 != set2
 * --------------------
 * Returns true if set1 and set2 are different.
 */

   bool operator!=(const Set & set2) const;

/*
 * Operator: +
 * Usage: set1 + set2
 *        set1 + value
 * --------------------
 * Returns the union of sets set1 and set2, which is the set of elements
 * that appear in at least one of the two sets.  The second form returns
 * the set formed by adding a single element.
 */

   Set operator+(const Set & set2) const;
   Set operator+(const ValueType & value) const;

/*
 * Operator: *
 * Usage: set1 * set2
 * --------------------
 * Returns the intersection of sets set1 and set2, which is the set of all
 * elements that appear in both.
 */

   Set operator*(const Set & set2) const;

/*
 * Operator: -
 * Usage: set1 - set2
 *        set1 - value
 * --------------------
 * Returns the difference of sets set1 and set2, which is all the
 * elements that appear in set1 but not set2.  The second form returns
 * the set formed by removing a single element.
 */

   Set operator-(const Set & set2) const;
   Set operator-(const ValueType & value) const;
```

FIGURE 17-2 Interface for the Set class (continued)

```
/*
 * Operator: +=
 * Usage: set1 += set2;
 *        set1 += value;
 * -----------------------
 * Adds all elements from set2 (or the single specified value) to set1.
 */

   Set & operator+=(const Set & set2);
   Set & operator+=(const ValueType & value);

/*
 * Operator: *=
 * Usage: set1 *= set2;
 * -----------------------
 * Removes any elements from set1 that are not present in set2.
 */

   Set & operator*=(const Set & set2);

/*
 * Operator: -=
 * Usage: set1 -= set2;
 *        set1 -= value;
 * -----------------------
 * Removes all elements from set2 (or a single value) from set1.
 */

   Set & operator-=(const Set & set2);
   Set & operator-=(const ValueType & value);
```

The private section of the class goes here.

```
};
```

The implementation of the class goes here.

```
#endif
```

Including high-level methods and operators as part of the **Set** class makes it easier to understand set-based algorithms, largely because the implementations of those algorithms end up looking very much like their mathematical formulations. This fact becomes particularly relevant in the discussion of graphs in Chapter 18. Graph algorithms are the most important—not to mention the most intellectually captivating—algorithms you will learn about from this book. Our experience at Stanford shows that you will learn these algorithms much more easily if the code uses the high-level operators that the expanded **Set** class provides.

Adding operators for union, intersection, and set difference requires investing some thought in the design. The fact that ∪ and ∩ don't appear on the standard keyboard suggests that it would be wise to use more conventional symbols for these operators, even if C++ allowed programmers to extend the operator set. As it happens, C++ restricts operator overloading to the *existing* operators, which means that it is necessary to choose appropriate symbols from the operators C++ already defines. Although union and set difference have intuitive representations as the operators **+** and **−**, choosing an operator to represent intersection is a bit harder.

Although the designers of the Stanford `set.h` interface considered other possibilities, the library implementation of the `Set` class uses the ***** operator to represent intersection. The ***** symbol is often used for this purpose in discussions of Boolean algebra, primarily because the result of applying multiplication to the values **0** and **1** suggests the idea of intersection:

*	0	1
0	0	0
1	0	1

As the binary multiplication table illustrates, the value of the product of two bit values is a **1** only if both input values are **1**s. In a similar way, an element is in the intersection of two sets only if it is a member of both.

Redefining the operators **+**, *****, and **−** inevitably leads clients to assume that they can use the shorthand assignment operators **+=**, ***=**, and **−=** as well. The extended `set.h` interface therefore includes these operators as well. These operators, moreover, take either a set or a single element as their right-hand side, which makes it possible, for example, to add the value **v** to a set **s** by writing

```
s += v;
```

◼ 17.3 Implementation strategies for sets

As was the case for maps, there are two common strategies for implementing the `Set` class. The approach chosen by the designers of the Standard Template Library was to use a balanced binary tree as the underlying representation. Other languages, however, typically implement sets using a hashing strategy, which is somewhat more efficient. The primary advantage of using a balanced binary tree is that doing so makes it easy to iterate through the elements of the set in sorted order.

The Java language seeks to satisfy as many clients as possible by offering both a `TreeSet` and a `HashSet` class. The `Set` class in the Stanford libraries, like its counterpart in the STL, corresponds to the `TreeSet` approach, although the libraries also export a **HashSet** class, which you will have a chance to implement in exercise 5.

The good news is that both the **TreeSet** and **HashSet** models are easy to implement in C++, as long as you make use of the classes you already have. The fundamental insight you need to develop a simple implementation is that sets and maps are essentially the same. You can easily build the **Set** class using the **Map** class. If you adopt this strategy, the private section of the **Set** class needs nothing beyond a single instance variable containing a map, as shown in Figure 17-3. The value field in the map is ignored; membership is determined by checking whether a key exists in the map. The **Map** class, however, requires a value field. As the comments in Figure 17-3 indicate, this implementation uses **bool** as the value type to suggest the idea that a particular element is either present or absent from the set.

When you define one abstraction in terms of another—as in the current proposal to implement sets by using maps—the resulting abstractions are said to be *layered.* Layered abstractions have a number of advantages. For one thing, they are usually easy to implement because much of the work can be relegated to the existing, lower-level interface.

This strategy of layering the implementation of sets on top of the implementation of maps is not in itself sufficient to write the code for the **Set** class, which exports the various high-level operations that are not part of the **Map** class. It does, however, provide a good start. Moreover, the high-level operations can easily be implemented by exploiting the existing capabilities of the **Map** class. The code for these operators appears in Figure 17-4.

FIGURE 17-3 Private section for the Set class

```
/*
 * Notes on the representation
 * ---------------------------
 * This implementation of the Set class uses a map as its underlying
 * data structure.  The value field in the map is ignored, but is
 * declared as a bool to suggest the presence or absence of a value.
 * The fact that this class is layered on top of an existing collection
 * makes it substantially easier to implement.
 */

private:

/* Instance variables */

    Map<ValueType,bool> map;                    /* Map used to store the elements    */
```

FIGURE 17-4 Implementation of the Set class

```
/*
 * Implementation notes: Set constructor and destructor
 * ----------------------------------------------------------
 * The constructor and destructor are empty because the Map class manages
 * the underlying representation.
 */

template <typename ValueType>
Set<ValueType>::Set() {
   /* Empty */
}

template <typename ValueType>
Set<ValueType>::~Set() {
   /* Empty */
}

/*
 * Implementation notes: size, isEmpty, add, remove, contains, clear
 * -----------------------------------------------------------------------
 * These methods forward their operation to the underlying Map object.
 */

template <typename ValueType>
int Set<ValueType>::size() const {
   return map.size();
}

template <typename ValueType>
bool Set<ValueType>::isEmpty() const {
   return map.isEmpty();
}

template <typename ValueType>
void Set<ValueType>::add(const ValueType & value) {
   map.put(value, true);
}

template <typename ValueType>
void Set<ValueType>::remove(const ValueType & value) {
   map.remove(value);
}

template <typename ValueType>
bool Set<ValueType>::contains(const ValueType & value) const {
   return map.containsKey(value);
}

template <typename ValueType>
void Set<ValueType>::clear() {
   map.clear();
}
```

FIGURE 17-4 Implementation of the Set class (continued)

```
/*
 * Implementation notes: isSubset
 * --------------------------------
 * This method simply checks to see whether each element of the current
 * set is an element of set2.
 */

template <typename ValueType>
bool Set<ValueType>::isSubsetOf(const Set & set2) const {
    for (ValueType value : map) {
        if (!set2.contains(value)) return false;
    }
    return true;
}

/*
 * Implementation notes: operator==, operator!=
 * ----------------------------------------------
 * These operators make use of the fact that two sets are equal only
 * if each set is a subset of the other.
 */

template <typename ValueType>
bool Set<ValueType>::operator==(const Set & set2) const {
    return isSubsetOf(set2) && set2.isSubsetOf(*this);
}

template <typename ValueType>
bool Set<ValueType>::operator!=(const Set & set2) const {
    return !(*this == set2);
}

/*
 * Implementation notes: operator+
 * --------------------------------
 * The union operator copies the current set and then adds the elements
 * from set2 to the result.
 */

template <typename ValueType>
Set<ValueType> Set<ValueType>::operator+(const Set & set2) const {
    Set<ValueType> set = *this;
    for (ValueType value : set2.map) {
        set.add(value);
    }
    return set;
}
```

FIGURE 17-4 Implementation of the Set class (continued)

```
Set<ValueType> Set<ValueType>::operator+(const ValueType & value) const {
   Set<ValueType> set = *this;
   set.add(value);
   return set;
}

/*
 * Implementation notes: operator*
 * -----------------------------------
 * The intersection operator adds elements to an empty set only if they
 * appear in both sets.
 */

template <typename ValueType>
Set<ValueType> Set<ValueType>::operator*(const Set & set2) const {
   Set<ValueType> set;
   for (ValueType value : map) {
      if (set2.contains(value)) set.add(value);
   }
   return set;
}

/*
 * Implementation notes: operator-
 * -----------------------------------
 * The set difference returns a new set consisting of the elements in
 * the current set that do not appear in set2.
 */

template <typename ValueType>
Set<ValueType> Set<ValueType>::operator-(const Set & set2) const {
   Set<ValueType> set;
   for (ValueType value : map) {
      if (!set2.contains(value)) set.add(value);
   }
   return set;
}

template <typename ValueType>
Set<ValueType> Set<ValueType>::operator-(const ValueType & value) const {
   Set<ValueType> set = *this;
   set.remove(value);
   return set;
}
```

FIGURE 17-4 Implementation of the Set class (continued)

```
/*
 * Implementation notes: shorthand assignment operators
 * -------------------------------------------------------
 * These operators modify the current set but are otherwise similar to
 * the operators that create new sets.  The only subtlety is that the
 * intersection operator must create a vector of elements that need to be
 * removed to avoid changing the set while cycling through its elements.
 */

template <typename ValueType>
Set<ValueType> & Set<ValueType>::operator+=(const Set & set2) {
   for (ValueType value : set2.map) {
      add(value);
   }
   return *this;
}

template <typename ValueType>
Set<ValueType> & Set<ValueType>::operator+=(const ValueType & value) {
   add(value);
   return *this;
}

template <typename ValueType>
Set<ValueType> & Set<ValueType>::operator*=(const Set & set2) {
   Vector<ValueType> toRemove;
   for (ValueType value : map) {
      if (!set2.contains(value)) toRemove.add(value);
   }
   for (ValueType value : toRemove) {
      remove(value);
   }
   return *this;
}

template <typename ValueType>
Set<ValueType> & Set<ValueType>::operator-=(const Set & set2) {
   for (ValueType value : set2.map) {
      remove(value);
   }
   return *this;
}

template <typename ValueType>
Set<ValueType> & Set<ValueType>::operator-=(const ValueType & value) {
   remove(value);
   return *this;
}
```

17.4 Optimizing sets of small integers

The implementation strategy in the preceding section works for any value type. That implementation, however, can be improved substantially for sets whose values are represented internally as small integers, such as enumeration types or characters.

Characteristic vectors

Suppose for the moment that you are working with a set whose elements always lie between 0 and **RANGE_SIZE** − 1, where **RANGE_SIZE** is a constant that specifies the size of the range to which element values are restricted. You can represent such sets efficiently using an array of Boolean values. The value at index position k in the array indicates whether the integer k is in the set. For example, if **elements[4]** has the value **true**, then 4 is in the set represented by the Boolean array **elements**. Similarly, if **elements[5]** is **false**, then 5 is not an element of that set.

Boolean arrays in which the elements indicate whether the corresponding index is a member of some set are called *characteristic vectors.* The following examples illustrate how the characteristic-vector strategy can be used to represent the indicated sets, assuming that **RANGE_SIZE** has the value 10:

∅

F	F	F	F	F	F	F	F	F	F
0	1	2	3	4	5	6	7	8	9

{1, 3, 5, 7, 9}

F	T	F	T	F	T	F	T	F	T
0	1	2	3	4	5	6	7	8	9

{2, 3, 5, 7}

F	F	T	T	F	T	F	T	F	F
0	1	2	3	4	5	6	7	8	9

The advantage of using characteristic vectors is that doing so makes it possible to implement the operations **add**, **remove**, and **contains** in constant time. For example, to add the element k to a set, all you have to do is set the element at index position k in the characteristic vector to **true**. Similarly, testing membership is simply a matter of selecting the appropriate element in the array.

Packed arrays of bits

Even though characteristic vectors allow highly efficient implementations in terms of their running time, storing characteristic vectors as explicit arrays can require a large amount of memory, particularly if **RANGE_SIZE** is large. To reduce the storage requirements, you can pack the elements of the characteristic vector into machine words so that the representation uses every bit in the underlying representation. Suppose, for example, that the type **unsigned long** is represented as a 32-bit value on your machine. You can then store 32 elements of a characteristic vector in a single value of type **unsigned long**, since each element of the characteristic vector requires only one bit of information. Moreover, if **RANGE_SIZE** is 256, you can store all 256 bits needed for a characteristic vector in an array of eight **unsigned long** values.

To understand how characteristic vectors can be packed into an array of machine words, imagine that you want to represent the integer set consisting of the ASCII code for the alphabetic characters. That set consists of the 26 uppercase letters with codes between 65 and 90 and the 26 lowercase letters with codes between 97 and 122. It can therefore be encoded as the following characteristic vector:

31	30	29	28	27	26	25	24	23	22	21	20	19	18	17	16	15	14	13	12	11	10	9	8	7	6	5	4	3	2	1	0	row
0	0	0	0	0	0	0	0	0	0	0	0	0	0	0	0	0	0	0	0	0	0	0	0	0	0	0	0	0	0	0	0	0
0	0	0	0	0	0	0	0	0	0	0	0	0	0	0	0	0	0	0	0	0	0	0	0	0	0	0	0	0	0	0	0	1
0	0	0	0	0	1	1	1	1	1	1	1	1	1	1	1	1	1	1	1	1	1	1	1	1	1	1	1	1	1	1	0	2
0	0	0	0	0	1	1	1	1	1	1	1	1	1	1	1	1	1	1	1	1	1	1	1	1	1	1	1	1	1	1	0	3
0	0	0	0	0	0	0	0	0	0	0	0	0	0	0	0	0	0	0	0	0	0	0	0	0	0	0	0	0	0	0	0	4
0	0	0	0	0	0	0	0	0	0	0	0	0	0	0	0	0	0	0	0	0	0	0	0	0	0	0	0	0	0	0	0	5
0	0	0	0	0	0	0	0	0	0	0	0	0	0	0	0	0	0	0	0	0	0	0	0	0	0	0	0	0	0	0	0	6
0	0	0	0	0	0	0	0	0	0	0	0	0	0	0	0	0	0	0	0	0	0	0	0	0	0	0	0	0	0	0	0	7

If you want to find the bit that corresponds to a particular integer value, the simplest approach is to use integer division and modular arithmetic. For example, suppose that you want to locate the bit corresponding to the character **'X'**, which has 88 as its ASCII code. The row number of the desired bit is 2, because there are 32 bits in each row and 88 / 32 is 2 according to the standard definition of integer division. Similarly, in row 2, you find the entry for **'X'** at bit number 24, which is the remainder of 88 divided by 32. Thus, the bit in the characteristic vector corresponding to the character **'X'** is the one highlighted in this diagram:

31	30	29	28	27	26	25	24	23	22	21	20	19	18	17	16	15	14	13	12	11	10	9	8	7	6	5	4	3	2	1	0	row
0	0	0	0	0	0	0	0	0	0	0	0	0	0	0	0	0	0	0	0	0	0	0	0	0	0	0	0	0	0	0	0	0
0	0	0	0	0	0	0	0	0	0	0	0	0	0	0	0	0	0	0	0	0	0	0	0	0	0	0	0	0	0	0	0	1
0	0	0	0	0	1	1	**1**	1	1	1	1	1	1	1	1	1	1	1	1	1	1	1	1	1	1	1	1	1	1	1	0	2
0	0	0	0	0	1	1	1	1	1	1	1	1	1	1	1	1	1	1	1	1	1	1	1	1	1	1	1	1	1	1	0	3
0	0	0	0	0	0	0	0	0	0	0	0	0	0	0	0	0	0	0	0	0	0	0	0	0	0	0	0	0	0	0	0	4
0	0	0	0	0	0	0	0	0	0	0	0	0	0	0	0	0	0	0	0	0	0	0	0	0	0	0	0	0	0	0	0	5
0	0	0	0	0	0	0	0	0	0	0	0	0	0	0	0	0	0	0	0	0	0	0	0	0	0	0	0	0	0	0	0	6
0	0	0	0	0	0	0	0	0	0	0	0	0	0	0	0	0	0	0	0	0	0	0	0	0	0	0	0	0	0	0	0	7

The fact that the highlighted bit is a **1** indicates that **'X'** is a member of the set.

Bitwise operators

In order to write code that works with arrays of bits stored in this tightly packed form, you need to learn how to use the low-level operators that C++ provides for manipulating the bits in a memory word. These operators, which are listed in Table 17-2, are called **bitwise operators.** They take values of any scalar type and interpret them as sequences of bits that correspond to their underlying representation at the hardware level.

To illustrate the behavior of the bitwise operators, let's consider a specific example. Suppose that the variables **x** and **y** have been declared as follows on a machine where the data type **short** requires 16 bits:

```
unsigned short x = 0x002A;
unsigned short y = 0xFFF3;
```

If you convert the initial values from hexadecimal to binary notation as described in Chapter 11, you can easily determine that the bit patterns for the variables **x** and **y** look like this:

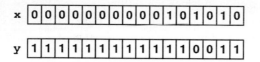

The **&**, **|**, and **^** operators each apply the logical operation specified in Table 17-2 to each bit position in the operand words. The **&** operator, for example, produces a result that has a **1** bit only in positions in which both operands have a **1** bit. Thus, if you apply the **&** operator to the bit patterns in **x** and **y**, you get this result:

```
x & y  0 0 0 0 0 0 0 0 0 0 1 0 0 0 1 0
```

TABLE 17-2 Bitwise operators in C++

x & y	Logical AND. The result has a **1** bit in positions where both x and y have a **1** bit.
x | y	Logical OR. The result has a **1** bit in positions where either x or y has a **1** bit.
x ^ y	Logical XOR. The result has a **1** bit in positions where the bits in x and y differ.
~x	Logical NOT. The result has a **1** bit where x has a **0** bit, and vice versa.
x << n	Left shift. The bits in x are shifted left n bit positions.
x >> n	Right shift. The bits in x are shifted right n bit positions.

The | and ^ operators produce the following results:

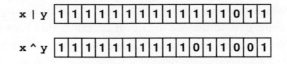

The ~ operator is a unary operator that reverses the state of every bit in its operand. For example, if you apply the ~ operator to the bit pattern in **x**, the result looks like this:

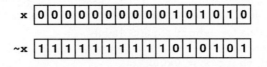

In programming, applying the ~ operation is called ***taking the complement*** of the single operand that follows the operator.

The operators **<<** and **>>** shift the bits in their left operand the number of positions specified by their right operand. The only difference between the two operations is the direction in which the shifting occurs. The **<<** operator shifts bits to the left; the **>>** operator shifts them to the right. Thus, the expression **x << 1** produces a new value in which every bit in the value of **x** is shifted one position to the left, as follows:

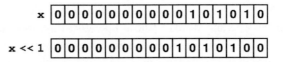

Similarly, the expression **y >> 2** produces a value in which the bits in **y** have been shifted two positions to the right, like this:

y   `1 1 1 1 1 1 1 1 1 1 1 1 0 0 1 1`

y >> 2   `0 0 1 1 1 1 1 1 1 1 1 1 1 1 0 0`

As long as the value being shifted is unsigned, bits that are shifted past the end of the word disappear and are replaced on the opposite end by 0 bits. If the value being shifted is signed, the behavior of the shift operators depends on the underlying characteristics of the hardware. For this reason, it is good practice to restrict your use of the shift operators to unsigned values, which thereby increases the portability of your code.

Implementing characteristic vectors

The bitwise operators introduced in the preceding section make it possible to implement operations on characteristic vectors in an extremely efficient way. If you want to test the state of an individual bit in a characteristic vector, all you have to do is create a value that has a 1 bit in the desired position and 0 bits everywhere else. Such a value is called a *mask* because you can use it to hide all the other bits in the word. If you apply the **&** operator to the word in the characteristic vector that contains the bit you're trying to find and the mask that corresponds to the correct bit position, all the other bits in that word will be stripped away, leaving you with a value that reflects the state of the desired bit.

To make this strategy more concrete, it helps to consider the underlying representation of a characteristic vector in more detail. The following code defines **CharacteristicVector** as a structure containing an array of words interpreted as a sequence of bits.

```
struct CharacteristicVector {
    unsigned long words[CVEC_WORDS];
};
```

where **CVEC_WORDS** is a constant defined as follows:

```
const int BITS_PER_BYTE = 8;
const int BITS_PER_LONG = BITS_PER_BYTE * sizeof(long);
const int CVEC_WORDS = (RANGE_SIZE + BITS_PER_LONG - 1)
                              / BITS_PER_LONG;
```

Given this structure, you can test a specific bit in a characteristic vector using the function **testBit**, which has the following implementation:

```
bool testBit(CharacteristicVector & cv, int k) {
    if (k < 0 || k >= RANGE_SIZE) {
        error("testBit: Bit index is out of range");
    }
    return cv.words[k / BITS_PER_LONG] & createMask(k);
}

unsigned long createMask(int k) {
    return unsigned long(1) << k % BITS_PER_LONG;
}
```

Suppose, for example, that you call **testBit(cv, 'X')**, where **cv** is bound to the characteristic vector corresponding to the set of all alphabetic characters. As discussed in the section on "Packed arrays of bits" earlier in the chapter, that characteristic vector looks like this:

```
0 0 0 0 0 0 0 0 0 0 0 0 0 0 0 0 0 0 0 0 0 0 0 0 0 0 0 0 0 0 0 0  0
0 0 0 0 0 0 0 0 0 0 0 0 0 0 0 0 0 0 0 0 0 0 0 0 0 0 0 0 0 0 0 0  1
0 0 0 0 0 1 1 1 1 1 1 1 1 1 1 1 1 1 1 1 1 1 1 1 1 1 1 1 1 1 1 0  2
0 0 0 0 0 1 1 1 1 1 1 1 1 1 1 1 1 1 1 1 1 1 1 1 1 1 1 1 1 1 1 0  3
0 0 0 0 0 0 0 0 0 0 0 0 0 0 0 0 0 0 0 0 0 0 0 0 0 0 0 0 0 0 0 0  4
0 0 0 0 0 0 0 0 0 0 0 0 0 0 0 0 0 0 0 0 0 0 0 0 0 0 0 0 0 0 0 0  5
0 0 0 0 0 0 0 0 0 0 0 0 0 0 0 0 0 0 0 0 0 0 0 0 0 0 0 0 0 0 0 0  6
0 0 0 0 0 0 0 0 0 0 0 0 0 0 0 0 0 0 0 0 0 0 0 0 0 0 0 0 0 0 0 0  7
31 30 29 28 27 26 25 24 23 22 21 20 19 18 17 16 15 14 13 12 11 10 9 8 7 6 5 4 3 2 1 0
```

The function `testBit` begins by choosing the appropriate word in the characteristic vector by evaluating the expression

```
cv.words[k / BITS_PER_LONG];
```

The subscript expression `k / BITS_PER_LONG` determines the index of the word in the characteristic vector that contains the kth bit in the entire structure. Because the character `'X'` has the ASCII value 88 and `BITS_PER_LONG` is 32, the subscript expression selects the word at index position 2, which consists of the following bits:

```
0 0 0 0 0 1 1 1 1 1 1 1 1 1 1 1 1 1 1 1 1 1 1 1 1 1 1 1 1 1 1 0
```

The function `createMask(k)` produces a mask that contains a **1** bit in the appropriate position. If `k`, for example, has the value 88, `k % BITS_PER_LONG` is 24, which means that the mask value consists of the value 1 shifted left 24 bit positions, as follows:

```
0 0 0 0 0 0 0 1 0 0 0 0 0 0 0 0 0 0 0 0 0 0 0 0 0 0 0 0 0 0 0 0
```

Because the mask has only a single **1** bit, the `&` operation in the code for `testBit` will return a nonzero value only if the corresponding bit in the characteristic vector is a **1**. If the characteristic vector contained a 0 in that bit position, there would be no bits common to both the vector and the mask, which means that the `&` operation would return a word containing only **0** bits. A word composed entirely of **0** bits has the integer value 0.

The strategy of using a mask also makes it easy to manipulate the state of individual bits in the characteristic vector. By convention, assigning the value **1** to a specific bit is called *setting* that bit; assigning the value **0** is called *clearing* the bit. You can set a particular bit in a word by applying the logical OR operation to the old value of that word and a mask containing the desired bit. You can clear a bit by applying the logical AND operation to the old value of the word and the complement of the mask. These operations are illustrated by the following definitions of the functions `setBit` and `clearBit`:

```
void setBit(CharacteristicVector & cv, int k) {
   if (k < 0 || k >= RANGE_SIZE) {
      error("setBit: Bit index is out of range");
   }
   cv.words[k / BITS_PER_LONG] |= createMask(k);
}

void clearBit(CharacteristicVector & cv, int k) {
   if (k < 0 || k >= RANGE_SIZE) {
      error("setBit: Bit index is out of range");
   }
   cv.words[k / BITS_PER_LONG] &= ~createMask(k);
}
```

Implementing the high-level set operations

Packing characteristic vectors into the bits in a word saves a large amount of space. As it happens, this same strategy also improves the efficiency of the high-level set operations of union, intersection, and set difference. The trick is to compute each word in the new characteristic vector using a single application of the appropriate bitwise operator.

As an example, the union of two sets consists of all elements that belong to either of its arguments. If you translate this idea into the realm of characteristic vectors, it is easy to see that any word in the characteristic vector of the set $A \cup B$ can be computed by applying the logical OR operation to the corresponding words in the characteristic vectors for those sets. The result of the logical OR operation has a **1** bit in those positions in which either of its operands has a **1** bit, which is exactly what you want to compute the union.

Template specialization

The characteristic vector model allows sets of characters to be implemented much more efficiently than more general sets in terms of both space and time. Despite that difference in efficiency, it doesn't make sense for the client to learn two different models for sets: one for characters and one for everything else. What you want to do instead is define two implementations of the template class and then have the compiler choose which version to use on the basis of the value type.

C++ allows you to define template classes in which you specify particular values for one or more of the template parameters of a more general type. This technique is called *template specialization.* If the client supplies a type that matches the specialized version, the compiler will use that definition instead of the more general one.

As an example, suppose that you wanted to define—as you will have a chance to do in exercise 8—a specialized implementation for the class **Set<char>** that uses a characteristic vector to store the data. The interface version of that class would look like this:

```
template <>
class Set<char> {
    class body for character sets
};
```

The empty template brackets tell the compiler that this version of the **Set** class is still defined as a template, but that there is no type variable for a client-specified type. The value type for this version of **Set** is always **char**. The same syntax applies to the implementations of the methods for the specialized class. The constructor for the **Set<char>** class therefore has the following stucture:

```
template <>
Set<char>::Set {
    implementation of the character set constructor
};
```

The private section and the implementation of the **Set<char>** class and the more general **Set<ValueType>** will certainly be different because those classes use different data models. Ideally, however, their interfaces will be the same.

Using a hybrid implementation

The predefined data type **char** has only 256 possible values. This fact makes it easy to use a characteristic vector as the underlying representation because that vector will require only 256 bits of storage. But what happens if you want to use this technique to streamline the class **Set<int>**? On a machine that uses 32-bit integers, the characteristic vector will require 2^{32} bits, which requires an unworkable amount of storage.

Even if characteristic vectors cannot represent all sets of integers, they can still be useful as long as the actual values in the set fall into a limited range. All you have to do is design a data structure that uses characteristic vectors as long as the integers stay small but then reverts to the more general binary-tree implementation if the client tries to store a value that is out of range. As a result, clients who only use integers in the restricted range get the enhanced performance associated with the characteristic vector strategy. Clients who need to define sets containing integers outside the optimal range can nonetheless use the same interface.

▰ Summary

In this chapter, you have learned about sets, which are important to computer science as both a theoretical and a practical abstraction. The fact that sets have a well-developed mathematical foundation—far from making them too abstract to be useful—increases their utility as a programming tool. Because of that theoretical foundation, you can count on sets to exhibit certain properties and obey specific rules. By coding your algorithms in terms of sets, you can build on that theoretical base to write programs that are easier to understand.

Important points in this chapter include:

- A set is an unordered collection of distinct elements. The set operations used in this book appear in Table 17-3, along with their mathematical symbols.

- Interactions among the various set operators are often easier to understand if you keep in mind certain identities that indicate that two set expressions are invariably equal. Using these identities can also improve your programming practice, because they provide you with tools to simplify set operations appearing in your code.

- The set class is straightforward to implement because much of it can be layered on top of the **Map** class, using either the tree-based or hash-based representation.

TABLE 17-3 Summary of the mathematical notation for sets

Empty set	$\emptyset$	The set containing no elements
Membership	$x \in S$	True if x is an element of S
Nonmembership	$x \notin S$	True if x is not an element of S
Equality	$A = B$	True if A and B contain exactly the same elements
Subset	$A \subseteq B$	True if all elements in A are also in B
Proper subset	$A \subset B$	True if A is a subset of B but the sets are not equal
Union	$A \cup B$	The set of elements in A, B, or both
Intersection	$A \cap B$	The set of elements in both A and B
Set difference	$A - B$	The set of elements in A that are not also in B

- Sets of integers can be implemented very efficiently using arrays of Boolean data called *characteristic vectors*. If you use the bitwise operators provided by C++, you can pack characteristic vectors into a small number of machine words and perform such set operations as union and intersection on many elements of the vector at a time.

Review questions

1. True or false: The elements of a set are unordered, so the set $\{3, 2, 1\}$ and the set $\{1, 2, 3\}$ represent the same set.

2. True or false: A set can contain multiple copies of the same element.

3. What sets are denoted by each of the following symbols: $\varnothing$, **Z**, **N**, and **R**?

4. What do the symbols $\in$ and $\notin$ mean?

5. Use an enumeration to specify the elements of the following set:

$$\{x \mid x \in \mathbf{N} \text{ and } x \leq 100 \text{ and } \sqrt{x} \in \mathbf{N}\}$$

6. Write a rule-based definition for the following set:

$$\{0, 9, 18, 27, 36, 45, 54, 63, 72, 81\}$$

7. What are the mathematical symbols for the operations union, intersection, and set difference?

8. Evaluate the following set expressions:

   a. $\{a, b, c\} \cup \{a, c, e\}$
   b. $\{a, b, c\} \cap \{a, c, e\}$
   c. $\{a, b, c\} - \{a, c, e\}$
   d. $(\{a, b, c\} - \{a, c, e\}) \cup (\{a, b, c\} - \{a, c, e\})$

9. What is the difference between a subset and a proper subset?

10. Give an example of an infinite set that is a proper subset of some other infinite set.

11. For each of the following set operations, draw Venn diagrams whose shaded regions illustrate the contents of the specified set expression:

   a. $A \cup (B \cap C)$ c. $(A - B) \cup (B - A)$
   b. $(A - C) \cap (B - C)$ d. $(A \cup B) - (A \cap B)$

12. Write set expressions that describe the shaded region in each of the following Venn diagrams:

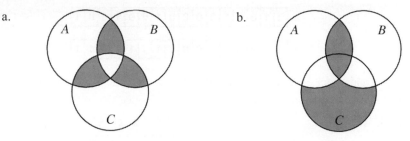

a.   b.

13. Draw Venn diagrams illustrating each of the identities in Table 17-1.

14. What is the *cardinality* of a set?

15. The general implementation of the **Set** class uses a data structure from an earlier chapter to represent the elements of a set. What is that structure? What properties make that structure useful for this purpose?

16. What is a characteristic vector?

17. What restrictions must be placed on a set in order to use characteristic vectors as an implementation strategy?

18. Assuming that **RANGE_SIZE** has the value 10, diagram the characteristic vector for the set $\{1, 4, 9\}$.

19. What set is represented by the following characteristic vector:

0	0	0	0	0	0	0	0	0	0	0	0	0	0	0	0	0	0	0	0	0	0	0	0	0	0	0	0	0	0	0	0	0
0	0	0	0	0	0	1	1	1	1	1	1	1	1	1	1	0	0	0	0	0	0	0	0	0	0	0	0	0	0	0	0	1
0	0	0	0	0	0	0	0	0	0	0	0	0	0	0	0	0	0	0	0	0	0	0	0	0	0	0	0	0	0	0	0	2
0	0	0	0	0	0	0	0	0	0	0	0	0	0	0	0	0	0	0	0	0	0	0	0	0	0	0	0	0	0	0	0	3
0	0	0	0	0	0	0	0	0	0	0	0	0	0	0	0	0	0	0	0	0	0	0	0	0	0	0	0	0	0	0	0	4
0	0	0	0	0	0	0	0	0	0	0	0	0	0	0	0	0	0	0	0	0	0	0	0	0	0	0	0	0	0	0	0	5
0	0	0	0	0	0	0	0	0	0	0	0	0	0	0	0	0	0	0	0	0	0	0	0	0	0	0	0	0	0	0	0	6
0	0	0	0	0	0	0	0	0	0	0	0	0	0	0	0	0	0	0	0	0	0	0	0	0	0	0	0	0	0	0	0	7

31 30 29 28 27 26 25 24 23 22 21 20 19 18 17 16 15 14 13 12 11 10 9 8 7 6 5 4 3 2 1 0

By consulting the ASCII chart in Table 1-2, identify the function in **<cctype>** to which this set corresponds.

20. In the diagrams used to represent characteristic vectors, an **unsigned long** is shown as taking 32 bits. Suppose that you have a machine on which a **long** takes 64 bits instead. Does the code given in the chapter continue to work?

21. Suppose that the variables **x** and **y** are of type **unsigned short** and contain the following bit patterns:

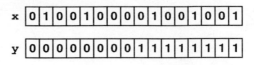

Expressing your answer as a sequence of bits, compute the value of each of the following expressions:

a. **x & y**   f. **x & ~y**

b. **x | y**   g. **~x & ~y**

c. **x ^ y**   h. **y >> 4**

d. **x ^ x**   i. **x << 3**

e. **~x**   j. **(x >> 8) & y**

22. Express the values of **x** and **y** from the preceding exercise as constants using both octal and hexadecimal notation.

23. Suppose that the variables **x** and **mask** are both declared to be of type **unsigned**, and that the value of **mask** contains a single **1** bit in some position. What expressions would you use to implement the following operations:

    a. Test the bit in **x** corresponding to the bit in **mask** to see if it is nonzero.

    b. Set the bit in **x** corresponding to the bit in **mask**.

    c. Clear the bit in **x** corresponding to the bit in **mask**.

    d. Complement the bit in **x** corresponding to the bit in **mask**.

24. Write an expression that constructs a mask of type **unsigned** in which there is a single **1** bit in bit position **k**, where bits are numbered from 0 starting at the right end of the word. For example, if **k** is 2, the expression should generate the following mask:

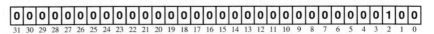

Exercises

1. To make it easier to write programs that use the **Set** class, it would be useful for the **set.h** interface to export an overloaded version of the **>>** operator to read sets from an input stream. Insofar as possible, the **>>** operator should maintain symmetry with the **<<** operator described in the chapter. In particular, the **>>** operator should require the elements of the set to be enclosed in curly braces and separated by commas.

2. Write a simple test program that uses the **>>** operator from the preceding exercise to read in two sets of strings and then display the result of calling the union, intersection, and set difference operators on those sets. A sample run of the program might look like this:

```
●○○                    SetOperations
Enter s1: {a, b, c}
Enter s2: {b, a, d}
s1 + s2 = {""}
s1 * s2 = {""}
s1 - s2 = {}
```

3. Write a function

```
Set<int> createPrimeSet(int max)
```

that returns a set of the prime numbers between 2 and **max**. A number N is prime if it has exactly two divisors, which are always 1 and the number N itself. Checking for primality, however, doesn't require you to try every possible divisor. The only numbers you need to check are the prime numbers between 2 and the square root of N. As it tests whether a number is prime, your code should make use of the fact that all potential factors must be in the set of primes you have already constructed.

4. The discussion in the chapter only sketches the implementation of the **Set** class. Complete the **Set** class by supplying the private section that defines the structure of a set and the code that implements the **Set** class as a layered abstraction on top of the tree-based version of maps.

5. As discussed in the chapter, the library implementation of sets uses balanced binary search trees to ensure that iterating over the set produces the keys in sorted order. If the order of iteration is not a concern, you can achieve better performance by using a hash table as the underlying representation. Write the interface and implementation for a **HashSet** class that adopts this strategy.

6. Write a program that implements the following procedure:

   • Read in two strings, each of which represents a sequence of bits. These strings must consist only of the characters **0** and **1** and must be exactly 16 characters long.

   • Convert each of these strings into a value of type **unsigned short** with the same internal pattern of bits. Assume that the variables used to store the converted result are named **x** and **y**.

   • Display the value of each of the following expressions as a sequence of 16 bits: **x & y, x | y, x ^ y, ~y, x & ~y**.

The operation of this program is illustrated by the following sample run:

```
● ○ ○                    BitOperations
Enter x: 0000000000101010
Enter y: 0000000000011011
  x & y = 0000000000001010
  x | y = 0000000000111011
  x ^ y = 0000000000110001
     ~y = 1111111111100100
 x & ~y = 0000000000100000
```

7. On most computer systems, the ANSI **<cctype>** interface introduced in Chapter 3 is implemented using the bitwise operators. The strategy is to use specific bit positions in a word to indicate properties that a character might have. For example, imagine that the three bits at the right end of a word are used to indicate whether a character is a digit, a lowercase letter, or an uppercase letter, as shown in this diagram:

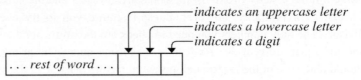

If you create an array consisting of 256 of these words—one for each character—you can implement the functions from **<cctype>** so that each function requires selecting the appropriate element of the array selection, applying one of the bitwise operators, and testing the result.

Use this strategy to implement a simplified version of the **<cctype>** interface that exports the functions **isdigit**, **islower**, **isupper**, **isalpha**, and **isalnum**. In your implementation, it is important to make sure that the implementations of **isalpha** and **isalnum** require no more operations than the other functions do.

8. Implement a template specialization of the **Set<char>** class that uses a characteristic vector instead of the usual binary tree.

9. Implement a template specialization of the **Set<int>** class that uses a characteristic vector as long as the elements are in the range 0 to 255 but that switches to the traditional representation if the client adds elements outside this range.

Chapter 18
Graphs

So I draw the world together link by link:
Yea, from Delos up to Limerick and back!

— Rudyard Kipling, "The Song of the Banjo," 1894

Many structures in the real world consist of a set of values connected by a set of links. Such a structure is called a ***graph.*** Common examples of graphs include cities connected by highways, web pages connected by hyperlinks, and courses in a college curriculum connected by prerequisites. Programmers typically refer to the individual elements—such as the cities, web pages, and courses—as ***nodes*** and the interconnections—the highways, hyperlinks, and prerequisites—as ***arcs,*** although mathematicians tend to use the terms ***vertex*** and ***edge*** instead.

Because they consist of nodes connected by a set of links, graphs are clearly similar to trees, which were introduced in Chapter 16. In fact, the only difference is that there are fewer restrictions on the structure of the connections in a graph than there are in a tree. The arcs in a graph, for example, often form cyclical patterns. In a tree, cyclical patterns are illegal because of the requirement that every node must be linked to the root by a unique line of descent. Because trees have restrictions that do not apply to graphs, graphs are a more general type that includes trees as a subset. Thus, every tree is a graph, but there are some graphs that are not trees.

In this chapter, you will learn about graphs from both a practical and a theoretical perspective. Learning to work with graphs as a programming tool is useful because they come up in a surprising number of contexts. Mastering the theory is extremely valuable as well, because doing so often makes it possible to find much more efficient solutions to problems with considerable practical importance.

18.1 The structure of a graph

The easiest way to get a sense of the structure of a graph is to consider a simple example. Suppose that you work for a small airline that serves 10 major cities in the United States with the routes shown in Figure 18-1. The labeled circles represent cities and constitute the nodes of the graph. The lines between the cities represent airline routes and constitute the arcs.

Although graphs are often used to represent geographical relationships, it is important to keep in mind that the graph is defined purely in terms of the nodes and connecting arcs. The layout is unimportant to the abstract concept of a graph. For example, the following diagram represents the same graph as Figure 18-1:

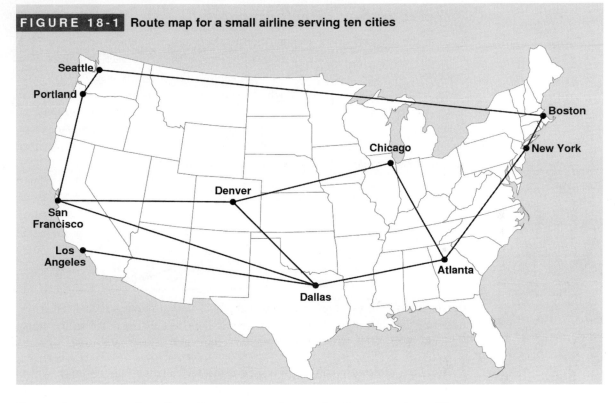

FIGURE 18-1   Route map for a small airline serving ten cities

The nodes representing the cities are no longer in the correct positions geographically, but the connections remain the same.

You can go one step further and eliminate the geometrical relationships altogether. Mathematicians use the tools of set theory to define a graph as the combination of two sets, which are typically called V and E after the mathematical terms *vertex* and *edge*. The airline graph, for example, consists of the following sets:

$V =$ { **Atlanta, Boston, Chicago, Dallas, Denver, Los Angeles,
New York, Portland, San Francisco, Seattle** }

$E =$ { **Atlanta↔Chicago, Atlanta↔Dallas, Atlanta↔New York,
Boston↔New York, Boston↔Seattle, Chicago↔Denver,
Dallas↔Denver, Dallas↔Los Angeles, Dallas↔San Francisco,
Denver↔San Francisco, Portland↔San Francisco,
Portland↔Seattle** }

Beyond its theoretical significance as a mathematical formalism, defining a graph in terms of sets also simplifies the implementation, because the `Set` class already implements many of the necessary operations.

Directed and undirected graphs

Because the diagram gives no indication to the contrary, the arcs in Figure 18-1 represent flights that operate in both directions. Thus, the fact that there is a connection between Atlanta and Chicago implies that there is also one between Chicago and Atlanta. A graph in which every connection runs both ways is called an **undirected graph.** In many cases, it makes sense to use **directed graphs,** in which each arc has a direction. For example, if your airline operates a plane from San Francisco to Dallas but has the plane stop in Denver on the return flight, that piece of the route map will look like this in a directed graph:

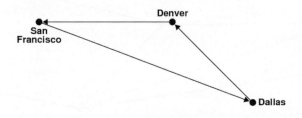

The diagrams in this text represent directed graphs only if the arcs include an arrow indicating their direction. If the arrows are missing—as they are in the airline graph in Figure 18-1—you can assume the graph is undirected.

Arcs in a directed graph are specified using the notation *start→finish,* where *start* and *finish* are the nodes on each side of the directed arc. Thus, the triangular route shown in the preceding diagram consists of the following arcs:

San Francisco→**Dallas**
Dallas→**Denver**
Denver→ **San Francisco**

Although arcs in an undirected graph are often written using a double-headed arrow, you don't actually need a separate symbol. If a graph contains an undirected arc, you can always represent it as a pair of directed arcs. For example, if a graph contains a bidirectional arc **Portland↔Seattle**, you can represent that fact by including both **Portland**→**Seattle** and **Seattle**→**Portland** in the set of arcs. Because it is always possible to simulate undirected graphs using directed ones, most graph packages—including the ones introduced in this chapter—define a single graph type that supports directed graphs. If you want to define an undirected graph, all you have to do is create two arcs for every connection, one in each direction.

Paths and cycles

The arcs in a graph represent direct connections, which correspond to nonstop flights in the airline example. The fact that the arc **San Francisco**→**New York** does not exist in the example graph does not mean that you cannot travel between those cities on this airline. If you want to fly from San Francisco to New York, you can use any of the following routes:

> **San Francisco** $\rightarrow$ **Dallas** $\rightarrow$ **Atlanta** $\rightarrow$ **New York**
> **San Francisco** $\rightarrow$ **Denver** $\rightarrow$ **Chicago** $\rightarrow$ **Atlanta** $\rightarrow$ **New York**
> **San Francisco** $\rightarrow$ **Portland** $\rightarrow$ **Seattle** $\rightarrow$ **Boston** $\rightarrow$ **New York**

A sequence of arcs that allow you to move from one node to another is called a *path.* A path that begins and ends at the same node, such as the path

> **Dallas** $\rightarrow$ **Atlanta** $\rightarrow$ **Chicago** $\rightarrow$ **Denver** $\rightarrow$ **Dallas**

is called a *cycle.* A *simple path* is a path that contains no duplicated nodes. Similarly, a *simple cycle* is a cycle that has no duplicated nodes other than the common node that appears at the beginning and the end.

Nodes in a graph that are connected directly by an arc are called *neighbors.* If you count the number of neighbors for a particular node, that number is called the *degree* of that node. In the airline graph, for example, **Dallas** has degree 4 because it has direct connections to four cities: **Atlanta**, **Denver**, **Los Angeles**, and **San Francisco**. By contrast, **Los Angeles**, has degree 1 because it connects only to **Dallas**. In the case of directed graphs, it is useful to differentiate the concepts of *in-degree,* which indicates the number of arcs coming into that node, and *out-degree,* which indicates the number of arcs leaving that node.

Connectivity

An undirected graph is *connected* if there is a path from each node to every other node. For example, the airline graph in Figure 18-1 is connected according to this rule. The definition of a graph, however, does not require that all nodes be connected in a single unit. For example, the graph

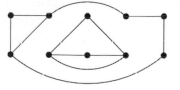

is an example of an unconnected graph, because no path links the cluster of four nodes in the interior of the diagram to any of the other nodes.

Given any unconnected graph, you can always decompose it into a unique set of subgraphs in which each subgraph is connected, but no arcs lead from one subgraph to another. These subgraphs are called the *connected components* of the graph. The connected components of the preceding graph diagram look like this:

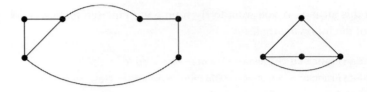

For directed graphs, the concept of connectivity is somewhat more complicated. If a directed graph contains a path connecting every pair of nodes, the graph is **strongly connected.** A directed graph is **weakly connected** if eliminating the directions on the arcs creates a connected graph. For example, the graph

is not strongly connected because you cannot travel from the node on the lower right to the node on the upper left moving only in the directions specified by the arcs. On the other hand, it is weakly connected because the undirected graph formed by eliminating the arrows is a connected graph. If you reverse the direction of the top arc, the resulting graph

is strongly connected.

18.2 Representation strategies

Like most abstract structures, graphs can be implemented in several different ways. The primary feature that differentiates these implementations is the strategy used to represent connections between nodes. In practice, the most common strategies are:

- Storing the connections for each node in an *adjacency list*
- Storing the connections for the entire graph in an *adjacency matrix*
- Storing the connections for each node as a *set of arcs*

These representation strategies are described in greater detail in the sections that follow.

Representing connections using an adjacency list

The simplest way to represent connections in a graph is to store within the data structure for each node a list of the nodes to which it is connected. This structure is called an **adjacency list.** For example, in the now-familiar airline graph

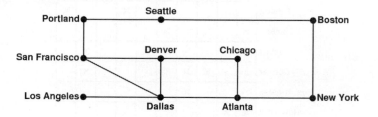

the adjacency lists for each node look like this:

Atlanta	→	(Chicago, Dallas, New York)
Boston	→	(New York, Seattle)
Chicago	→	(Atlanta, Denver)
Dallas	→	(Atlanta, Denver, Los Angeles)
Denver	→	(Chicago, Dallas, San Francisco)
Los Angeles	→	(Dallas)
New York	→	(Atlanta, Boston)
Portland	→	(San Francisco, Seattle)
San Francisco	→	(Dallas, Denver, Portland)
Seattle	→	(Boston, Portland)

Representing connections using an adjacency matrix

Although lists provide a convenient way to represent the connections in a graph, they can be inefficient when an operation requires searching through the list of arcs associated with a node. For example, if you use the adjacency list representation, determining whether two nodes are connected requires $O(D)$ time, where D represents the degree of the originating node. If the nodes in a graph all have a small number of neighbors, the cost of searching through this list is small. If, however, the nodes in a graph tend to have a large number of neighbors, the cost becomes more significant.

If efficiency becomes a concern, you can reduce the cost of checking for connections to constant time by representing the arcs in a two-dimensional array called an **adjacency matrix** that shows which nodes are connected. The adjacency matrix for the airline graph looks like this:

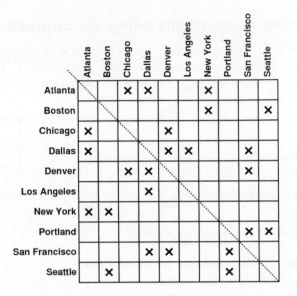

For an undirected graph of this sort, the adjacency matrix is *symmetric,* which means that the entries match when they are reflected across the main diagonal, which is shown in the figure as a dotted line.

To use the adjacency matrix approach, you must associate each node with an index number that specifies the column or row number in the table corresponding to that node. As part of the concrete structure for the graph, the implementation needs to allocate a two-dimensional grid with one row and one column for each node in the graph. The elements of the array are Boolean values. If the entry in `matrix[`*start*`][`*finish*`]` is `true`, there is an arc *start*→*finish* in the graph.

In terms of execution time, using an adjacency matrix is considerably faster than using an adjacency list. On the other hand, a matrix requires $O(N^2)$ storage space, where N is the number of nodes. For most graphs, the adjacency list representation tends to be more efficient in terms of space, although some graphs violate this principle. In the adjacency list representation, each node has a list of connections, which, in the worst case, will be D_{max} entries long, where D_{max} is the maximum degree of any node in the graph, which is therefore the maximum number of arcs emanating from a single node. The space cost for adjacency lists is therefore $O(N \times D_{max})$. If most of the nodes are connected to each other, D_{max} will be relatively close to N, which means that the cost of representing connections is comparable for the two approaches. If, on the other hand, the graph contains many nodes but relatively few interconnections, the adjacency list representation can save a considerable amount of space.

Although the dividing line is never precisely defined, graphs for which the value of D_{max} is small in comparison to N are said to be *sparse.* Graphs in which D_{max} is comparable to N are considered **dense.** Often, the algorithms and representation strategies you use for graphs depend on whether you expect those graphs to be sparse or dense. The analysis in the preceding paragraph, for example, indicates that the list representation is likely to be more appropriate for sparse graphs; if you are working with dense graphs, the matrix representation may well be a better choice.

Representing connections using a set of arcs

The motivation behind the third strategy for representing connections in a graph comes from the mathematical formulation of a graph as a set of nodes coupled with a set of arcs. If you were content to store no information with each node other than its name, you could define a graph as a pair of sets, as follows:

```
struct StringBasedGraph {
    Set<string> nodes;
    Set<string> arcs;
};
```

The set of nodes contains the names of every node in the graph. The set of arcs contains pairs of node names connected in some way that makes it easy to separate the node names representing the beginning and end of each arc.

The primary advantages of this representation are its conceptual simplicity and the fact that it mirrors so precisely the mathematical definition. The set-based representation does, however, have two important limitations. First, finding the neighbors for any particular node requires going through every arc in the entire graph. Second, most applications need to associate additional data with the individual nodes and arcs. For example, many graph algorithms assign a numeric value to each of the arcs that indicates the *cost* of traversing that arc, which may or may not refer to actual monetary cost. In Figure 18-2, for example, each arc in the airline graph is labeled with the distance in miles between the endpoints. You could use this information to implement a frequent-flier program that assigns points to travelers based on the distance flown.

Fortunately, neither of these problems is particularly difficult to solve. Iterating over the nodes and arcs in a graph is easy if you represent them using a collection class that supports iteration. You can, moreover, incorporate additional data into a graph by using structures to represent the nodes and arcs.

Given the fact that C++ is an object-oriented language, you would expect that graphs, nodes, and arcs would be represented as objects, with a new class definition for each level of the hierarchy. That design is certainly appropriate for this problem, and one possible implementation along these lines appears in section 18.5.

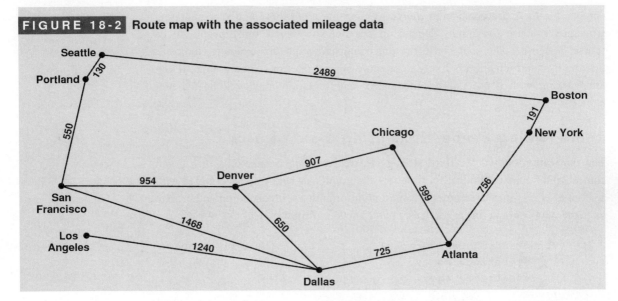

FIGURE 18-2 Route map with the associated mileage data

The following section, however, defines each of these types as structures rather than classes. There are two reasons for that decision. First, using structures results in a simpler implementation that makes it easier to focus on high-level operations rather than the details of object representation. Second, low-level structures are frequently used in practice because the contexts in which graphs arise vary so widely that it is hard to fit those applications into a common framework. For that reason, it often makes sense to add the relevant parts of the graph abstraction to the underlying implementation of some other data structure. If you do so, the code will probably resemble the structure-based implementation more closely than the object-based implementation presented later in the chapter.

18.3 A low-level graph abstraction

This section outlines the design of a low-level graph package in which the three levels of the hierarchy—the graph as a whole, the individual nodes, and the arcs that connect those nodes—are represented using C++ structure types. As a first cut at the final design, this section introduces a structure-based interface that defines three structures, as follows:

- A structure type called **SimpleGraph**, whose name is specifically chosen to differentiate this type from the **Graph** class introduced later in the chapter. As in the mathematical definition of a graph, a **SimpleGraph** contains two sets: one that specifies the nodes in the graph and one that specifies the arcs. Moreover, since nodes in this formulation have names, it is useful for the **SimpleGraph** structure to include a map that allows clients to translate from names into the corresponding node structure.

- A structure type called **Node** that contains the name of the node and a set that indicates which arcs extend from that node to other nodes in the graph.

- A structure type called **Arc** specifying the endpoints of the arc, along with a numeric value representing the cost.

This informal description of the data types provides almost enough information for you to write the necessary definitions, but there is one important consideration that needs to be included as part of the design process. The **SimpleGraph** structure conceptually "contains" **Node** values not only as part of its set of nodes but also as components of the elements in the set of arcs. Similarly, **Arc** values appear in two places because both the **SimpleGraph** and the **Node** structure specify a set of arcs. In each case, the nodes and arcs that appear in different parts of these structures must be identical whenever they refer to the same entity in the abstract structure. For example, the **Node** corresponding to **Atlanta** must be the *same* **Node** no matter whether it appears in the top-level set of nodes or in one of the internal arcs. These nodes cannot simply be copies of one another, because in that case changes to one copy would not be reflected in the others.

The critical implication of this observation is that the sets and structures used to represent the graph cannot contain **Node** and **Arc** values directly. The need to share common structures means that all the internal references to these structures must specify *pointers* to **Node** and **Arc** values. The sets in the **SimpleGraph** structure, therefore, must use **Node *** and **Arc *** as their element type and not the underlying structure types themselves. The same is true for the set of arcs in the **Node** structure and the references to nodes in the **Arc** structure. Figure 18-3 shows the structure of a low-level graph interface, which is called **graphtypes.h** to differentiate it from the more sophisticated **graph.h** interface that appears in section 18.5.

Figure 18-3 also illustrates a new feature of C++ that deserves some explanation. The structure types **Node** and **Arc** are defined so that each type refers to the other. The **Node** structure includes pointers to **Arc**s, and the **Arc** structure includes pointers to **Node**s. This mutual recursion in the definition of the type makes it impossible to declare either type in terms of types that have already been defined, as C++ requires. One of the definitions must come first and must include a pointer to a type that has yet to be defined.

C++ gets around this problem by allowing you to declare that an identifier is a class or a structure name without specifying the actual contents. All you have to do is replace the body of the class or structure with a semicolon, in much the same way that you write a function prototype. The lines

```
struct Node;
struct Arc;
```

FIGURE 18-3 Structure-based graph abstraction

```
/*
 * File: graphtypes.h
 * -------------------
 * This file defines low-level data structures that represent graphs.
 */

#ifndef _graphtypes_h
#define _graphtypes_h

#include <string>
#include "map.h"
#include "set.h"

struct Node;      /* Forward references to these two types so  */
struct Arc;       /* that the C++ compiler can recognize them. */

/*
 * Type: SimpleGraph
 * -----------------
 * This type represents a graph and consists of a set of nodes, a set of
 * arcs, and a map that creates an association between names and nodes.
 */

struct SimpleGraph {
   Set<Node *> nodes;
   Set<Arc *> arcs;
   Map<std::string,Node *> nodeMap;
};

/*
 * Type: Node
 * ----------
 * This type represents an individual node and consists of the
 * name of the node and the set of arcs from this node.
 */

struct Node {
   std::string name;
   Set<Arc *> arcs;
};

/*
 * Type: Arc
 * ---------
 * This type represents an individual arc and consists of pointers
 * to the endpoints, along with the cost of traversing the arc.
 */

struct Arc {
   Node *start;
   Node *finish;
   double cost;
};

#endif
```

in Figure 18-3 tell the compiler that **Node** and **Arc** are structure names. It is then possible to declare pointers to either of these structures before its definition appears. Such definitions are called *forward references.*

Defining graphs in terms of sets has many advantages. In particular, this strategy means that the data structure closely parallels the mathematical formulation of a graph, which is defined in terms of sets. The layered approach also has significant advantages in terms of simplifying the implementation. For example, defining graphs in terms of sets eliminates the need to define a separate iteration facility for graphs, because sets already support iteration. Thus, if you want to iterate over the nodes in the graph **g**, all you need to write is

```
for (Node *node : g.nodes) {
    code to process an individual node
}
```

In addition to simplifying the process of iteration, defining graphs in terms of sets makes it possible to apply higher-level set operations like union and intersection. Theoretical computer scientists often formulate graph algorithms in terms of these operations, and having them available to clients often makes those algorithms easier to code.

Unlike the interface files you've seen so far in this book, the **graphtypes.h** interface introduces three structure types but no classes or methods. As a result, it does not require an implementation, so there is no need for a **graphtypes.cpp** file. The fact that the interface does not provide a suite of methods for working with graphs, nodes, and arcs forces clients to define their own tools to create the required data structure. For example, the code in Figure 18-4 uses several helper functions to create the airline graph introduced earlier in the chapter and then calls the **printAdjacencyLists** function to cycle though each of the cities and display the names of the cities that can be reached in one step, as follows:

```
⊖ ⊝ ⊖                      AirlineGraph
Atlanta -> Chicago, Dallas, New York
Boston -> New York, Seattle
Chicago -> Atlanta, Denver
Dallas -> Atlanta, Denver, Los Angeles, San Francisco
Denver -> Chicago, Dallas, San Francisco
Los Angeles -> Dallas
New York -> Atlanta, Boston
Portland -> San Francisco, Seattle
San Francisco -> Dallas, Denver, Portland
Seattle -> Boston, Portland
```

FIGURE 18-4 Program to create the airline graph

```cpp
/*
 * File: AirlineGraph.cpp
 * -----------------------
 * This program initializes the graph for the airline example and then
 * prints the adjacency lists for each of the cities.
 */

#include <iostream>
#include <string>
#include "graphtypes.h"
#include "set.h"
using namespace std;

/* Function prototypes */

void printAdjacencyLists(SimpleGraph & g);
void initAirlineGraph(SimpleGraph & airline);
void addFlight(SimpleGraph & airline, string c1, string c2, int miles);
void addNode(SimpleGraph & g, string name);
void addArc(SimpleGraph & g, Node *n1, Node *n2, double cost);

/* Main program */

int main() {
   SimpleGraph airline;
   initAirlineGraph(airline);
   printAdjacencyLists(airline);
   return 0;
}

/*
 * Function: printAdjacencyLists
 * Usage: printAdjacencyLists(g);
 * ---------------------------------
 * Prints the adjacency list for each city in the graph.
 */

void printAdjacencyLists(SimpleGraph & g) {
   for (Node *node : g.nodes) {
      cout << node->name << " -> ";
      bool first = true;
      for (Arc *arc : node->arcs) {
         if (!first) cout << ", ";
         cout << arc->finish->name;
         first = false;
      }
      cout << endl;
   }
}
```

FIGURE 18-4 Program to create the airline graph (continued)

```
/*
 * Function: initAirlineGraph
 * Usage: initAirlineGraph(airline);
 * ------------------------------------
 * Initializes the airline graph to hold the flight data from Figure 18-2.
 * In a real application, the program would almost certainly read this
 * information from a data file.
 */

void initAirlineGraph(SimpleGraph & airline) {
   addNode(airline, "Atlanta");
   addNode(airline, "Boston");
   addNode(airline, "Chicago");
   addNode(airline, "Dallas");
   addNode(airline, "Denver");
   addNode(airline, "Los Angeles");
   addNode(airline, "New York");
   addNode(airline, "Portland");
   addNode(airline, "San Francisco");
   addNode(airline, "Seattle");
   addFlight(airline, "Atlanta", "Chicago", 599);
   addFlight(airline, "Atlanta", "Dallas", 725);
   addFlight(airline, "Atlanta", "New York", 756);
   addFlight(airline, "Boston", "New York", 191);
   addFlight(airline, "Boston", "Seattle", 2489);
   addFlight(airline, "Chicago", "Denver", 907);
   addFlight(airline, "Dallas", "Denver", 650);
   addFlight(airline, "Dallas", "Los Angeles", 1240);
   addFlight(airline, "Dallas", "San Francisco", 1468);
   addFlight(airline, "Denver", "San Francisco", 954);
   addFlight(airline, "Portland", "San Francisco", 550);
   addFlight(airline, "Portland", "Seattle", 130);
}

/*
 * Function: addFlight
 * Usage: addFlight(airline, c1, c2, miles);
 * ------------------------------------------
 * Adds an arc in each direction between the cities c1 and c2.
 */

void addFlight(SimpleGraph & airline, string c1, string c2, int miles) {
   Node *n1 = airline.nodeMap[c1];
   Node *n2 = airline.nodeMap[c2];
   addArc(airline, n1, n2, miles);
   addArc(airline, n2, n1, miles);
}
```

FIGURE 18-4 Program to create the airline graph (continued)

```
/*
 * Function: addNode
 * Usage: addNode(g, name);
 * --------------------------
 * Adds a new node with the specified name to the graph.
 */

void addNode(SimpleGraph & g, string name) {
   Node *node = new Node;
   node->name = name;
   g.nodes.add(node);
   g.nodeMap[name] = node;
}

/*
 * Function: addArc
 * Usage: addArc(g, n1, n2, cost);
 * -------------------------------
 * Adds a directed arc to the graph connecting n1 to n2.
 */

void addArc(SimpleGraph & g, Node *n1, Node *n2, double cost) {
   Arc *arc = new Arc;
   arc->start = n1;
   arc->finish = n2;
   arc->cost = cost;
   g.arcs.add(arc);
   n1->arcs.add(arc);
}
```

If you think carefully about the output shown in the sample run, the fact that the city names appear in alphabetical order might come as a surprise. The sets on which the graph is built are, at least in their mathematical form, unordered collections. The **for** loops in the algorithm process the **Node** and **Arc** pointers in the order of the memory addresses at which those structures appear. Since memory addresses bear no relation to the city names, the alphabetical ordering of the output is something of a mystery.

The reason for this seemingly odd behavior is that most C++ runtime systems allocate heap memory in the order in which the requests appear. The initialization code in Figure 18-4 creates the cities and connection information in alphabetical order, which means that the node for the second city appears at a higher memory address than the node for the first. Thus, the fact that the output is so nicely ordered is simply a coincidence and may not be true on all platforms. As you will see in Chapter 20, it is possible to extend the definition of the **Set** class so that its clients—like the **Graph** class in this example—can redefine the order in which elements appear.

18.4 Graph traversals

As you saw in the preceding example, it is easy to cycle through the nodes in a graph, as long as you are content to process the nodes in the order imposed by the set abstraction. Many graph algorithms, however, require you to process the nodes in an order that takes the connections into account. Such algorithms typically start at some node and then advance from node to node by moving along the arcs, performing some operation on each node. The precise nature of the operation depends on the algorithm, but the process of performing that operation—whatever it is—is called *visiting* the node. The process of visiting each node in a graph by moving along its arcs is called *traversing* the graph.

In Chapter 16, you learned that several traversal strategies exist for trees, of which the most important are preorder, postorder, and inorder traversals. Like trees, graphs also support more than one traversal strategy. For graphs, the two fundamental traversal algorithms are *depth-first search* and *breadth-first search,* which are described in the next two sections.

To make the mechanics of the algorithms easier to understand, the implementations of depth- and breadth-first search assume that the client has supplied a function called **visit** that takes care of whatever processing is required for each individual node. The goal of a traversal is to call **visit** once—and only once—on every node in an order determined by the connections. Because graphs often have many different paths that lead to the same node, ensuring that the traversal algorithm does not visit the same node many times requires additional bookkeeping. The implementations in the next two sections define a set of nodes called **visited** to keep track of the nodes that have already been processed. If the traversal algorithm encounters a node that is already in the **visited** set, that node must have been visited at an earlier point in the process.

Depth-first search

The depth-first strategy for traversing a graph is similar to the preorder traversal of trees and has the same recursive structure. The only additional complication is that graphs can contain cycles. As a result, it is essential to keep track of the nodes that have already been visited. The code that implements depth-first search starting at a particular node appears in Figure 18-5.

In this implementation, **depthFirstSearch** is a wrapper function whose only purpose is to introduce the **visited** set used to keep track of nodes that have already been processed. The function **visitUsingDFS** visits the current node and then calls itself recursively for each node directly accessible from the current one.

FIGURE 18-5 **Code to execute a depth-first search**

```
/*
 * Function: depthFirstSearch
 * Usage: depthFirstSearch(node);
 * ---------------------------------
 * Initiates a depth-first search beginning at the specified node.
 */

void depthFirstSearch(Node *node) {
   Set<Node *> visited;
   visitUsingDFS(node, visited);
}

/*
 * Function: visitUsingDFS
 * Usage: visitUsingDFS(node, visited);
 * ---------------------------------------
 * Executes a depth-first search beginning at the specified node that
 * avoids revisiting any nodes in the visited set.
 */

void visitUsingDFS(Node *node, Set<Node *> & visited) {
   if (visited.contains(node)) return;
   visit(node);
   visited.add(node);
   for (Arc *arc : node->arcs) {
      visitUsingDFS(arc->finish, visited);
   }
}
```

The depth-first strategy is most easily understood by tracing its operation in the context of a simple example, such as the airline graph introduced at the beginning of the chapter:

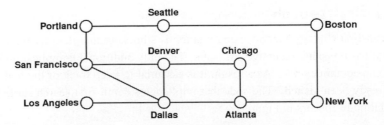

In this rendering of the graph, the nodes are drawn as open circles to indicate that they have not yet been visited. As the algorithm proceeds, each of these circles is marked with a number recording the order in which that node was processed.

Suppose that you initiate the depth-first search by making the following call:

```
depthFirstSearch(airline.nodeMap["San Francisco"]);
```

The call to the **depthFirstSearch** function itself creates an empty **visited** set and then hands control off to the recursive **visitUsingDFS** function. The first call visits the **San Francisco** node, which is recorded in the diagram as follows:

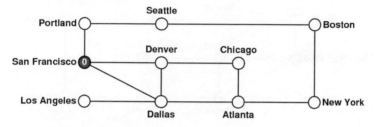

The code then makes several recursive calls to **visitUsingDFS**, one for each cycle of the loop

```
for (Arc *arc : node->arcs) {
    visitUsingDFS(arc->finish, visited);
}
```

The order in which these calls occur depends on the order in which the **for** statement steps through the arcs. Assuming that the **for** loop processes the nodes in alphabetical order, the first cycle of the loop calls **visitUsingDFS** with the **Dallas** node, which leads to the following state:

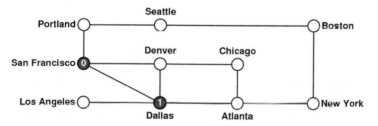

Given the way the code is written, the program must complete the entire call involving the **Dallas** node before it considers the other possible routes leaving the **San Francisco** node. The next node to be visited is therefore the city reachable from **Dallas** that appears first alphabetically, which is **Atlanta**:

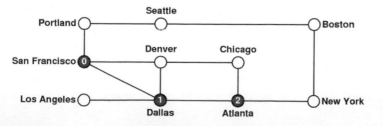

The overall effect of the depth-first search algorithm is to explore a single path in the graph as far as possible before backtracking to complete the exploration of paths at higher levels. From the **Atlanta** node, the process will continue to follow the path by choosing the starting point that appears first in the alphabetical list of neighbors. The depth-first exploration therefore continues with the nodes **Chicago** and **Denver**, which results in the following situation:

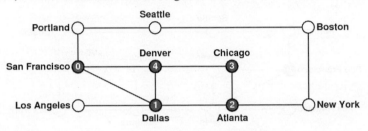

From **Denver**, however, forward progress becomes impossible. Every one of the connections from the **Denver** node has already been visited and therefore returns immediately. The recursive process therefore returns to **Chicago**, where it also finds no connections to unexplored territory. The recursive backtracking process then returns to **Atlanta**, where it can now pick up where it left off and explore the **New York** link. As always, the depth-first algorithm explores this path as far as it can, which leads to the following configuration:

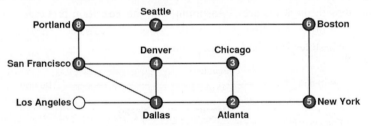

From here, the process will back up all the way to the **Dallas** node, from which it can pick up **Los Angeles**:

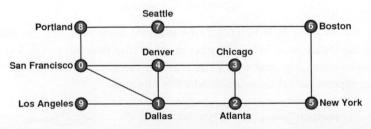

If you think about the depth-first algorithm in relation to other algorithms you've seen, you will realize that its operation is exactly the same as that of the maze-solving algorithm in Chapter 9. In that algorithm, it was necessary to mark squares along the path to avoid cycling forever around a loop in the maze. The marks in the maze are therefore analogous to the nodes in the `visited` set in the depth-first search implementation.

Breadth-first search

Although depth-first search has many important uses, the strategy has drawbacks that make it inappropriate for certain applications. The biggest problem with the depth-first approach is that it explores an entire path beginning at one neighbor before it goes back and looks at the other nearby neighbors. If you were trying to discover the shortest path between two nodes in a large graph, using depth-first search would take you all the way to the far reaches of the graph, even if your destination were one step away along a different path.

The breadth-first search algorithm gets around this problem by visiting each node in an order determined by how close it is to the starting node, measured in terms of the number of arcs along the shortest possible path. When you measure distance by counting arcs, each arc constitutes one *hop.* Thus, the essence of breadth-first search is that you visit the starting node first, then the nodes that are one hop away, followed by the nodes two hops away, and so on.

To get a more concrete sense of this algorithm, suppose that you want to apply a breadth-first traversal to the airline graph, again starting at the **San Francisco** node. The first phase of the algorithm simply visits the starting node:

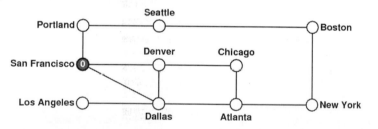

The next phase visits the nodes that are one hop away, as follows:

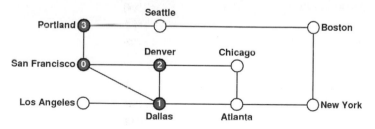

From here, the algorithm goes on to explore the nodes that are two hops away:

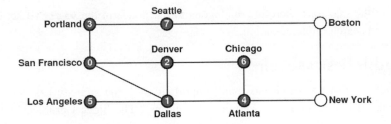

In the final phase, the algorithm completes its exploration of the graph by visiting the nodes that are three hops from the start:

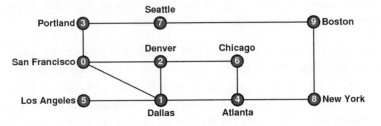

The easiest way to implement the breadth-first algorithm is to use a queue of unprocessed nodes. At each step in the process, you enqueue the neighbors of the current node. Because the queue is processed in order, all nodes that are one hop away from the starting node will appear earlier in the queue than nodes that are two hops away, and so forth. An implementation of this strategy appears in Figure 18-6.

FIGURE 18-6   Code to execute a breadth-first search

```
/*
 * Function: breadthFirstSearch
 * Usage: breadthFirstSearch(node);
 * ------------------------------------
 * Initiates a breadth-first search beginning at the specified node.
 */

void breadthFirstSearch(Node *node) {
    Set<Node *> visited;
    Queue<Node *> queue;
    queue.enqueue(node);
    while (!queue.isEmpty()) {
        node = queue.dequeue();
        if (!visited.contains(node)) {
            visit(node);
            visited.add(node);
            for (Arc *arc : node->arcs) {
                queue.enqueue(arc->finish);
            }
        }
    }
}
```

18.5 Defining a `Graph` class

The `graphtypes.h` interface, as it appears in Figure 18-3, leaves much to be desired. In particular, the existing version of the interface uses low-level structures to represent a graph and consequently takes no advantage of the object-oriented features of C++. The use of C-style structures, moreover, means that there are no methods associated with graphs, which forces clients to develop their own tools. The sections that follow outline two possible strategies for replacing the low-level graph package with a more sophisticated object-oriented design.

Using classes for graphs, nodes, and arcs

If the primary goal in redesigning the `graph.h` interface is to take maximum advantage of object-oriented design, the obvious strategy is to replace each of the low-level structures with a class. With this strategy, the interface would export a `Graph` class in the place of the `SimpleGraph` structure, along with classes corresponding to the `Node` and `Arc` types. The private fields in each of those classes would presumably match those in the corresponding structure. Clients, however, would gain access to those fields through method calls instead of through direct references.

Although this design is workable, it turns out to be cumbersome in practice. To understand why, it is important to note that graphs are typically used in a way that differs from the more familiar container classes such as arrays, stacks, queues, and sets. These more conventional collections contain values of some client-defined type. In this text, for example, you have seen programs that declare variables of type `Stack<double>` and `Set<string>`. The type within the angle brackets specifies the value type and is used as a template parameter for the class definition. The value type, however, plays no essential role in the implementation of the collection class itself.

For graphs, the situation is different. The elements of a graph are the nodes and arcs. Those structures, however, are an integral part of the graph and contain information required to maintain the overall data structure. Nodes, for example, must keep track of the set of arcs to other nodes; arcs need to keep track of their endpoints. At the same time, clients may want to associate additional data with each node or arc, depending on the application. Thus, nodes and arcs are hybrid structures that contain data required by the client along with data required by the implementation.

In most object-oriented languages, the usual strategy to use in situations of this kind is subclassing. In this model, the graph package itself would define base classes for nodes and arcs that contain the information necessary to represent the graph structure. Clients needing to include additional data would do so by extending these base classes to create new subclasses with additional fields and methods. For reasons that you will have a chance to explore more fully in Chapter 19, this approach is not ideal for C++. The fundamental problem is that dynamic memory allocation and inheritance don't always work together in C++ as seamlessly as they do in other languages, to the point that it is worth adopting a different approach.

Implementing `Graph` as a parameterized class

Fortunately, C++ templates make it possible to design a `Graph` class that takes advantage of the power of object-oriented design while retaining the simplicity of the low-level, structure-based approach. The basic idea behind this design is to export a parameterized `Graph` class that lets the client choose types for the nodes and arcs. Those types, however, cannot be chosen arbitrarily but must instead adhere to a few basic rules that allow them to function correctly in the context of a graph. The required fields are essentially the ones that appear in the low-level structures. Thus, the type the client chooses to represent a node must contain

- A string field called **name** that specifies the name of the node
- A field called **arcs** that specifies the set of arcs that begin at this node

The type chosen to represent an arc must contain

- Fields called **start** and **finish** that indicate the endpoints of the arc

Beyond the required fields, the types used to represent nodes and arcs may contain additional information required for the client's application.

The fields in the client-defined **Node** and **Arc** types must be internally consistent in the sense that all references to nodes and arcs must use the client type. Thus, the elements in the set of arcs contained in each node must be pointers to the client's arc type. In precisely the same way, the two node pointers in the arc structure must be declared as pointers to the client's node type.

The `Graph` class must have access to the required fields in the node and arc types. One way to provide that access is to make these fields public, as they are in any structure type. An alternative strategy that supports better encapsulation is to declare these fields in the private section of a class, but to give the `Graph` class access to them using a **friend** declaration.

A simple example will prove helpful in clarifying these rules. The code in Figure 18-7 defines two classes—**City** and **Flight**—each of which has no public instance variables. Each of these classes, however, contains the required private fields and defines **Graph<City,Flight>** as a friend.

FIGURE 18-7 Redefinition of the airline graph using classes

```cpp
class City;        /* Forward references to these two types so  */
class Flight;      /* that the C++ compiler can recognize them. */

/*
 * Class: City
 * -----------
 * This class defines the node type for the airport graph.
 */

class City {

public:
   string getName() {
      return name;
   }

private:
   string name;
   Set<Flight *> arcs;
   string airportCode;
   friend class Graph<City,Flight>;
};

/*
 * Class: Flight
 * -------------
 * This class defines the arc type for the airport graph.
 */

class Flight {

public:
   City *getStart() {
      return start;
   }

   City *getFinish() {
      return finish;
   }

   int getDistance() {
      return distance;
   }

   void setDistance(int miles) {
      distance = miles;
   }

private:
   City *start;
   City *finish;
   int distance;
   friend class Graph<City,Flight>;
};
```

Given these definitions of **City** and **Flight**, the airline graph itself is then an instance of the **Graph** template class specialized with the appropriate node and arc types, as follows:

```
Graph<City,Flight> airlineGraph;
```

Table 18-1 shows the methods exported by the **graph.h** interface in tabular form. Figure 18-8 shows the actual contents of the interface. As you can see from either format, the **graph.h** interface often exports more than one version of each method to make the methods as convenient as possible for clients to use.

TABLE 18-1 Entries exported by the **graph.h** interface

Constructor

Graph<*nodetype, arctype*>()	Creates an empty graph with no nodes and no arcs.

Methods

size()	Returns the number of nodes in the graph.
isEmpty()	Returns **true** if the graph contains no nodes.
clear()	Removes all the nodes and arcs from the graph.
addNode(*name*) **addNode**(*node*)	Adds the node to the graph. The first form constructs a new node from the name; the second adds a node constructed by the client.
removeNode(*name*) **removeNode**(*node*)	Removes a node from the graph, along with all arcs involving that node.
getNode(*name*)	Returns the node associated with *name*. If no node exists with the specified name, **getNode** returns **NULL**.
addArc(s_1, s_2) **addArc**(n_1, n_2) **addArc**(*arc*)	Adds an arc to the graph connecting the two nodes. The first two forms add an arc connecting the specified nodes; the third form adds an arc constructed by the client.
removeArc(s_1, s_2) **removeArc**(n_1, n_2) **removeArc**(*arc*)	Removes any arcs connecting the specified nodes.
isConnected(s_1, s_2) **isConnected**(n_1, n_2)	Returns **true** if there is an arc connecting the two nodes.
getNodeSet()	Returns the set of all nodes in a graph.
getArcSet()	Returns the set of all arcs in a graph.
getArcSet(*name*) **getArcSet**(*node*)	Returns the set of all arcs leaving the specified node.
getNeighbors(*name*) **getNeighbors**(*node*)	Returns the set of all nodes that are neighbors of the current node, in the sense that there is an arc from the specified node to the neighbor.

FIGURE 18-8 Interface for a parameterized Graph class

```
/*
 * File: graph.h
 * --------------
 * This file is the interface for a flexible graph package that exports
 * a parameterized Graph class.
 */

#ifndef _graph_h
#define _graph_h

#include <string>
#include "map.h"
#include "set.h"

/*
 * Class: Graph<NodeType,ArcType>
 * ------------------------------
 * This class represents a graph with the specified node and arc types.
 * The NodeType and ArcType parameters indicate the record or object types
 * used for nodes and arcs, respectively.  These types can contain any
 * fields or methods required by the client, but must contain the following
 * fields required by the Graph package itself:
 *
 * The NodeType definition must include:
 *   - A string field called name
 *   - A Set<ArcType *> field called arcs
 *
 * The ArcType definition must include:
 *   - A NodeType * field called start
 *   - A NodeType * field called finish
 */

template <typename NodeType,typename ArcType>
class Graph {

public:

/*
 * Constructor: Graph
 * Usage: Graph<NodeType,ArcType> g;
 * ---------------------------------
 * Creates an empty Graph object.
 */

   Graph();

/*
 * Destructor: ~Graph
 * ------------------
 * Frees the internal storage allocated to represent the graph.
 */

   ~Graph();
```

☞

FIGURE 18-8   Interface for a parameterized Graph class (continued)

```
/*
 * Method: size
 * Usage: int size = g.size();
 * ----------------------------
 * Returns the number of nodes in the graph.
 */

   int size() const;

/*
 * Method: isEmpty
 * Usage: if (g.isEmpty()) . . .
 * --------------------------------
 * Returns true if the graph is empty.
 */

   bool isEmpty() const;

/*
 * Method: clear
 * Usage: g.clear();
 * --------------------
 * Reinitializes the graph to be empty, freeing any heap storage.
 */

   void clear();

/*
 * Method: addNode
 * Usage: g.addNode(name);
 *        g.addNode(node);
 * -------------------------
 * Adds a node to the graph.  The first form creates the node from
 * the name.  The second form takes a node pointer created by the client.
 * Both forms return a pointer to the added node, although that value is
 * typically ignored.
 */

   NodeType *addNode(std::string name);
   NodeType *addNode(NodeType *node);

/*
 * Method: removeNode
 * Usage: g.removeNode(name);
 *        g.removeNode(node);
 * -----------------------------
 * Removes a node from the graph, where the node can be specified
 * either by its name or as a pointer value.  Removing a node also
 * removes all arcs that contain that node.
 */

   void removeNode(std::string name);
   void removeNode(NodeType *node);
```

FIGURE 18-8   Interface for a parameterized Graph class (continued)

```
/*
 * Method: getNode
 * Usage: NodeType *node = g.getNode(name);
 * -------------------------------------------
 * Looks up a node in the name table attached to the graph and
 * returns a pointer to that node.  If no node with the specified
 * name exists, getNode returns NULL.
 */

   NodeType *getNode(std::string name) const;

/*
 * Method: addArc
 * Usage: g.addArc(s1, s2);
 *        g.addArc(n1, n2);
 *        g.addArc(arc);
 * -----------------------
 * Adds an arc to the graph.  The endpoints of the arc can be specified
 * either as strings indicating the names of the nodes or as pointers to
 * the node structures.  All versions return a pointer to the added arc,
 * although that value is typically ignored.
 */

   ArcType *addArc(std::string s1, std::string s2);
   ArcType *addArc(NodeType *n1, NodeType *n2);
   ArcType *addArc(ArcType *arc);

/*
 * Method: removeArc
 * Usage: g.removeArc(s1, s2);
 *        g.removeArc(n1, n2);
 *        g.removeArc(arc);
 * -------------------------
 * Removes an arc from the graph, where the arc can be specified in any
 * of three ways: by the names of its endpoints, by the node pointers
 * at its endpoints, or as an arc pointer.  If more than one arc
 * connects the specified endpoints, all of them are removed.
 */

   void removeArc(std::string s1, std::string s2);
   void removeArc(NodeType *n1, NodeType *n2);
   void removeArc(ArcType *arc);
```

FIGURE 18-8 Interface for a parameterized Graph class (continued)

```
/*
 * Method: isConnected
 * Usage: if (g.isConnected(s1, s2)) . . .
 *        if (g.isConnected(n1, n2)) . . .
 * -----------------------------------------
 * Returns true if the graph contains an arc between the specified nodes.
 * Nodes can be specified either by name or as pointers to node objects.
 */

   bool isConnected(std::string s1, std::string s2) const;
   bool isConnected(NodeType *n1, NodeType *n2) const;

/*
 * Method: getNodeSet
 * Usage: for (NodeType *node : g.getNodeSet()) . . .
 * --------------------------------------------------
 * Returns the set of all nodes in the graph.
 */

   Set<NodeType *> & getNodeSet();

/*
 * Method: getArcSet
 * Usage: for (ArcType *arc : g.getArcSet()) . . .
 *        for (ArcType *arc : g.getArcSet(node)) . . .
 *        for (ArcType *arc : g.getArcSet(name)) . . .
 * -----------------------------------------------------
 * Returns the set of all arcs in the graph or, in the second and
 * third forms, the arcs that start at the specified node, which
 * can be indicated either as a pointer or by name.
 */

   Set<ArcType *> & getArcSet();
   Set<ArcType *> & getArcSet(NodeType *node);
   Set<ArcType *> & getArcSet(std::string name);

/*
 * Method: getNeighbors
 * Usage: for (NodeType *node : g.getNeighbors(node)) . . .
 *        for (NodeType *node : g.getNeighbors(name)) . . .
 * -------------------------------------------------------
 * Returns the set of nodes that are neighbors of the specified
 * node, which can be indicated either as a pointer or by name.
 */

   Set<NodeType *> getNeighbors(NodeType *node);
   Set<NodeType *> getNeighbors(std::string node);
```

☞

FIGURE 18-8 **Interface for a parameterized Graph class (continued)**

```
/*
 * Methods: copy constructor and assignment operator
 * --------------------------------------------------
 * These methods implement deep copying for graphs.
 */

   Graph(const Graph & src);
   const Graph & operator=(const Graph & src);
```

> The private section of the class goes here.

```
};
```

> The implementation of the class goes here.

```
#endif
```

The private section of the **Graph** class requires the sets of nodes and arcs, along with a map to translate node names into the corresponding node structures. The contents of the private section appear in Figure 18-9. The implementation of the **Graph** class is simpler than that of the other collection classes, given that much of the complexity has been shifted to the **Set** and **Map** classes on which **Graph** is based. The code for the **Graph** class appears in Figure 18-10.

FIGURE 18-9 **Private section for the Graph class**

```
/*
 * Notes on the representation
 * ---------------------------
 * The Graph class is built as a layered abstraction on top of the Set
 * and Map classes.  Most of the complexity appears in the underlying
 * implementations.
 */

private:

/* Instance variables */

   Set<NodeType *> nodes;                 /* The set of nodes in the graph */
   Set<ArcType *> arcs;                   /* The set of arcs in the graph  */
   Map<std::string,NodeType *> nodeMap;   /* A map from names and nodes    */

/* Private methods */

   void deepCopy(const Graph & src);
   NodeType *getExistingNode(std::string name) const;
```

FIGURE 18-10   Implementation of the Graph class

```
/*
 * Implementation notes: Graph constructor and destructor
 * ------------------------------------------------------
 * The only initialization required at this level is creating empty data
 * structures, which is performed automatically by the underlying classes.
 * The destructor, however, must free the individual arc and node
 * structures as well.  Calling clear is sufficient to accomplish this task.
 */

template <typename NodeType,typename ArcType>
Graph<NodeType,ArcType>::Graph() {
   /* Empty */
}

template <typename NodeType,typename ArcType>
Graph<NodeType,ArcType>::~Graph() {
   clear();
}

/*
 * Implementation notes: size, isEmpty
 * ------------------------------------
 * These methods are defined in terms of the node set, so the Graph
 * class simply forwards the requests to the Set class.
 */

template <typename NodeType,typename ArcType>
int Graph<NodeType,ArcType>::size() const {
   return nodes.size();
}

template <typename NodeType,typename ArcType>
bool Graph<NodeType,ArcType>::isEmpty() const {
   return nodes.isEmpty();
}

/*
 * Implementation notes: clear
 * ---------------------------
 * The implementation of clear frees all nodes and arcs.
 */

template <typename NodeType,typename ArcType>
void Graph<NodeType,ArcType>::clear() {
   for (NodeType *node : nodes) {
      delete node;
   }
   for (ArcType *arc : arcs) {
      delete arc;
   }
   arcs.clear();
   nodes.clear();
   nodeMap.clear();
}
```

FIGURE 18-10   Implementation of the Graph class (continued)

```
/*
 * Implementation notes: addNode
 * -------------------------------
 * The addNode method adds the node to the set of nodes for the graph and
 * to the map from names to nodes.
 */

template <typename NodeType,typename ArcType>
NodeType *Graph<NodeType,ArcType>::addNode(std::string name) {
   if (nodeMap.containsKey(name)) {
      error("addNode: Node " + name + " already exists");
   }
   NodeType *node = new NodeType();
   node->name = name;
   return addNode(node);
}

template <typename NodeType,typename ArcType>
NodeType *Graph<NodeType,ArcType>::addNode(NodeType *node) {
   nodes.add(node);
   nodeMap[node->name] = node;
   return node;
}

/*
 * Implementation notes: removeNode
 * -------------------------------
 * The removeNode method removes the specified node but must also
 * remove any arcs in the graph containing the node.  To avoid
 * changing the node set during iteration, this implementation
 * creates a vector of arcs that require deletion.
 */

template <typename NodeType,typename ArcType>
void Graph<NodeType,ArcType>::removeNode(std::string name) {
   removeNode(getExistingNode(name));
}

template <typename NodeType,typename ArcType>
void Graph<NodeType,ArcType>::removeNode(NodeType *node) {
   Vector<ArcType *> toRemove;
   for (ArcType *arc : arcs) {
      if (arc->start == node || arc->finish == node) {
         toRemove.add(arc);
      }
   }
   for (ArcType *arc : toRemove) {
      removeArc(arc);
   }
   nodes.remove(node);
}
```

FIGURE 18-10 Implementation of the Graph class (continued)

```cpp
/*
 * Implementation notes: getNode, getExistingNode
 * ------------------------------------------------
 * The getNode method simply looks up the name in the map, which correctly
 * returns NULL if the name is not found.  Other methods in the
 * implementation call the private method getExistingNode instead,
 * which checks for a NULL value and signals an error.
 */

template <typename NodeType,typename ArcType>
NodeType *Graph<NodeType,ArcType>::getNode(std::string name) const {
   return nodeMap.get(name);
}

template <typename NodeType,typename ArcType>
NodeType *Graph<NodeType,ArcType>::getExistingNode(std::string name) const {
   NodeType *node = nodeMap.get(name);
   if (node == NULL) error("No node named " + name);
   return node;
}

/*
 * Implementation notes: addArc
 * -----------------------------
 * The addArc method appears in three forms, as described in the interface.
 */

template <typename NodeType,typename ArcType>
ArcType *Graph<NodeType,ArcType>::addArc(std::string s1, std::string s2) {
   return addArc(getExistingNode(s1), getExistingNode(s2));
}

template <typename NodeType,typename ArcType>
ArcType *Graph<NodeType,ArcType>::addArc(NodeType *n1, NodeType *n2) {
   ArcType *arc = new ArcType();
   arc->start = n1;
   arc->finish = n2;
   return addArc(arc);
}

template <typename NodeType,typename ArcType>
ArcType *Graph<NodeType,ArcType>::addArc(ArcType *arc) {
   arc->start->arcs.add(arc);
   arcs.add(arc);
   return arc;
}
```

FIGURE 18-10	Implementation of the Graph class (continued)

```
/*
 * Implementation notes: removeArc
 * --------------------------------
 * These methods remove arcs from the graph, which is ordinarily a simple
 * matter of removing the arc from two sets: the set of arcs in the graph
 * as a whole and the set of arcs in the starting node.  The methods that
 * remove an arc specified by its endpoints, however, must take account of
 * the possibility that there is more than one arc and remove all of them.
 */

template <typename NodeType,typename ArcType>
void Graph<NodeType,ArcType>::removeArc(std::string s1, std::string s2) {
   removeArc(getExistingNode(s1), getExistingNode(s2));
}

template <typename NodeType,typename ArcType>
void Graph<NodeType,ArcType>::removeArc(NodeType *n1, NodeType *n2) {
   Vector<ArcType *> toRemove;
   for (ArcType *arc : arcs) {
      if (arc->start == n1 && arc->finish == n2) {
         toRemove.add(arc);
      }
   }
   for (ArcType *arc : toRemove) {
      removeArc(arc);
   }
}

template <typename NodeType,typename ArcType>
void Graph<NodeType,ArcType>::removeArc(ArcType *arc) {
   arc->start->arcs.remove(arc);
   arcs.remove(arc);
}

/*
 * Implementation notes: isConnected
 * ---------------------------------
 * Node n1 is connected to n2 if any of the arcs leaving n1 finish at n2.
 */

template <typename NodeType,typename ArcType>
bool Graph<NodeType,ArcType>::isConnected(std::string s1,
                                          std::string s2) const {
   return isConnected(getExistingNode(s1), getExistingNode(s2));
}

template <typename NodeType,typename ArcType>
bool Graph<NodeType,ArcType>::isConnected(NodeType *n1, NodeType *n2) const {
   for (ArcType *arc : n1->arcs) {
      if (arc->finish == n2) return true;
   }
   return false;
}
```

FIGURE 18-10   Implementation of the Graph class (continued)

```cpp
/*
 * Implementation notes: getNodeSet, getArcSet
 * --------------------------------------------
 * These methods simply return the set requested by the client.  For
 * efficiency, the sets are returned by reference, because doing so
 * eliminates the need to copy the set.
 */

template <typename NodeType,typename ArcType>
Set<NodeType *> & Graph<NodeType,ArcType>::getNodeSet() {
   return nodes;
}

template <typename NodeType,typename ArcType>
Set<ArcType *> & Graph<NodeType,ArcType>::getArcSet() {
   return arcs;
}

template <typename NodeType,typename ArcType>
Set<ArcType *> & Graph<NodeType,ArcType>::getArcSet(NodeType *node) {
   return node->arcs;
}

template <typename NodeType,typename ArcType>
Set<ArcType *> & Graph<NodeType,ArcType>::getArcSet(std::string name) {
   return getArcSet(getExistingNode(name));
}

/*
 * Implementation notes: getNeighbors
 * ----------------------------------
 * This implementation recomputes the set each time, which is reasonably
 * efficient if the degree of the node is small.
 */

template <typename NodeType,typename ArcType>
Set<NodeType *> Graph<NodeType,ArcType>::getNeighbors(NodeType *node) {
   Set<NodeType *> nodes;
   for (ArcType *arc : node->arcs) {
      nodes.add(arc->finish);
   }
   return nodes;
}

template <typename NodeType,typename ArcType>
Set<NodeType *> Graph<NodeType,ArcType>::getNeighbors(std::string name) {
   return getNeighbors(getExistingNode(name));
}
```

FIGURE 18-10 Implementation of the Graph class (continued)

```
/*
 * Implementation notes: copy constructor and assignment operator
 * ----------------------------------------------------------------
 * These methods ensure that copying a graph creates an entirely new
 * parallel structure of nodes and arcs.
 */

template <typename NodeType,typename ArcType>
const Graph<NodeType,ArcType> &
     Graph<NodeType,ArcType>::operator=(const Graph & src) {
   if (this != &src) {
      clear();
      deepCopy(src);
   }
   return *this;
}

template <typename NodeType,typename ArcType>
Graph<NodeType,ArcType>::Graph(const Graph & src) {
   deepCopy(src);
}

/*
 * Private method: deepCopy
 * --------------------------
 * This method reallocates all the nodes and arcs to ensure that the
 * structures are disjoint.
 */

template <typename NodeType,typename ArcType>
void Graph<NodeType,ArcType>::deepCopy(const Graph & other) {
   for (NodeType *oldNode : other.nodes) {
      NodeType *newNode = new NodeType();
      *newNode = *oldNode;
      newNode->arcs.clear();
      addNode(newNode);
   }
   for (ArcType *oldArc : other.arcs) {
      ArcType *newArc = new ArcType();
      *newArc = *oldArc;
      newArc->start = getExistingNode(oldArc->start->name);
      newArc->finish = getExistingNode(oldArc->finish->name);
      addArc(newArc);
   }
}
```

18.6 Finding shortest paths

Because graphs arise in many applications that have commercial importance, a considerable amount of research has been invested in developing effective algorithms for solving graph-related problems. Of these problems, one of the most interesting is that of finding a path in a graph from one node to another that has the smallest possible cost when evaluated according to some metric. This metric need not be economic. Although you might be interested in finding the least expensive path between two nodes for certain applications, you can use the same algorithm to find a path with the shortest overall distance, the smallest number of hops, or the least travel time.

As a concrete example, suppose that you want to find the path from San Francisco to Boston that has the shortest total distance, as computed by the mileage values shown on the arcs in Figure 18-2. Is it better to go through Portland and Seattle, or should you instead go through Dallas, Atlanta, and New York? Or is there perhaps some less obvious route that is shorter still?

With graphs as simple as the route map of this tiny airline, it is easy to compute the answer just by adding up the length of the arcs along all possible paths. As the graph grows larger, however, this approach can become unworkable. In general, the number of paths between two nodes in a graph grows in an exponential fashion, which means that the running time of the explore-all-paths approach is $O(2^N)$. As you know from the discussion of computational complexity in Chapter 10, problems whose solutions require exponential running time are considered to be intractable. If you want to find the shortest path through a graph in a reasonable time, it is essential to use a more efficient algorithm.

The most commonly used algorithm for finding shortest paths was discovered by Edsger W. Dijkstra in 1959. Dijkstra's algorithm for finding shortest paths is a particular example of a class of algorithms called *greedy algorithms,* in which you find the overall answer by making a series of locally optimal decisions. Greedy algorithms do not work for every problem, but are quite useful in solving the problem of finding the shortest path.

At its essence, the core of Dijkstra's algorithm for finding the shortest path—or, more generally, the path whose arcs have the minimum total cost—can be expressed as follows: explore all paths from the starting node in order of increasing total path cost until you encounter a path that takes you to your destination. This path must be the best one, because you have already explored all paths beginning at the starting node that have a lower cost. In the context of the specific problem of finding the shortest path, Dijkstra's algorithm can be implemented as shown in Figure 18-11.

FIGURE 18-11 Implementation of Dijkstra's algorithm for finding the shortest path

```
/*
 * Function: findShortestPath
 * Usage: Vector<Arc *> path = findShortestPath(start, finish);
 * ----------------------------------------------------------------
 * Finds the shortest path between the nodes start and finish using
 * Dijkstra's algorithm, which keeps track of the shortest paths in
 * a priority queue.  The function returns a vector of arcs, which is
 * empty if start and finish are the same node or if no path exists.
 */

Vector<Arc *> findShortestPath(Node *start, Node *finish) {
   Vector<Arc *> path;
   PriorityQueue< Vector<Arc *> > queue;
   Map<string,double> fixed;
   while (start != finish) {
      if (!fixed.containsKey(start->name)) {
         fixed.put(start->name, getPathCost(path));
         for (Arc *arc : start->arcs) {
            if (!fixed.containsKey(arc->finish->name)) {
               path.add(arc);
               queue.enqueue(path, getPathCost(path));
               path.remove(path.size() - 1);
            }
         }
      }
      if (queue.isEmpty()) {
         path.clear();
         return path;
      }
      path = queue.dequeue();
      start = path[path.size() - 1]->finish;
   }
   return path;
}

/*
 * Function: getPathCost
 * Usage: double cost = getPathCost(path);
 * ----------------------------------------------------------------
 * Returns the total cost of the path, which is just the sum of the
 * costs of the arcs.
 */

double getPathCost(const Vector<Arc *> & path) {
   double cost = 0;
   for (Arc *arc : path) {
      cost += arc->cost;
   }
   return cost;
}
```

The code for **findShortestPath** makes more sense if you think carefully about the data structures it uses. The implementation declares three local variables, as follows:

- The variable **path** keeps track of the minimum path and consists of a vector of arcs. The first arc in the vector starts at the origin and proceeds to the first intermediate stop. Each subsequent path begins where the preceding one left off, continuing on in this way until the final arc ends at the destination. If there is no path between the requested nodes, **findShortestPath** indicates that fact by returning an empty vector.

- The variable **queue** is a queue of paths, ordered so that paths in the queue are sorted in order of increasing cost. This queue therefore differs from the first-in/first-out discipline of traditional queues and is instead a *priority queue,* in which the client can specify a priority value for each element. The code for **findShortestPath** assumes that this functionality has been implemented in a class called **PriorityQueue**, as described in Chapter 16. This class operates identically to the standard **Queue** class with the exception of the **enqueue** method, which takes a second argument indicating the priority, as follows:

  ```
  void enqueue(ValueType element, double priority);
  ```

  As in conventional English usage, smaller priority numbers come first in the queue, so that elements entered with priority 1 are processed before any elements with priority 2. Because each path is entered into the priority queue in order of distance, each call to **dequeue** returns the shortest path remaining in the queue. The Stanford C++ libraries export the **PriorityQueue** class through the **pqueue.h** interface.

- The variable **fixed** is a map that associates each city name with the minimum distance to that city, as soon as that distance becomes known. Whenever a path is dequeued from the priority queue, you know the path must indicate the shortest route to the node at the end of that path, unless you have already found a shorter path ending at that node. Thus, whenever you dequeue a path from the priority queue, you can note that its distance is now known by storing the minimum distance in the map **fixed**.

The operation of **findShortestPath** is illustrated in Figure 18-12, which shows the steps involved in computing the shortest path from San Francisco to Boston in the airline graph from Figure 18-2.

FIGURE 18-12   Steps in the execution of Dijkstra's algorithm

Fix the distance to **San Francisco** at 0
Process the arcs out of **San Francisco (Dallas, Denver, Portland)**
     Enqueue the path: **San Francisco → Dallas** (1468)
     Enqueue the path: **San Francisco → Denver** (954)
     Enqueue the path: **San Francisco → Portland** (550)
Dequeue the shortest path: **San Francisco → Portland** (550)
Fix the distance to **Portland** at 550
Process the arcs out of **Portland (San Francisco, Seattle)**
     Ignore **San Francisco** because its distance is known
     Enqueue the path: **San Francisco → Portland → Seattle** (680)
Dequeue the shortest path: **San Francisco → Portland → Seattle** (680)
Fix the distance to **Seattle** at 680
Process the arcs out of **Seattle (Boston, Portland)**
     Enqueue the path: **San Francisco → Portland → Seattle → Boston** (3169)
     Ignore **Portland** because its distance is known
Dequeue the shortest path: **San Francisco → Denver** (954)
Fix the distance to **Denver** at 954
Process the arcs out of **Denver (Chicago, Dallas, San Francisco)**
     Ignore **San Francisco** because its distance is known
     Enqueue the path: **San Francisco → Denver → Chicago** (1861)
     Enqueue the path: **San Francisco → Denver → Dallas** (1604)
Dequeue the shortest path: **San Francisco → Dallas** (1468)
Fix the distance to **Dallas** at 1468
Process the arcs out of **Dallas (Atlanta, Denver, Los Angeles, San Francisco)**
     Ignore **Denver** and **San Francisco** because their distances are known
     Enqueue the path: **San Francisco → Dallas → Atlanta** (2193)
     Enqueue the path: **San Francisco → Dallas → Los Angeles** (2708)
Dequeue the shortest path: **San Francisco → Denver → Dallas** (1604)
Ignore **Dallas** because its distance is known
Dequeue the shortest path: **San Francisco → Denver → Chicago** (1861)
Fix the distance to **Chicago** at 1861
Process the arcs out of **Chicago (Atlanta, Denver)**
     Ignore **Denver** because its distance is known
     Enqueue the path: **San Francisco → Denver → Chicago → Atlanta** (2460)
Dequeue the shortest path: **San Francisco → Dallas → Atlanta** (2193)
Fix the distance to **Atlanta** at 2193
Process the arcs out of **Atlanta (Chicago, Dallas, New York)**
     Ignore **Chicago** and **Dallas** because their distances are known
     Enqueue the path: **San Francisco → Dallas → Atlanta → New York** (2949)
Dequeue the shortest path: **San Francisco → Denver → Chicago → Atlanta** (2460)
Ignore **Atlanta** because its distance is known
Dequeue the shortest path: **San Francisco → Dallas → Los Angeles** (2708)
Fix the distance to **Los Angeles** at 2708
Process the arcs out of **Los Angeles (Dallas)**
     Ignore **Dallas** because its distance is known
Dequeue the shortest path: **San Francisco → Dallas → Atlanta → New York** (2949)
Fix the distance to **New York** at 2949
Process the arcs out of **New York (Atlanta, Boston)**
     Ignore **Atlanta** because its distance is known
     Enqueue the path: **San Francisco → Dallas → Atlanta → New York → Boston** (3140)
Dequeue the shortest path: **San Francisco → Dallas → Atlanta → New York → Boston** (3140)

As you read through the implementation of Dijkstra's algorithm, it is useful to keep the following points in mind:

- *Paths are explored in order of the total distance rather than the number of hops.* Thus, the connections beginning with **San Francisco** → **Portland** → **Seattle** are explored before those of either **San Francisco** → **Denver** or **San Francisco** → **Dallas**, because the total distance is shorter.

- *The distance to a node is fixed when a path is dequeued, not when it is enqueued.* The first path to Boston stored in the priority queue is the one that goes through Portland and Seattle, which is not the shortest available path. The total distance along the path **San Francisco** → **Portland** → **Seattle** → **Boston** is 3169. Because the minimum distance is only 3140, the **San Francisco** → **Portland** → **Seattle** → **Boston** path is still in the priority queue when the algorithm finishes its operation.

- *The arcs from each node are scanned at most once.* The inner loop of the algorithm is executed only when the distance to that node is fixed, which happens only once for each node. As a result, the total number of cycles executed within the inner loop is the product of the number of nodes and the maximum number of arcs leading from a node. A complete analysis of Dijkstra's algorithm is beyond the scope of this text, but the running time is $O(M \log N)$, where N is the number of nodes and M is either N or the number of arcs, whichever is larger.

18.7 Algorithms for searching the web

As noted in the introduction to this chapter, the web is a graph in which the nodes are the individual pages and the arcs are the hyperlinks that take you from one page to another. In contrast to the graphs you have seen in this chapter, the graph for the web is huge. The number of pages on the web runs well into the billions, and the number of links is larger still.

In order to find something useful in that vast collection of pages, most people use a search engine to produce a list of those pages most likely to be of interest. Typical search engines operate by scanning the entire web—this process is called *crawling* and is carried out by many computers working in parallel—and then using that information to create an index indicating which pages contain a particular word or phrase. Given the scale of the web, however, the index alone is not sufficient. Unless the query terms are extremely specific, the list of all pages containing those terms will be unmanageably long. Search engines must therefore sort their results so pages that appear early in the list are the ones most likely to be of interest. Coming up with an algorithm to rank the importance of each page is the primary challenge in designing an effective search engine.

The Google PageRank algorithm

The best-known strategy for sorting web pages is Google's *PageRank algorithm,* which assigns each page a value that reflects the importance of that page based on the structure of the web graph as a whole. Although the name suggests the idea of ranking web pages, PageRank is in fact named after Larry Page, who designed the algorithm together with Google cofounder Sergey Brin while both were graduate students at Stanford University.

At one level, the idea behind the PageRank algorithm is simply that a page becomes more important if other pages link to it. In a sense, each page on the web represents an endorsement of the importance of the pages to which it links. All links, however, do not confer the same level of endorsement. A link from a page that is recognized as authoritative carries more weight than a link coming from a less credible source. This observation suggests a minor reformulation of the earlier characterization of importance: a page becomes more important if *important* pages link to it.

The fact that the importance of a page varies along with the importance of the pages that link to it suggests that the ranking of a page will fluctuate up and down as the rankings of other pages change. The PageRank algorithm therefore proceeds as a series of successive approximations. At the beginning, all pages are given equal weight. In subsequent iterations, the ranking of each page is used to adjust the rankings of the pages to which it points. Eventually, this process converges to a stable point in which the ranking of each page provides a measure of its importance as determined by the link structure of the web.

Another way to describe the effect of the PageRank algorithm is that the final ranking of each page represents the probability of reaching that page by following links on the web at random. Processes that proceed by making random choices without regard to previous decisions are called *Markov processes* after the Russian mathematician Andrei Markov (1856–1922) who was among the first to analyze their mathematical properties.

A tiny example of the PageRank calculation

Given that the actual web is too large to serve as an effective instructional example, it makes sense to start with a much smaller example. The diagram in Figure 18-13 shows the graph of a tiny web consisting of five pages, identified by the letters **A**, **B**, **C**, **D**, and **E**. The arcs in the graph represent the links between pages. For example, page **A** links to each of the other pages, while page **B** links only to page **E**.

The first step in the PageRank algorithm is to assign each page an initial ranking that is simply the probability of choosing that page at random out of the entire

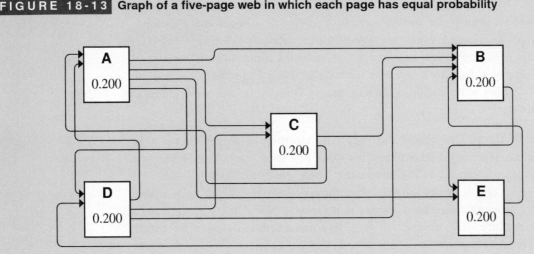

FIGURE 18-13 **Graph of a five-page web in which each page has equal probability**

collection of pages. There are five pages in this example, so the chance that any particular page gets chosen at random is one in five. This chance corresponds to a mathematical probability of 0.2, which appears at the bottom of each page.

On each of its iterations, the PageRank algorithm updates the probabilities assigned to each of the pages by computing the likelihood that the user reaches that page after following a random link from the end of the preceding cycle. For example, if you happen to be at node **A**, you have a choice to visit any of the other four nodes, because **A** has links to all of them. If you choose a link at random, you will go to node **B** a quarter of the time, node **C** a quarter of the time, and so on for nodes **D** and **E**. What happens, however, if you find yourself at node **B**? Given that there is only one link out of node **B**, any user who chooses a link from **B** will invariably end up at node **E**.

You can use this calculation to determine the likelihood of being at any node after following a random link. The are two ways, for example, to reach node **A** after following a link. You could have started at node **C** and chosen the link back to **A**, which was one of two links on the page. Alternatively, you could have started at node **D**, but in this case you had to be lucky enough to choose the link to **A** from three possibilities rather than two. The probability of reaching node **A** after following one random link is therefore one-half times the chance of being at **C** plus one-third times the chance of being at **D**. If you express this calculation as a formula using primed letters to indicating probabilities on the next cycle, the result looks like this:

$$\mathbf{A'} = \tfrac{1}{2}\,\mathbf{C} + \tfrac{1}{3}\,\mathbf{D}$$

A similar analysis yields the following formulas for the other pages in the graph:

$$\mathbf{B'} = \tfrac{1}{4}\mathbf{A} + \tfrac{1}{2}\mathbf{C} + \tfrac{1}{3}\mathbf{D} + \tfrac{1}{2}\mathbf{E}$$
$$\mathbf{C'} = \tfrac{1}{4}\mathbf{A} + \tfrac{1}{3}\mathbf{D}$$
$$\mathbf{D'} = \tfrac{1}{4}\mathbf{A} + \tfrac{1}{2}\mathbf{E}$$
$$\mathbf{E'} = \tfrac{1}{4}\mathbf{A} + \mathbf{B}$$

Each iteration of the PageRank algorithm replaces the probabilities for the pages **A**, **B**, **C**, **D**, and **E** with the values **A'**, **B'**, **C'**, **D'**, and **E'** computed by these formulae. The results of executing two iterations of the PageRank algorithm are shown in Figure 18-14.

FIGURE 18-14 **Probabilities after the first two iterations of the PageRank algorithm**

After the first cycle:

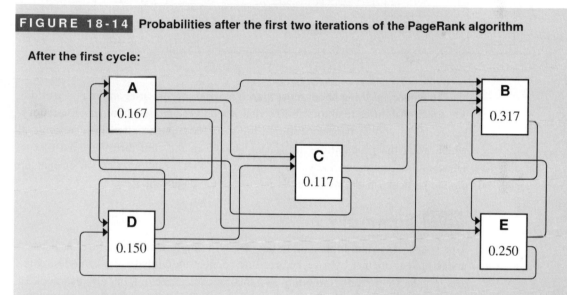

After the second cycle:

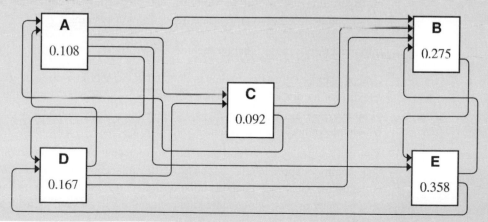

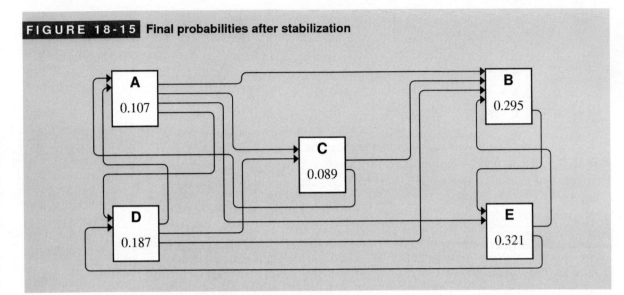

FIGURE 18-15 Final probabilities after stabilization

The wonderful thing about most Markov processes that arise in the real world is that the probabilities tend to stabilize after a relatively modest number of iterations. Figure 18-15 shows the probabilities for these five pages after 16 iterations, at which point the probabilities no longer change in the first three decimal places. These values, therefore, indicate the probability that a random web surfer ends up on that particular page, which is the essence of the PageRank idea.

Summary

This chapter has introduced you to the idea of a graph, which is defined as a set of nodes linked together by a set of arcs that connect individual pairs of nodes. Like sets, graphs are not only important as a theoretical abstraction, but also as a tool for solving practical problems that arise in many application domains. For example, graph algorithms are useful in studying the properties of connected structures ranging from the Internet to large-scale transportation systems.

Important points in this chapter include:

- Graphs may be either directed or undirected. The arcs in a directed graph run in one direction only, so the existence of an arc $n_1 \rightarrow n_2$ does not imply the existence of an arc $n_2 \rightarrow n_1$. You can represent undirected graphs using directed graphs in which the connected pairs of nodes are linked by two arcs, one in each direction.

- You can adopt any of several strategies to represent the connections in a graph. One common approach is to construct an adjacency list, in which the data structure for each node contains a list of the connected nodes. You can also use an adjacency matrix, which stores the connections in a two-dimensional array of

Boolean values. The rows and columns of the matrix are indexed by the nodes in the graph; if two nodes are connected in the graph, the corresponding entry in the matrix contains the value `true`.

- The `graph.h` interface can be implemented easily by layering it on top of the set package. Although it is possible to define such an interface using either a low-level, structure-based approach or a high-level, entirely object-oriented style, it is better to adopt an intermediate approach that defines a `Graph` class but leaves the client free to define the structures used for nodes and arcs.

- The two most important traversal orders for a graph are depth-first search and breadth-first search. The depth-first algorithm chooses one arc from the starting node and then recursively explores all paths beginning with that arc until no additional nodes remain. Only at that point does the algorithm return to explore other arcs from the original node. The breadth-first algorithm explores nodes in order of their distance from the original node, measured in terms of the number of arcs along the shortest path. After processing the initial node, breadth-first search processes all the neighbors of that node before moving on to nodes that are two hops away.

- You can find the minimum-cost path between two nodes in a graph by using Dijkstra's algorithm, which is vastly more efficient than the exponential strategy of comparing the cost of all possible paths. Dijkstra's algorithm is an example of a larger class of algorithms called *greedy algorithms,* which select the locally best option at any decision point.

Review questions

1.   What is a graph?

2.   True or false: Trees are a subset of graphs, which form a more general class.

3.   What is the difference between a directed and an undirected graph?

4.   If you are using a graph package that supports only directed graphs, how can you represent an undirected graph?

5.   Define the following terms as they apply to graphs: *path, cycle, simple path, simple cycle.*

6.   What is relationship between the terms *neighbor* and *degree?*

7.   What is the difference between a strongly connected and a weakly connected graph?

8.   True or false: The term *weakly connected* has no practical relevance to undirected graphs because all such graphs are automatically strongly connected if they are connected at all.

9.   What terms do mathematicians typically use in place of the words *node* and *arc?*

10.   Suppose that the computer science offerings at some university consisted of eight courses with the following prerequisite structure:

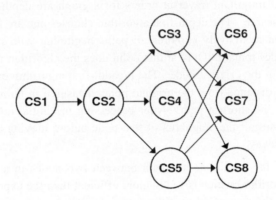

      Using the mathematical formulation for graphs described in this chapter, define this graph as a pair of sets.

11.   Draw a diagram showing the adjacency list representation of the graph in the preceding question.

12.   Given the prerequisite graph shown in question 10, what are the contents of the corresponding adjacency matrix?

13.   What is the difference between a sparse and a dense graph?

14.   If you were asked to choose the underlying representation of a graph for a particular application, what factors would you consider in deciding whether to use adjacency lists or adjacency matrices in the implementation?

15.   Why is it unnecessary to implement a separate iterator facility for the graph package?

16.   Why do the sets used in either version of the `graph.h` interface use pointers to arcs and nodes as their element types?

17.   What are the two fundamental traversal strategies for graphs?

18. Write down both the depth-first and the breadth-first traversal of the airline graph in Figure 18-1, starting from Atlanta. Assume that iteration over nodes and arcs always occurs in alphabetical order.

19. What problem does this chapter cite as the most significant problem with including class definitions for **Node** and **Arc** in the **graph.h** interface?

20. What rules does the **graph.h** interface impose on the client-defined types used to represent nodes and arcs?

21. What is a greedy algorithm?

22. Explain the operation of Dijkstra's algorithm for finding minimum-cost paths.

23. Show the contents of the priority queue at each step of the trace of Dijkstra's algorithm shown in Figure 18-11.

24. Using Figure 18-12 as a model, trace the execution of Dijkstra's algorithm to find the shortest path from Portland to Atlanta.

Exercises

1. Using the low-level, structure-based version of the **graph.h** interface, design and implement a function

```
void readGraph(SimpleGraph & g, istream & infile);
```

that reads a text description of a graph from **infile** into the graph **g** passed by the client. The input stream, which must already be open, consists of lines that can be in any of these three forms:

x	Defines a node with name x
$x - y$	Defines the bidirectional arc $x \leftrightarrow y$
$x \rightarrow y$	Defines the directional arc $x \rightarrow y$

The names x and y are arbitrary strings that do not contain a hyphen. Either of the two connection formats should also allow the user to specify the cost of the arc by enclosing a number in parentheses at the end of the line. If no parenthesized value appears, the cost of the arc should be initialized to 1. The definition of the graph ends with a blank line or the end of the file.

New nodes are defined whenever a new name appears in the data file. Thus, if every node is connected to some other node, it is sufficient to include only the arcs in the data file, because defining an arc automatically defines the nodes at its endpoints. If you need to represent a graph containing isolated nodes, you must specify the names of those nodes on separate lines somewhere in the data file.

When reading in an arc description, your implementation should discard leading and trailing spaces from the node names, but retain any internal spaces. The line

```
San Francisco - Denver (954)
```

should therefore define nodes with the names `"San Francisco"` and `"Denver"`, and then create connections between the two nodes in each direction, initializing both arcs to have a cost of 954.

As an example, calling `readGraph` on the following data file would produce the airline graph that appears in the chapter as Figure 18-2:

```
AirlineGraph.txt
Atlanta - Chicago (599)
Atlanta - Dallas (725)
Atlanta - New York (756)
Boston - New York (191)
Boston - Seattle (2489)
Chicago - Denver (907)
Dallas - Denver (650)
Dallas - Los Angeles (1240)
Dallas - San Francisco (1468)
Denver - San Francisco (954)
Portland - Seattle (130)
Portland - San Francisco (550)
```

2. As a counterpart to the `readGraph` function from the preceding exercise, implement a function

```
void writeGraph(SimpleGraph & g, ostream & outfile);
```

that writes a text description of a graph to the specified output file. You may assume that the data field in each node of the graph contains its name, just as if `readGraph` had created the graph. The output of the `writeGraph` function must be readable using `readGraph`.

3. Eliminate the recursion from the implementation of `depthFirstSearch` in Figure 18-5 by using a stack to store the unexplored nodes. At the beginning of the algorithm, you simply push the starting node on the stack. Then, until the stack is empty, you repeat the following operations:

1. Pop the topmost node from the stack.

2. Visit that node.

3. Push its neighbors on the stack

4. Take your solution from the preceding exercise and replace the stack with a queue. Describe the traversal order implemented by the resulting code.

5. The `depthFirstSearch` and `breadthFirstSearch` traversal functions given in the chapter are written to emphasize the structure of the underlying algorithms. If you want to include these traversal strategies as part of the graph package, you need to reimplement the functions so that they no longer depended on a client-supplied `visit` function. One approach is to implement these two algorithms by adding the following methods to `graph.h`:

```
void mapDFS(void (*fn)(NodeType *), NodeType *start);
void mapBFS(void (*fn)(NodeType *), NodeType *start);
```

In each case, the functions should call `fn(node)` for every node reachable from `start` in the specified traversal order.

6. The implementation of breadth-first search given in the chapter generates the correct traversal but ends up adding a large number of unnecessary paths to the queue. The problem is that the code adds new paths to the queue even when the final node in the chain has already been visited, which means that it will simply be ignored whenever that path is removed from the queue. You can fix this problem simply by checking to see whether the final node has been visited before adding it to the queue.

    Write a program to test assess the relative efficiency of the implementations with and without this test. Your program should read in several large graphs that vary in their average degree and then run each of these algorithms starting at random nodes in each graph. Your program should keep track of both the average queue length during the execution of the algorithm and the total running time necessary to visit each of the nodes.

7. Write a function

```
bool pathExists(Node *n1, Node *n2);
```

that returns `true` if there is a path in the graph between the nodes `n1` and `n2`. Implement this function by using depth-first search to traverse the graph from `n1`; if you encounter `n2` along the way, then a path exists. Reimplement your function so that it uses breadth-first search instead. In a large graph, which implementation is likely to be more efficient?

8. Write a function

```
int hopCount(Node *n1, Node *n2);
```

that returns the number of hops in the shortest path between the nodes **n1** and **n2**. If **n1** and **n2** are the same node, **hopCount** should return 0; if no path exists, **hopCount** should return −1. This function is easily implemented using breadth-first search.

9.   Complete the implementation of the **Graph** class from Figure 18-7 by writing the files **graphpriv.h** and **graphimpl.cpp**.

10. Define and implement a **graphio.h** interface that exports the methods **readGraph** and **writeGraph** from exercises 1 and 2, updated to use the template version of the **Graph** class.

11. Although the section entitled "Finding shortest paths" includes an implementation of Dijkstra's algorithm, there is no surrounding infrastructure to turn that algorithm into an application. Create one by writing a C++ program that performs the following operations:

   • Reads in a graph from a file

   • Allows the user to enter the names of two cities

   • Uses Dijkstra's algorithm to find and display the minimum path

12. Several important graph algorithms operate on a special class of graphs in which the nodes can be divided into two sets in such a way that all the arcs connect nodes in different sets, with none of the arcs running between nodes in the same set. Such graphs are said to be *bipartite.* Write a template function

```
template <NodeType,ArcType>
bool isBipartite(Graph<NodeType,ArcType> & g);
```

that takes an arbitrary graph and returns **true** if it has the bipartite property.

13. Although Dijkstra's algorithm for finding minimum-cost paths has considerable practical importance, there are other graph algorithms that have comparable commercial significance. In many cases, finding a minimum-cost path between two specific nodes is not as important as minimizing the cost of a network as a whole.

   As an example, suppose that you are working for a company that is building a new cable system that connects 10 large cities in the San Francisco Bay area. Your preliminary research has provided you with cost estimates for laying new cable lines along a variety of possible routes. Those routes and their associated costs are shown in the graph on the left side of Figure 18-16. Your job is to find the most economical way to lay new cables so that all the cities are connected through some path.

FIGURE 18-16   **A graph and its minimum spanning tree**

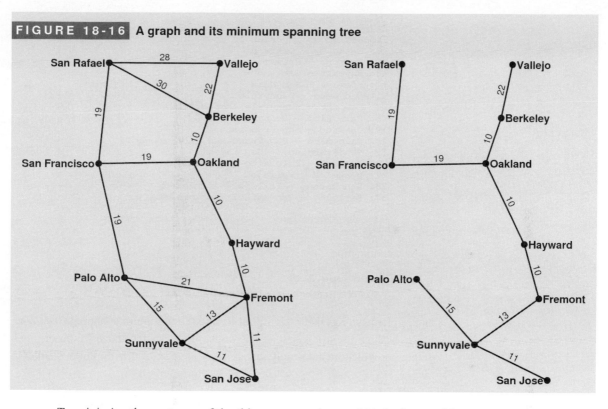

To minimize the cost, one of the things you need to avoid is laying a cable that forms a cycle in the graph. Such a cable would be unnecessary, because the cities it would connect are already linked by some other path. If your goal is to find a set of arcs that connects the nodes of a graph at a minimum cost, you might as well leave such edges out. The remaining graph, given that it has no cycles, forms a tree. A tree that links all the nodes of a graph is called a *spanning tree.* The spanning tree in which the total cost associated with the arcs is as small as possible is called a ***minimum spanning tree.*** The cable-network problem described earlier in this exercise is therefore equivalent to finding the minimum spanning tree of the graph, which is shown in the right side of Figure 18-16.

There are many algorithms in the literature for finding a minimum spanning tree. One of the simplest was devised by Joseph Kruskal in 1956. In Kruskal's algorithm, all you do is consider the arcs in the graph in order of increasing cost. If the nodes at the endpoints of the arc are unconnected, then you include this arc as part of the spanning tree. If, however, the nodes are already connected by a path, you ignore the arc entirely. The steps in the construction of the minimum spanning tree for the graph in Figure 18-16 are shown in the following sample run:

```
○ ○ ○                    MinimumSpanningTree
Process edges in order of cost:
10: Berkeley - Oakland
10: Fremont - Hayward
10: Hayward - Oakland
11: Fremont - San Jose
11: San Jose - Sunnyvale
13: Fremont - Sunnyvale (not needed)
15: Palo Alto - Sunnyvale
19: Oakland - San Francisco
19: Palo Alto - San Francisco (not needed)
19: San Francisco - San Rafael
21: Fremont - Palo Alto (not needed)
22: Berkeley - Vallejo
28: San Rafael - Vallejo (not needed)
30: Berkeley - San Rafael (not needed)
```

Write a function

```
Graph<Node,Arc>
    findMinimumSpanningTree(Graph<Node,Arc> & g);
```

that implements Kruskal's algorithm to find the minimum spanning tree. The function should return a new graph whose nodes match those in the original graph, but which includes only the arcs that are part of the minimum spanning tree.

14. A *dominating set* of a graph is a subset of the nodes such that those nodes along with their immediate neighbors constitute all graph nodes. That is, every node in the graph is either in the dominating set or is a neighbor of a node in the dominating set. In the graph diagrammed below—in which each node is labeled with the number of neighbors to facilitate tracing the algorithm—the filled-in nodes constitute a dominating set for the graph. Other dominating sets are also possible.

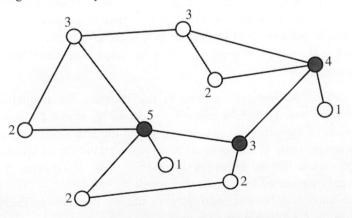

Ideally, you would like to be able to find the smallest possible dominating set, but that is known to be a computationally difficult task—too expensive for most graphs. The following algorithm usually finds a relatively small dominating set, even though it does not always produce the optimal result:

1. Start with an empty set *S*.

2. Consider each graph node in order of decreasing degree. In other words, you want to start with the node that has the most neighbors and then work down through the nodes with fewer neighbors. If two or more nodes have the same degree, you can process them in any order.

3. If the node you chose in step 2 is not redundant, add it to *S*. A node is *redundant* if it and all of its neighbors are neighbors of some node already in *S*.

4. Continue until *S* dominates the entire graph.

    Write a template function

```
template <NodeType,ArcType>
Set<NodeType *>
    findDominatingSet(Graph<NodeType,ArcType> & g);
```

that uses this algorithm to find a small dominating set for the graph **g**.

15. Graph algorithms are often well suited to distributed implementations in which processing is performed at each node in the graph. In particular, such algorithms are used to find optimal transmission routes in a computer network. As an example, the following graph shows the first 10 nodes in the ARPANET—the network created by the Advanced Research Projects Agency (ARPA) of the U.S. Department of Defense—which was the forerunner of today's much more sophisticated Internet:

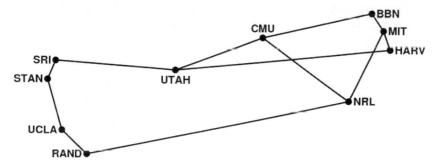

Each node in the early ARPANET consisted of a small computer called an *Interface Message Processor,* or *IMP.* As part of the network operation, each IMP sent messages to its neighbors indicating the number of hops from that node to every other node, to the extent that the IMP possessed that information. By monitoring the messages coming in, each IMP could quickly develop useful routing information about the network as a whole.

To make this idea more concrete, imagine that every IMP maintains an array in which each index position corresponds to one of the nodes. When the entire network is up and running, the array in the Stanford IMP (**STAN**) should have the following contents:

4	3	3	4	3	2	1	0	1	2
BBN	CMU	HARV	MIT	NRL	RAND	SRI	STAN	UCLA	UTAH

The interesting question, however, is not so much what the array contains but rather how the network computes and maintains these counts. When a node is restarted, it has no knowledge of the complete network. In fact, the only information the Stanford node can determine on its own is that its own entry is 0 hops away. Thus, at start-up time, the array in the **STAN** node looks like this:

?	?	?	?	?	?	?	0	?	?
BBN	CMU	HARV	MIT	NRL	RAND	SRI	STAN	UCLA	UTAH

The routing algorithm then proceeds by letting each node forward its routing array to its neighbors. The Stanford IMP, for example, sends its array off to SRI and UCLA. It also receives similar messages from its neighbors. If the IMP at UCLA has just started up as well, it might send a message containing the array

?	?	?	?	?	?	?	?	0	?
BBN	CMU	HARV	MIT	NRL	RAND	SRI	STAN	UCLA	UTAH

This message provides the Stanford node with some interesting information. If its neighbor can get to UCLA in 0 hops, then the Stanford node can get there in 1. As a result, the Stanford node can update its own routing array as follows:

?	?	?	?	?	?	?	0	1	?
BBN	CMU	HARV	MIT	NRL	RAND	SRI	STAN	UCLA	UTAH

In general, whenever any node gets a routing array from its neighbor, all it has to do is go through each of the known entries in the incoming array and replace the corresponding entry in its own array with the incoming value plus one, unless its own entry is already smaller. In a very short time, the routing arrays throughout the entire network will have the correct information.

Write a program that uses the graph package to simulate the calculations of this routing algorithm on a network of nodes.

Chapter 19
Inheritance

Beware how you trifle with your marvelous inheritance.
— Henry Cabot Lodge, "League of Nations," 1919

As you know from the discussion of the stream hierarchy in Chapter 4, one of the defining properties of object-oriented languages like C++ and Java is that they allow you to define hierarchical relationships among classes. Whenever you have a class that provides some of the functionality you need for a particular application, you can define new subclasses that are derived from the original class, but which specialize its behavior in some way. Each subclass inherits behavior from its superclass, which in turn inherits the behavior of its superclasses, all the way up the class hierarchy. Although you have seen inheritance used in the stream libraries, you have not yet had occasion to use inheritance in your own classes. This chapter gives you that opportunity by defining several class hierarchies in which inheritance plays a central role.

At the same time, it is important to recognize that using inheritance is more problematic in C++ than it is in many other programming languages. In particular, if you have already had experience with Java, you will almost certainly have preconceptions about inheritance that don't apply in the C++ world. It is therefore just as important to learn about the limitations of inheritance in C++ as it is to learn about its strengths.

19.1 Simple inheritance

Before moving on to consider more sophisticated applications of inheritance, it makes sense to begin with a few simple examples. In its most basic form, the definition of a subclass in C++ looks like this:

```
class subclass : public superclass {
    new entries for the subclass
};
```

In this pattern, *subclass* inherits all the public entries in *superclass*. The entries in the private section of *superclass* remain private. Subclasses therefore have no direct access to the private methods and instance variables of their superclasses.

Specifying types in a template class

In C++, it is possible to create useful subclasses that contain no code other than the class header, particularly if the superclass is a template class. For example, you can define a **StringMap** class that maps strings to strings by writing the following definition:

```
class StringMap : public Map<string,string> { };
```

Using the simple type name **StringMap** makes programs shorter and more readable because it is no longer necessary to write out the template arguments everywhere the type name appears.

The advantage of specifying the types of the template parameters increases along with the sophistication of the classes involved. You might certainly want to define a new **Graph** subclass to represent the airline graph from Chapter 18, particularly given that the application already defines its own **City** and **Flight** classes. The following definition creates a new **AirlineGraph** class that specifies **City** and **Flight** as the types for the nodes and arcs:

```
class AirlineGraph : public Graph<City,Flight> { };
```

Defining an Employee class

Suppose that you have been given the task of designing an object-oriented payroll system for a company. You might begin by defining a general class called **Employee** that encapsulates the information about an individual worker along with methods that implement operations required for the payroll system. These operations might include simple methods like **getName**, which returns the name of an employee, along with more complicated methods like **getPay**, which calculates the pay for an employee according to data stored within each **Employee** object. In many companies, however, employees fall into several different classes that are similar in certain respects but different in others. For example, a company might have hourly employees, commissioned employees, and salaried employees on the same payroll. In such companies, it might make sense to define subclasses for each employee category as illustrated by the UML diagram in Figure 19-1.

The root of this hierarchy is the **Employee** class, which defines the methods that are common to all employees. The **Employee** class therefore exports methods like **getName**, which the other classes simply inherit. All employees, after all, have a

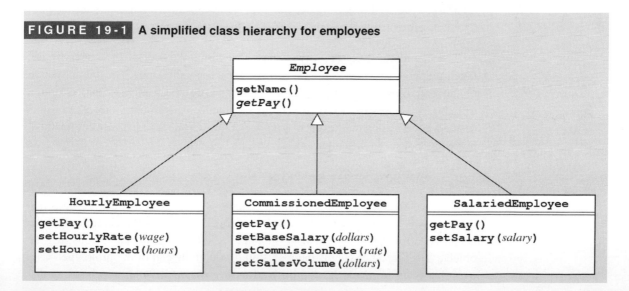

FIGURE 19-1 A simplified class hierarchy for employees

name. On the other hand, it is almost certainly necessary to write separate `getPay` methods for each of the subclasses, because the computation is different in each case. The pay of an hourly employee depends on the hourly wage and the number of hours worked. For a commissioned employee, the pay is typically the sum of some base salary plus a commission on the sales volume for which that employee is responsible. At the same time, it is important to note that every employee has a `getPay` method, even though its implementation differs for each of the subclasses. It therefore makes sense to *specify* that method at the level of the `Employee` class and then to *override* that definition in each of the subclasses.

If you look closely at the typography in Figure 19-1, you'll notice that the name of the `Employee` class and its `getPay` method appear in italics. In UML, italic type is used to indicate that a class or method is ***abstract,*** which indicates that definitions at this level of the hierarchy provide only a specification for definitions that appear in the subclasses. There are, for example, no objects whose primary type is `Employee`. Every `Employee` must instead be constructed as an `HourlyEmployee`, a `CommissionedEmployee`, or a `SalariedEmployee`. Any object belonging to one of these subclasses is still an `Employee` and therefore inherits the `getName` method along with the prototype for the virtual method `getPay`.

Figure 19-2 provides a skeleton for a set of class definitions based on the classes in the `Employee` hierarchy. As with the C++ interfaces you have seen in this text, the implementation of the `Employee` class and its subclasses appear in a separate `.cpp` file. Even taking that fact into account, the class definitions in Figure 19-2 are still too fragmentary to be useful in practice, since they are missing such details as the contents of the private sections, the format of any constructors needed to create these objects, and all of the commentary that would be essential in an interface. The goal of the figure, however, is to illustrate the use of subclasses in C++, and the example is certainly sufficient for that purpose.

The definition of the `Employee` class that forms the root of the hierarchy has much the same structure as the classes you have seen all along. The public section of the `Employee` class declares two methods: a `getName` method that returns a `string` and a `getPay` method that returns a double. The prototype for `getName` is defined just as you would expect. The declaration of the abstract `getPay` method, however, looks a bit different:

```
virtual double getPay() = 0;
```

This declaration introduces two new features of C++. The first difference is that the prototype begins with the keyword `virtual`, which tells the compiler that the actual code for this method will be supplied by the subclass used to construct the object. The second change is the inclusion of `= 0` at the end of the prototype. C++ uses this syntax to mark the definition of a ***pure virtual method,*** which is one that

| FIGURE 19-2 | Simplified definitions for the `Employee` class hierarchy |

```
/*
 * Class: Employee
 * ----------------
 * This class defines the root of the Employee hierarchy.  Employee is
 * an abstract class, which means that there are no objects whose primary
 * type is Employee.  Every object is constructed as one of the subclasses.
 * The getPay method is declared using the virtual keyword, which means
 * that it can be overridden by its subclasses.  The "= 0" notation at the
 * end of the prototype marks getPay as a "pure virtual" method, which
 * is implemented only in the subclasses.
 */

class Employee {
public:
   std::string getName();
   virtual double getPay() = 0;
};

/*
 * Subclasses: HourlyEmployee, CommissionedEmployee, SalariedEmployee
 * ------------------------------------------------------------------
 * These classes represent the concrete manifestations of the abstract
 * Employee class.  Each subclass inherits the getName method from
 * Employee, but defines its own version of the getPay method.
 */

class HourlyEmployee : public Employee {
public:
   virtual double getPay();
   void setHourlyRate(double rate);
   void setHoursWorked(double hours);
};

class CommissionedEmployee : public Employee {
public:
   virtual double getPay();
   void setBaseSalary(double dollars);
   void setCommissionRate(double rate);
   void setSalesVolume(double dollars);
};

class SalariedEmployee : public Employee {
public:
   virtual double getPay();
   void setSalary(double salary);
};
```

has no definition in the base class and can therefore come only from a subclass. Not all virtual methods, however, are pure virtual. In many hierarchies, the base class provides a default definition, which is then overridden only in those subclasses that need to change it.

If you are used to inheritance in other languages, the idea of marking a method with the **virtual** keyword seems unnecessary. In most languages that support inheritance, *all* methods are virtual in the way that C++ uses that term. If a subclass overrides a method in its superclass, programmers used to the usual model of inheritance expect the new definition supplied by the subclass to be used for any object that has that type. This rule, however, is not applied automatically in C++. If you leave out the **virtual** keyword, the compiler determines which version of a method to call on the basis of how the object is *declared*, not how the object is *constructed*. For example, even if you were to override the **getName** method in the **SalariedEmployee** subclasses, calling **getName** on a variable declared to be an **Employee** would call the original version of **getName** defined in the employee class. The new version of **getName** is used only on a value explicitly declared to be a **SalariedEmployee**.

The class definitions for the three subclasses of **Employee** each have a common form. The class header indicates the inheritance relationship by adding a colon, the keyword **public**, and the superclass name after the name of the subclass. Thus, the header line for **HourlyEmployee** is

```
class HourlyEmployee : public Employee
```

The **HourlyEmployee** class automatically inherits the public methods from the **Employee** class and therefore has a **getName** method that comes directly from the superclass. The definition of the **getPay** method, however, must come from the subclass, because it is defined as a pure virtual method in the **Employee** class. Each subclass definition must therefore inform the compiler that it is overriding the **getPay** method by including the following virtual prototype:

```
virtual double getPay();
```

The implementation of **getPay** appears in the **.cpp** file, tagged with the name of the subclass to which it applies. The implementation of **getPay** for the **HourlyEmployee** class would therefore look something like this, assuming that the class includes private instance variables called **hoursWorked** and **hourlyRate**:

```
double HourlyEmployee::getPay() {
    return hoursWorked * hourlyRate;
}
```

The limitations of subclassing in C++

One of the basic principles that underlies object-oriented design is that subclasses are instances of their superclass. Thus, in the **Employee** hierarchy introduced in the preceding section, an **HourlyEmployee** is also an instance of the more general

Employee class. That fact, however, may lead you to make incorrect assumptions about the operations you can perform on instances of hierarchical data structures, particularly if you have had previous exposure to languages like Java that behave very differently in C++.

The most confusing aspect of inheritance in C++ arises in the implementation of assignment. Given that every **HourlyEmployee** is also an **Employee**, it seems logical to assume that one could assign—as you could in Java, for example—an object of type **HourlyEmployee** to a variable of type **Employee**, as the following lines seem to do:

```
HourlyEmployee bobCratchit;
Employee clerk;
clerk = bobCratchit;
```

The first line declares **bobCratchit** to be a variable of type **HourlyEmployee**; the second declares **clerk** to be of type **Employee**. The trouble comes on the third line, which attempts to assign the value of **bobCratchit**. Although the code is perfectly legal in C++, the bug icon is there to warn you that the code is unlikely to do what you expect or want.

In C++, local variables are always allocated on the stack, even if they are instances of a class type. To create the stack frame, the compiler must know how much space to allocate for each of the local variables. In this example, the compiler assigns **bobCratchit** enough space to hold an object of type **HourlyEmployee** and **clerk** enough space to hold one of type **Employee**. The **HourlyEmployee** class extends the **Employee** class, which means that it presumably has fields that are not present in the base class. A subclass always requires at least as much space as its superclass, and typically requires more. Thus, the picture of the stack frame containing these two variables will look something like this:

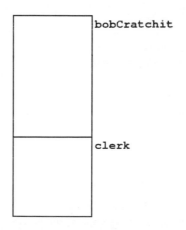

In C++, assigning one object to another—in the absence of a new definition of assignment—is implemented by copying all the fields. The assignment statement

```
clerk = bobCratchit;
```

therefore tries to copy the data from **bobCratchit** into the space reserved for **clerk**, which corresponds to trying to hammer a large peg into a small hole.

What C++ does in this situation is to copy only those parts of the object that fit into the smaller space, which are simply those fields that **HourlyEmployee** inherits from **Employee**. The actual data transfer therefore looks something like this:

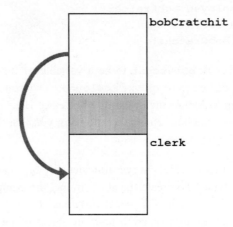

The part of the **HourlyEmployee** class shown in gray is left behind. This behavior—copying only part of an object during assignment—is called *slicing.*

The inability to copy a subclass instance into space reserved for the superclass creates other problems as well. You might, for example, want to store a list of employees in a vector. Unfortunately, you can't make any headway if you try to use a declaration of the following form:

```
Vector<Employee> payroll;
```

As in the assignment example, the elements of the **payroll** vector only have space to fit an object of the **Employee** class. If you try to execute the statement

```
payroll.add(bobCratchit);
```

the implementation of the **add** method will slice away all the data in **bobCratchit** that isn't part of the **Employee** base class.

The traditional way to get around these problems in C++ is to use pointers to objects rather than the objects themselves. It is, for example, perfectly appropriate to declare the **payroll** vector as follows:

```
Vector<Employee *> payroll;
```

All pointers to **Employee** objects are the same size and therefore fit in the same vector. What's more, if you dereference one of the elements of **payroll** and then call a virtual method in the **Employee** class, C++ invokes the version of the method appropriate to that object subtype. Thus, if you execute the code

```
for (Employee *ep : payroll) {
    cout << ep->getName() << ": " << ep->getPay() << endl;
}
```

you get a list of all the employees in the payroll vector along with the pay each employee should receive. The call to **getPay** invokes the version of the method appropriate to the actual **Employee** subclass for that element.

Unfortunately, using pointers complicates the process of memory management, which is already a difficult challenge in C++. As long as each class defines a destructor that frees any allocated memory, it is possible to keep the nightmares of memory management under control. As soon as you let pointers cross the boundary to the client side of the interface, however, you can no longer guarantee that the destructors will be called at the appropriate time, and the overall complexity skyrockets.

When you design an abstraction in C++, it is important to keep this tradeoff in mind. In most cases, the best approach is to avoid the use of inheritance and create independent classes that manage their own heap memory. If you decide that you need inheritance, however, you face a difficult choice. One approach is to define private versions of the copy constructor and assignment operator so that copying objects in that inheritance hierarchy is prohibited. Although this strategy eliminates the possibility of losing data through slicing, disallowing assignment makes it harder to embed objects in larger data structures. If you don't prohibit assignment, however, clients must then assume the responsibility for memory management. More often than not, clients do a terrible job in this regard.

The designers of the C++ libraries made different choices in different situations. The collection classes are implemented as independent classes that do not form an inheritance hierarchy. The stream classes, by contrast, form a sophisticated hierarchy but do not allow assignment. In each case, the designers chose to keep the details of memory management hidden from the client. You would be wise to do the same in your own designs.

▐▐▐ 19.2 A hierarchy of graphical objects

One of the contexts in which inheritance hierarchies are worth the added complexity is the design of graphical interfaces. Graphical user interfaces are ubiquitous in systems today and typically rely on inheritance hierarchies to define the associated *application programming interface* (or *API* for short) that implementers use to write the necessary code. Within the context of a particular API, inheritance hierarchies come up at a variety of levels. The windows, dialogs, and panels displayed by applications form one hierarchy. Within the components of this hierarchy, most window systems allow programs to display text, images, and various graphical shapes that form an inheritance hierarchy of their own.

The Stanford libraries include an interface called **gobjects.h** that allows clients to display objects in a graphics window. This section implements a simplified version of **gobjects.h** that exports the classes shown in Figure 19-3, which are limited to lines, rectangles, and ovals.

As you can see from Figure 19-3, the classes in **gobjects.h** form a hierarchy. The abstract class **GObject** represents the root of the inheritance tree. The methods exported by the **GObject** class apply to all graphical objects. Given any **GObject**, you can set its location in the graphics window or specify its color. The **GObject** class also specifies a method called **draw**, which is used by the implementation to display the object on the graphics window. In the **GObject** class itself, **draw** is declared as a pure virtual method, which means that it is unimplemented at this level of the hierarchy. The implementation of **draw** is supplied by the concrete subclasses **GLine**, **GRect**, and **GOval**. Figure 19-4 shows the contents of the simplified **gobjects.h** interface.

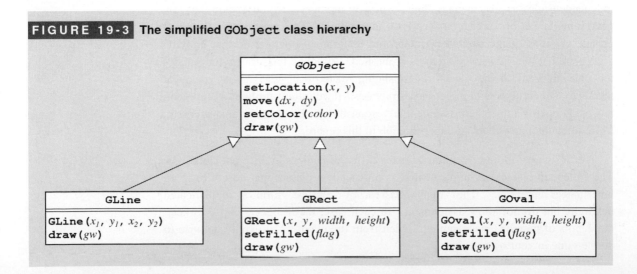

FIGURE 19-3 **The simplified GObject class hierarchy**

FIGURE 19-4 The `gobjects.h` interface

```
/*
 * File: gobjects.h
 * -----------------
 * This file defines a simple hierarchy of graphical objects.
 */

#ifndef _gobjects_h
#define _gobjects_h

#include <string>
#include "gwindow.h"

/*
 * Class: GObject
 * ---------------
 * This class is the root of the hierarchy and encompasses all objects
 * that can be displayed in a window.  Clients typically use a pointer
 * to a GObject rather than the GObject itself.
 */

class GObject {

public:

/*
 * Method: setLocation
 * Usage: gobj->setLocation(x, y);
 * -----------------------------------
 * Sets the x and y coordinates of gobj to the specified values.
 */

   void setLocation(double x, double y);

/*
 * Method: move
 * Usage: gobj->move(dx, dy);
 * ------------------------------
 * Adds dx and dy to the coordinates of gobj.
 */

   void move(double x, double y);

/*
 * Method: setColor
 * Usage: gobj->setColor(color);
 * -------------------------------
 * Sets the color of gobj.
 */

   void setColor(std::string color);
```

☞

FIGURE 19-4 The `gobjects.h` interface (continued)

```
/*
 * Abstract method: draw
 * Usage: gobj->draw(gw);
 * -----------------------
 * Draws the graphical object on the GraphicsWindow specified by gw.
 * This method is implemented by the specific GObject subclasses.
 */

   virtual void draw(GWindow & gw) = 0;

protected:

/* The following methods and fields are available to the subclasses */

   GObject();                           /* Superclass constructor      */
   std::string color;                   /* The color of the object     */
   double x, y;                         /* The coordinates of the object */

};

/*
 * Subclass: GLine
 * ---------------
 * The GLine subclass represents a line segment on the window.
 */

class GLine : public GObject {

public:

/*
 * Constructor: GLine
 * Usage: GLine *lp = new GLine(x1, y1, x2, y2);
 * ----------------------------------------------
 * Creates a line segment that extends from (x1, y1) to (x2, y2).
 */

   GLine(double x1, double y1, double x2, double y2);

/* Prototypes for the overridden virtual methods */

   virtual void draw(GWindow & gw);

private:
   double dx;                           /* Horizontal distance from x1 to x2 */
   double dy;                           /* Vertical distance from y1 to y2   */

};
```

FIGURE 19-4　The `gobjects.h` interface (continued)

```
/*
 * Subclass: GRect
 * --------------
 * The GRect subclass represents a rectangle.
 */

class GRect : public GObject {

public:

/*
 * Constructor: GRect
 * Usage: GRect *rp = new GRect(x, y, width, height);
 * --------------------------------------------------------
 * Creates a rectangle of the specified size whose upper left corner is (x, y).
 */

   GRect(double x, double y, double width, double height);

/*
 * Method: setFilled
 * Usage: rp->setFilled(flag);
 * ---------------------------
 * Indicates whether the rectangle is filled.
 */

   void setFilled(bool flag);

/* Prototypes for the overridden virtual methods */

   virtual void draw(GWindow & gw);

private:
   double width, height;          /* Dimensions of the rectangle   */
   bool filled;                   /* True if the rectangle is filled */

};

/*
 * Subclass: GOval
 * --------------
 * The GOval subclass represents an oval defined by a bounding rectangle.
 */

class GOval : public GObject {

public:
```

FIGURE 19-4 **The `gobjects.h` interface (continued)**

```
/*
 * Constructor: GOval
 * Usage: GOval *op = new GOval(x, y, width, height);
 * -----------------------------------------------------
 * Creates an oval inscribed in the specified rectangle.
 */

   GOval(double x, double y, double width, double height);

/*
 * Method: setFilled
 * Usage: op->setFilled(flag);
 * -----------------------------
 * Indicates whether the oval is filled.
 */

   void setFilled(bool flag);

/* Prototypes for the overridden virtual methods */

   virtual void draw(GWindow & gw);

private:
   double width, height;          /* Dimensions of the bounding rectangle */
   bool filled;                   /* True if the oval is filled           */

};

#endif
```

Each of the subclasses in the `gobjects.h` interface defines a constructor whose arguments match those in the method from the `GWindow` class that draws the same shape. The `GLine` constructor, for example, takes the coordinates of the endpoints and therefore has the following prototype:

```
GLine(double x1, double y1, double x2, double y2);
```

These arguments are the same as those for the `drawLine` method in `GWindow`.

The code in Figure 19-4 introduces one important new feature of C++. In many interface hierarchies, it is useful to give subclasses access to the instance variables of the superclass, mostly because doing so can streamline the code. The `GObject` class accomplishes this goal by using the `protected` keyword to label the section in which those instance variables appear. Entries in the `protected` section are accessible to any subclasses but remain off-limits to clients.

The code needed to implement the `GObject` hierarchy is straightforward and appears in Figure 19-5.

FIGURE 19-5 Implementation of the `GObject` class hierarchy

```cpp
/*
 * File: gobjects.cpp
 * --------------------
 * This file implements the gobjects.h interface.
 */

#include <string>
#include "gwindow.h"
#include "gobjects.h"
using namespace std;
/*
 * Implementation notes: GObject class
 * -----------------------------------
 * The constructor for the superclass sets the default color (BLACK).
 */

GObject::GObject() {
   setColor("BLACK");
}

void GObject::setLocation(double x, double y) {
   this->x = x;
   this->y = y;
}

void GObject::move(double dx, double dy) {
   x += dx;
   y += dy;
}

void GObject::setColor(string color) {
   this->color = color;
}

/*
 * Implementation notes: GLine class
 * ---------------------------------
 * The constructor for the GLine class has to change the specification
 * of the line from the endpoints passed to the constructor to the
 * representation that uses a starting point along with dx/dy values.
 */

GLine::GLine(double x1, double y1, double x2, double y2) {
   this->x = x1;
   this->y = y1;
   this->dx = x2 - x1;
   this->dy = y2 - y1;
}

void GLine::draw(GWindow & gw) {
   gw.setColor(color);
   gw.drawLine(x, y, x + dx, y + dy);
}
```

FIGURE 19-5 Implementation of the GObject class hierarchy (continued)

```
/*
 * Implementation notes: GRect and GOval classes
 * ----------------------------------------------
 * The constructors for these classes store their arguments in the
 * corresponding instance variables.  The draw method forwards the
 * appropriate request to the GWindow class.
 */

GRect::GRect(double x, double y, double width, double height) {
   this->x = x;
   this->y = y;
   this->width = width;
   this->height = height;
   filled = false;
}

void GRect::setFilled(bool flag) {
   filled = flag;
}

void GRect::draw(GWindow & gw) {
   gw.setColor(color);
   if (filled) {
      gw.fillRect(x, y, width, height);
   } else {
      gw.drawRect(x, y, width, height);
   }
}

GOval::GOval(double x, double y, double width, double height) {
   this->x = x;
   this->y = y;
   this->width = width;
   this->height = height;
   filled = false;
}

void GOval::setFilled(bool flag) {
   filled = flag;
}

void GOval::draw(GWindow & gw) {
   gw.setColor(color);
   if (filled) {
      gw.fillOval(x, y, width, height);
   } else {
      gw.drawOval(x, y, width, height);
   }
}
```

Calling superclass constructors

Constructors are responsible for initializing the fields of an object to ensure that it is created in a consistent state. To maintain this consistency through the entire inheritance hierarchy, each subclass constructor must invoke some constructor in its superclass. In the absence of any other specification, this responsibility falls to the default constructor for the superclass. Thus, before initializing their own local fields, the constructors for the **GLine**, **GRect**, and **GOval** objects will call the default constructor in **GObject** class.

Declaring the **GObject** constructor in the protected section of the **GObject** class means that subclasses have access to the **GObject** constructor, but that clients do not. Adopting this strategy prohibits clients from declaring a **GObject** variable or using **GObject** as a template parameter for any of the collection classes. As noted in the section entitled "The limitations of subclassing in C++" earlier in this chapter, any clients who try to use the **GObject** class in these ways can only get themselves into trouble. Making such uses illegal is therefore something of a public service. Clients are instead allowed to use *pointers* to **GObject**s in these contexts, exactly as they should.

In some cases, however, it may be useful to call some other variant of the constructor besides the parameterless default version. C++ allows you to do so by including in the code for the subclass constructor an additional specification called an ***initializer list***. The initializer list appears just before the brace that begins the body of the constructor and is set off from the parameter list by a colon. The elements of the initializer list should be in one of the following forms:

- The name of the superclass, followed by a parenthesized list of arguments that match the prototype for some variant of the superclass constructor

- The name of a field in the superclass, followed by an initializer for that field enclosed in parentheses

Both styles are used in professional C++ programming, but the examples in this book use only the first style.

The easiest way to illustrate the use of an initializer list is in the context of a simple example. Suppose that you want to extend the **GObject** hierarchy by adding a **GCircle** class as a subclass of **GOval**. Every circle is, of course, just an oval in which the width and height are the same. Circles, however, are usually defined by specifying the radius and the coordinates of the center. It would therefore make things easier for clients if the constructor for the **GCircle** class took as arguments those values rather than the bounding rectangle used for the **GOval** class. Figure 19-6 shows the interface entry for a **GCircle** subclass that adopts this convention.

FIGURE 19-6 Interface entry for the `GCircle` class

```
/*
 * Subclass: GCircle
 * ------------------
 * The GCircle subclass represents a circle.
 */

class GCircle : public GOval {

public:

/*
 * Constructor: GCircle
 * Usage: GCircle circle(x, y, r);
 *        GCircle *cp = new GCircle(x, y, r);
 * --------------------------------------------
 * Creates a circle of radius r centered at the point (x, y).
 */

   GCircle(double x, double y, double r);

};
```

The only issue that arises in the implementation of the **GCircle** class is how to initialize the **GOval** from which the **GCircle** is derived. The **GCircle** class can't take the usual approach of calling the default constructor for **GOval**, because **GOval** doesn't have a default constructor. The constructor for **GCircle** must instead invoke the **GOval** constructor with the arguments that **GOval** expects. Fortunately, these arguments are easy to calculate from the values **x**, **y**, and **r**. Figure 19-7 shows the implementation of the **GCircle** class, in which the only code appears in the initializer list.

FIGURE 19-7 Implementation of the `GCircle` class showing the use of an initializer list

```
/*
 * Implementation notes: GCircle
 * -----------------------------
 * The GCircle class is a subclass of GOval for which the constructor
 * interprets its arguments in a different way.  This constructor uses
 * an initialization list to call the GOval constructor with the
 * correct arguments.
 */

GCircle::GCircle(double x, double y, double r)
         : GOval(x - r, y - r, 2 * r, 2 * r) {
   /* Empty */
}
```

Storing `GObject` pointers in a vector

One of the advantages of defining the **GObject** hierarchy is that doing so makes it possible to store graphical objects in collections, as long as you remember to use pointers to the **GObject**s rather than the objects themselves. Figure 19-8 shows a program that assembles a collection of **GObject**s into a vector and then draws those objects on the window, producing a copy of the image from the **GraphicsExample** program in Chapter 2, which appears on page 110. This version of the program takes care to free the heap memory it has allocated.

FIGURE 19-8 Test program that stores graphical objects in a vector

```
/*
 * File: TestDisplayList.cpp
 * ---------------------------
 * This program tests the GObject classes by storing pointers to several
 * graphical objects in a vector and then drawing them all at once.  The
 * picture is the same as the GraphicsExample.cpp program from Chapter 2.
 */

#include <iostream>
#include "gwindow.h"
#include "gobjects.h"
#include "vector.h"
using namespace std;

int main() {
   GWindow gw;
   double width = gw.getWidth();
   double height = gw.getHeight();
   GRect *rp = new GRect(width / 4, height / 4, width / 2, height / 2);
   GOval *op = new GOval(width / 4, height / 4, width / 2, height / 2);
   rp->setColor("BLUE");
   op->setColor("GRAY");
   Vector<GObject *> displayList;
   displayList.add(new GLine(0, height / 2, width / 2, 0));
   displayList.add(new GLine(width / 2, 0, width, height / 2));
   displayList.add(new GLine(width, height / 2, width / 2, height));
   displayList.add(new GLine(width / 2, height, 0, height / 2));
   displayList.add(rp);
   displayList.add(op);
   for (GObject *sp : displayList) {
      sp->draw(gw);
   }
   for (GObject *sp : displayList) {
      delete sp;
   }
   displayList.clear();
   return 0;
}
```

19.3 A class hierarchy for expressions

Another context in which class hierarchies occur naturally is in the representation of arithmetic expressions in a programming language. As it reads your programs, the C++ compiler must analyze expressions to figure out which operators apply to which operands and to determine the order in which those operators are evaluated. Compilers typically store this information in a tree structure in which the individual nodes are part of a class hierarchy used to represent different expression types.

The goal of this section is to explore this strategy for representing arithmetic expressions by walking through the implementation of a simple application that repeatedly executes the following steps:

1. Read an expression entered by the user into a tree-structured internal form.
2. Evaluate the tree to compute the expression value.
3. Print the result of the evaluation on the console.

This iterated process is called a *read-eval-print loop.* Read-eval-print loops are characteristic of *interpreters,* which are applications that execute programs by performing the necessary operations without ever translating the program into machine language. Although interpreted programs are generally less efficient than compiled ones, interpreters are substantially easier to write and understand.

The operation of reading an expression and converting it to its internal form can also be decomposed into three phases, as follows:

1. *Input.* The input phase consists of reading in a line of text from the user, which can be accomplished with a simple call to the `getline` function.
2. *Lexical analysis.* The lexical analysis phase consists of dividing the input line into individual units called *tokens,* each of which represents a single logical entity, such as an integer constant, an operator, or a variable name. The `TokenScanner` class from Chapter 6 provides the ideal tool for this phase of the process.
3. *Parsing.* Once the line has been broken down into its component tokens, the parsing phase consists of determining whether the individual tokens represent a legal expression and, if so, what the structure of that expression is. To do so, the parser must determine how to construct a valid parse tree from the individual tokens in the input.

The main program for a simple interpreter that incorporates these phases appears in Figure 19-9.

FIGURE 19-9 Main module for the interpreter

```
/*
 * File: Interpreter.cpp
 * -----------------------
 * This program simulates the top level of an expression interpreter.  The
 * program reads an expression, evaluates it, and then displays the result.
 */

#include <iostream>
#include <string>
#include "error.h"
#include "exp.h"
#include "parser.h"
#include "tokenscanner.h"
using namespace std;

int main() {
   EvaluationContext context;
   TokenScanner scanner;
   Expression *exp;
   scanner.ignoreWhitespace();
   scanner.scanNumbers();
   while (true) {
      exp = NULL;
      try {
         string line;
         cout << "=> ";
         getline(cin, line);
         if (line == "quit") break;
         scanner.setInput(line);
         Expression *exp = parseExp(scanner);
         int value = exp->eval(context);
         cout << value << endl;
      } catch (ErrorException ex) {
         cerr << "Error: " << ex.getMessage() << endl;
      }
      if (exp != NULL) delete exp;
   }
   return 0;
}
```

A sample run of the program might look like this:

```
⊖ ⊖ ⊖                    Interpreter
=> x = 6
6
=> y = 10
10
=> 2 * x + 3 * y
42
=> quit
```

As the sample run makes clear, the interpreter allows assignment to variables and adheres to C++'s precedence conventions by evaluating multiplication before addition.

The heart of the implementation is the **Expression** class, which represents an arithmetic expression. The **Expression** class is defined in the **exp.h** interface. Even before you study this interface, you can make reasonable inferences about its structure from looking at the code for the interpreter. From the declaration of the variable **exp**, you know that the code works with pointers to **Expression** objects rather than with the objects directly. One implication of this design is that any methods applied to expression variables like **exp** will use the **->** operator. Also, you can infer from the code that the **Expression** class has a method called **eval**, even though you don't know the details of that operation. That, of course, is how it should be. As a client of the expression package, you are less concerned with how expressions are implemented than you are with how to use them. As a client, you need to think of the **Expression** class as an abstract data type. The underlying details become important only when you have to modify the implementation.

Another thing you might notice in Figure 19-9 is that the **eval** method takes a parameter called **context**, which is an object of type **EvaluationContext**. The primary purpose of the **EvaluationContext** parameter is maintain a *symbol table,* which keeps track of what value is currently assigned to each variable name. As you might expect, the code for the **EvaluationContext** class uses a **Map** to implement these associations. That fact, however, is an implementation detail. The methods in the **EvaluationContext** class frame the symbol table operations in terms that make sense in the context of a programming language.

Exception handling

As with many of the programs you have seen in this book, the modules in the interpreter report errors by calling the **error** function, which was introduced in Chapter 2. As you have used it up to now, the **error** function prints a message and terminates the execution of the program. If the interpreter died while you were typing a long and complicated expression, you would have every right to be annoyed. Just think how you feel when an application dies and you lose everything you have entered up to that point. As with most interactive programs, it is better for the interpreter to respond by displaying an appropriate error message and then letting you correct the invalid input.

The interpreter program in Figure 19-9 responds to errors gracefully by relying on a feature of C++ called *exception handling,* which allows programmers to respond when events occur that are considered to fall outside of normal program operation. As it is implemented in the Stanford libraries, the **error** function generates a signal that something is amiss, which makes it possible for other functions to respond to the error condition, even when the error occurs in a function deeply nested within the function that implements the response. The only requirement is that the code that responds to the exception must appear somewhere in the chain of function calls that precede the point at which the error occurs. The code that signals the unusual condition is said to ***throw an exception.*** To be consistent with that metaphor, the code that responds is said to *catch* that exception.

The feature of C++ that allows this style of exception handling is the **try** statement, which has the following paradigmatic form:

```
try {
    code under the control of the try statement
} catch (type var) {
    code to respond to an exception with the specified value type
}
```

The syntactic pattern used to throw an exception is simply

```
throw value;
```

When this statement appears inside any function nested within the **try**, the program stops executing the current function and climbs back up the chain of function calls, popping and discarding stack frames until it reaches the frame containing the **try** statement. Assuming that the value in the **throw** statement matches the type in the **catch** clause, that value is assigned to the variable *var,* and control continues with the statements in the **catch** clause. In more sophisticated applications, a **try** statement can have several **catch** clauses, which are differentiated by the type of variable. The **try** statements in this book are used only to catch the **ErrorException** thrown by **error** and therefore need just one **catch** clause.

The structure of expressions

Before you can complete the implementation of the interpreter, you need to understand what expressions are and how they can be represented as objects. As is often the case when you are thinking about a programming abstraction, it helps to begin with the insights you have acquired about expressions from your experience as a C++ programmer. For example, you know that the lines

```
0
2 * 11
3 * (a + b + c)
x = x + 1
```

represent legal expressions in C++. At the same time, you also know that the lines

```
2 * (x - y
17 k
```

are not expressions. The first has unbalanced parentheses, and the second is missing an operator. An important part of understanding expressions is articulating what constitutes an expression so that you can differentiate legal expressions from malformed ones.

A recursive definition of expressions

As it happens, the best way to define the structure of a legal expression is to adopt a recursive perspective. A sequence of symbols is an expression if it has one of the following forms:

1. An integer constant

2. A variable name

3. An expression enclosed in parentheses

4. A sequence of two expressions separated by an operator

The first two possibilities represent the simple cases. The last two possibilities define an expression recursively in terms of simpler expressions.

To see how you might apply this recursive definition, consider the following sequence of symbols:

```
y = 3 * (x + 1)
```

Does this sequence constitute an expression? You know from experience that the answer is yes, but you can use the recursive definition of an expression to justify that answer. The integer constants 3 and 1 are expressions according to rule #1. Similarly, the variable names **x** and **y** are expressions as specified by rule #2. Thus, you already know that the expressions marked by the symbol *exp* in the following diagram are expressions, as defined by the simple-case rules:

```
 exp     exp          exp    exp
  |       |            |      |
  y   =   3   *   (    x  +   1    )
```

At this point, you can start to apply the recursive rules. Given that **x** and **1** are both expressions, you can tell that the string of symbols **x + 1** is an expression by applying rule #4, because it consists of two expressions separated by an operator. You can record this observation in the diagram by adding a new expression marker tied to the parts of the expression that match the rule, as shown:

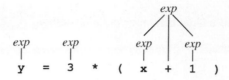

The parenthesized quantity can now be identified as an expression according to rule #3, which results in the following diagram:

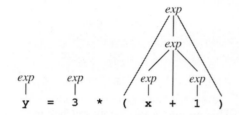

By applying rule #4 two more times to take care of the remaining operators, you can show that the entire set of characters is indeed an expression, as follows:

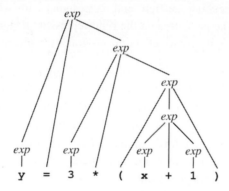

As you can see, this diagram forms a tree. A tree that demonstrates how a sequence of input symbols fits the syntactic rules of a programming language is called a *parse tree.*

Ambiguity

Generating a parse tree from a sequence of symbols requires a certain amount of caution. Given the four rules for expressions outlined in the preceding section, it is possible to generate more than one parse tree for the expression

        y = 3 * (x + 1)

Although the tree structure shown at the end of the last section presumably represents what the programmer intended, it is just as valid to argue that y = 3 is an expression according to rule #4, and that the entire expression therefore consists of the expression y = 3, followed by a multiplication sign, followed by the

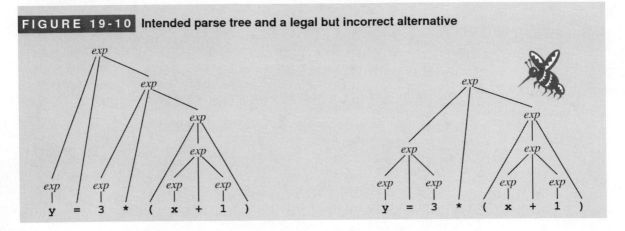

FIGURE 19-10 Intended parse tree and a legal but incorrect alternative

expression **(x + 1)**. This argument ultimately reaches the same conclusion about whether the input line represents an expression, but generates a different parse tree. Both parse trees are shown in Figure 19-10. The parse tree on the left is the one generated in the preceding section and corresponds to what the expression presumably means. The parse tree on the right represents a legal application of the expression rules but is unlikely to reflect the programmer's intent.

The problem with the second parse tree is that it ignores the precedence rule that multiplication should be performed before assignment. The recursive definition of an expression indicates only that a sequence of two expressions separated by an operator is an expression; it says nothing about the relative precedence of the various operators and therefore admits both the intended and unintended interpretations. Because it allows multiple interpretations of the same string, the informal definition of *expression* given in the preceding section is said to be **ambiguous.** To resolve the ambiguity, the parsing algorithm must include some mechanism for determining the order in which operators are applied.

The question of how to resolve the ambiguity in an expression is discussed in the section on "Parsing an expression" later in this chapter. At the moment, the point of introducing parse trees is to provide some insight into how you might represent an expression as a data structure. To this end, it is important to note that the parse trees in Figure 19-10 are not ambiguous. The structure of each tree explicitly represents the structure of a valid expression. The ambiguity exists only in deciding how to generate the parse tree from the input string. Once you have the correct parse tree, its structure contains everything you need to understand the order of the operators.

Expression trees

In fact, parse trees contain more information than you need in the evaluation phase. Parentheses are useful in determining how to generate the parse tree but play no role in the evaluation of an expression once its structure is known. If your concern is simply to find the value of an expression, you do not need to include parentheses within the structure. This observation allows you to simplify a complete parse tree into an abstract structure called an ***expression tree*** that is more appropriate for the evaluation phase. In the expression tree, nodes in the parse tree that represent parenthesized subexpressions are eliminated. Moreover, it is convenient to drop the *exp* labels from the tree and instead mark each node in the tree with the appropriate operator symbol. For example, the intended interpretation of the expression

```
y = 3 * (x + 1)
```

corresponds to the following expression tree:

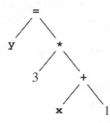

The structure of an expression tree is similar in many ways to the binary search tree from Chapter 16, but there are also some important differences. In the binary search tree, every node had the same structure. In an expression tree, there are three different types of nodes, as follows:

1. ***Constant nodes*** represent integer constants, such as 3 and 1 in the example tree.
2. ***Identifier nodes*** represent the names of variables, such as **x** and **y**.
3. ***Compound nodes*** represent the application of an operator to two operands, each of which is an arbitrary expression tree.

Each of these node types corresponds to one of the rules in the recursive formulation of an expression. The definition of the **Expression** class itself must make it possible for clients to work with expression nodes of all three types. Similarly, the underlying implementation must somehow make it possible for different expression types to coexist within the tree.

To represent such a structure, you need to define a representation for expressions that allows them to have different structures depending on their type. An integer expression, for example, must include the value of the integer as part of its internal structure. An identifier expression must include the name of the identifier. A compound expression must include the operator along with the left and right subexpressions. Defining a single abstract type that allows expressions to take on these different underlying structures requires you to implement a class hierarchy in which a general **Expression** class becomes the superclass for three subclasses, one for each of the expression types.

Creating an inheritance hierarchy is an appropriate way to represent the different types of expression trees. The top of the hierarchy is occupied by the **Expression** class, which specifies the features that are common to each of the expression types. The **Expression** class has three subclasses, one for each expression type. The definitions for all four of these classes—the high-level **Expression** class and the lower-level subclasses **ConstantExp**, **IdentifierExp**, and **CompoundExp**—are all included as part of the **exp.h** interface.

As is typical for a class hierarchy, many of the most common methods are defined at the level of the **Expression** class but implemented individually in each of the subclasses. Every **Expression** object implements the following methods:

- The **eval** method determines the value of the expression, which is always an integer in this application. For constant expressions, **eval** simply returns the value of the constant. For identifier expressions, **eval** determines the value by looking up the identifier name in the symbol table. For compound expressions, **eval** begins by calling itself recursively on the left and right subexpressions and then applying the appropriate operator.

- The **toString** method converts an expression into a string that makes the structure explicit by adding parentheses around every subexpression, even if those parentheses are not required. Although the **toString** method is not used in the interpreter, it will prove useful in debugging. If you are unsure whether an expression has the correct form, you can use **toString** to verify its structure.

- The **getType** method makes it possible to determine the type of an existing expression. The return value is one of the enumeration constants defined for the type **ExpressionType**: **CONSTANT**, **IDENTIFIER**, and **COMPOUND**.

- The **Expression** class exports a set of getter methods that return various parts of the expression structure. In **exp.h**, the getter methods are defined at the level of the abstract class because doing so makes them considerably easier to use.

In the **Expression** class itself, each of these methods is declared as virtual. When the program runs, it chooses which version of the method to call by looking at the actual type of the expression.

The **exp.h** interface

Figure 19-11 shows the interface for the **Expression** class and its subclasses. Each **Expression** subclass must implement the three pure virtual methods declared in the superclass: **eval**, **toString**, and **getType**. While the superclass specifies the prototype, each subclass is free to implement those methods in its own way.

FIGURE 19-11   The exp.h interface

```
/*
 * File: exp.h
 * ------------
 * This interface defines a class hierarchy for arithmetic expressions.
 */

#ifndef _exp_h
#define _exp_h

#include <string>
#include "map.h"
#include "tokenscanner.h"

/* Forward reference */

class EvaluationContext;

/*
 * Type: ExpressionType
 * --------------------
 * This enumerated type is used to differentiate the three different
 * expression types: CONSTANT, IDENTIFIER, and COMPOUND.
 */

enum ExpressionType { CONSTANT, IDENTIFIER, COMPOUND };

/*
 * Class: Expression
 * -----------------
 * This class is used to represent a node in an expression tree.
 * Expression itself is an abstract class, which means that there are
 * never any objects whose primary type is Expression.  All objects are
 * instead created using one of the three concrete subclasses:
 *
 *   1. ConstantExp   -- an integer constant
 *   2. IdentifierExp -- a string representing an identifier
 *   3. CompoundExp   -- two expressions combined by an operator
 *
 * The Expression class defines the interface common to all expressions;
 * each subclass provides its own implementation of the common interface.
 */

class Expression {

public:

/*
 * Constructor: Expression
 * -----------------------
 * Specifies the constructor for the base Expression class.  Each subclass
 * defines its own constructor as well.
 */

   Expression();
```

FIGURE 19-11 The `exp.h` interface (continued)

```
/*
 * Destructor: ~Expression
 * Usage: delete exp;
 * -------------------
 * Deallocates the storage for this expression.  This method must be
 * declared virtual to ensure that the correct subclass destructor
 * is called when deleting an expression.
 */

   virtual ~Expression();

/*
 * Method: eval
 * Usage: int value = exp->eval(context);
 * ---------------------------------------
 * Evaluates this expression and returns its value in the context of
 * the specified EvaluationContext object.
 */

   virtual int eval(EvaluationContext & context) = 0;

/*
 * Method: toString
 * Usage: string str = exp->toString();
 * --------------------------------------
 * Returns a string representation of this expression.
 */

   virtual std::string toString() = 0;

/*
 * Method: getType
 * Usage: ExpressionType type = exp->getType();
 * ---------------------------------------------
 * Returns the type of the expression, which must be one of the constants
 * CONSTANT, IDENTIFIER, or COMPOUND.
 */

   virtual ExpressionType getType() = 0;

/*
 * Getter methods for convenience
 * -------------------------------
 * The following methods get the fields of the appropriate subclass.  Calling
 * these methods on an object of the wrong subclass generates an error.
 */

   virtual int getConstantValue();
   virtual std::string getIdentifierName();
   virtual std::string getOperator();
   virtual Expression *getLHS();
   virtual Expression *getRHS();

};
```

FIGURE 19-11 The exp.h interface (continued)

```
/*
 * Subclass: ConstantExp
 * ------------------------
 * This subclass represents an integer constant.
 */

class ConstantExp : public Expression {

public:

/*
 * Constructor: ConstantExp
 * Usage: Expression *exp = new ConstantExp(value);
 * ----------------------------------------------------
 * Creates a new integer constant expression.
 */

   ConstantExp(int value);

/* Prototypes for the virtual methods overridden by this class */

   virtual int eval(EvaluationContext & context);
   virtual std::string toString();
   virtual ExpressionType getType();
   virtual int getConstantValue();

private:
   int value;                       /* The value of the integer constant */

};

/*
 * Subclass: IdentifierExp
 * ------------------------
 * This subclass represents an identifier used as a variable name.
 */

class IdentifierExp : public Expression {

public:

/*
 * Constructor: IdentifierExp
 * Usage: Expression *exp = new IdentifierExp(name);
 * ----------------------------------------------------
 * Creates an identifier expression with the specified name.
 */

   IdentifierExp(std::string name);
```

FIGURE 19-11 The exp.h interface (continued)

```
/* Prototypes for the virtual methods overridden by this class */

    virtual int eval(EvaluationContext & context);
    virtual std::string toString();
    virtual ExpressionType getType();
    virtual std::string getIdentifierName();

private:
    std::string name;                 /* The name of the identifier */

};

/*
 * Subclass: CompoundExp
 * -----------------------
 * This subclass represents a compound expression consisting of
 * two subexpressions joined by an operator.
 */

class CompoundExp : public Expression {

public:

/*
 * Constructor: CompoundExp
 * Usage: Expression *exp = new CompoundExp(op, lhs, rhs);
 * -------------------------------------------------------------
 * Creates a new compound expression composed of the operator (op)
 * and the left and right subexpressions (lhs and rhs).
 */

    CompoundExp(std::string op, Expression *lhs, Expression *rhs);

/* Prototypes for the virtual methods overridden by this class */

    virtual ~CompoundExp();
    virtual int eval(EvaluationContext & context);
    virtual std::string toString();
    virtual ExpressionType getType();
    virtual std::string getOperator();
    virtual Expression *getLHS();
    virtual Expression *getRHS();

private:

    std::string op;                   /* The operator string (+, -, *, /)  */
    Expression *lhs, *rhs;            /* The left and right subexpression  */

};
```

FIGURE 19-11 The `exp.h` interface (continued)

```
/*
 * Class: EvaluationContext
 * ----------------------------
 * This class encapsulates the information that the evaluator needs to
 * know in order to evaluate an expression.
 */

class EvaluationContext {

public:

/*
 * Method: setValue
 * Usage: context.setValue(var, value);
 * ----------------------------------------
 * Sets the value associated with the specified var.
 */

   void setValue(std::string var, int value);

/*
 * Method: getValue
 * Usage: int value = context.getValue(var);
 * ----------------------------------------------
 * Returns the value associated with the specified variable.
 */

   int getValue(std::string var);

/*
 * Method: isDefined
 * Usage: if (context.isDefined(var)) . . .
 * ----------------------------------------------
 * Returns true if the specified variable is defined.
 */

   bool isDefined(std::string var);

private:

   Map<std::string,int> symbolTable;

};

#endif
```

Representing the Expression subclasses

The abstract **Expression** class declares no data members. This design makes sense because no data values are common to all node types. Each specific subclass has its own unique storage requirements—an integer node needs to store an integer constant, a compound node stores pointers to its subexpressions, and so on. Each subclass declares the specific data members that are required for its particular expression type. Each subclass also defines its own constructor whose arguments provide the information needed to represent an expression of that type. To create a constant expression, for example, you need to specify the value of the integer. To construct a compound expression, you need to provide the operator and the left and right subexpressions.

All **Expression** objects are immutable, which means that any **Expression** object, once created, will never change. Although clients are free to embed existing expressions in larger ones, the interface offers no facilities for changing the components of any existing expression. Using an immutable type to represent expressions helps enforce the separation between the implementation of the **Expression** class and its clients. Because clients are prohibited from making changes in the underlying representation, they are unable to change the internal structure in a way that violates the requirements for expression trees.

Diagramming expressions

To reinforce your understanding of how **Expression** objects are stored, you can visualize how the concrete structure is represented inside the computer's memory. The representation of an **Expression** object depends on its specific subclass. You can diagram the structure of an expression tree by considering the three classes independently. A **ConstantExp** object simply stores an integer value, shown here as it would exist for the integer 3:

CONSTANT
3

An **IdentifierExp** object stores a string representing a variable name, illustrated here for the variable **x**:

IDENTIFIER
x

A **CompoundExp** object stores the binary operator along with two pointers that indicate the left and right subexpressions:

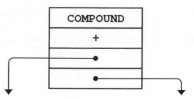

Because compound nodes contain subexpressions that can themselves be compound nodes, expression trees can grow to an arbitrary level of complexity. Figure 19-12 illustrates the internal data structure for the expression

$$y = 3 * (x + 1)$$

which includes three operators and therefore requires three compound nodes. The parentheses do not appear explicitly in the expression tree because the structure of the tree correctly reflects the desired order of operations.

Implementing the methods

The methods in the various expression classes are straightforward to implement. The implementation of the **Expression** class hierarchy appears in Figure 19-13.

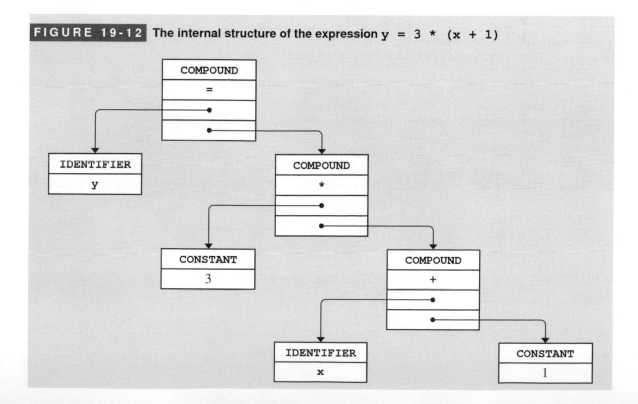

FIGURE 19-12 The internal structure of the expression y = 3 * (x + 1)

FIGURE 19-13   Implementation of the exp.h interface

```
/*
 * File: exp.cpp
 * -------------
 * This file implements the exp.h interface.
 */

#include <string>
#include "error.h"
#include "exp.h"
#include "strlib.h"
using namespace std;

/*
 * Implementation notes: Expression
 * --------------------------------
 * The Expression class itself implements only those methods that
 * are not designated as pure virtual methods.
 */

Expression::Expression() {
   /* Empty */
}

Expression::~Expression() {
   /* Empty */
}

int Expression::getConstantValue() {
   error("getConstantValue: Illegal expression type");
   return 0;
}

std::string Expression::getIdentifierName() {
   error("getIdentifierName: Illegal expression type");
   return "";
}

std::string Expression::getOperator() {
   error("getOperator: Illegal expression type");
   return "";
}

Expression *Expression::getLHS() {
   error("getLHS: Illegal expression type");
   return NULL;
}

Expression *Expression::getRHS() {
   error("getRHS: Illegal expression type");
   return NULL;
}
```

FIGURE 19-13 Implementation of the exp.h interface (continued)

```
/*
 * Implementation notes: ConstantExp
 * ----------------------------------
 * The ConstantExp subclass represents an integer constant.  The eval
 * method simply returns that value.
 */

ConstantExp::ConstantExp(int value) {
   this->value = value;
}

int ConstantExp::eval(EvaluationContext & context) {
   return value;
}

string ConstantExp::toString() {
   return integerToString(value);
}

ExpressionType ConstantExp::getType() {
   return CONSTANT;
}

int ConstantExp::getConstantValue() {
   return value;
}

/*
 * Implementation notes: IdentifierExp
 * -----------------------------------
 * The IdentifierExp subclass represents a variable name.  The
 * implementation of eval looks up that name in the evaluation context.
 */

IdentifierExp::IdentifierExp(string name) {
   this->name = name;
}

int IdentifierExp::eval(EvaluationContext & context) {
   if (!context.isDefined(name)) error(name + " is undefined");
   return context.getValue(name);
}

string IdentifierExp::toString() {
   return name;
}

ExpressionType IdentifierExp::getType() {
   return IDENTIFIER;
}

string IdentifierExp::getIdentifierName() {
   return name;
}
```

FIGURE 19-13 Implementation of the exp.h interface (continued)

```cpp
/*
 * Implementation notes: CompoundExp
 * ---------------------------------
 * The implementation of eval for CompoundExp evaluates the left and right
 * subexpressions recursively and then applies the operator.  Assignment is
 * treated as a special case because it does not evaluate the left operand.
 */
CompoundExp::CompoundExp(string op, Expression *lhs, Expression *rhs) {
   this->op = op;
   this->lhs = lhs;
   this->rhs = rhs;
}

CompoundExp::~CompoundExp() {
   delete lhs;
   delete rhs;
}

int CompoundExp::eval(EvaluationContext & context) {
   int right = rhs->eval(context);
   if (op == "=") {
      context.setValue(lhs->getIdentifierName(), right);
      return right;
   }
   int left = lhs->eval(context);
   if (op == "+") return left + right;
   if (op == "-") return left - right;
   if (op == "*") return left * right;
   if (op == "/") {
      if (right == 0) error("Division by 0");
      return left / right;
   }
   error("Illegal operator in expression");
   return 0;
}

string CompoundExp::toString() {
   return '(' + lhs->toString() + ' ' + op + ' ' + rhs->toString() + ')';
}

ExpressionType CompoundExp::getType() {
   return COMPOUND;
}

string CompoundExp::getOperator() {
   return op;
}

Expression *CompoundExp::getLHS() {
   return lhs;
}

Expression *CompoundExp::getRHS() {
   return rhs;
}
```

| FIGURE 19-13 | Implementation of the `exp.h` interface (continued) |

```
/*
 * Implementation notes: EvaluationContext
 * ----------------------------------------------
 * The methods in the EvaluationContext class simply call the appropriate
 * method on the map used to represent the symbol table.
 */

void EvaluationContext::setValue(string var, int value) {
    symbolTable.put(var, value);
}

int EvaluationContext::getValue(string var) {
    return symbolTable.get(var);
}

bool EvaluationContext::isDefined(string var) {
    return symbolTable.containsKey(var);
}
```

The implementation of the **Expression** class consists of an empty constructor, an empty destructor, and default implementations for the getter methods. In the **exp.h** interface, the destructor is marked using the **virtual** keyword, as it should be in any inheritance hierarchy that involves dynamic memory allocation. Making a destructor virtual ensures that subclasses can provide their own destructors that are called along with the destructor for the base class. The implementations for the getter methods simply report an error if a client ever invokes them. Each subclass can therefore override the getter methods that apply to that class, inheriting the others from **Expression**.

The implementation of each subclass in Figure 19-13 follows a common pattern. Each of the subclasses defines a constructor that takes the arguments specified by its interface and uses those arguments to initialize the appropriate instance variables. The implementation of most of the remaining methods then follows directly from the structure of that subclass.

The implementation of **eval** differs significantly for each expression type. The value of a constant expression is the value of the integer stored in that node. The value of an identifier expression comes from the symbol table in the evaluation context. The value of a compound expression requires a recursive computation. Each compound expression consists of an operator and two subexpressions. For the arithmetic operators (+, −, *, and /), **eval** uses recursion to evaluate the left and right subexpressions and then applies the appropriate operation. For the assignment operator (=), however, **eval** updates the symbol table by assigning the value of the right-hand side to the identifier that appears to the left of the assignment operator.

19.4 Parsing an expression

The problem of building the appropriate parse tree from a stream of tokens is not an easy one. To a large extent, the underlying theory necessary to build an efficient parser lies beyond the scope of this text. Even so, it is possible to make some headway on the problem and solve it for the limited case of arithmetic expressions.

Parsing and grammars

In the early days of programming languages, programmers implemented the parsing phase of a compiler without thinking very hard about the nature of the process. As a result, early parsing programs were difficult to write and even harder to debug. In the 1960s, however, computer scientists studied the problem of parsing from a more theoretical perspective, which simplified it greatly. Today, a computer scientist who has taken a course on compilers can write a parser for a programming language with very little work. In fact, most parsers can be generated automatically from a simple specification of the language for which they are intended. In the field of computer science, parsing is one of the areas in which it is easiest to see the profound impact of theory on practice. Without the theoretical work necessary to simplify the problem, programming languages would have made far less headway than they have.

The essential theoretical insight necessary to simplify parsing is actually borrowed from linguistics. Like human languages, programming languages have rules of syntax that define the grammatical structure of the language. Moreover, because programming languages are much more regular in structure than human languages, it is usually easy to describe the syntactic structure of a programming language in a precise form called a *grammar.* In the context of a programming language, a grammar consists of a set of rules that show how a particular language construct can be derived from simpler ones.

If you start with the English rules for expression formation, it is not hard to write down a grammar for the simple expressions used in this chapter. Partly because it simplifies things a little in the parser, it helps to incorporate into the parser the notion of a *term* as any single unit that can appear as an operand to a larger expression. For example, constants and variables are clearly terms. Moreover, an expression in parentheses acts as a single unit and can therefore also be regarded as a term. Thus, a term is one of the following possibilities:

• An integer constant

• A variable

• An expression in parentheses

An expression is then either of the following:

- A term

- Two expressions separated by an operator

This informal definition can be translated directly into the following grammar, presented in what programmers call **BNF**, which stands for Backus-Naur Form, named after its inventors John Backus and Peter Naur:

$$E \ \rightarrow \ T \qquad\qquad\qquad T \ \rightarrow \ integer$$
$$E \ \rightarrow \ E \ op \ E \qquad\qquad T \ \rightarrow \ identifier$$
$$\qquad\qquad\qquad\qquad\qquad T \ \rightarrow \ (\ E \ )$$

In the grammar, uppercase letters like E and T are called **nonterminal symbols** and stand for an abstract linguistic class, such as an expression or a term. The specific punctuation marks and the italicized words represent the **terminal symbols,** which are those that appear in the token stream. Explicit terminal symbols, such as the parentheses in the last rule, must appear in the input exactly as written. The italicized words represent placeholders for tokens that fit their general description. Thus, the notation *integer* stands for any string of digits returned by the scanner as a token. Each terminal corresponds to exactly one token in the scanner stream. Nonterminals typically correspond to a sequence of tokens.

Taking precedence into account

Like the informal rules for defining expressions presented in the section on "A recursive definition of expressions" earlier in the chapter, grammars can be used to generate parse trees. Just like those rules, this grammar is ambiguous as written and can generate several different parse trees for the same sequence of tokens. Once again, the problem is that the grammar does not take into account how tightly each operator binds to its operands. Generating the correct parse tree from an ambiguous grammar therefore requires the parser to have access to the precedence information.

The easiest way to specify precedence is to assign each operator a numeric value that indicates its precedence, with higher precedence values corresponding to operators that bind more tightly to their operands. For the arithmetic operators and assignment, this precedence information can be encoded in the following function:

```
int precedence(string token) {
   if (token == "=") return 1;
   if (token == "+" || token == "-") return 2;
   if (token == "*" || token == "/") return 3;
   return 0;
}
```

If you call **precedence** on a token that does not match one of the legal operators, the function returns 0. You can therefore use **precedence** to determine whether a token is an operator by checking for a nonzero result.

Recursive-descent parsers

Most parsers today are created automatically from a grammar for the language through the use of programs called *parser generators.* For simple grammars, however, it is not difficult to implement a parser by hand. The general strategy is to write a function that is responsible for reading each of the nonterminal symbols in the grammar. The expression grammar uses the nonterminals E and T, which suggests that the parser needs the functions **readE** and **readT**. Each of these functions takes the token scanner as an argument so that it can read tokens from the input source. By checking those tokens against the rules of the grammar, it is usually possible—at least for simple grammars—to determine which rule to apply, particularly if the **readE** function has access to the current precedence level.

The **readE** and **readT** functions are mutually recursive. When the **readE** function needs to read a term, it does so by calling **readT**. Similarly, when **readT** needs to read an expression enclosed in parentheses, it calls **readE** to accomplish that task. Parsers that use mutually recursive functions in this fashion are called *recursive-descent parsers.*

As the mutual recursion proceeds, the **readE** and **readT** functions build up the expression tree by calling the constructors for the appropriate expression class. For example, if **readT** discovers an integer token, it can allocate a **ConstantExp** node that contains that value. This expression tree is then returned up the chain of recursive calls through the return value of these functions.

The implementation of the parser module appears in Figure 19-14. The only complex part of the parser implementation is the code for **readE**, which needs to take precedence into account. As long as the precedence of the operators it encounters is greater than the current precedence provided by its caller, **readE** can create a compound expression node from the subexpressions to the left and right of the operator, after which it can loop back to check the next operator. When **readE** encounters the end of the input or an operator whose precedence is less than or equal to the current precedence, it returns to the next higher level in the chain of **readE** calls, where the prevailing precedence is lower. Before doing so, **readE** must put the as-yet-unprocessed operator token back into the scanner input stream so that it can be read again at the appropriate level. This task is accomplished by calling the **saveToken** method in the **TokenScanner** class.

FIGURE 19-14 Implementation of the expression parser

```cpp
/*
 * File: parser.cpp
 * ----------------
 * This file implements the parser.h interface.
 */

#include <iostream>
#include <string>
#include "error.h"
#include "exp.h"
#include "parser.h"
#include "strlib.h"
#include "tokenscanner.h"
using namespace std;

/*
 * Implementation notes: parseExp
 * ------------------------------
 * This code just reads an expression and then checks for extra tokens.
 */

Expression *parseExp(TokenScanner & scanner) {
   Expression *exp = readE(scanner, 0);
   if (scanner.hasMoreTokens()) {
      error("Unexpected token \"" + scanner.nextToken() + "\"");
   }
   return exp;
}

/*
 * Implementation notes: readE
 * Usage: exp = readE(scanner, prec);
 * ------------------------------
 * The implementation of readE uses precedence to resolve the ambiguity in
 * the grammar.  At each level, the parser reads operators and subexpressions
 * until it finds an operator whose precedence is greater than that of the
 * prevailing one.  When a higher-precedence operator is found, readE calls
 * itself recursively to read that subexpression as a unit.
 */

Expression *readE(TokenScanner & scanner, int prec) {
   Expression *exp = readT(scanner);
   string token;
   while (true) {
      token = scanner.nextToken();
      int tprec = precedence(token);
      if (tprec <= prec) break;
      Expression *rhs = readE(scanner, tprec);
      exp = new CompoundExp(token, exp, rhs);
   }
   scanner.saveToken(token);
   return exp;
}
```

FIGURE 19-14 Implementation of the expression parser (continued)

```
/*
 * Implementation notes: readT
 * ----------------------------
 * This function scans a term, which is either an integer, an identifier,
 * or a parenthesized subexpression.
 */

Expression *readT(TokenScanner & scanner) {
   string token = scanner.nextToken();
   TokenType type = scanner.getTokenType(token);
   if (type == WORD) return new IdentifierExp(token);
   if (type == NUMBER) return new ConstantExp(stringToInteger(token));
   if (token != "(") error("Unexpected token \"" + token + "\"");
   Expression *exp = readE(scanner, 0);
   if (scanner.nextToken() != ")") {
      error("Unbalanced parentheses");
   }
   return exp;
}

/*
 * Implementation notes: precedence
 * ---------------------------------
 * This function checks the token against each of the defined operators
 * and returns the appropriate precedence value.
 */

int precedence(string token) {
   if (token == "=") return 1;
   if (token == "+" || token == "-") return 2;
   if (token == "*" || token == "/") return 3;
   return 0;
}
```

In my experience, it is nearly impossible to understand the code for **readE** without walking through at least one example. The rest of this section traces through what happens if you call **parseExp** when the scanner contains the string

```
odd = 2 * n + 1
```

In this expression, the multiplication is performed first, followed by the addition, and then finally by the assignment. The interesting question is how the parser determines this ordering and assembles the appropriate expression tree.

The process of parsing this expression is too complicated to trace one line at a time. A more practical approach is to show the execution history at a few interesting points along the way. In particular, it should be possible to predict what will happen on each call to **nextToken** and **readT** without tracing them in detail.

In the initial call to **readE**, the code reads the first term and the token that follows it, which is the assignment operator. The = operator has a precedence value of 1, which is greater than the prevailing precedence of 0. The code therefore reaches the following point in the first **readE** call:

```
Expression *readE(TokenScanner & scanner, int prec) {
   Expression *exp = readT(scanner);
   string token;
   while (true) {
      token = scanner.nextToken();
      int tprec = precedence(token);
      if (tprec <= prec) break;
      Expression *rhs = readE(scanner, tprec);
      exp = new CompoundExp(token, exp, rhs);
   }
   scanner.saveToken(token);
   return exp;
}
```

				exp	rhs
				odd	
scanner	prec	tprec	token		
odd = 2 * n + 1	0	1	"="		

From here, the parser needs to read the right operand of the assignment operator, which requires a recursive call to **readE**. This call proceeds similarly, but with a new precedence value of 1. Execution of the call soon reaches the following state:

```
Expression *readE(TokenScanner & scanner, int prec) {
   Expression *readE(TokenScanner & scanner, int prec) {
      Expression *exp = readT(scanner);
      string token;
      while (true) {
         token = scanner.nextToken();
         int tprec = precedence(token);
         if (tprec <= prec) break;
         Expression *rhs = readE(scanner, tprec);
         exp = new CompoundExp(token, exp, rhs);
      }
      scanner.saveToken(token);
      return exp;
   }
```

				exp	rhs
				2	
scanner	prec	tprec	token		
odd = 2 * n + 1	1	3	"*"		

This level of the process is concerned only with reading the subexpression starting with the token **2**. The stack frame underneath the current one keeps track of what the parser was doing prior to making the recursive call.

At this point, the parser makes yet another recursive call to **readE**, passing in the precedence of the * operator, which has the value 3. On this call, however, the precedence of the **+** operator that comes next in the token stream is less than the current precedence, which causes the loop to exit at the following point:

```
Expression *readE(TokenScanner & scanner, int prec) {
  Expression *readE(TokenScanner & scanner, int prec) {
    Expression *readE(TokenScanner & scanner, int prec) {
       Expression *exp = readT(scanner);
       string token;
       while (true) {
          token = scanner.nextToken();
          int tprec = precedence(token);
          if (tprec <= prec) break;
          Expression *rhs = readE(scanner, tprec);
          exp = new CompoundExp(token, exp, rhs);
       }
☞     scanner.saveToken(token);
       return exp;
    }
```

scanner	prec	tprec	token	exp	rhs
odd = 2 * n + 1	3	2	"+"	n	

The parser saves the **+** operator in the token stream and returns the identifier expression **n** to the point at which the most recent call occurred. The result of the **readE** call is assigned to the variable **rhs**, as follows:

```
Expression *readE(TokenScanner & scanner, int prec) {
  Expression *readE(TokenScanner & scanner, int prec) {
     Expression *exp = readT(scanner);
     string token;
     while (true) {
        token = scanner.nextToken();
        int tprec = precedence(token);
        if (tprec <= prec) break;
        Expression *rhs = readE(scanner, tprec);
☞      exp = new CompoundExp(token, exp, rhs);
     }
     scanner.saveToken(token);
     return exp;
  }
```

scanner	prec	tprec	token	exp	rhs
odd = 2 * n + 1	1	3	"*"	2	n

From here, the parser creates a new compound expression by combining **exp** and **rhs**. That value is not yet returned as the value from this level but is instead assigned to the variable **exp**. The parser then makes another pass through the **while** loop in which it reads the **+** token a second time. On this cycle, however, the precedence of **+** is greater than the precedence set by the assignment operator. The execution therefore reaches the following state:

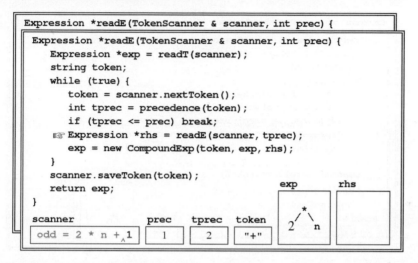

Although you can go through the steps in detail if you need to, you should be able to apply the recursive leap of faith by now. The scanner contains a single token, which is the integer 1. Given that you've already watched the parser read the integer 2, you should be able to skip ahead to the next line in the execution:

```
Expression *readE(TokenScanner & scanner, int prec) {
    Expression *readE(TokenScanner & scanner, int prec) {
        Expression *exp = readT(scanner);
        string token;
        while (true) {
            token = scanner.nextToken();
            int tprec = precedence(token);
            if (tprec <= prec) break;
            Expression *rhs = readE(scanner, tprec);
      ☞    exp = new CompoundExp(token, exp, rhs);
        }
        scanner.saveToken(token);
        return exp;
    }
```

The parser again assembles the values of **exp** and **rhs** into a new compound expression and cycles back for another iteration of the **while** loop.

On the next iteration, **token** is the empty string marking the end of the token stream. The empty string is not a legal operator, so the **precedence** function returns the value 0, which is less than the prevailing precedence at this level. The parser therefore exits from the `while` loop, which leads to the following configuration:

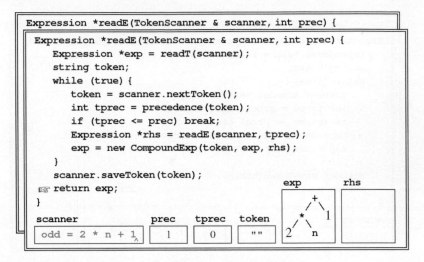

When control returns to the first `readE` call, all the necessary information is now in place, as follows:

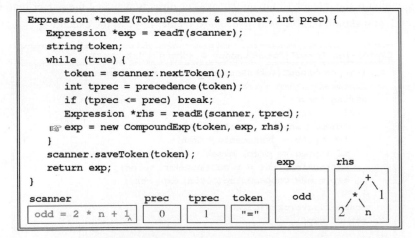

All `readE` has to do is create the new compound and—after reading the empty token one more time—return the final version of the expression tree to `parseExp`:

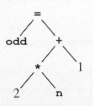

19.5 Multiple inheritance

One of the features that sets C++ apart from most other object-oriented languages is that classes can inherit behavior from more than one superclass. This property is called *multiple inheritance.* Although multiple inheritance can make hierarchies more difficult to understand, it appears in several classes in the C++ library and is therefore worth including in this book.

Multiple inheritance in the stream libraries

Although Chapter 4 introduces the stream class hierarchy, it stops short of describing those features that use multiple inheritance. As it happens, the stream libraries include classes that are both input and output streams. Figure 19-15 updates the UML diagram from Figure 4-7 to show how these classes fit into the stream hierarchy as a whole. The **fstream** class at the bottom is an **iostream**, which is in turn—if you follow the arrow leading up and to the left—an **istream**.

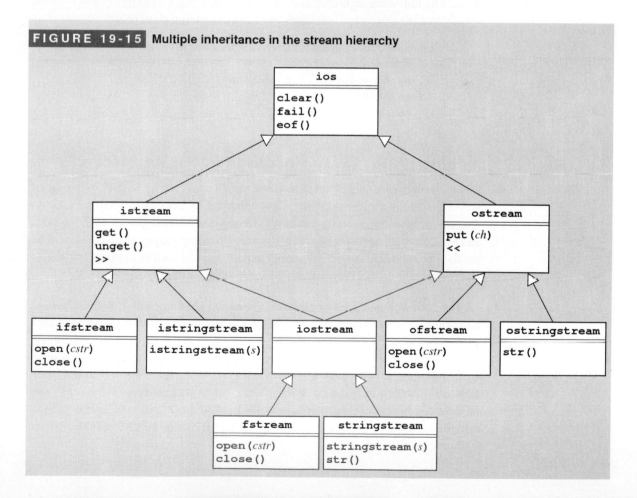

FIGURE 19-15 Multiple inheritance in the stream hierarchy

The **fstream** class therefore inherits all the methods that pertain to **istream**s. If you instead follow the arrow up and to the right, you discover that the **fstream** class is an **ostream**, which means that it inherits these methods as well.

As an example of how you might use these bidirectional streams, suppose that you have been asked to write a function **roundToSignificantDigits** that takes a floating-point value *x* and, as its name implies, rounds it to some specified number of significant digits. For example, if you call

```
roundToSignificantDigits(3.14159265, 5)
```

the function should return the value of π rounded to 5 significant digits, which is 3.1416. Although it is possible to write this function in other ways, the simplest strategy is to use the facilities already provided by streams. All you need to do is write the value of *x* to an output stream after setting the precision to the desired number of digits, and then read that same value back to convert it to its numeric form. The following implementation does just that using a **stringstream**—which is both an **istream** and an **ostream**—to store the intermediate string:

```
double roundToSignificantDigits(double x, int nDigits) {
   stringstream ss;
   ss << setprecision(nDigits) << x;
   ss >> x;
   return x;
}
```

Adding a `GFillable` class to the `GObject` hierarchy

As an example of how multiple inheritance might prove useful in your own code, it is worth returning to the **GObject** class hierarchy introduced in section 19.2. As that class hierarchy currently exists, the **GRect** and **GOval** classes each export a **setFilled** method that lets clients specify whether a graphical object should be outlined or solid. By default, rectangles and ovals are drawn as outlines, but clients can change that assumption by invoking the method **setFilled(true)**.

The code in Figure 19-4 implements the **setFilled** method in both the **GRect** and **GOval** classes, even though the code for the method is exactly the same in each case. As a general rule, experienced programmers avoid duplicating code unless doing so is absolutely necessary. Multiple inheritance offers a strategy for avoiding such duplication. The **GRect** and **GOval** classes already inherit behavior from **GObject**; if they also inherit from a class called **GFillable**, the **setFilled** method can be defined in that class instead. The UML diagram for the revised **GObject** hierarchy appears in Figure 19-16, and the code for **GFillable** appears in Figure 19-17.

FIGURE 19-16   The Shape class hierarchy with a GFillable class

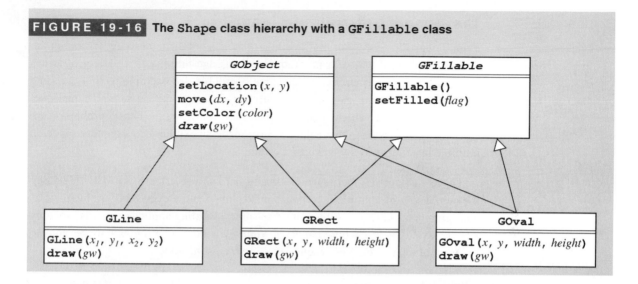

FIGURE 19-17   The GFillable class

```
class GFillable {

public:

/*
 * Constructor: GFillable
 * _____
 * Ensures that fillable shapes are created as outlines by default.
 */

   GFillable() {
      fillFlag = false;
   }

/*
 * Method: setFilled
 * Usage: shape.setFilled(flag);
 * _____
 * Sets the fill status for shape, where false is outlined and true is filled.
 */

   void setFilled(bool flag) {
      fillFlag = flag;
   }

protected:

   bool fillFlag;            /* Flag is false for outline, true for solid fill */

};
```

The dangers of multiple inheritance

Even though the concept of multiple inheritance is not difficult to understand in the abstract, making it part of a programming language introduces a variety of issues that can get extremely tricky. One source of trouble, for example, is that the same method or field name can appear in more than one superclass, which makes it difficult to decide which version should be inherited. These problems are sufficiently serious that the creators of Java made an explicit decision not to include multiple inheritance in the language design.

Given that single inheritance is already hard to use effectively in C++, adding the complexity of multiple inheritance makes this feature even more problematic as a programming strategy. Although it has some appealing applications, it is probably best to avoid multiple inheritance in your own programming but to be able to understand what's going on when you see it in existing code.

▨ Summary

In this chapter, you have learned how to use inheritance in C++ and have seen several practical applications of the concept. In particular, sections 19.3 and 19.4 offer a brief glimpse of how compiler writers can use inheritance hierarchies to represent arithmetic expressions.

Important points in this chapter include:

- C++ allows subclasses to inherit the public behavior of the superclasses. In its simplest form, the C++ syntax for defining a subclass looks like this:

      class *subclass* : **public** *superclass* {
          new entries for the subclass
      };

- In contrast to most object-oriented languages, C++ does not make it possible to assign subclass objects to variables of their superclass type without incurring a loss of data. In practice, inheritance is most useful if you work with *pointers* to objects instead of with the objects themselves. Unfortunately, exposing pointers forces clients to assume more responsibility for memory management, which often makes using inheritance in C++ more trouble than it is worth.

- Methods are not automatically overridden by definitions in their subclasses. In C++, only methods marked with the keyword **virtual** can be overridden in this way.

- Methods that are implemented only by subclasses are said to be *pure virtual*. Such methods are marked in their interface description by adding the notation = 0 before the semicolon at the end of the prototype.

- C++ classes include a **protected** section along with the **public** and **private** sections you have used all along. Declarations in the **protected** section are available to subclasses but inaccessible to clients.

- Calling the constructor for a subclass always invokes a constructor for its superclass. In the absence of any other specification, C++ calls the default constructor although clients can supply an *initializer list* to call a different one.

- C++ includes a **try** statement that lets programmers respond to exceptional conditions that occur during the execution of a program. In its simplest form, the **try** statement looks like this:

```
try {
    code under the control of the try statement
} catch (type var) {
    code to respond to an exception with the specified value type
}
```

To throw an exception, you use the **throw** keyword followed by a value.

- Expressions in a programming language have a recursive structure. There are simple expressions, which consist of constants and variable names. More complex expressions combine simpler subexpressions into larger units, forming a hierarchical structure that can be represented as a tree.

- Inheritance makes it easy to define a class hierarchy to represent the nodes of an expression tree.

- The process of reading an expression from the user can be divided into the phases of *input, lexical analysis,* and *parsing*. The input phase is the simplest and consists of reading a string from the user. Lexical analysis involves breaking a string into component tokens in a fashion similar to that used in the **TokenScanner** class from Chapter 6. Parsing consists of translating the collection of tokens returned from the lexical analysis phase into its internal representation, following a set of syntactic rules called a *grammar*.

- For many grammars, it is possible to solve the parsing problem using a strategy called *recursive descent*. In a recursive-descent parser, the rules of the grammar are encoded as a set of mutually recursive functions.

- Once parsed, expression trees can be manipulated recursively in much the same way as the trees in Chapter 16. In the context of the interpreter, one of the most important operations is evaluating an expression tree, which consists of walking the tree recursively to determine its value.

- C++ allows classes to inherit behavior from more than one superclass. This technique is called *multiple inheritance*. Although multiple inheritance can be useful in certain contexts, it adds considerable complexity, both to the C++ language and to applications that use this feature.

▰ Review questions

1. In C++, what header line would you use to define a class named **Sub** that inherited the public behavior from a class named **Super**?

2. True or false: The superclass specification in a new class definition may not be a template class with specific instantiation of the template types.

3. True or false: As in most object-oriented languages, a new definition of a method in a C++ subclass automatically overrides the definition of that method in its superclass.

4. In your own words, describe the effect of the **virtual** keyword.

5. What is a *pure virtual method?* Why is such a construct useful?

6. What syntactic marker does C++ use to indicate that a method is pure virtual?

7. What is an *abstract class?* Is it possible for an abstract class to provide its own implementation of its exported methods?

8. What is meant by the term *slicing?*

9. When you store values from an inheritance hierarchy in a collection, does it make more sense to store the values themselves or pointers to those values allocated elsewhere?

10. What classes and methods are virtual in the **GObject** class hierarchy shown in Figure 19-3?

11. How does the visibility of entries in the **protected** section of a class differ from those in its **public** and **private** sections?

12. What is an *initializer list?* Where do initializer lists appear in a C++ program?

13. What is the difference between an *interpreter* and a *compiler?*

14. What is a *read-eval-print loop?*

15. What are the three phases involved in reading an expression?

16. What is an *exception?*

17. In its simplest form that catches only one exception type, what is the syntax of the **try** statement in C++?

18. State the recursive definition for an expression as given in this chapter.

19. Identify which of the following lines constitutes an expression according to the definition used in this chapter:

    a. `(((0)))`

    b. `2x + 3y`

    c. `x - (y * (x / y))`

    d. `-y`

    e. `x = (y = 2 * x - 3 * y)`

    f. `10 - 9 + 8 / 7 * 6 - 5 + 4 * 3 / 2 - 1`

20. For each of the legal expressions in the preceding question, draw a parse tree that reflects the standard precedence assumptions of mathematics.

21. Of the legal expressions in question 19, which ones are ambiguous with respect to the simple recursive definition of expressions?

22. What are the differences between parse trees and expression trees?

23. What are the three types of expressions that can occur in an expression tree?

24. True or false: The methods in the `exp.h` interface do not work with **Expression** objects directly but instead use pointers to **Expression** objects.

25. What are the public methods of the **Expression** class?

26. Using Figure 19-12 as a model, draw a complete structure diagram for the following expression:

    `y = (x + 1) / (x - 2)`

27. Why are grammars useful in translating programming languages?

28. What do the letters in *BNF* stand for?

29. In a grammar, what is the difference between a *terminal symbol* and a *nonterminal symbol?*

30. What is a *recursive-descent parser*?

31. What is the significance of the second argument to the `readE` function in the implementation of the parser?

32. If you look at the definition of `readT` in Figure 19-14, you will see that the function body does not contain any calls to `readT`. Is `readT` a recursive function?

33. In the implementation of the **CompoundExp** subclass, why is the = operator handled differently from the arithmetic operators?

34. What is *multiple inheritance?*

35. True or false: Multiple inheritance proved so useful in C++ that the designers of Java incorporated it into their language design.

Exercises

1. Complete the definition of the **Employee** class hierarchy by adding the necessary instance variables to the private sections and the implementations for the various methods. Design a simple program to test your code.

2. Add a new **Square** subclass to the **GObject** hierarchy, whose constructor takes the coordinates of the upper left corner and a size as parameters.

3. Add the pure virtual method

   ```
   virtual bool contains(double x, double y) = 0;
   ```

   to the **GObject** class presented in Figure 19-5 and then implement that method for each of the subclasses. For the **GRect** and **GOval** subclasses, the **contains** method should return **true** if the specified point is inside the object, and false if it is outside. For the **GLine** class, **contains** should return **true** if the point is within half a pixel distance of the line. If you are unsure of how to determine whether a point is inside a **GOval** or how to calculate the distance from a point to a line, you should do what professional programmers do in such circumstances: look the answer up on the web.

4. The **TestGObjects** program in Figure 19-8 uses a vector to hold the list of graphical objects. That technique is useful enough that it makes sense to encapsulate it in a class. Implement a new **DisplayList** class that extends **Vector<GObject *>** but also provides additional methods that are useful in working with graphical objects, as shown in Figure 19-18.

5. Starting with the implementation of the **DisplayList** class from exercise 4, add a method **getElementAt**(*x*, *y*) that returns a pointer to the **GObject** closest to the front of the graphics window containing the point (*x*, *y*). To do so, you need to use the **gobjects.h** interface from exercise 3 so that you have access to the **contains** method.

6. Integrate the code for **GFillable** from Figure 19-17 into the **GObject** hierarchy. Write a test program that displays both filled and outlined shapes.

FIGURE 19-18 The `displaylist.h` interface

```cpp
/*
 * File: displaylist.h
 * --------------------
 * This file defines a DisplayList class that maintains a list of graphical
 * objects.
 */

#ifndef _displaylist_h
#define _displaylist_h

#include "gobjects.h"
#include "gwindow.h"

/*
 * Class: DisplayList
 * --------------------
 * This class is a vector of graphical objects arranged from back to front.
 * The individual elements of the DisplayList are pointers to GObjects.
 */

class DisplayList : public Vector<GObject *> {

public:

/*
 * Methods: moveToFront, moveToBack, moveForward, moveBackward
 * Usage: list.moveToFront(obj);
 *        list.moveToBack(obj);
 *        list.moveForward(obj);
 *        list.moveBackward(obj);
 * --------------------------------
 * These methods change the position of obj in the DisplayList.  The first
 * two methods move the object all the way to the specified end.  The last
 * two move it one position in the indicated direction, if possible.  Each
 * of these method signals an error if obj is not in the DisplayList.
 */

   void moveToFront(GObject *obj);
   void moveToBack(GObject *obj);
   void moveForward(GObject *obj);
   void moveBackward(GObject *obj);

/*
 * Method: draw
 * Usage: list.draw(gw);
 * -------------------------
 * Draws the GObjects in the DisplayList on the graphics window.  The
 * objects are drawn from back to front, so that objects closer to the
 * front seem to cover those further back.
 */

   void draw(GWindow & gw) const;

};

#endif
```

7. In its discussion of recursive backtracking, Chapter 9 offered a general outline for creating two-player games based on the minimax algorithm. At that point in the text, it was difficult to encapsulate the code for the minimax algorithm in a way that would allow the code to be shared by many different games. The combination of templates and inheritance make it much easier to define a base class for two-player games that is easy to extend for particular games.

   Design and implement a template class called **TwoPlayerGame** that takes the type used to represent a move as a template parameter. Specific games can then extend that class by overriding the methods that pertain only to that game, leaving intact the methods that implement the minimax algorithm itself. For example, the class definition for the simple Nim game described in Chapter 9 would look like this:

   ```
   class NimGame : public TwoPlayerGame<NimMove> {
       code specific to the Nim game
   };
   ```

   The **NimMove** type is defined in the same way that the **Move** type was in the implementation of the Nim game. In Chapter 9, the code for the minimax algorithm required that type to be named **Move**. Specifying template parameters makes it possible to use a name that is more descriptive.

   Test your implementation of the **TwoPlayerGame** class by completing the definition of the Nim class. Once you have a working implementation of Nim, demonstrate the flexibility of your class by using it to implement one of the other two-player games described in the exercises in Chapter 9.

8. Make the necessary changes to the interpreter introduced in section 19.3 so that expressions can include the remainder operator **%**, which has the same precedence as ***** and **/**.

9. Make the changes you would need to have the interpreter work with values of type **double** instead of type **int**.

10. Using the **Expression** class hierarchy exported by **exp.h**, write a function

    ```
    void listVariables(Expression *exp);
    ```

    that prints the variable names in that expression. The variables should appear in alphabetical order with one variable name per line. For example, if you parse the expression

    ```
    3 * x * x - 4 * x - 2 * a + y
    ```

calling **listVariables** on the resulting expression should produce the following output:

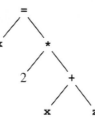

11. In mathematics, there are several common procedures that require you to replace all instances of a variable in a formula with some other variable. Working entirely as a client of the **exp.h** interface, write a function

```
Expression *changeVariable(Expression *exp,
                           string oldName,
                           string newName);
```

that returns a new expression which is the same as **exp** except that every occurrence of the identifier **oldName** is replaced with **newName**. For example, if **exp** is the expression

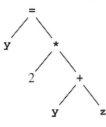

calling

```
Expression *newExp = changeVariable(exp, "x", "y");
```

will assign the following expression tree to **newExp**:

When you implement this function, it is important that the new expression tree does not share any nodes with the original one. If nodes are shared, it becomes impossible to free the heap storage using the **delete** operator because doing so will free nodes that are needed by the other tree.

12. In the expression interpreter introduced in section 19.3, every operator is a binary operator in the sense that it takes two operands, one on each side. Most programming languages also allow unary operators that take a single operand. Make the changes to the interpreter necessary to support the unary – operator.

13. Write a function

```
bool expMatch(Expression *e1, Expression *e2);
```

that returns **true** if **e1** and **e2** are matching expressions, which means that they have exactly the same structure, the same operators, the same constants, and the same identifier names, in the same order. If there are any differences at any level of the expression tree, your function should return **false**.

14. Write a program that reads expressions from the user in their standard mathematical form and then displays those same expressions using reverse Polish notation, in which the operators follow the operands to which they apply. (Reverse Polish notation, or RPN, was introduced in the discussion of the calculator application in Chapter 4.) Your program should be able to duplicate the following sample run:

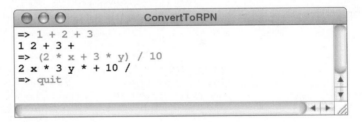

15. After it parses an expression, a commercial compiler typically looks for ways to simplify that expression so that it can be computed more efficiently. This process is part of a more general technique called *optimization,* in which the compiler seeks to make the code it generates as efficient as possible. One common technique used in the optimization process is *constant folding,* which consists of identifying subexpressions that are composed entirely of constants and replacing them with their value. For example, if a compiler encounters the expression

```
days = 24 * 60 * 60 * sec
```

there is no point in generating code to perform the first two multiplications when the program is executed. The value of the subexpression 24 * 60 * 60 is constant and might as well be replaced by its value (86400) before the compiler actually starts to generate code.

Write a function **foldConstants(exp)** that takes an expression pointer and returns a pointer to an entirely new expression in which all subexpressions composed entirely of constants are replaced by the computed value.

16. The process of turning the internal representation of an expression back into its text form is generally called ***unparsing*** the expression. Write a function **unparse(exp)** that displays the expression **exp** on the screen in its standard mathematical form. Parentheses should be included in the output only if they are required by the precedence rules. Thus, the expression represented by the tree

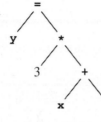

should be unparsed as

> y = 3 * (x + 1)

17. Although the interpreter program that appears in this chapter is considerably easier to implement than a complete compiler, it is possible to get a sense of how a compiler works by defining one for a simplified computer system called a ***stack machine.*** A stack machine performs operations on an internal stack, which is maintained by the hardware, in much the same fashion as the Reverse Polish calculator from Chapter 5. For the hypothetical stack machine used in this problem, the available instructions appear in Figure 19-19.

FIGURE 19-19 Instructions implemented by the stack machine

LOAD #*n*	Pushes the constant *n* on the stack.
LOAD *var*	Pushes the value of the variable *var* on the stack.
STORE *var*	Stores the top stack value in *var* without actually popping it.
DISPLAY	Pops the stack and displays the result.
ADD **SUB** **MUL** **DIV**	These instructions pop the top two values from the stack and apply the indicated operation, pushing the final result back on the stack. The top value is the right operand; the next one down is the left.

Write a function

```
void compile(istream & infile, ostream & outfile);
```

that reads expressions from **infile** and writes to **outfile** a sequence of instructions for the stack machine that have the same effect as evaluating each of the expressions in the input file and displaying their result. For example, if the file opened as **infile** contains

```
x = 7
y = 5
2 * x + 3 * y
```

calling **compile(infile, outfile)** should write a file containing the following code:

```
LOAD #7
STORE x
DISPLAY
LOAD #5
STORE y
DISPLAY
LOAD #2
LOAD x
MUL
LOAD #3
LOAD y
MUL
ADD
DISPLAY
```

18. The symbol table in the **EvaluationContext** class maps identifier names directly to their values. In a real compiler, the symbol table maps identifier names to *addresses* that contain the values. You can simulate this process by changing **EvaluationContext** so that it exports the following methods:

```
int getAddress(string name);
int getValue(int addr);
void setValue(int addr, int value);
```

The first method looks up the identifier name in an internal symbol table and returns a numeric address associated with that value. If the name has not previously appeared, **getAddress** should generate a new address and return that value. The **getValue** and **setValue** methods now take numeric addresses rather than names but otherwise work as they did in the original version of the interface.

Modify the interpreter from section 19.3 so that it uses this design.

19. Starting with the address-based interpreter from exercise 18, add the unary operators **&** and ***** that manipulate pointer values. Once you have added these operators, your interpreter should be able to produce a sample run that looks something like this:

```
PointerInterpreter
=> x = 1
1
=> y = 2
2
=> ptr = &x
1000
=> *ptr
1
=> ptr = &y
1004
=> *ptr
2
=> *ptr = 3
3
=> y
3
=>
```

The address values are arbitrary and depend on how your implementation of **getAddress** assigns new addresses. This implementation uses four-digit integers as addresses to make those values easier to recognize.

20. Using tree structures to represent expressions makes it possible to perform sophisticated mathematical operations by transforming the structure of the tree. For example, it is not hard to write a function that differentiates an expression by applying the standard rules that express the derivative of an expression in terms of the derivatives of its parts. The most common rules for differentiating an arithmetic expression are shown in Figure 19-20.

FIGURE 19-20 Standard formulas for differentiation

$x' = 1$

$c' = 0$

$(u + v)' = u' + v'$

$(u - v)' = u' - v'$

$(uv)' = uv' + vu'$

$(u / v)' = \dfrac{uv' - vu'}{v^2}$

where:

x is the variable used as the basis for the differentiation

c is a constant or variable that does not depend on x

u and v are arbitrary expressions

Write a recursive function `differentiate(exp, var)` that uses the rules in Figure 19-20 to find the derivative of `exp` with respect to the variable `var`. The result of `differentiate` is an `Expression` pointer that you can use in any context. You could, for example, evaluate that expression or pass it to `differentiate` to calculate the second derivative.

21. Expand the power of the interpreter by turning it into a simple programming language along the lines of the BASIC language developed in the mid-1960s by John Kemeny and Thomas Kurtz. In BASIC, programs consist of lines beginning with a number that determines the order of execution. Each line contains a statement chosen from those in Figure 19-21. Entering the `RUN` command in place of a statement runs the program, starting with the lowest numbered line and continuing until the program reaches the `END` statement marking the end of the program. As an example, the following session prints the powers of 2 less than 500:

```
○ ○ ○                     Basic
10 LET n = 1
20 PRINT n
30 LET n = 2 * n
40 IF n < 500 THEN 20
50 END
RUN
1
2
4
8
16
32
64
128
256
```

FIGURE 19-21　Simple statements in the BASIC language

`LET` *var* `=` *exp*	Assigns the value of *exp* to the variable *var*.
`INPUT` *var*	Requests an input value from the user and assigns it to *var*.
`PRINT` *exp*	Prints the value of *exp* on the console.
`GOTO` *line*	Jumps to the specified line number and continues execution from there.
`IF` e_1 *op* e_2 `THEN` *line*	Transfers control to the specified line number if the specified test is true. The operator may be any of the standard relational operators.
`END`	Marks the end of the program.

Chapter 20
Strategies for Iteration

What needs this iteration?

— William Shakespeare, *Othello,* ~1603

One of the most important operations on a collection is iterating through each of its elements. Up to now, you've used a range-based **for** loop for this purpose, which leads to extremely concise, highly readable code. That feature, however, is new to C++ as of the 2011 standard. Prior to the introduction of the extended version of **for**, looping though the elements of a C++ collection typically involved using an *iterator,* which is an object that refers to a particular element in a collection but can also step through additional elements one at a time.

Since the range-based **for** loop was unavailable for most of C++'s history, iterators are extremely common in existing code. In addition, many of the most useful library functions for working with collections use iterators to specify the portion of a collection to which those functions apply. For these reasons, it is necessary to understand the use of iterators in order to program effectively in C++. It is not, however, essential to understand the underlying implementation details. This chapter therefore focuses primarily on how iterators work from the client's perspective and how to use them in applications. The implementation details appear in the final section of the chapter, which is relevant only if you need to implement classes that support iteration.

In between the client- and implementation-focused discussions of iterators, the chapter introduces a different model for applying an operation to every element in a collection. Instead of using iterators or the range-based **for** loop to cycle through the individual elements, an alternative strategy is to allow clients to apply a function to each element of the collection in turn. Functions that are used in this way are called *mapping functions.* Mapping functions are less convenient than iterators and are consequently used less often. They are, however, easier to implement. Mapping functions, moreover, are increasingly important to computer science, particularly with the development of massively parallel applications.

20.1 Using iterators

In both the STL and the Stanford libraries, every collection class exports a class named **iterator** that implements an iterator for that class. Syntactically, iterators in C++ resemble pointers. Iterators use, for example, the ***** operator to retrieve the value of the current element and **++** to advance the iterator to the next element. If you are feeling rusty on these operators, it's worth reviewing Chapter 11, which introduces the idiomatic patterns you need to make iterators work.

A simple example of iterators

Before diving into a detailed discussion of the **iterator** class and its operation, it is useful to consider a simple example that uses an iterator to step through the elements in a collection. The first example of the range-based **for** loop back in

Chapter 5 used the following code to list the two-letter words from the lexicon stored in **EnglishWords.dat**:

```
int main() {
   Lexicon english("EnglishWords.dat");
   for (string word : english) {
      if (word.length() == 2) {
         cout << word << endl;
      }
   }
   return 0;
}
```

Using iterators, the **TwoLetterWords** program looks like this:

```
int main() {
   Lexicon english("EnglishWords.dat");
   for (Lexicon::iterator it = english.begin();
                          it != english.end(); it++) {
      string word = *it;
      if (word.length() == 2) {
         cout << word << endl;
      }
   }
   return 0;
}
```

The heart of this implementation is the **iterator** type, which is used to declare the loop index variable **it**. The iterator **it** starts at the beginning of the **english** lexicon and continues through it, one word at a time, until it reaches the end.

Unlike most of the types you have seen so far, **iterator** is not an independent type but is instead exported as part of a collection class. Types defined in this way are called *nested types*. Each collection class defines its own version of **iterator** as a nested type. Because the name **iterator** does not uniquely identify the collection class to which it belongs, clients must use the fully qualified name. Thus, the iterator for the **Lexicon** class is called **Lexicon::iterator**. Similarly, the iterator for the class **Vector<int>** is called **Vector<int>::iterator**.

In addition to the **iterator** type specific to that collection, every collection class exports two methods that return iterator values. The **begin** method returns an iterator initialized so that it refers to the first element of the collection. The **end** method returns an iterator that refers to a nonexistent element that follows the last element. The **begin** and **end** iterators therefore describe a range in a form reminiscent of the half-open interval introduced in Chapter 2. The elements in the collection start with the element indicated by **begin** and extend up to but do not include the element indicated by **end**.

In C++, the operators used for iterators are the same as those for pointers. Given an iterator, you find the value to which it refers by using the ***** operator, in just the same way you would dereference a pointer. Thus, the statement

```
string word = *it;
```

initializes the variable **word** so it contains the string from the lexicon at the current position of the iterator.

The expression **it++** at the end of the **for** loop advances the iterator so that it refers to the next entry in the lexicon. Once again, the syntax mirrors the programming model used for pointers, where the **++** operator increments the pointer value so that it refers to the next element in an array.

Iterators support the various shorthand forms that C++ implements for pointers. For example, some programmers might—although doing so seems like a poor choice in terms of style—choose to combine the increment and dereference operators by using the declaration

```
string word = *it++;
```

and then leave out the increment operation at the end of the **for** header line. Other programmers might eliminate the local variable **word** by dereferencing the iterator value in the **if** test and the output statement, as follows:

```
for (Lexicon::iterator it = english.begin();
                       it != english.end(); it++) {
   if (it->length() == 2) {
      cout << *it << endl;
   }
}
```

As with pointers, the idiomatic pattern ***it++** means to increment the pointer but to dereference its current value before the increment occurs. Similarly, the expression **it->length()** is shorthand for **(*it).length()**, which calls the **length** method on the current entry in the lexicon.

The iterator hierarchy

At a minimum, every iterator in C++ supports the ***** and **++** operators outlined in the preceding section, along with the relational operators **==** and **!=**. Those operators are sufficient to implement the range-based **for** loop that moves forward through each element of the collection, one element at a time. Some collection classes, however, define iterators that support more general operations.

The varying levels at which iterators support extended operations follow the inheritance hierarchy shown in Figure 20-1. The most primitive styles of iterator are **InputIterator**, which allows reading values, and **OutputIterator**, which allows writing by assigning a new value to the dereferenced iterator. The **ForwardIterator** class combines these capabilities and supports both reading and writing. The **BidirectionIterator** model adds the **--** operator, which makes it possible to move the iterator forward or backward. The **RandomAccessIterator** is the most general form and includes operators for advancing the iterator by *n* elements as well as the full complement of relational operators.

The **Lexicon** class supports only the **InputIterator** level of service, which means, for example, that it is impossible to iterate through the words in a **Lexicon**

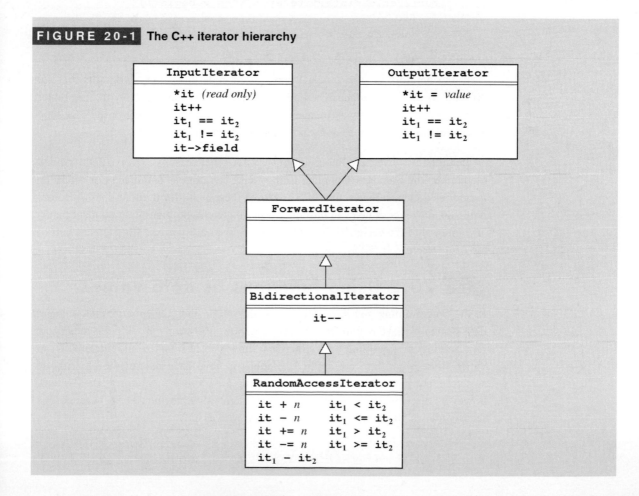

FIGURE 20-1 The C++ iterator hierarchy

backwards without first putting them into some more general structure. By contrast, the iterator for the **Vector** class is a **RandomAccessIterator**. As a consequence, it is possible to iterate backwards through the elements of the vector **v** using the following code, which prints the elements on the console in reverse order:

```
Vector<int>::iterator it = v.end();
while (it != v.begin()) {
   cout << *--it << endl;
}
```

In this code fragment, it is essential to decrement the iterator before dereferencing it. The initial value of **it** refers to the nonexistent element that follows the end of the vector. The decrement operator moves the iterator back one position, which therefore aligns it with the last element. Similarly, you can print every other element of **v** using the following code:

```
for (Vector<int>::iterator it = v.begin();
                           it < v.end(); it += 2) {
   cout << *it << endl;
}
```

Using iterators in such unusual ways often ends up making programs that are difficult to maintain, much like code that tries to be too clever with its pointer manipulation. The best way to specify iteration is to use the range-based **for** loop whenever you can, because doing so hides the iterators altogether.

Iterators, however, are important in C++ for other reasons. Many functions and methods in the Standard Template Library take iterators as parameters or return an iterator as their result. Section 20.4 explores these facilities in more detail. Before doing so, however, it helps to introduce a more general programming concept that is also integral to the design of the STL, which is the ability to use functions as part of the data structure.

20.2 Using functions as data values

In the programming you have done up to this point, the concepts of functions and data structures have remained relatively separate. Functions provide the means for representing an algorithm; data structures allow you to organize the information to which those algorithms are applied. Functions have been part of the algorithmic structure, not part of the data structure. Being able to use functions as data values, however, often makes it much easier to design effective interfaces, because this facility allows clients to specify operations as well as data.

Pointers to functions

In the earliest days of computing, programs were represented in a form that kept code and data entirely separate. Typically, instructions were punched on paper tape and then fed into the machine, which would then execute the instructions in sequence. If you needed to change the program, you had to punch a new tape. One of the most important characteristics of modern computers is that the same memory words used to store data values are also used to store the machine-language instructions executed by the hardware. This technique of storing instructions in the memory addresses used for data values is called the ***von Neumann architecture,*** after the mathematician John von Neumann. Although computing historians now believe that von Neumann did not invent the idea, he seems to have been the first to publish it, and the concept continues to bear his name.

One of the important implications of the von Neumann architecture is that every machine-language instruction in a program has an address in memory. This fact makes it possible to create a ***pointer to a function,*** which is simply the address of its first instruction. Most modern programming languages use pointers to functions internally but hide the details from the programmer. In contrast to those languages, C++ makes it possible for programmers to declare pointers to functions and then use those functions as data values in an application.

A simple plotting application

Before looking at the details of how C++ incorporates pointers to functions into its syntax, it helps to consider an example that shows how this technique is used in practice. One of the easiest examples to explain is the problem of generating a graphical plot of a client-specified function. Suppose, for example, that you want to write a program that plots the value of a function $f(x)$ for values of x in a specified range. For example, if f is the trigonometric sine function, you would like your program to produce a sample run that looks like something like this:

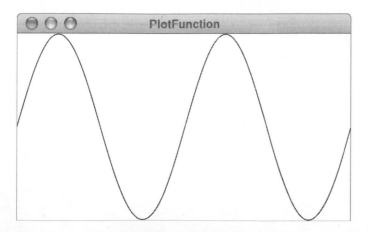

The graphical output shows only the shape of the graph and does not indicate any units along the *x*- and *y*-axes. In this diagram, the values of *x* vary from -2π to 2π, and the values of *y* extend from -1 to 1. The `plot` function called by the client would need to include these ranges as parameters, which means that the call that produces this output would look something like this, assuming the appropriate definition of the constant `PI`:

```
plot(gw, sin, -2 * PI, 2 * PI, -1, 1);
```

The interesting parameter here is the argument just after the graphics window, which is the name of the function you want to plot. In this example, the function is the trigonometric function `sin` from the `<cmath>` library.

If `plot` is designed in a general way, however, it should be possible to plot a different function by changing the second argument. For example, the call

```
plot(gw, sqrt, 0, 4, 0, 2);
```

should plot the `sqrt` function on a graph that extends from 0 to 4 along the *x*-axis and from 0 to 2 along the *y*-axis, as follows:

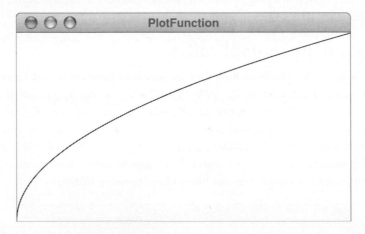

At the same time, the function that is passed to `plot` can't be just any old function. It wouldn't make sense, for example, to use a string function, because graphical plots on an *x*-*y* grid make sense only for functions that apply to numbers. What's more, it also wouldn't make sense to call `plot` with a numeric function that takes several arguments. The function argument makes sense only if it takes one real number (presumably a `double`) and returns a real number as well. Thus, you can say that the second argument to `plot` must be chosen from the general class of functions that map one `double` into another `double`.

That argument, moreover, must be a data value that is part of the C++ type system. Although functions themselves are not data values, pointers to functions are. The second argument to **plot** is therefore a pointer to a function that takes a **double** as its argument and returns a **double** as a result. The client provides the address of the function to the **plot** utility. The **plot** implementation then calls that client-supplied function to calculate each new *y* value in the graph. Because the **plot** utility makes a call that crosses back over the abstraction barrier that separates the implementation of **plot** from its caller, the function supplied by the client is called a *callback function.*

Declaring pointers to functions

The only new language feature you need to learn before coding the **plot** function is the declaration syntax for the second argument, which you know is a pointer to a function taking and returning a **double**. When you first encounter it, the syntax for declaring a function pointer seems confusing, even though it is consistent with the declaration model used elsewhere in C++. The key to understanding the declaration of function pointers lies in recognizing that the declaration of a variable mirrors its use and not its structure. This principle is illustrated by the examples in Table 20-1.

TABLE 20-1 Reading declarations in C++

Declarations in C++ adopt the syntax of their use

`double x;`	In this simple declaration, the variable **x** is of type **double**.
`double list[n];`	This declaration indicates that when **list** is followed by an integer in square brackets, the result is a **double**. The variable **list** is therefore an array of **double**s.
`double *dp;`	The expression ***dp** is of type **double**, which means that **dp** must be a pointer to a **double**.
`double **dpp;`	The expression ****dpp** is of type **double**, which means that **dpp** must be a pointer to a pointer to a **double**.
`double f(double);`	If **f**(*exp*) appears with an argument of type **double**, the result of the function call is a **double**. This declaration is therefore the prototype for a function **f** that takes one **double** argument and returns a result of type **double**.
`double *g(double);`	If the expression ***g**(*exp*) appears in the code, the result is a **double**. Because parentheses take precedence over the asterisk, this declaration is a prototype for a function **g** that returns a pointer to a **double**.
`double (*fn)(double);`	In contrast to the preceding entry, the dereference operator is now applied before the function call. The variable **fn** is therefore a pointer to a function returing a **double**. C++ automatically dereferences function pointers, so calls to the function are usually written as **fn**(*exp*).

The last line in Table 20-1, which declares **fn** as a pointer to a function taking and returning a **double**, is exactly what you need to complete the prototype for the **plot** function, which looks like this:

```
void plot(GWindow & gw, double (*fn)(double),
                        double minX, double maxX,
                        double minY, double maxY);
```

The arguments are the graphics window, the function to be plotted, and the limits of the plot in both the *x* and the *y* direction.

Implementing the plot function

Once you have defined the prototype, you can write a simple implementation of **plot** using the graphics library introduced in Chapter 2, as shown in Figure 20-2. The implementation cycles through each pixel coordinate across the graphics window, transforming each *x* coordinate into the corresponding position in the

FIGURE 20-2 Implementation of the **plot** function

```
/*
 * Function: plot
 * Usage: plot(gw, fn, minX, maxX, minY, maxY);
 * -----------------------------------------------
 * Plots the specified function (which must map one double to another
 * double) on the screen.  The remaining arguments indicate the range
 * of values in the x and y directions, respectively.
 */

template <typename FunctionClass>
void plot(GWindow & gw, FunctionClass fn,
                        double minX, double maxX,
                        double minY, double maxY) {
   double width = gw.getWidth();
   double height = gw.getHeight();
   double nSteps = int(width);
   double dx = (maxX - minX) / nSteps;
   double sx0 = 0;
   double sy0 = height - (fn(minX) - minY) / (maxY - minY) * height;
   for (int i = 1; i < nSteps; i++) {
      double x = minX + i * dx;
      double y = fn(x);
      double sx1 = (x - minX) / (maxX - minX) * width;
      double sy1 = height - (y - minY) / (maxY - minY) * height;
      gw.drawLine(sx0, sy0, sx1, sy1);
      sx0 = sx1;
      sy0 = sy1;
   }
}
```

interval between **minX** and **maxX**. For example, the point halfway across the window corresponds to the value halfway between **minX** and **maxX**. The program then calls the function **fn** to compute the value of *y*, as follows:

```
double y = fn(x);
```

The final step consists of converting the *y* value to the appropriate vertical position on the screen by scaling this value with respect to **minY** and **maxY**. This operation is essentially the inverse of the transformation to derive the value of *x*. The only difference is that the *y*-axis on the screen is inverted from the traditional Cartesian coordinate plane, which makes it necessary to subtract the computed value from the height of the graphics window.

The implementation of **plot** begins by computing the coordinates of the point at the left edge of the window, storing the result in the variables **sx0** and **sy0**. From there it computes the coordinates of the curve one pixel further to the right, storing these coordinates in the variables **sx1** and **sy1**. The graphics library call then connects these points with a call to

```
gw.drawLine(sx0, sy0, sx1, sy1);
```

Each additional cycle of the loop connects the current point to its predecessor. This process has the effect of approximating the graph of the function by connecting a sequence of line segments, each of which extends one pixel in the *x* direction.

The **plot** function in Figure 20-2 is almost certainly too primitive to be used in a practical application. It nonetheless makes a useful first example of how treating functions as data values can be useful in an application.

Mapping functions

Callback functions provide another strategy for iterating over the elements of a collection. If a class exports a method that allows a client to call a function on every element of a collection, clients can use that method as an alternative to using an iterator or a range-based **for** loop. Functions that allow you to call a function on every element in a collection are called ***mapping functions.***

As an example, the **Lexicon** class exports the function

```
void mapAll(void (*fn)(string));
```

This mapping function takes as its argument a pointer to a function with one argument of type **string**. The effect of **mapAll** is to call the specified function on each word in the lexicon, processing the words in the same order as the **Lexicon** iterator.

The existence of **mapAll** in the **Lexicon** class makes it possible to recode the **TwoLetterWords** program as

```
int main() {
    Lexicon english("EnglishWords.dat");
    english.mapAll(printTwoLetterWords);
    return 0;
}
```

where **printTwoLetterWords** is defined as

```
void printTwoLetterWords(string word) {
    if (word.length() == 2) {
        cout << word << endl;
    }
}
```

The **mapAll** method calls **printTwoLetterWords** for every entry in the lexicon. The callback function checks to see if **word** has length 2 and, if so, prints it.

In the Stanford libraries, every collection class defines a mapping function called **mapAll** that applies a callback function to every element. The order of the calls is the same as the order guaranteed when using the range-based **for** loop to iterate over the elements of the collection. Thus, **mapAll** invokes the callback function in index order for a **Vector**, in row-major order for a **Grid**, in alphabetical order for a **Lexicon**, in ascending key order for a **Map**, and in ascending value order for a **Set**.

The callback functions themselves ordinarily take one argument whose type matches the value type for the class. The exceptions to this rule are the classes that map keys into values. For both the **Map** class and the **HashMap** class, the callback function takes two arguments, which represent a key and its corresponding value. For example, you can use the **listMap** function in Figure 20-3 to list all key-value pairs in a **Map<string,int>**.

In addition to the by-value parameters used in Figure 20-2, the **mapAll** methods in the Stanford collection class library also accept mapping functions that use constant reference parameters. Thus, if you want to increase the efficiency of the code by eliminating the need to make copies of the key values, you can use the following prototype for **listMapEntry**:

```
void listMapEntry(const string & key, const int & value);
```

These two function types have different signatures in C++, and the **mapAll** method is designed to work with either type.

FIGURE 20-3 Function to list the entries in a `Map<string,int>`

```
/*
 * Function: listMap
 * Usage: listMap(map);
 * --------------------
 * Displays the key-value pairs in the map.  The output appears in
 * lexicographic order because the Map class uses the ordering of
 * the key type.
 */

void listMap(const Map<string,int> & map) {
   map.mapAll(listMapEntry);
}

/*
 * Function: listMapEntry
 * Usage: listMap(key, value);
 * ---------------------------
 * Prints a single key-value pair.  This function is designed to be
 * used as a callback function for the mapAll method in the Map class.
 */

void listMapEntry(string key, int value) {
   cout << key << " = " << value << endl;
}
```

Implementing mapping functions

In comparison to the iterators you will have a chance to consider more closely in section 20.6, mapping functions are relatively easy to implement. Assuming that you are using the array-based implementation of **Vector** from Figure 14-11, you can implement **mapAll** as shown in Figure 20-4. As long as you define a recursive helper method, implementing **mapAll** for the **Map** class is almost as simple. The

FIGURE 20-4 Implementation of the `mapAll` function for the `Vector` class

```
/*
 * Implementation notes: mapAll
 * ----------------------------
 * This method uses a for loop to call fn on every element.
 */

template <typename ValueType>
void Vector<ValueType>::mapAll(void (*fn)(ValueType)) const {
   for (int i = 0; i < count; i++) {
      fn(array[i]);
   }
}
```

FIGURE 20-5 Implementation of the `mapAll` function for the `Map` class

```
/*
 * Implementation notes: mapAll
 * -----------------------------
 * The exported version of mapAll uses a private helper method that takes
 * the tree as an argument and performs a standard inorder traversal,
 * calling fn(key, value) for every key-value pair.
 */

template <typename KeyType,typename ValueType>
void Map<KeyType,ValueType>::mapAll(void (*fn)(KeyType, ValueType)) const {
   mapAll(root, fn);
}

template <typename KeyType,typename ValueType>
void Map<KeyType,ValueType>::mapAll(BSTNode *t,
                                    void (*fn)(KeyType, ValueType)) const {
   if (t != NULL) {
      mapAll(t->left, fn);
      fn(t->key, t->value);
      mapAll(t->right, fn);
   }
}
```

code in Figure 20-5 makes only the following assumptions about the implementation of the **Map** class: that it is based on binary search trees as described in Chapter 16, that the root of the binary search tree is stored in the instance variable **root**, and that the **BSTNode** type includes fields for the key and the value.

The limitations of callback functions

In the simple form in which you have seen them used so far, callback functions are not too difficult to understand. In fact, separating the task of iterating through the elements of a collection and the code that gets executed on each cycle has advantages in terms of program structure. This strategy, however, also has serious limitations. The fundamental problem is that clients usually need to pass information to the callback function beyond the parameters supplied by the collection class. Using callback functions makes that process difficult.

To illustrate this problem, it helps to generalize the **TwoLetterWords** problem so that the program lists all the words of a specified length that is not necessarily two. More specifically, the goal in this example is to write a function

```
void listWordsOfLengthK(const Lexicon & lex, int k)
```

which, as its name implies, lists the words in the lexicon whose length is **k**.

If you use the range-based **for** loop, this function is straightforward to code:

```
void listWordsOfLengthK(const Lexicon & lex, int k) {
   for (string word : lex) {
      if (word.length() == k) {
         cout << word << endl;
      }
   }
}
```

If you try to use the **mapAll** method instead, you run into a bit of a problem. The callback function needs access to the value of **k**, but there is no obvious way to convey that information using **mapAll**. To make sure that the callback function has the information it needs, the client must somehow pass **k** to the mapping function, which must then turn around and pass that same value back to the function that lists the words. In a way, the situation is reminiscent of the Red Queen's observation in Lewis Carroll's *Through the Looking Glass* that "it takes all the running you can do, to keep in the same place." The client needs to provide the supplemental data the callback function needs, but must rely on the collection class to deliver the data to the client's callback function. Fortunately, C++ offers an elegant solution to this problem, as described in the following section.

20.3 Encapsulating data with functions

Function pointers are limited in their utility because they offer no way to supply client-supplied data along with the function. For most applications, what you need is a strategy that encapsulates the callback function and the client-supplied data as a single unit. In computer science, this combination of a function and its associated data is called a *closure.*

Some languages support closures automatically by giving functions access to the local variables in effect at the time that function was defined. C++ does not support that model. To use closures in C++, you need to create the necessary data structures yourself. Although that process is more complex than passing a simple function pointer, closures are sufficiently important that it is well worth spending some time to understand how they work.

Simulating closures using objects

Before revealing the strategy that C++ programmers use to create the effect of closures, it's worth noting that C++ already offers a mechanism for encapsulating data and code in a single entity. That mechanism is called an object. For the most part, providing that encapsulation is precisely what objects are for. The instance variables store the data, and the methods provide the code.

To solve the problem of listing all words with k letters, all you need to do is define a new class that stores k in an instance variable, but also exports a method that prints the current word from the lexicon if its length matches the stored value of k. In the implementation of `listWordsOfLengthK`, you could create an object initialized to contain the desired value of k. If it were then possible to pass that object to the mapping function, you'd have a complete solution to the problem.

The only stumbling block to this solution is that the mapping function needs to know the name of the method it should call for every value in the collection. To ensure that the mapping function is as general as possible, it makes sense to define a consistent method name for this purpose. Although any method name would do, the most convenient strategy is to have the object itself serve as the method by overloading `operator()`, which defines what it means to "call" an object as a function. In C++, classes that overload this operator are called **function classes**. Instances of those classes are called **function objects** or **functors**.

A simple example of a function object

To make sure that you understand how function objects work, it makes sense to start with a simple example unconnected to the idea of mapping functions. Suppose that you want to allow clients to create and call a function-like object that takes a single integer argument and returns the argument value after adding some increment chosen by the client. Given any constant increment, that function is easy to write in C++. For example, the function that adds 1 to its argument is

```
int add1(int x) {
    return x + 1;
}
```

The goal in this example is different in a way that may at first seem subtle. Given an integer constant k, you want to allow the client to define the function

```
int addk(int x) {
    return x + k;
}
```

You can't implement all possible functions of this form, because there would have to be as many of them as there are integers. What you need to do instead is create a function class that encapsulates two components: an instance variable that keeps track of the value of k and an overloaded binding of `operator()` that adds the stored value of k to its argument. The implementation of the `AddKFunction` class appears in Figure 20-6. The constructor creates a new instance of `AddKFunction` for a specific increment value; the overloaded binding of `operator()` adds that stored value to the client-supplied argument.

FIGURE 20-6 **Function class that adds a constant to its argument**

```
/*
 * Class: AddKFunction
 * --------------------
 * This class defines a function object that takes a single integer x and
 * computes the value x + k, where k is a constant specified by the client.
 */

class AddKFunction {

public:

/*
 * Constructor: AddKFunction
 * Usage: AddKFunction addk = AddKFunction(k);
 * -------------------------------------------
 * Creates a function object that adds k to its argument.
 */

   AddKFunction(int k) {
      this->k = k;
   }

/*
 * Operator: ()
 * ------------
 * Defines the behavior of an AddKFunction object when it is called
 * as a function.
 */

   int operator()(int x) {
      return x + k;
   }

private:

   int k;       /* Instance variable that keeps track of the increment value */

};
```

The following main program offers a simple illustration of the **AddKFunction** class in operation:

```
int main() {
   AddKFunction add1 = AddKFunction(1);
   AddKFunction add17 = AddKFunction(17);
   cout << "add1(100) -> " << add1(100) << endl;
   cout << "add17(25) -> " << add17(25) << endl;
   return 0;
}
```

Running this program with the definition of **AddKFunction** from Figure 20-6 produces the following output on the console:

```
●○○                    AddKFunction
add1(100) -> 101
add17(25) -> 42
```

Function objects are useful in C++ because clients can invoke them using the conventional syntax for function calls. In the test program for the **AddKFunction** class, for example, the local variables **add1** and **add17** are bound to different instances of the **AddKFunction** class. The calls to those function objects, however, look exactly like traditional function calls. The expression **add1(100)** calls **add1** on the value 100, just as if it had been defined as a function in the usual way.

Passing function objects to mapping functions

The strategy of using function objects makes it possible to solve the problem of passing additional information to a callback function. In addition to function pointers, the **mapAll** functions for the Stanford collection classes—and their counterparts in the Standard Template Library—allow the argument to be a function object whose **operator()** method is overloaded to take the same arguments that you would pass to a mapping function. For example, you can call the **mapAll** method for the **Lexicon** class with a function object that takes a string, which means that the corresponding function class must overload the method

```
void operator()(string);
```

Figure 20-7 defines the function class you need to write **listWordsOfLengthK**, which itself requires just a single line of code:

```
void listWordsOfLengthK(const Lexicon & lex, int k) {
    lex.mapAll(ListKLetterWords(k));
}
```

Writing functions that take functional parameters

From the various implementations of mapping functions presented earlier in the chapter, you know that the method header for the **mapAll** method in the **Lexicon** class must look like this if you pass it a function pointer:

```
void mapAll(void (*fn)(string));
```

This prototype indicates that the argument to **mapAll** must be a pointer to a function that takes a string and returns no result.

FIGURE 20-7 Function class that displays only *k*-letter words

```
/*
 * Class: ListKLetterWords
 * ------------------------
 * This class defines a function object that takes a word and prints it
 * on the console if it has length k, where k is specified by the client.
 */

class ListKLetterWords {

public:

/*
 * Constructor: ListKLetterWords
 * Usage: ListKLetterWords fn = ListKLetterWords(k);
 * --------------------------------------------------
 * Creates a function object that prints its argument only if it has
 * length k.  This function object is used as the argument to the mapAll
 * method in the Lexicon class.
 */

   ListKLetterWords(int k) {
      this->k = k;
   }

/*
 * Operator: ()
 * -------------
 * Defines the behavior of a ListKLetterWords object when it is called
 * as a function.
 */

   int operator()(string word) {
      if (word.length() == k) {
         cout << word << endl;
      }
   }

private:

/* Instance variables */

   int k;       /* Length of desired words */

};
/*
 * Function: listWordsOfLengthK
 * Usage: listWordsOfLengthK(lex, k);
 * -----------------------------------
 * Lists all words in the specified lexicon whose length is equal to k.
 */

void listWordsOfLengthK(const Lexicon & lex, int k) {
   lex.mapAll(ListKLetterWords(k));
}
```

The interesting question to ask at this point is how to declare the version of **mapAll** that takes a function object instead of a function pointer. C++ offers a concise—if sometimes confusing—syntax for declaring the type of a function pointer. If you want **mapAll** to take a function object, how would you declare the type of that parameter? This question is difficult because a function object can be an instance of any class that overloads the function call operator. Given that you can overload this operator in any class at all, there doesn't seem to be any obvious way to declare its type.

C++ circumvents this problem by using template functions to implement any functions that take function objects as parameters. The prototype for this version of **mapAll** therefore looks like this:

```
template <typename FunctionClass>
void mapAll(FunctionClass fn)
```

The value passed to **mapAll** can be of any type. If that type fails to override the function call operator with a method taking the expected arguments, the compiler will generate an error message when the compiler attempts to expand the **mapAll** template function.

20.4 The STL algorithm library

Although iterators are certainly useful for their original purpose of stepping through the elements of a collection, they have even greater importance in C++ because so many of the functions in the Standard Template Library take iterators as parameters. Suppose, for example, that you need to sort the elements of a vector and want to take advantage of the extensive engineering work that the designers of the C++ library have invested in creating an efficient library implementation of a general sorting algorithm. The STL does indeed include a function named **sort** for this purpose. That function, however, does not take a **Vector** argument as you might expect, especially after seeing the various implementations of a **sort** function in Chapter 10. The library version of the **sort** function instead takes two iterators that define the subrange of the vector you want to sort. To sort all the elements of a vector **v**, you call

```
sort(v.begin(), v.end());
```

If you wanted to sort only the first **k** elements of **v**, you could call

```
sort(v.begin(), v.begin() + k);
```

The **iterator** class for **Vector** implements the **RandomAccessIterator** model, which means that adding **k** to an iterator produces an iterator pointing to the value **k** elements farther along.

The **sort** function in the Standard Template Library is only one of many useful functions exported by the **<algorithm>** interface. Although the capabilities available through this interface are quite extensive, you can make considerable headway using the functions listed in Table 20-2. As you can see from the usage patterns in the first column, many of these functions take a pair of iterators as arguments in exactly the same way that the **sort** function does. For example, you can randomly shuffle the elements of the vector **v** by calling

```
random_shuffle(v.begin(), v.end());
```

The functions grouped at the bottom of Table 20-2 take functional arguments that operate on the value type of a collection. The **for_each** function generalizes the idea of mapping functions and works with any collection that supports iteration. You can, for example, list all two-letter words in a lexicon called **lex** by calling

```
for_each(lex.begin(), lex.end(), printTwoLetterWords);
```

where **printTwoLetterWords** is the callback function defined in the section on "Mapping functions" earlier in this chapter. The callback function can also be a function object, which means that you can list the **k**-letter words by calling

```
for_each(lex.begin(), lex.end(), ListKLetterWords(k));
```

You can use the functions in the **<algorithm>** interface as building blocks for more sophisticated operations. As an example, the code in Figure 20-8 implements the selection sort algorithm from Chapter 10 using several high-level functions from the **<algorithm>** library as tools.

FIGURE 20-8 Implementation of selection sort that uses the **<algorithm>** library

```
/*
 * Function: sort
 * Usage: sort(vec);
 * ------------------
 * Sorts the elements in the vector by combining high-level operations
 * from the <algorithm> interface.  The selection sort algorithm is
 * described in Chapter 10.
 */

void sort(Vector<int> & vec) {
   for (Vector<int>::iterator lh = vec.begin(); lh != vec.end(); lh++) {
      Vector<int>::iterator rh = min_element(lh, vec.end());
      iter_swap(lh, rh);
   }
}
```

TABLE 20-2	Selected functions in the `<algorithm>` library

Simple polymorphic functions

`max(x, y)`	Returns the larger of x and y.
`min(x, y)`	Returns the smaller of x and y.
`swap(x, y)` `iter_swap(i₁, i₂)`	Swaps the values in the reference parameters x and y or the values pointed to by the iterators i_1 and i_2.

Functions that operate on an iterator range

`binary_search(begin, end, value)`	Returns `true` if the iterator range from *begin* to *end* contains the specified value.
`copy(begin, end, out)`	Copies the values from the specified iterator range into the iterator that starts at *out*.
`count(begin, end, value)`	Returns the number of values in the specified iterator range that are equal to *value*.
`fill(begin, end, value)`	Sets every element in the specified iterator range to *value*.
`find(begin, end, value)`	Returns an iterator pointing to the first element in the iterator range that is equal to *value*, or *end* if none exists.
`merge(begin₁, end₁, begin₂, end₂, out)` `inplace_merge(begin, middle, end)`	Merges the consecutive sorted subsequences in the two ranges into a completely sorted sequence starting at *out*. The `inplace_merge` version merges two subsequences from the same collection, using *middle* to indicate the beginning of the second sequence.
`min_element(begin, end)` `max_element(begin, end)`	Returns an iterator pointing to the minimum or maximum element in the iterator range.
`random_shuffle(begin, end)`	Shuffles the elements in the iterator range.
`replace(begin, end, old, new)`	Replaces all instances of *old* in the iterator range with *new*.
`reverse(begin, end)`	Reverses the elements in the specified iterator range.
`sort(begin, end)`	Sorts the elements in the iterator range into ascending order.

Functions that take functional arguments, which may be either function objects or function pointers

`for_each(begin, end, fn)`	Calls *fn* on each element in the iterator range.
`count_if(begin, end, pred)`	Returns the number of values in the iterator range for which calling *pred* on that value returns `true`.
`replace_if(begin, end, pred, new)`	Substitutes *new* for all values in the iterator range for which calling *pred* on that value returns `true`.
`partition(begin, end, pred)`	Rearranges the elements in the range so that all elements for which *pred* returns `true` come at the beginning. The function returns an iterator pointing at the boundary.

20.5 Functional programming in C++

As you learned in Chapter 1, the developers of C++ added object-oriented features on top of the imperative programming language C. Given that history, one expects C++ to include both object-oriented and imperative features. By contrast, C++ was not designed to support another popular paradigm called *functional programming,* which is characterized by the following properties:

- Programs are expressed in the form of nested function calls that perform the necessary computation without performing any operations (such as assignment) that change the program state.

- Functions are data values and can be manipulated by the programmer just like other data values.

Even though functional programming was not a goal of the language design, the fact that C++ includes both templates and function objects make it possible to adopt a programming style that is remarkably close to the functional programming model.

The STL `<functional>` interface

The Standard Template Library offers rudimentary support for the functional programming paradigm through the `<functional>` interface, which exports a variety of classes and methods, including those that appear in Table 20-3. The classes generally fall into two categories represented by the first section of the table. The template class `binary_function<`arg_1`,`arg_2`,`*result*`>` is the common superclass for all function classes in the `<functional>` library that take two arguments—the first of type arg_1 and the second of type arg_2—and return a value to type *result*. The class `unary_function<`*arg*`,`*result*`>` plays the same role for function classes that take a single argument.

The classes in the next three sections act as object-oriented counterparts of the standard arithmetic, relational, and logical operators provided by C++. It is important to remember that these entries refer to *classes* rather than *objects*. For example, if you want to create a function object that adds two integer values, you need to invoke the constructor of the `plus<int>` class, like this:

```
plus<int>()
```

Leaving out the parentheses is an easy mistake to make, but one that is likely to produce cryptic error messages from the compiler.

The `bind1st` and `bind2nd` functions make it possible to incorporate constant arguments into a function object. For example, the expression

```
bind2nd(plus<int>(), 1)
```

TABLE 20-3 Selected classes and functions in the `<functional>` library

Base classes

`binary_function<`*arg₁ type,*
        arg₂ type,
        result type>
	Superclass for function classes that take two parameters of the specified types and return a value of the indicated result type.

`unary_function<`*argument type,* *result type>*	Superclass for function classes that take one parameter of the specified argument type and return the indicated result.

Classes implementing the arithmetic operators

`plus<`*argument type>*	Binary function class implementing the + addition operator.
`minus<`*argument type>*	Binary function class implementing the – subtraction operator.
`multiplies<`*argument type>*	Binary function class implementing the * multiplication operator.
`divides<`*argument type>*	Binary function class implementing the / division operator.
`modulus<`*argument type>*	Binary function class implementing the % remainder operator.
`negate<`*argument type>*	Unary function class implementing the – negation operator.

Classes implementing comparison operations

`equal_to<`*argument type>*	Function class implementing the == relational operator.
`not_equal_to<`*argument type>*	Function class implementing the != relational operator.
`less<`*argument type>*	Function class implementing the < relational operator.
`less_equal<`*argument type>*	Function class implementing the <= relational operator.
`greater<`*argument type>*	Function class implementing the > relational operator.
`greater_equal<`*argument type>*	Function class implementing the >= relational operator.

Classes implementing the logical connectives

`logical_and<`*argument type>*	Function class implementing the `&&` operator.
`logical_or<`*argument type>*	Function class implementing the `||` operator.
`logical_not<`*argument type>*	Function class implementing the `!` operator.

Functions that produce function objects

`bind1st` (*fn, value*) `bind2nd` (*fn, value*)	Returns a new unary function object that calls the binary function object *fn* with either its first parameter (`bind1st`) or its second parameter (`bind2nd`) bound to *value*.
`not1` (*fn*) `not2` (*fn*)	Returns a new function object that returns `true` if the unary function object (`not1`) or the binary function object (`not2`) returns `false` and vice versa.
`ptr_fun` (*fnptr*)	Returns a new function object that calls the specified function pointer, which may take either one argument or two arguments of the same type.

returns a unary function object that adds the constant 1 to its argument. This value is therefore similar to the function object produced by calling `AddKFunction(1)` that you saw earlier in the chapter. The advantage of the functional form is that you can assemble what you need by combining various pieces from the `<functional>` interface and no longer need to define the `AddKFunction` class.

The `bind1st` and `bind2nd` functions are particularly useful in conjunction with the high-level methods of the `<algorithm>` library. As an example, you can count the number of negative values in an integer vector **v** by making the following call:

```
count_if(v.begin(), v.end(), bind2nd(less<int>(), 0))
```

The `ptr_fun` function makes it possible to integrate the concepts of function pointers and function objects. If *fnptr* is a pointer to a function that takes either a single argument or two arguments of the same type, `ptr_fun`(*fnptr*) returns a function object that has the same effect. You can use this function to avoid duplicating code when you want to define a function that takes—as the functions in the `<algorithm>` library do—either a function pointer or a function object.

To get a sense of how you might apply this technique, suppose that you want to enhance the definition of the `plot` function from section 20.2 so that the second argument could be a function object as well as a function pointer. To do so, all you would have to do is copy the code from Figure 20-2 and then change the header of the function to

```
template <typename FunctionClass>
void plot(GWindow & gw, FunctionClass fn,
                        double minX, double maxX,
                        double minY, double maxY)
```

The body of the function doesn't need to change at all. Moreover, these two versions of the `plot` function can happily coexist because the compiler can tell which version to apply by looking at the arguments the caller supplies.

It is, however, inelegant to have two identical copies of the same code. To avoid doing so, you can reimplement the function-pointer version as follows:

```
void plot(GWindow & gw, double (*fn)(double),
                        double minX, double maxX,
                        double minY, double maxY) {
    plot(gw, ptr_fun(fn), minX, maxX, minY, maxY);
}
```

The call to `fun_ptr` produces a function object from the function pointer, which can then be passed to the other version of the `plot` function.

Comparison functions

The comparison function classes in the `<functional>` library are particularly important because they make it possible for clients to define their own ordering relationships. The functions in the `<algorithm>` library that involve sorting, which include `sort`, `merge`, `inplace_merge`, `binary_search`, `min_element`, and `max_element` from Table 20-2, take an optional functional parameter that defines the ordering. By default, this parameter is generated by calling the `less` constructor appropriate to the value type. To use a different ordering, clients supply their own function pointer or function object instead. That function, which is called a *comparison function,* should take two arguments of the value type and return a Boolean value, which is `true` if the first value comes before the second.

As a simple example, you can arrange the integer vector **vec** in reverse order by making the following call:

```
sort(vec.begin(), vec.end(), greater<int>());
```

In this call, the comparison function is an instance of `greater<int>` instead of the default `less<int>`, which means that the order is reversed.

You can use either function pointers or function objects as comparison functions. For example, if you define the function

```
bool lessIgnoringCase(string s1, string s2) {
    return toLowerCase(s1) < toLowerCase(s2);
}
```

you can sort the string vector **names** without regard to case by calling

```
sort(names.begin(), names.end(), lessIgnoringCase());
```

In much the same way, you can sort the string vector **words** from shortest to longest by defining the function

```
bool isShorter(string s1, string s2) {
    return s1.length() < s2.length();
}
```

and then calling

```
sort(words.begin(), names.end(), isShorter());
```

You can also pass a comparison function to the constructors for the **Map** and **Set** classes to define the order in which elements appear. The **Graph** class depends on this facility to ensure that nodes and arcs appear in order by the names of the nodes.

20.6 Implementing iterators

In the first section of this chapter, you learned how to use iterators in the Standard Template Library. For completeness, it is important to look at how those types are implemented, so that you have some idea of what is going on behind the scenes.

Implementing an iterator for the `Vector` class

Implementing `iterator` for the `Vector` class presents a relatively straightforward challenge. The underlying structure of the vector is defined in terms of a simple dynamic array, and the only state information the iterator needs to maintain is the current index value, along with a pointer back to the `Vector` object itself. The private instance variables of the `iterator` class can therefore be declared like this:

```
const Vector *vp;
int index;
```

The variable `vp` is declared here as a pointer to a `const Vector` to let the compiler know that the operations of the iterator don't change the vector itself. The `begin` function in the `Vector` class needs to return an iterator in which the variable `vp` points to the vector itself and the variable `index` is set to 0. The `end` function must return an iterator in which `vp` is initialized in the same way and the variable `index` is set to the number of elements in the vector, which is stored in the variable `count`. Both of these functions can be implemented easily if the `iterator` class includes a constructor that takes these two values and uses them to initialize the corresponding instance variables, like this:

```
iterator(const Vector *vp, int index) {
   this->vp = vp;
   this->index = index;
}
```

The `Vector` class needs access to this constructor, but it should not be available to clients. The easiest way to accomplish this goal is to have the `iterator` class declare `Vector` as a friend. The implementations of `begin` and `end` are then just

```
iterator begin() const {
   return iterator(this, 0);
}

iterator end() const {
   return iterator(this, count);
}
```

   From this point, all that remains is to implement the various operators. The code for the `Vector` implementation of the `iterator` class appears in Figure 20-9.

FIGURE 20-9   Implementation of the `iterator` class for `Vector`

```
/*
 * Nested class: iterator
 * ----------------------
 * This nested class implements a standard iterator for the Vector class.
 */

   class iterator {

   public:

/*
 * Implementation notes: iterator constructor
 * -------------------------------------------
 * The default constructor for the iterator returns an invalid iterator
 * in which the vector pointer vp is set to NULL.  Iterators created by
 * the client are initialized by the constructor iterator(vp, k), which
 * appears in the private section.
 */

      iterator() {
         this->vp = NULL;
      }

/*
 * Implementation notes: dereference operator
 * -------------------------------------------
 * The * dereference operator returns the appropriate index position in
 * the internal array by reference.
 */

      ValueType & operator*() {
         if (vp == NULL) error("Iterator is uninitialized");
         if (index < 0 || index >= vp->count) error("Iterator out of range");
         return vp->array[index];
      }

/*
 * Implementation notes: -> operator
 * ---------------------------------
 * Overrides of the -> operator in C++ follow a special idiomatic pattern.
 * The operator takes no arguments and returns a pointer to the value.
 * The compiler then takes care of applying the -> operator to retrieve
 * the desired field.
 */

      ValueType *operator->() {
         if (vp == NULL) error("Iterator is uninitialized");
         if (index < 0 || index >= vp->count) error("Iterator out of range");
         return &vp->array[index];
      }
```

FIGURE 20-9 Implementation of the `iterator` class for `Vector` (continued)

```
/*
 * Implementation notes: selection operator
 * -----------------------------------------
 * The selection operator returns the appropriate index position in
 * the internal array by reference.
 */

    ValueType & operator[](int k) {
        if (vp == NULL) error("Iterator is uninitialized");
        if (index + k < 0 || index + k >= vp->count) {
            error("Iterator out of range");
        }
        return vp->array[index + k];
    }

/*
 * Implementation notes: relational operators
 * -------------------------------------------
 * These operators compare the index field of the iterators after making
 * sure that the iterators refer to the same vector.
 */

    bool operator==(const iterator & rhs) {
        if (vp != rhs.vp) error("Iterators are in different vectors");
        return vp == rhs.vp && index == rhs.index;
    }

    bool operator!=(const iterator & rhs) {
        if (vp != rhs.vp) error("Iterators are in different vectors");
        return !(*this == rhs);
    }

    bool operator<(const iterator & rhs) {
        if (vp != rhs.vp) error("Iterators are in different vectors");
        return index < rhs.index;
    }

    bool operator<=(const iterator & rhs) {
        if (vp != rhs.vp) error("Iterators are in different vectors");
        return index <= rhs.index;
    }

    bool operator>(const iterator & rhs) {
        if (vp != rhs.vp) error("Iterators are in different vectors");
        return index > rhs.index;
    }

    bool operator>=(const iterator & rhs) {
        if (vp != rhs.vp) error("Iterators are in different vectors");
        return index >= rhs.index;
    }
```

FIGURE 20-9 Implementation of the `iterator` class for `Vector` (continued)

```
/*
 * Implementation notes: ++ and -- operators
 * ------------------------------------------
 * These operators increment or decrement the index.  The suffix versions
 * of the operators, which are identified by taking a parameter of type
 * int that is never used, are more complicated and must copy the original
 * iterator to return the value prior to changing the count.
 */
    iterator & operator++() {
        if (vp == NULL) error("Iterator is uninitialized");
        index++;
        return *this;
    }

    iterator operator++(int) {
        iterator copy(*this);
        operator++();
        return copy;
    }

    iterator & operator--() {
        if (vp == NULL) error("Iterator is uninitialized");
        index--;
        return *this;
    }

    iterator operator--(int) {
        iterator copy(*this);
        operator--();
        return copy;
    }

/*
 * Implementation notes: arithmetic operators
 * -------------------------------------------
 * These operators update the index field by the increment value k.
 */
    iterator operator+(const int & k) {
        if (vp == NULL) error("Iterator is uninitialized");
        return iterator(vp, index + k);
    }

    iterator operator-(const int & k) {
        if (vp == NULL) error("Iterator is uninitialized");
        return iterator(vp, index - k);
    }

    int operator-(const iterator & rhs) {
        if (vp == NULL) error("Iterator is uninitialized");
        if (vp != rhs.vp) error("Iterators are in different vectors");
        return index - rhs.index;
    }
```

FIGURE 20-9   Implementation of the `iterator` class for `Vector` (continued)

```
/* Private section */

    private:
        const Vector *vp;                  /* Pointer to the Vector object */
        int index;                         /* Index for this iterator      */

/*
 * Implementation notes: private constructor
 * ------------------------------------------
 * The begin and end methods use the private constructor to create iterators
 * initialized to a particular position.  The Vector class must therefore be
 * declared as a friend so that begin and end can call this constructor.
 */

        iterator(const Vector *vp, int index) {
            this->vp = vp;
            this->index = index;
        }

        friend class Vector;

    };
```

The functions in Figure 20-9 include a number of checks to make sure that iterators are used appropriately. If a client tries to use an uninitialized iterator, to dereference an iterator that is out of range, or to compare iterators from different vectors, the implementation calls **error** to report the problem. Although some implementations of the Standard Template Library do the same, many do not. Using an implementation that performs little or no error checking makes the debugging process much more difficult.

On the other hand, if you are willing to give up some amount of error checking to simplify the code, you can implement **iterator** for the **Vector** class by using only a few lines of code in contrast to the four pages taken up by Figure 20-9. Understanding how to do so requires looking at the requirements for C++ iterators in a different way, as discussed in the following section.

Using pointers as iterators

Much of the reason that Figure 20-9 is so long is that the level of service provided by **RandomAccessIterator** requires the definition of so many operators. In order to make sure that an iterator operates as clients expect, the implementation must define each of the following operators:

```
    *   ->   []   ==   !=   <   <=   >   >=   ++   --   +   -
```

There is, however, no requirement that the implementation provide these operators by defining methods in a class. If you have a type that already implements these operators in an appropriate way, you can use that type as an iterator. In C++, pointer types implement every one of those operators in just the right way, which means that you can use pointer values as iterators.

One of the implications of this reinterpretation of iterators is that you can use traditional C++ arrays with the functions exported by the **<algorithm>** interface. For example, if you have an array named **array** whose effective size is stored in the variable **n**, you can sort that array by calling

```
sort(array, array + n);
```

The name of the array is treated as a pointer to its first element, and pointer addition is defined so that **array + n** points to the element just after the end of the valid data.

The fact that iterators can be pointers offers another strategy for implementing **iterator** for the **Vector** class. If the iterator were simply a pointer to the appropriate element of the array, all you would need to do is define **begin** and **end** like this:

```
ValueType *begin() const {
   return array;
}

ValueType *end() const {
   return array + count;
}
```

The definitions of all the operators come for free.

There is, however, one additional definition you have to include in the definition in order to make the range-based **for** statement work in conjunction with the **Vector** class. The C++ compiler translates the range-based **for** loop

```
for (type var : collection) {
   body of the loop
}
```

into the following traditional **for** loop, where *ctype* represents the type of the collection and **it** is a private iteration variable not used elsewhere:

```
for (ctype::iterator it = collection.begin();
                     it != collection.end(); it++) {
    type var = *it;
    body of the loop
}
```

To make this translation work, there has to be a nested type within the **Vector** class named **iterator**. In this implementation, that type should simply be a pointer to the value type, but it must be named **iterator**, because that is what the compiler expects. Fortunately, C++ makes it possible to assign new names to existing types, as described in the following section.

The `typedef` keyword

C++ includes a mechanism—inherited from its predecessor language C—that allows programmers to assign new names to existing types. If you take any variable declaration and precede it with the keyword **typedef**, the compiler defines each of the names in that declaration as a synonym for the type it would have had as a variable. As an illustration of this principle, the declaration

```
char *cstring;
```

defines the variable **cstring** as a pointer to a **char**. The **typedef** statement

```
typedef char *cstring;
```

defines the type name **cstring** as "pointer to **char**" and therefore as a synonym for the **char *** type.

Although it is easy to overuse the **typedef** keyword, it can be extremely useful in certain circumstances. One common application consists of providing a concise name for function pointer types. As you have presumably noticed over the course of reading this chapter, the declaration of function pointer arguments often become so long and convoluted that providing a simple type name for those arguments makes a big difference in readability. To reduce this complexity, you can, for example, define the type name **mapCallback** so it is a synonym for the type "pointer to a function taking arguments of type **KeyType** and **ValueType** and returning no result" by including the following line in the definition of the **Map** class:

```
typedef void (*mapCallback)(KeyType, ValueType);
```

The prototype for the **mapAll** function then becomes

```
void mapAll(mapCallback fn)
```

instead of the following longer—although arguably more informative—version:

```
void mapAll(void (*fn)(KeyType, ValueType))
```

The **typedef** keyword is also just what you need to complete the streamlined implementation of the **iterator** type for the **Vector** class. All you have to do is export the following definition from the public section of **Vector**:

```
typedef ValueType *iterator;
```

Implementing iterators for the other collection classes

Even though the **Vector** class implements the most sophisticated level of iterator functionality, it is considerably easier to implement the **iterator** class for **Vector** than it is for most of the other collection classes. Defining iterators for classes like **Grid** and **HashMap** is not too difficult, and you will have a chance to do so in the exercises. Defining an iterator for a tree-structured class like **Map**, however, turns out to be tricky, mostly because the implementation has to translate the recursive structure of the data into an iterative form. As a general rule, it is wise to leave the implementation of iterators to experts, just as it is better to rely on professionals to write random number generators, hash functions, and sorting algorithms.

Summary

This chapter has used the problem of iterating over the elements of a collection class as a framework for introducing a variety of interesting topics including iterators, function pointers, function objects, the STL **<algorithm>** library, and techniques for using the functional programming paradigm in C++. Important concepts in this chapter include:

- The collection classes in both the Stanford libraries and the Standard Template Library export a nested **iterator** class, which supports cycling through the elements in a collection.

- In C++, the syntax for iterators is based on pointer arithmetic and uses the same set of operators. Not all iterators, however, support the full set of operators that apply to pointers. Instead, iterators offer different levels of service depending on the capabilities of the collection for which they are defined. The hierarchy of iterator functionality appears in Figure 20-1 on page 891.

- In addition to the **iterator** type itself, each class exports the methods **begin** and **end**, which return iterators pointing to the first element and just beyond the last one.

- The C++ compiler translates the range-based **for** loop

  > **for** (*type var* : *collection*) {
  >   *body of the loop*
  > }

  into the following **for** loop, where *ctype* represents the type of the collection and **it** is a private iteration variable not used elsewhere:

  > **for** (*ctype*::**iterator it** = *collection*.**begin()**;
  >   **it** != *collection*.**end()**; **it++**) {
  >   *type var* = ***it;**
  >   *body of the loop*
  > }

- In the von Neumann architecture used in most modern computers, every function is stored in memory and therefore has an address. In C++, pointers to functions are legitimate data values.

- A *mapping function* applies a client-specified callback function to every element of a collection. Mapping functions can therefore be used in many of the same contexts as iterators or the range-based **for** loop.

- Traditional mapping functions make it difficult to pass additional data to the callback function. To get around this problem, C++ supports *function objects,* which encapsulate the necessary data and operations in a class instance that implements the function-call operator.

- The STL **<algorithm>** library includes implementations of several common algorithms that operate on collections. Most of these functions take iterators to specify a range of elements.

- Even though C++ was designed to use both the imperative and object-oriented paradigms, it can also be used—particularly with the help of the **<functional>** library—to support certain aspects of the functional programming model.

- Comparison functions make it possible to specify new ordering relationships for the functions in the **<algorithm>** library and for collection classes like **Map** and **Set**, which need to determine the relative order of elements.

- C++ includes the **typedef** keyword, which makes it possible to define new names for existing types. The easiest way to understand how **typedef** works is to remember that the types a **typedef** statement defines are the variables that statement would declare if you took the **typedef** keyword away.

- Implementing an iterator for a new class requires considerable care and a surprising amount of code. In general, it is probably wise to leave this job to experts.

Review questions

1. Suppose that you have a **Set<int>** variable called **primes**. How would you use an iterator to display every element in **primes** in ascending order, without using a range-based **for** loop?

2. Assuming that the variable **it** is an iterator, describe the effect of the expression ***it++**.

3. True or false: If **c** is a nonempty collection, calling **c.begin()** returns an iterator pointing at the first element of that collection.

4. True or false: If **c** is a nonempty collection, calling **c.end()** returns an iterator pointing at the last element of that collection.

5. In the UML diagram for the iterator hierarchy in Figure 20-1, the list of methods in the **ForwardIterator** box is empty. Why does this level of the hierarchy exist?

6. True or false: If **c** is a nonempty collection, calling **c.end()** returns an iterator pointing at the last element of that collection.

7. What feature of the von Neumann architecture makes it possible to define pointers to functions?

8. Describe the difference between the declarations

   ```
   char *f(string);
   ```

   and

   ```
   char (*f)(string);
   ```

9. How would you declare a variable **fn** as a pointer to a function taking two integers and returning a Boolean value?

10. What is a *callback function?*

11. What is a *mapping function?*

12. In your own words, describe the difference between a *function pointer* and a *function object.*

13. By definition, every function class implements one particular operator. Which operator is it?

14. What are the two arguments to the **sort** function exported by the STL **<algorithm>** library?

15. What are the primary attributes of the functional programming paradigm, as it is described in this chapter?

16. True or false: The types of the two arguments in a function class that inherits from **binary_function** must be the same.

17. What is the purpose of including the **bind1st** and **bind2nd** functions in the **<functional>** library?

18. Use the capabilities of the **<functional>** library to write a single call to **count_if** that returns the number of even values in the integer vector **vec**.

19. What is a *comparison function?*

20. Describe the type introduced by the following **typedef** statement:

```
typedef void (*proc)();
```

21. List the complete set of operators implemented by an iterator offering the level of service provided by **RandomAccessIterator**.

22. True or false: Pointers in C++ define all the operators necessary to implement a **RandomAccessIterator**.

▮ Exercises

1. Rewrite the **WordFrequency** program from Figure 5-11 so that it uses iterators instead of the range-based **for** loop, which appears three times in the implementation.

2. In Figure 20-2, **plot** appears as a freestanding function. To make it easier for clients to use, it would be better to put this function in a library. Create the files **plot.h** and **plot.cpp** necessary to export the two versions of the **plot** function—one that takes a function pointer and one that takes a function object—through that interface. Since you already have the code, the challenge in this exercise is to figure out which parts of that code need to be in **plot.h** and which need to be in **plot.cpp**.

    Use your new **plot.h** interface to plot a graph showing the growth curves of the most common complexity classes: constant, logarithmic, linear, $N \log N$, quadratic, and exponential. If you use an x range of 1 to 15 and a y range of 0 to 50, this graph looks like this:

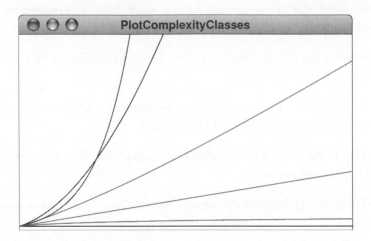

3. In its current design, the **plot** function takes six arguments: the graphics window, the function to be plotted, and two pairs of values indicating the range of the plot in both the *x* and the *y* dimension. You can eliminate the last two parameters by having **plot** compute the limits of the *y* range from the displayed valued. All you need to do is execute the computation twice, once to find the minimum and maximum values of the function and once to plot the function using those values as the limits of the range. Starting with the **plot** library you wrote for exercise 2, add new versions of **plot** that compute the *y* limits automatically.

4. You can use function pointers to maintain a map of mathematical functions by name. For example, if you start with the declarations

    ```
    typedef double (*doubleFn)(double);
    Map<string,doubleFn> functionTable;
    ```

    you can then store functions under their conventional names simply by adding entries to **functionTable**. For example, the following lines add the **sin** and **cos** functions from the **<cmath>** library:

    ```
    functionTable["sin"] = sin;
    functionTable["cos"] = cos;
    ```

    Use this technique to add the standard mathematical functions to the expression interpreter from Chapter 19. This change requires you to make several extensions to the existing framework, as follows:

    • The interpreter must use real numbers rather than integers in its computation. You had the opportunity to make this change in exercise 8 from Chapter 19.

- The function table needs to be integrated into the **EvaluationContext** class so that the interpreter has access to the functions by name.

- The parser module needs to include a new grammatical rule for expressions that represents a function call with a single argument.

- The **eval** method for the new function class must look up the function name in the function table and then apply that function to the result of evaluating the argument.

Your implementation should allow functions to be combined and nested just as in C++. For example, if your interpreter defines the functions **sqrt**, **sin**, and **cos**, your program should be able to produce the following sample run:

```
●●● ○               Interpreter
=> sqrt(2)
1.41421
=> sqrt(sqrt(sqrt(256)))
2
=> cos(0)
1
=> PI = 3.14159265358
3.14159
=> sin(PI / 2)
1
=> sin(PI / 6)
0.5
=> x = 5
5
=> y = 12
12
=> sqrt(x * x + y * y)
13
```

5. Starting with the extended version of the **Expression** class you implemented in exercise 4, create a function class called **ExpressionFunction** that turns an expression string into a function object that maps the value of the variable **x** into its evaluated result. For example, if you call the constructor

        ExpressionFunction("2 * x + 3")

    the result should be a function that you can apply to a single argument. Thus, if you call

        ExpressionFunction("2 * x + 3")(7)

    the result should be the value of the expression **2 * 7 + 3**, or 14.

6. Combine the **ExpressionFunction** facility from exercise 5 with the **plot** function from exercise 3 so that the function argument to **plot** can be a string

that represents an expression involving the variable **x**. For example, after making these extensions to the **plot.h** interface, you should be able to call

```
plot(gw, "sin(x)", -2 * PI, 2 * PI, 1, 1)
```

to produce the sine wave plot shown at the bottom of page 893. The string expression, however, can use any of the facilities recognized by the expression parser, so you could use it to plot more complicated functions, as illustrated by the following call:

```
plot(gw, "sin(2 * x) + cos(3 * x)", -PI, PI)
```

This statement uses **ExpressionFunction** to produce a function object that evaluates the expression **sin(2 * x) + cos(3 * x)** and then uses that function object to generate the following plot:

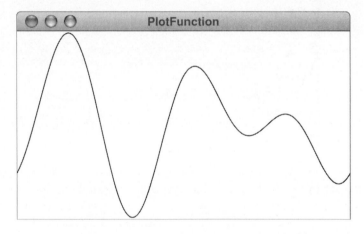

7. In calculus, the *definite integral* of a function is defined to be the area bounded horizontally by two specified limits and vertically by the x-axis and the value of the function. For example, the definite integral of the trigonometric sine function in the range 0 to π is the area of the shaded region in the following diagram:

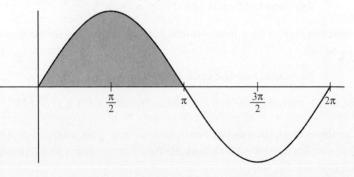

You can compute an approximation of this area by adding up the area of small rectangles of a fixed width, where the height is given by the value of the function at the midpoint of the rectangle:

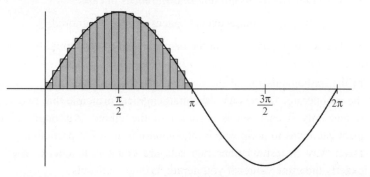

Design the prototype and write the code for a function named **integrate** that approximates the definite integral by summing the areas of the rectangles. For example, to calculate the area of the shaded region in the earlier example, the client would write

```
double value = integrate(sin, 0, PI, 20);
```

The last argument is the number of rectangles into which the area gets divided; the larger this value, the more accurate the approximation.

Note that any region that falls below the *x*-axis is treated as negative area. Thus, if you compute the definite integral of **sin** from 0 to 2π, the result would be 0 because the areas above and below the axis cancel each other out.

8.   Implement the function

```
template <typename IterType>
IterType max_element(IterType begin, IterType end);
```

from the **<algorithm>** library, which returns an iterator pointing to the largest element in the iterator range. Since many of the standard libraries include **<algorithm>**, you may have to give your function a different name.

9.   Write the prototype for and then implement the template function **count_if** from the **<algorithm>** library.

10. The code for **lessIgnoringCase** on page 912 is inefficient because it always converts strings to lowercase even if it is possible to determine the relative ordering by looking only at the first character. Write a more efficient version of **lessIgnoringCase** that looks at as few characters as possible to determine the result.

11. Write a comparison function **titleComesBefore** that takes two strings and compares them, subject to the following rules:

    • The comparison should ignore differences in case.

    • All punctuation marks except spaces should be ignored.

    • The words *a, an,* or *the* at the beginning of a title should be ignored.

12. In the implementation of the **Set** class presented in Figure 17-4, the code for the **==** operator for sets uses the mathematical principle that two sets are equal if and only if each set is a subset of the other. Although relying on that principle leads to a concise implementation, it is not particularly efficient. A faster way to test whether two sets are equal is to check whether you get exactly the same values if you iterate through both sets.

    The only problem you have to tackle before you try to solve this problem is that the **Set** implementation from Chapter 17 doesn't include an iterator. That implementation, however, is layered on top of the **Map** class from the Stanford libraries, which does export an **iterator** class. You can therefore create the necessary iterators from the **map** instance variable in each set. Given the arcane rules for declarations involving template classes in C++, the declarations of **Map** iterators inside the **Set** class need to be marked with the **typename** keyword, which forces you to write declarations like this:

    ```
    typename Map<ValueType,bool> it = map.begin();
    ```

    Use this strategy to reimplement the **==** operator in the **set.h** interface.

13. Implement an iterator for the **StringMap** class, as it appears in Figure 15-8 on page 676. This class is a specialized version of **HashMap**, which means that the iterator can process elements in any order.

14. Implement an iterator for the **Grid** class that processes the elements in row-major order.

15. To give yourself an even bigger challenge, implement an iterator for the **Map** class from Chapter 16, which is based on binary search trees. The **Map** iterator always processes elements in ascending order, which corresponds to an inorder walk of the tree. When you implement this behavior using an iterator, however, you can no longer rely on the magic of recursion, because the iterator needs to operate sequentially, one step at a time. The code for the **Map** iterator must therefore perform all the bookkeeping that occurs automatically when you implement the inorder walk recursively. Keeping track of that state will require you to maintain a stack of as-yet-unvisited nodes.

Index